Lawrenceville Press

A Guide to Microsoft® Office 2003

for Information and Communication Technologies

Beth Brown

Elaine Malfas

Jan Marrelli

All orders including educational, Canadian, foreign, FPO, and APO may be placed by contacting:

Lawrenceville Press, Inc.
P.O. Box 704
Pennington, NJ 08534-0704
(609) 737-1148
(609) 737-8564 fax

This text is available in hardcover and softcover editions.

16 15 14 13 12 11 10 9 8 7 6 5 4 3 2

W e have strived to make this the most comprehensive and easy to understand Microsoft Office 2003 text available. Our primary objective in this text is to teach 21st century skills through a project-based, hands-on approach. To meet this objective, we correlated the text to the National Standards for Business Education and used our teaching experiences, as well as the feedback, comments, and suggestions from other experienced educators to determine how best to present application concepts.

For the best classroom experience for both student and teacher, our comprehensive text includes hands-on practices, critical-thinking review questions, and exercises of varying difficulty levels. The exercises are designed to broaden student knowledge in core content areas as well as teach global awareness and financial, economic, and business literacy. Learning opportunities are extended outside of school through exercises that require community interaction.

A Guide to Microsoft Office 2003 is written for a one-term or two-term course. The text is written in a style appropriate for students at a variety of levels. The text starts with a Microsoft Office Basics chapter and then covers Outlook, Word, Excel, Access, and PowerPoint. The integration of data between the Office applications is covered throughout the text.

This text is available in hardcover and softcover editions. The softcover edition has a sewn lay-flat binding, which keeps the text open at any page and gives the book additional strength.

Design and Features

Hands-on Practices Concepts are presented, discussed, and then followed by a "hands-on" practice that requires the student to test newly learned skills using the computer. The practices also serve as excellent reference guides for review. Answers to all the practices are included in the Teacher Resource Materials.

Sidebars and Tips Additional topics and tips that complement the text are in boxes in the margin.

Chapter Summaries Concepts covered in the chapter are reviewed.

Vocabulary Sections At the end of each chapter is a list of new terms and definitions and a list of commands and buttons covered in the chapter.

Review Questions Numerous review questions provide immediate reinforcement of new concepts. Answers to all review questions are included in the Teacher Resource Materials.

Exercises Numerous exercises of varying difficulty are appropriate for students with a wide range of abilities. Cross-curricular content is integrated into the exercises. Answers to all exercises are included in the Teacher Resource Materials.

Appendices Using Microsoft Office Help features and digital cameras are presented in appendices at the end of the text.

Online Resources Materials that complement and extend this text are free for download and distribution in your class. Supplemental chapters cover operating systems, personal finances, introduction to computers, and keyboarding skills. Students can download all the files needed to complete the practices and exercises from www.lpdatafiles.com.

Teacher Resource Materials

Our Teacher Resource Materials correlate directly to the text book and provide all the additional materials required to offer students an excellent computer applications course. The Teacher Resource Materials feature:

- **cd_contents.htm** Help files and a guide for using the text and resource materials.

- **Lesson Plans** Lessons in PDF format keyed to the chapters in the text. Each lesson includes assignments, teaching notes, worksheets, and additional topics.

- **Tutorials** Flash movie files that guide you and your student through tasks. Each movie is keyed to sections in the text.

- **PowerPoint Presentations** Topics keyed to the text are in PowerPoint files for presentation.

- **Vocabulary** Word files of the vocabulary presented in the text.

- **Rubrics** Rubrics keyed to exercises in the text for assessment.

- **Worksheets** Problems that supplement the exercises in the text provide additional reinforcement of concepts.

- **Critical Thinking Worksheets** Thought-provoking written-response questions keyed to concepts practiced in the text.

- **Review Question Answers** Answers for the review questions presented in the text.

- **Data files** All files the student needs to complete the practices and exercises in the text, as well as the files needed to complete the worksheets, quizzes, and tests.

- **Exam***View*® **Software** Question banks keyed to the text and the popular **Exam***View*® software are included to create multiple tests, quizzes, and additional assessment materials.

- **Answer files** Answers to the practices, exercises, worksheets, quizzes, and tests.

Acknowledgments

The authors are especially grateful to the many instructors and their students who classroom test our texts as they are being written. Their comments and suggestions have been invaluable.

The success of this and many of our other texts is due to the efforts of Heidi Crane, Vice President of Marketing at Lawrenceville Press. She has developed the promotional material which has been so well received by instructors around the world, and coordinated the comprehensive customer survey which led to many of the features in this edition. Joseph DuPree and Christina Albanesius run our Customer Relations Department and handle the thousands of orders we receive in a friendly and efficient manner. Richard Guarascio and Michael Porter are responsible for the excellent service Lawrenceville Press offers in shipping orders.

We thank Kevin Werdehausen of Von Hoffmann Inc. who supervised the printing of this text.

We also thank Nanette Hert, computer science teacher at Saint Andrew's School, for all her input on this text. She has edited the text for accuracy and contributed to other aspects of development. We thank Daniel Kopp for his contribution, including the Alaska photographs.

Finally, we would like to thank our students, for whom and with whom this text was written. Their candid evaluation of each lesson and their refusal to accept anything less than perfect clarity in explanation have been the driving force behind the creation of *A Guide to Microsoft Office 2003*.

About the Authors

Beth A. Brown, a Computer Science graduate of Florida Atlantic University, is director of development at Lawrenceville Press where she has coauthored a number of applications and programming texts and their accompanying Teacher Resource Materials. She has taught computer applications and programming at the high school level.

Elaine Malfas is a graduate of Hartwick College and earned an M.S. degree in Technical Communication from Rensselaer Polytechnic Institute. Ms. Malfas has coauthored several computer texts and their accompanying Teacher Resource Materials. She has taught computer applications and desktop publishing at the high school level.

Jan Marrelli has a Bachelor of Science in Business Administration from Lake Superior State University and a Bachelor of Education from the University of Western Ontario. She has been a Business Coordinator and taught computer applications and programming for the Algoma District School Board as well as participating in curriculum development and assessment projects for the Ontario Ministry of Education.

Microsoft Office Basics

After completing Chapter 1, students will be able to:

1. Describe the Microsoft Office applications.
2. Identify the different parts of a Windows application interface.
3. Enter data into a document.
4. Use menus and toolbars.
5. Identify dialog box options.
6. Save files.
7. Create headers and footers.
8. Open, save, print, and close files.
9. Quit an application.
10. Multitask.

Using a Communications Application

After completing Chapter 2, students will be able to:

1. Define terminology associated with the World Wide Web.
2. Describe several categories and purpose of Web sites.
3. Evaluate Web sites.
4. Explain how a Web browser interprets an HTML document.
5. Demonstrate the basic features of Internet Explorer.
6. Use search engines and subject trees.
7. Cite a Web page.
8. Use Outlook to send e-mail messages.
9. Display the Address Book.
10. Add a signature to e-mail messages.
11. Organize and search for e-mail messages.
12. Block messages from specific senders.
13. Discuss how to avoid getting a virus.
14. Follow e-mail etiquette rules.
15. Describe instant messaging.

Personal Information Management

After completing Chapter 3, students will be able to:

1. Explain how a personal information manager can simplify the organization of personal and business activities.
2. Display Calendar in different views.
3. Add events and appointments to Calendar.
4. Work with multiple calendars.

5. Integrate the Outlook Calendar and e-mail tools.
6. Add tasks to TaskPad.
7. Print a calendar.
8. Create an electronic address book.

Using a Word Processor

After completing Chapter 4, students will be able to:

1. Explain why the word processor is ideal for producing a variety of different documents.
2. Identify the different parts of the Word window.
3. Use the word processor to enter and modify text.
4. Insert symbols into a document.
5. Understand automatic spelling and grammar checking.
6. Use smart tags.
7. Find and replace text and special characters in a document.
8. Use the thesaurus to display a list of synonyms.
9. Demonstrate techniques for selecting, copying, and moving text.
10. Use the Office Clipboard.
11. Apply character and paragraph formats.
12. Print preview and print a document.
13. Create hyperlinks to a Web page and to an e-mail address.
14. Use document collaboration features to peer edit a document.
15. E-mail a document from Word.
16. Use Reading Layout view to read a document on the screen.

Formatting Documents

After completing Chapter 5, students will be able to:

1. Display and use the Reveal Formatting task pane.
2. Apply page formats, such as margins and headers and footers.
3. Insert page numbers into headers and footers.
4. Position text using tabs and tab stops.
5. Select and format a vertical block of text in a table.

6. Apply paragraph formats, such as line spacing and indents.
7. Format hanging indents and first line indents.
8. Format bulleted and numbered lists.
9. Create footnotes and endnotes.
10. Search for clip art and add pictures to a document.
11. Create and use templates.
12. Save a Word document as an HTML file.

Long Documents and Desktop Publishing

After completing Chapter 6, students will be able to:

1. Create and format a table.
2. Apply styles to text.
3. Hyphenate a document.
4. View and modify a document in Outline view.
5. Create a table of contents.
6. Divide a document into sections.
7. Create different headers and footers for a document that is divided into sections.
8. Create diagrams and organization charts.
9. Format a document in columns.
10. Create a brochure and a newsletter in Word.

Using a Spreadsheet

After completing Chapter 7, students will be able to:

1. Describe tasks a spreadsheet would be used for.
2. Identify the different parts of the Excel spreadsheet window.
3. Enter and edit data in a worksheet.
4. Demonstrate techniques for selecting cells.
5. Preview and set print options for a worksheet.
6. Use formulas to perform calculations.
7. Understand relative cell references.
8. Copy and paste data between Word and Excel.
9. E-mail a worksheet for collaboratation.
10. Add a picture to a worksheet.
11. Create hyperlinks to a Web page and to an e-mail address.
12. Apply cell formatting, such as cell borders, patterns, and color.
13. Apply conditional formatting to help make spreadsheet data easier to evaluate.
14. Create and use templates.
15. Save Excel data in HTML format.

Working with Functions and Organizing Data

After completing Chapter 8, students will be able to:

1. Determine how changing data impacts results by asking "What If" questions.
2. Use the SUM, AVERAGE, MAX, MIN, and ROUND functions.
3. Understand absolute cell references.
4. Identify common error values.
5. Sort the data in a spreadsheet.
6. Insert and delete rows and columns.
7. Use the IF function.
8. Change the print orientation and margins of a worksheet.
9. Print part of a worksheet.
10. Use text in the IF function.
11. Create an amortization table using the PMT function.
12. Organize data using multiple sheets in a workbook.

Creating Charts

After completing Chapter 9, students will be able to:

1. Explain how a chart can enhance and simplify the understanding of numerical data in a worksheet.
2. Identify the different chart objects.
3. Create pie, bar, and line charts.
4. Move, size, and delete charts.
5. Print a chart.
6. Copy a chart object into a Word document.
7. Apply chart formatting.
8. Identify various other types of charts that can be created.

Advanced Spreadsheet Techniques

After completing Chapter 10, students will be able to:

1. Use the CHOOSE and VLOOKUP functions.
2. Name a cell or range.
3. Freeze selected rows and columns.
4. Create hyperlinks to a worksheet location.
5. Embed and link objects.
6. Use dates and times in formulas.
7. Protect worksheets and workbooks from changes.
8. Apply data entry criteria.

9. Create a data form.
10. Create an Excel list that can be sorted and filtered.
11. Perform repetitive tasks using macros.

Using a Relational Database

After completing Chapter 11, students will be able to:
1. Describe a relational database and its structure.
2. Identify the different parts of the Access database window.
3. Define fields and records.
4. Select a primary key.
5. Develop a database schema.
6. Create a table and a form.
7. Enter records using forms.
8. View tables in Design view and Datasheet view.
9. Sort, update, and delete records.
10. Preview and print records.
11. Modify a table and form.
12. Copy Access data to Excel and Word.
13. Export Access table data to HTML format.

Relational Database Techniques

After completing Chapter 12, students will be able to:
1. Define relationships.
2. View subdatasheets.
3. Create and use select queries.
4. Create a range query.
5. Create and use complex queries.
6. Use fields and wildcards in query criteria.
7. Create form letters and mailing labels from Access data.
8. Create parameter and update queries.

Analyzing Data in a Database

After completing Chapter 13, students will be able to:
1. Create a report.
2. Add summary values to a report.
3. Use Design view to modify a report.
4. Distribute a report.
5. Create a calculated field.
6. Export an Access table to an Excel workbook.
7. Import an Excel worksheet to Access.
8. Link Access data to a Word document.

Creating Presentations

After completing Chapter 14, students will be able to:
1. Explain the purpose of a presentation.
2. Identify the different parts of the PowerPoint window.
3. Plan a presentation.
4. Add and delete slides, and change the order of slides.
5. Display a presentation in different views.
6. Change the design of a presentation using a design template.
7. Apply a different color scheme to a template.
8. Print a presentation.
9. Add footers to slides.
10. Use the Slide Master.
12. Apply formatting and add a picture to a slide.
13. Create and print speaker notes.
14. Collaborate on a presentation.
15. E-mail a presentation from PowerPoint.

Advanced PowerPoint Presentations

After completing Chapter 15, students will be able to:
1. Add animation and slide transitions.
2. Move and duplicate data within the same presentation and between presentations.
3. Add a chart from an Excel workbook to a slide.
4. Use ink during a slide show presentation.
5. Create and use templates.
6. Add sound and a movie to a slide.
7. Explain a variety of ways to deliver a presentation.
8. Assign a password to protect a presentation.
9. Create hyperlinks to a Web page and to an e-mail address.
10. Save a PowerPoint presentation in HTML format.
11. Publish a presentation to the Web.
12. Create a photo album.

Table of Contents

Chapter 1 – Microsoft Office Basics

Chapter 2 – Using a Communications Application

Chapter 3 – Personal Information Management

Chapter 4 – Using a Word Processor

Chapter 5 – Formatting Documents

Chapter 13 – Analyzing Data in a Database

Chapter 14 – Creating Presentations

Chapter 15 – Advanced PowerPoint Presentations

Appendix A – Using Microsoft Office Help

Appendix B – Digital Images

Microsoft Office Basics

This chapter discusses features common to Microsoft Office applications and how to effectively use these features.

What is Microsoft Office?

Office 2003 Editions

Some editions of Office 2003 include additional applications, such as Publisher 2003 and FrontPage 2003.

Microsoft Office 2003 is a Windows application that consists of several applications, each designed to perform specific tasks:

- **Outlook 2003** is a personal information manager and communications application that has tools for keeping track of contacts, organizing appointments, managing e-mail, and listing tasks.

- **Word 2003** is a word processor application that is used to produce easy-to-read, professional-looking documents such as letters, résumés, and reports.

- **Excel 2003** is a spreadsheet application that is used to organize, analyze, and chart data.

- **Access 2003** is a database application that is used to generate forms, queries, and reports from the data it stores.

- **PowerPoint 2003** is a presentation application that is used to create professional-looking visuals.

What is a Windows Application?

TIP When purchasing software, a Windows application usually has the notation "for Windows" after the software name.

Windows applications are programs or software written by professional programmers to perform specific tasks and to run under the Windows operating system.

Most Windows applications have a similar interface. The *interface* of an application is the way it looks on the screen and the way in which the user provides input to the application. For example, the Word 2003 interface is called a *window* and looks similar to:

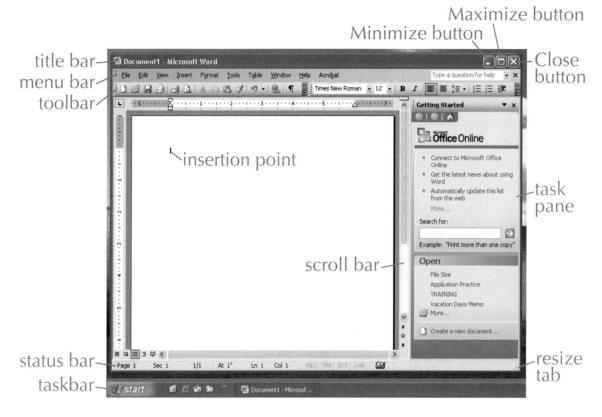

title bar
menu bar
toolbar

Minimize button
Maximize button
Close button

insertion point

task pane

scroll bar

status bar
taskbar

resize tab

- The file name and type of document are displayed in the **title bar**. In Microsoft Word, the name Document1 is used temporarily until the document is saved with a descriptive name. Drag the title bar to move a window.

- Select commands from menus in the **menu bar**.

- Click a button on the **toolbar** to perform an action.

- The vertical line is the **insertion point** that indicates where the next character typed will be placed.

- View information about the document in the **status bar**.

- Open applications and files are indicated on the **taskbar**.

- Drag the **resize tab** to size the window.

- Links based on the current user selection are displayed in the **task pane**.

- Drag the **scroll bar** to bring unseen parts of the document into view.

- Click the **Close button** (▣) to close the window.

- Click the **Maximize button** (▣) to expand the window to fill the screen.

- Click the **Restore button** (▣) to restore the window to its previous size. The Restore button is displayed instead of the Maximize button when a window has been maximized.

- Click the **Minimize button** (▬) to reduce the application window to a button on the taskbar.

Practice: Manipulating a Window

You will start the Microsoft Word 2003 application and manipulate the Word window.

① *START THE WORD 2003 WINDOWS APPLICATION*

Ask your instructor for the appropriate steps to start Microsoft Word 2003.

② *MANIPULATE THE WINDOW*

a. Look at the Word window. Locate the features of the window that are common to all Windows applications.

b. If the window is maximized, click the Restore button (⬒) to decrease the size of the window, otherwise click the Maximize button (⬜).

c. Click the Minimize button (▬) to reduce the Word window to a button on the taskbar.

d. On the taskbar, click [Document1 - Microso...] to again display the Word window.

③ *CLOSE THE WINDOW*

In the upper-right corner of the window, click the Close button (✖). The window is removed and the Word application is closed.

Keyboard Layout

Most keyboards use the QWERTY keyboard layout which was originally designed to prevent the keys from jamming on mechanical typewriter keyboards.

TIP The numeric keypad, located on the right-hand side of most keyboards, can make the entering of large amounts of numeric data more efficient. It also allows easy access to the mathematical operators +, −, *, and /. Most keyboards require pressing the Num Lock key on the numeric keypad before numbers can be entered.

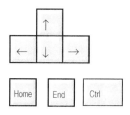

Entering Data

Data is entered into a Windows application using an input device. Examples of input devices include the keyboard, mouse, scanner, CD/DVD drive, and disk drive. On the keyboard, keys are used to type text and enter numeric data. A standard keyboard has a layout similar to:

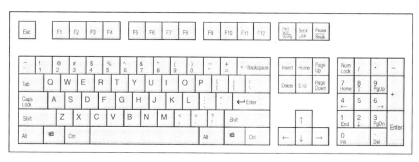

Typed text is placed at the insertion point. Press and hold the Shift key while pressing a character key to insert uppercase letters or the character shown above a number or symbol on a key.

Certain keys and key combinations can increase productivity:

* Press an <u>arrow key</u> to move the insertion point within existing text without erasing or entering text. Press and hold an arrow key to keep moving the insertion point in that direction.

* Press the <u>Home key</u> or <u>End key to</u> move the insertion point to the beginning or end of a line of text, respectively. <u>Ctrl+Home</u> moves the insertion point to the beginning of the document, Ctrl+End to the end.

- Press the Delete key to erase the character directly to the right of the insertion point.

- Press the Backspace key to erase the character directly to the left of the insertion point.

- Press the Esc (Escape) key to cancel (escape from) the current operation. The specific effect of the Esc key depends on the current operation.

- Press the Enter key to end a paragraph or to terminate a line of text. Press Enter twice to create a blank line after a paragraph.

- Press the Page Up or Page Down key to move a document in a window.

The mouse is an input device that is used to select commands and respond to application prompts. Sliding the mouse to move the pointer on the screen is called *pointing*. Point to an object on the screen and press the left mouse button and release it quickly to select an object. This type of selection is called *clicking*. The insertion point can also be positioned by clicking in a specific location in a document.

Double-clicking means to point to an object and press the left mouse button twice in rapid succession. *Right-clicking* means to point to an object and press and release the right mouse button quickly. A mouse may contain a *scroll wheel*, which can be rolled to scroll quickly through a document. Most handheld computers use a *stylus pen* to perform the same functions as a mouse.

Notebook Computers

Notebook computers may be equipped with a touchpad, trackball, or pointing stick instead of a separate mouse.

Optical Mouse

An optical mouse uses lasers to detect the movement of the mouse instead of mechanical sensors.

Using Menus and Toolbars

An application window contains menus and toolbars. Click a menu name to display a menu of commands:

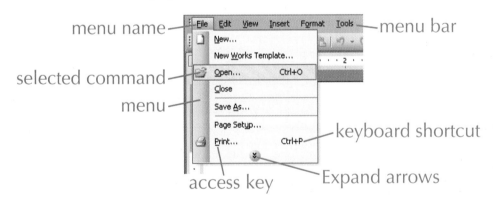

The Expand arrows (⊻) at the bottom of a menu indicate that there are more commands available. Point to the arrows to expand the menu and view additional commands. The commands in an unexpanded menu will vary because an unexpanded menu displays the most commonly used commands.

A command is executed by clicking it. A command can also be executed with a keyboard shortcut or keyboard accelerator. A *keyboard shortcut* is a sequence of keys that executes a command. For example, the keyboard shortcut for the Open command is Ctrl+O. Press and hold the Ctrl key while pressing the O key to execute the Open command. A *keyboard accelerator*

The → Symbol

In this text, the → symbol indicates the location of a command. For example, "select File → Open" means to select the File menu and then select the Open command from the File menu.

uses the Alt key and a series of access keys to execute a command. An *access key* is indicated by the underlined character in a command or menu name. For example, F is the access key for the File menu and O is the access key for the Open command. Press Alt, then press F, and then press O to execute the Open command.

Dimmed commands indicate that they cannot be selected at this time. To remove a menu from the screen, click outside the displayed menu or press the Esc key.

Toolbars contain buttons that represent different actions, such as saving a document. Click a button to perform an action. Point to a button to display a ScreenTip, which is the action that the button will perform:

If a toolbar displays a Toolbar Options button (⋮) at the far right, click this button to display more toolbar buttons. Toolbars may vary in appearance because the most frequently used buttons are displayed.

Dialog Boxes

In a menu, an ellipsis (…) after a command name indicates that a dialog box will appear when the command is selected. Some buttons also display a dialog box when clicked. A *dialog box* contains a series of options users select to communicate with an application:

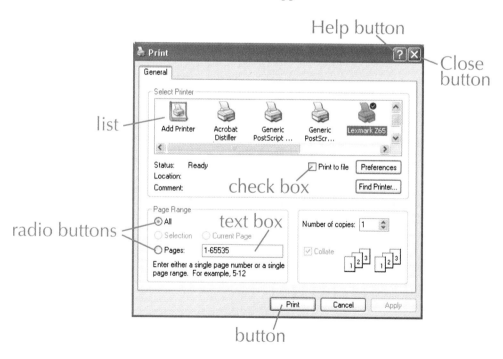

- Select text or icons from scrollable **lists**.
- Select a **radio button** to indicate a choice from a set of options.
- Click **check boxes** to select options.
- Enter values into a **text box**.

- Click a **button** to initiate an action.
- Click the **Help button** (⊙) to display information about dialog box elements.
- Click the **Close button** (✕) to remove a dialog box without applying any options. Select Cancel or press the Esc key to perform the same function.

The default button in a dialog box is displayed with a thicker border and can be selected by pressing the Enter key. In the dialog box on the previous page, Print is the default button.

Additional options that can be displayed in a dialog box include:

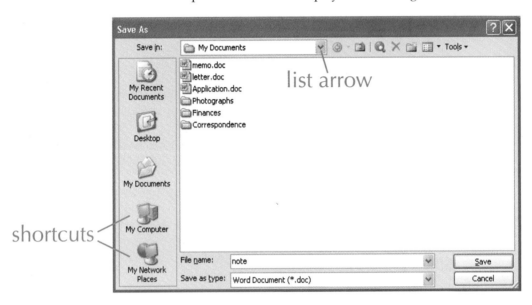

- Click the **list arrow** to display a list of items to choose from.
- Click a **shortcut** to perform an action. In the dialog box above, the shortcuts change a folder location.

Practice: Working with a Document – part 1 of 3

You will start the Word application, add text, display ScreenTips, and display a menu.

① **START WORD**

Maximize the Word window.

② **ENTER DATA**

a. Type the following without pressing the Enter key: The Office 2003 applications are considered business productivity tools because they give users the ability to process large amounts of data in a short time.

b. Press Home. The insertion point moves to the start of the line.

c. Press End. The insertion point moves to the end of the line.

d. Press ↵Enter to end the paragraph. Press ↵Enter again to create a blank line and then type your first and last name.

e. Press the appropriate arrow keys to move the insertion point to the left of the "O" in "Office."

f. Press ⌫ the appropriate number of times to delete the words "Office 2003" and the space that follows the words.

③ *DISPLAY SCREENTIPS*

a. On the toolbar, point to the left-most button. A ScreenTip is displayed. What action does this button perform?

b. On the toolbar, point to the various buttons and note the ScreenTips.

④ *DISPLAY A MENU*

a. On the menu bar, click File. The File menu is displayed. Note the commands in the menu.

b. In the File menu, which commands will display a dialog box when the command is selected?

c. What is the keyboard shortcut for the Print command?

d. Press the Esc key. The File menu is removed.

Storage Media

Files can be stored for later retrieval on various types of storage media, such as a disk, CD, DVD, hard disk, or Zip disk.

TIP A document should be saved often to prevent accidental loss due to factors such as a power interruption or network problem.

Saving Files

Once a document has been created in an application, it should be saved as a file. A *file* is a collection of related data stored on a lasting medium, such as a hard disk. A saved file can be loaded into memory for further editing at a later time.

A file must be given a name to identify it. A *file name* is a unique name for a file stored on disk. When a new document is created, a temporary generic file name, such as Document1 or Book1 is displayed in the title bar until the document is saved. Select File → Save or click the Save button (🖫) on the toolbar to save a document. The Save As dialog box is displayed the first time a file is saved:

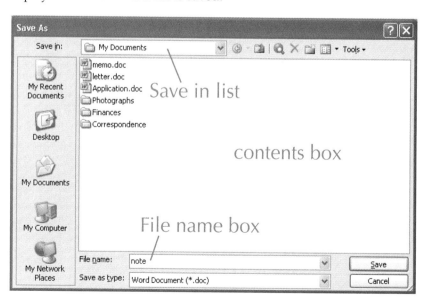

• The Save in list displays the location where the file will be saved. To change the location, click the Save in list arrow to display a list of available drive and folder locations. The shortcuts can also be used to change the folder location.

Creating a New Folder

Click the New Folder button (⬜) in the dialog box and then type a descriptive name for the folder.

File Name Extensions

Microsoft Office file name extensions include:

.doc Word document
.xls Excel workbook
.ppt PowerPoint presentation
.mdb Access database

- The contents box displays folders and files. *Folders* are used to organize commonly related files. Double-click a folder in the contents box to place that folder name in the Save in list and display the files and other folders in that folder.

- Windows applications automatically place a file name in the File name box. This file name should be changed to a name that is valid and descriptive of the file's contents. A valid file name can contain letters, numbers, spaces, and the underscore character (_), but cannot contain colons (:), asterisks (*), question marks (?), and some other special characters. Examples of valid, descriptive file names are Biology Paper, CHAPTER 5 EXERCISE, and Application Letter 2006 02 08.

Applications automatically add an extension to the file name when saved. An *extension* indicates what application the file was created in. For example, Word 2003 automatically adds the .doc extension to the file name.

Any changes made to a document after saving are not automatically stored in the file on disk. The file must be saved again, which *overwrites* the original file with the changed file.

Headers and Footers

Documents can be made more informative and organized by including text at the top and bottom of each page in areas called the *header* and *footer*. Headers and footers are often used to include the document title, chapter title, chapter number, student name, or a graphic, such as a company logo. Headers and footers can also include information that updates automatically, such as the current date. To add information to a header or footer, select View → Header and Footer, which displays header and footer areas where text is typed.

Printing a Document

TIP Select File → Print Preview before printing to display the document as it will appear when printed.

TIP Always save before printing.

To print a document, select File → Print, which displays the Print dialog box. In the Print dialog box, select Print to print one copy of the document. To print more than one copy of the document, type a number in the Number of copies box and then select Print. To print specific pages, select Pages and then type the appropriate page number or range of pages in the Pages box and then select Print.

The Print button (🖨) on the toolbar may also be used to print a document. However, clicking the Print button prints one copy of the document using the default settings without displaying the Print dialog box.

Closing a Document

When finished working on a document, it should be saved and then closed. *Closing a document* means that its window is removed from the Desktop and the file is no longer in the computer's memory. Select File → Close or click the Close button (☒) in the upper-right corner of the document window to close a document. A warning dialog box is displayed if the document has been modified since it was last saved.

Practice: Working with a Document – part 2 of 3

You will save, print, and close a document. Word should already be started with the document from the "Working with a Document — part 1 of 3" practice displayed.

① SAVE THE DOCUMENT

a. Select File → Save. The Save As dialog box is displayed. Note the Save in folder and files listed in the contents box will vary:

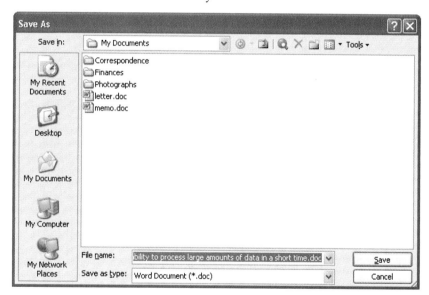

b. Use the Save in list and the contents box below it to select the appropriate location for the file to be saved.

Note: You may have to ask your instructor for instructions on navigating to the appropriate folder.

c. Windows applications automatically place a file name in the File name box, which should be replaced with a descriptive file name. In the File name box, type:
Application Practice

d. Select Save. The file is saved in the selected location with the name Application Practice. Note that the file name is now displayed in the title bar of the document window.

② *ADD A HEADER*

a. Select View → Header and Footer. The insertion point is placed in the Header area and the Header and Footer toolbar is displayed:

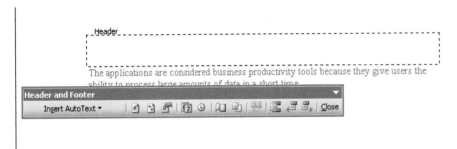

b. On the Header and Footer toolbar, click the Insert Date button (▣). The current date is displayed in the header.

c. On the Header and Footer toolbar, click Close.

③ *PRINT THE DOCUMENT*

a. Save the modified Application Practice.

b. Select File → Print. The Print dialog box is displayed. The appearance and options available in the Print dialog box will vary depending on the printer or printers connected to your workstation or network:

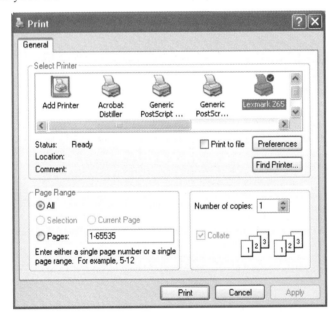

c. Select Pages and then type 1 in the Pages box. Set the Number of copies to 1, if it is not already.

d. Select Print. Page 1 of the document is printed.

④ *SAVE THE MODIFIED APPLICATION PRACTICE CLOSE THE DOCUMENT*

Quitting an Application

Quitting an application means that the application window is removed from the Desktop and the program is no longer in the computer's memory. To quit an application, select File → Exit or click the Close button in the upper-right corner of the application window.

Opening a File

Recently Used File List

Recently used files can be opened by selecting the file name from the File menu.

Opening a file transfers a copy of the file contents to the computer's memory and then displays it in a window. To open a file, select File → Open or click the Open button ( ) on the toolbar to display the Open dialog box. Use the Look in list and contents box to display the appropriate file. Click the appropriate file and then select Open to display the file in a window.

Practice: Working with a Document – part 3 of 3

You will open a file and quit an application. Word should already be started.

① *OPEN A DOCUMENT*

a. Select File → Open. The Open dialog box is displayed. The Look in folder and files listed in the contents box will vary:

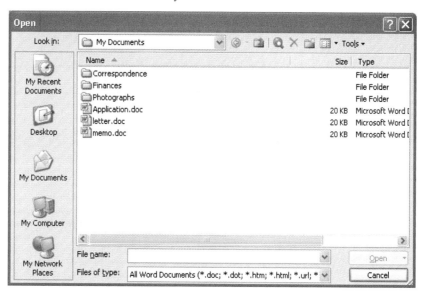

b. Use the Look in list and the contents box below it to display the file name Application Practice.

Note: You may have to ask your instructor for instructions on navigating to the appropriate folder.

c. In the contents box, click Application Practice and select Open. The Application Practice document is displayed in a window.

Multitasking

TIP When more than one document is open in an application, the **Window** menu can be used to switch between open documents.

Multitasking is an operating system feature that allows more than one application to run at a time. Any of the Microsoft Office applications can be running at the same time. For example, a report may require typing a document in a word processor application, creating charts in a spreadsheet application, and researching information using a Web browser application.

The taskbar displays buttons for each open file or application:

Click a button on the taskbar to either display or minimize the window containing the file or application.

Office applications allow a user to multitask within the application by allowing more than one document to be open within the application. For example, it is possible to have two or more Word documents open at the same time.

Practice: Multitasking and Viewing Files

You will multitask by working with two Word documents. You will also change the way files are viewed. Word should already be started with the Application Practice document displayed.

① CREATE A NEW DOCUMENT

a. On the toolbar, click the New Blank Document button (⬜). A new blank document is displayed. Note that the taskbar indicates there are two Word documents running.

b. On the taskbar, click [Application Practice - ...]. The Application Practice document is displayed.

c. On the taskbar, click the button for the new Word document. The new blank document is again displayed.

d. In the new blank document, type: When a document is saved as a file, the size of the file is measured in bytes. Files that consist of text and are relatively small can be measured in kilobytes (K), for example 128K. The K comes from the word kilo and represents 1,024 bytes. Larger files are measured in megabytes (MB), which represents 1,048,576 bytes.

e. Press Enter twice and type your first and last name.

② SAVE THE DOCUMENT

a. Select File → Save. The Save As dialog box is displayed.

1. Use the **Save in** list and the contents box below it to select the appropriate location for the file to be saved.

2. In the **File name** box, type: File Size

3. Select **Save**. The file is saved in the selected location with the name File Size. Note that the file name is now displayed in the title bar of the document window.

③ *CLOSE THE APPLICATION PRACTICE DOCUMENT*
   a. Use the taskbar to switch to the Application Practice document.
   b. Close the Application Practice document.

④ *CLOSE THE FILE SIZE DOCUMENT*

⑤ *OPEN THE FILE SIZE DOCUMENT*
   a. Select File → Open. The Open dialog box is displayed. If necessary, use the Save in list to navigate to the location where the File Size document is saved.
   b. Files can be viewed in different ways. In the Open dialog box, click the Views button arrow. A menu is displayed:

   1. Select Details. The file list in the contents box is displayed in Details view and the list now contains the file size, file type, and date modified. Scroll if necessary to view the file details.
   2. Select the other commands in the Views menu and note how the file list is displayed.
   3. In the Views menu, select Details.
   4. The sequence the files are displayed can be changed to make files easier to locate. At the top of the contents box, click the Name header:

   The folders and files are listed in descending alphabetical order.
   5. Click the Name header again. The folders are displayed in ascending alphabetic order, followed by the file names in ascending alphabetic order. How would this feature be helpful?
   6. Scroll if necessary to view the Date Modified header at the top of the contents box. Click the Date Modified header:

   The folders and files are displayed in chronological order. How would this feature be helpful?
   7. In the contents box, click File Size and select Open. The File Size document is displayed in a window.

⑥ *QUIT THE WORD APPLICATION*
   a. Close File Size.
   b. Select File → Exit.

Microsoft Office 2003 is a Windows application that consists of applications including Outlook, Word, Excel, Access, and PowerPoint. Most Windows applications have a similar interface.

Data is entered into an application using an input device, such as the keyboard, mouse, or scanner.

An application window contains menus and toolbars. Click a menu name to display a menu with a series of commands. Toolbars contain buttons that represent different actions, such as saving a document. A dialog box may be displayed when a command is selected. A dialog box contains a series of options users select to communicate with an application.

Once a document has been created in an application, it should be saved as a file and given a descriptive name. To save a document, select File → Save or click the Save button on the toolbar. Applications automatically add an extension to a file name. Folders are used to organize commonly related files.

To print a document, select File → Print or click the Print button on the toolbar.

Quitting an application means that the application window is removed from the Desktop and the program is no longer in the computer's memory. Opening a file transfers a copy of the file contents to the computer's memory and then displays it in a window. Closing a document means that its window is removed from the Desktop and the file is no longer in the computer's memory.

Multitasking is an operating system feature that allows more than one application to run at a time. The taskbar displays buttons that represent each open file or application.

Vocabulary

Access The Microsoft database application.

Access key A key that is indicated by the underlined character in a command or menu name.

Alt key Used to execute a keyboard accelerator.

Button An element in a dialog box that initiates an action when clicked.

Check box An element in a dialog box that allows the user to select options.

Clicking Selecting an object by pointing to it and pressing the left mouse button and releasing it quickly.

Closing a document Removing the document's window from the Desktop and the file from the computer's memory.

Double-clicking Pointing to an object and pressing the left mouse button twice in rapid succession.

Excel The Microsoft spreadsheet application.

Extension Added to a file name by an application to indicate what application the file was created in.

Field code A holding place for a piece of information in a header or footer that Word updates automatically.

File A collection of related data stored on a lasting medium, such as a hard disk.

File name A unique name for a file.

Folder Used to organize commonly related files.

Footer Text that appears at the bottom of every page in a document.

Header Text that appears at the top of every page in a document.

Insertion point A blinking vertical line in a document that indicates where the next character typed will be placed.

Interface The way an application looks on the screen and the way in which the user provides input to the application.

Keyboard accelerator A sequence of keys that executes a command.

List An element in a dialog box that displays a list of items to choose from.

Menu A list of commands.

Menu bar A horizontal bar that displays command names.

Microsoft Office A Windows application that consists of several applications, each designed to perform specific tasks.

Multitasking An operating system feature that allows more than one application to run at a time.

Opening a file Transfers a copy of the file contents to the computer's memory and then displays it in a window.

Outlook The Microsoft personal information manager and communications application.

Overwrites Replaces the original file with the changed file when changes are made to a document and it is saved again.

Pointing Sliding the mouse to move the pointer on the screen.

PowerPoint The Microsoft presentation application.

Quitting an application The application window is removed from the Desktop and the program is no longer in the computer's memory.

Radio button An element in a dialog box that allows the user to choose from a set of options.

Resize tab Dragged to size the window. Located in the bottom-right corner of the window.

Right-clicking Pointing to an object and pressing and releasing the right mouse button quickly.

Scroll bar Dragged to bring unseen parts of the document into view.

Scroll wheel A feature of a mouse that can be rolled to scroll quickly through a long document.

Shortcut Icon in a dialog box that performs an action.

Status bar Displays information about a document.

Stylus pen A device on a handheld computer that performs the same functions as a mouse. Also called a pen.

Task pane Displays varying links based on the current user selection. The pane is found on the right side of the window.

Taskbar Displays buttons that represent each open file or application.

Text box An element in a dialog box that allows the user to enter values.

Title bar A horizontal bar that displays the name and type of document.

Toolbar A horizontal bar that contains buttons that are clicked to perform an action.

Window The interface of a Windows application.

Windows application Programs or software written by professional programmers to perform specific tasks and run under the Windows operating system.

Word The Microsoft word processor application.

Close button Closes the document window dialog box or removes the application from the screen. Found in the upper-right corner of a window.

Exit **command** Used to quit an application. Found in the File menu. The Close button in the upper-right corner of the application window can be used instead of the command.

Expand arrows Indicates that there are more commands available in a menu. Found in the bottom of a menu.

Help button Displays information about the dialog box elements. Found in a dialog box.

Maximize button Expands the window to fill the screen. Found in the upper-right corner of a window.

Minimize button Reduces an application's window to a button on the taskbar. Found in the upper-right corner of a window.

Open **command** Displays a dialog box used to open an existing document. Found in the File menu. The Open button on the toolbar can be used instead of the command.

Print command Displays a dialog box used to print a document. Found in the File menu. The Print button on the toolbar can be used instead of the command.

Restore button Restores the window to its previous size. Found in the upper-right corner of a window.

Save **command** Saves a document. Found in the File menu. The Save button on the toolbar can be used instead of the command.

Toolbar Options button Displays more buttons in a toolbar. Found at the far right of a toolbar.

Views button arrow Displays a menu with commands that can be used to view files in different ways. Found on the dialog box toolbar.

1. a) What is a Windows application?
   b) What is the interface of a Windows application called?
   c) List three examples of Windows applications available on your computer.

2. a) List four features common to a Windows application.
   b) How is a window moved?
   c) What does the toolbar contain?
   d) What does the status bar display?
   e) What button is used to expand a window to fill the screen?

3. a) List three examples of input devices.
   b) List one example of an input device not mentioned in the text.

4. a) List the step required to insert an uppercase "k" at the insertion point.
   b) Which keyboard key is used to move the insertion point to the beginning of a line of text?
   c) Which keyboard key is used to erase the character directly to the left of the insertion point?
   d) Which key is pressed to end a paragraph?

5. a) List the step required to position the insertion point using the mouse.
   b) What is double-clicking?

6. List three ways to execute the Open command in the File menu.

7. a) What do the Expand arrows at the bottom of a menu indicate?
   b) When can certain menu commands not be selected?
   c) Which key is used to remove a menu from the screen?

8. a) List the step required to find out what action a button on the toolbar will perform?
   b) Why do toolbars sometimes vary in the buttons they contain?

9. a) What is a dialog box used for?
   b) What is a radio button?
   c) Which element in a dialog box initiates an action when clicked?

10. a) What is a file?
    b) What are folders used for?
    c) Can a valid file name contain spaces?
    d) What does the extension at the end of a file name indicate?

11. What is the difference between selecting the Print command and selecting the Print button on the toolbar?

12. What happens when a document is closed?

13. What happens when an application is quit?

14. What happens when a file is opened?

15. a) What is multitasking?
    b) List an example of a classroom assignment which would require multitasking.

16. What do the buttons on the taskbar represent?

True/False

17. Determine if each of the following are true or false. If false, explain why.
    a) Most Windows applications have a similar interface.
    b) The title bar displays the file name and type of document.
    c) Commands are selected from menus in the title bar.
    d) Press the End key to move the insertion point to the end of a line of text.
    e) Press the Alt key to cancel the current operation.
    f) The commands in an unexpanded menu will never vary.
    g) A dialog box may contain check boxes.
    h) Answer to History ? is an example of a valid, descriptive file name.
    i) Any changes made to a document after saving are automatically stored in the file on disk.
    j) A header is often used to include the document title, chapter title, or student name.
    k) A word processor application and a spreadsheet application can be running at the same time.
    l) Only one Word document can be opened at a time.

Exercise 1 ——————————————————————— Computer Lab

Research your classroom computer lab and workstation by typing the answers to a series of questions.

a) In a new Word document, type Class Computer Lab and Workstation and press Enter twice.

b) Type Microsoft Office Applications and press Enter.

c) Type the names of the Microsoft Office applications available from your computer workstation, pressing Enter after each application name.

d) Press Enter to leave a blank line, type Input Devices and press Enter.

e) Data is entered into a Windows application using an input device. Examples of input devices include the keyboard, mouse, scanner, CD/DVD drive, and disk drive. Type the input devices connected to your computer workstation, pressing Enter after each device.

f) Press Enter to leave a blank line, type Storage Media and press Enter.

g) Files can be stored for later retrieval on various types of storage media, such as a disk, CD/DVD, or Zip disk. Type the types of storage media you are able to save your files on, pressing Enter after each type of storage media.

h) Press Enter to leave a blank line, type Output Devices and press Enter.

i) Output devices display or store processed data. Monitors and printers are examples of display output devices. The CD-RW and disk drives are examples of output devices used for storing data. Type the output devices connected to your computer, pressing Enter after each device.

j) Press Enter to leave a blank line, type Printer and press Enter.

k) Common classifications of printers include laser and dot matrix. A laser printer uses a laser and toner to generate characters and graphics on paper. An ink jet printer uses an ink cartridge to place very small dots of ink onto paper to create characters and graphics. Classify the type of printer that is connected to your classroom computer lab.

l) Press Enter twice.

m) Type your first and last name.

n) Add a header with the current date.

o) Save the document naming it Computer Lab and print a copy.

Exercise 2 ————————————————————————Keyboard Shortcuts

A keyboard shortcut is a sequence of keys that executes a command. Using the keyboard shortcuts instead of a mouse can increase productivity because the hands do not have to leave the keyboard. Create a keyboard shortcut reference sheet by completing the following steps:

a) Create a new Word document.

b) Display the File menu. Expand the menu. Make a list of all the keyboard shortcuts and their corresponding command. Type File, press Enter and then type each command and its shortcut on a separate line. After the last command is typed, press Enter again to add a blank line.

c) Display the Edit menu. Expand the menu. Make a list of all the keyboard shortcuts and the corresponding command. Type Edit, press Enter and then type each command and its shortcut on a separate line. After the last command is typed, press Enter again to add a blank line.

d) Display the View menu. Expand the menu. Make a list of all the keyboard shortcuts and the corresponding command. Type View, press Enter and then type each command and its shortcut on a separate line. After the last command is typed, press Enter again to add a blank line.

e) Display the Insert menu. Expand the menu. Make a list of all the keyboard shortcuts and the corresponding command. Type Insert, press Enter and then type each command and its shortcut on a separate line. After the last command is typed, press Enter again to add a blank line.

f) Display the Format menu. Expand the menu. Make a list of all the keyboard shortcuts and the corresponding command. Type Format, press Enter and then type each command and its shortcut on a separate line. After the last command is typed, press Enter again to add a blank line.

g) Display the Tools menu. Expand the menu. Make a list of all the keyboard shortcuts and the corresponding command. Type Tools, press Enter and then type each command and its shortcut on a separate line. After the last command is typed, press Enter again to add a blank line.

h) Display the Help menu. Expand the menu. Make a list of all the keyboard accelerators and the corresponding command. Type Help, press Enter and then type each command and its shortcut on a separate line.

i) Save the document naming it Keyboard Shortcuts and print a copy.

Exercise 3

Dialog boxes are used to communicate with an application. Become familiar with dialog box elements by completing the following steps:

a) In new Word document, display the Open dialog box.

b) Identify the elements found in the Open dialog box.

c) Click Cancel to remove the dialog box without applying any options.

d) Display the Print dialog box.

e) The name of the default printer attached to the workstation or network is listed in the Printer Name box. What is the name of the default printer?

f) Some workstations and networks have more than one printer connected. If more than one printer is connected, they will be listed in the Printer Name list. Click the Name list and write the names of any other printers in the list.

g) What would be typed in the Pages box to print pages 5, 6, and 7 of the current document?

h) In the Print range section, is it possible to select more than one radio button?

i) Click Cancel to remove the dialog box without applying any options.

Exercise 4 ——————————————————————————— Passwords

It is important to keep your computer password a secret. Learn tips on password security by completing the following steps.

a) In a new Word document, type the title Computer Passwords and press Enter twice.

b) Type the following without pressing the Enter key: It is important to keep your password a secret so that other individuals cannot gain unauthorized access to your computer. Do not share your password with anyone and if you receive an e-mail requesting your password, even if it looks like it is from a legitimate source, do not provide the requested information.

c) Press Enter twice.

d) Type the following without pressing the Enter key: When selecting a password, do not select a password that is easy to guess. Passwords should also be changed frequently.

e) Press Enter twice and then type your first and last name.

f) Save the document naming it Passwords.

g) Close the file.

h) Open Passwords.

i) Add the current date in a header.

j) Save the modified Passwords and print a copy.

Exercise 5 ——————————————————————E-COMMERCE

E-commerce Web sites are created by businesses for the purpose of selling their products or services to consumers online. Learn more about e-commerce by completing the following exercise.

a) Open E-COMMERCE, which is a Word data file for this text. Read the document.

b) Press the Page Down key.

c) Press the Page Up key.

d) Position the insertion point at the start of the last paragraph, which starts "Wireless technology…"

e) Press the End key.

f) Press the Home key.

g) Position the insertion point after the period in the last sentence in the last paragraph.

h) Press Enter twice.

i) Type your first and last name.

j) Add a header with the current date.

k) Display the File menu using the appropriate access key.

l) Save the modified E-COMMERCE and print a copy.

m) Minimize the window to a button on the taskbar.

n) Maximize the E-COMMERCE window.

o) Close the document.

p) Quit the Word application.

Exercise 6 ——————————————————— Reflection Chapter 1

Reflect on what you have learned in this chapter by completing the following exercise.

a) In a new Word document, type three entries from the vocabulary list that you were previously unfamiliar with. Press Enter after each word.

b) Below the three vocabulary words, press Enter, type one property about menus and toolbars that you were previously unfamiliar with and then press Enter twice.

c) Type one property about dialog boxes that you were previously unfamiliar with and then press Enter twice.

d) Many users follow a consistent practice when naming files. For example, all documents for a club could begin with the club name, as in Computer Club May Newsletter. Explain one way you could be consistent in naming files and give an example. Press Enter twice after typing your explanation.

e) Which file view in the Open dialog box do you prefer? Why? Press Enter twice after typing your answer.

f) Type your first and last name.

g) Save the document naming it Reflection Chapter 1 and print a copy.

Chapter 2

Using a Communications Application

This chapter discusses the Internet Explorer Web browser and using Outlook to send e-mail.

What is the Web?

The *World Wide Web* is the total collection of Web pages that are stored on Web servers located all over the world. Schools, companies, and other organizations often have their own Web server. *Web servers*, which are computers that deliver Web pages, are also provided by Web hosting companies or *Web hosts*. Web authors post their Web sites to a Web server and the site becomes part of the World Wide Web. *Posting* is the process of copying Web site files to a Web server.

Web sites contain pages with information on a wide variety of topics. For example, the CNN Web site provides news about current events:

A Web page has similar features to a page you might see in a printed book or magazine, such as formatted text and colorful pictures. A Web page's purpose is the same as any printed material, which is to communicate with the reader. What makes a Web page so different from printed materials is that it can contain hyperlinks. A *hyperlink*, or *link*, is text or graphics on a Web page that can be clicked to display another portion of that same page or another Web page.

hyperlink, link

A series of related Web pages that are connected by hyperlinks make up a *Web site*. The main page is designated as the *home page* and is the starting point of the Web site. The home page usually contains links to the rest of the pages of the Web site.

Web site, home page

What is on the Web?

The Web offers access to a multitude of information, and most Web sites fall into one of the following categories: personal, commercial, informational, media, and portal:

- **Personal Web sites**, are created by individuals for the purpose of displaying information about themselves. A personal Web site might contain pages about the individual's hobbies, pets, family members, or links to their favorite Web sites.

- **Commercial Web sites** include *corporate presence Web sites*, which are created by companies and organizations for the purpose of displaying information about their products or services. It also includes *e-commerce Web sites*, which are created by businesses for the purpose of selling their products or services to consumers online.

- **Informational Web sites** are created for the purpose of displaying factual information about a particular topic and are often created by educational institutions, governments, and organizations.

- **Media Web sites** are online newspapers and periodicals that are created by companies for the purpose of informing readers about current events and issues.

- **Portal Web sites** are created by businesses for the purpose of creating a starting point for people to enter the Web. Portals contain hyperlinks to a wide range of topics, such as sport scores and top news stories, and most portals include access to a search engine.

Information found at a Web site, regardless of the category, should be evaluated for accuracy. Anyone can post a Web site on the Web. There are no rules as to the accuracy or reliability of the information. This means that you must discriminate, read carefully, and check sources.

A few topics to think about and questions to answer when evaluating a source are:

evaluating a source

- **Up-to-date**. On what date was the Web page last updated? Is the information current?

- **Bias**. Is the information incorrect or incomplete in order to give a particular or slanted view of a topic?

- **Validity**. Is the information truthful and trustworthy? What is the primary source of the information? Information posted by NASA or Yale University is more likely to be valid than information posted by a high school student who cites no sources.

Surfing the Net

"Surfing the net" means to browse Web pages looking for information on topics of interest. The phrase was coined in 1992 when a librarian named Jean Armour Polly used a mouse pad with a picture of a surfer on it.

Blog

Blog is short for Weblog and is a type of Web site where users can post entries in a journal format.

TIP The Web categories listed in the "What is on the Web?" section are very general and not all Web sites fall under exactly one category.

- **Author**. Does the author present his or her credentials? A well established authority in the field you are researching is probably a trustworthy source.

While the Internet and Web were originally developed to help the academic and scientific communities, the Web is being used more and more for advertising and e-commerce. It is common to find advertisements, called *banner ads*, on Web sites:

A banner ad is designed to entice a user to click it, which in turn displays the advertiser's page. Most Web sites host banner ads for a fee.

Web Browsers

Web page
HTML document

A *Web page* is a document created with <u>HyperText Markup Language</u> (HTML) and possibly other code, and published to a Web server. An *HTML document* defines the content and layout of a Web page with tags that are surrounded by angle brackets (<>). The following HTML document contains five different tags:

```
<html>

<head>
<title>Example HTML Document</title>
</head>

<body>
<p>This is an example HTML document.</p>
</body>

</html>
```

This HTML document contains <html>, <head>, <title>, <body>, and <p> tags

A *Web browser* interprets an HTML document to display a Web page. When the HTML document shown above is interpreted by the Web browser Internet Explorer, it is displayed as:

Note the text enclosed by the <title> tags of the HTML document is displayed on the title bar of the browser window. The text enclosed by the <body> tags is displayed as the Web page content.

TIP In Internet Explorer, select View → Source to view the HTML associated with the displayed Web page.

Types of Web Browsers

Internet Explorer is just one example of a Web browser. Other Web browsers include Netscape Navigator, Mozilla, Opera, and Lynx.

HTML documents are interpreted similarly regardless of the browser, but each browser has its own features and capabilities that can account for differences in the way a Web page is displayed.

URLs

TIP It is not usually necessary to type the http:// of a URL because the browser will automatically add it.

Every Web page has a URL (Uniform Resource Locator) associated with it. A *URL* is an address that is interpreted by a Web browser to identify the location of a page on the Web. For example, consider the URL for the Earth Day Network:

http://www.earthday.net — Domain Name

- **http** is the Web protocol used to handle requests and the transmission of pages between a Web server and a Web browser.

- **//** separates the protocol from the domain name.

- **www.earthday.net** is the domain name. A *domain name* identifies a particular Web page and is made up of a sequence of parts, or subnames, separated by a period. The *subnames* are called labels and may represent a server or organization. The suffix of a domain name is called the *top-level domain* and identifies the type of Web site. In this case .net indicates the site is a network organization.

Top-level Domains

Top-level domains include:
.gov - government agency
.edu - educational institution
.org - non profit organization
.com - commercial business

Each country also as a 2 character top-level domain, such as .uk - United Kingdom.

Internet Explorer

A Web browser, such as Internet Explorer, is needed to view Web pages. Starting Internet Explorer displays a browser window:

title bar
menu bar
toolbar
Address bar

- The Web page title and name of browser are displayed in the **title bar**.

- Select commands from menus in the **menu bar**.

- Click a button on the **toolbar** to perform an action.

- Click the **Back button** to display the previously displayed Web page.

- Click the **Forward button** to display the next Web page from the previously selected pages.

Home Page

To change the home page that appears when Internet Explorer is started, select **Tools → Internet Options**, select the **General** tab, and then specify a URL in the **Address** box.

Research Task Pane

The Research button (![icon]) displays the Research task pane, which can be used to look up definitions, synonyms, encyclopedia articles, and to translate words. The Research task pane is discussed further in Chapter 4.

TIP To replace the existing URL in the Address bar, highlight the URL and then type the new URL.

TIP In Internet Explorer, typing the name of a Web site and then pressing Ctrl+Enter automatically adds www. and .com to the Web site name.

- ![icon] Click the **Stop button** to stop the transmission of a Web page.
- ![icon] Click the **Refresh button** to update the displayed Web page.
- ![icon] Click the **Home button** to display a preselected Web page, which is the Web page that is displayed when Internet Explorer is first started.
- ![icon] Search Click the **Search button** to display a pane used to locate Web pages that contain particular information.
- ![icon] Favorites Click the **Favorites button** to display the *Favorites list*, which is used to maintain a list of Web pages.
- ![icon] Media Click the **Media button** to display the Media bar, which can be used to listen to media files and Internet radio stations.
- ![icon] Click the **History button** to display the *History list*, which lists the URLs of Web sites that have been visited in the previous days and weeks.
- ![icon] Click the **Print button** to print the currently displayed Web page(s).
- Type a URL in the **Address bar** and then press Enter or click the **Go button** (![icon] Go) to open a Web page. Select a previously typed URL from the Address bar list.
- Drag the **scroll bar** to bring unseen parts of the document into view.
- View the progress of a loading Web page in the **status bar**.

Practice: Using Internet Explorer – part 1 of 2

You will view Web pages and use the features of Internet Explorer. This practice requires Internet access.

① *START INTERNET EXPLORER*

    a. Ask your instructor for the appropriate steps to start Internet Explorer. The preselected home page is displayed.

    b. Maximize the window.

    c. What is the URL of the home page?

② *GO TO THE MSNBC HOME PAGE*

    a. In the Address bar, replace the existing URL with www.msnbc.com, the URL for the MSNBC home page.

    b. Press Enter. The Web page is opened.

    c. Use the scroll bar to scroll through the home page.

    d. What is displayed in the title bar?

③ *VIEW MSNBC STORIES*

    a. Click a hyperlink that interests you.

    b. Continue to surf MSNBC Web pages. Realize that a hyperlink may display a Web page at a site other than MSNBC. To return to the MSNBC site, click ![icon] Back ▾ on the toolbar.

    c. Which Web site category would the MSNBC Web site fall into?

④ *GO TO THE CNN HOME PAGE*

    a. In the Address bar, replace the existing URL with www.cnn.com, the URL for the CNN home page.

    b. Press Enter. The Web page is opened. Use the scroll bar to scroll through the CNN home page.

    c. Which Web site category would the CNN Web site fall into?

⑤ *GO TO THE FLORIDA ATLANTIC UNIVERSITY HOME PAGE*

    a. In the Address bar, replace the existing URL with www.fau.edu, the URL for the Florida Atlantic University home page.

    b. Press Enter. The Web page is opened. Use the scroll bar if necessary to scroll through the Florida Atlantic University home page.

    c. Which Web site category would this Web site fall into?

⑥ *USE THE HISTORY LIST TO ACCESS WEB PAGES*

    a. On the toolbar, click the History button (⊘). The History pane is displayed on the left side of the window.

    b. Point to the History pane border to display a double-headed arrow (↔) and then drag the pane to size the History pane so that it is a little wider.

    c. The View button in the History pane can be used to specify how the History list is displayed. In the History pane, click the View button and then select By Order Visited Today:

    d. Click CNN.com. The CNN home page is displayed.

    e. In the History pane, click the View button and then select By Date.

    f. Click the Today folder (🖿 Today) if the Today folder is not expanded. In the Today folder, note that a folder is displayed for each of the sites visited today.

    g. Click the fau folder:

    The title of the home page is displayed as a hyperlink to the home page. Click the link to display the Florida Atlantic University home page.

    h. A pane, such as the History pane, will be displayed in the left side of the window until closed. Click the Close button (✕) in the top-right corner of the History pane. The History pane is closed and the Web page in the right pane is expanded to fill the space.

⑦ *GO TO THE GAP HOME PAGE*

    a. In the Address bar, replace the existing URL with www.gap.com, the URL for the Gap home page.

    b. Press Enter. The Web page is opened. Use the scroll bar if necessary to scroll through the Gap's home page.

⑧ ADD A WEB PAGE TO THE FAVORITES LIST

a. On the toolbar, click ⭐ Favorites . The Favorites pane is displayed in the left side of the window. The Favorites pane contains the *Favorites list*, which is used to maintain a list of Web pages. Selecting any of the Web pages in the list will access that page and display it in the pane in the right side of the window.

b. What pages are displayed in your Favorites list?

c. A Favorites list can be organized using folders. In the Favorites pane, click 📑 Add... . The Add Favorites dialog box is displayed:

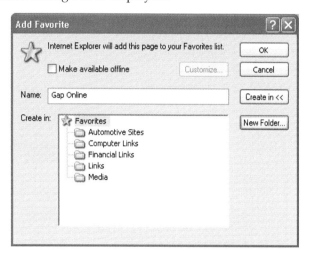

1. Click New Folder... . (If the New Folder button is not displayed, click Create in >> .) The Create New Folder dialog box is displayed:

2. In the Folder name box, type: Shopping Sites

3. Select OK. The dialog box is removed.

4. Select OK. The dialog box is removed and the current page is added to the Shopping Sites folder in the Favorites list.

⑨ GO TO ANOTHER WEB PAGE

a. In the Address bar, replace the existing URL with www.roots.com, the URL for the Roots home page.

b. Press Enter. The Web page is opened.

⑩ *RETURN TO A FAVORITE WEB PAGE*

    a. In the Favorites pane, click the Shopping Sites folder to display the page that was added:

    b. Click the link for Gap Online. The selected page is displayed in the right pane.

⑪ *DELETE A FOLDER FROM THE FAVORITES LIST*

    The Organize button in the Favorites pane is used to display a dialog box where folders can be created and renamed, moved, or deleted. The URLs can also be renamed, moved, or deleted.

    a. In the Favorites pane, click ⬚ Organize... . The Organize Favorites dialog box is displayed.

    b. Click the Shopping Sites folder to select it:

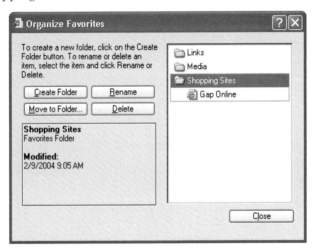

    c. Select ⬚ Delete . A warning is displayed. Select Yes to delete the folder and its contents.

    d. Select ⬚ Close . The dialog box is removed.

⑫ *CLOSE THE FAVORITES PANE*

Printing a Web Page

Web pages do not always print on a single sheet of paper. Therefore, it is important to preview a Web page before printing to avoid printing unwanted pages. Select File → Print Preview to display the Print Preview window, which indicates the number of pages that will be printed. Click the Page Setup button (🖼) on the Print Preview window toolbar to add a header and footer to the Web page printout. Click Print... to display the Print dialog box. Options in the Print dialog box can then be used to specify which pages should be printed.

Header and Footer Codes

Header and footer codes include &d to display the current date, &u to display the page address, &w to display the Web page title, &t to display the current time, &p to display the page number, &P to display the total number of pages, and &b to right-align text.

You will preview and then print a Web page. You will also add your name to the printout. Internet Explorer should already be started.

① PRINT A WEB PAGE

a. In the Address bar, replace the existing URL with www.earthday.net, the URL for the Earth Day Network home page. Press Enter.

b. Select File → Print Preview to display the Earth Day Network page as it will appear when printed. The Print Preview window is displayed:

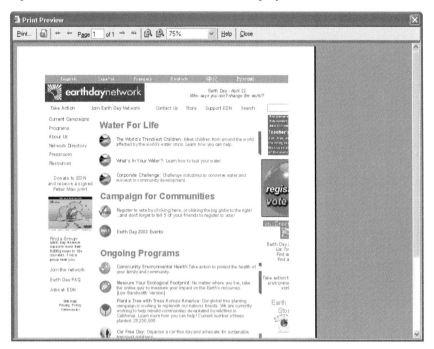

1. How many pages will be printed?

2. Click 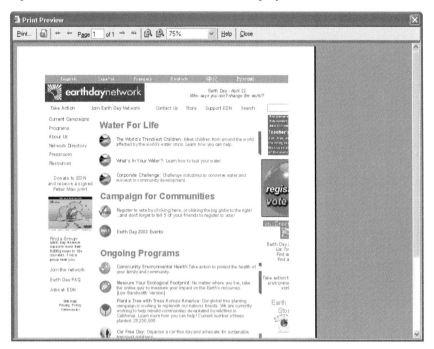. The magnification of the document is viewed at is increased.

3. Click 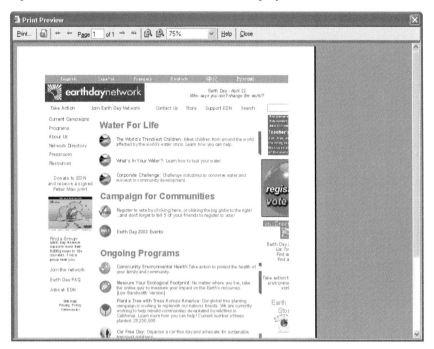. The magnification of the document is viewed at is decreased.

4. It is important to add your name to a Web page printout especially if you are printing to a network printer. Select the Page Setup button ( ) on the Print Preview toolbar. The Page Setup dialog box is displayed.

5. Internet Explorer automatically places codes in the Header and Footer boxes. In the Footer box, replace the existing codes with your first and last name:

6. Select OK. The dialog box is removed.
7. In the Print Preview window, scroll to the bottom of the page and notice your name displayed as a footer in the bottom-left corner of the page.
8. On the Print Preview toolbar, click Print... . A dialog box is displayed.

   a. Select Print to accept the default print settings. The Web page is printed.

   b. Refer to the printout and the "Header and Footer Codes" sidebar to determine the meaning of the four codes in the Header box.

Searching the Web

Search Engines

A search engine usually works by sending out an agent, such as spider. A spider is an application that gathers a list of available Web page documents and stores this list in a database that users can search by keywords.

When displaying information, search engines often show "Sponsored Sites Results" first. These are sites that contain the information being searched for but have paid the search engine to list their sites at the top of the list.

A *search engine* is a program that searches a database of Web pages for keywords and then lists hyperlinks to these pages that contain the keywords. Commonly used search engines include:

Yahoo! (www.yahoo.com)
Google (www.google.com)
MSN (www.msn.com)
AOL (www.aol.com)
Excite (www.excite.com)
Ask Jeeves (www.ask.com)
Overture (www.overture.com)
Lycos (www.lycos.com)
WebCrawler (www.webcrawler.com)
FAST Search (www.alltheweb.com)
About.com (www.about.com)
AltaVista (www.altavista.com)
Looksmart (www.looksmart.com)

search criteria

match

Search engines are queried by entering *search criteria*, which can include single words or phrases that are then used by the engine to determine a match. A *match* is a Web page that contains the search criteria. Surrounding phrases with quotation marks finds Web pages that contain the entire phrase. The more specific the search criteria, the better the chance the information will be found.

Most searches yield far too many matches to be useful. Limiting the number of matches to a reasonable number can usually be accomplished by using Boolean logic in the search criteria:

- The + (plus sign) is used in search criteria to limit a search to only Web pages that contain all of the specified words. For example, a search for florida +hotel or florida hotel returns only links to pages containing both words. AND can be used in place of + in most search engines.

- OR can be used in most search engines to find Web pages that contain any one of the words in the criteria. For example, the criteria florida OR hotel returns links to pages containing either of the words.

- The – (minus sign) is used to exclude unwanted Web pages. For example, the search for shakespeare –play returns hyperlinks to pages containing the word shakespeare, but eliminates pages that also contain the word play. NOT can be used in place of – in most search engines.

Boolean Logic

Boolean logic uses three logical operators:

AND   locates pages that include both words

OR locates pages that include one word or the other or both

NOT   locates pages that include the first word, but not the second word

A boolean expression always evaluates to TRUE or FALSE with pages that match the search condition evaluating to TRUE.

Practice: Searching the Web – part 1 of 2

You will search the Web using a search engine. Internet Explorer should already be started.

① *GO TO THE YAHOO! SEARCH ENGINE*

In the Address bar, replace the existing URL with www.yahoo.com, the URL for Yahoo!'s home page, and then press Enter. The Yahoo! home page is displayed.

② *TYPE SEARCH CRITERIA*

a. In the Search text box, type: shakespeare

b. Click Yahoo! Search to start the search. After a few moments a list of Web site hyperlinks are displayed. How many Web Results matches are there?

c. Scroll down to display the results of the search, then click one of the hyperlinks that interests you. A new page is opened.

③ *SELECT OTHER WEB PAGES LOCATED IN THE SEARCH*

a. On the toolbar, click ⦿ Back ▾ . The Web site hyperlinks are again displayed. Click a different Web page hyperlink.

b. Continue this process to access additional pages.

④ *DEFINE CRITERIA USING BOOLEAN OPERATORS*

a. Refine the search criteria to: shakespeare OR "Globe Theatre" and see how many Web page matches there are.

b. Refine the search criteria to: shakespeare +"Globe Theatre" and see how many Web page matches there are. Note that there is no space after the + sign.

c. Further refine the criteria to: shakespeare +"Globe Theatre" +reconstruction –usa and see how many Web page matches there are.

d. Click a few of the hyperlinks to determine if their Web pages include the information that is being searched for.

Searching by Category

Some search engines provide a *subject tree*, or *Web directory*, which is a list of sites separated into categories. The term subject tree is used because many of the categories "branch" off into subcategories. These subcategories allow the user to narrow down the subject and display a list of appropriate hyperlinks, which are at the lowest level of the tree.

Practice: Searching the Web – part 2 of 2

You will search the Web using Google's subject tree. Internet Explorer should already be started.

① *GO TO THE GOOGLE SEARCH ENGINE*

a. In the Address bar, replace the existing URL with www.google.com, the URL for Google's home page, and then press Enter. The Google home page is displayed.

b. Click the Directory link. The Google Directory page is displayed.

② *FIND A SOFTWARE RETAILER USING A SUBJECT TREE*

a. Scroll down if necessary and click the <u>Computers</u> link in the list of Google Directory categories. Links to Computers subcategories are displayed.

b. Scroll down if necessary and click the <u>Shopping</u> link.

c. In the Computer Shopping subcategories list, click the <u>Software Retailers</u> link. A list of hyperlinks to appropriate sites is displayed.

d. Click one of the hyperlinks. The corresponding home page is displayed.

Citing Web Pages

If information from a Web site is to be referenced or quoted in a report, essay, or other document, a citation must be used to give credit to the original author and allow the reader to locate the cited information. A widely accepted form for citation is published by the Modern Language Association (MLA) in its publication *MLA Handbook for Writers of Research Papers, Fourth Edition*.

In general, a citation for material located at a Web site should look similar to:

Author's Last Name, First Name MI. Site Title. Access date. Organization name. <URL>.

Citing Online Sources

Online sources of information that are used to support research must be cited. This includes e-mail messages, graphics, sounds, video clips, and newsgroups. The MLA's Web site (www.mla.org) contains information on how to cite online sources.

A citation of a personal Web site could look similar to:

> Rawlings, Julie. Home page. 23 Dec. 2006. <http://www.lpdatafiles.com/jrawlings/index.htm>.

A citation of an article in an online magazine could look similar to:

> Schiffman, Paula. "Making Vinegar at Home." Vinegar Monthly. 4 May 2006. <http://www.lpdatafiles.com/vinegarassoc/journal.asp>.

A citation of a posting to a discussion list could look similar to:

> Cruz, Anthony. "Are Orchestras Going Downhill?" online posting. 10 Oct. 2006. Tuscon Annual Ballet Conf. <http://www.lpdatafiles.com/tuscontoes/downhill.txt>.

Practice: Citing a Web Site

In this practice you will cite a Web page. Internet Explorer should already be started.

① *SEARCH FOR INFORMATION*

Use one of the search engines listed in the "Searching the Web" section to search for Web pages about the Egyptian Step Pyramid of Djoser.

② *EVALUATE WEB SITES*

Browse the links to find a Web page that contains reliable information. Refer to the "What is on the Web?" section for a few topics to think about and questions to answer when evaluating a source.

③ *CITE THE WEB PAGE*

Use the information on the Web page to write an example citation.

What is E-mail?

E-mail means electronic mail and is the sending and receiving of messages and computer files over a communications network such as a LAN (Local Area Network) or the Internet. An e-mail address is required in order to send and receive e-mail messages. E-mail addresses are provided when you sign up with an ISP or an online service. A typical e-mail address is similar to:

christina@lpdatafiles.com

user name   host or domain name   top-level domain

E-mail software is also required for sending and receiving e-mail messages. Examples of e-mail software include Outlook, Outlook Express and Eudora. Free e-mail accounts, known as *browser-based e-mail*, are also available through numerous sites such as Yahoo! and Hotmail. These accounts require only a Web browser such as Internet Explorer.

E-mail Protocols

POP3 is an e-mail protocol that connects to an e-mail server to download messages to a local computer.

IMAP is an e-mail protocol that connects to an e-mail server to read message headers and then the user selects which e-mail messages to download to a local computer.

HTTP is used as an e-mail protocol when a Web page is used to access an e-mail account.

Using Outlook to Send E-mail

Microsoft Outlook is a personal information manager application that has tools for organizing appointments, listing tasks, and managing e-mail messages. Organizing appointments and listing tasks are discussed in Chapter 3.

Outlook Today is displayed when Outlook is started:

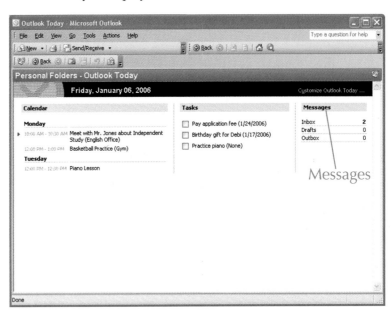

Outlook Today

If Outlook Today is not displayed when Outlook is started, click the Outlook Today button (📋) on the Advanced toolbar. Display the Advanced toolbar by selecting View → Toolbars → Advanced.

TIP Outlook is also accessible by clicking the Mail button (📧) on the Internet Explorer toolbar.

The Outlook Today window displays a summary of e-mail messages under the Messages title. Click the Messages title to display the Inbox window:

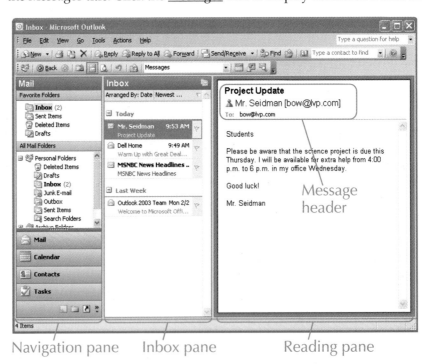

Navigation pane   Inbox pane   Reading pane

Mail Formats

Outlook can send and receive e-mail messages in HTML, plain text, and Outlook Rich Text format.

HTML is the default and recommended format because it is used by most e-mail programs. Plain text format is understood by most e-mail software, but it does not support formatting, such as bold. Outlook Rich Text Format is a Microsoft format that supports numerous formatting options, but is only understood by certain e-mail programs.

Select Tools → Options and then select the Mail Format tab to change the mail format.

The *Inbox window* contains three panes. The pane on the left is the Navigation pane. The *Navigation pane* lists e-mail folders where e-mail messages are stored and contains links to other Outlook tools which are

TIP To preview the first three lines of each message in the Inbox, select View → AutoPreview.

TIP Select Tools → Spelling and Grammar to check spelling before sending a message.

discussed in Chapter 3. The *Inbox pane* displays the e-mail messages stored in the Inbox folder arranged by date. The *Reading pane* displays the selected message. The selected message is displayed with a *Message header*, which contains the subject of the message, the recipients, and the sender.

To create a new e-mail message, click New on the toolbar or select File → New → Mail Message. A Message form for composing an e-mail message is displayed. Type the e-mail address of the recipient in the To box. If an e-mail message is to be sent to more than one individual, separate e-mail addresses with a semi-colon (;). In the Cc box, type the e-mail address of recipients that are receiving a copy of the e-mail message. In the Subject box, type a title that is descriptive of the message contents. Compose the message in the Message body and click Send to send the message.

Practice: E-mail Messages – part 1 of 3

You will send an e-mail message. This practice requires Internet access and an e-mail account.

① *START OUTLOOK AND DISPLAY THE INBOX WINDOW*

   a. Ask your instructor for the appropriate steps to start Outlook and display Outlook Today.

   b. Click the <u>Messages</u> link. The Inbox window is displayed.

② *CREATE AN E-MAIL MESSAGE*

   a. Click New on the toolbar. A Message form is displayed. Complete the Subject box and type the message as shown:

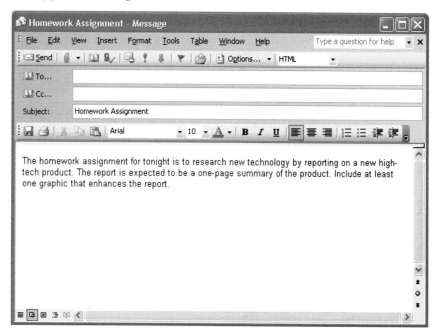

   b. Exchange e-mail addresses with a partner. Type your partner's e-mail address in the To box.

   c. On the Message toolbar, click Send. The e-mail message is sent.

③ RECEIVE AND PRINT AN E-MAIL MESSAGE

a. When an e-mail message is sent, it resides in an electronic mailbox on an e-mail server until it is retrieved. On the toolbar, click ⌸ Send/Receive ▾. Messages are received from the e-mail server and placed in the Inbox.

b. In the Inbox, select the message from your partner. The message is displayed in the Reading pane.

c. On the toolbar, click the Print button (🖨). The e-mail message is printed.

④ REPLY TO AN E-MAIL MESSAGE

a. The Reply button is used to respond to an e-mail message so that the recipient can refer to the original message. On the toolbar, click 📧 Reply. A Reply Message form is displayed with the original message and the sender's e-mail address in the To box. Note that the prefix "RE:" has been added to the start of the subject line.

b. In the Message body, type: Thank you for sending me the homework assignment. I think I will research Smartphones.

c. Click ⌸ Send.

⑤ FORWARD AN E-MAIL MESSAGE

a. The Forward button is used to send a selected e-mail message to another e-mail address. On the toolbar, click 📧 Forward. A Forward Message form is displayed with the original e-mail message and the original sender's e-mail address. Note that "FW:" has been added to the start of the subject line.

b. In the To box, type the e-mail address of another student in the class.

c. In the Message body, type: Hi, I am forwarding the homework assignment.

d. Click ⌸ Send.

The Address Book

The *Address Book* is an Outlook tool that stores contact names and e-mail addresses. The Address Book is updated automatically as contacts are added to the Outlook Contacts tool, which is discussed in Chapter 3.

Click the Address Book button (📖) on the toolbar to view entries in the Address Book:

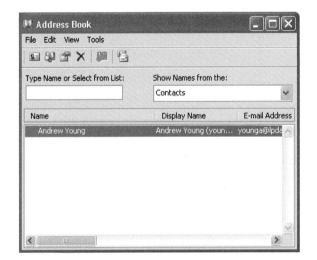

Distribution List

A distribution list consists of a group of related contacts, such as the Photography Club Members. A distribution list can be used to send messages to a group of people.

To create a distribution list in Outlook, select File → New → Distribution List and then select members for the distribution list from the displayed Address Book.

Click the New Entry button (▣) to display a Contact form. Contact information can then be typed in the appropriate fields. Click 🖫 Save and Close to save the contact information in the Address Book.

Contacts in the Address Book are automatically recognized by Outlook. As an e-mail address is typed in the To or Cc box of a message form, Outlook displays the complete address using the Address Book. Press Tab to insert the entry. An e-mail address can also be selected from the Address Book by clicking ☐ To... ☐ or ☐ Cc... ☐ in the Message form.

E-mail Attachments

E-mail provides a way to quickly send a file. The Insert File button (🖉) on the Message form toolbar displays a dialog box where an *attachment file* is selected. Files can be attached to messages in their *native format*, which is the original form the file was saved in. However, the recipient must have the software the file was created in or a compatible software application that can convert the file in order to view the attachment. To avoid problems with viewing attachments, files can be sent in text format, which most users can view, or PDF format, which requires Adobe Reader, a free application from Adobe Systems that most users have.

Practice: E-mail Messages – part 2 of 3

You will add an entry to the Address Book and select a contact from the Address Book. Outlook should already be started.

① *ADD AN ENTRY TO THE ADDRESS BOOK*

    a. On the toolbar, click the Address Book button (▣). The Address Book is displayed.

        1. On the Address Book toolbar, click the New Entry button (▣). Another dialog box is displayed:

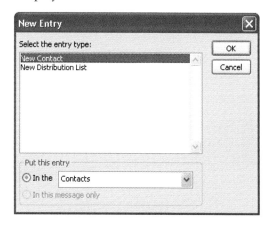

        2. In the Select the entry type box, select New Contact and then select OK. A Contact form is displayed.

        3. Complete the Full Name box and E-mail box entries as shown on the next page. Note that Outlook automatically creates an entry for the File as box:

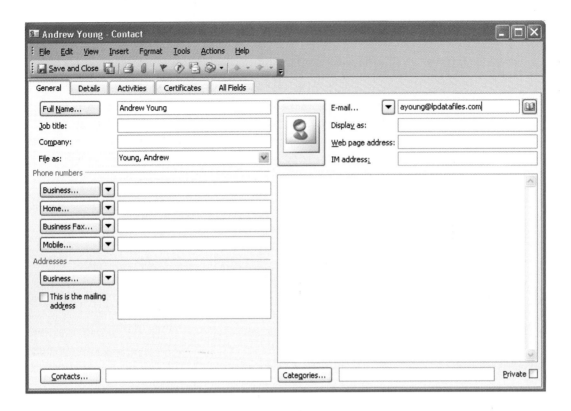

4. Click Save and Close . The Contact form is removed and the contact appears in the Address Book.

5. Close the Address Book.

② *CREATE AN E-MAIL MESSAGE AND ADD AN ATTACHMENT*

a. On the toolbar, click New ▾ . A Message form is displayed.

b. Click To... . A dialog box is displayed:

1. In the Name list, select Andrew Young and then click OK. The dialog box is removed and Andrew Young's e-mail address is placed in the To box.

c. In the Subject box, type: My Assignment

d. In the Message body, type: Here is a copy of my homework assignment. Can you proofread it for me? Thank you.

e. On the Message form toolbar, click the Insert File button (📎). A dialog box is displayed.

    1. Use the Look in list and contents box to select HOMEWORK, which is a data file for this text.

    2. Select Insert. The file is attached to the message.

    3. The file size of the attachment is displayed to the right of the file name. What is the file size of the HOMEWORK file?

f. Click 📨 Send .

Adding a Signature to E-mail Messages

vCards

vCards are the Internet standard for creating and sharing business cards.

E-mail messages often contain similar text. For example, the sender's name, title, and company name. A user can compose e-mail messages faster when text that would be typed over and over again is stored as a named signature. A *named signature* is saved in Outlook and then inserted, rather than typed, saving time and avoiding typing errors. A *signature* is simply text. More than one signature can be created for different audiences, such as a business signature and a personal signature.

Practice: Creating an E-mail Signature

You will create a named signature. Outlook should already be started.

① *CREATE A NAMED SIGNATURE*

a. Select Tools → Options. A dialog box is displayed.

    1. Select the Mail Format tab to display those options:

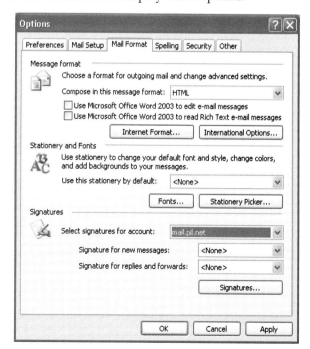

2. Select Signatures. The Create Signature dialog box is displayed.

3. Select New. The Create New Signature dialog box is displayed:

4. In the Enter a name for your new signature box, type your first and last name.

5. Select the Start with a blank signature option if it is not already selected.

6. Select Next. The Edit Signature dialog box is displayed:

7. In the Signature text box, type your first and last name. Note that if this was a business signature, information such as a job title, name of the business, contact number, and e-mail address could be typed as well.

8. Select Finish. The signature is added to Outlook and displayed in the Preview box.

9. Select OK. The dialog box is removed.

10. Select OK. The dialog box is removed. The signature will be automatically added to any outgoing e-mail messages.

Organizing E-mail Messages

Related e-mail messages should be organized into folders. The folder list is displayed in the Navigation pane. Outlook automatically creates some folders and rules that direct specific e-mail messages to the appropriate folders:

- **Inbox** folder stores received messages.

- **Sent Items** folder stores messages that have been sent.

- **Deleted Items** folder stores messages that have been deleted until they are permanently deleted or retrieved. Messages stored in the Deleted Items folder are permanently deleted by right-clicking the Deleted Items folder and selecting Empty "Deleted Items" Folder from the displayed menu. Messages can be retrieved from this folder by dragging the appropriate message to another folder.

- **Drafts** folder stores unfinished messages that have been automatically saved by Outlook because they have been left open for a period of time.

- **Outbox** folder stores messages that have been created offline until they are sent.

The Inbox arranges e-mail messages by date. This arrangement can be changed to display e-mail messages alphabetically by sender, by recipient, or by subject. Changing the arrangement may help locate a message. However, related e-mail messages in the Inbox should be organized into folders with descriptive names to avoid an Inbox full of unrelated messages and to make it easy to locate messages.

Messages can also be searched for using the Find feature. On the toolbar, click [Find] to display the Find pane:

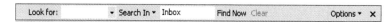

Type criteria, such as a word, a sender name, or a date in the Look for box, and then click Find Now.

Favorite Folders

E-mail folders that are frequently used are displayed in the Favorite Folders list. To move a folder to the Favorites list, drag the folder in from the All Mail Folders list.

Rules

Rules help manage e-mail messages by automatically performing an action based on a condition. For example, move all messages from Susan Thompson to the Sales folder. To create a rule, select Tools → Rules and Alerts.

Flagging Messages

Right-click a message and select Follow Up from the displayed menu to add a colored flag and/or reminder to a message.

Practice: E-mail Messages – part 3 of 3

You will organize e-mail messages. Outlook should already be started.

① *CHANGE ARRANGEMENT OF INBOX MESSAGES*

    a. Display the Inbox window if it is not already showing.

    b. At the top of the Inbox pane, click `Arranged By: Date`. A menu is displayed:

c. In the menu, select **From**. Scroll to view all of the messages. Note that the e-mail messages are arranged in alphabetic order by the sender's name.

d. Arrange the messages by **Subject**.

e. Arrange the messages by **Date**.

② *CREATE A NEW FOLDER*

a. Select **Tools → Organize**. The Ways to Organize Inbox pane is displayed:

b. Select New Folder... . A dialog box is displayed:

c. In the Name box, type Homework:

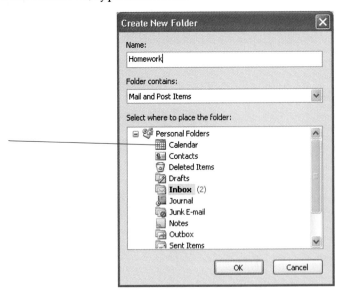

d. Select **OK**. The new folder is created and displayed in the All Mail Folders List.

③ *MOVE A FOLDER TO THE FAVORITE FOLDERS LIST*

Drag the Homework folder to the Favorite Folders pane. A copy of the Homework folder is placed in the Favorite Folders list for easy access.

④ *SEARCH FOR A MESSAGE AND MOVE A MESSAGE TO A FOLDER*

a. On the toolbar, click 🔍Find. Search options are displayed.

b. In the **Look for** box, type: Homework Assignment

c. Click Find Now. Outlook displays messages that meet the search criteria in a list.

d. Select the Homework Assignment message and then drag the message to the Homework folder in the Favorites list. The message is placed in the Homework folder.

e. Click 🔍Find again. Search options are removed. The Inbox displays all e-mail messages.

⑤ *QUIT OUTLOOK*

E-mail Security

<table>
<tr><td>

IRM

E-mail messages can include restricted permissions that can help prevent messages from being forwarded, printed, or copied using Outlook's Information Rights Management (IRM). To set restricted permission, select the Permissions button (▣) on the toolbar of a message form. Note that this feature requires the Windows Rights Management Client to be installed.

</td></tr>
</table>

E-mail is an effective way to communicate. Unfortunately, along with personal and business messages, most people also receive a lot of "junk e-mail". Outlook has a Junk E-mail filter, which catches obvious junk mail and automatically places it the Junk E-Mail folder. This folder should be checked periodically to ensure a legitimate message has not accidentally been filtered to this folder. If a legitimate message is located in this folder, right-click the message and select Junk E-Mail → Mark as Not Junk and then select OK to move the message to the Inbox.

It is also possible to block messages from specific senders. Right-click a message from the sender to be blocked and select Junk E-mail → Add Sender to Blocked Senders List. To view and edit the Blocked Senders list, select Tools → Options, which displays the Options dialog box. Select Junk E-mail and then select the Blocked Senders tab to display those options:

TIP The Safe Senders tab in the Junk E-mail Options dialog box can be used to add e-mail addresses of individuals to ensure that their e-mail messages will not be treated as junk e-mail.

To remove a name from the Blocked Senders list, select the name and then select Remove. Blocked senders can also be added in this dialog box by selecting Add and typing the sender's e-mail address.

Many computer viruses have been associated with e-mail attachments. A *virus* is a program that is designed to reproduce itself by copying itself into other programs stored on a computer without the user's knowledge. Viruses have varying effects, such as displaying annoying messages, causing programs to run incorrectly, and erasing the contents of the hard drive.

Outlook provides some protection from e-mail viruses by automatically blocking attachment files that contain code that can run without warning, such as .bat, .exe, .vbs, and .j files. However, precautions still need to be taken to avoid getting a virus:

- Invest in antivirus software. Antivirus software will detect many types of viruses by scanning incoming e-mail messages before they are opened. If a virus is detected, the software will display a warning and try to remove the virus.

- Update the antivirus software frequently. New viruses are continually being created and new virus definitions must be downloaded on a regular basis in order for the antivirus software to be effective.

- Always save an attachment file and then virus-check the file before opening it. This precaution should be taken for all messages from known and unknown sources, since many viruses target address books and fool users into thinking the e-mail is from someone familiar.

E-mail Composition and Etiquette

Rules to follow when composing e-mail messages include:

- Use manners. Include "please" and "thank you" and appropriately address individuals as Mr., Ms., Mrs., Dr., and so on.

- Be concise. Write in short, complete sentences.

- Be professional, which includes using the proper spelling and grammar. Outlook includes a Spelling Checker in the Tools menu.

- Re-read a message before it is sent. Always fill in the To box last to avoid sending a message before it is complete.

E-mail messages are not private. An e-mail message goes through several mail servers before it reaches the recipient, making it easily accessible for others to read. Therefore, sending e-mail messages requires following a certain etiquette:

- Send messages through your account only.

- Use appropriate subject matter and language.

- Be considerate of other people's beliefs and opinions.

Worm

A worm is a type of virus that can reproduce itself and use the memory of a computer, but it cannot attach itself to a program.

Encryption

One way to protect the privacy of an e-mail message is to encrypt the message, which converts the message to scrambled or cipher text. The recipient of the message needs a key to unscramble the message.

Message Importance

Icons can be added to an e-mail message to note that the message is of high importance (!) or low importance (↓). These icons should only be used sparingly to catch the user's attention in special cases. If every message sent has a high importance icon, the user will ignore the meanings of the icons.

When sending e-mail at work or school, it is important to remember that employers and school administrators have the right to read any e-mail messages sent over the corporate or school network, as well as the right to track online activity.

Instant Messaging

TIP Instant message addresses can be stored in the Contacts list, which is discussed in Chapter 3.

Personal Information

Personal information and data that is considered confidential should never be passed in an on-line chat.

Instant messaging (IM) is a communication tool that allows for *real time*, or immediate text-based communication. Instant messaging allows for private on-line chat sessions and is useful for brief communication that is faster than e-mail.

Sending instant messages requires registering with an instant messaging service, such as Microsoft Windows Messenger or Microsoft MSN Messenger Service, and then adding the instant messaging addresses of the people you want to send instant messages to. These individuals also have to add your instant messaging address to their instant messaging program in order to accept messages from your address. Once this setup is complete, the instant messaging service will automatically indicate which contacts are online to send messages to.

Outlook supports instant messaging using Microsoft Windows Messenger and Microsoft MSN Messenger Service. When an e-mail from a contact is displayed in the Reading pane, a Person Names Smart Tag icon (▨) appears in the Message header. An instant message can be sent as long as the individual's status is not "offline."

To send an instant message from Outlook, click the Person Names Smart Tag and select **Send Instant Message** from the displayed menu. A window is displayed where an instant message can be composed.

Chapter Summary

The World Wide Web is the total collection of Web pages that are stored on Web servers located all over the world. A series of related Web pages that are connected by hyperlinks make up a Web site. The main page is designated as the home page.

Most Web sites fall into one of the following categories: personal, commercial, informational, media, and portal. Information found at a Web site should be evaluated for accuracy. Web sites often host banner ads for a fee.

A Web page is a document created with Hypertext Markup Language (HTML). A Web browser interprets the HTML to display a Web page. A URL is an address that is interpreted by a Web browser to identify the location of a page on the Web.

A Web browser, such as Internet Explorer, is needed to view Web pages. In Internet Explorer, the History list is a list of the pages that have been visited in the last 20 days and the Favorites list is used to maintain a list of Web pages. Select File → Print Preview to displays the Web page as it will appear when printed, indicating the number of pages.

A search engine is a program that searches a database of Web pages for keywords and then lists hyperlinks to pages that contain those keywords. Search criteria is entered, which is used by the search engine to determine a match. Limiting the number of matches to a reasonable number can be accomplished using Boolean logic in the search criteria. Some search engines also provide a subject tree, or Web directory.

There are guidelines for citing electronic material on the Internet. The primary purpose of a citation is to give credit to the original author and allow the reader to locate the cited information.

E-mail is the sending and receiving of messages and computer files over a communications network such as a LAN or the Internet. E-mail software is required for online communications.

Microsoft Outlook is a personal information manager application that has tools for organizing appointments, listing tasks, and managing e-mail. The Address Book in Outlook stores contact names and e-mail addresses. The Insert File button on the Message form toolbar is used to send a file with an e-mail message. Named signatures can be created and stored in Outlook so that signature text does not have to be retyped over and over again. Related e-mail messages should be organized into folders.

Outlook has a Junk E-mail Filter, which catches obvious junk mail and automatically places it in the Junk E-mail folder. It is also possible to block messages from specific senders.

Many computer viruses have been associated with e-mail attachments. Precautions need to be taken to avoid getting a virus. A certain etiquette should be followed when composing and sending e-mail messages.

Instant messaging is a communication tool that allows for real time or immediate text-based communication. Outlook supports instant messaging using Microsoft Windows Messenger and Microsoft MSN Messenger Service.

Address Book An Outlook tool that stores contact names and e-mail addresses.

Attachment A file sent along with an e-mail message to the recipient.

Banner ad One type of advertisement on Web sites.

Browser-based e-mail A free e-mail account.

Commercial Web site A business-related Web site such as corporate presence or e-commerce.

Corporate Presence Web site A Web site created by companies and organizations for the purpose of displaying information about their products or services.

Domain name Part of the URL that identifies a particular Web page and is made up of a sequence of parts, or subnames, separated by a period.

E-commerce Web site A Web site created by businesses for the purposes of selling their products or services to consumers online.

E-mail (electronic mail) The sending and receiving of messages and computer files over a communications network such as a LAN or the Internet.

Favorites list A list of Web pages that have been added to the Internet Explorer Favorites list.

History list A list of URLs of Web sites that have been visited in the previous days and weeks.

Home page The main page of a Web site.

HTML document A document that defines the content and layout of a Web page with tags that are surrounded by angle brackets (<>).

Hyperlink Text or graphics on a Web page that can be clicked to display another portion of that same page or another Web page.

Inbox pane Displays the e-mail messages stored in the Inbox folder arranged by date.

Informational Web site A Web site created by educational institutions, governments, and organizations for the purpose of displaying information about a particular topic.

Instant messaging (IM) A communication tool that allows for real time, or immediate text-based communication.

Link *See* Hyperlink.

Match A Web page that contains the search criteria.

Media Web site Online newspaper and periodicals that are created by companies for the purpose of informing readers about current events and issues.

Minus sign (–) Used in search criteria to exclude unwanted Web pages.

Native format The original form a file is saved in.

Outlook The Microsoft personal information manager application.

Personal Web site A Web site created by an individual for the purpose of displaying information about themselves.

Plus sign (+) Used in search criteria to limit a search to only those Web pages containing two or more specified words.

Portal Web site A Web site created by businesses for the purpose of creating a starting point for people to enter the Web.

Post The process of copying Web site files to a Web server.

Search criteria A single word or phrase that is used by the search engine to match Web pages.

Search engine A program that searches a database of Web pages for keywords and then lists hyperlinks to pages that contain those keywords.

Signature Text that is added to an e-mail message.

Subject tree A list of sites separated into categories.

Subname Part of the URL that represents a server or organization. Also called a label.

Top-level domain Part of the URL that identifies the type of Web site.

URL An address that is interpreted by a Web browser to identify the location of a page on the Web.

Virus A program that is designed to reproduce itself by copying itself into other programs stored on a computer without the user's knowledge.

Web browser Interprets an HTML document to display a Web page.

Web directory *See* Subject tree.

Web host A company that provides a Web server for Web authors to post their Web sites to.

Web page A document created with HyperText Markup Language (HTML) and possibly other code, and published to a Web server.

Web server A computer that delivers Web pages.

Web site A series of related Web pages that are connected by hyperlinks.

World Wide Web The total collection of Web pages that are stored on Web servers located all over the world.

Back button Displays the previously selected Web page. Found on the toolbar.

Favorites button Displays a pane with the Favorites list, which can be used to quickly view Web pages frequently accessed. Found on the toolbar.

Forward button Displays the next Web page from the previously selected pages. Found on the toolbar.

Go button Opens the Web page that has the URL that was typed in the Address bar. Found on the Address bar.

History button Displays a pane with the URLs of Web sites that have been visited in the previous days and weeks. Found on the toolbar.

Home button Displays a preselected Web page, which is the Web page that is displayed when Internet Explorer is first started. Found on the toolbar.

Media button Displays the Media bar, which can be used to listen to media files and Internet radio stations.

Print button Prints the currently displayed Web page. Found on the toolbar.

Print Preview **command** Displays the Web page as it will appear when printed. Found in the File menu.

Refresh button Updates the displayed Web page. Found on the toolbar.

Search button Displays a pane used to locate Web pages that contain particular information. Found on the toolbar.

Stop button Turns red when Internet Explorer is loading a Web page. Can be used to stop the transmission of a Web page. Found on the toolbar.

Add Sender to Blocked Senders List command Blocks messages from specific senders. Found in the menu displayed by right-clicking a message.

Address Book button Displays the Address Book. Found on the toolbar of the Inbox window.

Cc button Displays the Address Book, which is used to select an e-mail address. Found in a Message form.

Empty "Deleted Items" Folder command Permanently deletes e-mail messages in the Deleted Items folder. Found in the menu displayed by right-clicking the Deleted Items folder.

Find button Displays and removes a pane used to search for messages. Found on the toolbar of the Inbox window.

Forward button Sends a selected e-mail message to another e-mail address. Found on the toolbar of the Inbox window.

Insert File button Displays a dialog box that is used to send a file with an e-mail message. Found on the toolbar of a Message form.

Mail Message command Used to create a new e-mail message. Found in File → New. The New Mail Message button on the Inbox window toolbar can be used instead of the command.

Mark as Not Junk command Removes e-mail messages from the Junk E-Mail folder. Found in the menu displayed by right-clicking a message.

New Entry button Adds a new entry to the Address book. Found on the toolbar of the Address Book window.

Options command Displays a dialog box used to create a signature and view and edit the Blocked Senders list. Found in the Tools menu.

Organize command Displays a pane used to organize the Inbox. Found in the Tools menu.

Person Names Smart Tag icon Displays a menu used to send an instant message to a contact. Found in the message header in the Reading pane in the Inbox window.

Print button Prints the selected e-mail message. Found on the toolbar of the Inbox window.

Reply button Displays an e-mail message form that includes the original message and the sender's e-mail address in the To box. Found on the toolbar of the Inbox window.

Save and Close button Saves entered contact information and closes the form. Found on the toolbar of a Contact form.

Send button Used to send e-mail messages. Found on the toolbar of a Message form.

Send/Receive button Sends and Receives messages from the e-mail server. Found on the toolbar of the Inbox window.

To button Displays the Address Book, which is used to select an e-mail address. Found in a Message form.

1. a) What is the World Wide Web?
   b) What does a Web host provide?
   c) What is meant by posting a Web site?

2. a) What is a hyperlink?
   b) What is a Web site?
   c) What is the main page of a Web site called?

3. What is the purpose of a personal Web site?

   Answer question 4 and 5 using Internet search skills or by discussing the answers with a partner.

4. a) E-commerce Web sites are often an extension of a traditional or "brick-and-mortar " business. List one traditional business that uses an e-commerce Web site as a method of extending their business.
   b) Amazon.com is an example of a business that only does transactions on-line. List an example of another business that only conducts business through their Web site.
   c) Compare shopping at an e-commerce Web site with traditional shopping. List two advantages and two disadvantages of shopping at an e-commerce Web site.

5. a) List an example of a media Web site.
   b) Yahoo! is an example of a portal Web site. List another example of a portal Web site.

6. Why is it difficult to determine if information on the Web is accurate?

7. How can you attempt to determine the accuracy of information on a Web page?

8. Why do Web sites host banner ads?

9. a) What language is used to create Web pages?
   b) What is displayed when a Web browser interprets an HTML document?

10. a) What is a URL?
    b) Label and describe each part of the URL http://www.lpdatafiles.com.

11. a) What is the History list?
    b) What is the Favorites list used for?

12. a) What is a search engine?
    b) List three commonly used search engines.
    c) Which search engine do you prefer to use? Why?
    d) What is search criteria?
    e) What is a match?

13. Write search criteria to locate Web pages that contain the following information:
    a) restaurants in Los Angeles
    b) art museums in Boston
    c) auto repair jobs in Montreal, Canada
    d) mosquitoes and bees, but not ants
    e) the English author Jane Austen
    f) the phrase *to each his own*
    g) George Washington and John Adams, but not Thomas Jefferson
    h) travel to Ireland, but not Dublin

14. What is the purpose of a subject tree?

15. a) Why is it necessary to cite sources?
    b) On August 2, 2006 you accessed Tara Perez's Ivy University master's degree thesis titled *Bird Watching in South Florida's Soccer Fields* on a Web page at http://www.tarap.ufl.edu. Write a citation for a research paper that quotes Tara's thesis.

16. Write your e-mail address and label the parts of the address.

17. a) What are the two requirements for sending and receiving e-mail messages?
    b) List two examples of e-mail software.
    c) List one example of a browser-based e-mail site.

18. What type of application is Microsoft Outlook?

19. a) What is the Address Book?
    b) When is the Address Book automatically updated?
    c) When typing an e-mail address in the To box of a message form, Outlook will automatically complete the address if the recipient is in the Address Book. What key is pressed to accept the completed address?

20. a) What software must an e-mail recipient have on their computer to view a Word document attached to a message?
    b) Which formats are best for attachments? Why?

21. a) What is a signature?
    b) Why would you create a named signature?
    c) List the steps required to create a signature named Samuel Perez that automatically adds Samuel Perez, Project Manager to every new e-mail message.

22. List the name of five folders automatically created by Outlook and describe the messages each of the folders store.

23. a) Why is it important to organize the Inbox into folders with descriptive names?
    b) List the names of two folders that could be added to your Inbox to organize your messages.

24. List one way junk e-mail is dealt with in Outlook.

25. a) What is a virus?
    b) Give two examples of effects that viruses may have.
    c) How does Outlook provide some protection from e-mail viruses?
    d) List three precautions that should be taken to avoid getting a virus.
    e) What precautions against viruses are taken in your computer lab?

26. List three rules to follow when composing e-mail messages.

27. a) Sending an e-mail message should be thought of the same as sending a postcard. Explain this statement.
    b) List three examples of e-mail etiquette.

28. a) What is instant messaging?
    b) What is required to send instant messages?
    c) List two instant messaging services.
    d) List one advantage of sending an instant message instead of an e-mail message.

True/False

29. Determine if each of the following are true or false. If false, explain why.
    a) Copying Web site files to a Web server is called hosting.
    b) The main page of a Web site is called the home page.
    c) HTML tags are surrounded by curly brackets ({ }).
    d) The http part of a URL is called the domain name.
    e) A search engine is a program that searches a database of Web pages.
    f) A Web directory lists sites by creation date.
    g) Web pages should never be included in citations because there is no need to give credit to the original author.
    h) Files can be sent as attachments in an e-mail message.
    i) More than one named signature can be created.
    j) Viruses are always harmless programs.
    k) Antivirus software never needs updating.
    l) Instant messaging is a real-time communication tool.

Exercises

Note that the exercises below require written answers. If a word processor is used, be sure to use an appropriate title, header, and file name.

Exercise 1

Become familiar with different categories of Web sites by completing the following steps.

a) Locate an example of a personal Web site. List the URL and briefly describe the content at the site.

b) Locate an example of an e-commerce Web site. List the URL and briefly describe the products that can be purchased at this site.

c) Locate an example of an informational Web site. List the URL and briefly describe the information available at the site.

d) Locate an example of a media Web site. Print the home page of the media Web site and note how up-to-date the content is.

e) Locate an example of a portal Web site. Print the home page of the portal Web site and circle four hyperlinks available on the portal home page.

Exercise 2

Examine and evaluate Web site content by completing the following steps.

a) In Internet Explorer, enter the URL: www.cnn.com

b) Read the content on the home page.

c) On what date was the Web page last updated?

d) Is the information incorrect or incomplete in order to give a particular or slanted view of a topic. Explain your answer.

e) Is the information truthful and trustworthy? Explain your answer.

f) Describe a banner ad displayed on this site.

g) In Internet Explorer, enter the URL: www.earthday.net

h) Repeat steps (b) through (g) for the Earth Day Network Web site.

Exercise 3

You are interested in finding a job in Los Angeles, California and are skilled in Web site design. A full-time position with a local Web site design company would be ideal.

a) Conduct a search on the Internet using at least two search engines to find two possible positions. On a separate sheet titled References, cite each source.

b) Write a brief description of each of the positions that you found.

c) Once you have found the position of your choice, you need information on making the move to Los Angeles. First, you will want to rent an apartment and cannot afford more than $1,500 a month. Conduct a search on the Internet to come up with brief descriptions of three apartments in Los Angeles that rent for $1,500 or less.

d) Add a paragraph that describes all three apartments, including number of bedrooms and bathrooms and rent per month.

Exercise 4

Your English instructor has assigned a report on the American authors Kurt Vonnegut, Jr. and Ernest Hemingway. Keep in mind that knowledge of information like the titles of their books might help in your search. Because people maintain Web pages as homages to their favorite authors, but are not obligated to check their facts for accuracy, it is a good idea to double check the information you find with more than one Web page.

a) Conduct a search on the Internet using at least two search engines to find biographical data on each author.

b) Create a folder named American Authors in the Favorites list and add relevant Web pages to this folder.

c) Write a paragraph of biographical information for each author.

d) On a separate sheet titled References, cite each source.

Exercise 5

You have decided to purchase an automobile that costs $20,000 or less. A used car will probably give you the best value.

a) Conduct a search on the Internet using at least two search engines to find four used cars in your price range. On a separate sheet titled References, cite each source.

b) List each car's specifications and price.

c) Select one of the four cars for purchase and explain your choice in a paragraph.

d) You will need automobile insurance for your used car. Search the Internet and find two insurance companies that offer automobile insurance.

e) List the contact information for the two insurance companies.

Exercise 6

A good friend has been diagnosed with Carpal Tunnel Syndrome and would like you to find out as much as you can about her injury.

a) Conduct a search on the Internet using at least two search engines to find three Web pages that have information about Carpal Tunnel Syndrome.

b) Create a folder named: Carpal Tunnel Syndrome in the Favorites list and add relevant Web pages to this folder.

c) Write a one-paragraph description of the injury.

d) In a second paragraph, write about possible treatments for the injury.

e) On a separate sheet titled References, cite each source.

Exercise 7

You and a friend have decided to take a trip to Australia. Before you go you should find out about airfare, hotels, climate, travel documents, and restaurants. Information about Australia's museums and tourist attractions would also be helpful in planning the trip.

a) Conduct a search on the Internet using at least two search engines to find six Web pages that have information about Australia.

b) Write a one-paragraph description of the country.

c) In a second paragraph, write about the places that you might visit.

d) On a separate sheet titled References, cite each source.

Exercise 8

You have decided to investigate marine biology as a possible career path.

a) Conduct a search on the Internet using at least two search engines to find six degree programs in marine biology.

b) List each program location (college name), the degree, the number of credits required to finish the degree, and some of the costs involved.

Exercise 9

Update your Address Book and organize your Inbox by completing the following steps.

a) Collect e-mail addresses from six people you would be likely to send e-mail messages to and are not in your Address Book.

b) Create six new entries in the Address Book.

c) Send an e-mail to a classmate working on the same exercise with Address Book Completed as the subject and the message: I am finished typing the information for my Address Book. Have you finished? Please reply using the Reply button.

d) Reply to the classmate's e-mail message using the Reply button. Note that you may have to click the Send/Receive button on the Inbox toolbar to receive the message from the e-mail server.

e) Organize your e-mail messages by creating two new folders, naming the folders appropriately, and then moving messages to the new folders.

f) Create a named signature that you could use for professional correspondence, such as sending college applications or resumes.

Exercise 10

Many computer viruses have been associated with e-mail attachments.

a) Conduct a search on the Internet to find information about a virus associated with e-mail attachments.

b) Write a one-paragraph description of the virus. Include details, such as the damage caused by the virus and steps necessary to remove the virus.

c) On a separate sheet titled References, cite each source.

Exercise 11

Each of the following people has made a major contribution to the world of art or music. Select one of the six artists listed below and then find a minimum of five Web pages that provide information about the artist, including pictures of his or her works. Using the information you find, write a two-page report. On a separate sheet titled References, cite each source.

- Mary Cassatt
- Georgia O'Keeffe
- Maxfield Parrish
- Frederic Remington
- Pablo Picasso
- Annie Leibovitz

Exercise 12

Select one of the six topics listed below and then find a minimum of five Web pages that provide information on your topic. Using the information you find, write a two-page report. On a separate sheet titled References, cite each source.

- hurricanes
- the ocean floor
- earthquakes
- tornadoes
- the ozone layer
- solar energy

Chapter 3

Personal Information Management

Outlook is the Microsoft personal information manager. This chapter introduces Outlook for organizing appointments, tasks, and contacts.

What is a Personal Information Manager?

Outlook Today

If Outlook Today is not displayed when Outlook is started, click the Outlook Today button (⌕) on the Advanced toolbar. Display the Advanced toolbar by selecting **View → Toolbars → Advanced.**

Developing good organizational skills can help contribute to success in both school and work. A *personal information manager* (PIM), such as Microsoft Outlook, can simplify the organization of personal and business activities. Outlook has tools for keeping track of contacts, organizing appointments, managing e-mail, and listing tasks.

Outlook Today is displayed when Outlook is started:

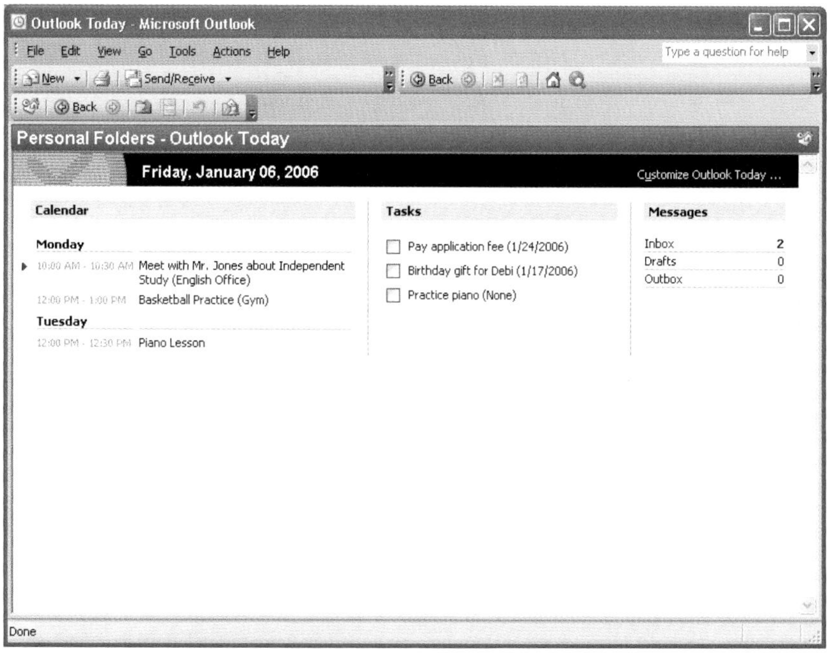

Outlook Today displays the current date, calendar appointments for the next few days, tasks, and a summary of e-mail messages. The titles <u>Calendar</u>, <u>Tasks</u>, and <u>Messages</u> are links to those Outlook tools.

Calendar

Effective time management skills can help lead to success in school and work. One aspect of managing time involves keeping an organized schedule. *Calendar* is an Outlook scheduling tool that can be used to keep track of assignment due dates, create reminders about events, and schedule appointments and meetings. Click the <u>Calendar</u> link in Outlook Today to display Calendar:

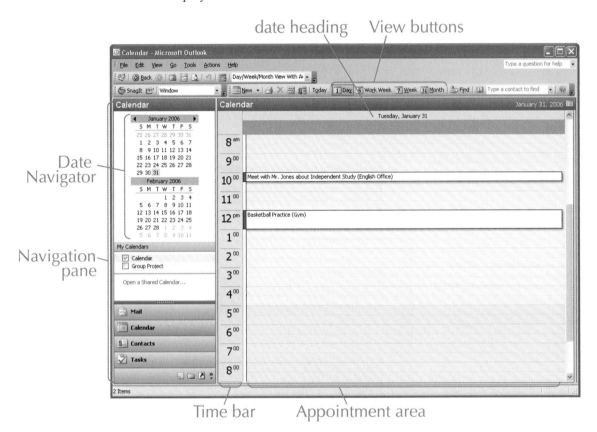

- The **View buttons** on the toolbar change the way Calendar is displayed. Day view (1 Day) is shown above, and displays the calendar for the current day. Work Week view (5 Work Week) displays the calendar for Monday through Friday of the current week. Week view (7 Week) displays the calendar for Monday through Sunday of the current week. Month view (31 Month) displays a scrollable calendar for the month.

- The **Appointment area** contains details and reminders of appointments. The **date heading** at the top of the Appointment area displays the date that the calendar is referring to.

- The **Time bar** displays a series of time intervals indicating the time of day.

- The **Navigation Pane** contains Date Navigator and links to other Outlook tools. **Date Navigator** displays a calendar for the current and next month. Days are highlighted depending on the view. In Calendar above, Day view is selected, so Date Navigator highlights the current day. Click a day in Date Navigator to display appointments for that day.

TIP The number of calendars displayed in Date Navigator can be expanded by dragging the right border of the Navigation pane or by making the Calendar window larger.

You will start Microsoft Outlook and display Calendar in different views.

① *START OUTLOOK AND DISPLAY CALENDAR*

    a. Ask your instructor for the appropriate steps to start Microsoft Outlook 2003.

    b. Click the Calendar link. Calendar is displayed.

    c. On the toolbar, click ▣Day if it is not already selected. Calendar is displayed in Day view. Note the features of Calendar including the Navigation pane, Date Navigator, the View buttons, the Appointment area and the date heading.

② *CHANGE THE DATE NAVIGATOR DISPLAY*

    a. In Date Navigator, click the arrow to the left of the current month:

    The previous month is displayed and the current month moves below the previous month. Your Date Navigator may display different months.

    b. In Date Navigator, click the arrow to the right of the previous month. The current month is displayed on top with the next month displayed below.

    c. In Date Navigator, click and hold the current month's name:

    A list is displayed that includes the past three months and the next three months. In the list, select the month that is three months ahead of the current month. Date Navigator displays the selected month.

③ *DISPLAY THE CALENDAR FOR A DIFFERENT DAY*

    a. Note the date heading at the top of the Appointment area.

    b. In Date Navigator, click a different date. The selected date is displayed.

    c. On the toolbar, click Today. The current day is displayed.

④ *DISPLAY THE CALENDAR IN DIFFERENT VIEWS*

    a. On the toolbar, click ▣Work Week. Monday through Friday of the current week is displayed:

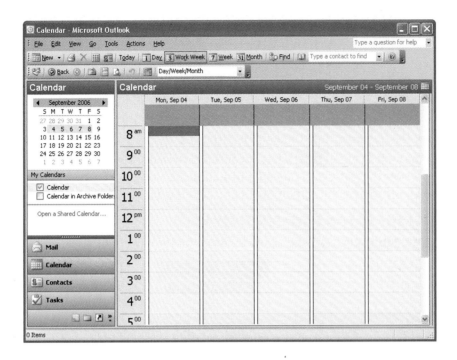

b. On the toolbar, click [7 Week]. Monday through Sunday of the current week is displayed.

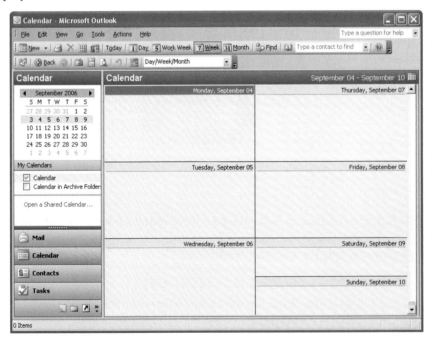

c. On the toolbar, click [31 Month]. A scrollable calendar with one week per row is displayed:

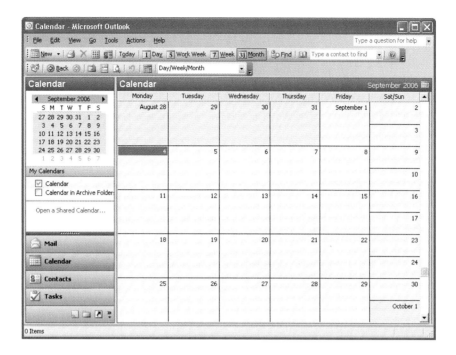

d. Drag the scroll bar to scroll beyond the current month.

e. On the toolbar, click Today. The calendar automatically scrolls to display the current date in Month view.

f. On the toolbar, click 1 Day. Calendar displays the current date in Day view.

Holidays

Holidays can be added and displayed in a banner on the appropriate calendar day. To add holidays, select Tools → Options and then select Calendar Options in the Preferences tab to display those options. Select Add Holidays and then select the check box of the appropriate country.

TIP In a form, press the Tab key to move the insertion point from field to field. Press Shift+Tab to move the insertion point to the previous field.

Calendar Events

An *event* is an activity that is scheduled for a specific day but is not assigned a start or an end time. Events are displayed in a banner at the top of the Appointment area. In the example below, Vacation Day is displayed as an event on Wednesday January 18:

To add an event to Calendar, first use Date Navigator to display the appropriate calendar day and then double-click the date heading or select Actions → New All Day Event to display an Event form.

To remove an event from the Event banner, right-click the event and select Delete from the menu or select the event and then click the Delete button (X) on the toolbar. To edit an event, double-click the event to display its form.

Practice: Adding an Event to Calendar

You will add an event to Calendar. Calendar should already be displayed.

① *USE DATE NAVIGATOR TO DISPLAY A DATE*

In Date Navigator, click the date three days from today. The calendar for the selected day is displayed.

② *ADD AN EVENT*

a. In the Appointment area, double-click the date heading. An Event form is displayed.

b. Complete the Subject box, change the Label to Personal, select the All day event check box, and clear the Reminder check box:

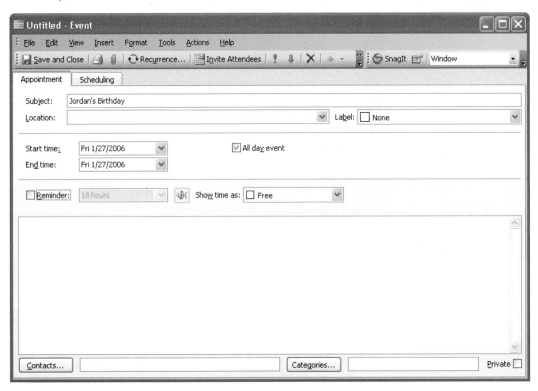

c. On the Event form toolbar, click [💾 Save and Close]. The form is removed and the event is displayed in a banner:

Jordan's Birthday

Arranging the Calendar

To arrange Calendar by active appointments or by events select View → Arrange By → Current View and then select the appropriate arrangement.

Calendar Appointments

An *appointment*, just like an event, is an activity scheduled on a specific day. However, an appointment differs from an event in that it has a specific starting and ending time. For example, in the calendar on the next page, there is an event and an appointment. Vacation Day is an event that occurs for the whole day. Beach Volleyball Game is an appointment because it has a starting and ending time:

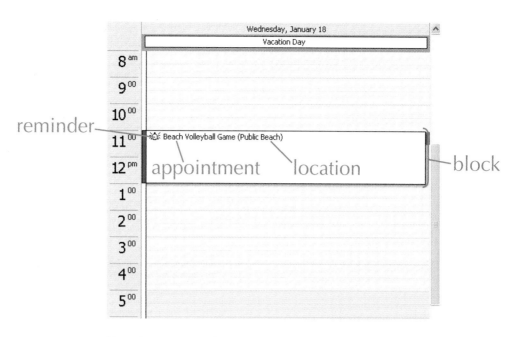

reminder

appointment location block

If an appointment location is specified, it is shown in parentheses next to the appointment information. In this example, Public Beach is the location of the appointment that is scheduled from 11:00 a.m. to 12 p.m. The bell to the left of each appointment indicates a sound will play and a reminder about the appointment will be displayed at a set time:

TIP Outlook should remain running, even when working in another application, so that the Reminder window will be displayed.

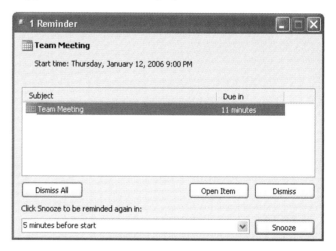

TIP The Snooze button works just like an alarm clock snooze button. Another reminder window will appear in the specified time.

The Reminder window displays the appointment with the time left before the appointment starts (Due in). The Due in time is automatically updated. In the example above, the Reminder window was displayed 15 minutes before the appointment time and now indicates the team meeting starts in 11 minutes. Click Dismiss to delete the reminder and close the window.

adding an appointment

Appointments can be added in any view. Click New on the toolbar to display an Appointment form. In Day view, double-click in the appropriate Appointment area to display a form. Information such as location, date and time can be specified in the Appointment form. For appointments that occur on a regular basis, recurrence information can also be added.

deleting an appointment

editing an appointment

To remove an appointment, right-click the appointment in any view and select Delete from the menu or select the appointment and then click the Delete button ([X])on the toolbar. To edit an appointment, double-click the appointment to display its form.

Practice: Adding an Appointment to Calendar

You will add appointments to Calendar. Calendar should already be displayed.

1. **USE DATE NAVIGATOR TO DISPLAY A DATE**

    In Date Navigator, click the date five days from today. The calendar for the selected day is displayed.

2. **ADD AN APPOINTMENT**

    a. Double-click the 4:00 PM slot. An Appointment form is displayed.

    b. Complete the Subject box and Location box, change the Label to Personal, change the End time to 6:00 PM, and select the Reminder check box, and change the reminder time, as shown:

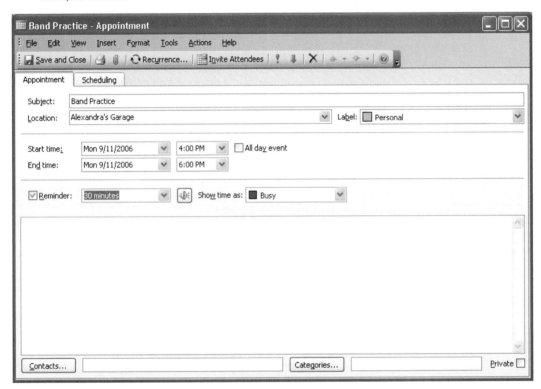

    c. On the Appointment form toolbar, click [💾 Save and Close]. The form is removed and the appointment is displayed in the Appointment area of Calendar.

3. **ADD A RECURRING APPOINTMENT**

    a. In Date Navigator, click the date for next Friday. The calendar for the selected day is displayed.

    b. Double-click the 4:00 PM slot. An Appointment form is displayed.

    c. Complete the Subject box and Location box, change the Label to Must Attend, select the Reminder check box, and change the reminder time, as shown:

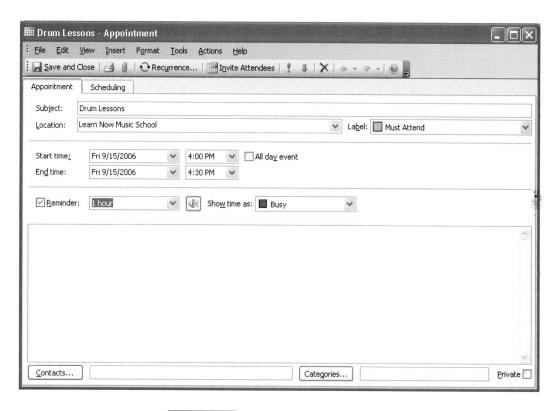

d. On the toolbar, click ⟲ Recurrence... . A dialog box is displayed.

e. Change the End time, select the Recurrence pattern options: Weekly, Recur every 1 week on Friday, and change the Range of recurrence to End after 15, as shown:

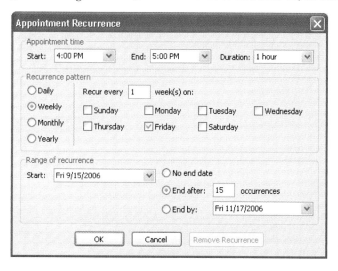

f. Select OK. The dialog box is removed.

g. On the Appointment form toolbar, click 🖫 Save and Close . The form is removed and the appointment is added. The ⟲ symbol indicates a recurring appointment:

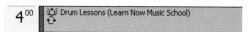

h. Use Date Navigator to select the date two Fridays from now. Note the recurring appointment. Select the date eight Fridays from now and note the recurring appointment. Also note the Friday dates containing the recurring appointment are displayed in bold in Date Navigator.

Working with Multiple Calendars

It is sometimes useful to keep a separate calendar for a specific purpose, such as a group project. Select File → New → Folder to display the Create New Folder dialog box with options for creating a new Calendar Items folder. Check boxes in My Calendars allow for more than one calendar to be viewed at the same time:

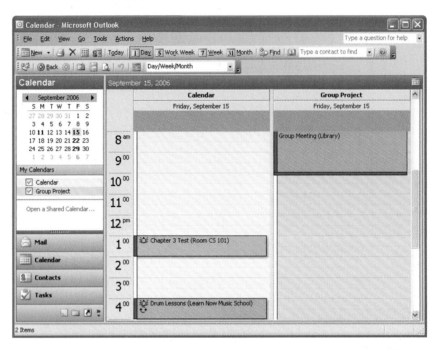

Calendar and a Group Project Calendar

Calendars are listed in the Navigation pane under My Calendars:

The check boxes to the left of the Calendar names are used to select calendars to display.

Sharing a Calendar

An Outlook Calendar can be shared with other people over a network only if the individuals have a Microsoft Exchange Server E-mail account.

Practice: Working with Multiple Calendars

You will create a second calendar. Outlook should already be started.

① **CREATE A SECOND CALENDAR**

    a. Select File → New → Folder. A dialog box is displayed.

    b. Complete the Name box and select Calendar Items in the Folder contains box, as shown on the next page:

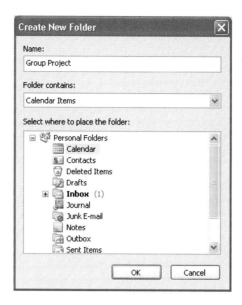

c. Select **OK**. The Group Project calendar is added to the My Calendars list in the Navigation pane.

d. In the Navigation pane, click the **Group Project** check box. The Group Project calendar is displayed beside Calendar.

② *ADD AN APPOINTMENT TO THE GROUP PROJECT CALENDAR*

a. Select the Day button on the toolbar, if it is not already selected. Both calendars are displayed in Day view.

b. Select the Today button on the toolbar. Both calendars now display the current date in the date heading.

c. On the Group Project calendar, add an 8 PM appointment. In the **Subject** box, type: Internet Research and change the **End time** to 10:00 PM.

d. Click ![Save and Close].

③ *COPY AN APPOINTMENT*

Appointments can be copied from one calendar to the other.

Position the pointer on top of the Internet Research appointment and then click the right mouse button and drag the appointment to the 8 PM time slot on Calendar. Release the mouse and then select **Copy** from the displayed menu. The appointment now appears on both calendars.

④ *CHANGE CALENDAR DISPLAY*

In the Navigation pane, click the **Group Project** check box to clear it. The Group Project calendar is removed.

⑤ *DISPLAY OUTLOOK TODAY*

a. Select View ➡ Toolbars ➡ Advanced, if the Advanced toolbar is not displayed.

b. Click the Outlook Today button (![icon]). Outlook Today is displayed. Note the list of events and appointments.

Sending Meeting Requests

Chapter 2 discusses using Outlook to send e-mail. Sending meeting requests is one way to integrate the Outlook Calendar and E-mail tools. A *meeting request* can be used to set up a time for members of a club to meet, notify individuals of a project due date, or schedule a group project meeting. Recipients can add it to their calendar or decline the request. Note that the individual receiving the request must have Outlook installed if they want to add the request to their calendar.

TIP To invite more than one person to a meeting, separate e-mail addresses with a semi-colon.

To create a meeting request, first display Calendar and then select File → New → Meeting Request to display a Meeting form. Information is added the same way an appointment is added. Invitees are then invited to attend the meeting by specifying their e-mail addresses.

Each individual receiving the meeting request is able to accept, tentatively accept, decline, or propose a new meeting time by clicking the appropriate button at the top of the e-mail message.

Practice: Sending Meeting Requests

You will send a meeting request. This practice requires Internet access. Outlook should already be started.

① *USE DATE NAVIGATOR TO DISPLAY A DATE IN CALENDAR*

    a. In Date Navigator, click the date five days from today. The calendar for the selected day is displayed.

② *CREATE A MEETING REQUEST*

    a. Select File → New → Meeting Request. A Meeting form is displayed.

    b. Complete the Subject box and Location box, change the Label to Business, change the Start time to 9:00 AM and the End time to 11:30 AM, select the Reminder check box, change the reminder time to 1 hour, and type a message as shown:

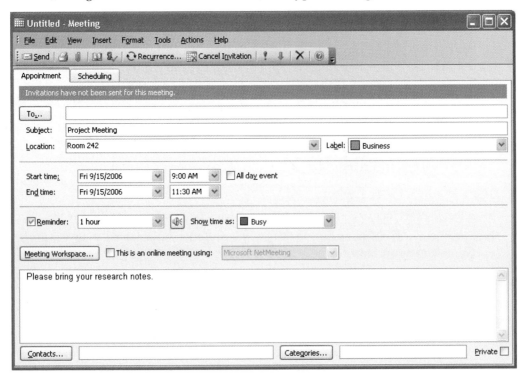

c. Exchange e-mail addresses with a partner. In the To box, type the e-mail address of your partner.

d. Click . The message request is sent to your partner.

③ *RECEIVE AND ACCEPT A MEETING REQUEST*

a. In the Navigation pane, click the Mail shortcut:

b. In a few minutes, click ⟨Send/Receive ▾⟩. The e-mail from your partner is delivered to Inbox. Note that the e-mail message header includes:

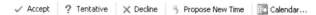

Accept places the meeting request information on the calendar. Decline sends a response to the sender declining the request. Propose New Time sends a response that proposes a new time for the meeting.

c. In the Message header, click Accept. The meeting information is added to the calendar. If a dialog box is displayed, click Do not respond.

d. In the Navigation pane, click the Calendar shortcut:

Calendar

Calendar is displayed. Locate the Project Meeting appointment.

Outlook Tasks

Outlook includes a Tasks tool which can be used to list and monitor tasks that need to be completed. A *task* is a job, chore, or errand that needs to be completed. Tasks can be entered and tracked in the TaskPad area of Calendar. Display TaskPad by selecting View → TaskPad:

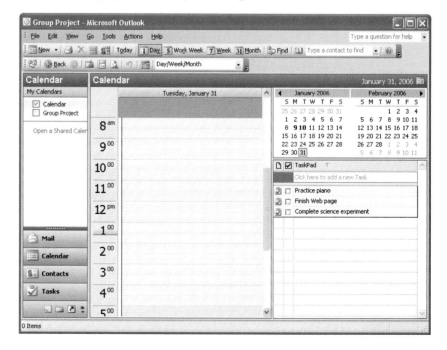

TIP Tasks added to the TaskPad will automatically appear in the Outlook Today summary under the Tasks heading.

Double-click a task to view its Task form, where modifications can be made. A Task form also allows additional information to be recorded, such as a due date or notes.

Once a task has been completed, select its check box or right-click the task and select Mark Complete from the menu, which displays the task as complete:

completing a task
deleting a task

A completed task remains in the TaskPad and is displayed with a line through it. To delete a task, right-click the task and select Delete from the displayed menu or click the task and then click the Delete button (☒) on the toolbar.

 Tasks

The Tasks list can also be displayed and organized in the Tasks window. Click Tasks in the Navigation pane to display the Tasks window:

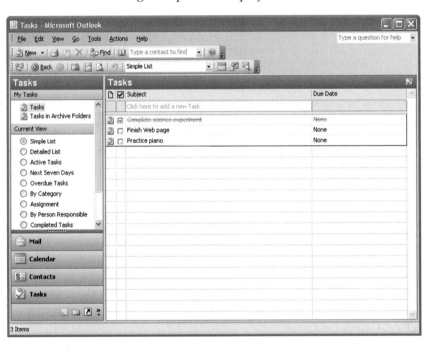

Outlook Tasks Window displayed in Simple List View

Select a Current View option to change the way tasks are displayed.

Practice: Adding Tasks to TaskPad

You will add tasks to the TaskPad, modify a task, mark a task complete, and delete a task from the TaskPad. Outlook should already be started.

① *DISPLAY TASKPAD*
   a. Display Calendar in Day view.
   b. Select View → TaskPad. The TaskPad is displayed. Date Navigator may now appear above TaskPad.

② *ADD TWO TASKS*

   a. Click the Click here to add a new Task row in the TaskPad. The insertion point appears.

   b. Type Pay student activity fee and press Enter. The task is added to the TaskPad.

   c. Type Update Web page and press Enter. The new task is added to the top of the list in the TaskPad.

   d. Double-click the new task. The Update Web page Task form is displayed:

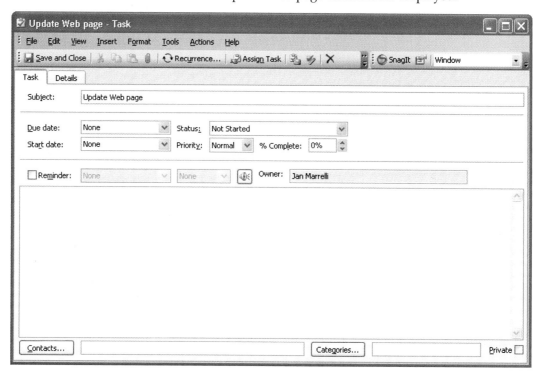

   e. Click the Due date arrow. A calendar is displayed.

   f. Click the date that represents Monday of next week. The selected date is displayed in the Due date box.

   g. On the Task form toolbar, click 🔲 Save and Close . The form is removed and the modified task is displayed on the TaskPad. Note that there is no difference in the way the task is displayed in the TaskPad.

   h. Click the Outlook Today button (🗒). Outlook Today is displayed. Note the Tasks list. The due date for the Update Web page task is displayed in parentheses.

③ *MARK A TASK AS COMPLETE AND DELETE IT FROM THE TASKPAD*

   a. In Outlook Today, click the check box to the left of the Pay student activity fee task. The task is displayed as complete.

   b. Switch to Calendar. Note the completed task in the TaskPad.

   c. Right-click the Pay student activity fee task. A menu is displayed.

   d. Select Delete from the menu. The task is removed from the TaskPad.

Previewing and Printing a Calendar

A calendar can be printed so that the information can be used as a reference away from the computer. *Previewing* displays the calendar as it will appear when printed. Select a view button on the toolbar and then select File → Print Preview to display the calendar in the Print Preview window.

Practice: Printing a Calendar

You will preview and then print a calendar. Outlook should already be started.

   ① *CHANGE CALENDAR DISPLAY AND PRINT PREVIEW*

      a. In Calendar, display the calendar for today's date in Day view if it is not already displayed.

      b. Select File → Print Preview. Calendar is displayed as it will appear when printed.

      c. Add your name to Calendar before printing. On the toolbar, click Page Setup... . A dialog box is displayed. Click the Header/Footer tab to display those options.

      d. In the right-most Header box, type: your first and last name and then select OK.

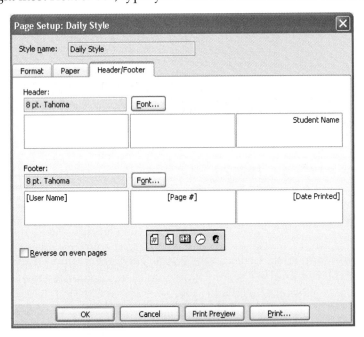

      e. On the toolbar, click Print... . The Print dialog box is displayed.

      f. Select OK. The dialog box is removed and Calendar for today's date is printed.

      g. Display Calendar in Week view and then print preview Calendar.

      h. In the Print Preview window, click Close to return to Calendar without printing.

      i. Display Calendar in Month view and then Print Preview Calendar. How many months will be printed in this view?

      j. In the Print Preview window, click Close to return to Calendar without printing.

Outlook Contacts

Contacts is an Outlook tool that is used to create an electronic address book that stores information such as addresses and phone numbers of individuals and businesses:

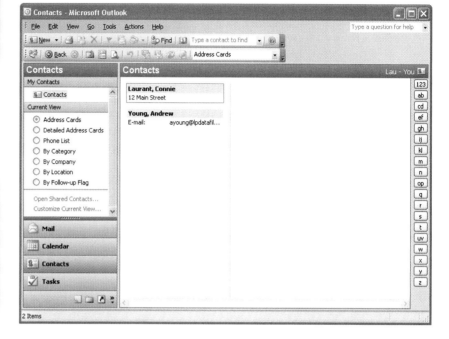

adding a contact

Select a **Current View** option to change the way contacts are displayed. To add a new contact, click New on the toolbar or double-click a blank area of Contacts, which displays a Contact form.

deleting a contact

To remove a contact from the contacts list, right-click the contact and select **Delete** from the menu or select the contact and then click the Delete button (X) on the toolbar. To edit a contact, double-click the contact to display its form.

editing a contact

printing contacts

Contacts can be printed so that the information can be used as a reference away from the computer. Select **File → Print Preview** to display the calendar as it will appear printed. To print preview, click Print... to display a dialog box with print options.

Practice: Adding Contacts

You will add contacts to the Contacts list, modify a contact, and delete a contact. Outlook should already be started.

① DISPLAY CONTACTS

In the Navigation pane, click the Contacts shortcut. Contacts is displayed. Note the features of Contacts including the Contacts Index. A message may be displayed indicating there are no items to show in this view.

② ADD A CONTACT

a. On the toolbar, click 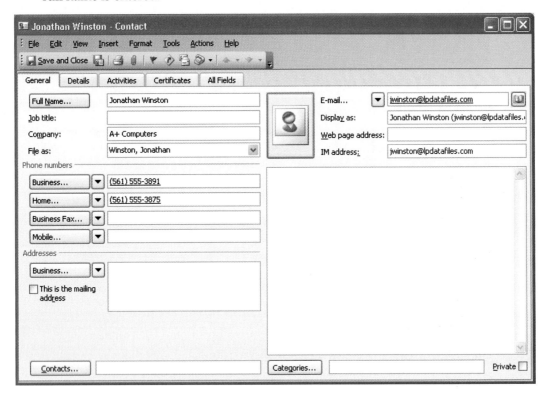 New. A Contact form is displayed.

b. Complete the Full Name box, Company box, Business and Business Fax phone numbers, E-mail box, and IM address box. The File as box is completed automatically after the full name is entered:

c. Click the Details tab. Note the additional fields that could be added for a contact.

d. Click the General tab.

e. On the Contact form toolbar, click Save and Close. The form is removed and the contact is displayed in the contacts list.

③ ADD A SECOND CONTACT

a. On the toolbar, click New.

b. In the Company box, type Lake Worth Hockey Rink and then press Tab. Note that Lake Worth Hockey Rink is displayed in the File as box and Lake Worth Hockey Rink – Contact is displayed in the title bar. If a company name is entered in the Company field and the Full Name box is left blank, Outlook files the contact by the company name as it is typed.

c. In the Business box in the Phone numbers section, type: (561) 555-3545

d. In the Web page address box, type: www.lwhockeyrink.lpdatafiles.com

e. Click Save and Close.

④ ADD A THIRD CONTACT

a. On the toolbar, click New.

b. In the Full Name box, type: Catherine Richmond

c. In the Job title box, type: Manager

d. In the Company box, type: The Grand Beach Hotel

e. In the Business box in the Phone numbers section, type: (561) 555-8765

f. In the Home box in the Phone numbers section, type: (561) 555-0002

g. In the Business Fax box in the Phone numbers section, type: (561) 555-0006

h. In the Mobile box in the Phone numbers section, type: (561) 555-0004

i. In the E-mail box, type: richmondc@lpdatafiles.com

j. In the Web page address box, type: www.thegrandbeachhotel.lpdatafiles.com

k. Click [Save and Close].

⑤ *ADD A FOURTH CONTACT*

a. On the toolbar, click [New ▾].

b. In the Full Name box, type your name.

c. In the Addresses area, click the Business arrow to display a list of address types:

Select Other and then enter your school address.

d. In the E-mail box, type your e-mail address.

e. In the IM address box, type your instant messaging address, if you have one.

f. On the Contact form toolbar, click [Save and Close].

⑥ *MODIFY CONTACT INFORMATION*

a. Double-click the Catherine Richmond contact. The Catherine Richmond Contact form is displayed.

b. In the Business box in the Phone numbers section, change the phone number to: (561) 555-4343

c. On the Contact form toolbar, click [Save and Close]. The modified contact information is saved and the updated Contacts list is displayed.

⑦ *DELETE A CONTACT*

a. In Contacts, click the Jonathan Winston contact to select it.

b. On the toolbar, click the Delete button ([X]). The contact is deleted.

⑧ *CHANGE CURRENT VIEW*

a. In the Navigation pane, in the Current View options, select Address Cards if it is not already selected. Note that Address Cards view displays selected contact information and is a quick way to reference frequently used information, such as phone numbers and e-mail addresses.

b. In the Navigation pane, in the Current View options, select Phone List. Note that Phone List view displays phone and fax numbers.

c. Change the Current View to Detailed Address Cards. Note that Detailed Address Cards view displays all the contact information in an expanded address card format.

⑨ *PRINT PREVIEW AND PRINT*

a. Select File ➛ Print Preview. The Print Preview window is displayed.

b. Click the Actual Size button ([🔍]). The Contacts list is displayed as it will appear when printed.

c. Scroll to the bottom of the page. Note that Outlook automatically adds a footer to the bottom of each printed page. The footer contains the user name, the page number, and the current date and time.

d. The status bar displays a Page indicator that displays "Page 1 of 2", which indicates page 1 is currently displayed and the contacts list will be printed on 2 pages. Click the Multiple Pages button ( ) to view both pages side by side. Note that the second page contains a form for writing contact entries down so that they can be added to the contacts list at a later time.

e. Click Print... . A dialog box is displayed:

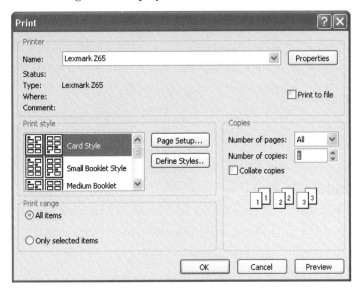

The view the Contacts list is displayed in determines the Print style, which is displayed in the Print dialog box. For example, Address Cards view is printed in Card Style and Phone List view is printed in Table Style. Note that booklets can be printed on both sides of the paper, but only if the printer supports double-sided printing. If the printer does, the double-sided printing option must be selected in the Print dialog box

1. In the Print dialog box, select Small Booklet Style.

2. Select OK. A warning box may appear:

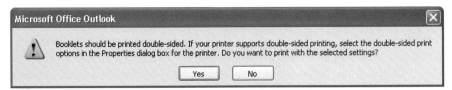

If the warning box appears, select Yes. The dialog is removed and the Contacts list is printed.

⑩ *VIEW THE ADDRESS BOOK*

"The Address Book" section in Chapter 2 in the text explained that the Address Book is created automatically as contacts are added to the Outlook Contacts tool. Note that the contacts are only added if the E-mail box in the Contacts form is filled in. In this practice, you added four contacts to the contact list. View the Address Book to see if these individuals have been automatically added to the Contacts list by completing the following steps:

a. In the Navigation pane, click Mail. The Inbox window is displayed.

b. On the toolbar, click the Address Book button (). The Address Book is displayed. Note that the contacts have automatically been added to the contacts list.

c. Click the Close button in the upper-right corner of the Address Book. The Address Book is closed.

⑪ *QUIT OUTLOOK*

Chapter Summary

A personal information manager (PIM), such as Microsoft Outlook, can simplify the organization of personal and business activities.

Calendar is an Outlook scheduling tool that can be used to keep track of assignment due dates, create reminders about events, and schedule appointments and meetings. An event is an activity that is scheduled for a specific day, but is not assigned a start or end time. Events are displayed in a banner at the top of the Appointment area. An appointment is an activity scheduled on a specific day that has a specific start and ending time. An appointment is displayed in the Appointment area of Calendar in the appropriate time slot. A recurring appointment is an appointment that occurs on a regular basis. An additional calendar can be created for a specific purpose, such as a group project.

A meeting request can be used to set up a time for members of a club to meet, notify individuals of a project due date, or schedule a group project meeting. Recipients can add it to their calendars or decline the request.

Outlook includes a Tasks tool which can be used to list and monitor tasks that need to be completed in TaskPad. A task is a job, chore, or errand that needs to be completed.

A calendar can be printed so that the information can be used away from the computer. Previewing displays the calendar as it will appear when printed. Select a View button on the toolbar and then select the Print Preview command to display the calendar in the Print Preview window.

Contacts is an Outlook tool that is used to create an electronic address book that stores information such as addresses and phone numbers of individuals and businesses. The Contact list can be displayed in several different views and printed so that the information can be used as a reference away from the computer.

Vocabulary

Appointment An activity scheduled on a specific day that has a specific starting and ending time.

Appointment Area An area of Calendar that contains details and reminders of appointments.

Calendar An Outlook tool that can be used to keep track of assignment due dates, create reminders about events, and schedule appointments and meetings.

Contacts An Outlook tool that is used to create an electronic address book that stores information such as addresses and phone numbers of individual and businesses.

Date Heading Area in the Appointment area of Calendar that displays the date that the calendar is referring to.

Date Navigator Area in the Navigation Pane of Calendar that displays a calendar for the current and next month.

Event An activity that is scheduled for a specific day but is not assigned a start or an end time.

Meeting Request An electronic invitation that can be accepted or declined by the recipient.

Navigation Pane Area of Calendar that contains Date Navigator and links to other Outlook tools.

Personal information manager An application such as Microsoft Outlook, that can simplify the organization of personal and business activities.

Previewing Displays the calendar as it will appear when printed.

Task A job, chore, or errand that needs to be completed.

Time bar Displays a series of time intervals indicating the time of the day.

Outlook Commands and Buttons

Advanced **command** Displays the advanced toolbar. Found in the Toolbars submenu in the View menu.

1 Day Displays the calendar for the current day in Day view. Found on the Calendar toolbar.

X Delete **command** Deletes an event, appointment, or task. Found in the menu displayed by right-clicking an event, appointment, or task. The Delete button on the toolbar can be used instead of the command.

Folder **command** Displays a dialog box used to create an additional calendar. Found in the New submenu in the File menu.

Meeting Request **command** Displays a Meeting form. Found in the New submenu in the File menu.

31 Month Displays a scrollable calendar with one week per row. Found on the Calendar toolbar.

New All Day Event **command** Displays an Event form used to add an event to Calendar. Found in the Actions menu.

New ▾ **New Appointment button** Displays an Appointment form used to add a new appointment. Found on the Calendar toolbar.

New ▾ **New Contact button** Displays a Contact form used to add a new contact. Found on the Contacts toolbar.

Outlook Today button Displays Outlook Today. Found on the Advanced toolbar.

Print Preview command Displays Calendar and the Contacts list as it will appear when printed. Found in the File menu.

Recurrence... Displays a dialog box with appointment recurrence options. Found on the Appointment form toolbar.

Save and Close Saves information typed in the Event, Appointment, and Task forms and removes the window. Found on the Event, Appointment, and Task forms toolbar.

Send/Receive ▾ Sends and Receives messages from the e-mail server. Found on the Message form and Meeting form toolbars.

Today Selects and displays the calendar for the current day regardless of the view. Found on the Calendar toolbar.

7 Week Displays the calendar for Monday through Sunday of the current week. Found on the Calendar toolbar.

5 Work Week Displays the calendar for Monday through Friday of the current week. Found on the Calendar toolbar.

1. a) What is a personal information manager?
    b) List three Outlook tools.

2. List three uses for the Outlook tool Calendar.

3. List two uses of Date Navigator.

4. List the step required to change Date Navigator to display the month four months ahead of the current month.

5. a) List the four views Calendar can be displayed in.
    b) How is Calendar changed from Day view to Month view?
    c) What view displays Monday through Sunday of the current week?
    d) How is Calendar changed to display the current day?
    e) Which Calendar view do you prefer to work in? Why?

6. a) What is an event?
    b) Where are events displayed?
    c) List the steps required to add the event "Alumni Basketball Game" on May 15, 2006.

7. What is the difference between an appointment and an event?

8. a) How is an appointment location displayed?
    b) What does a bell symbol to the left of an appointment indicate?

9. a) List the steps required to add the appointment "Hair Cut" from 5:00 p.m. to 5:45 p.m. on January 21, 2006, from Day view.
    b) List the step required to delete the "Hair Cut" appointment added in step (a).
    c) List the steps required to add a recurring appointment "Volleyball Practice" from 3:00 p.m. to 4:00 p.m. starting March 8, 2006 and occurring every Wednesday for 10 weeks.

10. a) List an example of a situation where it would be useful to have more than one calendar.
    b) List the step required to turn on the display of an additional calendar named "Business Calendar."

11. a) What two Outlook tools are used when sending meeting requests?
    b) List three examples of when you might send a meeting request.
    c) List the steps required to send a meeting request.
    d) What options does an individual that receives a meeting request have?

12. a) What is a task?
    b) Where are tasks entered and tracked?
    c) List the step required to display the Tasks window?
    d) In the Task window, list four ways the tasks list can be displayed.

13. a) List the steps required to add the task "Study for Java test" with a due date of April 11, 2006.
    b) List the steps required to modify the task in part (a) to include the note, "Test covers chapters 1 through 7."

14. a) How is a task marked complete?
    b) How is a completed task displayed in the TaskPad?
    c) How is a completed task deleted?

15. What is displayed when a calendar is previewed?

16. What is Contacts?

17. What does the information in the File as box determine?

18. a) List the steps required to add a new contact with the name Manuel Burgos, job title IT Systems Administrator, and business telephone number (954) 555-6230.
    b) List the steps required to delete the contact added in part (a).

19. List three views that the Contacts list can be displayed in.

20. List one reason why you would print the Contacts list.

True/False

21. Determine if each of the following are true or false. If false, explain why.
    a) Work Week view displays the calendar for Monday through Sunday of the current week.
    b) An event has a specific start time and end time.
    c) An appointment can occur on a regular basis.
    d) A meeting request uses e-mail to notify invitees of a scheduled meeting.
    e) A task is an event that is scheduled for more than one day.

Exercise 1

You will organize your personal and school schedule in Outlook by completing the following steps:

a) Add relevant school events to Calendar. These may include sports events, picture day, and school holidays.

b) Add appropriate personal events to Calendar. These may include family birthdays, anniversaries, and trips.

c) Using the course syllabus for each of your courses, add relevant school appointments to Calendar. These may include group work and study sessions, as well as assignment, project, test, and exam dates. Add reminders and notes as necessary.

d) Add appropriate personal appointments to Calendar. These may include hair appointments, workout schedule, and dates.

e) On the TaskPad, add school-related tasks that need to be completed. Add additional information as necessary. These may include returning a library book, paying an activity fee, and completing a project.

f) On the TaskPad, add appropriate personal tasks that need to be completed. These may include purchasing a birthday gift, practicing an instrument, and completing chores.

g) Print a copy of the current month's calendar to be used as a reference away from the computer.

h) Maintain the calendar throughout the school year. This includes modifying events and appointments and marking tasks as complete when appropriate.

Exercise 2

You will create a separate calendar in Outlook for your basketball team's schedule by completing the following steps:

a) On the TaskPad, add the task: Create basketball schedule

b) Create a new calendar folder named: Basketball Schedule

c) On the Basketball Schedule calendar, add a recurring appointment that occurs from 3:00 p.m. to 5:00 p.m. every Tuesday, starting on the next Tuesday, for 10 weeks. Set the reminder time to 1 hour. Appropriately color code the appointment.

d) Add a Team Meeting appointment on the next Wednesday from 7:00 p.m. to 9:00 p.m. Set the reminder time to 30 minutes. Appropriately color code the appointment.

e) Add a Basketball Tournament event two Saturdays from now. The location of the event is the Community Center Gym.

f) On the TaskPad, add the task: Pick up basketballs for tournament

g) On the TaskPad, mark the "Create basketball schedule" task complete.

h) Print a copy of the Basketball Schedule calendar to be posted for team members.

Exercise 3

Use the Outlook Contacts tool to complete the following steps:

a) In the Contacts window, add contact information for at least ten individuals or businesses. These may include friends, coaches, restaurants, and family members.

b) Display the contacts list in Detailed Address Card view and then print a copy in Small Booklet Style.

c) Display the Address Book and note the information that has been automatically added from the contacts list.

d) Exchange e-mail messages with a classmate who is not in your Contacts list. Update your Contacts list to include this new information.

e) Check the Address Book and note that the new contact was automatically added.

f) Send a meeting request to the classmate in part (d). The subject of the meeting is Yearbook Meeting. The meeting will occur three days from today and will last from 11 a.m. until 3 p.m. The meeting will be held in the library.

Chapter 4

Using a Word Processor

Word is the Microsoft Office word processor application. This chapter introduces Word for creating letters and simple documents. Modifying a document and collaborating on a document are explained.

What is a Word Processor?

A *word processor* is a computer application for creating, modifying, printing, and e-mailing documents. It is used to produce easy-to-read, professional-looking documents such as letters, résumés, and reports. The Microsoft Word 2003 window looks similar to:

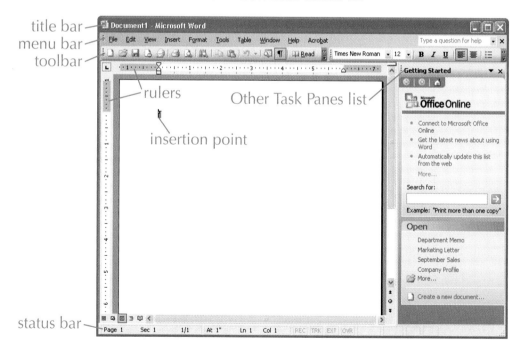

The Word window displays information about a document and includes tools for working with documents:

- The file name of the current document is displayed in the **title bar**. The name Document1 is used temporarily until the document is saved with a descriptive name.

- Select commands from menus in the **menu bar**.

Overtype Mode

Overtype mode means that as text is typed it replaces existing text, instead of inserting characters. Overtype mode is on if the OVR indicator on the status bar is not dimmed:

REC   TRK   EXT   OVR

To turn off overtype mode, double-click OVR on the status bar or press the Insert key on the keyboard.

TIP Press and hold an arrow key to move the insertion point in that direction.

One Space After a Period

How many spaces are typed after a period? Only one space is needed because the distance between each character is adjusted proportionally, making text easy to read.

inserting symbols

- Click a button on the **toolbar** to perform an action. Click the New Blank Document button ( ) to create a new document.

- The **rulers** show the paper size. Markers on the rulers are used for formatting text.

- The vertical line is the **insertion point** that indicates where the next character typed will be placed. In a new document the insertion point is in the upper-left corner. It blinks to draw attention to its location.

- View information about the current document in the **status bar**.

- Links for opening a document or creating a new document are in the **Getting Started task pane**. Click the arrow in the **Other Task Panes list** to select a different task pane to display. Click the Create a new document link for new document options.

Creating Document Text

In a word processor document, typed text is placed at the insertion point. Press a letter, number, or symbol key to place that character in the document at the insertion point. Press and hold the Shift key while pressing a key to insert uppercase letters or the character shown above a number or symbol.

Some keys on the keyboard are used to perform actions, such as moving the insertion point or deleting text. The arrow keys move the insertion point within existing text without erasing or entering text.

Together, the Ctrl key (Control) and an arrow key move the insertion point from word to word in a document. For example, press and hold the Ctrl key and then press the right arrow key to move the insertion point to the beginning of the next word to the right.

Press the Home key or End key to move the insertion point to the beginning or end of a line of text, respectively. Ctrl+Home moves the insertion point to the beginning of the document, and Ctrl+End to the end.

To erase the character directly to the right of the insertion point, press the Delete key. Deleting a character moves the characters to its right to fill the gap.

Press the Backspace key to erase the character directly to the left of the insertion point. Characters to the right move over to fill the gap.

To end a paragraph or to terminate a line of text, press the Enter key. Pressing Enter ends the current paragraph and creates a new one. Press Enter twice to create a blank line after the current paragraph.

There are symbols that do not appear on the keyboard, such as the copyright (©) and degree (°) symbols. To insert such symbols into a document, select Insert ➞ Symbol to display the Symbol dialog box. Click a symbol and then select Insert to place the symbol at the insertion point. Other symbols are displayed in the dialog box by selecting a font in the Font list.

Editing Text in a Document

A word processor document is *edited*, or modified, on the screen. When editing, first position the insertion point where text is to be typed or deleted. One way to position the insertion point is by pressing an arrow key to move the insertion point. To position the insertion point with the mouse, move the pointer into the document until it changes from an arrow shape to the *I-beam pointer* (I). Click the I-beam pointer where the insertion point should appear.

When text is typed, existing text automatically moves to the right to make room for the new text. Word automatically determines if the words to the right will fit on the end of the current line or if some words must go on the next line. This process is called *word wrap.*

word wrap

When text is deleted, remaining text automatically moves to fill the space. The word wrap process may also cause words to move up from the lines below when text is deleted.

Select Edit → Undo (⟲ ▾) to reverse an edit. Select Edit → Redo or Edit → Repeat (⟳ ▾) to repeat the last action performed. Click the arrow in the Undo or Redo button to display a list of the last actions performed. Select an option from the list to undo or redo that particular action.

TIP When editing, use the Enter key to end a paragraph only. Within a paragraph, allow the word wrap process to wrap text from line to line.

Spaces, tabs (discussed later in the text), and paragraphs are not normally displayed as characters in a document, but they can be displayed as special symbols. These symbols are called *formatting marks* and do not appear on paper when a document is printed:

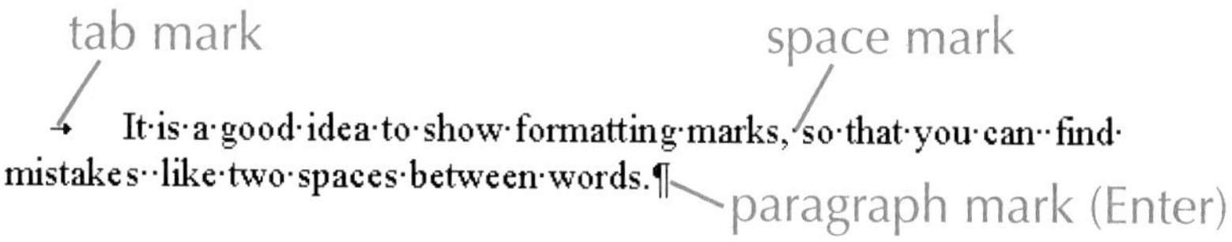

The ¶ Button

The Show/Hide ¶ button may not initially appear on the toolbar. In this case, click the Toolbar Options button (⁝) on the toolbar and then click ¶. Once selected, the button is added to the toolbar.

tab mark   space mark

→ It·is·a·good·idea·to·show·formatting·marks,·so·that·you·can··find·
mistakes··like·two·spaces·between·words.¶ paragraph mark (Enter)

It is much easier to edit a document when formatting marks are visible. Display formatting marks by clicking the Show/Hide ¶ button (¶) on the toolbar. Click ¶ again to hide the formatting marks.

Practice: Request – part 1 of 2

You will create and save a new Word document. The document is a letter in the block style as defined in *The Gregg Reference Manual Ninth Edition* by William Sabin (copyright 2001 Glencoe/McGraw-Hill).

① *START WORD*

 a. Ask your instructor for the appropriate steps to start Microsoft Word 2003.

 b. Look at the word processor window. Note the title bar, menu bar, toolbar, rulers, status bar, and Getting Started task pane.

 c. The blinking insertion point is in the upper-left of the document. Press the right arrow key. The insertion point does not move because there is no text in the document.

② TYPE THE LETTER HEADING

A block style letter is a letter style that is often used in business. The block style should also be used by individuals writing to a company or professional organization. A *block style letter* contains a heading, opening, body, and closing with all lines beginning at the left side of the page.

a. On the Toolbar, click the Show/Hide ¶ button (¶) to display formatting marks, if they are not already showing. A ¶ marker is displayed to the right of the insertion point.

Note: If you do not see ¶ on the Toolbar, click the Toolbar Options button:

b. A letter heading includes a return address and date. Press Enter 6 times to move the insertion point down about 1 inch (2.54 cm).

c. Type the following address and date, and then press Enter 4 times. Ignore the purple dotted line:

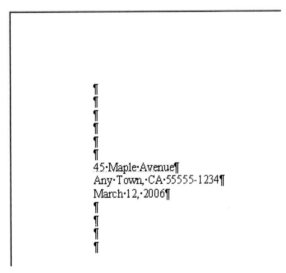

③ SAVE THE LETTER

Select File → Save. The Save As dialog box is displayed.

1. Use the **Save in** list and the contents box below it to select the appropriate location for the file to be saved.

2. In the **File name** box, replace existing text with Request and then select Save.

④ TYPE THE LETTER OPENING

The letter opening includes an inside address and salutation. Type the following letter opening and then press Enter twice. Ignore the red wavy line and purple dotted line:

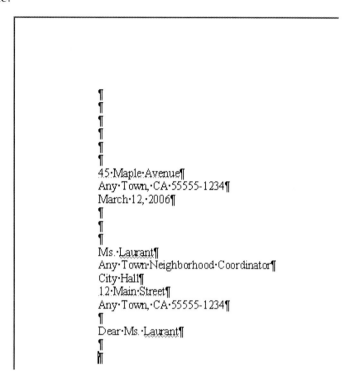

⑤ TYPE THE LETTER BODY

Type the following letter body and then press Enter 2 times after the last paragraph. Red wavy lines and purple dotted lines may appear. Ignore them for now:

Dear·Ms.·Laurant¶

¶

I·represent·the·Arbor·Neighborhood·Association,·which·includes·families·from·1ˢᵗ·Street·through·8ᵗʰ·Street,·east·of·Oak·Avenue·and·west·of·Poplar·Avenue.·We·would·like·to·participate·in·the·"Neighborhood·Cleanup"·campaign.·I·am·writing·to·request·that·a·representative·from·your·organization·speak·at·our·next·association·meeting.·Our·next·meeting·is·scheduled·for·Saturday,·April·16,·2006·at·the·Lake·pavilion·in·Poplar·Park.¶

¶

We·have·already·started·the·campaign·by·picking·up·a·brochure·and·free·trash·bags·from·your·office.·Our·association·is·relying·on·a·representative·to·offer·suggestions·on·a·cleanup·schedule·and·an·incentives·program·for·the·neighborhood·children.¶

¶

Thank·you·for·your·time.·I·look·forward·to·hearing·from·you·soon.¶

¶

¶

⑥ *TYPE THE LETTER CLOSING*

   a. The letter closing includes a complimentary closing and a signature line. Type Sincerely and then press Enter 4 times.

   b. Type Blaine Trevi and then select Insert → Symbol. A dialog box is displayed.

      1. In the Subset list, select Latin-1. (You may need to first change the Font list to (normal text).) In the Latin characters, click ñ:

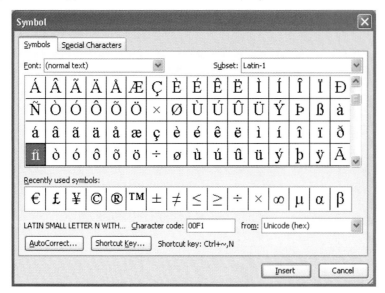

      2. Select Insert and then select Close. ñ has been added to the name.

   c. Type o to complete the name. The closing should look similar to:

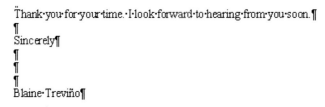

⑦ *EDIT THE LETTER*

   a. In the body of the letter, the time of the meeting needs to be specified. Place the insertion point just before "Saturday" and then type 2:00 p.m. followed by a space.

   b. Below Blaine Treviño's name, type your name.

   c. Save the modified Request.

⑧ *PRINT THE LETTER*

Spelling and Grammar Checking

Word includes a *spelling checker* that automatically checks words as they are typed. Words typed in a document are compared to those in a dictionary file. If a word is spelled incorrectly or is not in the dictionary file, a red wavy line appears below it. To correct the word, right-click it to display suggested words, and then click the correct spelling from the menu:

red wavy line

TIP If the wrong menu appears, the pointer may not have been over the word.

AutoCorrect

The AutoCorrect feature will automatically correct typing mistakes, misspelled words, and incorrect capitalization as you type. Point to the corrected text and then point to the blue bar below the text to display the AutoCorrect Options button (⚡ ▾). Click this button to display options for reversing the correction.

Right-click a word with a red wavy underline to display a menu of word choices

Because the dictionary file does not contain every word in the English language, a red wavy line may appear below a correctly spelled word, such as a proper name. When this happens, the wavy line can be ignored. It will not appear on paper when the document is printed. To remove the red wavy line from all occurrences of that word in the document, right-click the word and select Ignore All from the menu.

green wavy line

Word also has a *grammar checker* that displays a green wavy line below a phrase or sentence when a possible grammatical error is detected. Right-click the text that has a green wavy line to display suggested corrections:

Proofreading

Spelling and grammar checkers can increase the accuracy of a document. However, proofreading a document is still a very important step in the editing process. For example, a word may be spelled correctly but used inappropriately. Having a person other than the author proofread a document increases the chances of finding spelling, grammar, and punctuation errors.

Right-click a word with a green wavy underline to display a menu of grammar options

A green wavy line may appear below an acceptable sentence. When this happens, the wavy line can be ignored, or it can be removed from the document by selecting Ignore Once from the menu.

Smart Tags

TIP Smart tags can save time because they perform actions in Word that would otherwise require opening another application.

Word automatically evaluates text as it is typed to determine if it is data that can be used in other applications. For example, a person's name typed in a document may be useful stored as part of an Outlook contact for future use. Text recognized as data is marked with a purple dotted underline, which is called a *smart tag indicator*.

Jade Boticelli
1137 Main Street ——smart tag indicator
Holyoke, NC 02401

Move the pointer over the smart tag indicator to display the Smart Tag Actions button (ⓢ). Click ⓢ to display a menu with commands for adding the data as an Outlook contact or removing the smart tag.

Practice: Request – part 2 of 2

You will correct mispelled words and remove the red wavy line from correctly spelled words in a business letter. Grammar will also be corrected. A contact will be added to Outlook. Word should already be started with the Request document displayed from the last practice.

① *REMOVE THE RED WAVY LINE FROM CORRECTLY SPELLED LAST NAMES*

   a. Right-click either "Laurant." A menu is displayed.

   b. Select **Ignore All**. The red wavy line disappears from both occurrences of "Laurant."

   c. At the bottom of the letter, right-click "Treviño" and select **Ignore All**.

② *ADD A CONTACT TO OUTLOOK*

   a. Point to the address "12 Main Street", which is marked with a smart tag indicator. The Smart Tag Actions button is displayed.

   b. Click the Smart Tag Actions button (ⓢ) and then select **Add to Contacts**. A dialog box is displayed.

       1. In the **Full Name** box, type Connie Laurant:

       2. On the dialog box toolbar, click 🖫 Save and Close. A contact is created.

③ *REMOVE SMART TAGS*

   a. Point to "45 Maple Avenue" at the top of the letter. The Smart Tag Actions button is displayed.

   b. Click the Smart Tag Actions button (ⓢ) and then select **Remove this Smart Tag**. The purple dotted line is no longer displayed.

   c. Remove the other smart tags from the letter.

④ *SAVE AND CLOSE THE MODIFIED REQUEST*

Finding and Replacing Text

finding text

A word processor document can be easily searched for a specified character, word, or phrase. In Word, Edit → Find displays a Find and Replace dialog box where search text is entered. Word searches a document starting at the position of the insertion point. If a match is found, Word stops searching and selects the text. The search can be continued until the entire document has been scanned.

replacing text

Text can be replaced with other text by using the Replace command, also in the Edit menu. In this case, search text as well as replace text are entered in the Find and Replace dialog box.

refining a search

To make a text search more specific, options such as Match case and Find whole words only can be selected in the Find and Replace dialog box. Match case selects text with the same capitalization as the search text. For example, a search for Cat will not find CAT or cat. Find whole words only selects text that entirely matches the search text. For example, a search for fin will not find finer, stuffing, or muffin.

finding formatting marks

Formatting marks and other special characters are entered as search text by making a selection from the Special list at the bottom of the Find and Replace dialog box. For example, it may be helpful to find all the occurrences of the word tip at the beginning of a paragraph. Since all (except the first) paragraphs in a document have a paragraph mark before them, precise search text is entered by selecting Paragraph Mark from Special and then typing tip.

The More Button

If additional search options, such as Match case, are not displayed, then select the More button in the Find and Replace dialog box.

Using a Thesaurus

synonyms

antonyms

Research task pane

TIP The thesaurus shows similar phrases when a phrase is selected rather than a single word.

A *thesaurus* is a collection of *synonyms*, which are words that have similar meanings. For example, "chilly" is a synonym for "cool." A thesaurus also provides related words, phrases, and *antonyms*, which are words with opposite meaning. For example, "hot" is an antonym for "cool." In Word, place the insertion point in a word and then select Tools → Language → Thesaurus to display the Research task pane with Thesaurus results. To replace the selected word with one from the Research task pane, click the arrow to the right of the word and select Insert from the displayed menu. Thesaurus results can also be displayed by right-clicking a word, which displays a menu with a Synonyms command.

Word uses a file for the thesaurus which does not contain every possible word in the English language. If the selected word cannot be found, suggested spellings are displayed in the Research task pane.

Practice: HANDBOOK

You will customize a company employee handbook. Word should already be started.

① *OPEN HANDBOOK*

Open the HANDBOOK document, which is a Word data file for this text. Company etiquette rules are listed.

② *FIND TEXT*

    a. Select Edit ➔ Find. The Find and Replace dialog box is displayed.

       Note: Your dialog box may show additional find options.

    b. In the Find what box, type: telephone

    c. Select Find Next. The first occurrence of "telephone" after the insertion point is selected.

    d. Select Find Next. Another occurrence is selected.

    e. Continue to select Find Next until Word has finished searching the document. Did you notice that "telephone" with a lowercase t as well as "Telephone" with an uppercase T were found?

③ *MODIFY SEARCH CRITERIA*

    a. In the Find and Replace dialog box, select More if the search options are not displayed.

    b. Select the Match case check box:

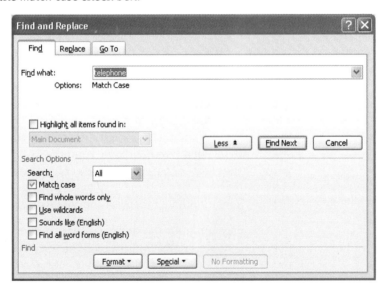

    c. Select Find Next. A lowercase "telephone" is found.

    d. Continue to select Find Next until all occurrences have been located. Select OK to remove the dialog box. Did any of the selected words contain an uppercase T?

④ *FIND A SPECIAL CHARACTER*

    a. In the Find what box, replace "telephone" with: e-mail

    b. Select Special and then select Paragraph Mark:

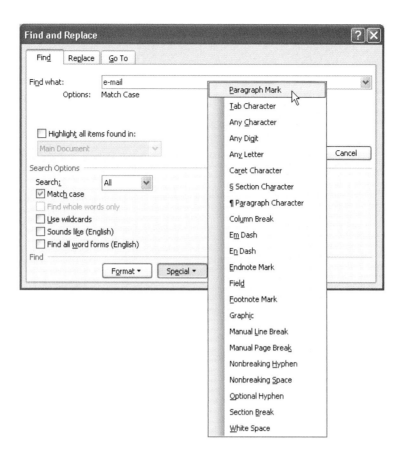

c. Check that the Find what criteria is: e-mail^p

d. Clear the Match case option.

e. Select Find Next. "E-mail" followed by a paragraph marker is selected.

f. Continue to select Find Next until all occurrences have been located. Select OK to remove the dialog box. Were there any other occurrences of e-mail at the end of a paragraph?

g. Select Cancel. The dialog box is removed.

⑤ *CUSTOMIZE THE HANDBOOK*

a. Select Edit → Replace. The Find and Replace dialog box is displayed.

Note: Your dialog box may show additional find and replace options.

b. In the Find what box, type: XYZ Company

c. In the Replace with box, type: Widget Corporation

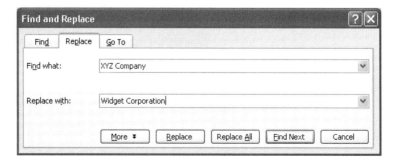

d. Select Find Next. The first occurrence is located and selected.

e. Select Replace. The selected text is replaced with Widget Corporation and the rest of the text is scanned for another occurrence.

f. Continue to select Replace to change all occurrences of XYZ Company to Widget Corporation. Select OK to remove the dialog box.

g. Close the Find and Replace dialog box.

⑥ *USE A THESAURUS*

a. Place the insertion point in the word "Gathering," which is the third subheading of the document.

b. Select Tools → Language → Thesaurus. The Research task pane is displayed with thesaurus results for "Gathering."

c. In the task pane, point to "meeting," click the arrow, and then select Insert:

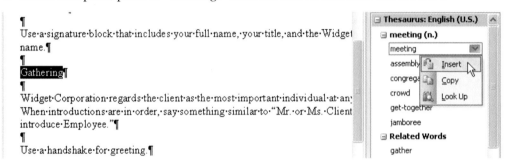

The word "Gathering" is replaced by "Meeting." Note that Word used the appropriate capitalization.

d. Find and replace all other occurrences of "gathering" with "meeting." Close the dialog box when done.

⑦ *FIND A SYNONYM FOR THE WORD ESCORT*

a. In the last paragraph, right-click the word "escort." A menu is displayed.

b. In the menu, select Synonyms and then select accompany. The word "accompany" replaces "escort."

⑧ *SAVE, PRINT, AND THEN CLOSE THE MODIFIED HANDBOOK*

a. Type your name after the last paragraph in the document.

b. Save the modified HANDBOOK, print a copy, and then close the file.

Selecting Text

Editing is faster when text to delete or change is selected first. Select text by dragging the I-beam pointer over any amount of text, from a single character to several pages. *Selected text* is shown highlighted on the screen:

> The·Lollipop·River·Troupe·will·perform·their·version·of·"Green·Grass·in·Ohio"·next· weekend.·Tickets·are·on·sale·at·the·box·office·and·are·priced·at·$5·for·adults,·$1·for· children·12·and·under.·The·box·office·is·open·from·2·p.m.·to·9·p.m.·every·Thursday· through·Sunday.¶

The second sentence is selected

Type to replace selected text with new text. Press the Backspace key or Delete key to remove the selected text. Click anywhere in the document or press an arrow key to remove the selection without deleting the text.

In addition to dragging the I-beam pointer, other ways to select text include:

- **Double-click a word** to extend the selection from the first character to the space after the word.

- **Hold down the Shift key and click a character** to extend the selection from the insertion point to the character clicked.

- **Hold down the Shift key and press an arrow key** to extend the selection from the insertion point to the character in the direction of the arrow key. **Hold down both the Ctrl and Shift keys and press an arrow key** to extend the selection from the insertion point to the word in the direction of the arrow key.

- **Hold down the Ctrl key and click** to select the sentence clicked.

- **Move the pointer to the left of the text (near the left edge of the page) until the pointer turns into a right-pointing arrow (⇗) and click** to select the line of text to the right. **Double-click** to select the entire paragraph, and **triple-click** to select the entire document. **Drag up or down** to select multiple lines of text.

- Edit → Select All to select all the text in the document.

Cut, Copy, and Paste

TIP Using Ctrl key shortcuts for Cut (Ctrl+X), Copy (Ctrl+C), and Paste (Ctrl+V) may improve productivity because your hands do not need to leave the keyboard.

The Paste Options Button

Click the Paste Options button ([⬚ ▾]) to display formatting options after pasting text.

Editing a document often requires moving and duplicating text. *Moving text* means that selected text is "cut" from one place in a document and then "pasted" into another place. *Duplicating text* means that selected text is "copied" from one place in a document and the copy "pasted" into another place. The Cut ([✂]), Copy ([▨]), and Paste ([▨]) commands from the Edit menu are used to move and duplicate text.

There are four steps to move or duplicate text:

1. Select the text to be moved or copied.

2. Select either Cut or Copy.

3. Place the insertion point in the document where the text is to be inserted.

4. Select Paste.

Clipboard

Cut or copied text is placed on the *Clipboard*, which is a designated area in memory. Paste places the most recent contents of the Clipboard at the insertion point. Text on the Clipboard remains there until different text is cut or copied or the computer is turned off.

Office Clipboard

The *Office Clipboard* stores the last 24 cut or copied items. Select Edit → Office Clipboard to display the Clipboard task pane. Point to an item and then click the arrow to display Paste and Delete commands.

moving and duplicating between documents

Text can be moved and duplicated between two or more documents. For example, cut text from one document can be pasted into a different document. Similarly, copied text can be pasted into a different document. After cutting or copying from one document, display the second document, position the insertion point, and then paste.

You will edit a company orientation handout. Word should already be started.

① *OPEN ORIENTATION*

    a. Open the ORIENTATION document, which is a Word data file for this text. The Widget Corporation employee orientation document is displayed.

    b. Display all characters, if they are not already showing.

② *MOVE A PARAGRAPH*

    a. Select the second paragraph of text after the "Introduction" heading. Also include the blank paragraph marker before the paragraph of text. To select the paragraphs, drag the pointer from the blank paragraph to the paragraph marker at the end of the text, similar to:

> ¶
> Now·in·our·twentieth·year·of·business,·Widget·Corporation·is·dedicated·to·educating· employees·so·that·our·customers·are·served·in·the·best·way·possible.·As·a·Widget· employee,·you·are·expected·to·implement·the·skills·and·information·that·you·will·be· given·at·the·orientation.·A·company·is·only·as·strong·as·its·weakest·link.·Help·keep·us· strong!¶

    b. On the toolbar, click the Cut button (✄). The paragraph is removed from the document and placed on the Clipboard.

    c. Place the insertion point just after the last paragraph in the Introduction, which starts "Our orientation is...."

    d. On the toolbar, click the Paste button (📋). The paragraph from the Clipboard is pasted into the document.

    e. Save the modified ORIENTATION.

③ *PASTE TEXT FROM ANOTHER DOCUMENT*

    a. Open the HANDBOOK document, which was modified in an earlier practice in this chapter.

    b. Scroll to view the "Meeting" information at the bottom of the page.

    c. Place the insertion point just to the left of the second etiquette rule that reads "Use a handshake...."

    d. Press and hold the Shift key and then click at the end of the text that reads "...on the right shoulder." The selection includes:

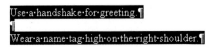

> Use·a·handshake·for·greeting.¶
> ¶
> Wear·a·name·tag·high·on·the·right·shoulder.¶

    e. On the toolbar, click the Copy button (📋). The text is copied to the Clipboard.

    f. Close HANDBOOK. The ORIENTATION document is again displayed.

    g. Select Edit → Office Clipboard. The Clipboard task pane is displayed with the copied etiquette rules.

    h. Scroll the ORIENTATION document to display the first paragraph in the "What You Need to Know" section.

    i. Place the insertion point in the second blank paragraph after "...please be sure to:"

j. In the Clipboard task pane, click the etiquette rules. The etiquette paragraphs are copied into the ORIENTATION document:

¶
A·Networking·Breakfast:··The·morning·begins·with·a·continental·breakfast.·During·this· time·you·should·introduce·yourself·to·other·employees.·As·per·the·Widget·Handbook,· please·be·sure·to:¶
¶
Use·a·handshake·for·greeting.¶
¶
Wear·a·name·tag·high·on·the·right·shoulder.¶
¶
Morning·Sessions:··A·binder·with·the·Widget·Handbook,·handouts·about·ethics·in·the·

k. Type your name after the last paragraph in the document.

l. Save the modified ORIENTATION and print a copy.

Formatting Characters

The way text appears on a page is called its *format*. Font, size, and style define a character's format. A *font* or *typeface* refers to the shape of characters. The default font in Word is Times New Roman. There are also special fonts, such as Wingdings, that contain pictures called *dingbats*. Note how each font shapes characters differently:

Tahoma: ABCDEF abcdef 1234567890

Times New Roman: ABCDEF abcdef 1234567890

Comic Sans MS: ABCDEF abcdef 1234567890

Courier: ABCDEF abcdef 1234567890

Wingdings: ✌✋☜☞☝☟ ✁✂✃✄✆✈✉✎✐✌

The size of text is measured in points, and there are 72 points to an inch. For example:

This is an example of 8 point Tahoma.

This is an example of 10 point Tahoma.

This is an example of 12 point Tahoma.

This is an example of 14 point Tahoma.

The way in which a character is emphasized is called its *style*. The most common styles are bold, italic, and underline:

Bold text is printed darker so that words and phrases stand out on a page. It is often used for titles and headings.

Italic text is slanted and is mostly used for emphasis. It is sometimes used for headings.

Underline text has a line under it and is mostly used for emphasis. It is sometimes used for the title of a publication.

Regular text, sometimes called normal text, is the default style.

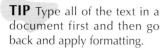

Using Fonts and Sizes Effectively

Using too many different fonts can make a document look cluttered and unprofessional. Keep it simple by using only two or three fonts per document. The size of text also affects the look of a document. To help the reader distinguish between headings and body text, body text is usually 8 to 14 points and headings are at least 2 points larger than the body text, usually 12 to 72 points.

TIP Type all of the text in a document first and then go back and apply formatting.

Marks for Footnotes and Endnotes

Footnotes and endnotes are usually marked with superscripted text. Creating footnotes and endnotes is described in Chapter 5.

TIP To keep your hands on the keyboard while formatting, use the Ctrl key to bold (Ctrl+B), italicize (Ctrl+I), underline (Ctrl+U), superscript (Ctrl+Shift+=), and subscript (Ctrl+=) text. Pressing Ctrl+spacebar removes any applied styles from selected text.

TIP Always preview a document before printing to see document formatting because print preview displays an entire page at once.

Another text style is *superscript*, which reduces the size of the text and raises it to the top of the current line. *Subscript* is a text style that reduces the size of the text and lowers it to the bottom of the current line. In the following example, the "th" after the 5 is a superscript, and the "2" in H_2O is a subscript:

> In her 5th Avenue boutique, Dina Johannsen sold her designer perfume called "DJ's H_2O."

Text color can also be changed to emphasize headings, subheadings, and other text. Color should be applied with readability in mind. Bright colors and many colors in a single document are not usually recommended.

Format characters by first selecting the text. Next, select Format → Font to display the Font dialog box with options for changing the font, style, size, and color of selected text. The Font dialog box is also displayed by right-clicking selected text and then selecting Font from the menu.

The Font box (Times New Roman) and Font Size box (12) on the toolbar can also be used to change the font and size of selected text. The Bold (**B**), Italic (*I*), and Underline (U) buttons on the toolbar can be used to apply or remove character styles from selected text. The Font Color button (A) can be used to change the font color. More than one button can be used at a time text to apply multiple styles.

Previewing a Document

A document can be previewed to see how it will appear when printed. Select File → Print Preview or click the Print Preview button ( ) on the toolbar to display the Print Preview window:

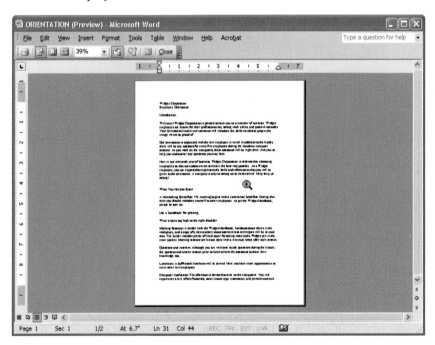

Once in print preview, the document can be viewed in different ways:

- Press the **Page Up key** or **Page Down key** to display the previous or next page, respectively.

- Use the **vertical scroll bar** to view previous and next pages.

- Move the pointer onto the document and then **click the magnifying glass** (🔍) to zoom into that portion of the page. Click again to display the entire page.

Click the Print button (🖨) on the toolbar to print a copy of the document using the default printer settings. Click Close on the toolbar or press the Esc key to return to the document window.

Practice: ORIENTATION – part 2 of 4

You will format a company orientation handout. Word should already be started with the ORIENTATION document displayed from the last practice.

① *FORMAT THE ENTIRE TITLE*

a. At the top of the document, select the entire title "Widget Corporation Employee Orientation."

b. Select Format → Font. A dialog box is displayed.

c. Change the Font to Arial, the Font style to Bold, the Size to 16, and the color to green:

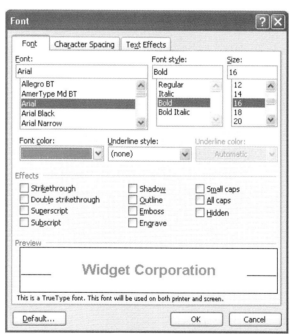

d. Select OK. The title is formatted:

> **Widget·Corporation¶**
> **Employee·Orientation¶**
> ¶
> Introduction¶

② FORMAT TEXT USING THE TOOLBAR

a. In the next line, select the "Introduction" title.

b. On the toolbar, click the Italic button (**I**). The selected text is italic.

c. On the toolbar, click the Bold button (**B**). The selected text is now both bold and italic.

d. Click anywhere in the document to remove the selection.

③ FORMAT THE REMAINING TWO TITLES AS BOLD AND ITALIC

a. Scroll down page 1 until the "What You Need to Know" title is displayed, and then select the title.

b. Right-click the selected text. A menu is displayed.

c. Select Font from the menu. A dialog box is displayed.

    1. In the Font style list, select Bold Italic.

    2. Select OK. The dialog box is removed and the selected text is bold and italic.

d. Click anywhere to remove the selection.

e. Use either of the methods in Steps 2 and 3 to format the "See You Soon" title as bold and italic.

④ UNDERLINE A PHRASE IN THE INTRODUCTION

a. Scroll to the top of page 1.

b. Select the words "pleased to have you" in the second sentence of the paragraph that begins "Welcome! ...."

c. On the toolbar, click the Underline button (**U**). The selected text is underlined.

d. Click anywhere to remove the selection.

⑤ REMOVE FORMATTING

a. Place the insertion point just to the right of the "d" in "pleased to have you" in the underlined text.

b. Hold down the Shift key and then press the right-arrow key until "to have you" is selected.

c. On the toolbar, click the Underline button. The selected text is no longer underlined.

d. Click anywhere to remove the selection. Only the word "pleased" is underlined.

Check – Your document should look similar to:

Widget·Corporation¶
Employee·Orientation¶
¶
Introduction¶
¶
Welcome!·Widget·Corporation·is·<u>pleased</u>·to·have·you·as·a·member·of·our·team.·Widget·employees·are·known·for·their·professionalism,·strong·work·ethics,·and·positive·attitudes.·Your·orientation·leaders·and·assistants·will·introduce·the·skills·needed·to·project·the·image·we·are·so·proud·of.¶
¶
Our·orientation·is·organized·with·the·new·employee·in·mind.·In·addition·to·the·leader,·there·will·be·one·assistant·for·every·five·employees·during·the·hands-on·computer·sessions.·As·you·work·on·the·computers,·these·assistants·will·be·right·there·with·you·to·help·you·and·answer·any·questions·you·may·have.¶
¶
Now·in·our·twentieth·year·of·business,·Widget·Corporation·is·dedicated·to·educating·

6. **PREVIEW THE DOCUMENT**

 a. Save the modified document.

 b. On the toolbar, click the Print Preview button (). ORIENTATION is displayed in the Print Preview window.

 c. Point to the middle of the page. The pointer changes to a magnifying glass (🔍).

 d. Click in the middle of the page. The document is magnified.

 e. Click again in the middle of the page. The entire page is displayed in the window.

 f. Scroll down, if necessary, to display the second page of ORIENTATION.

7. **PRINT THE DOCUMENT**

 a. Press the Page Up key to display page 1 of the document.

 b. On the toolbar, click the Print button (🖨). The document is printed.

 c. On the toolbar, click `Close`. The Print Preview window is closed and the document window is displayed.

Paragraph Alignment

The _alignment_ of text in a paragraph refers to its position relative to the sides of the page:

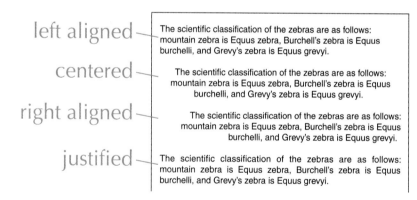

left aligned — The scientific classification of the zebras are as follows: mountain zebra is Equus zebra, Burchell's zebra is Equus burchelli, and Grevy's zebra is Equus grevyi.

centered — The scientific classification of the zebras are as follows: mountain zebra is Equus zebra, Burchell's zebra is Equus burchelli, and Grevy's zebra is Equus grevyi.

right aligned — The scientific classification of the zebras are as follows: mountain zebra is Equus zebra, Burchell's zebra is Equus burchelli, and Grevy's zebra is Equus grevyi.

justified — The scientific classification of the zebras are as follows: mountain zebra is Equus zebra, Burchell's zebra is Equus burchelli, and Grevy's zebra is Equus grevyi.

> **Format Painter**
>
> To copy entire paragraph formats from one paragraph to another, place the insertion point in the paragraph that contains the formatting to be copied and click the Format Painter button (🖌) on the toolbar. The formats are copied and the pointer changes to 🔳. Click another paragraph to apply the formatting.

TIP Right-click a paragraph to display the Paragraph command.

Left aligned is the default and means that the left edge of a paragraph is straight and the right edge of the paragraph is jagged. This format is most often used in letters and research papers. _Centered_ means that the left and right edges of the paragraph are equally distant from the left and right sides of the page. Headings and titles are often centered. _Right aligned_ means that the right edge of the paragraph is straight and the left edge is jagged. _Justified_ alignment creates straight edges at both sides of a paragraph and is often used in newspapers and books.

The Align Left (≣), Center (≣), Align Right (≣), and Justify (≣) buttons on the toolbar can be used to apply a paragraph alignment. To format multiple paragraphs together, first select the paragraphs and then click an alignment button.

The Paragraph dialog box can also be used to format paragraphs. Select Format → Paragraph to display the dialog box. Click the Indents and Spacing tab to display options for changing alignment.

You will continue to format ORIENTATION. Word should already be started with the ORIENTATION document displayed from the last practice.

① *CENTER THE FIRST TWO LINES IN THE DOCUMENT*

    a. At the top of page 1, place the insertion point anywhere in the "Widget Corporation" title.

    b. Select Format ➜ Paragraph. A dialog box is displayed.

    c. Change the Alignment to Centered:

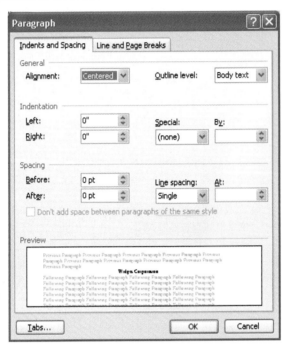

    d. Select OK. The dialog box is removed and the text is centered.

    e. Place the insertion point in the next line of the document: "Employee Orientation"

    f. On the toolbar, click the Center button (⬚). The text is centered.

② *JUSTIFY THE PARAGRAPHS IN THE INTRODUCTION*

    a. Place the insertion point anywhere in the paragraph that begins "Welcome! Widget Corporation…."

b. Hold down the Shift key and click in the last paragraph of the introduction, which begins "Now in our twentieth year…." Each paragraph in the Introduction now contains some selected text:

> Welcome!·Widget·Corporation·is·<u>pleased</u>·to·have·you·as·a·member·of·our·team.·Widget·employees·are·known·for·their·professionalism,·strong·work·ethics,·and·positive·attitudes.·Your·orientation·leaders·and·assistants·will·introduce·the·skills·needed·to·project·the·image·we·are·so·proud·of.¶
>
> ¶
>
> Our·orientation·is·organized·with·the·new·employee·in·mind.·In·addition·to·the·leader,·there·will·be·one·assistant·for·every·five·employees·during·the·hands-on·computer·sessions.·As·you·work·on·the·computers,·these·assistants·will·be·right·there·with·you·to·help·you·and·answer·any·questions·you·may·have.¶
>
> ¶
>
> Now·in·our·twentieth·year·of·business,·Widget·Corporation·is·dedicated·to·educating·employees·so·that·our·customers·are·served·in·the·best·way·possible.·As·a·Widget·employee,·you·are·expected·to·implement·the·skills·and·information·that·you·will·be·given·at·the·orientation.·A·company·is·only·as·strong·as·its·weakest·link.·Help·keep·us·strong!¶

c. On the toolbar, click the Justify button (▤). The paragraphs are justified.

d. Click anywhere to remove the selection.

③ SAVE THE MODIFIED ORIENTATION

Hyperlinks in a Document

TIP If your hyperlink isn't automatic, select **Tools →** **AutoCorrect Options** to display a dialog box. Select the **AutoFormat As You Type** tab and then select the **Internet and network paths with hyperlinks** check box.

When a Web site address is typed in a document, Word automatically turns it into a blue, underlined <u>hyperlink</u>. For example, after the URL www.lpdatafiles.com is typed, Word formats that text as blue underlined characters. A reader viewing the Word document on screen can press the Ctrl key and then click the link to follow a hyperlink. Holding down the Ctrl key changes the pointer to 🖑. Clicking 🖑 displays the Web page in a browser window if there is an Internet connection.

Word also recognizes an e-mail address and formats it as blue underlined characters. A reader viewing the Word document on screen can press the Ctrl key and then click the link to display a new e-mail message window.

TIP Refer to Chapter 2 for more information on the Internet and URLs.

The Insert Hyperlink dialog box contains options for inserting a hyperlink into a document. To use this dialog box, select Insert → Hyperlink or click the Insert Hyperlink button (🖼) on the toolbar. Select a type of link from the Link to list and then type a label in the Text to display box. For Web page links, type a URL in the Address box. For an e-mail address link, type an address in the E-mail address box. The label is placed at the insertion point, but the URL will be followed when the reader clicks the label.

removing a hyperlink

To remove the blue underline from text, right-click the link and then select Remove Hyperlink from the menu. The text remains, but is no longer a hyperlink.

You will add an e-mail contact and Web site address to ORIENTATION. Word should already be started with the ORIENTATION document displayed from the last practice.

① **ADD AN E-MAIL CONTACT AND A WEB SITE ADDRESS**

   a. Scroll to the end of the document.

   b. Place the insertion point just before the period in the last sentence that ends "human resources at extension #3872...."

   c. Type a space and then type: or e-mail widget@lpdatafiles.com

   d. Place the insertion point after the period following the e-mail address and type a space. The e-mail address becomes blue and underlined.

   e. Type the sentence: You may also download this document from our Web site at www.lpdatafiles.com/widget.

   f. Type a space after the period. The link becomes blue and underlined.

   g. Save the modified ORIENTATION.

   Check – Your document should look similar to:

> ***See·You·Soon!***¶
> ¶
> Widget·Corporation·is·glad·to·have·you·on·board.·We·look·forward·to·a·productive· orientation.·If·you·have·any·questions,·please·call·human·resources·at·extension·#3872·or· e-mail·<u>widget@lpdatafiles.com</u>.·You·may·also·download·this·document·from·our·Web· site·at·<u>www.lpdatafiles.com/widget.htm</u>.·¶

② **TEST THE HYPERLINK**

   This step requires a browser and Internet access. If either of these are not available, then skip this step.

   a. Press and hold the Ctrl key and then click <u>www.lpdatafiles.com/widget.htm</u>. A browser window is opened and the Web site displayed.

   b. Close the browser window.

③ **SAVE, PRINT, AND CLOSE THE MODIFIED ORIENTATION**

Document Collaboration

<u>*Document collaboration*</u> means working with others to create, review, and revise a document to achieve the desired result. One form of collaboration is *peer editing*. It is always a good idea to have a peer edit a document because it is often difficult to catch mistakes, especially in a lengthy document that has been worked on for an extended time. Peer editing often involves "suggested" changes instead of changes that have to be made, such as spelling errors.

The peer editing process can involve providing a printout for a peer to mark edits, but this can be inefficient and inconvenient. Another way to gather input from a reviewer is to provide the document as a file which tracks changes. This method allows the reviewer to type edits and com-

TIP The TRK indicator on the Status bar is bold when tracking changes.

(handwritten margin note: Important for exchanging & reviewing other persons doc.)

ments directly into the document itself. Changes will be recorded as they are made so that the original author can later decide which changes to keep and which to discard. To modify a document to track changes, select Tools → Track Changes. When the reviewer makes changes in a document that is tracking changes, edits appears similar to:

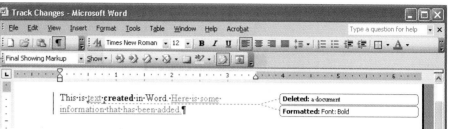

Reviewing toolbar—

When tracking changes, a Reviewing toolbar is displayed at the top of the Word window. The Insert Comment button (▢) can be used by the reviewer. Other buttons are used by the original author to select the previous (▢) or next (▢) edit, to accept a change and merge it into the selected document (▢▾), and to reject a change or delete a comment (▢▾).

E-Mailing a Document

TIP Refer to Chapter 2 for more on e-mail and attachments.

(handwritten note: How to e-mail directly)

E-mail is a fast and efficient message delivery system. In Word, the content of a document can be e-mailed as a message. To e-mail a message, open the document in Word and then click the E-mail button (▢) on the toolbar, which displays the address information boxes. Type the e-mail address of the recipient in the To box. The file name of the document automatically appears as the Subject. Type text in the Introduction box if additional information should appear in the e-mail message and then click Send a Copy to send the message.

Messages e-mailed from Word appear directly in the body of the e-mail. To send a document as a separate file to an e-mail recipient, the document should be sent as an e-mail attachment. Select File → Send To → Mail Recipient (as Attachment) to display an e-mail window with the document included as an attachment file.

(handwritten note: collaborating doc. through email →)

When collaborating on a document, select File → Send To → Mail Recipient (for Review) to send a document as an attachment that will track changes when opened by the recipient. After the reviewer has made edits, Reply with Changes... on the Reviewing toolbar is clicked to e-mail the document back as an attachment. The original author will be prompted to merge any changes into the existing document. Selecting Yes overwrites the existing file with the new. Selecting No displays the new document with a name similar to the old, allowing the new version to be saved separately from the existing version.

Reading a Document on Screen

Reading Layout view   *Reading Layout view* makes it easier to read a document that is displayed on the screen. In this view, text is larger and word wrap is changed so that fewer words appear on a line. The reader can use the Page Up and Page Down keys or the scroll bar to scroll through the pages of the document. Reading Layout view is the default view when an e-mail attachment is opened in Word. Make edits in Reading Layout view or click the Close button to switch to Page Layout view.

Practice: Benefit

You will e-mail a document to a peer for editing. This practice requires Outlook and Internet access. You are also required to work with a classmate and exchange documents through e-mail. Word should already be started.

① *CREATE NEW A DOCUMENT*

     a. On the toolbar, click the New Blank Document button (⬚). A new document is displayed.

     b. In a new document, type the following:

        I am looking forward to my Widget Corporation orientation. I believe I will benefit most from

     c. Complete the document by reading the ORIENTATION printout from the last practice and then writing about one thing that will occur at the orientation that you feel will be beneficial if you were the new employee.

     d. Save the document naming it Benefit *Name* where *Name* is your name.

② *E-MAIL A DOCUMENT FOR REVIEW*

     a. Select File → Send To → Mail Recipient (for Review). After a few seconds, an e-mail window is created with the Benefit document as an attachment.

     b. If the e-mail window is not displayed, click the "Please review" button on the Windows taskbar. The e-mail window is displayed. Note the body of the e-mail contains a "Please review the attached document." sentence.

     c. In the To box, type the e-mail address of a classmate.

     d. On the Outlook toolbar, click ⬚Send. The e-mail is sent to your classmate for review.

③ *REVIEW A DOCUMENT*

     a. Check your e-mail.

     b. Open the e-mail from your classmate. Note that the e-mail message asks you to review the attached document.

     c. Open the attachment. A dialog box may be displayed with information about the Reading Layout feature.

     d. Read through the document and type any suggestions.

     e. Place the insertion point at the very beginning of the document.

     f. On the Reviewing toolbar, click the Insert Comment button (⬚). The insertion point is moved to the comment.

     g. Type Reviewed by and then your name.

h. On the Reviewing toolbar, click [Reply with Changes...]. After a few seconds, an Outlook e-mail window is displayed. (If you do not see the Reply with Changes button, click the Toolbar Options button to display it.)

i. On the Outlook toolbar, click [Send]. The document is e-mailed back to the sender. You may get a warning dialog box. Select Yes.

④ *REVIEW CHANGES*

a. Check your e-mail.

b. Open the e-mail reply from your classmate. The e-mail message includes the reviewed document as an attachment.

c. Open the attachment. You may get a message about merging changes. Select Yes. Note that the document is in Reading Layout view.

d. On the toolbar, click [Close] to view the document in Page Layout view.

e. Place the insertion point at the very beginning of the document.

f. On the Reviewing toolbar, click the Next button ([→]). The comment is selected.

g. On the Reviewing toolbar, click the Reject Change/Delete Comment button ([×▼]).

h. On the Reviewing toolbar, click the Next button ([→]). An edit is selected.

i. Evaluate the edit and then on the Reviewing toolbar, click either the Accept Change ([✓▼]) or Reject Change/Delete Comment button ([×▼]).

j. Continue clicking the Next button ([→]) and then accept or delete edits for all the tracked changes.

k. Save the modified Benefit document. If prompted to overwrite an existing document, select OK.

⑤ *CLOSE BENEFIT*

⑥ *QUIT WORD*

Chapter Summary

This chapter introduced the word processor, which can be used to produce easy-to-read, professional-looking documents. Microsoft Word is the word processor application in Microsoft Office.

Keys on the keyboard are used to type text and perform actions in Word. The Symbol command is used to insert a symbol that does not appear on the keyboard.

Move the pointer into a document to change it from an arrow shape to the I-beam pointer. Click the I-beam pointer in text to move the insertion point to that position.

Word automatically determines if the next word will fit on the end of the current line or the next line in a process called word wrap.

The last action can be reversed by selecting the Undo command. Select the Redo or Repeat commands to perform the same action again. Buttons on the toolbar can be used instead.

Spaces, tabs, and paragraphs are called formatting marks. Formatting marks are displayed by clicking the Show/Hide ¶ button.

Word includes a spelling checker and a grammar checker. A red wavy line appears below a misspelled word and a green wavy line below a phrase when a grammatical error is detected. Right-click a wavy line to display a menu of suggestions.

If text in a document is one of several types of data commonly used in other applications, Word designates the text as a smart tag. Move the pointer over a smart tag indicator to display the Smart Tag Actions button, which displays a menu of actions when clicked.

To scan a document for search text, use the Find command. Special characters can be included in search text. Use the Replace command to change search text to other text.

The Thesaurus command is used to display a the Research task pane with a list of synonyms and antonyms for a selected word.

Select text by dragging the I-beam pointer over it. Selected text can be moved or copied using the Copy, Cut, and Paste buttons on the toolbar. Cut or copied text is placed on the Clipboard. The Office Clipboard is available in Microsoft Office applications. Clicking an item in the Clipboard task pane pastes a copy of it at the insertion point.

A font refers to the shape of characters, and the size of text is measured in points. The way a character is emphasized is called its style. Common styles are bold, italic, and underline, superscript and subscript. The Font command is used to format the font, size, style, and color of selected text. The Font box, Font Size box, and the Bold, Italic, Underline, and Font Color buttons on the toolbar can also be used.

A document can be previewed to see how it will appear when printed by selecting the Print Preview command or the Print Preview button.

The alignment of text in a paragraph refers to its position relative to the sides of the page. The Align Left, Center, Align Right, and Justify buttons on the toolbar are used to change paragraph alignment. The Paragraph command displays a dialog box with alignment options.

A document can include hyperlinks to a Web page or to an e-mail address. A hyperlink in a Word document is automatically formatted as blue and underlined when it is typed. A hyperlink can also be created using the Insert Hyperlink button.

To e-mail an open document from Word, click the E-mail button, type information in the address boxes, and then click Send a Copy. A document can also be e-mailed as an attachment. E-mailing attached documents allows for collaboration and peer editing.

Alignment The position of text relative to the sides of the page. Left, right, centered, and justified are alignments.

Antonym A word that has the opposite meaning of another word.

Bold text A format that prints text darker.

Center alignment A format where the left and right edges of the paragraph are equally distant from the left and right sides of the page.

Clipboard A designated area in memory where cut and copied text is placed.

Dingbat A picture created by a special font such as Wingdings.

Document collaboration Working with others to create, review, and revise a document.

Duplicate text To make a copy of text and then place that copy at a different location in the document or into a completely different document.

Edit To modify the contents of a document on the screen.

Font The shape of a set of characters.

Format The way text appears on a page.

Formatting marks Special symbols, representing spaces, tabs, and paragraphs, that do not appear on paper when a document is printed.

Getting Started task pane A task pane shown in the Word window with options for creating a new document.

Grammar checker A feature of Word that automatically checks a document for possible grammatical errors.

I-beam pointer The shape of the pointer when it is moved into a document.

Insertion point A blinking vertical line in a document that indicates where the next character typed will be placed.

Italic text A format that makes text slanted.

Justified alignment A format where both sides of the paragraph are straight.

Left alignment The default format where the left edge of the paragraph is straight and the right edge is jagged.

Microsoft Word The word processor application in Microsoft Office.

Move text Delete text from a document and then place that text at a different location in the document of into a completely different document.

Office Clipboard Stores the last 24 cut or copied items.

Peer editing A form of collaboration where a peer edits a document.

Point The unit used to measure the size of text. There are 72 points to an inch.

Reading Layout view A Word view that makes reading a document on screen easier because text is larger.

Right alignment A format where the right edge of the paragraph is straight and the left edge is jagged.

Rulers Located at the top and left side of the document window, they are used for measuring and also contain markers for formatting text.

Selected text Text that is shown highlighted on the screen.

Smart tag Text in a document that has been designated by Word to be one of several types of data commonly used in other applications.

Smart tag indicator A purple dotted underline that appears under text that has been designated by Word as a smart tag.

Spelling checker A feature of Word that automatically compares words to those in a dictionary file to determine if they are spelled correctly.

Status bar A bar at the bottom of the screen that displays information about the current document.

Style The way a character is emphasized.

Subscript Text that is reduced in size and lowered to the bottom of the current line.

Superscript Text that is reduced in size and raised to the top of the current line.

Synonym A word that has a similar meaning to another word.

Thesaurus A collection of synonyms.

Title bar A bar at the top of the Word window that displays the file name of the current document.

Toolbar A bar at the top of the Word window that contains buttons that are clicked to perform an action.

Typeface Commonly referred to as font. *See* font.

Underline text A format that puts a line under text.

Word The Microsoft word processing application.

Word processor A computer application for creating, modifying, printing, and e-mailing documents.

Word wrap The process Word uses to determine if the next word will fit on the end of the current line or if it must go on the next line.

Accept Change button Makes a tracked change permanent. Found on the toolbar.

Add to Contacts **command** Displays a contact form. Found in the menu displayed by clicking the Smart Tag Actions button.

Align Left button Left aligns the text in the selected paragraph. Found on the toolbar.

Align Right button Right aligns the text in the selected paragraph. Found on the toolbar.

Bold button Formats selected text as bold. Found on the toolbar.

Center button Center aligns the text in the selected paragraph. Found on the toolbar.

Close button Returns to the document window from the Print Preview window. Found on the toolbar in the Print Preview window.

Copy **command** Adds a copy of the selected text to the Clipboard, leaving the selected text at its original location. Found in the Edit menu. The Copy button on the toolbar can be used instead of the command.

Cut **command** Moves the selected text to the Clipboard. Found in the Edit menu. The Cut button on the toolbar can be used instead of the command.

Delete **command** Deletes an item from the Clipboard. Found in the clipboard.

E-mail button Displays address information boxes for sending a document as an e-mail. Found on the toolbar.

Find **command** Displays a dialog box used to scan a document for search text. Found in the Edit menu.

Font **command** Displays a dialog box used to change the font, style, and size of selected text. Found in the Format menu. Also found in the menu displayed by right-clicking text.

Font box Changes the font of selected text. Found on the toolbar.

Font Size box Changes the size of selected text. Found on the toolbar.

Hyperlink **command** Displays a dialog box used for inserting a hyperlink into a document. Found in the Insert menu. The Insert Hyperlink button on the toolbar can be used instead of the command.

Ignore All **command** Removes the red wavy line from all occurrences of that word in the document. Found in the menu displayed by right-clicking a word that has a red wavy line.

Ignore Once **command** Removes the green wavy line from a sentence that contains a possible grammatical error. Found in the menu displayed by right-clicking a phrase or sentence that has a green wavy line.

Insert Comment button Adds a comment to a document. Found on the toolbar.

Italic button Formats selected text as italic. Found on the toolbar.

Justify button Justify aligns the text in the selected paragraph. Found on the toolbar.

Mail Recipient (as Attachment) **command** Used to e-mail a document as an attachment. Found in File → Send To.

Mail Recipient (for Review) **command** Used to e-mail a document as an attachment that will track changes when opened by the recipient. Found in File → Send To.

New Blank Document button Creates a new document. Found on the toolbar.

New Document task pane Contains links for opening a document or creating a new document.

Next button Selects the next tracked change. Found on the toolbar.

Office Clipboard **command** Displays the Clipboard task pane with the last 24 cut or copied items. Found in the Edit menu.

Other Task Panes list List of available task panes. Found at the top a task pane.

Paragraph **command** Displays a dialog box used to apply paragraph formats. Found in the Format menu. Also found in the menu displayed by right-clicking text.

⊡ Paste **command**   Places the contents of the Clipboard at the insertion point. Found in the Edit menu. The Paste button on the toolbar can be used instead of the command.

⊡ **Previous button**   Selects the previous tracked change. Found on the toolbar.

⊡ Print **button** Prints a copy of the document. Found on the toolbar in the Print Preview window.

⊡ Print Preview **command**   Displays the document in the Print Preview window. Found in the File menu. The Print Preview button on the toolbar can be used instead of the command.

⊡▾ Redo **command or** Repeat **command** Performs the last action again. Found in the Edit menu. The Redo button on the toolbar can be used instead of the command.

⊡▾ **Reject Change/Delete Comment button** Ignores a tracked change or removes a comment. Found on the toolbar.

Remove Hyperlink **command** Removes the blue underline from a hyperlink. Found in the menu displayed by right-clicking the link.

Remove this Smart Tag **command** Removes the purple dotted smart tag indicator from text. Found in the menu displayed by clicking the Smart Tag Actions button.

Replace **command**   Displays a dialog box used to search a document for search text and change it to specified text. Found in the Edit menu.

⊡ Reply with Changes...   Found on the toolbar after a document sent for review has been opened.

Select All **command** Selects all the text in a document. Found in the Edit menu.

⊡ Send a Copy   Sends the content of a document as an e-mail message. Found on the toolbar after the E-mail button has been clicked.

¶ **Show/Hide ¶ button**   Displays formatting marks. Found on the toolbar.

⊡ **Smart Tag Actions button**   Displays the type of data, the smart tag data, and a menu of actions. Displayed by moving the pointer over a smart tag indicator.

Symbol **command**   Displays a dialog box used to insert symbols not found on the keyboard into a document. Found in the Insert menu.

Synonyms **command**   Displays a list of synonyms and an antonym for a word. Found in the menu displayed by right-clicking a word.

Thesaurus **command** Displays the Research task pane with synonyms. Found in Tools ➜ Language.

Track Changes **command** Marks additions, deletions, and other changes in a document as they are made. Found in the Tools menu.

⊡ **Underline button**   Formats selected text as underlined. Found on the toolbar.

⊡▾ Undo **command**   Reverses the effects of the last action. Found in the Edit menu. The Undo button on the toolbar can be used instead of the command.

1. What is a word processor?

2. a) What is the insertion point?
   b) How can the insertion point be moved down 3 lines and then 10 places to the right without deleting or entering text?
   c) What is the difference between pressing the Backspace key four times and the left-arrow key four times when the insertion point is located in the middle of a line of text?
   d) How can symbols not represented by a key on the keyboard be added to a document?

3. a) What is the shape of the pointer when it is in a document?
   b) How can the mouse be used to move the insertion point?

4. What is word wrap?

5. a) What toolbar button is used to reverse the last action performed?
   b) Can an action be repeated? If so, how?

6. a) What are formatting marks?
   b) How are formatting marks useful when editing a document?

7. a) What does a red wavy line under a word indicate?
   b) List the steps required to correct a misspelled word.
   c) What does a green wavy line under a sentence indicate?

8. a) What does a purple dotted line under text indicate?
   b) What is displayed when the Smart Tag Actions button is clicked?

9. What is the search text for finding Jerome? What option should be used to find only occurrences with an uppercase "J"?

10. a) In a search for the word hat, how can you avoid finding the word that?
    b) What is the search text for finding the word The at the beginning of a paragraph?

11. a) What is replace text?
    b) List the steps required to find each occurrence of day and replace it with week.

12. a) What is a thesaurus?
    b) What is a synonym?
    c) What is an antonym?
    d) List two places to find a list of synonyms for the word house in a document.

13. a) How is selected text shown on the screen?
    b) What happens if text is selected and then the Backspace key is pressed?

14. List two methods for selecting an entire paragraph of text.

15. List the steps required to copy the third paragraph in a document to the end of the document.

16. What is the difference between moving and duplicating text?

17. List the steps required to paste an item from the Office Clipboard to the location of the insertion point in a document.

18. a) What does "font" refer to?
    b) List five fonts available on your computer.

19. Fonts can be divided into three categories: serif, sans serif, and decorative. *Serif fonts* have small strokes at the ends of characters that help the reader's eye recognize each letter. The horizontal and vertical strokes of the letters often vary in thickness. Serif fonts are more conventional and are used in large amounts of text. *Sans serif fonts* lack the decorative flourishes of serif fonts. Sans serif fonts are often used in headings to contrast with the body text:

    Decorative fonts have letters that are specially shaped and are neither serif nor sans serif. Some decorative fonts have a picture, rather than a letter, that corresponds to characters.

    a) Refer to the "Formatting Characters" section in this chapter and then list the font name and category for each of the fonts presented in the fonts example in that section.
    b) List an appropriate use for each type of font.

20. a) What is character size measured in?
    b) What kind of text would be appropriate in size 24?
    c) Would text in the body of a letter be better as size 10 or size 18? Why?

21. Can text be formatted as both bold and italic? If so, how?

22. List the step required to remove bold formatting from a selected paragraph.

23. Underlined text is sometimes confused for a hyperlink. Why?

24. List two instances of when the subscript or superscript format should be used.

25. a) How does a document appear in Print Preview?
    b) Which keys are used to scroll through a document in print preview?
    c) What does it mean to change the magnification of a document? How is this done?

26. List the steps required to preview an open document, print a copy, and then return to the document window.

27. List the four paragraph alignments and describe each one.

28. List the appropriate paragraph style for the following documents. Use each of the four alignments (right, left, center, justify) only once:
    a) A birth announcement.
    b) A term paper.
    c) A promotional flyer for a very contemporary advertising agency.
    d) A newspaper article.

29. a) What does Word do when a Web site address is typed in a document?
    b) How can a hyperlink be followed from the Word document on screen?

30. a) How does Word format an e-mail address?
    b) What happens when a reader presses the Ctrl key and clicks an e-mail hyperlink?

31. a) What does document collaboration mean?
    b) What are two forms of collaboration?

32. What feature does Word have that allows for reviewing and editing a document between two or more people?

33. Can comments be added to a document being reviewed? If so, how?

34. a) List three ways a document can be e-mailed from Word.
    b) When should a document be e-mailed as an attachment?
    c) How should a document be e-mailed to a reviewer who is collaborating on the document? Why?

35. What is Reading Layout view?

True/False

36. Determine if each of the following are true or false. If false, explain why.
    a) Pressing and holding the Ctrl key and then pressing the left arrow key moves the insertion point to the beginning of the previous word to the left.
    b) Pressing the End key moves the insertion point to the beginning of a line of text.
    c) There is no way to create a © symbol in a Word document.
    d) The Enter key should be pressed when a line of text reaches the right edge of the document, even when a new paragraph is not being started.
    e) Double-clicking a word selects that word and the line of text that it appears in.
    f) Text cannot be copied from one document to another.

Exercise 1 ─────────────────── Ceramics Info Request

When writing a letter that requests a response or information, the first paragraph should introduce the writer and explain the purpose of the letter. The second paragraph should explain any necessary details of the request and ask any additional questions. The third paragraph should thank the reader for his or her consideration and emphasize the request.

a) In a new document create the following letter, allowing Word to wrap the text. Create the letter using the block style. Be sure to press Enter 6 times before typing the return address. Refer to the Request practices for more information.

72 Simple Lane
Plain City, FL 33101-1234
September 20, 2006

Ms. Marcia Paloma
Periwinkle Ceramics
Big Pine Lane
Sunport, FL 33568

Dear Ms. Paloma

I am enrolled in the introductory ceramics class that you are teaching this spring. My experience in creating ceramic pieces is limited, but I have admired your artwork for many years. I am honored and excited to participate in your class.

My friend would also like to enroll in your ceramics program. She would like to be in the same class that I am signed up for, if there are still openings. Please send a brochure and availability information to the following address:

Kaitlin Pruitt
44 Simple Lane
Plain City, FL 33101-1234
pruittk@lpdatafiles.com

I understand your classes fill quickly. My friend is eagerly awaiting your reply so that she may enroll in your class. Thank you very much for your time.

Sincerely

Kallie Gavrilos

b) Check the document on screen and correct any errors and misspellings. Remove the red wavy line from correctly spelled words.

c) Save the document naming it Ceramics Info Request and print a copy.

d) Make the following changes to the letter:

- Change the word introductory to advanced in the first sentence.
- Change the words a brochure to an application in the second paragraph.
- Use the thesaurus to change the word quickly in the fourth paragraph to an appropriate synonym.
- Change Kallie Gavrilos to your name.

e) Save the modified Ceramics Info Request and print a copy.

Exercise 2 ———————————————— Donation Thanks

You have been asked to write a thank you letter to Mrs. Kristine LeBon for her donation.

a) In a new document create the following letter, allowing Word to wrap the text. Create the letter using the block style:

123 Whippo Lane
Butler, PA 16001-7896
January 9, 2006

Mrs. Kristine LeBon
17 North Main St.
Reedsburg, GA 04459-2233

Dear Mrs. LeBon

I am writing to thank you for your very generous donation to the Sarah Bernstein Memorial Library. We are always appreciative of donations, both monetary and otherwise.

As you are well aware, our library has needed new carpeting for several years now. The old rugs were an ugly avocado color. The new carpeting not only looks beautiful, but will also help keep the environmental conditions good for books.

Thanks again from the gang at the Sarah Bernstein Memorial Library.

Sincerely

Chris Warheit
Library Assistant

b) Check the document on screen and correct any errors and misspellings. Remove the red wavy line line from correctly spelled words.

c) Save the letter naming it Donation Thanks.

d) Make the following changes:

- Delete the word very in the first sentence.
- Use the thesaurus to change the word appreciative in the first paragraph to an appropriate synonym.
- Add the following sentence to the end of the first paragraph in the body of the letter: Your donation was truly a welcome surprise.
- Delete the sentence The old rugs were an ugly avocado color. in the second paragraph in the body of the letter.
- Change good for books to favorable for printed materials at the end of the second paragraph in the body of the letter.
- Change the gang to all of us in the third paragraph in the body of the letter.
- Change Chris Warheit to your name.

e) Check the document on screen and correct any errors and misspellings.

f) Save the modified Donation Thanks and then print a copy.

Exercise 3 ———————————————— Leadership

Effective leaders are key to a successful business. Learn more about leadership skills by completing the following exercise.

a) In a new document, type the following essay, allowing Word to wrap the text:

Leaders in any business environment are viewed as role models and visionaries for those who work with them. Effective leaders tend to possess similar characteristics, such as approachable, responsible, wise, and sensitive.

An effective leader is always organized and enthusiastic. An effective leader knows how to delegate and utilize the strengths of their employees.

b) Check the document on screen and correct any errors and misspellings.

c) Save the document naming it Leadership.

d) Make the following changes:

- Change the word wise to knowledgeable in the first paragraph.
- Change the word effective to successful in the second paragraph. Use the grammar checker to correct the grammatical error that occurs as a result of changing the word.
- Add a third paragraph with the text: Leadership skills can be learned. Individuals who would like to become leaders should become accessible and approachable, be willing to share the credit with colleagues, and take initiative.

e) Save the modified Leadership, preview the document, and then print a copy.

Exercise 4 ———————————————————————— Cover Letter

It is common practice to include a cover letter with a résumé or portfolio when applying for a job. A cover letter should be in the block style and addressed to a specific individual and company. The first paragraph should indicate the position being applied for and give the location and date of the advertisement. The second and possibly third paragraph should expand in detail upon qualifications pertinent to the job. The concluding paragraph should request an interview, state contact information, and thank the reader for his or her time and consideration.

   a) Given the following job advertisement from the Sun News on August 24, 2006, create a cover letter:

      Part-Time Sales Position
      Great opportunity for a student. Part-time position in busy retail clothing store. Hours are 5–9 p.m. three days a week and 9–5 p.m. on Saturdays. Need to be motivated and a self-starter. Salary includes wage plus commission. Send or e-mail cover letter and résumé to:
      Ms. Jessica Wilson, Manager
      Clothes and More
      678 Palm Blvd.
      Boca Raton, FL 33427-5314
      clothesandmore@lpdatafiles.com

   b) Check the document on screen and correct any errors and misspellings.

   c) Save the document naming it Cover Letter *Name* where *Name* is your name.

   d) Collaborate with another student in the class. E-mail or give your peer a copy of the file so that it can be proofread with tracking turned on.

   e) Evaluate your peer's letter. With tracking turned on, make at least three "suggested" edits along with any necessary edits, such as formatting or grammatical errors.

   f) Use the Reviewing toolbar to accept and reject suggestions by your peer.

   g) Save the modified letter, preview the document, and then print a copy.

Exercise 5 ———————————————————————— Complaint Letter

You have recently organized the senior prom. The catered food at the prom arrived an hour late, was cold, and the menu was different than what was agreed to. You have decided to write a letter of complaint to the manager of the catering company asking for a refund.

A letter of complaint should be brief and to the point. All relevant facts should be included, the action wanted should be clear, and the tone of the letter should be reasonable. One appropriate format is to write about the problem in the first paragraph, state the solution in the second paragraph, and then give a deadline for a response in the last paragraph.

   a) In a new document create a letter of complaint in the block style. Address the letter to:

      Mr. William Thomas
      Catering Manager
      Catering For All Occasions
      43-901 Airport Way
      Detroit, MI 48225

b) Check the document on screen and correct any errors and misspellings.

c) Save the document naming it Complaint Letter *Name* where *Name* is your name.

d) Collaborate with another student in the class. E-mail or give your peer a copy of the file so that it can be proofread with tracking turned on.

e) Evaluate your peer's letter. With tracking turned on, make at least three "suggested" edits along with any necessary edits, such as formatting errors or spelling mistakes.

f) Save the edited letter and return it to your peer.

g) Use the Reviewing toolbar to accept and reject suggestions by your peer. Save the modified letter.

h) Preview the document and print a copy.

Exercise 6 ——————————————————————— Poem

An occasional poem is a poem written for a special occasion, such as a birth, wedding, inauguration, victory, or dedication.

a) In a new document create an occasional poem. The poem should be from four to 16 lines. Use the thesaurus in Word to find synonyms and antonyms.

b) Check the document on screen and correct any errors and misspellings.

c) Save the document naming it Poem, preview the document, and then print a copy.

Exercise 7 ——————————————————— COMPUTER MAINTENANCE

A regular maintenance routine will help keep your computer in good condition. A maintenance routine should include cleaning the computer, maintaining the hard disk, and regularly updating virus protection and operating system software. COMPUTER MAINTENANCE contains some tips about keeping a computer in good condition. Open COMPUTER MAINTENANCE, which is a Word data file for this text, and complete the following steps:

a) Type your name below the "Computer Maintenance" title.

b) Center align and bold the title "Computer Maintenance" and format it as Tahoma 14 point.

c) Left align and bold the following headings and format them as Tahoma 12 point:

"Cleaning the Computer"
"Disk Maintenance"
"Updating Virus Protection and Operating System Software"

d) Input devices are devices from which the computer can accept data. Two input devices are discussed in the "Cleaning the Computer" section. Format the first occurrence of each input device name as italic.

e) Output devices are devices that display or store processed data. One output device is discussed in the "Cleaning the Computer" section. Bold the first occurrence of the output device name.

f) The "Disk Maintenance" section lists an example of an operating system. Format the name of the listed operating system as bold and italic.

g) The "Updating Virus Protection and Operating System Software" section explains what must be downloaded on a regular basis to protect against new viruses. Format the name of the download as bold and italic.

h) Save the modified COMPUTER MAINTENANCE and print a copy.

Exercise 8 — Entertainment Review

The local newspaper has an opening for an entertainment critic. A review should include:

- Title
- Name of movie, concert, play, art show, or event
- Date of review
- Intended audience (young children, children, teen, young adult, adult)
- Rating, if applicable (G, PG, PG-13, and so on)
- Type of movie, music, play, art, or event
- Name of producer or gallery
- Name of director, if applicable
- Name of actors, band members, artist, headliner, or main attraction
- Summary of the movie or play, without giving away surprise moments or the ending
- Comparison to similar movies, concerts, plays, art shows, or events
- Your overall rating

a) In a new document create a half-page review of a recent movie, concert, play, art show, or similar event that you attended. A review should be written based on facts and without bias. Be sure to include the appropriate information as listed above.

b) Create a center aligned, bold title that has the name of the event that was reviewed. Be sure there is a blank paragraph between the title and the first paragraph.

c) Format any titles in the review as italic, such as the title of a movie or a song title.

d) Justify the body of the review.

e) Select Tools → Word Count to display the number of words in the document. Add a paragraph to the end of the review that includes your name and the number of words in the article.

f) Check the document on screen and correct any errors and misspellings.

g) Save the document naming it Entertainment Review and print a copy.

Exercise 9 ——————————————————————— PROPOSAL

Dr. Ellie Peterson and Dr. Jeremy Prow are studying coral reefs off the coast of Florida. They have created a funding proposal for their coral research.

a) Open PROPOSAL, which is a Word data file for this text, and make the following changes:

- Change the heading so it reads A PROPOSAL FOR CORAL RESEARCH at the top of the page.
- Change the word effect to affect in the "Summary" paragraph.
- Change the word accomplish to complete in the "Summary" paragraph.
- Delete the text state of the art in the "Purpose and Description" paragraph.

b) Check the document on screen and correct any errors and misspellings.

c) Center align and bold the headings "A PROPOSAL FOR CORAL RESEARCH" and "GROWTH STUDIES OF CORAL ON SOUTH FLORIDA REEFS."

d) Format the headings "Summary," "Purpose and Description," "Coral," and "Computerized Guide" as italic.

e) Center align and bold the "BUDGET" heading and format it in a larger font size.

f) Find the word greater in the proposal and then use the thesaurus to replace it with a synonym.

g) Replace all occurrences of aging with growth.

h) Save the modified PROPOSAL.

i) Print only page 1. (Refer to Chapter 1 for information on printing single pages.)

Exercise 10 ——————————————————————— Vacation

In a new document create a one-page description of your last vacation. Describe where you went, how you traveled, what you saw, and what you did. Include a hyperlink to a Web site that contains additional information about the vacation area. Check the document on screen for errors and misspellings and make any corrections. Save the document naming it Vacation and print a copy.

Exercise 11 ——————————————————————— TAKING TESTS

The TAKING TESTS document gives directions on how to take a test, but the steps are listed out of order. Open TAKING TESTS, which is a Word data file for this text, and complete the following steps:

a) Use the Cut and Paste buttons on the toolbar to place the directions in proper order. Be sure there is a blank line between each step.

b) Save the modified TAKING TESTS, preview the document, and then print a copy.

Exercise 12 —————————————————————— SCULPTORS

Five sculptors that lived during the late 19th and early 20th centuries are:

Sculptor	Country
Constantin Brancusi	Romania
Ronald Moody	Jamaica
Ivan Mestrovic	Croatia
Jacques Lipchitz	Lithuania
Pablo Gargallo	Spain

These sculptors were born in different countries and their art was influenced by events, movements, and cultures of those years common to the artists.

a) Open SCULPTORS, which is a Word data file for this text. It contains information about the five artists listed above. Cut and paste the paragraphs so that the country, artist's name, and description are in alphabetical order by country.

b) Save the modified SCULPTORS and print a copy.

c) Cut and paste the paragraphs so that the country, artist's name, and description are in chronological order by artist's birth date.

d) Save the modified SCULPTORS and print a copy.

e) Use books or the Internet to research each artist and find the name of a work (a sculpture), the materials used, and the year it was completed. Between each artist's name and biography, add the information about the artist's work and include a hyperlink to a Web site that contains additional information about the artist.

f) Save the modified SCULPTORS and print a copy.

Exercise 13 —————————————————————— Short Soccer

The sports editor for your college newspaper likes the soccer article that you submitted. However, space limitations require that the article be between 150 and 160 words.

a) Open SOCCER, which is a Word data file for this text.

b) Carefully read the article and determine which sentences and words are extraneous and which are necessary to maintain the focus of the article.

c) In a new document, paste the text from the SOCCER article that still make a complete story without losing the focus of the original article.

d) Select Tools → Word Count to display the number of words. Continue to edit the article to meet the space limitations.

e) Save the document naming it Short Soccer.

f) E-mail the Short Soccer article as a document for review to: editor@lpdatafiles.com

g) Preview the document and print a copy.

Exercise 14 ——————————— Water Conservation

You have been asked to write an article about an environmental issue.

a) In Word, open and then print a copy of the WATER, CONSERVATION, and XERISCAPE documents, which are Word data files for this text.

b) In a new document create an article based soley on the documents printed in step (a). Include a title, introductory paragraph, supporting paragraph(s), a closing paragraph, and your name.

c) Under the title, type by *Student Name* replacing *Student Name* with your name and then press Enter twice. You may need to point to the blue bar below "by" and then click the AutoCorrect Options button and select Undo Automatic Capitalization if the word "by" does not remain lowercase.

d) Bold the document's title and format it as 14 point. Bold the byline and format it as italic.

e) Justify the text in the body of the article.

f) Check the document on screen and correct any errors and misspellings.

g) Save the document naming it Water Conservation, preview the document, and then print a copy.

Exercise 15 ——————————— Grand Opening

You have opened a retail store. Your store could sell jewelry, clothing, sporting goods, or anything else you wish. You will need a flyer to promote the grand opening of your new store. A *flyer* is a one-page document that is sent in the mail, hand delivered, or left out for pick up. The intended audience is prospective customers residing in the area of the business location. A flyer should have large elements to catch the reader's attention so that the reader immediately knows the general topic. The rest of the flyer should contain as much information as possible, including business name, address, phone number, e-mail address, Web site address, and fax number. These elements can be smaller because the flyer already has the reader's attention. A flyer should also include coupons or other promotions to draw the prospective customer into the store.

a) In a new document create a flyer that will be sent to prospective customers announcing your grand opening.

b) Assume the flyer will be printed in color and format the text appropriately. Decide which text should be used to get the reader's attention and make that text much larger. Experiment with different fonts for the larger text, and choose one that is easy to read and compliments your business. Experiment with different ways of emphasizing the text.

c) Bold all occurrences of the store's name. Be sure each occurrence of the store's name is in the same color.

d) Format appropriate paragraph alignments throughout the flyer.

e) Check the document on screen and correct any errors and misspellings.

f) Save the document naming it Grand Opening.

Chapter 5

Formatting Documents

This chapter covers formatting options that improve the appearance and readability of documents. Tabs, tab stops, indenting text, adding images, and converting documents to HTML are covered.

The Reveal Formatting Task Pane

A document may have many formats applied. A listing of the formats for selected text or text around the insertion point can be viewed in the Reveal Formatting task pane. Select Format → Reveal Formatting to display the task pane:

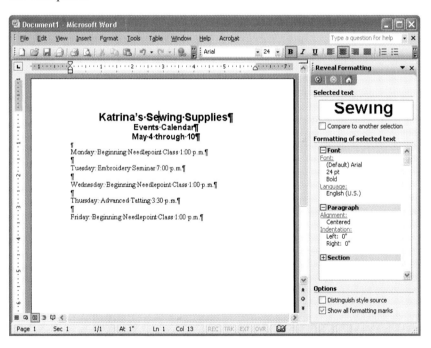

Applied formatting is listed under headings that are links. Clicking a link displays the appropriate dialog box so that the formatting may be changed. For example, clicking <u>Alignment</u> displays the Paragraph dialog box.

The Reveal Formatting task pane is also useful for comparing formats. Select the Compare to another selection check box in the task pane, which adds another Selected text box and changes the Formatting of selected text list to Formatting differences. Select text in the document to display it in the second Selected text box and list the formatting differences:

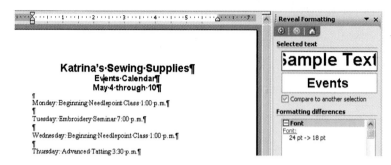

Margins and Pagination

Within a document, text is divided into pages. *Margins* are the white region around the text on a page. *Pagination* is how a document is divided into pages:

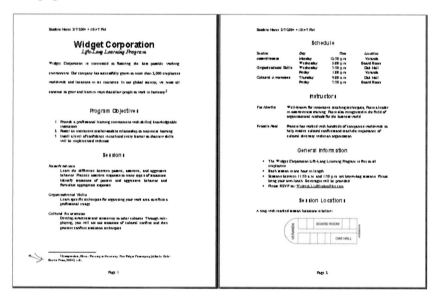

A document page has top, bottom, left, and right margins. Text is divided into pages.

Margin size affects the amount of text that a page can contain. Smaller margins leave more room for text. Wider margins mean less text. For example, widening the left and right margins decreases the number of characters that fit on a line and may increase pagination. Narrowing the same margins increases the amount of text in a line and may decrease pagination. Similarly, larger top and bottom margins decrease the number of lines of text a page can contain and smaller top and bottom margins increase the amount of text on a page, also affecting pagination.

The default margins in Word for an 8.5-inch by 11-inch page are 1.25 inches for the left and right and 1 inch for the top and bottom. Select File → Page Setup to display the Page Setup dialog box and then select the Margins tab to display options for changing margins.

Paper Sizes

The size of paper used for a document can be changed using the Paper size list in the Paper tab options in the Page Setup dialog box:

Size	Measurements
Letter	8.5" x 11"
Tabloid	11" x 17"
Legal	8.5" x 14"
Executive	7.25" x 10.5"
A3	297mm x 420mm
A4	210mm x 297mm
A5	148mm x 210mm
B4 (JIS)	257mm x 364mm
B5 (JIS)	182mm x 257mm

Word automatically determines how much text will fit on a page based on the amount of text and the document formatting. As a document is edited, Word automatically updates the pagination. To change pagination, insert a *page break*. Inserting a page break moves the text after the insertion point to the next page. To insert a break, press Ctrl+Enter or select Insert → Break to display a dialog box with the Page break option.

To delete a page break, place the insertion point to the left of the page break and press the Delete key. The document repaginates and text from the next page moves up to fill the current page.

Practice: TRAINING – part 1 of 7

You will display formatting and change margins and pagination for a two-page document.

① *OPEN TRAINING*
   a. Start Word.
   b. Open TRAINING, which is a Word data file for this text.

② *REVEAL FORMATTING*
   a. Select Format → Reveal Formatting. The Reveal Formatting task pane is displayed.
   b. Place the insertion point in the heading, which reads "Widget Corporation." Note the formatting listed in the task pane.
   c. Move the insertion point to other paragraphs and note the formatting listed in the task pane.

③ *CHANGE FORMATTING WITH THE TASK PANE*
   a. At the top of the document, select the text "Life-Long Learning Program."
   b. In the Reveal Formatting task pane, click <u>Font</u>. A dialog box is displayed.
      1. In the Font style list, click Bold Italic.
      2. In the Size list, click 16.
      3. Select OK. The text formatting is changed. Note the task pane lists the new formats.

④ *CHANGE THE MARGINS*
   a. On the toolbar, click the Print Preview button (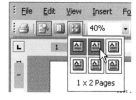).
   b. On the toolbar, click the Multiple Pages button and select 1x2 Pages:

Note the pagination of the TRAINING document.
   c. Close the Print Preview window. The document window is again displayed.
   d. In the Reveal Formatting task pane, click the ⊞ next to Section to expand the list of formats.
   e. In the Reveal Formatting task pane, click <u>Margins</u>. A dialog box is displayed.

f. Change the Left and Right margin options as shown:

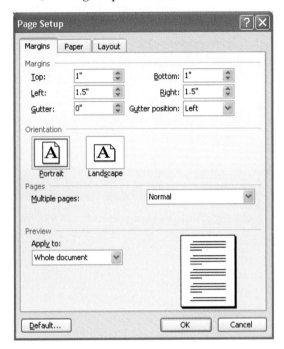

g. Select OK. The left and right margins are wider, leaving more white space on the sides of the document text.

h. Print preview the TRAINING document. The margins are wider and the pagination has changed.

i. Close the Print Preview window. The document window is again displayed.

j. Save the modified TRAINING.

⑤ *CHANGE THE PAGINATION*

a. Scroll to the "Schedule" title in the document.

b. Place the insertion point just to the left of the "S" in "Schedule."

c. Press Ctrl+Enter. A page break is inserted, and text after the break is moved to the next page:

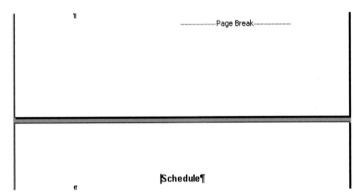

d. Print preview the TRAINING document. Note the change in pagination.

e. Close the Print Preview window. The document window is again displayed.

⑥ *SAVE THE MODIFIED TRAINING DOCUMENT*

Headers and Footers

A *header* is a special area at the top of a page and a *footer* is a special area at the bottom of the page. A header or footer is often used to include the current page number, the file name of the document, the author's name, or the date. Select View → Header and Footer to display the Header and Footer toolbar. The document text dims and the insertion point moves into the header area, shown with a dashed border at the top of the page:

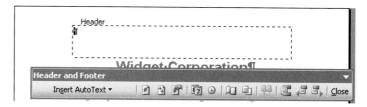

Type text in the header area and then format it, if needed.

To move the insertion point to the footer, click the Switch Between Header and Footer button ([icon]) on the Header and Footer toolbar. Clicking this button again moves the insertion point back to the header.

different first page

Text typed in the header or footer is printed on each page of the document. However, it is possible to have a different header and footer printed on the first page than on the rest of the pages. Select File → Page Setup to display a dialog box and then select the Layout tab. Select the Different first page check box to remove the contents from both the header and the footer on the first page of the document. Different text can then be added to the header and footer area on the first page, or those areas can be left empty so that nothing prints in the header and footer on page 1.

adding page numbers

Page numbers are often used in documents that have more than one page. Click the Insert Page Number button ([icon]) to add a page number. The page number is added at the insertion point, and can then be formatted. When the document is printed, the appropriate page number will appear on every page in the document. To change the numbering style, click the Format Page Number button ([icon]). To delete a page number, select it and press the Delete key.

The Header and Footer toolbar includes the Insert Date ([icon]) and Insert Time ([icon]) buttons. It is easier to keep track of document revisions when printouts include the date and time they were printed. Click [icon] to insert the current date and [icon] to insert the current time. The date and time are automatically updated when a document is printed or opened. To delete the date or time, select it and press the Delete key.

To return to the document text, double-click the document or click [Close] on the Header and Footer toolbar.

Editing Existing Headers and Footers

Double-click an existing header or footer to place the insertion point in the text. The Header and Footer toolbar is automatically displayed.

TIP To change the format of a date or time in a header or footer, right-click the date or time and then select Edit Field from the menu.

The Date and Time Command

To insert the date and time in the document, rather than the header or footer, select Insert → Date and Time. Selecting the Update automatically check box will insert a time stamp composed of a code that is automatically updated when the file is later opened or printed.

Practice: TRAINING – part 2 of 7

You will add headers and footers to a document. Word should already be started with the TRAINING document displayed from the last practice.

① *ADD NAME, DATE, AND TIME INFORMATION TO A HEADER*

    a. Select View → Header and Footer. The insertion point is placed in the header area and the Header and Footer toolbar is displayed.

    b. Type your name followed by a space.

    c. On the Header and Footer toolbar, click the Insert Date button (🗓). The current date is displayed in the header.

    d. Type a space after the date.

    e. On the Header and Footer toolbar, click the Insert Time button (🕐). The current time is displayed in the header.

      Check — Your header should look similar to:

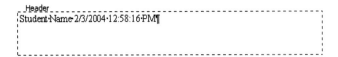

② *ADD THE PAGE NUMBER TO A FOOTER*

    a. On the Header and Footer toolbar, click the Switch Between Header and Footer button (📑). The insertion point is placed in the Footer area.

    b. Type Page followed by a space.

    c. On the Header and Footer toolbar, click the Insert Page Number button (🔢). The current page number is inserted in the footer.

    d. On the toolbar, click the Center button (☰). The footer information is centered:

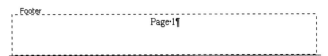

    e. On the Header and Footer toolbar, click Close. The header and footer are now dimmed.

③ *SAVE, PREVIEW, AND THEN PRINT THE DOCUMENT*

    a. Save the modified TRAINING.

    b. Print preview the TRAINING document. The header and footer information is displayed. Note the page numbers are correct for each of the pages.

    c. Print the TRAINING document.

    d. Close print preview.

Tabs are used to position text within a line. Press the Tab key to insert a tab and move any text to the right of the insertion point over to the position of the next tab stop. Delete a tab by placing the insertion point to the left of the tab and pressing the Delete key. Any text is automatically moved to the left to fill the space previously created by the tab.

A *tab stop* specifies a location within the line of text. In Word, tab stops are displayed on the ruler above the document. A set of default tab stops are located at every half inch, but they do not appear on the ruler.

formatting a table

Tabs can be used to create a table of data. New tab stops are created at the appropriate intervals to align the data in columns:

Name	Age	Kennel	Feeding Time	Weight (kg)
Peach	12	29B	4 p.m	7.75
Jessie	3	6C	6 p.m	8.5
Duffy	10	20A	4:30 p.m	9
Indy	7	5A	7 p.m	16

A tab stop can be set at any position on the ruler within the margins. When a tab stop is set, Word automatically removes the default tab stops to the left. For example, a tab stop set at 1.4 inches automatically removes the default tab stops at 0.5 and 1.0 inches. The default stop at 1.5 inches is not affected.

Text is aligned to a tab stop according to the type of tab stop:

- **Left tab stop** (**L**) aligns the beginning of the text at the stop.

- **Right tab stop** (**⌐**) aligns the end of the text at the stop.

- **Center tab stop** (**⊥**) centers the text equidistant over the stop.

- **Decimal tab stop** (**⊥**) aligns the decimal point (a period) at the stop.

Each tab stop is used in the text shown below. Note the markers on the ruler:

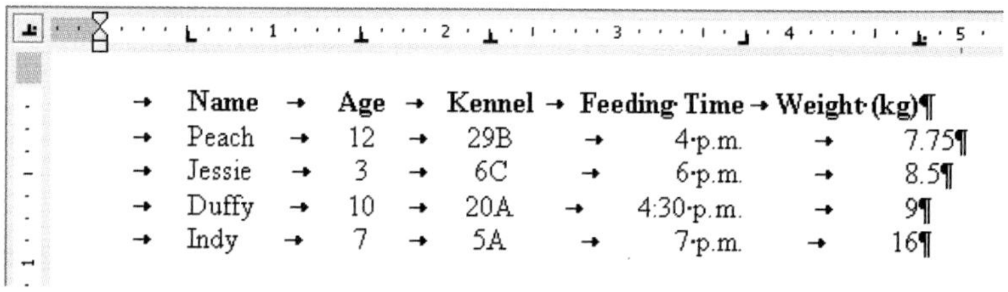

Tab stops are applied to the paragraph that contains the insertion point or to multiple paragraphs selected together. When the insertion point is moved through the text, the ruler changes to show the tab stops for the current paragraph.

Set a tab stop by first clicking the Tab Selection button on the ruler until the type of tab stop to be created is displayed:

Tab Selection button

TIP Select View → Ruler to display the rulers.

Click the white area of the ruler above the document to place a tab stop. The tab stop can be dragged to a new location if needed. For example, click the Tab Selection button until the Right tab stop button (▫) is displayed and then click the ruler to create a right tab stop at that location.

To remove a tab stop, drag its marker downward, off the ruler and into the document. Any text that was aligned at a deleted stop is then aligned to the next tab stop.

Tab stops can also be set by selecting Format → Tabs, which displays the Tabs dialog box. In the dialog box, type the Tab stop position that corresponds to the markings on the ruler, select the appropriate Alignment, and then select Set to create a tab stop at that position. Repeat this procedure to create as many tab stops as needed. To remove a tab stop, select it from the Tab stop position list in the Tabs dialog box and then select Clear. Selecting Clear All removes all the tab stops.

Tab Leaders

A tab leader is a character that is repeated to fill the space spanned by a tab. Examples of tab leaders are ...., ----, and _ __. The dotted pattern is often used in a table of contents or index. The solid line is used to represent a blank on a form or a test. Select a tab leader in the Tabs dialog box in the Leader section.

Selecting a Vertical Block of Text

Tables of data often have formatting applied to a column of data. To select a vertical block of text, hold down the Alt key and drag:

Name	→	Age	→	Kennel	→	Feeding Time	→	Weight (kg)	¶
Peach	→	12	→	29B	→	4 p.m	→	7.75	¶
Jessie	→	3	→	6C	→	6 p.m	→	8.5	¶
Duffy	→	10	→	20A	→	4:30 p.m	→	9	¶
Indy	→	7	→	5A	→	7 p.m	→	16	¶

Formatting can then be applied to the selected text. For example, click the Italic button to format selected data as italic:

Name	→	Age	→	Kennel	→	Feeding Time	→	Weight (kg)	¶
Peach	→	12	→	29B	→	*4 p.m*	→	7.75	¶
Jessie	→	3	→	6C	→	*6 p.m*	→	8.5	¶
Duffy	→	10	→	20A	→	*4:30 p.m*	→	9	¶
Indy	→	7	→	5A	→	*7 p.m*	→	16	¶

Practice: TRAINING – part 3 of 7

You will set tab stops in a document and format a column of text. Word should already be started with the TRAINING document displayed from the last practice.

① **SELECT A TABLE**

  a. Display formatting marks if they are not already showing.

  b. Scroll to the "Schedule" section at the top of page 2. In this table, there is a single tab between each column: one tab after "Session," "Day," and "Time." The table is difficult to read because tab stops have not been set.

c. Select all the paragraphs in the table. The selection should look similar to:

Schedule¶

Session → Day → Time→ Location¶
Assertiveness→Monday → 12:30·p.m → Veranda¶
→ Wednesday→ 5:00·p.m → Board·Room¶
Organizational·Skills→Wednesday→ 3:30·p.m → Oak·Hall¶
→ Friday→1:00·p.m → Veranda¶
Cultural·Awareness→ Thursday → 9:00·a.m. → Oak·Hall¶
→ Friday→3:30·p.m → Board·Room¶

② *SET TAB STOPS FOR THE TABLE*

a. At the far left of the ruler, click the Tab Selection button until the left tab stop button (🔳) is displayed, if it is not already showing.

b. Click the ruler near the 2" mark. A left tab stop is created and the "Day" column is aligned at the stop.

c. On the ruler, drag the left tab stop marker to the 1.75" mark. The column of text is moved closer to the session names.

d. Click the Tab Selection button until the right tab stop button (🔳) is displayed.

e. Click the ruler at the 3.75" mark. A right tab stop is created and the "Time" column is aligned at the stop.

f. Click the Tab Selection button until the center tab stop button (🔳) is displayed.

g. Click the ruler at the 4.75" mark. A center tab stop is created and the "Location" column is aligned at the stop.

h. Click anywhere in the document to remove the selection.

Check — Your table should look similar to the following. Click in the table and compare your markers to those shown below:

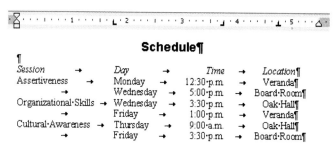

② *FORMAT A VERTICAL BLOCK OF TEXT*

a. Press and hold the Alt key and drag from the beginning of the "Assertiveness" title to the end of the data in the first column:

b. On the toolbar, click the Bold button. The column of text is formatted as bold:

Schedule¶

¶
Session	→	Day	→	Time	→	Location¶
Assertiveness	→	Monday	→	12:30·p.m	→	Veranda¶
→		Wednesday	→	5:00·p.m	→	Board·Room¶
Organizational·Skills	→	Wednesday	→	3:30·p.m	→	Oak·Hall¶
→		Friday	→	1:00·p.m	→	Veranda¶
Cultural·Awareness	→	Thursday	→	9:00·a.m.	→	Oak·Hall¶
→		Friday	→	3:30·p.m	→	Board·Room¶

④ *SAVE AND THEN PRINT THE MODIFIED TRAINING*

Line Spacing

The space between lines of text in a paragraph can be changed. *Single spacing* is the default. *Double spacing* adds more space between lines of text for notes or comments and can make a document easier to read:

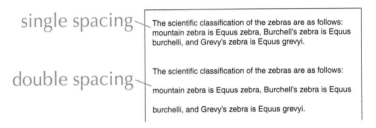

single spacing

double spacing

TIP Right-click a paragraph to display the Paragraph command.

The Line Spacing button (⬆≡▾) on the toolbar can be used to change the amount of space between lines of text in a paragraph. Click the arrow in the Line Spacing button and then click the spacing. Click More in the button list to display the Paragraph dialog box, which has additional spacing options. The Paragraph dialog box can also be displayed by selecting Format → Paragraph. Click the Indents and Spacing tab in the dialog box to display those options. To format multiple paragraphs together, first select the paragraphs.

Indenting Paragraphs

Margin settings apply to an entire document and cannot change from paragraph to paragraph. However, *indents* decrease the width of lines of text in a specific paragraph. Indents are often used to set off paragraphs such as a quotation.

The default indents are 0 inches, meaning that lines of text extend from the left margin to the right margin. Specify left and right indents to give a paragraph shorter line lengths:

The Indent Buttons

The Increase Indent button (⬚) on the toolbar increases the left indent of a paragraph by 0.5 inches. Similarly, the Decrease Indent button (⬚) decreases a paragraph's left indent by 0.5 inches.

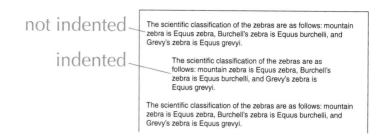

not indented — The scientific classification of the zebras are as follows: mountain zebra is Equus zebra, Burchell's zebra is Equus burchelli, and Grevy's zebra is Equus grevyi.

indented — The scientific classification of the zebras are as follows: mountain zebra is Equus zebra, Burchell's zebra is Equus burchelli, and Grevy's zebra is Equus grevyi.

The scientific classification of the zebras are as follows: mountain zebra is Equus zebra, Burchell's zebra is Equus burchelli, and Grevy's zebra is Equus grevyi.

To indent a paragraph, select Format → Paragraph to display the Paragraph dialog box and then select the Indents and Spacing tab to display those options. Setting indents affects only the paragraph that contains the insertion point, or multiple paragraphs selected together.

Indents can also be set by dragging markers on the ruler:

TIP Select View → Ruler to display the rulers.

left indent marker   right indent marker

When an indent marker is dragged, a dotted line appears that helps line up text. This method of changing indents is usually less precise than using options in the Paragraph dialog box.

Practice: TRAINING – part 4 of 7

You will indent paragraphs and change line spacing in a document. Word should already be started with the TRAINING document displayed from the last practice.

① *CHANGE PARAGRAPH LINE SPACING*

   a. Near the top of the document, place the insertion point in the paragraph of text beginning "Widget Corporation is committed…."

   b. On the toolbar, click the arrow next to the Line Spacing button (⬚). (You may need to click the Toolbar Options button to display the Line Spacing button.) A list is displayed.

   c. In the Line Spacing list, select 2.0. The paragraph of text is double-spaced:

Widget·Corporation¶
Life-Long·Learning·Program¶
¶
Widget· Corporation· is· committed· to· fostering· the· best· possible· working·

environment.·Our·company·has·successfully·grown·to·more·than·2,000·employees·

worldwide· with· locations· in· six· countries.· In· our· global· society,·we· must· all·

continue·to·grow·and·learn·in·ways·that·allow·people·to·work·in·harmony.¶

② *INDENT A PARAGRAPH*

   a. In the "Sessions" section, place the insertion point in the paragraph that begins "Learn the difference…."

   b. In the Reveal Formatting task pane, click <u>Indentation</u>. The Paragraph dialog box is displayed.

c. Change the Left and Right indentation options as shown:

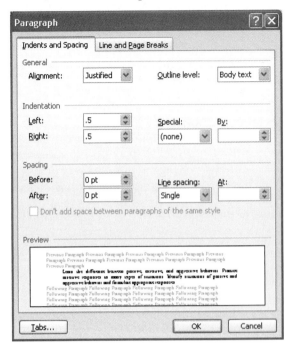

d. Select OK. The paragraph is indented.

③ **INDENT ANOTHER PARAGRAPH**

a. In the "Sessions" section, place the insertion point in the paragraph that begins "Learn specific techniques…."

b. On the toolbar, drag the Left Indent marker to the 0.5" mark:

The left side of the paragraph is indented.

c. On the toolbar, drag the Right Indent marker to the 5" mark:

The right side of the paragraph is indented. Note the Reveal Formatting task pane displays the new indent amounts.

④ **INDENT A THIRD PARAGRAPH**

a. In the "Sessions" section, place the insertion point in the paragraph that begins "Develop awareness…."

b. Create 0.5" left and right indents.

⑤ **SAVE AND THEN PRINT THE MODIFIED TRAINING**

Hanging and First Line Indents

hanging indent

A paragraph can be formatted so that the first line is indented differently from the rest of the paragraph. When the first line of a paragraph is farther to the left than the rest of the paragraph, it is formatted with a *hanging indent*. A hanging indent is often used for lists, outlines, or for a bibliography entry:

> Riggi, Donna. *The Complete Guide to Stocking and Selling Mattresses*. Chicago: Winding Staircase Press, 1993.

Create a hanging indent by selecting Format ➞ Paragraph to display the Paragraph dialog box. Select the Indents and Spacing tab to display those options and then select Hanging in the Special list. The By box is used to specify the amount the text hangs out from the rest of the paragraph.

Markers on the ruler show the hanging indent:

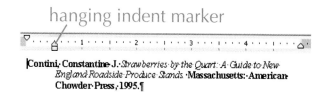

Drag the hanging indent marker to create or change a hanging indent.

first line indent

Another paragraph format is the *first line indent*, which indents the first line of the paragraph farther to the right than the rest of the paragraph. A first line indent is often used for text in a published book or paper. For example, this paragraph is formatted with a first line indent.

Create a first line indent by selecting Format ➞ Paragraph to display the Paragraph dialog box. Select the Indents and Spacing tab to display those options and then select First line in the Special list. Use the By box to specify the amount the text indents in from the rest of the paragraph. First line indents can also be created by dragging the first line indent marker (▽) on the ruler.

Creating Lists

bulleted list

One use for hanging indents is in the creation of *bulleted lists*. In a bulleted list, each item is a separate paragraph formatted with a hanging indent, a special character such as a bullet (•), and a tab. To create a bulleted list, first select the paragraphs in the list

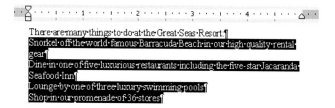

and then click the Bullets button (▤) on the toolbar:

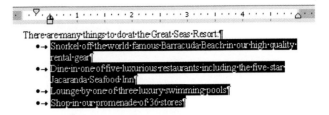

Word automatically formats the paragraph with a hanging indent and adds a bullet character and a tab to each paragraph.

numbered list   Bulleted lists are used when each item is equally important. *Numbered lists* show a priority of importance and are used, for example, for the steps in a recipe. To create a numbered list, first select the paragraphs and then click the Numbering button (▤) on the toolbar:

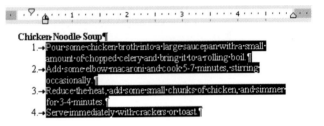

Word automatically formats the paragraph with a hanging indent and adds a number followed by a period and a tab to each paragraph.

Click the Increase Indent button (▤) on the toolbar to increase the indent of bulleted or numbered items. To remove the bullets or numbering formats, select the formatted paragraphs and then click the Bullets or Numbering button on the toolbar, respectively.

Practice: TRAINING – part 5 of 7

You will create lists in a document. Word should already be started with the TRAINING document displayed from the last practice.

① *FORMAT A NUMBERED LIST*

   a. Scroll to the "Program Objectives" in the middle of page 1.

   b. Select the paragraphs containing the objectives:

> **Program·Objectives¶**
>
> ¶
> Provide·a·professional·learning·environment·with·skilled,·knowledgeable·instructors.¶
> Foster·an·interactive·teacher-student·relationship·to·maximize·learning.¶
> Instill·a·level·of·confidence·in·each·and·every·learner·so·that·new·skills·will·be·implemented·with·ease.¶
> ¶

   c. On the toolbar, click the Numbering button (▤). The paragraphs are formatted with numbers and a hanging indent.

② *FORMAT A HANGING INDENT*

a. Scroll to the "Instructors" section on page 2 and then select the paragraphs about the instructors:

Instructors¶

Pat·Merlin·Well-known·for·innovative·teaching·techniques,·Pat·is·a·leader·in·assertiveness·training.·Pat·is·also·recognized·in·the·field·of·organizational·methods·for·the·business·world.¶

Francis·Neal·Francis·has·worked·with·hundreds·of·companies·world-wide·to·help·resolve·cultural·conflicts·and·teach·the·importance·of·cultural·diversity·within·an·organization.¶

b. Select Format → Paragraph. A dialog box is displayed.

c. In the Special list, select Hanging and change the By option to 1.5:

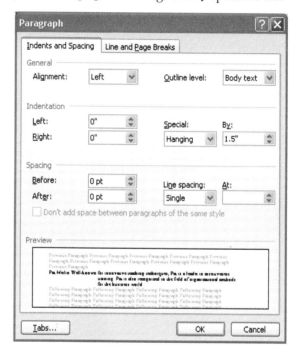

d. Select OK. The paragraphs have hanging indents, but are still not formatted properly.

e. Place the insertion point just after "Merlin" in the first instructor paragraph.

f. Delete the space and then press the Tab key.

g. Replace the space after the second instructor's last name with a tab.

③ *MODIFY THE HANGING INDENT*

a. Again select the paragraphs about the instructors.

b. On the ruler, drag the hanging indent marker (△) to the 1.25" mark. Click anywhere in the document to remove the selection. Your document should look similar to:

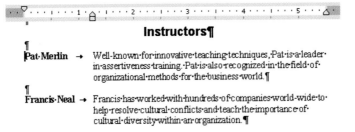

Instructors¶

Pat·Merlin → Well-known·for·innovative·teaching·techniques,·Pat·is·a·leader· in·assertiveness·training.·Pat·is·also·recognized·in·the·field·of· organizational·methods·for·the·business·world.¶

Francis·Neal → Francis·has·worked·with·hundreds·of·companies·world-wide·to· help·resolve·cultural·conflicts·and·teach·the·importance·of· cultural·diversity·within·an·organization.¶

④ *FORMAT A BULLETED LIST*

    a. Scroll to the "General Information" section on page 2. The section contains a list.

    b. Select all the paragraphs in the list:

General·Information¶

The·Widget·Corporation·Life-Long·Learning·Program·is·free·to·all·employees.¶
Each·session·is·one·hour·in·length¶
Sessions·between·11:30·a.m.·and·1:30·p.m.·are·brown-bag·sessions.·Please·bring· your·own·lunch.·Beverages·will·be·provided.¶
Please·RSVP·to·WidgetLLL@lpdatafiles.com¶

    c. On the toolbar, click the Bullets button (⊞). The items in the list are formatted with bullets and a hanging indent. Click anywhere in the document to remove the selection:

General·Information¶

  •→ The·Widget·Corporation·Life-Long·Learning·Program·is·free·to·all· employees.¶
  •→ Each·session·is·one·hour·in·length¶
  •→ Sessions·between·11:30·a.m.·and·1:30·p.m.·are·brown-bag·sessions.·Please· bring·your·own·lunch.·Beverages·will·be·provided.¶
  •→ Please·RSVP·to·WidgetLLL@lpdatafiles.com¶

⑤ *SAVE THE MODIFIED TRAINING AND THEN PRINT A COPY*

Creating Footnotes and Endnotes

TIP Double-click the footnote number in the text to move the insertion point to the footnote at the bottom of the page.

Research papers and reports often include *footnotes* to document sources. To add a footnote, place the insertion point in the text where the footnote number should appear and select Insert → Reference → Footnote to display the Footnote and Endnote dialog box. Footnotes appear at the bottom of the page by default. In Print Layout view, a footnote looks similar to:

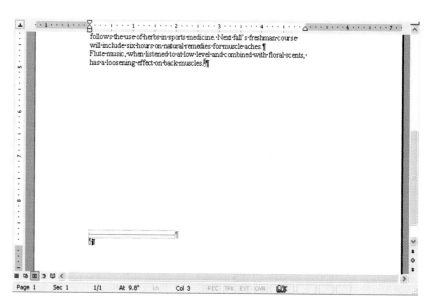

follows·the·use·of·herbs·in·sports·medicine.·Next·fall's·freshman·course·
will·include·six·hours·on·natural·remedies·for·muscle·aches.¶
Flute·music,·when·listened·to·at·low·level·and·combined·with·floral·scents,·
has·a·loosening·effect·on·back·muscles.¶

A line separates footnotes from the rest of the text

footnote standard format

In a new footnote, the insertion point automatically moves to the right of the footnote number at the bottom of the page so that the footnote information can be typed and formatting applied. The standard format for footnotes is a 0.5 inch first line indent and a blank line after the horizontal line and a blank line between footnotes.

Word sequentially numbers footnotes, and automatically renumbers footnotes when one is moved, inserted, copied, or deleted. Delete a footnote by deleting the footnote number in the text, which automatically removes the reference from the bottom of the page.

endnotes

Endnotes appear separately on the last page of a document and are sometimes used instead of footnotes. Select the Endnotes option in the Footnote and Endnote dialog box to create endnotes instead of footnotes.

Practice: TRAINING – part 6 of 7

You will add a footnote to a document and apply the standard format as defined in *The Gregg Reference Manual Ninth Edition* by William Sabin (copyright 2001 Glencoe/McGraw-Hill). Word should already be started with the TRAINING document displayed from the last practice.

① *CREATE A FOOTNOTE*

  a. In the first paragraph of the document, place the insertion point after the period after the last word, which reads "…harmony."

  b. Select Insert → Reference → Footnote. A dialog box is displayed.

  c. Select Insert to accept the default options. Word inserts a 1 at the insertion point and then the insertion point is moved to the bottom of the page where the footnote text can be typed. Note the line separating the reference from the rest of the text.

② *ENTER THE FOOTNOTE TEXT*

  a. Move the insertion point to the left of the footnote number and then press Enter.

  b. Move the insertion point after the footnote number and type the following text, allowing Word to wrap the text:

  Kemperstein, Chris. Working in Harmony: The Widget Philosophy (Atlanta: Calo-Brown Press, 2004) 110.

③ **FORMAT THE FOOTNOTE TEXT**

a. Select the book title, "Working in Harmony: The Widget Philosophy."

b. On the toolbar, click the Italic button (I). The book title is now italic.

c. Click anywhere in the footnote text. The book title is no longer selected and the insertion point is placed in the footnote.

d. With the insertion point in the footnote text, drag the first line indent marker (▽) on the ruler to the 0.5" mark. The footnote now has a first line indent of 0.5 inches.

Check – The footnote should look similar to:

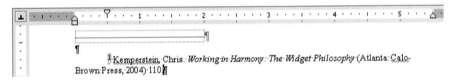

④ **SAVE THE MODIFIED TRAINING, PRINT PREVIEW, AND THEN PRINT A COPY**

Adding Images to a Document

Images can be used to make a document more interesting and informative. Images in digital format come from various sources, including scanned artwork, digital camera pictures, screen captures, and illustration software. Select Insert → Picture → From File to display the Insert Picture dialog box with a list of image files.

clip art

Clip art is an image file with a general-purpose picture created by an artist using illustration software. Select Insert → Picture → Clip Art to display the Clip Art task pane:

keyword   Type a *keyword*, which is a descriptive word, in the Search for box and select Go to find all the clip art that have the keyword in their description. To narrow a search, use the options in the Search in list, which contains clip art collection names, and the Results should be list, which contains file formats. For example, type needlepoint in the Search for box and then select Go to display pictures similar to:

To place a clip art image into the document, click the arrow to the right of the image and select Insert from the menu.

An image may need to be sized. Click a picture in a document to select it and display handles:

Point to a corner handle, which changes the pointer to a double-headed arrow shape, and then drag to size the picture.

Drag the center of a picture (not a handle) to move the picture. Wherever a picture is moved, text moves to make room. The Cut, Copy, and Paste buttons on the toolbar can be used to create copies or move a selected picture. Press the Delete key to delete the selected picture. Click anywhere in the document other than on the picture to remove the handles.

In a document, a picture can have formats applied to the paragraph it is in. For example, to center a picture, place the insertion point in the paragraph that contains the picture and click the Center button on the toolbar.

You will add a picture file to a document. Word should already be started with the TRAINING document displayed from the last practice.

① **INSERT A PICTURE**

    a. Scroll to the bottom of page 2.

    b. Place the insertion point in the blank paragraph at the very end of the document.

    c. Select Insert → Picture → From File. A dialog box is displayed.

        1. Use the Look in list and contents box below to select WIDGET MAP, which is an image data file for this text.

        2. Select Insert. The picture is displayed at the insertion point.

    d. On the toolbar, click the Center button. The map is centered.

② **SAVE THE MODIFIED TRAINING, PREVIEW, AND THEN PRINT PAGE 2**

③ **CLOSE TRAINING**

Templates

Supplied Templates

A variety of templates are supplied with Word. The Templates dialog box separates templates into tabbed categories.

A *template* is a master document that includes the basic elements for particular types of documents. Templates are used again and again whenever a document of that type is needed. For example, office memos usually contain the same layout (To:, From:, Subject:, company logo, and so on), with only the topic changing for each new memo. Instead of typing the text, setting tab stops, and applying the formatting every time, a more efficient approach would be to create a template that contains the unchanging elements and then use this template each time a new memo is needed.

To create a template, type text in a new document and apply formatting. Select File → Save As to display a dialog box. Type a file name in the File name box and select Document Template in the Save as type list. To open a template, click the <u>On my computer</u> link in the New Document task pane, which displays the Templates dialog box. The new template appears in the General tab.

TIP Select View → Task Pane and then select New Document from the Other Task Panes list.

TIP Word templates have the .dot file name extension.

When a template is used, Word creates a new, blank, untitled document that contains the same formatting and text as the template. This prevents accidentally saving over and changing the original template.

Practice: Widget Memo

You will create a template and then create a new document based on the template. The document is a memo in the professional style as defined in *The Gregg Reference Manual Ninth Edition* by William Sabin (copyright 2001 Glencoe/McGraw-Hill).

① **CREATE A NEW WORD DOCUMENT**

② **TYPE TEXT AND FORMAT THE DOCUMENT**

    a. Press Enter 6 times to move the insertion point down about 1 inch (2.54 cm) from the top margin.

b. Type the following text, pressing Tab after each colon. Use the Enter key to include a blank line between each line of text and two blank lines after the "SUBJECT" line:

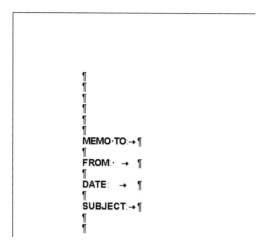

c. Format each of the words as Arial and bold. Do not include the tab character or colon in the formatting.

d. Select the paragraphs that contain text, and then set a left-aligned tab stop at 1".

e. Click anywhere to remove the selection.

③ **SAVE THE TEMPLATE**

a. Select File → Save. The Save As dialog box is displayed.

b. In the File name box, type Widget Memo and in the Save as type list, select Document Template. Note that the Save in list has changed to display the Templates folder:

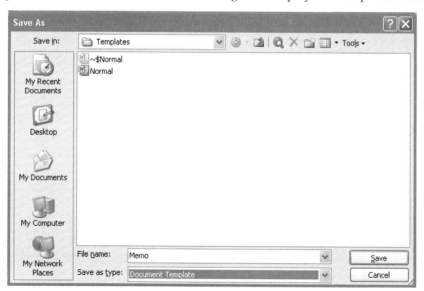

c. Select Save. The document is saved as a template.

④ **CLOSE THE TEMPLATE**

⑤ CREATE A NEW DOCUMENT USING THE TEMPLATE

   a. If a task pane is not showing, select View → Task Pane.

   b. From the Other Task Panes list, select New Document:

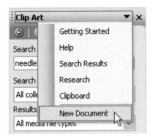

   c. In the New Document task pane, click <u>On my computer</u>. The Templates dialog box is displayed.

        1. Select the General tab if those icons are not already displayed.

        2. Click the Widget Memo icon and then select OK. A new document with the Widget Memo template text is displayed.

⑥ CREATE A MEMO USING THE TEMPLATE

   a. Type the following information into the memo headings, using the arrow keys to move the insertion point in the text:

        MEMO TO: All Employees

        FROM: Assistant Manager

        DATE: March 16, 2006

        SUBJECT: Vacation Days

   b. Press the down-arrow key until the insertion point is in the last line of the document.

   c. Complete the memo by typing the following text for the body of the memo:

        Effective April 15, each employee will be allotted two vacation days per month.

⑦ SAVE, PRINT, AND THEN CLOSE THE DOCUMENT

   a. Select File → Save. The Save As dialog box is displayed.

        1. Use the Save in list and the contents box below it to select the appropriate location for the file to be saved.

        2. In the File name box, replace existing text with Vacation Days Memo and then select Save.

   b. Print the memo and then close the document.

Creating an HTML File

HTML is the file format for documents viewed using a browser, such as documents on the Web. A document in HTML format is more versatile because Word is not needed to view it, just a browser, such as Internet Explorer. Select File → Save as Web Page to save a document in Web format. The Save As dialog box includes a Change Title button. Click this button to give the Web page a descriptive *title*, which is text displayed in the title bar of the browser window.

Word displays a document saved as a Web page in Web Layout view. To preview a document as it will appear in a browser, select File → Web Page Preview.

Saving a document as a Web page creates a copy of the file with the extension .mht. To view the file in a Web browser, open a browser, such as Internet Explorer and select File → Open.

MHTML

The Save as Web Page command saves a document in MHTML (MIME HTML) format, which means that all the information for the document, including pictures, is saved within one single file.

Practice: Widget Picnic

You will create a new document and then save it as a Web page. The Web page document will then be viewed in a browser. This practice requires browser software. Internet access is not required.

① CREATE A NEW WORD DOCUMENT

In a new document, type the following, replacing *Student Name* with your name:

Widget Corporation Annual Picnic

All employees and their families are invited to attend. Join together at Foliage Park on Saturday from 11:30 a.m. until 3:00 p.m. for food, fun, and games.

Food includes:

Hot dogs, hamburgers, and veggie burgers
Potato salad and green salad
Baked beans and coleslaw

Games include horse shoes, softball, and a three-legged race

Student Name

② FORMAT TEXT

a. Bold the title "Widget Corporation Annual Picnic" and make it 24 points in size.

b. Format the three food items as a bulleted list.

③ INSERT CLIP ART

a. Add four blank paragraphs after the "…three-legged race" paragraph.

b. With the insertion point in the last blank paragraph, select Insert → Picture → Clip Art. The Clip Art task pane is displayed.

1. In the Search for box, type picnic and then click Go. Clip art images are displayed.

2. Point to an appropriate clip art image and then click the arrow that appears beside the image.

3. In the menu, select Insert. The clip art is placed at the insertion point.

c. Center the paragraph containing the image.

④ SAVE THE DOCUMENT AND PRINT A COPY

a. Save the document naming it: Widget Picnic

b. Print a copy.

⑤ SAVE THE DOCUMENT AS HTML

a. Select File → Save as Web Page. A dialog box is displayed.

1. Click Change Title. A dialog box is displayed. Type a title as shown:

2. Select OK.

b. Select Save. The dialog box is removed and the document is displayed in Web Layout view.

⑥ PREVIEW THE HTML DOCUMENT IN A BROWSER

a. Select File → Web Page Preview. A browser window opens with the Web page document displayed.

b. Expand the window, if necessary, to view the entire document. Note the title in the title bar.

c. Close the browser window.

⑦ CLOSE WIDGET PICNIC AND QUIT WORD

Chapter Summary

This chapter discussed formatting documents to improve appearance and readability. The Reveal Formatting task pane displays a list of formats that have been applied to text, and can be used to compare the formats of two selections of text.

Margins are the white region around text on a page. Pagination is how a document is divided into pages. The Page Setup command is used to change margins, and the Break command is used to set pagination.

A header is a special area at the top of a page and the footer is a special area at the bottom of the page. The Header and Footer command displays the header and footer areas.

Tabs are used to position text within a line. A tab stop specifies a location within a line of text and is displayed on the ruler above a document. The Tab Selection button is used to set a tab stop.

A vertical block of text in a table is selected by holding down the Alt key and dragging. Once selected, formatting can be applied to the entire column.

The space between lines of text in a paragraph is changed by using the Line Spacing button on the toolbar or the Paragraph command.

Indents, hanging indents, and first line indents affect the width of lines of text in a paragraph. Indents are set by using the Paragraph command or by dragging markers on the ruler.

Bulleted and numbered lists are paragraphs formatted with a hanging indent, a number or bullet, and a tab. The Bullets button, Numbering button, and the Increase Indent button on the toolbar are used to format lists.

The Footnote command creates footnotes and endnotes. Remove a footnote by deleting its number from the text.

Pictures can be either images from a file or clip art. Images come from a number of sources, including digital camera images and scanned images. Clip art is an image file created using illustration software. The Clip Art task pane is used to display clip art. Use the From File command to add an image to a document.

A template contains the basic elements for a particular type of document. A template is created by saving a document as type Document Template. To open a document based on a template, click the On my computer link in the New Document task pane.

HTML documents are used for Web sites and for distributing documents to individuals that have browser software and do not have Microsoft Word. Select the Save as Web Page command to convert a document to a Web page.

Vocabulary

Bulleted list List created with each item as a separate paragraph formatted with a hanging indent, a special character such as a bullet (•), and a tab.

Clip art An image file with a general-purpose picture created by an artist using illustration software.

Double spacing Paragraph format that adds more space between each line of text.

Endnote Used to document a source. Found on the last page of a document.

First line indent First line of a paragraph that is farther to the right than the rest of the paragraph.

Footer Text that is printed at the bottom of each page.

Footnote Used to document a source. Usually located at the bottom of the page that contains the footnoted material.

Hanging indent First line of a paragraph that is farther to the left than the rest of the paragraph.

Header Text that is printed at the top of each page.

HTML The file format for documents viewed using a browser.

Indent Paragraph format that decreases the width of lines of text in a specific paragraph.

Keyword A descriptive word used to search for clip art.

Margins The white region around the text on a page.

Numbered list List created with each item as a separate paragraph formatted with a hanging indent, a number, and a tab. Each number indicates an item's priority in the list.

Page break Changes the pagination in a document.

Pagination How a document is divided into pages.

Single spacing The default paragraph format that does not add extra space between each line of text.

Tab Used to position text within a line.

Tab stop Specifies a location within a line of text.

Template A master document that includes the basic elements for a particular type of document.

Title Text displayed in the title bar of a Web browser.

Break command Displays a dialog box used to add a page break at the insertion point. Found in the Insert menu.

Bullets button Formats a paragraph with a hanging indent and inserts a bullet and a tab to create a bulleted item in a list. Found on the toolbar.

Clip Art command Displays the Clip Art task pane, which is used to insert clip art into a document at the insertion point. Found in Insert → Picture.

Close Closes the Header and Footer toolbar. Found on the Header and Footer toolbar.

Footnote command Displays a dialog box used to create footnotes or endnotes. Found in Insert → Reference.

Format Page Number button Displays a dialog box used to change the page numbering style. Found on the Header and Footer toolbar.

From File command Displays a dialog box used to add an image at the insertion point. Found in Insert → Picture.

Header and Footer command Displays the Header and Footer toolbar, dims the text in the document, and moves the insertion point to the header area at the top of the page. Found in the View menu.

Increase Indent button Indents an item farther in a bulleted or numbered list. Found on the toolbar.

Insert command Inserts a clip art image into a document. Found in the menu displayed by clicking the arrow to the right of an image in the Clip Art task pane.

Insert Date button Inserts the current date at the insertion point in a header or footer. Found on the Header and Footer toolbar.

Insert Page Number button Adds a page number at the insertion point in a header or footer. Found on the Header and Footer toolbar.

Insert Time button Inserts the current time at the insertion point in a header or footer. Found on the Header and Footer toolbar.

Line Spacing button Used to change the amount of space between lines of text in a paragraph. Found on the toolbar.

Numbering button Formats a paragraph with a hanging indent and inserts a number and a tab to create a numbered item in a list. Found on the toolbar.

Open command Used to open an HTML file. Found in the File menu of the browser window.

Page Setup command Displays a dialog box used to apply formats to pages. Found in the File menu.

Paragraph command Displays a dialog box used to apply paragraph formats. Found in the Format menu.

Reveal Formatting command Displays the Reveal Formatting task pane. Found in the Format menu.

Save as Web Page command Displays a dialog box used to save a document in HTML format. Found in the File menu.

Switch Between Header and Footer button Moves the insertion point to either the header or footer area in a document. Found on the Header and Footer toolbar.

Tab Selection button Used to select the type of tab stop that will be created by clicking the ruler. Found on the ruler.

Tabs command Displays a dialog box used to set or clear individual tab stops. Found in the Format menu.

Web Page Preview command Opens a browser window to preview a Web page. Found in the File menu.

1. How can a list of format differences between the first paragraph and last paragraph in a document be compared?

2. a) What are margins?
   b) What are the default margins in Word?

3. a) How can the margins of a document be changed so the left margin is 2″ and the right margin 3″?
   b) How long is a line of text after these margins have been set? (Assume an 8.5-inch x 11-inch sheet of paper.)

4. a) What is pagination?
   b) How is pagination changed?
   c) What else (other than changing margins) can affect a document's pagination?

5. List two ways to insert a page break.

6. How does the pagination differ between a document with 1″ top, bottom, left, and right margins and a document with 2″ top, bottom, left, and right margins?

7. a) What is a header?
   b) What is a footer?
   c) List three kinds of information that is often included in a header or footer.
   d) How can the insertion point be quickly moved from the header to the footer?

8. List the steps required to have Word print the text Proposal in the header and a page number in the footer on each page in a document.

9. Explain why including the date and time in the header is helpful.

10. a) What are tabs used for?
    b) What does a tab stop do?
    c) How can you tell where tab stops have been set?

11. What default tab stops will automatically be removed when a tab stop is set at 3″ on the ruler?

12. List the four types of tab stops and describe each one.

13. a) List the steps required to set a center tab stop at 2.25".
    b) How can the tab stop described in part (a) be moved to 3"?
    c) How can the tab stop described in part (a) be removed?

14. How can a center tab stop at 2.5" be changed to a left tab stop at 3"?

15. What type of data would be best aligned using a decimal tab stop?

16. List the steps to select only the second column of data in a table and format it as italic.

17. a) What is double spacing?
    b) Why would double spacing paragraphs in a document be helpful?

18. What button on the toolbar can be used to change the formatting of a paragraph from double spaced to single spaced?

19. a) Do indents increase or decrease the width of lines of text in a paragraph?
    b) Explain what a paragraph formatted with left and right indents of 2" looks like compared to a paragraph with no indents.
    c) Which type of indent formats the first line of a paragraph farther to the left than the rest of the paragraph?

20. What is the difference between formatting a paragraph with 0.5" left and right indents using the Paragraph dialog box and by dragging markers on the ruler.

21. a) List the steps required to format a paragraph with a hanging indent of 0.25".
    b) Give an example of when a hanging indent is useful.

22. Draw what the markers on the ruler would look like after a paragraph has been formatted with a first line indent of 0.5".

23. Compare and contrast hanging and first line indents.

24. List the steps required to format six paragraphs as a bulleted list of six items.

25. When would a numbered list be used instead of a bulleted list?

26. How can steps 2 and 3 of a numbered list of five items be indented farther?

27. a) What are footnotes used for?
    b) List the steps required to create a footnote for a paragraph in a document.

28. a) How can a footnote be deleted?
    b) What happens to the numbers of the other footnotes when one is deleted?

29. Compare and contrast footnotes and endnotes.

30. a) What is clip art?
    b) List the steps required to add clip art about education at the insertion point in a document.

31. a) List the steps required to size a picture smaller and center it.
    b) How can a picture be deleted?
    c) Once inserted, can a picture be moved? If so, how?

32. a) What is a template?
    b) Give an example of when using a template could be helpful. Explain why.

33. a) Describe the usefulness of being able to save a Word document to be viewed on the Web.
    b) How can the title of a Word document saved as HTML be changed?

True/False

34. Determine if each of the following are true or false. If false, explain why.
    a) A list of the character and paragraph formats that have been applied to text can be displayed in a task pane.
    b) Once inserted, page breaks cannot be deleted from a document.
    c) It is possible to have a different header and footer printed on the first page than on the rest of the pages.
    d) The date and time in a header (created using the Insert Date and Insert Time buttons on the Header and Footer toolbar) need to be manually updated every time a document is printed or opened.
    e) Default tab stops are located at every inch on the ruler.
    f) A right tab stop aligns the end of the text at the stop.
    g) A paragraph in a new document is double spaced by default.
    h) Margin settings can change from paragraph to paragraph.
    i) Indents are often used to set off paragraphs such as a quotation.
    j) A hanging indent is part of the standard footnote format.
    k) The steps in a recipe should be formatted as a bulleted list.
    l) Footnotes appear at the bottom of the page by default.
    m) The text cars would be an appropriate keyword when searching for clip art of musical instruments.
    n) The Cut, Copy, and Paste buttons on the toolbar can be used to create copies of or move a selected picture.
    o) A Web page title is text displayed in the title bar of the Web browser.

Exercise 1 ——————————————————————————————— Portfolio

A portfolio is a collection of work that clearly illustrates effort, progress, and achievement of knowledge and skills. A portfolio can take the form of a file folder, a three-ring binder, or it can be stored in digital format. Create a portfolio using samples of work created from the exercises in this text. Use a file folder to store the work samples. The portfolio should contain:

- an inventory of the works produced
- exemplary samples of work
- a learning journal, which documents the skills acquired as a result of working through this text

a) Open INVENTORY, which is a Word data file for this text. Replace Student Name with your name in the footer. Print a copy and place the hard copy at the front of the portfolio. Each time a sample of work is added to the portfolio, it should be documented on the inventory sheet. The documentation can be done in pencil or pen initially. When the portfolio is complete, the entries can be typed into the data file.

b) As exercises are completed, select samples for the portfolio. The samples selected for the portfolio should be "polished copies." This may require making edits to work that has already been assessed. Select samples that illustrate a range of skills and knowledge learned.

c) Each time a sample is selected, open LEARNING JOURNAL, which is a Word data file for this text, and make an entry in the learning journal to document and reflect on the skills acquired as a result of completing the sample exercise. In the footer, replace Student Name with your name. When the portfolio is complete, place a copy of LEARNING JOURNAL after the samples of work.

Exercise 2 ——————————————————————————————— OPENINGS

The OPENINGS document contains several introductions that can be used to start a paragraph. Open OPENINGS, which is a Word data file for this text, and complete the following steps:

a) Choose one of the introductions, delete the rest, then write a paragraph using the remaining introduction as the beginning of the paragraph.

b) Justify and double-space the paragraph.

c) Create a header with a title for the story and center align the header text. Format the title as 18 point and bold.

d) Create a footer with your name and right align the footer text.

e) Check the document on screen and correct any errors and misspellings.

f) Save the modified OPENINGS and print a copy.

Exercise 3 ——————————————————————— WELCOME

The WELCOME document contains a letter for new customers. Open WELCOME, which is Word data file for this text, and complete the following steps:

a) Insert BARBELL, which is an image data file for this text, to the left of the title "Marrelli's Gym" and size the picture appropriately.

b) Format the title "Marrelli's Gym" as 18 point, bold, and in a different font.

c) Change the top and left margins to 2".

d) Justify all the paragraphs of the letter except for the "Marrelli's Gym" title.

e) Create a footer with your name and right align the footer text.

f) Format the entire table at the bottom of the letter with the following tab stops:

- at 1.25" create a left tab stop (for the hours on Monday – Friday)

- at 2.75" create a left tab stop (for the hours on Saturday)

- at 4.25" create a left tab stop (for the hours on Sunday)

g) Format the column titles in the table as bold and italic.

h) Save the modified WELCOME and print a copy.

Exercise 4 ——————————————————————TELECOMMUTING

The TELECOMMUTING document contains information about the advantages of telecommuting. Open TELECOMMUTING, which is a Word data file for this text, and complete the following steps:

a) Center align the following headings and format them as 14 point, bold, Tahoma:

"Computers in the Home Office"

"The Process of Telecommuting"

"Advantages of Telecommuting"

"Telecommuting in Coral County"

b) Underline the first sentence of the second paragraph that begins "Telecommuting is possible because…."

c) Justify the first paragraph that begins "The invention of the microcomputer…."

d) Change the left and right margins to 0.75".

e) Insert a page break before the heading "Telecommuting in Coral County."

f) Create a header with the text TELECOMMUTING and center the header text.

g) Create a footer with your name and right align the footer text.

h) Format the table on page 2 with the following tab stops:

- at 2" create a right tab stop (for the number of people)

- at 3.5" create a right tab stop (for the percentage of population)

i) The column headings should be centered above the text in the columns. Format the column titles "Number of People" and "Percentage of Population" in the table to have only the following tab stops:

- at 1.75" create a center tab stop (for "Number of People")
- at 3.5" create a center tab stop (for "Percentage of Population")

j) Bold the column titles in the table.

k) Format the last line in the table that contains the totals as italic.

l) Create 0.5" left and right indents for the last paragraph on page 1, the one that begins "…if 10% to 20%…."

m) Place a footnote after the period ending the quote indented in part (l). Create the following footnote for the quote, formatting it in the standard format as practiced earlier in this chapter:

[1] Effy Oz, *Ethics for the Information Age* (Wm. C. Brown Communications, Inc., 1994).

n) Insert an appropriate clip art picture in a new paragraph above the heading "Computers in the Home Office." Center align the picture and size the picture smaller so that the document prints on two pages.

o) Save the modified TELECOMMUTING and print a copy.

Exercise 5 ———————————————Vitamins

In a new document create the following table, separating the columns with single tabs (do <u>not</u> precede the first column with a tab). Your table will not look like the one below until tab stops have been set:

Vitamin	Usage in Body	Common Food Sources
A	skeletal growth, skin	green leafy or yellow vegetables
B1	metabolism of carbohydrates	whole grains, liver
B12	production of proteins	liver, kidney, lean meat
C	resistance to infection	citrus fruits, tomatoes
E	antioxidant	peanut or corn oils

a) Save the document naming it Vitamins.

b) Format the entire table with the following tab stops:

- at 1.25" create a left tab stop (for the usage in body)
- at 3.5" create a left tab stop (for the common food sources)

c) Format the entire "Common Food Sources" column of data as italic.

d) At the top of the document, create a bold title with the text Vitamins and Their Usage. Insert a blank paragraph between the title and the table.

e) Bold the column titles in the table.

f) Subscript the "1" in "B1" and subscript the "12" in "B12."

g) Insert an appropriate clip art image to the left of the title at the top of the document.

h) Create a footer with your name and right align the footer text.

i) Check the document on screen and correct any errors and misspellings.

j) Save the modified Vitamins and print a copy.

Exercise 6 ——————————————— U.S. PRESIDENTS

The U.S. PRESIDENTS document contains a list of all the presidents of the United States, which needs formatting with tab stops. Open U.S. PRESIDENTS, which is Word data file for this text, and complete the following steps:

a) Format the entire document with left tab stops at 0.75" and 4" and a right tab stop at 3.5". The table should appear similar to the following:

Number	President	Years in Office	Party
1.	George Washington	1789-1797	(none)
2.	John Adams	1797-1801	Federalist
3.	Thomas Jefferson	1801-1809	Democratic-Republican
…	…	…	…

b) Save the modified U.S. PRESIDENTS.

c) Bold the column titles in the table.

d) Double space the entire table.

e) Create a header with your name and center the header text.

f) Create a footer with the page number and center the footer text.

g) Save the modified U.S. PRESIDENTS and print a copy.

h) Save the document as a Web page and then preview the document in a Web browser.

Exercise 7 ——————————————— PROPOSAL

The Coral Research proposal modified in Chapter 4, Exercise 9 needs to be formatted. Open PROPOSAL and complete the following steps:

a) Change the top and bottom margins to 1.25" and the left and right margins to 1.5".

b) Insert a page break before the heading "Computerized Guide."

c) Format the table below the "BUDGET" heading with the following tab stops:

- at 0.75" create a left tab stop
- at 4.5" create a decimal tab stop

d) Format the three numbered paragraphs of stages on page 2 as a numbered list.

e) Insert a page break before the heading "Notes" at the bottom of page 2.

f) Create a header with your name and center the header text.

g) Create a footer with the page number and center the footer text.

h) Save the modified PROPOSAL and print a copy.

Exercise 8   Entertainment Review

The review created in Chapter 4, Exercise 8 needs additional formatting before the article can be submitted. Open Entertainment Review and complete the following steps:

a) Double space the body of the review.

b) Create a header with the text CRITIC'S CHOICE and center the text.

c) Create a footer with your name and right align the footer text.

d) Save the modified Entertainment Review and print a copy.

e) Save the document as a Web page and then preview the document in a Web browser.

Exercise 9   Hawaiian Islands

In a new document create the following table, separating the columns with single tabs (do not precede the first column with a tab). Your table will not look like the one below until tab stops have been set:

Island	Area (km2)	Tallest Peak	Peak Height (m)
Hawaii	6,501	Mauna Kea	4,139
Maui	1,174	Haleakala	3,007
Oahu	979	Kaala	1,208
Kauai	890	Kawaikini	1,573
Molokai	420	Kamakou	1,491
Lanai	225	Lanaihale	1,011
Niihau	118	Paniau	384
Kahoolawe	72	Lua Makika	443

a) Save the document naming it Hawaiian Islands.

b) Format the entire table with the following tab stops:

- at 1" create a left tab stop (for the area)

- at 2.5" create a center tab stop (for the tallest peak)

- at 4" create a right tab stop (for the peak height)

c) In the paragraph with the column titles, change the right tab stop at 4" to a center tab stop at 3.75".

d) Bold the column titles "Island," "Area (km2)," "Tallest Peak," and "Peak Height (m)" in the table.

e) Format the entire "Tallest Peak" column of data as italic.

f) At the top of the document, create a bold title with the text The Hawaiian Islands. Insert a blank paragraph between the title and the table.

g) Superscript the "2" in the column title "Area (km2)."

h) Format the entire document as 11 point Tahoma.

i) Create a footer with your name and center the footer text.

j) Check the document on screen and correct any errors and misspellings.

k) Save the modified Hawaiian Islands and print a copy.

Exercise 10 ——————————————— Science Review

In a new document create the following table, separating the columns with single tabs (do <u>not</u> precede the first column with a tab). Your table will not look like the one below until tab stops have been set:

Measurement	Units	Symbol	Formula
Area	square meter	m2	m2
Heat	joule	J	N x m
Power	watt	W	J/s
Force	newton	N	kg x m/s2
Pressure	pascal	Pa	N/m2
Velocity	meter per second	m/s	m/s

a) Save the document naming it Science Review.

b) Format the entire table with the following tab stops:

- at 1.5" create a left tab stop (for the units)

- at 3.5" create a center tab stop (for the symbol)

- at 5" create a right tab stop (for the formula)

c) Superscript all four occurrences of "2" in the table.

d) Format the Formula data as Courier.

e) Insert three blank paragraphs after the first table, then create the following table, separating the columns with single tabs (do not precede the first column with a tab). Your table will not look like the one below until tab stops have been set:

Formula	Name
C2H2	acetylene
H2O	water
K2SO4	potassium sulfate
NH3	ammonia
CH4	methane
C6H6	benzene

f) Format the entire second table to have only one tab stop, a left tab stop at 1".

g) In the second table, subscript all occurrences of numbers.

h) Format the Formula data as Courier font.

i) At the top of the document, create a title with the text Science Review Sheet. Bold and center align the title. Insert a blank paragraph between the title and the first table.

j) Bold all of the column titles in both tables.

k) Create a header with your name and left align the header text.

l) Check the document on screen and correct any errors and misspellings.

m) Save the modified Science Review and print a copy.

Exercise 11 —————————————————————————— E-tail

E-tail stands for electronic retailing. An e-tailer sells goods and products online. Many e-tailers, such as amazon.com, do not have a corresponding "brick and mortar" establishment. E-tail is considered a B2C (business to consumer) form of e-commerce.

a) In a new document, type E-tail and press Enter.

b) Type by *Student Name* replacing *Student Name* with your name and then press Enter twice. You may need to point to the blue bar below "by" and then click the AutoCorrect Options button and select Undo Automatic Capitalization if the word "by" does not remain lowercase.

c) Type the text:

    E-tail is a form of e-commerce where a retailer sells goods and products online. There are advantages and disadvantages to shopping on-line.

    Advantages include:

d) Brainstorm with another student to come up with advantages and disadvantages of purchasing goods and products online.

e) Below "Advantages include:" create a bulleted list that lists three advantages of purchasing goods and products online and then press Enter twice.

f) Type Disadvantages include: and then press Enter.

g) Create a bulleted list with three disadvantages of purchasing goods and products online.

h) Add a header with your name and left align the header text.

i) Save the document naming it E-tail and print a copy.

Exercise 12 —————————————————————————— Frozen Desserts

Many cultures have a frozen dessert that is considered a special treat for both children and adults. Four frozen desserts and their countries of origin are:

Dessert	Country
kulfi	India
ais kacang	Malaysia
gelato	Italy
limber	Puerto Rico

a) Use books and the Internet to research two of the four frozen desserts listed above. Find information on the typical ingredients, flavors, how the dessert is made, and other facts. Keep track of the sources.

b) In a new document, write an introductory paragraph that indicates the report is about frozen desserts. After the introductory paragraph, write a paragraph for each of the two desserts, discussing cultural traditions and describing the dessert.

c) After the descriptive paragraphs, include a recipe for each dessert. Format the steps in the recipes as numbered lists and apply any other formatting to make the recipes attractive and easily readable.

d) Cite the sources of information, including the recipe sources, using footnotes. Format footnotes in the standard format as practiced earlier in this chapter.

e) Add page breaks where needed to make the document more readable.

f) Add a header with your name and left align the header text.

g) Save the document naming it Frozen Desserts and print a copy.

Exercise 13 ———————————————————Etiquette

Using electronic communication devices requires following a certain etiquette. For example:

Telephone Calls
Always state your name and the purpose of the call.

Cellular Phone
Refrain from talking on the phone while driving.

Speakerphone
Be sure there is no background noise.

Voicemail
Speak slowly and clearly.

E-mail
Use meaningful subject lines.

a) In a new document type the title Electronic Communication Etiquette, press Enter, and then type the devices and rules above.

b) Center align the title and format it as 20 point, bold, Tahoma. Bold the device names.

c) Brainstorm in small groups to generate three additional etiquette rules that apply to each device.

d) Add the additional etiquette rules in separate paragraphs below the appropriate device name.

e) Format the etiquette rules under each title as a bulleted list.

f) Create a header with your name and right align the header text. Add a footer with the date and center the footer text.

g) Save the document naming it Etiquette and print a copy.

Exercise 14 ——————————————— CAMPING TIPS

The CAMPING TIPS document contains a list of helpful information on camping. Open CAMPING TIPS, which is a Word data file for this text, and complete the following steps:

a) Find the word unwind in the document and then use the thesaurus to replace it with a synonym.

b) Format the entire document, except the title, as a numbered list.

c) Format the list of items after the first camping tip as a bulleted list. Use the Increase Indent button on the toolbar to indent the entire list farther so that it is a sublist of the first camping tip.

d) Create a header with your name and right align the header text.

e) Save the modified CAMPING TIPS and print a copy.

Producing a movie requires a screenplay, which is a document that includes the script for the actors and descriptions of what the audience will see. A screenplay is formatted in a particular way:

- Courier font, 12 point
- 8.5-inch x 11-inch paper
- a header with a page number in the upper-right corner on all pages except page 1
- top and bottom margins set between 0.5" and 1"
- left margin set to between 1.2" and 1.6" (wider than right margin to allow for binding)
- right margin set between 0.5" and 1"

The Courier font in size 12 is used as a way to measure the length of the screenplay. A one-page screenplay in this font and size with the margin settings stated above averages one minute of screen time. A screenplay averages 110 pages. The start of a screenplay could look similar to:

FADE IN:

A DREARY DAY

Susan is sitting at her computer. She has been trying to compose her weekly advice column but she doesn't have much to work. She is restless and complaining out loud.

          NANCY
Hi Susan. Are you finished your column yet?

          SUSAN
No, I have not even started. My readers have not sent me any material to work with this week.

          NANCY
Well can't you invent some questions?

          SUSAN
I really don't like to do that, but I might have to today. Unless of course you need some advice?

Nancy slumps down in the chair and starts to look very distraught.

          NANCY
Well Susan, now that you mention it.

a) Develop an appropriate story idea for a screenplay. The screenplay should include dialogue between at least two characters.

b) In a new Word document, apply the appropriate screenplay formatting as listed above.

c) Compose a screenplay that is a minimum of five pages in length. Note that the name of the scene and the character names are typically typed in capital letters.

d) Type your name after the last paragraph of the screenplay.

e) Save the document naming it Screenplay and print a copy.

f) A rubric can be used to assess the quality of a document. Open SCREENPLAY RUBRIC, which is a Word data file for this text. It currently lists two assessment criteria. Brainstorm in small groups to generate three additional assessment criteria.

g) Place the insertion point in the blank paragraph above "Additional Comments." Add the additional assessment criteria and corresponding scale. Format the three additional assessment criteria as a numbered list.

h) Create a header with your name and right align the header text. Add a footer with the date and center the footer text.

i) Save the modified SCREENPLAY RUBRIC and print a copy.

j) Exchange screenplays with a classmate. Use the rubric to peer-edit your classmate's screenplay.

k) Reflect on the design of the rubric? Does it appropriately assess the screenplay? Make any appropriate revisions.

Exercise 16 ——————————————————SCIENCE MUSEUM

The SCIENCE MUSEUM document contains information on a museum. Open SCIENCE MUSEUM, which is a Word data file for this text, and complete the following steps:

a) Format the exhibits under each of the five departments in the museum as bulleted lists.

b) Create 0.5" left and right indents for the paragraph that begins "It is my dream that the Sunport Science Museum…."

c) Place a footnote after the period ending the quote indented in part (b). Create the following footnote for the quote, formatting it in the standard format as practiced earlier in this chapter:

> [1] Elaine Diver, Keynote address, Sunport Science Museum Dedication, Sunport, FL, 15 Feb. 1965.

d) Insert an appropriate clip art picture below the title and center align it. Size the picture if necessary so that all the information fits on one page.

e) Create a header with your name and right align the header text.

f) Save the modified SCIENCE MUSEUM and print a copy.

Exercise 17 ——————————————————— SUNPORT CAMPING

The SUNPORT CAMPING document contains a short article on the recent Sunport Camping Symposium. Open SUNPORT CAMPING, which is a Word data file for this text, and complete the following steps:

a) Format the symposium specials, starting with "Johnson Cooking" and ending with "The Camp Grounds Company," as a bulleted list.

b) Format the two book titles in the paragraph after the bulleted list as italic.

c) Place footnotes after the punctuation marks at the end of each book title. Create the following footnotes, formatting each in the standard format as practiced earlier in this chapter:

[1] Gordon Washington, *Mountain Streams are Nice but Ponds are Better* (New Haven: Persimmons Publishing, 1994) 133.

[2] Henrietta Lebon, *Good Dirt Bad Dirt* (Minneapolis: Baked Zucchini Press, 1995) 54.

d) Create a header with your name and right align the header text.

e) Save the modified SUNPORT CAMPING and print a copy.

Exercise 18 ———————————————— Birthday Traditions

Birthdays are celebrated in different ways around the world:

Africa	Instead of celebrating a child's birthday, in African nations an initiation ceremony is held for a group of children. During the ceremony they learn about the customs and beliefs of their tribe.
Brazil	The earlobe of the birthday child is pulled once for each year they have been alive.
China	The birthday child pays respect to the parents and receives a money gift. The birthday is celebrated at a lunch with friends and relatives, and noodles are served to represent a long life.
Denmark	A flag is flown outside the house when someone is having a birthday. The birthday child wakes up to find gifts around their bed.
Mexico	A piñata is filled with surprises. The birthday child, blindfolded, hits the hanging piñata until it breaks open.
Nepal	For good luck, rice yogurt with coloring in it is placed on the forehead of the birthday child.
Russia	A birthday pie with a birthday greeting carved into the crust is the traditional food.
Scotland	The birthday child receives one pound note (money) for each year they have been alive plus an additional pound for good luck.
Vietnam	Everybody celebrates their birthday on New Year's day. Children receive "lucky" money in red envelopes.

Within each country, families also have their own traditions. In the United States, common family birthday traditions are:

- The birthday child chooses the restaurant or dinner menu for that evening.
- The birthday child receives a rose or other item for each year they have been alive.
- Two parties are planned, one for the family and one for friends.
- The cake or a meal is served on a special birthday plate.

a) Use books and the Internet to research birthday traditions in four locations in the world. You may choose those listed above or other locations. Find information on the typical celebrations, gifts, and food served. Keep track of the sources.

b) In a new document, write an introductory paragraph that indicates the report is about birthday traditions in your country and other areas of the world. After the introductory paragraph, write a paragraph for each area's birthday traditions, discussing the celebrations, typical gifts, and foods served if appropriate.

c) Discuss birthday traditions with other students and write four more paragraphs, each describing a unique birthday tradition that you learned about from other students.

d) Cite the sources of information, including student names, using footnotes. Format footnotes in the standard format as practiced earlier in this chapter.

e) Create a header with your name and right align the header text.

f) Save the document naming it Birthday Traditions and then print a copy.

Exercise 19 ✎ ———————————————— Geology Schedule

You have enrolled in an independent study of the geologic eras of the earth and your instructor wants a schedule of topics and due dates for your research papers.

a) Create a new document using the Widget Memo template from a practice completed earlier in this chapter. In the new document create the following memorandum, substituting your name for Your Name and allowing Word to wrap the text:

MEMO TO: Dr. Janet Sung, Geology Department

FROM: Your Name

DATE: January 15, 2006

SUBJECT: Geologic eras topics and due dates

The following schedule outlines the research paper topics and due dates for my independent study on the geologic eras of the earth:

Topic Due Date
Precambrian 1/29
Paleozoic 2/12
Mesozoic 2/26
Cenozoic 3/12

One week before each due date I will submit an outline containing a specific topic and a list of sources for each paper.

b) Check the document on screen and correct any errors and misspellings.

c) Create a header with the text Independent Study in Geology and center the header text.

d) Create a footer with your name and right align the footer text.

e) Edit the data and column titles in the listing of research papers so that there is a single tab between each paper topic and due date. Delete any spaces that were previously used to separate the columns.

f) Format the entire table with a center tab stop at 1.5".

g) Format the column titles "Topic" and "Due Date" in the table as italic.

h) Bold the data in the "Topic" column.

i) Save the document naming it Geology Schedule and print a copy.

Exercise 20 ———————————————————— Scannable Resume

A résumé summarizes accomplishments, education, and work experience. Many large companies scan résumés using an optical character reader (OCR) into a computerized database and then search the database for resumes that contain keywords that describe the qualifications required for the position. This is an efficient way for companies to sort through hundreds of résumés. When submitting a résumé, it is a good idea to check with the company's Human Resources department to see if the company scans résumés since the content and format of a scannable résumé differs greatly from that of a traditional résumé.

Scannable résumés consist of keyword summaries that contain job-related acronyms and terminology and are written using nouns instead of action verbs.

A scannable résumé should contain little punctuation and if punctuation is used with a word that may be a keyword, a space should be placed before the punctuation mark because if the computer is searching for the word management, it might not recognize management, or management.

A scannable résumé has to be formatted so that it can be read properly by the OCR. Formatting used on traditional résumés, such as shading and lines, should be avoided because it can be misinterpreted.

Guidelines for a scannable résumé include:

- Use white or other light-colored paper
- Send the original copy, not photocopies
- Avoid graphics, shading, bold, italics, and underlining
- Avoid horizontal and vertical lines
- Use standard fonts, such as Arial
- Do not fold or staple the resume
- Put your name at the top of each page
- Use left alignment
- Use separate lines for address information
- Avoid columns
- Use – or * for bullets because a • could be interpreted as the letter "o"

In a new document, create a scannable résumé by completing the following steps:

a) In a scannable résumé, the heading is single-spaced and centered. All capital letters are used for the name. Type the heading below:

THOMAS YOUNG
43 Main Street
Miami FL 33056
305-555-7879
youngt@lpdatafiles.com

b) Résumé side headings vary depending on the résumé content. Example side headings include: Objective, Education, Experience, Computer Skills, Volunteer Experience, Hobbies, Leadership Skills, Organizational Skills, Awards, Accomplishments, and References. In a scannable résumé, side headings are typed in all capitals with one blank line above and below each side heading. Formatting such as bold or italic should not be applied to a side heading. Type the side heading OBJECTIVE and press Enter twice.

c) Type the following objective:

A technical writing position where my writing and computer skills are used to produce clear and accurate technical training manuals.

d) The experience and skills sections below are written using keyword nouns instead of action verbs which are typically found on a traditional resume. Press Enter twice and then type the rest of the résumé. You may need to point to the blue bar below the dash and then click the AutoCorrect Options button and select Undo Automatic Bullets if the bullets automatically indent:

TECHNICAL WRITING EXPERIENCE

- Preparation of technical training manuals for cell phone users
- Preparation of technical training manuals for several brands of DVD players
- Preparation of sales brochures
- Production of customer viewable copy

COMPUTER SKILLS

- Mastery of Adobe Acrobat, Adobe InDesign, Microsoft Word
- Creation and maintenance of company Web sites
- Programming experience in Java, Pearl, and C++

ADMINISTRATIVE SKILLS

- Manage project teams
- Control of project expense budgets
- Deliver technical training
- Team player
- Excellent communication skills
- Customer oriented

EDUCATION

- BA in Visual Communication Design Ohio State University 2000

e) Save the document naming it Scannable Resume and print a copy.

f) A résumé is often the only impression an employer has of the application. Therefore, it is important to ensure that a résumé is error-free before it is submitted. Proofread the hard copy carefully and if necessary, edit and print a new copy of the résumé.

g) In a new document, create your own scannable résumé following the format outlined in this exercise.

Exercise 21 —————————————————— Basic Resume

A résumé summarizes accomplishments, education, and work experience. A traditional résumé is a printed document that is typically one page in length and lists a person's educational background, previous job experiences, skills obtained through education and work experience, and accomplishments, such as memberships, awards, and activities.

In a new document create a résumé for yourself. Your résumé should contain the following:

- Four sections of information with the following titles: Education, Experience, Skills, and Accomplishments. The information in each section should be indented paragraphs.
- At least one bulleted or numbered list.
- A header with your name, address, and phone number.
- A footer with the text References available upon request.

Format the résumé appropriately, using emphasized text, two different fonts, two or three different sizes, and tabs and tab stops. Check the document on screen for errors and misspellings and make any corrections. Save the document naming it Basic Resume and print a copy.

Exercise 22 —————————————————— Research Paper

A widely accepted format for research papers is defined by the Modern Language Association (MLA) in its publication *MLA Handbook for Writers of Research Papers, Fourth Edition*. A research paper that follows the MLA guidelines has the following format:

- 8.5-inch x 11-inch paper
- 1 inch top, bottom and side margins
- Paragraphs with a first line indent of 0.5"
- Double-spaced body

A research paper does not require a title page, instead the student name, teacher name, course, and date appear double-spaced at the top of page 1. The header contains the student's last name followed by the page number, all right aligned. The page number is not preceded by "page" or "p." The page number may or may not appear on the first page.

Sources are cited in the body of the paper by typing the author's last name and page number in parentheses at the end of the cited text. For example, (Burns 767). The Works Cited list appears as the last page of the paper with the centered title "Works Cited." A citation for a book is structured as follows:

Burns, K. Cellular Biology. New York: Ivy Press, 2003.

A citation for material located at a Web site is structured as follows:

Rawlings, Julie. Cellular Biology Online. 23 Dec. 2004. Ivy University.
<http://www.lpdatafiles.com>.

a) Select a research topic from one of the following weather-related topics:

- Typhoons
- Hurricanes
- Tornados
- Tropical Cyclones

b) Use the Internet and books to research the selected topic.

c) In a new document, format the paper size and margins as outlined in the beginning of this exercise.

d) At the top of the document, type the information that follows, replacing Student Name with your name, Teacher Name with your teacher's name, Course Code with your course code or name, and Date with the current date. Note that these paragraphs should not have an indent:

Student Name

Teacher Name

Course Code

Date

e) Press Enter after the date and then type an appropriate title for the research paper. Center align the title.

f) From your research, compose a report that is at least 2 pages in length. The paragraphs of the report should have a 0.5" first line indent. Be sure to appropriately cite all sources within the body of the paper by typing the author's last name and page number in parentheses at the end of the cited text. Include at least two citations in the paper.

g) Add a header with *Student Last Name* followed by the page number, replacing *Student Last Name* with your last name.

h) At the end of the document, insert a page break and type the title Works Cited. Center the title.

i) Create the appropriate citation entries.

j) Save the report naming it Research Paper and print a copy.

Exercise 23 ———————————————————Logo Proposals

The Picture toolbar is displayed in Word when an image is selected:

- The Color button (⬛) converts an image to grayscale, black and white, or washout.

- The contrast buttons (◑ and ◐) increase or decrease the difference between light and dark colors, and the brightness buttons (☀ and ☀) increase or decrease the lightness of colors.

- Click the Crop button (⌗) and then drag a handle to remove part of the image.

- Rotate the image by clicking the Rotate by 90° button (⬔).

- The Line Style button (☰) is used to add a border.

- The Compress Pictures button (▨) deletes cropped areas and make file sizes smaller.

- The Text Wrapping button (▣) determines how an image should be placed in the text in a document.

- The Format Picture button (▨) displays a dialog box with formatting options.

- The Set Transparent Color button (✎) converts a specified color to transparent.

In a new document create three logo proposals by completing the following steps:

a) In the first paragraph, insert the picture LOGO, which is an image data file for this text. Press Enter twice and insert the LOGO picture file again. Press Enter twice and then insert the LOGO picture file a third time. Your document should contain three picture files, one above the other with a blank paragraph between each.

b) Use the Picture toolbar to modify each of the logos. Experiment with all the options to come up with three very different logos. Crop at least one of the images.

c) In the blank paragraph below each image, describe the modifications. Include the buttons and options selected in your descriptions.

d) Create a footer with your name and right align the footer text.

e) Save the document naming it Logo Proposals and print a copy.

Exercise 24 —————————————— Return Address Labels

Multiple labels that contain the same text can easily be created in Word. This feature is useful for creating return address labels for use on envelopes. When printing a labels document, special adhesive paper with multiple labels on each page is used in the printer. The Avery® brand of adhesive labels is widely used, and the dimensions of many of its labels have been included in Word.

In a new document create a sheet of return address labels by completing the following steps:

a) Select Tools → Letters and Mailings → Envelopes and Labels. A dialog box is displayed.

b) In the Labels tab of the dialog box, select Options. A dialog box is displayed.

c) In the Options dialog box, select 5267 - Return Address and then select OK. The dialog box is removed.

d) In the large Address box, type your first and last name and then press Enter. The insertion point is moved to the next line.

e) Below your first and last name, type your street address and then press Enter.

f) Below your street address, type your city, state, and zip (or province or postal code).

g) In the dialog box, select New Document. The dialog box is removed and a new document with labels is displayed.

h) Select Edit → Select All. All of the text in the document is selected. Change the font size to 8. The label text is now completely displayed in each label.

i) Save the document naming it Return Address Labels and print a copy.

Chapter 6

Long Documents and Desktop Publishing

Brochures and newsletters are introduced in this chapter. Tables, styles, hyphenation, sections, and columns are explained. Diagrams and organization charts are also covered.

Using Tables

Tables can be created by using tabs and tab stops similar to:

Element	Symbol	Atomic Number	Atomic Mass¶
Calcium	Ca	20	40.1¶
Gold	Au	79	197.0¶

Tables are also created in Word using rows and columns of cells. Cells have borders, which makes the information easier to read:

Element	Symbol	Atomic Number	Atomic Mass
Calcium	Ca	20	40.1
Gold	Au	79	197.0

row
column
cell

The table above has three rows and four columns. *Rows* are horizontal and, in this example, the first row contains the titles. *Columns* are vertical. The intersection of a row and column is called a *cell*. Cells can contain text and clip art.

creating a table

A table is created by clicking the Insert Table button (⊞) on the toolbar, which displays a grid of squares that represent cells. Move the pointer over the grid to select the squares:

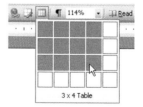

3 x 4 Table

The Table Command

Another way to create a table is to select Table → Insert → Table, which displays a dialog box with options for creating a table.

Click to create a table at the insertion point. Text is then typed into the individual cells:

Element¤	¤	¤	¤	¤
¤	¤	¤	¤	¤
¤	¤	¤	¤	¤

Click a cell to place the insertion point in that cell. Press the Tab key to move the insertion point to the next cell in the row. In the last cell of a row, press the Tab key to move to the first cell in the next row. The arrow keys are used to move the insertion point from cell to cell. Press Enter to create a new paragraph within the cell instead of moving to another cell.

Formatting Cell Contents

selecting cells

Tables of cells are much easier to format than a table that uses tabs and tab stops. Cells can be selected individually, by row, by column, or by table, and then formatting applied:

- Point to the left edge of a cell, the pointer changes to ⬈, and then click to select the cell's contents.

- Point to the left of a row, the pointer changes to ⬈, and then click to select the row. Drag to select multiple rows.

- Point to the top of a column, the pointer changes to ⬇, and then click to select the column. Drag to select multiple columns.

- Click ⊞ in the upper-left corner of a table to select the table.

TIP Select Table ➝ Select to display commands for selecting the table, column, row, or cell that contains the insertion point.

formatting cells

Formats such as alignment, indents, and fonts can be applied to selected cells. Note that some formats affect the row height, for example formatting text in a larger font size increases the row height.

When a table is created, Word automatically adjusts the column widths to be equal so that the table fills the space between the left and right margins. The lines separating the row and column are called *boundaries* and are used to change the width of a column or the height of a row:

column width and row height

- Point to the right boundary, the pointer changes to ⊣⊢, and then drag the boundary to change the column's width.

- Point to the bottom boundary of a row, the pointer changes to ⬍, and then drag to change the row's height.

- Double-click a boundary to change the height or width just enough to display the data entirely.

adding and deleting rows and columns

After creating a table, a row or column may need to be added. Click the Insert Rows button (⊟) on the toolbar to add a row above the selected row. Click the Insert Columns button (⊟) to add a column to the left of the selected column. These buttons are only available if a row or column is selected. Rows and columns can also be added using Table ➝ Insert. Delete a row, column, or entire table using Table ➝ Delete.

You will insert a table into a document and format it.

① **START WORD AND OPEN VOLCANOES**

Open VOLCANOES, which is a Word data file for this text, and display formatting marks if they are not already displayed.

② **INSERT A TABLE**

a. In the bottom half of page 2, place the insertion point in the blank paragraph after the sentence that ends "…the last eruption:"

b. On the toolbar, click the Insert Table button (▦). Empty squares are displayed.

c. Move the pointer over the squares until four rows and three columns are selected (a 4 x 3 table) and then click. The table is inserted into the document.

③ **ENTER DATA**

a. Click the first cell of the first row to place the insertion point if it is not already there.

b. Type Name and then press the Tab key. The insertion point is now in the second cell of the first row.

c. Type Country and then press the Tab key.

d. Type Last Erupted and then press the Tab key. The insertion point is now in the first cell of the second row.

e. Enter the remaining data so that your table looks similar to:

Name¤	Country¤	Last·Erupted¤
Mt.·Saint·Helens¤	United·States¤	1980¤
Mt.·Etna¤	Italy¤	2001¤
Mt.·Hekla¤	Iceland¤	2000¤

④ **FORMAT THE DATA**

a. Point to the top of the third column until the pointer changes to ↓ and then click. The last column is selected.

b. On the toolbar, click the Align Right button. The data is right aligned.

c. Point to the left of the first row until the pointer changes to ⇗ and then click. The first row is selected.

d. Format the data as 14 point and bold. The row height increases with the larger font size.

e. Click anywhere to remove the selection.

⑤ **FORMAT THE TABLE**

a. Point to the boundary between the first and second column until the pointer changes to ◄▮►.

b. Drag the boundary to the left until the first column is just slightly wider than the data. Word automatically changes the column width of the second column so that the table still fills the space between the left and right margin.

c. Repeat step 6, parts (a) and (b) for the second and third columns. The table no longer fills the space between the left and right margin:

ground.·The·exact·location·of·where·they·come·out·of·is·called·a·vent.·A·volcano·usually·has·

more·than·one·vent.·The·following·table·lists·three·volcanoes·and·the·date·of·the·last·eruption:¶

Name☐	Country☐	Last·Erupted☐☐
Mt.·Saint·Helens☐	United·States☐	1980☐☐
Mt.·Etna☐	Italy☐	2001☐☐
Mt.·Hekla☐	Iceland☐	2000☐☐

¶
Eruptions·can·be·violent·or·quiet.·Some·eruptions·send·lava·high·above·the·surface·in·spectacular·

fountain·shapes.·Violent·eruptions·such·as·these·often·include·chunks·of·solid·rock·that·were·

⑥ **ADD A COLUMN AND FORMAT IT**

a. Select the third column.

b. On the toolbar, click the Insert Columns button (📁). A new column is inserted.

c. Enter data into the new column:

Name☐	Country☐	Height·(m)☐	Last·Erupted☐☐
Mt.·Saint·Helens☐	United·States☐	2,549☐	1980☐☐
Mt.·Etna☐	Italy☐	3,323☐	2001☐☐
Mt.·Hekla☐	Iceland☐	1,491☐	2000☐☐

d. Double-click the boundary between the third and fourth columns. The column is widened just enough to display the data.

⑦ **SAVE THE MODIFIED VOLCANOES**

Styles

heading
body text

A *style* is a named set of formats which makes it easy to have consistent formatting in a document. For example, long documents usually contain *headings*, which are titles that are often bold and in a larger and different font than the *body text*, which are the main paragraphs in a document. A style is used to apply all the formats to a heading in one step.

Word includes several built-in styles for formatting text:

Normal	Times New Roman, 12 point, left-aligned
Heading 1	**Arial, 16 point, bold, left-aligned**
Heading 2	***Arial, 14 point, bold italic, left-aligned***
Heading 3	**Arial, 13 point, bold, left-aligned**

Normal style is automatically applied to paragraphs in a new document. A style is applied using the Styles and Formatting task pane. Select Format → Styles and Formatting to display the task pane:

TIP Click the Styles and Formatting button (🔲) on the toolbar to display the task pane.

TIP The Show list is used to change the listed styles to all those available or those in use.

TIP A style can be applied by selecting it from the Style list (Normal ▾) on the toolbar.

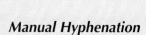

Available styles are listed in the Pick formatting to apply list. Clicking a style applies the style to the paragraph that contains the insertion point. Click Clear Formatting in the list to change the formatting of the paragraph to Normal style.

A new style can be created when the built-in styles are not appropriate. Click New Style... in the Styles and Formatting task pane, which displays the New Style dialog box.

Hyphenating a Document

Manual Hyphenation

In the Hyphenation dialog box, select Manual to display each word as it is selected for hyphenation.

Hyphenating a document is a process that divides words, if necessary, at the end of lines with a hyphen (-) so that part of a word wraps to the next line. Hyphenation can smooth out very ragged right edges in left-aligned text and can lessen the space between words in justified text.

Once a document is otherwise complete, hyphenation can be performed. Select Tools → Language → Hyphenation to display a dialog box. Select the Automatically hyphenate document check box to hyphenate the document.

Practice: VOLCANOES – part 2 of 4

You will apply styles, create a new style, and hyphenate a document. Word should already be started with VOLCANOES open from the last practice.

① *APPLY STYLES*

a. Select Format → Styles and Formatting. The Styles and Formatting task pane is displayed. Note the styles in the Pick formatting to apply list. Some styles were created just for this document, and have "Volcano" in the name of the style.

b. At the top of page 2, place the insertion point in the "Introduction" heading.

c. In the Styles and Formatting task pane, click Heading 1. The Heading 1 style is now applied to the "Introduction" heading.

d. Below the "Introduction" paragraph on page 1, place the insertion point in the "Volcano Facts" heading.

e. In the Styles and Formatting task pane, click Heading 1.

f. Scroll to the bottom of page 4 and apply the Heading 1 style to the "Conclusion" heading.

② *CREATE A NEW STYLE*

a. In the Styles and Formatting task pane, click New Style... . A dialog box is displayed. Type a style name and select options as shown below:

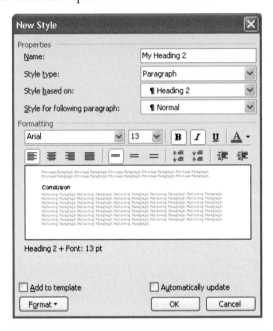

b. Select OK. The dialog box is removed and the new "My Heading 2" style is added to the Styles and Formatting task pane.

③ *APPLY STYLES TO THE OTHER HEADINGS*

a. Scroll to the middle of page 2 and place the insertion point in the "Stages of Volcanic Activity" heading.

b. In the Styles and Formatting task pane, click the My Heading 2 style.

c. Scroll through the rest of the document and apply the My Heading 2 style to the "Types of Volcanoes" and "Types of Lava Rocks" headings.

d. Scroll to the middle of page 2 and place the insertion point in the "Eruption Stage" heading.

e. In the Styles and Formatting task pane, click the Heading 3 style.

f. Scroll through the rest of the document and apply the Heading 3 style to the "Cooling and Inactive Stage," "Cinder Cones," "Shield Volcanoes," "Composite Volcanoes," "Basalt," "Obsidian," and "Andesite" headings.

④ *HYPHENATE THE DOCUMENT*

a. Select Tools → Language → Hyphenation. A dialog box is displayed. Select the options as shown:

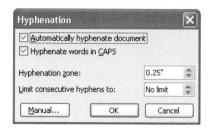

b. Select OK. The dialog box is removed and Word hyphenates the document. Scroll through the document and look for hyphenated words.

⑤ *SAVE THE MODIFIED VOLCANOES*

Using Outline View

Outline view displays the organization of a document. A document is displayed in Outline view by selecting View → Outline:

·Our·Solar·System¶

·Planets¶

·Mercury¶
Mercury·is·the·closest·planet·to·the·sun·at·57.9·million·km. ·Unlike·Earth,·which·has·one·orbiting· satellite,·Mercury·does·not·have·any·known·satellites. ·The·core·of·Mercury·is·a·large·dense·iron· core. ·The·surface·is·lunar·like·and·contains·craters·from·earlier·collisions·of·asteroids. ·Mercury· takes·approximately·58.7·days·to·rotate·about·its·axis.¶

·Venus¶
Venus·is·the·second·planet·from·the·sun·at·108.2·million·km. ·It·also·has·no·known·satellites. ·Its· atmosphere's·primary·gas·is·carbon·dioxide. ·A·thick·cloud·layer·made·mostly·of·sulfuric·acid· covers·the·surface. ·Venus·takes·approximately·243·days·to·rotate·about·its·axis.¶

·Earth¶
Earth·is·the·third·planet·from·the·sun·at·150·million·km·and·the·only·known·planet·that·contains· life. ·It·has·one·orbiting·satellite·called·the·moon. ·The·inner·core·is·believed·to·be·solid·with·a· liquid·outer·core. ·The·surrounding·atmosphere·is·made·up·mostly·of·oxygen·and·nitrogen. ·The· Earth·takes·24·hours·to·rotate·about·its·axis.¶
¶

○ **Our·Solar·System¶**
   ○ **Planets¶**
      ○ **Mercury¶**
         □ Mercury·is·the·closest·planet·to·the·sun·at·57.9·million·km. ·Unlike· Earth,·which·has·one·orbiting·satellite,·Mercury·does·not·have·any· known·satellites. ·The·core·of·Mercury·is·a·large·dense·iron·core. · The·surface·is·lunar·like·and·contains·craters·from·earlier·collisions· of·asteroids. ·Mercury·takes·approximately·58.7·days·to·rotate· about·its·axis.¶
      ○ **Venus¶**
         □ Venus·is·the·second·planet·from·the·sun·at·108.2·million·km. ·It· also·has·no·known·satellites. ·Its·atmosphere's·primary·gas·is· carbon·dioxide. ·A·thick·cloud·layer·made·mostly·of·sulfuric·acid· covers·the·surface. ·Venus·takes·approximately·243·days·to·rotate· about·its·axis.¶
      ○ **Earth¶**
         □ Earth·is·the·third·planet·from·the·sun·at·150·million·km·and·the· only·known·planet·that·contains·life. ·It·has·one·orbiting·satellite· called·the·moon. ·The·inner·core·is·believed·to·be·solid·with·a·liquid· outer·core. ·The·surrounding·atmosphere·is·made·up·mostly·of· oxygen·and·nitrogen. ·The·Earth·takes·24·hours·to·rotate·about·its· axis.¶

Print Layout view

Outline view

In Outline view, Word uses styles to determine heading levels and body text. Paragraphs are indented according to their levels, for example the Heading 1 style is at a higher level than Heading 2. In the example shown above, "Our Solar System" is in the Heading 1 style and "Planets" is Heading 2 style. Paragraphs with the Normal style are the lowest level.

Outlining toolbar

The Outlining toolbar is displayed when a document is in Outline view. Buttons on the Outlining toolbar affect the paragraph containing the insertion point:

- Promote button (⬅) or Demote button (➡) applies the next higher or lower level style, respectively. Demote to Body Text button (⏩) applies the Normal style. Promote to Heading 1 (⏪) applies the Heading 1 style.

- Move Up button (⬆) or Move Down button (⬇) moves the paragraph before or after the preceding paragraph, respectively.

- Expand button (⊞) or Collapse button (⊟) displays or hides the body text under the heading containing the insertion point, respectively.
- Show Level list (Show All Levels ▾) displays different heading levels. Body text is only displayed when Show All Levels is selected.

Icons next to text in the document in Outline view indicate levels:

◻ Body text

✚ Headings followed by a paragraph with a lower level

▭ Headings followed by a paragraph with the same level

selecting and moving a topic   Entire topics can be selected by clicking ✚ next to a heading, which selects that heading and the text under it. Use the Move Up or Move Down buttons or drag ✚ to move a selected topic. A document printed in Outline view include the same headings and body text as displayed on the screen.

Practice: VOLCANOES – part 3 of 4

You will display a document in Outline view, modify the document, and print the outline. Word should already be started with VOLCANOES open from the last practice.

① *DISPLAY VOLCANOES IN OUTLINE VIEW*

    a. At the top of page 2 and place the insertion point in the "Introduction" heading.

    b. Select View ➜ Outline. The document is displayed in Outline view. Note the different levels in the document.

② *DISPLAY DIFFERENT LEVELS OF HEADINGS*

    a. On the Outlining toolbar, in the Show Level list select Show Level 1:

    Only the headings with the Heading 1 style are displayed.

    b. On the Outlining toolbar, in the Show Level list select Show Level 2. Heading levels 1 and 2 are displayed.

    c. On the Outlining toolbar, in the Show Level list select Show Level 3. All three heading levels are displayed.

③ *MOVE THE "TYPES OF LAVA ROCKS" TOPIC*

    a. Click ✚ next to the "Types of Lava Rocks" heading. The entire topic, including lower level headings, is selected.

    b. On the Outlining toolbar, click the Move Up button (⬆). The selected topic is moved before the "Composite Volcanoes" heading.

    c. On the Outlining toolbar, click the Move Up button three more times. The selected topic is moved before the "Types of Volcanoes" topic and its headings:

- **Introduction**¶
- **Volcano·Facts**¶
  - *Stages·of·Volcanic·Activity*¶
    - Eruption·Stage¶
    - Cooling·and·Inactive·Stage¶
  - *Types·of·Lava·Rocks*¶
    - Basalt¶
    - Obsidian¶
    - Andesite¶
  - *Types·of·Volcanoes*¶
    - Cinder·Cones¶
    - Shield·Volcanoes¶
    - Composite·Volcanoes¶
- **Conclusion**¶

d. On the Outlining toolbar, in the Show Level list select Show All Levels. Note that the text under each heading also moved.

e. On the Outlining toolbar, in the Show Level list select Show Level 3.

f. Click anywhere to remove the selection.

④ *SAVE AND THEN PRINT THE DOCUMENT IN OUTLINE VIEW*

a. Save the modified VOLCANOES.

b. On the toolbar, click the Print button. An outline of the document is printed with only the headings displayed.

c. Select View → Print Layout. The document is again displayed in Print Layout view.

d. Save the modified VOLCANOES.

Creating a Table of Contents

TOC A *table of contents*, or *TOC*, is a list of headings and corresponding page numbers in a document. A table of contents can be created automatically based on heading styles. Select Insert → Reference → Index and Tables to display a dialog box. Select the Table of Contents tab in the dialog box to display those options. Select formatting options and the levels of headings to include. The table of contents is placed at the insertion point.

Each entry in a table of contents is a hyperlink to the corresponding heading. Point to a table of contents entry to display a ScreenTip:

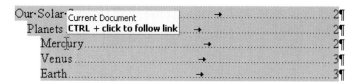

Hold down the Ctrl key, the pointer changes to ☝, and click a TOC entry to scroll the document and place the insertion point in the corresponding heading.

Word does not automatically update a table of contents when changes are made to a document. Click a table of contents and then press the F9 key, which displays the Update Table of Contents dialog box. Select Update entire table to update any headings and corresponding page numbers.

Creating a Hyperlink to a Heading

A hyperlink can be used to quickly scroll to a heading. For example, entries in a table of contents are hyperlinks to headings in the same document, but are not blue and underlined. The Insert Hyperlink dialog box contains options for inserting a hyperlink to a heading. To use this dialog box, select Insert → Hyperlink or click the Insert Hyperlink button (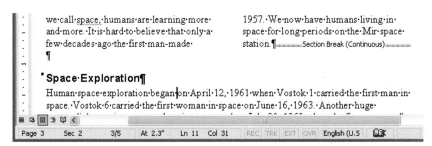) on the toolbar. Select Place in This Document displays the outline for the document. Click a heading in the outline to select the destination for the hyperlink.

Creating Sections in a Document

Long documents often need to have different formatting applied to portions of the document. For example, pages two and three of a document may need to be formatted with two columns, while page one needs only one column. A document can be divided into portions called *sections*, which allows different page formats to be applied to each section.

section break

A *section break* is used to divide a document into sections. Select Insert → Break to display the Break dialog box. Select Next page to start the next section on a new page, or select Continuous to start the next section on the same page.

The status bar at the bottom of the document window indicates the section that contains the insertion point. When formatting marks are displayed, section breaks are identified by a double line and the type of break:

For example, a continuous section break was added to the document shown above. The status bar indicates that the insertion point is in section 2 (Sec 2) of this five page document. Section 1 is formatted with two columns, and section 2 is in one column.

Formatting that applies to pages, such as margins and columns, affect only the section that contains the insertion point.

deleting a section break

Place the insertion point to the left of a section break and press the Delete key to delete a section break.

Section Headers and Footers

A document divided into sections can have different headers and footers in each section. For example, in a report, the page numbers in the footer should start on the first page of the body of the report, not the title page.

By default, each section header and footer contains the same text as the previous section. For example, if Solar System is entered as the header text in section 1, the header in section 2 automatically contains Solar System and is noted with the text Same as Previous above the header area:

```
Header -Section 1-
Solar·System¶


Header -Section 2-                                          Same as Previous
Solar·System¶
```

To create a different header or footer in a section, select View → Header and Footer and then place the insertion point in the header or footer area. Next, click the Link to Previous button ( ) on the Header and Footer toolbar so that it is no longer selected. The text in the header area can then be changed and will appear on all pages in that section.

Different page numbering may be required for different parts of a document. *Front matter* is information that comes before the body of a report, such as the title page and table of contents, which are often numbered with small Roman numerals (i, ii, iii, and so on). The *body* of a report contains the information being presented and is usually numbered with Arabic numerals (1, 2, 3, and so on) starting at 1. To format different page numbers, click the Format Page Number button ( ) to display a dialog box. Select a format in the Number format list. Page numbering can be started at a different number by selecting Start at and then typing the new number.

Page X of X

Click the Insert Number of pages button ( ) to insert the total number of pages in the document.

Number Formats

Format	Type
1, 2, 3, …	Arabic
- 1 -, - 2 -, - 3 -,…	Arabic
a, b, c, …	letters
A, B, C, …	letters
i, ii, iii, …	Roman
I, II, III,…	Roman

Practice: VOLCANOES – part 4 of 4

You will create a table of contents for VOLCANOES, divide the document into two sections, and insert and format different page numbers in the footers of section 1 and section 2. Word should already be started with VOLCANOES open from the last practice.

① *CREATE A HYPERLINK TO A HEADING*

   a. At the top of page 2, in the first sentence of the introduction select the word "erupted."

   b. Click the Insert Hyperlink button ( ) on the toolbar. The Insert Hyperlink dialog box is displayed.

   c. Select Place in This Document to display those options and then click Eruption Stage in the outline:

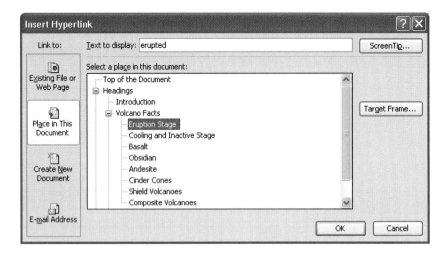

d. Select OK. The word "erupted" is now a hyperlink and is blue and underlined.

e. Point to the hyperlink, hold down the Ctrl key until the pointer changes to 🖑 and then click. The document is scrolled to the Eruption Stage heading, and the insertion point is placed in the heading.

② *INSERT A TABLE OF CONTENTS*

a. Scroll to the top of page 2 and place the insertion point in the paragraph above the "Introduction" heading.

b. Type TABLE OF CONTENTS and then press Enter.

c. Select Insert → Reference → Index and Tables. A dialog box is displayed.

d. Select the Table of Contents tab and then select the options as shown below:

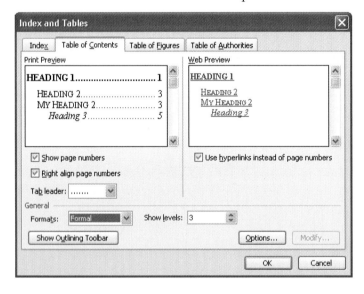

e. Select OK. A table of contents is inserted at the insertion point.

f. Bold and center align the "TABLE OF CONTENTS" title.

③ *USE A HYPERLINK IN THE TABLE OF CONTENTS*

a. Point to "Obsidian" in the table of contents until a ScreenTip is displayed.

b. Hold down the Ctrl key until the pointer changes to 🖑 and then click the Obsidian entry. The document is scrolled to the Obsidian heading, and the insertion point is placed in the heading.

④ *INSERT A SECTION BREAK*

   a. Scroll to page 2 and place the insertion point to the left of the "I" at the beginning of the "Introduction" heading, below the table of contents.

   b. Select Insert ➜ Break. A dialog box is displayed. Select Next page:

   c. Select OK. A section break is inserted between pages 2 and 3 and the main text of the report is moved to page 3. Note that the status bar displays Sec 2 because the insertion point is currently in section 2 of the document.

⑤ *INSERT A PAGE NUMBER IN THE FOOTER*

   a. At the top of page 2, place the insertion point in the "TABLE OF CONTENTS" title. The insertion point is now in section 1.

   b. Select File ➜ Page Setup. A dialog box is displayed.

      1. Select the Layout tab to display those options.

      2. Select the Different first page option and then OK.

   c. Select View ➜ Header and Footer. The header area of section 1 is displayed.

   d. On the Header and Footer toolbar, click the Switch Between Header and Footer button (⊞). The insertion point is placed in the footer of section 1.

   e. On the Header and Footer toolbar, click the Insert Page Number button (⊡). The page number is inserted in the footer.

   f. On the toolbar, click the Center button. The footer text is center aligned.

   g. On the Header and Footer toolbar, click the Format Page Number button (⊡). A dialog box is displayed. Change the Number format to i, ii, iii, ...:

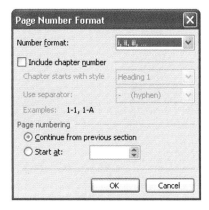

   h. Select OK. The dialog box is removed.

   i. Close the Header and Footer toolbar.

⑥ FORMAT THE PAGE NUMBER IN THE FOOTER OF SECTION 2

   a. Scroll through the document to view the dimmed footer text. Note that the page numbers in the footer in section 2 need to be formatted to start numbering at 1.

   b. Place the insertion point anywhere in section 2 if it is not already there. The status bar indicates the section that currently contains the insertion point.

   c. Select View → Header and Footer. The header area of section 2 is displayed.

   d. On the Header and Footer toolbar, click the Switch Between Header and Footer button (◫). The insertion point is placed in the footer of section 2.

   e. On the Header and Footer toolbar, click the Link to Previous button (▦) to deselect it. The footer in section 2 will not be the same as the footer in section 1.

   f. On the Header and Footer toolbar, click the Format Page Number button (▦). A dialog box is displayed. Select the options as shown below:

   g. Select OK. The dialog box is removed.

   h. Close the Header and Footer toolbar and preview the document. Zoom in and note the different page numbers, then close the Print Preview window.

⑦ UPDATE THE TABLE OF CONTENTS

   a. At the top of page 2, place the insertion point in the table of contents.

   b. Press the F9 key. A dialog box is displayed.

   c. Select Update entire table and then OK. The table of contents now shows the correct page numbers:

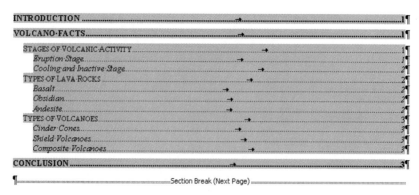

⑧ SAVE, PRINT, AND THEN CLOSE THE MODIFIED VOLCANOES

Creating Diagrams and Organization Charts

Diagrams are illustrations that show relationships between elements and are used to supplement information in documents. *Elements* may be people, companies, tasks, goals, statistics, or practically anything. In a Word diagram, elements are represented by shapes. To create a diagram at the insertion point, select Insert → Diagram which displays a dialog box:

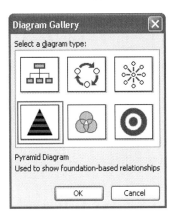

Organization Chart Shows a hierarchy.

Cycle Diagram Shows steps in an ongoing process.

Radial Diagram Shows relationships to a central element.

Pyramid Diagram Shows relationships with a foundation.

Venn Diagram Shows overlap between two or more elements.

Target Diagram Shows the steps that lead to a goal.

When a diagram is added to a Word document, the Diagram toolbar is displayed:

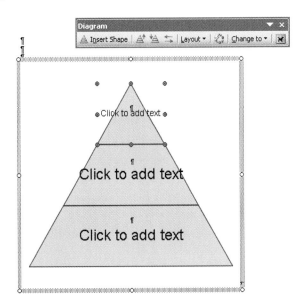

The top element is selected in this pyramid diagram

The pyramid diagram has three elements, and the top element is selected. Click the edge of an element to select it and display handles. Press the Delete key to remove a selected element. Depending on the type of diagram, the buttons in the Diagram toolbar change. For most diagrams, click △ Insert Shape to insert a new element and click Layout ▾ to display options to expand or resize the bordered area surrounding the diagram. Move a selected element to a different level in the diagram using the Move Shape Backward (△↑) and Move Shape Forward (↰) buttons.

To size the entire diagram, drag a corner handle on the bordered area around the diagram.

text in an element

Click in an element to place the insertion point and type text. The font, font size, alignment, and font color of selected text in an element can be formatted.

organization chart

An *organization chart* shows the hierarchy of the employees or departments in a company. Creating an organization chart displays the Organization Chart toolbar:

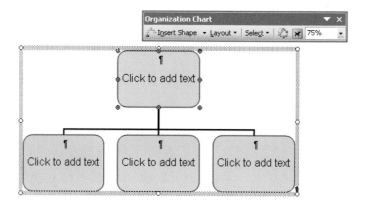

Click Insert Shape ▾ to display a list of elements to add, and click Layout ▾ to display options for changing the arrangement of elements in the chart. Click Select ▾ to select entire rows or sections of the chart.

Formatting a Document in Columns

Columns are commonly used in newspapers, magazines, and other long publications to make lines of text easier to read. Columns are also used to format brochures. Select Format → Columns to display a dialog box:

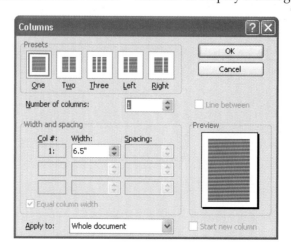

Select the number of columns per page in the Presets options or type a number in the Number of columns box. The Line between check box is used to include a line between the columns. Column widths are changed in the Width and spacing options. The Apply to list options determine the portion of the document that the column formatting is applied to.

The Columns button (▦) on the toolbar can also be used to format a document into columns.

column break

To control the flow of text between columns, place a *column break* where a column of text should end. Text after a column break is moved to the next column. To insert a column break, select Insert → Break and then select Column break from the displayed dialog box.

Creating a Brochure

Brochures are often used as advertising or as informative publications. A *brochure* is typically a single sheet of paper, printed on both sides, and folded two or three times to create a smaller publication that can be handed out, mailed, or placed in a strategic location where interested people can pick one up.

two-fold brochure

One common brochure layout is a *two-fold brochure*, which has six panels of information:

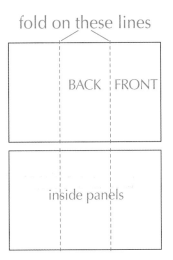

In Word, a two-page document is set up in landscape orientation with all margins 0.5" and three equal columns 1" apart. Column breaks are used to start a new column, and a next page section break is used at the bottom of the "FRONT" panel (above) to start the second page.

purpose

audience

Text and pictures are added to the document and formatted with the purpose and the audience of the brochure in mind. The *purpose* of the brochure is the goal, for example to inform people about preparing taxes properly or to encourage people to hire you for your services. The *audience* of the brochure are the people that will read it.

The text and pictures in a brochure are restricted to narrow columns, and the design should consider the column width:

- Use left alignment for paragraphs of text. Headings are usually left aligned or centered.

- A font size of 8 to 12 point is best for paragraphs of text.

- Pictures should be high-quality and appropriate for the purpose and audience.

printing a brochure When the brochure is finished, print a copy, fold it, and review it thoroughly before printing copies to distribute. If a printer does not have the capability to print both sides of the paper, print one side then put the paper back in the printer and print the other side. The Word document can also be brought to a printing company for professional printing on a variety of paper, and most companies have folding and mailing services.

Practice: TUTORING

You will create a brochure and a diagram. Word should already be started.

① *OPEN TUTORING*

Open TUTORING, which is a Word data file for this text, and display formatting marks if they are not already displayed.

② *INSERT A PYRAMID DIAGRAM*

a. Locate the words "Get to the TOP!" about halfway down the first page and place the insertion point in the blank paragraph below the words.

b. Select Insert → Diagram. A dialog box is displayed.

   1. Select the pyramid diagram (▲).

   2. Select OK. A pyramid diagram is created and the Diagram toolbar is displayed.

c. In the top element of the pyramid, click the "Click to add text" and type: A

d. Select the letter A and format the font size as 36 points.

e. In the middle element of the pyramid, click the "Click to add text" and type: B Student

f. Select the text "B Student" and format the font size as 36 points.

g. In the bottom element of the pyramid, click the "Click to add text," type C Student and format the text as 36 points.

h. Drag a corner handle on the bordered area around the diagram and size the entire diagram smaller. The diagram should be no wider than the two tables in the document. Scroll up or down to view the tables and adjust the size of the diagram if necessary.

i. Click outside the diagram. The diagram is no longer selected:

¶
Karen¶
Can·Help·You¶
Get·to·the·TOP!¶

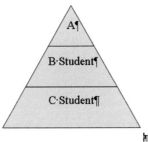

Services¶
Tutoring·helps·any·student·understand·their·schoolwork·better.·Whether·you·just·need·a·little·
help·to·get·through·a·difficult·project,·or·steady·assistance·with·an·entire·subject,·Karen·can·help.·
Through·tutoring·you·gain·knowledge·and·insight·to·different·ways·to·attack·problems·and·find·
the·correct·answers·fast.·Tutoring·saves·time,·too,·by·helping·you·focus·on·your·work·during·
scheduled·sessions.¶

③ *FORMAT THE DOCUMENT FOR A BROCHURE*

   a. Select File ➡ Page Setup. A dialog box is displayed.

       1. Click the Margins tab to display those options, and change the Top, Bottom, Left, and Right margins to 0.5".

       2. Click the Landscape option.

       3. Select OK.

   b. Select Format ➡ Columns. A dialog box is displayed. Change the Number of columns to 3 and the Spacing to 1. When the spacing is changed, the Width may automatically adjust:

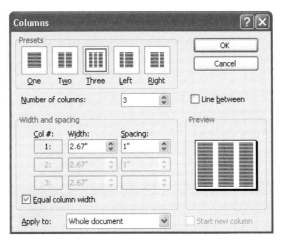

   c. Select OK. The document is now set up for a brochure.

④ *FORMAT TEXT*

   a. At the top of the page, format the text "Your Report Card could look like:" as Arial 22 point bold.

   b. Select the text from "Your Report Card…" to "Get to the TOP!" and click the Center button on the toolbar. The text is centered.

   c. In the upper-left corner of the report card table, click ⊞ to select the entire table and then click the Center button on the toolbar. The table is centered.

   d. Place the insertion point to the left of the "Your" in "Your Report Card could look like:" and press Enter six times. The text is moved down.

   e. Place the insertion point in the blank paragraph below the report card table.

f. Select Insert ➔ Break. A dialog box is displayed.

g. Select Column break and then OK. A column break is inserted and the text below the break is moved to the next column, which is the middle column:

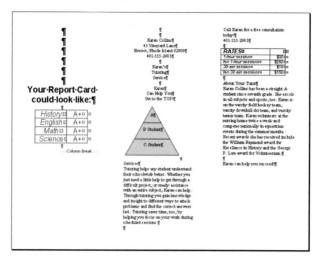

h. Place the insertion point at the top of the middle column and press Enter until the name and address are moved down near the middle of the column.

i. Place the insertion point in the blank paragraph below the phone number in the middle column.

j. Select Insert ➔ Break. A dialog box is displayed.

k. Select Column break and then OK. A column break is inserted and the "Karen's Tutoring Service" paragraphs are moved to the next column.

l. Format the "Karen's Tutoring Service" paragraphs as 48 point and italic.

m. Place the insertion point in the paragraph above "Karen's Tutoring Service" and press Enter until "Karen's Tutoring Service" is near the middle of the column.

⑤ *FORMAT THE SECOND PAGE OF THE BROCHURE*

a. Place the insertion point in the blank paragraph below the "Karen's Tutoring Service" paragraphs.

b. Select Insert ➔ Break. A dialog box is displayed.

c. Select Next page and then OK. A section break is inserted and text is moved to the next page.

d. At the top of the next page, format the text "Karen Can Help You Get to the TOP!" as Arial 22 point bold.

e. Place the insertion point in the paragraph above "Karen Can Help…" and press Enter six times.

f. Place the insertion point in the paragraph with the diagram and click the Center button on the toolbar. The diagram is centered.

g. Select Insert ➔ Break. A dialog box is displayed.

h. Select Column break and then OK. A column break is inserted.

i. Format the "Services" heading as 22 point.

j. Place the insertion point in the blank paragraph above the "Call Karen for a free consultation…" and press Enter four times.

k. Format the text "Call Karen for a free consultation…" and the phone number below it as 22 point.

l. Place the insertion point in the blank paragraph below the phone number and press Enter four times.

m. Place the insertion point in the blank paragraph below the Rates table and select Insert → Break. A dialog box is displayed.

n. Select Column break and then OK. A column break is inserted.

o. Format the "About Your Tutor" heading as 22 point.

p. Format the "Karen can help you succeed!" as Arial, 22 point, bold, and center align the text.

q. Place the insertion point in the blank paragraph above the "Karen can help you succeed!" and press Enter six times.

⑥ *SAVE, PREVIEW, AND PRINT THE BROCHURE*

a. Save the modified TUTORING.

b. Print preview the brochure. It should look similar to:

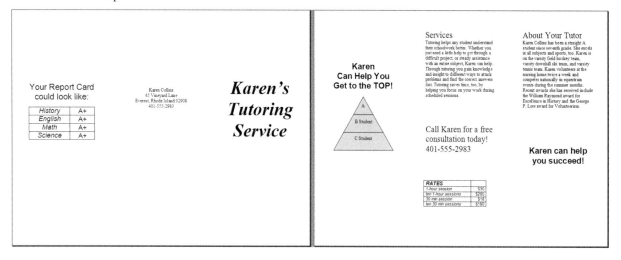

c. Add a footer to the document with your name centered.

d. Print a copy, then put the pages with the non-printed sides back to back. Fold in thirds, so that "Karen's Tutoring Service" is on the front and her address and phone number are on the back.

Creating a Newsletter

Companies, clubs, and organizations often produce monthly newsletters to inform their employees or members of upcoming events and issues.

title area

Newsletters have several common elements. Most newsletters have a title area, some text, and graphics. A *title area* is the section at the top of the first page that contains publication information such as the title and date. The pages in a newsletter are usually formatted in two or three columns with informative headers and footers. A table of contents is usually included on the first page.

Sections are used in a newsletter created in Word to allow for different formats such as columns. The first page can be divided into sections with the title area in one section and the text in another section. The rest of the newsletter is in a third section. Additional sections can be added as needed for different page formats.

Practice: SPACE TRANSMISSIONS

You will create a format a newsletter. Word should already be started.

① *OPEN SPACE TRANSMISSIONS*

Open SPACE TRANSMISSIONS, which is a Word data file for this text, and display formatting marks if they are not already displayed.

② *CREATE THE TITLE AREA*

a. Near the top of page 1, place the insertion point to the left of the "I" at the beginning of the "In This Issue" heading.

b. Select Insert ➞ Break. A dialog box is displayed.

c. Select Continuous and then OK. A section break is inserted. Section 1 is now the title area of the newsletter.

③ *FORMAT SECTION 2 IN TWO COLUMNS*

a. Place the insertion point in section 2 of the document.

b. Select Format ➞ Columns. A dialog box is displayed.

   1. In the Number of columns box, type 2.

   2. Select OK. The text in section 2 is formatted in two columns.

④ *FORMAT THE REMAINING PAGES IN THREE COLUMNS*

a. Scroll to the top of page 2.

b. Insert a Continuous section break just before "Space Exploration Facts."

c. Format section 3 of the document in three columns.

⑤ *SAVE THE MODIFIED SPACE TRANSMISSIONS*

⑥ *PREVIEW, PRINT, AND THEN CLOSE SPACE TRANSMISSIONS*

Chapter Summary

This chapter explained how to create tables, brochures, and newsletters and introduced features that help organize and format long documents.

A table consists of rows and columns of cells and is created using the Insert Table button. Text is entered in a cell and can be formatted. Rows or columns can be selected and then formatted, deleted, or added.

A document can be hyphenated to improve the look of a document. A style is a named set of formatting. Styles are applied using the Styles and Formatting task pane

Outline view displays the organization of a document. In Outline view, Word uses styles to determine heading levels and body text.

A table of contents, or TOC, is created by selecting Insert ➞ Reference ➞ Index and Tables. A table of contents can be updated by selecting it and then pressing the F9 key.

A document can include a hyperlink to another part of the document. A hyperlink in a Word document is formatted as blue and underlined.

A document is divided into sections by inserting section breaks. The status bar displays the section of the document that contains the insertion point. Sections can have different headers and footers by clicking the Link to Previous button. Different page numbering can be applied to each section using the Format Page Number button.

A document or a section is formatted in columns by selecting Format → Columns. Diagrams and organization are created by selecting Insert → Diagram. Brochures and newsletters can be created in Word using sections and columns.

Vocabulary

Audience The people that read the publication.

Body The information presented in a report.

Body text The main paragraphs in a document.

Boundary The line separating a row and column in a table.

Brochure A single sheet of paper with information on both sides and folded two or three times to create a smaller publication.

Cell The intersection of a row and column in a table.

Column Vertical cells in a table.

Column break Used to end a column of text. Text after the break is moved into the next column.

Diagrams Illustrations that show relationships between elements.

Elements Parts of a diagram.

Front matter Information that comes before the body of a report.

Headings Titles that are often bold and in a larger and different font than the body text.

Hyphenating A process that divides a word, when necessary, at the end of a line with a hyphen (-) so part of the word wraps to the next line.

Organization Chart A diagram that shows the hierarchy of the employees or departments in a company.

Outline view Displays the organization of a document.

Purpose The goal of a publication.

Row Horizontal cells in a table.

Section break Used to divide a document into sections.

Sections Parts of a document that can have different formatting.

Style A named set of formats.

Table of contents A list of the headings and their corresponding page numbers in a document.

Title area A section at the top of a newsletter that contains information about the publication.

TOC *See* Table of contents.

Two-fold brochure A brochure layout that has six panels of information.

Break command Displays a dialog box used to insert a section break. Found on the Insert menu.

Collapse button Hides the body text under the heading containing the insertion point. Found on the Outlining toolbar.

Columns command Displays a dialog box used to format text in columns. Found in the Format menu. The Columns button on the toolbar can be used instead of the command.

Delete command Selected to delete a row, column, or an entire table. Found on the Table menu.

Demote button Applies the next lower level style to the paragraph containing the insertion point. Found on the Outlining toolbar.

Demote to Body Text button Applies the Normal style to the paragraph containing the insertion point. Found on the Outlining toolbar.

Diagram command Displays a dialog box used to add a diagram or organization chart to a document. Found in the Insert menu.

Expand button Displays the body text under the heading containing the insertion point. Found on the Outlining toolbar.

Format Page Number button Displays a dialog box used to format the numbering. Found on the Header and Footer toolbar.

Header and Footer command Places the insertion point in the header area. Found in the View menu.

Hyperlink command Displays a dialog box used to insert a hyperlink. Found in the Insert menu. The Insert Hyperlink button on the toolbar can be used instead of the command.

Hyphenation command Displays the Hyphenation dialog box. Found in Tools → Language.

Index and Tables command Displays a dialog box used to insert a table of contents. Found in Insert → Reference.

Insert Columns button Adds a column to the left of the selected column in a table. Found on the toolbar when a column is selected.

Insert Rows button Adds a row above the selected row in a table. Found on the toolbar when a row is selected.

Insert Shape Inserts a new element in a diagram. Found on the Diagram toolbar.

Insert Shape Displays a list of elements to add to an organization chart. Found on the Organization Chart toolbar.

Insert Table button Clicked to create a table. Found on the toolbar,.

Layout Displays options to expand or resize the bordered area surrounding a diagram or organization chart. Found on the Diagram toolbar and the Organization Chart toolbar.

Link to Previous button Allows for different section headers or footers. Found on the Header and Footer toolbar.

Move Down button Moves the paragraph containing the insertion point to after the preceding paragraph. Found on the Outlining toolbar.

Move Shape Backward button Moves a selected element backwards to a different level in a diagram. Found on the Diagram toolbar.

Move Shape Forward button Moves a selected element forward to a different level in a diagram. Found on the Diagram toolbar.

Move Up button Moves the paragraph containing the insertion point to before the preceding paragraph. Found on the Outlining toolbar.

Outline command Displays a document in Outline view. Found in the View menu.

Promote button Applies the next higher level style to the paragraph containing the insertion point. Found on the Outlining toolbar.

Promote to Heading 1 button Applies the Heading 1 style to the paragraph containing the insertion point. Found on the Outlining toolbar.

Select Contains options for selecting rows or sections of an organization chart. Found on the Organization Chart toolbar.

Show All Levels **Show Level list** Displays different heading levels. Found on the Outlining toolbar.

Styles and Formatting command Displays the Styles and Formatting task pane. Found in the Format menu.

1. What is a cell?

2. How is a table with four columns and three rows created using the toolbar?

3. a) What happens when the Tab key is pressed if the insertion point is in the first cell in a table?
   b) What happens when the Tab key is pressed if the insertion point is in the last cell of a row in a table?

4. a) How is a row selected?
   b) How is a column selected?

5. a) What is a boundary?
   b) What happens when the boundary of a column is double-clicked?

6. How is a row inserted between rows two and three of a table?

7. How is a row deleted from a table?

8. a) What is a style?
   b) What are headings?

9. a) What formatting does the Normal style apply to a paragraph?
   b) What formatting does the Heading 1 style apply to a paragraph?

10. List the steps required to apply the Heading 2 style to a paragraph.

11. List the steps required to create a new style named Caption, based on the Normal style, that center aligns a paragraph.

12. List the steps required to hyphenate the open document.

13. a) What does Outline view display?
    b) How do you display the open document in Outline view?

14. List the steps required to select a topic in Outline view and move it to after the topic below it.

15. a) What is a TOC?
    b) How is a table of contents created?

16. List the steps required to use an entry in the table of contents to display the corresponding heading in the document.

17. a) How is a document divided into sections?
    b) List the steps required to insert a Next page section break at the insertion point.

18. List the steps required to have Cats in the header on page 2 of a document and Dogs in the header on page 3.

19. a) List the steps required to have a footer with Roman numeral page numbers in section 1 and Arabic page numbers in section 2.
    b) List the steps required to start page numbering at 1 on the third page of a document.

20. a) What is a diagram?
    b) What is an element?

21. List the steps required to insert a Venn diagram at the insertion point and remove an element.

22. List the steps required to format a document in three columns.

23. Describe how to set up a two-fold brochure in Word.

24. Find a two-fold brochure and describe the purpose and audience of the brochure.

25. a) What is the title area of a newsletter?
    b) Why is a newsletter created in Word divided into sections?

True/False

26. Determine if each of the following are true or false. If false, explain why.
    a) An organization chart shows relationships among employees of a company.
    b) A font size of 14 is best for paragraphs of text in a brochure.
    c) A brochure created in Word can be printed at a professional printing company.
    d) Styles are used to create tables.
    e) A document should be formatted in sections in order to effectively create and use styles.

Exercise 1 ——————————————— ELEMENTS

The ELEMENTS document contains information on elements and chemical formulas. Open ELEMENTS, which is a Word data file for this text, and complete the following steps:

a) Insert a table with four rows and three columns (a 4 x 3 table) in the second blank paragraph after the "Alkali Metals" heading.

b) Enter the following data into the table starting in the first cell:

Element	Symbol	Atomic Number
Lithium	Li	3
Sodium	Na	11
Potassium	K	19

c) Insert a table with five rows and three columns (a 5 x 3 table) in the second blank paragraph after the "Nonmetals" heading.

d) Enter the following data into the table starting in the first cell:

Element	Symbol	Atomic Number
Carbon	C	6
Nitrogen	N	7
Oxygen	O	8
Fluorine	F	9

e) Insert a table with four rows and three columns (a 4 x 3 table) in the second blank paragraph after the "Noble Gases" heading.

f) Enter the following data into the table starting in the first cell:

Element	Symbol	Atomic Number
Helium	He	2
Neon	Ne	10
Argon	Ar	18

g) Bold and increase the size of the text in the first row of all the tables.

h) Decrease the width of the columns in each table appropriately.

i) Apply the Heading 1 style to the "Elements" heading and the Heading 2 style to the "Alkali Metals," "Nonmetals," and "Noble Gases" headings.

j) Create a header with your name right aligned.

k) Save the modified ELEMENTS and print a copy of the document in Outline view with the first and second level headings displayed.

l) Print a copy in Print Layout view.

Exercise 2 —————————————————————————— SOLAR SYSTEM

The SOLAR SYSTEM document contains a report on our solar system. Open SOLAR SYSTEM, which is a Word data file for this text, and complete the following steps:

a) Have Word hyphenate the document.

b) Apply the Heading 1 style to the "Introduction," "Our Solar System," and "Conclusion" headings.

c) Apply the Heading 2 style to the "Planets," "Objects," and "Stars" headings.

d) Apply the Heading 3 style to each planet and to the "Meteoroids" and "Comets" headings.

e) Use Outline view to move the topic "Objects" (including the headings and text below it) to after the "Stars" heading and text.

f) Save the modified SOLAR SYSTEM and print a copy of the document in Outline view with the first, second, and third level headings displayed.

g) Have Word insert a Formal format table of contents above the "Introduction" heading at the top of page 2. Include a title for the table of contents and format the title appropriately.

h) Insert a Next page section break after the table of contents you just inserted.

i) Create a section 1 footer with your name followed by a space and a page number in the i, ii, iii, ... format. Center align the footer. No footer should appear on the first page in section 1.

j) Create a section 2 footer with your name followed by a space and a page number in the 1, 2, 3, … format. The page numbers in the section 2 footers should start at 1 and be center aligned.

k) Update the table of contents to reflect the new page numbering.

l) At the bottom of the first page of the document, change "Your Name" to your name.

m) Save the modified SOLAR SYSTEM and print a copy.

Exercise 3 —————————————————————————— Take-Out Menu

In a new document create a take-out menu in the form of a two-fold brochure for a restaurant. Your brochure should contain the following:

- The name of the restaurant
- At least one clip art picture
- At least one table
- Your name

Check the document on screen and correct any errors and misspellings. Save the document naming it Take-Out Menu and print a copy. Assemble the brochure and fold it properly.

Exercise 4 ——————————————————————————— Hierarchy

Ask a parent or another adult for information about the company they work for. Discuss the company organization, also called the hierarchy. Take notes about the hierarchy.

    a) In Word, create an organization chart that reflects the hierarchy in the company that you discussed with the parent or other adult.

    b) Create a footer with your name.

    c) Save the document naming it Hierarchy and print a copy.

    d) Take the printout to the parent or adult and ask them to assess it for accuracy.

    e) Make any changes to the document, and print a new copy.

Exercise 5 ——————————————————————— Charity Brochure

Identify a local charity and meet with an adult at that charity. Offer to create a brochure that focuses on one aspect of their choice about the charity. Discuss the purpose and audience of the brochure, the contents, and how the brochure will be printed. Ask the adult to e-mail content and a logo to you.

    a) In Word, create a brochure for the charity. Copy and paste text and graphics from the e-mail into the brochure. Format the brochure appropriately.

    b) Check the document on screen and correct any errors and misspellings.

    c) Save the document naming it Charity Brochure and print a copy.

    d) Take the printout to the adult and ask them to assess it. Discuss any changes for the brochure with the adult.

    e) Make any changes to the document, and print a new copy.

Exercise 6 ——————————————————————— HONORS HANDOUT

The HONORS HANDOUT document contains information on different honors clubs at Ivy University. Open HONORS HANDOUT, which is a Word data file for this text, and complete the following steps:

    a) Insert a table with four rows and four columns (a 4 x 4 table) in the blank paragraph after the last sentence under the "Fraternities" heading on page 3.

    b) Enter the following data into the table starting in the first cell, using Insert → Symbol to insert the Greek letters into the table:

Name	Greek Letters	College	Members
Delta Epsilon Phi		Business	45
Lambda Pi Sigma		Liberal Arts	56
Xi Psi Zeta		Engineering	34

    c) Bold and increase the size of the text in the first row.

    d) Decrease the width of the columns appropriately.

    e) Apply the Heading 1 style to the "Honors Program," "Honors Societies," and "Honors Classes" headings.

    f) Apply the Heading 2 style to the "Clubs" and "Fraternities" headings.

g) Apply the Heading 3 style to the following headings:

Business Honors Society   Delta Epsilon Phi
Honors Computer Club   Lambda Pi Sigma
Science Club of Honors   Xi Psi Zeta

h) Have Word insert a Formal format table of contents above the "Honors Program" heading at the top of page 2. Include a title for the table of contents and format the title appropriately.

i) Insert a Next page section break after the table of contents you just inserted.

j) Create a section 1 footer with your name followed by a space and a page number in the i, ii, iii, ... format. Center align the footer. No footer should appear on the first page in section 1.

k) Create a section 2 footer with your name followed by a space and a page number in the 1, 2, 3, … format. The page numbers in the section 2 footers should start at 1 and be center aligned.

l) Update the table of contents to reflect the new page numbering.

m) Save the modified HONORS HANDOUT and print a copy.

Exercise 7 — Favorite Recipe

Recipes in a cookbook often appear with different page formats. In a new document enter your favorite recipe. Format the document into three continuous sections as follows:

Section 1:   include the name of the recipe, your name, and a clip art graphic
Section 2:   list the ingredients for the recipe and format the section in two columns
Section 3:   a numbered list of the recipe steps

Save the document naming it Favorite Recipe and print a copy.

Exercise 8 — Instructional Manual

In a new document create an instructional manual on a topic of your choice. Knowledge or experience about the selected topic is necessary. Example topics include creating a portfolio, building a model airplane, learning to play the piano, or making maple syrup. The instructional manual should contain the following:

- A cover page with an appropriate title, your name, your teacher's name, and the date.

- An introduction page that describes the importance of reading the manual and captures the reader's attention.

- At least one page outlining the process, keyed using numbered steps with an explanation following each step. Graphics may be used to enhance the explanation.

- A conclusion that summarizes the process as a whole and can include any advantages, cautions, or limitations. Sources can also be cited on this page, if applicable.

Format the instructional manual appropriately, using emphasized text, different fonts, different sizes, tabs and tab stops, and numbered and bulleted lists. Check the document on screen for errors and misspellings and make any corrections. Save the document naming it Instructional Manual and print a copy.

Exercise 9 ———————————————————————————Technology Research

Research a technology topic of your choice using the Internet. Write a report based on the information you found. The report should include a title page, a table of contents, the body of the report, and footnotes where appropriate. Include at least two hyperlinks, and create and use your own style using the Style dialog box. Save the report naming it Technology Research and print a copy.

Exercise 10 ——————————————————————————————— Newsletter

In a new document create a newsletter on any topic. Save the document naming it Newsletter and print a copy when complete. Be sure to check the document on screen for errors and misspellings and make any corrections. Your newsletter should contain the following:

- At least two pages, formatted in two columns per page.
- At least four different stories and two advertisements.
- Appropriate character formatting. The titles of each article should be bold and in a larger font size than the text of the article. Titles of books, magazines, songs, etc. should be italicized.
- At least one numbered or bulleted list.
- A header with the title of the newsletter.
- A footer with a centered page number.
- At least one table of information. Be sure that tabs and tab stops are used to align the information in the tables.
- At least one footnote.
- At least two clip art pictures.

Page one of an example newsletter could look similar to the following:

Exercise 11 ——————————— Software Assessment Rubric

A rubric is a scoring tool used to assess the quality of student work. The criteria column of a rubric should clearly state what is being assessed and the level descriptors should describe what the criteria looks like at that level. Create a rubric that could be used to assess the quality of a software package installed on a computer by completing the following steps:

a) In a new Word document, type: Rubric for Assessing Software

b) Press Enter twice and insert a table with seven rows and five columns.

c) Format the title "Rubric for Assessing Software" as 20 point, bold, Tahoma, and centered.

d) Enter the following data into the table as shown below:

Criteria	Level 1 Unacceptable	Level 2 Fair	Level 3 Good	Level 4 Excellent
The interface is visually attractive	The interface is not visually attractive due to features such as screen clutter, colors that strain the eye and so forth	The interface has some attractive features	The interface has mostly attractive features	The interface is very attractive
The software is user-friendly				
The software is able to interface with other installed software				
The software is appropriate for the curriculum or grade-level				

e) In the two blank cells in the Criteria column, type two additional criteria that should be examined when assessing the quality of a software package.

f) Complete the rubric by writing level descriptors for the criteria. Note that the level descriptors should be written using parallel language so it is easy to differentiate between the levels.

g) Create a header with your name centered.

h) Save the document naming it Software Assessment Rubric and then print the rubric.

Chapter 7

Using a Spreadsheet

Excel is the Microsoft Office spreadsheet application. This chapter introduces Excel for storing and analyzing data. E-mailing a worksheet, converting to HTML, and templates are also explained.

What is a Spreadsheet?

A *spreadsheet* is a computer application for storing and analyzing data. It is used in many different ways, for payroll and inventory, for data collection, and for personal budgets and cost calculations. The Microsoft Excel 2003 spreadsheet window looks similar to:

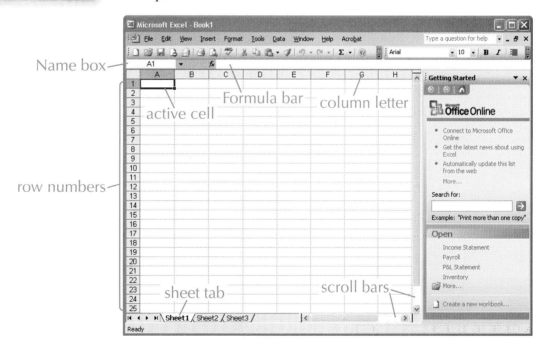

workbook
worksheets, sheets

An Excel spreadsheet document is called a *workbook*. Each new workbook contains three *worksheets*, also called *sheets*. The Excel window displays information about a workbook and includes tools for working with one:

- The file name of the current workbook is displayed in the **title bar**. The name Book1 is used temporarily until the workbook is saved with a descriptive name.

- Select commands from menus in the **menu bar**.

- Click a button on the **toolbar** to perform an action. Click the New button (⬜) to create a new workbook.

- Click a **sheet tab** to display a worksheet in the workbook.

- **Letters** at the top of the worksheet identify columns. **Columns** are lettered from A to Z and then AA to IV for a total of 256 columns. In the worksheet shown, only columns A through H are displayed.

- **Numbers** down the left side of the worksheet identify **rows**, which are numbered from 1 to 65,536. In the worksheet shown, only rows 1 through 25 are displayed.

- **Scroll bars** are used to display rows and columns that are not currently visible in the worksheet.

- A **cell** is the intersection of a row and column. Each cell can store a single item of data.

- A **cell reference** is the column letter and row number that identify a single cell. For example, A1 is the cell reference of the selected cell in the worksheet shown. A cell reference can be thought of as a cell's name.

- The **selected cell** is called the **active cell** and is displayed with a bold border. In the worksheet shown, cell A1 is the active cell. The column letter and row number corresponding to the active cell are orange. Type data to place it into the active cell.

- The **Name box** displays the cell reference of the active cell, which is A1 in the worksheet shown.

- The active cell contents are displayed on the **Formula bar**.

- Links for opening a workbook or creating a new workbook are in the **Getting Started task pane**. Click the arrow in the **Other Task Panes list** to select a different task pane to display. Click the Create a new workbook link for new workbook options.

Cell Reference vs. Cell Contents

Each cell is identified by its cell reference, such as A3 or C2, and each cell can contain data, such as the number 5 or the label Total. This system is similar to mailboxes at the post office where each box (or cell) has a name and can store information. Be careful not to confuse the cell reference with the data it stores.

Entering Data into a Worksheet

planning a spreadsheet

Before entering data into a worksheet, develop a plan for the spreadsheet. A carefully planned spreadsheet presents data in a logical, organized, and easy-to-understand format. The planning process involves three major steps:

1. What is the purpose of the spreadsheet? Determine what information the spreadsheet is to produce.

2. What information is needed for the purpose of the spreadsheet? Determine the data to include.

3. What labels are needed to make the information easy to understand? Which information should be in rows and which should be in columns? Design the organization of the spreadsheet.

After developing a spreadsheet plan, enter data into a new worksheet. Worksheet *data* is categorized as either a label, value, or time/date. *Labels* are text and cannot be used in calculations. *Values* are numeric and can be used in calculations. *Times/dates* are either a time, such as 12:10 PM, or

TIP Click the Spelling button () on the toolbar to check the spelling of labels in a spreadsheet.

TIP To efficiently enter large amounts of numeric data, use the numeric keypad. Before typing numbers on the numeric keypad, press the Num Lock key.

TIP To display the Formula bar, select View → Formula Bar.

a date, such as 6/5/2006. A time/date entry may be used in some calculations. Labels are left aligned and values and times/dates are right aligned in cells:

	A	B	C	D
1	Inventory	9/8/2006	1:30 PM	789
2				

Use the keyboard or keypad to type data. As data is typed, it appears in the active cell and on the Formula bar, and the Cancel and Enter buttons are activated:

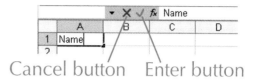

Cancel button   Enter button

Click the Enter button (✓) to enter data in the active cell. Click the Cancel button (✗) to restore the original contents of the active cell. On the keyboard:

- **Press the Enter key** to enter data and make the next cell in the column active.

- **Press the Tab key** to enter data and make the next cell in the row active. Use the Tab key to efficiently enter data across a row. Once the row is complete, press Enter, which selects the cell in the first column that contains data in the next row.

- **Press an arrow key** to enter the data and make the next cell in the direction of the arrow key active.

- **Press the Esc key** to cancel data entry and restore the original contents of the active cell.

Some data may extend beyond the width of a cell. For example, a long label is truncated when the next cell contains data:

C2	▼	fx	This is a long label		
	A	B	C	D	E
1					
2			This is a lo	Label 2	
3					

Cell C2 stores This is a long label, as shown on the Formula bar, but only the characters that fit in the width of the cell are displayed. To change the width of a column, point to the *boundary*, the bar separating the column letters at the top of the worksheet, until the pointer changes to ✛:

C2	▼	fx	This is a long label		
	A	B	C ✛	D	E
1					
2			This is a lo	Label 2	
3					
4					

Drag the boundary to the right to increase the width of the column, and drag it to the left to decrease the width. The width of the entire column is changed because the width of a single cell cannot be changed.

AutoComplete

Excel uses a feature called AutoComplete to guess the current entry based on data in the cells above:

	A
1	Inventory
2	Inventory
3	

Press Enter to accept the entry, or continue to type to replace the AutoComplete entry.

TIP To change the width of a column so that it is just wide enough to display the data it contains, double-click the right boundary of the column.

Editing Cell Contents

TIP Press Ctrl+Home to select cell A1. Press the Page Up or Page Down key to select a cell one screen up or one screen down, respectively.

TIP Press Ctrl+Backspace to scroll to the active cell.

To change data in a cell, the cell must be active. To select a cell, press the arrow keys to move to the cell. The mouse may also be used to select a cell. When the pointer is moved onto the worksheet, it changes to ⊕. Click a cell to make it the active cell.

The contents of the active cell are displayed on the Formula bar. To delete the data in the active cell, press the Delete key. To edit the data in the active cell, click the Formula bar to place the insertion point. The *insertion point* is a blinking vertical line that indicates where the next character typed will be placed. Use the Backspace key to delete data one character at a time. After editing the data, click the Enter button or press the Enter key.

Select Edit → Undo (⟲▾) to reverse an edit made by mistake. Select Edit → Repeat (⟳▾) to repeat the last action performed. Click the arrow in the Undo or Redo button to display a list of the last actions performed. Select an option from the list to undo or redo that particular action.

Practice: Grades – part 1 of 5

You will create a new workbook and enter data. The spreadsheet plan is:

1. The purpose of the spreadsheet is to organize student test grades. Later the spreadsheet will be expanded to produce student and test averages.

2. The data needed is student names, test grades, test names, and test dates.

3. The spreadsheet will be organized with one student per row and one test per column. Labels will be needed to identify each student, test, and date.

① *START EXCEL*

a. Ask your instructor for the appropriate steps to start Microsoft Excel 2003.

b. Look at the spreadsheet window. Note the title bar, menu bar, toolbar, rows, columns, and Getting Started task pane.

c. Note the bold border around the active cell. In a new workbook, the active cell is cell A1.

② *ENTER COLUMN LABELS IN ROW 1*

a. In cell A1, type Name and then click the Enter button (✓). Cell A1 now contains the label Name. Note that the active cell's contents are displayed on the Formula bar.

b. Press the right-arrow key to select cell B1, and then type: Test 1

c. Press the Tab key. The label is entered and the next cell in the row is active.

d. Type: Test 2

e. Press the Tab key. The label is entered and cell D1 is the active cell.

f. Continue this procedure to place the labels Test 3 in cell D1 and Test 4 in cell E1:

	A	B	C	D	E
1	Name	Test 1	Test 2	Test 3	Test 4
2					
3					

③ ENTER THE TEST DATES

a. Press Enter. Cell B2 is selected because the Tab key was used to enter the data in cells B1 through D1.

b. In cell B2, type the date 9/4/2006 and press Tab. The date is right aligned.

c. In cell C2, type 9/14/2006 and then press the Tab key.

d. In cell D2, enter the date: 9/20/2006

e. In cell E2, enter the date: 10/9/2006

④ ENTER THE STUDENT NAMES AND GRADES

Enter the following labels and values starting in cell A4 by typing the label or value and pressing the Tab key to enter the data and move to the next cell in the row. Press Enter at the end of the row.

Garcia, E.	85	73	88	95
Neave, C.	92	88	85	91
Jones, D.	72	63	67	72
McCallister, T.	87	92	85	93
Smith, L.	94	91	93	84
Bell, M.	70	74	80	85

⑤ WIDEN COLUMN A

a. Point to the boundary between columns A and B. The pointer changes to ✛.

b. Drag the boundary to the right approximately halfway across column B. The labels in column A should be entirely displayed. If they are not, continue to widen column A until all labels are completely displayed.

⑥ EDIT A GRADE

a. Select cell E9.

b. On the Formula bar, click to the right of the number 5. The insertion point appears.

c. Press the Backspace key once to delete the number 5.

d. Type a 3 and then press Enter. The grade is now an 83:

	A	B	C	D	E
1	Name	Test 1	Test 2	Test 3	Test 4
2		9/4/2006	9/14/2006	9/20/2006	10/9/2006
3					
4	Garcia, E.	85	73	88	95
5	Neave, C.	92	88	85	91
6	Jones, D.	72	63	67	72
7	McCallister, T.	87	92	85	93
8	Smith, L.	94	91	93	84
9	Bell, M.	70	74	80	83
10					

⑦ SAVE THE WORKBOOK

Save the workbook naming it: Grades

Formatting Cells

Formatting is applied to cells to make the data easier to understand and read. Formatting does not change the value of data stored in a cell, only the way it is displayed.

Unless cells are formatted otherwise, labels are left aligned and values and times/dates are right aligned. For this reason, labels and values displayed in the same column do not line up. For example, the test labels and dates in the Grades worksheet do not align in the column.

The Align Left (▤), Center (▤), and Align Right (▤) buttons on the toolbar can be used to change cell alignment. The Format Cells dialog box can also be used to change cell alignment. Select Format → Cells to display the dialog box. Click the Alignment tab to display options for changing alignment. Select the Wrap text check box to allow for more than one line of text within a cell. This feature is useful for long column headings.

Character formatting can also be applied to cell data. The default font in Excel is Arial. Select Format → Cells and then the Font tab to display those formatting options.

The Font box (Arial ▾) and Font Size box (10 ▾) on the toolbar can also be used to change the font and size of selected cells. The Bold (**B**), Italic (*I*), and Underline (U) buttons on the toolbar can be used to apply or remove character styles from selected cells. More than one button can be used at a time text to apply multiple styles.

Font Size

Changing the font size of worksheet labels can help distinguish between labels, such as titles and column headings, and numeric data. The row height adjusts automatically when the font size is changed.

TIP Right-click a cell to display the Format Cells command.

Formatting Numeric Data

Cells that store numeric data should be properly formatted to reflect the type of value stored. For example, values that represent money should display $ and two decimal places. Currency and other cell formats are shown below. Each of the cells storing numeric data contain the value 1.5:

	A	B	C	D	E
1					
2	Number	Currency	Accounting	Percentage	Scientific
3	1.50	$1.50	$ 1.50	150.00%	1.50E+00
4					
5			Currency Style button	Percent Style button	
6			$ 1.50	150%	
7					

To format the active cell, select Format → Cells and then the Number tab to display number formatting options, which include:

- **Number** displays a value with two decimal places.

- **Currency** displays a value with a dollar sign and two decimal places.

- **Accounting** is similar to Currency except the dollar sign aligns itself at the left edge of the cell. The Currency Style button ($) on the toolbar can also be used to apply the Accounting format.

- **Percentage** displays a value as a percentage with two decimal places. The Percent Style button (%) on the toolbar can be used to format a cell as percentage with no decimal places.

- **Scientific** displays a value in scientific notation with two decimal places.

The Format Cells dialog box also contains options for changing the number of decimal places (the Decimal places box), for including a thousands separator (the Use 1000 Separator (,) check box), and for formatting negative numbers (the Negative numbers list).

A cell is automatically formatted if a $, %, or a decimal position is typed with the number. For example, entering $45.67 in a cell formats that cell to display any number as currency and two decimal places. If 34 is then entered in that cell, $34.00 is displayed. Entering 45% in a cell formats that cell to display any number with a percent sign and no decimal places. If 55.3 is then entered in that cell, 55% is displayed.

Formatting a cell does not change the value that is stored in the cell, only how that value is displayed. Number signs (####) are displayed if a cell is not wide enough to display the formatted number.

Time/date values can also be formatted by selecting one of the many Date or Time options in the Format Cells dialog box. Examples of date formats include 3/14/01 and March 14, 2001. Examples of time formats include 1:30:55 PM and 1:30 PM.

Format Painter

Cell formats can be copied from one cell to another. Select the cell that contains the formatting to be copied and click the Format Painter button (✓) on the toolbar to change the pointer to ✚. Click another cell to apply the copied formatting to that cell.

Selecting Cells

Formatting multiple cells is faster when cells are selected together first. Adjacent worksheet cells can be selected together to form a range. *Adjacent cells* are cells that are next to each other. A *range* is a selection of two or more cells. Drag the pointer from one cell to another to select a range:

Drag from cell B2 to cell D5 to create this range

Another way to select a range is to first select the starting cell, then hold down the Shift key and click the last cell in the range. A third way to select a range is to press and hold the Shift key while pressing an arrow key to move create a range in the direction of the arrow.

To select all the cells in a row or column, click the row number or column letter, respectively. Click the Select All button to select the entire worksheet:

Selecting Non-adjacent Cells

A range can consist of non-adjacent cells by selecting the first cell or range of cells and then holding down the Ctrl key and selecting other cells or ranges.

Select All button

Previewing and Setting Print Options

A worksheet should be previewed before printing. Select File → Print Preview or click the Print Preview button (⌖) on the toolbar to display the Print Preview window. Once in print preview, the worksheet can be viewed in different ways:

- Press the **Page Up key** or **Page Down key** to display the previous or next page, respectively.

- Use the **vertical scroll bar** to view previous and next pages.

- Move the pointer onto the document and then **click the magnifying glass** (⌕) to zoom into that portion of the page. Click again to display the entire page.

Click Print... on the toolbar to print a copy of the worksheet using the default printer settings. Click Close on the toolbar or press the Esc key to return to the worksheet window.

gridlines
row and column headings

Gridlines and row and column headings can make a worksheet printout easier to read. *Gridlines* are solid lines that mark off the rows and columns, similar to what appears on in the Excel window. *Row and column headings* are the row numbers and column letters. Select File → Page Setup to display the Page Setup dialog box. Select the Sheet tab to display options for gridlines and row and column headings.

Information such as the date or the file name can be included in a header or footer to help identify printouts. Headers and footers are automatically printed at the top and bottom of each worksheet page, respectively. To add header or footer information, select File → Page Setup to display the Page Setup dialog box. Select the Header/Footer tab and then select an option from the Header and Footer lists. If additional information is needed in the header and footer, select the Custom Header or Custom Footer button.

Practice: Grades – part 2 of 5

You will format cells and numeric data and then preview and print a workbook. Excel should already be started with the Grades spreadsheet displayed from the last practice.

① *BOLD THE NAME LABEL*

   a. Select cell A1.

   b. On the toolbar, click the Bold button (**B**). The label is now bold.

② *RIGHT ALIGN AND BOLD THE TEST LABELS*

   a. Drag the pointer from cell B1 to cell E1. Cells B1 through E1 are selected as a range:

	A	B	C	D	E
1	Name	Test 1	Test 2	Test 3	Test 4
2		9/4/2006	9/14/2006	9/20/2006	10/9/2006

   b. On the toolbar, click the Align Right button (☰). The contents of the cells are right aligned.

   c. On the toolbar, click the Bold button (**B**). The cell contents are now bold and right aligned.

③ **FORMAT THE DATES**

    a. Select cell B2.

    b. Hold the Shift key down and then click cell E2. Cells B2 through E2 are selected as a range.

    c. Select Format → Cells. A dialog box is displayed. The Date options are selected.

    d. In the Type list, select a format similar to 3/14/01:

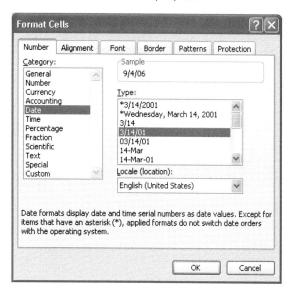

    e. Select OK. The cells are formatted:

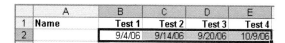

④ **CREATE A HEADER AND A FOOTER**

    a. Select File → Page Setup. A dialog box is displayed.

    b. Select the Header/Footer tab. In the Header list, select an option similar to "Grades, Page 1":

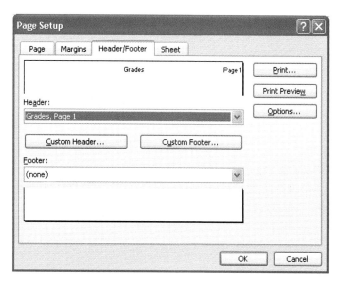

    c. Select the Custom Footer button. The Footer dialog box is displayed.

d. Click in the Right section box and then type your name, similar to:

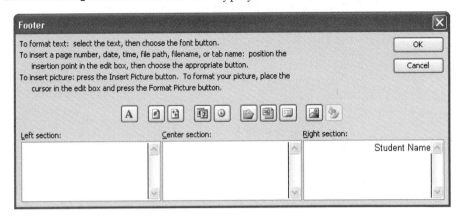

e. Select OK. The dialog box is removed.

f. Select OK. The Page Setup dialog box is removed.

⑤ *PREVIEW AND PRINT THE WORKSHEET*

a. Select File → Print Preview. The worksheet is displayed in a Print Preview window.

b. Move the pointer onto the preview and click the magnifying glass pointer to zoom in. Note the header and footer. Also note how it is difficult to read the worksheet data because there are no gridlines or row and column headings.

c. Select ⌈ Close ⌉ to return to Normal view.

d. Select File → Page Setup. A dialog box is displayed.

e. Select the Sheet tab and then select the Gridlines and the Row and column headings check boxes:

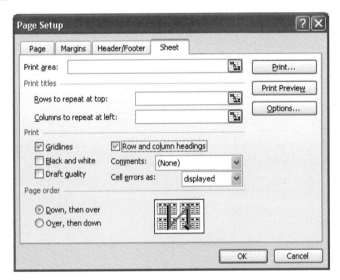

f. Select OK. The dialog box is removed.

g. Save the modified Grades workbook.

h. On the toolbar, click the Print Preview button (🔍). Note how much easier the worksheet is to read.

i. Select ⌈ Print... ⌉ and then select OK to print a copy of the worksheet.

⑥ *CLOSE GRADES*

formulas

One feature of a spreadsheet application is its ability to store formulas. *Formulas* are mathematical statements used to calculate values. In an Excel worksheet, a formula must begin with an equal sign (=). For example, entering the formula =25 * 3 in a cell displays the value 75.

The following mathematical operators can be used in a formula:

Exponentiation   ^

Multiplication   *

Division   /

Addition   +

Subtraction   –

Exponentiation means to raise a value to a power and is represented by the caret (^) symbol. For example, 2^3 is expressed as 2^3.

order of operations

Excel evaluates a mathematical expression using a specific *order of operations*. Exponentiation is performed first, multiplication and division next, and then addition and subtraction. Two operators of the same precedence are evaluated in order from left to right. For example, the expression =5 + 2 * 3 – 1 evaluates to 10 because multiplication is performed first and then the addition and subtraction from left to right. For example:

Formula	Resulting value
=2*2+3*2	10
=25*8/4	50
=35+12/3	39
=3+5*8+7	50

The order in which Excel evaluates a mathematical expression can be changed by including parentheses in the expression. Operations within parentheses are evaluated first. For example, the result of =(5 + 2) * 3 – 1 is 20 because 5 and 2 were added before the multiplication and subtraction were performed. For example:

Formula	Resulting value
=(3+5)*(8+7)	120
=3^2*8-4	68
=6+2^2	10
=(6+2)^2	64

errors

Excel automatically checks a formula for errors when it is entered into a cell. A cell with an invalid formula displays an error value and a green triangle in the upper-left corner of the cell. For example, a number cannot be divided by zero because the result is mathematically undefined. Therefore, entering =10/0 displays #DIV/0! in the cell. Select the cell with the error to display the Trace Error button (◈ ▾). Click this button to display a description of the error and a list of options.

TIP When spreadsheet results are not as expected, check the Formula bar to verify cell contents.

Displaying Formulas

To display the formulas stored in cells, press Ctrl+` (grave accent):

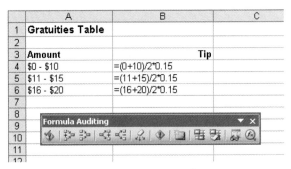

	A	B	C
1	**Gratuities Table**		
2			
3	**Amount**	**Tip**	
4	$0 - $10	$0.75	
5	$11 - $15	$1.95	
6	$16 - $20	$2.70	
7			

Before pressing Ctrl+`

	A	B	C
1	**Gratuities Table**		
2			
3	**Amount**	**Tip**	
4	$0 - $10	=(0+10)/2*0.15	
5	$11 - $15	=(11+15)/2*0.15	
6	$16 - $20	=(16+20)/2*0.15	
7			
8			
9	Formula Auditing		
10			
11			
12			

After pressing Ctrl+`

When formulas are displayed, adjust column widths as necessary to view formulas entirely. The Formula Auditing toolbar, which contains advanced formula editing features, is automatically displayed.

Displaying formulas does not change the worksheet, only the way it is displayed. Print the worksheet when formulas are displayed to print the formulas stored in the cells rather than the values. Press Ctrl+` again to remove the Format Auditing toolbar and display values in each cell. Columns that were widened to view formulas will need to be narrowed.

Practice: Examples

You will enter formulas into the cells of a new, empty workbook to perform calculations. Excel should already be started.

① **CREATE A NEW WORKBOOK**

On the toolbar, click the New button ( ). A new workbook is displayed.

② **ENTER LABELS**

a. In cell A1, enter the label: Example Formulas

b. Bold the label. Note that the text extends into the next cell.

c. Double-click the boundary between columns A and B. Column A is widened just enough to display the label.

d. Select cell A2 and enter the label: Formula

e. Select cell B2 and enter the label: Result

f. Format both labels as italic and right align the label in cell B2:

	A	B
1	**Example Formulas**	
2	*Formula*	*Result*
3		

③ ENTER A LABEL AND A FORMULA

    a. Select cell A3.

    b. Type 20/50 and then click the Enter button. The result is a label because it is not preceded by an equal sign.

    c. Select cell B3.

    d. Type =20/50 and then click the Enter button. The result 0.4 is displayed. Note that the formula is displayed on the Formula bar, and the result of the formula is shown in the cell:

B3	▼	*fx* =20/50	
	A	B	C
1	Example Formulas		
2	Formula	Result	
3	20/50	0.4	
4			

④ ENTER FORMULAS

    a. Enter the labels and formulas in the cells indicated. Note the resulting values:

In cell			In cell		to display	
A4 enter	20*50		**B4** enter	=20*50	to display	1000
A5	20–50		**B5**	=20–50		–30
A6	2+20*5+50		**B6**	=2+20*5+50		152
A7	(2+20)*(5+50)		**B7**	=(2+20)*(5+50)		1210
A8	20/0		**B8**	=20/0		#DIV/0!

⑤ VIEW FORMULAS

    a. Save the worksheet naming it: Examples

    b. Press Ctrl+` (located above the Tab key). Worksheet formulas are displayed at their cell locations and the Formula Auditing toolbar is displayed.

    c. Print the worksheet.

    d. Press Ctrl+` to again display only the values of each cell.

⑥ SAVE AND THEN CLOSE EXAMPLES

Using Cell References in Formulas

Formulas often require values stored in other cells. To use, or refer to, a value in a cell, type its cell reference in the formula. The formula looks in the cell for the value to use in the calculation. For example, cell D2 contains a formula that references values in cells B2 and C2:

D2	▼		*fx* =B2*C2		
	A	B	C	D	E
1	Item	Price	Quantity	Total	
2	Pen	$1.00	100	$100.00	
3					
4					

Formulas that contain cell references are automatically recalculated when the value in a referenced cell changes. If the value in cell B2 or C2 changes, the formula automatically recalculates.

As a cell reference is typed into a formula, Excel outlines the referenced cell in a colored border. Cell references can be typed in uppercase or lowercase letters. However, Excel automatically converts a cell reference to uppercase letters.

Pointing is the best method for entering cell references into a formula because typing errors are avoided. To use this technique, type a formula up to where a cell reference should appear and then click a cell, which places its reference in the formula.

A formula cannot reference the cell it is stored in. For example, the formula in the worksheet on the previous page cannot be stored in cells B2 or C2 because this would cause an error called a *circular reference*.

Cut, Copy, and Paste

TIP Right-click a cell to display the Cut, Copy, and Paste commands.

Organizing and expanding a worksheet often requires moving and duplicating data. *Moving data* means that selected cell contents are "cut" from the worksheet and then "pasted" into other cells. *Duplicating data* means that selected cell contents are "copied" and this copy "pasted" into other cells. Data can be moved and duplicated within the same worksheet or between two or more worksheets.

The Cut (✂), Copy (▤), and Paste (▤▾) commands from the Edit menu are used to move and duplicate data.

Office Clipboard

Cut and Copy place selected cell contents on the *Clipboard*, which is a designated area in memory. Paste places the contents of the Clipboard at the selected cell. The Office Clipboard stores the last 24 cut or copied items. Select Edit → Office Clipboard to display the Clipboard task pane. Any of the items in the Clipboard task pane can be pasted into a worksheet or deleted from the Office Clipboard.

---

1. Select the *source*, which is the cell or range to be duplicated or moved.

2. Select either Cut or Copy. The source displays a moving dashed border.

3. Select the *destination*, which is the upper-left cell of the range where the data is to be pasted.

4. Select Paste. The data as well as the source formatting is pasted. Any pre-existing cell contents are replaced with the pasted data. Press the Esc key to remove the dashed border.

To copy cell contents to adjacent cells, use the Fill handle. The *Fill handle* is the solid square in the lower-right corner of a selected cell or range:

	A	B	C	D
1	Pizza Delray			
2	Cost Analysis			
3				
4	Ingredients	Cheese	Pepperoni	Vegetarian
5	Pizza Dough	$1.00	$1.00	$1.00
6	Cheese	$2.00	$1.50	$1.50
7	Pepperoni		$1.50	
8	Sauce	$0.50		
9				

—Fill handle

Point to the Fill handle until the pointer changes to **+**. Drag the Fill handle to copy the contents of the selected cell or range to adjacent cells:

The Paste Options and Auto Fill Options Buttons

Depending on how data is copied from one cell to another, either the Paste Options (▤) or the Auto Fill Options button (▤) will be displayed. Click the button to display a list of options for newly pasted data.

	A	B	C	D	E
1	Pizza Delray				
2	Cost Analysis				
3					
4	Ingredients	Cheese	Pepperoni	Vegetarian	
5	Pizza Dough	$1.00	$1.00	$1.00	
6	Cheese	$2.00	$1.50	$1.50	
7	Pepperoni		$1.50		
8	Sauce	$0.50	$0.50	$0.50	
9					
10					

Drag the Fill handle from cell B8 to cell D8 to copy the contents of B8 to cells C8 and D8

When a formula is copied, cell references automatically change relative to the new row or column. For example, if cell B10 contains the formula =B8+B9, copying this cell to cells C10 and D10 creates the formula =C8+C9 in cell C10 and =D8+D9 in cell D10. Cell references that reflect the row or column they have been copied to are called *relative cell references*.

relative cell reference

Practice: Grades – part 3 of 5

You will add formulas to a worksheet that contains data. Excel should already be started.

① *OPEN GRADES*

② *ENTER A FORMULA*

a. In cell F1, enter the label: Average

b. Bold and right align the label in cell F1, if it is not already.

c. In cell F4, start typing a formula to average the student's grades. Type =(and then click cell B4:

	A	B	C	D	E	F	G
1	Name	Test 1	Test 2	Test 3	Test 4	Average	
2		9/4/06	9/14/06	9/20/06	10/9/06		
3							
4	Garcia, E.	85	73	88	95	=(B4	
5	Neave, C.	92	88	85	91		
6	Jones, D	72	63	67	72		

d. Enter the remainder of the formula, as shown on the Formula bar, by typing and pointing:

F4   ▾   *fx* =(B4+C4+D4+E4)/4

	A	B	C	D	E	F	G
1	Name	Test 1	Test 2	Test 3	Test 4	Average	
2		9/4/06	9/14/06	9/20/06	10/9/06		
3							
4	Garcia, E.	85	73	88	95	85.25	
5	Neave, C.	92	88	85	91		
6	Jones, D	72	63	67	72		

③ *COPY A FORMULA*

a. Select cell F4 and drag the Fill handle to cell F9. The formula is copied to the cells below with the cell references automatically changing:

	A	B	C	D	E	F	G
1	Name	Test 1	Test 2	Test 3	Test 4	Average	
2		9/4/06	9/14/06	9/20/06	10/9/06		
3							
4	Garcia, E.	85	73	88	95	85.25	
5	Neave, C.	92	88	85	91	89	
6	Jones, D.	72	63	67	72	68.5	
7	McCallister, T.	87	92	85	93	89.25	
8	Smith, L.	94	91	93	84	90.5	
9	Bell, M.	70	74	80	83	76.75	
10							
11							
12							

④ *CREATE ANOTHER LABEL AND FORMULA*

    a. Select cell F1.

    b. On the toolbar, click the Copy (⊞) button. The selected cell displays a moving dashed border.

    c. Select cell A10.

    d. On the toolbar, click the Paste (⊞▾) button. A copy of the label is pasted in the cell.

    e. Press Esc. The moving dashed border is no longer displayed.

    f. With cell A10 selected, edit the label on the Formula bar to read: Test Average

    g. In cell B10, start typing a formula to average the test grades. Type =(and then click cell B4:

	A	B	C
1	Name	Test 1	Test 2
2		9/4/06	9/14/06
3			
4	Garcia, E.	85	73
5	Neave, C.	92	88
6	Jones, D.	72	63
7	McCallister, T.	87	92
8	Smith, L.	94	91
9	Bell, M.	70	74
10	Test Average	=(B4	
11			

    h. Enter the remainder of the formula, as shown on the Formula bar, by typing and pointing:

B10   ▾ f_x =(B4+B5+B6+B7+B8+B9)/6

	A	B	C	D	E	F	G
1	Name	Test 1	Test 2	Test 3	Test 4	Average	
2		9/4/06	9/14/06	9/20/06	10/9/06		
3							
4	Garcia, E.	85	73	88	95	85.25	
5	Neave, C.	92	88	85	91	89	
6	Jones, D.	72	63	67	72	68.5	
7	McCallister, T.	87	92	85	93	89.25	
8	Smith, L.	94	91	93	84	90.5	
9	Bell, M.	70	74	80	83	76.75	
10	Test Average	83.33333					
11							
12							

⑤ *COPY ANOTHER FORMULA*

    Select cell B10 and drag the Fill handle to cell E10. The formula is copied to the cells to the right with the cell references automatically changing:

	A	B	C	D	E	F	G
1	Name	Test 1	Test 2	Test 3	Test 4	Average	
2		9/4/06	9/14/06	9/20/06	10/9/06		
3							
4	Garcia, E.	85	73	88	95	85.25	
5	Neave, C.	92	88	85	91	89	
6	Jones, D.	72	63	67	72	68.5	
7	McCallister, T.	87	92	85	93	89.25	
8	Smith, L.	94	91	93	84	90.5	
9	Bell, M.	70	74	80	83	76.75	
10	Test Average	83.33333	80.16667	83	86.33333		
11							
12							
13							

⑥ *FORMAT CELLS*

    a. Select cells B10 through E10.

    b. Select Format → Cells. A dialog box is displayed. Select the Number options.

        1. In the Decimal places list, select 1.

        2. Select OK. The averages are displayed with one decimal place.

    c. Format cells F4 through F9 to Number with one decimal place.

⑦ *CHANGE A GRADE*

    Change the grade in cell C6 to 81. Note how the formulas automatically recalculate the averages.

⑧ *SAVE THE MODIFIED GRADES AND PRINT A COPY*

Copying and Pasting Data Between Word and Excel

Spreadsheet data is often presented in a Word document. Rather than retype the spreadsheet data, which could introduce typing errors, data should be copied and pasted directly into the document from the spreadsheet. To copy and paste selected cells from a worksheet to a Word document, click the Copy button (🗐) on the Excel toolbar, display the Word document, place the insertion point where the data is to appear, and then click the Paste button (📋▾) on the Word toolbar.

Data copied from Excel is pasted as a table into a Word document:

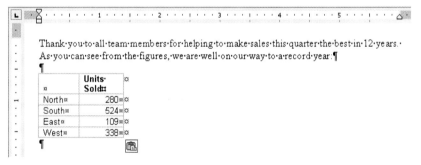

TIP Refer to Chapter 1 for more information on multi-tasking.

Click the Paste Options button (📋▾) to display a list of formatting options for the pasted data. Select Match Destination Table Style to format the data in the default Word table style with solid borders and Times New Roman font.

Information organized in a table or aligned with tabs and tab stops in a Word document can be copied to a spreadsheet. To copy and paste selected information to a spreadsheet, click the Copy button on the Word toolbar, display the Excel worksheet, select the upper-left cell of the range where data is to be placed, and then click the Paste button on the Excel toolbar. Pasted data is automatically arranged into rows and columns similar to the way it appeared in the Word document.

You will copy worksheet data to a Word document. Excel should already be started with the Grades spreadsheet displayed from the last practice.

① *OPEN DEPT MEMO*

    a. Start Word.

    b. Open DEPT MEMO, which is a Word data file for this text. Read the unfinished memo.

② *COPY DATA TO THE CLIPBOARD*

    a. Use the taskbar to display the Grades workbook.

    b. Select cells B1 through E10. All the grades and test averages are selected.

    c. On the toolbar, click the Copy button. The data is copied to the Clipboard.

③ *PASTE DATA*

    a. Use the taskbar to display the DEPT MEMO document.

    b. Place the insertion point in the second blank paragraph after the text that reads "First quarter grades for the Business Applications class are:"

    c. On the toolbar, click the Paste button. The worksheet data is pasted.

    d. Click the Paste Options button (📋▾) and select Match Destination Table Style. The memo looks similar to:

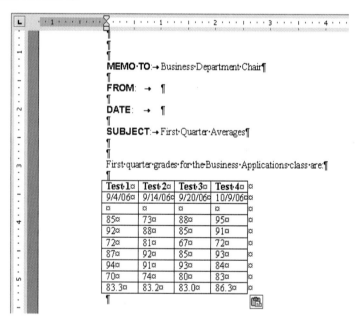

④ *COMPLETE THE MEMO*

    a. In the FROM: line, type your name.

    b. In the DATE: line, type today's date.

⑤ *SAVE THE MODIFIED DEPT MEMO AND PRINT A COPY*

⑥ *CLOSE DEPT MEMO AND CLOSE GRADES*

⑦ *QUIT WORD*

Spreadsheet Collaboration

A worksheet often requires data from several individuals or departments. To allow for collaboration while keeping track of modifications, select Tools → Track Changes → Highlight Changes and then select the Track changes while editing. check box. Changes will be recorded as they are made so that the original creator can later decide which changes to keep and which to discard.

TIP Use the options in the Highlight Changes dialog box to specify which changes to track.

When Highlight Changes has been selected, a modified cell displays a dark blue triangle in the upper-left corner of the cell. The row number and column letter of a modified cell are displayed in red:

	A	B	C
1		**Units Sold**	
2	North	280	
3	South	504	
4	East	109	
5	West	338	
6			

Tracks Changes

The contents of cell B3 have changed

Point to a cell with changes to display information about the change. Select Tools → Track Changes → Accept or Reject Changes, which displays a dialog box prompting for which changes to review. Next, each change is displayed in a dialog box where the change can be accepted or rejected.

To stop tracking changes, select Tools → Track Changes → Highlight Changes and then clear the Track changes while editing. check box.

E-mailing a Spreadsheet

E-mail is a fast and efficient message delivery system. To e-mail worksheet contents, open the workbook and then click the E-mail button (🖃) on the toolbar, which displays the address information boxes. Type the e-mail address of the recipient in the To box. The file name automatically appears as the Subject. Type text in the Introduction box if additional information should appear in the e-mail message and then click 🖃Send this Sheet to send the worksheet. To e-mail just a range of cells, first select the range on the worksheet and then click the E-mail button.

Data from a worksheet e-mailed from Excel appears directly in the body of the e-mail. In Outlook, right-click the message area of the e-mail and select Open in Microsoft Excel 11 to start Excel and open the worksheet.

To send a worksheet as a separate file to an e-mail recipient, the worksheet should be sent as an e-mail attachment. Select File → Send To → Mail Recipient (as Attachment) to display an e-mail window with the workbook included as an attachment file.

When collaborating on a worksheet, select File → Send To → Mail Recipient (for Review) to send a file as an attachment. When a worksheet is sent for review, a dialog box prompts to designate the workbook as shared. Changes are tracked in a shared workbook. The reviewer adds or modifies data and then clicks `Reply with Changes...` on the Reviewing toolbar to e-mail the worksheet back as an attachment. The original author will be prompted to merge any changes into the existing document. Selecting Yes to merge changes overwrites the existing file with the new. Selecting No displays the new worksheet with a name similar to the old, allowing the new version to be saved separately from the existing version.

Practice: Widget Sales

You will e-mail a document to a peer for collaboration. This practice requires Outlook and Internet access. You are also required to work with a classmate and exchange documents through e-mail. Excel should already be started.

① *CREATE NEW A WORKBOOK*

   a. On the toolbar, click the New button (⬜). A new workbook is displayed.

   b. Enter the following data and format it as shown:

	A	B	C	D
1	Widget Corporation			
2	2006 Sales			
3				
4	Division	Fall	Winter	Spring
5	North	1,467	2,310	1,682
6	South	1,200	1,196	890
7	East	640	994	1,245
8	West	1,067	875	1,011
9				

   c. Save the workbook naming it Widget Sales *Name* where *Name* is your name.

② *E-MAIL A WORKSHEET FOR COLLABORATION*

   a. Select File → Send To → Mail Recipient (for Review). A dialog box prompts to share the spreadsheet.

   b. Select Yes. The Save As dialog box is displayed so that the workbook can be saved as shared.

   c. Select Save. A dialog box warns that the current file will be overwritten.

   d. Select Yes. After several seconds, an e-mail window is displayed with the Widget Sales document as an attachment.

   e. If the e-mail window is not displayed, click the "Please review" button on the Windows taskbar. The e-mail window is displayed. Note that the body of the e-mail contains a "Please review the attached document." sentence.

   f. In the To box, type the e-mail address of a classmate.

   g. In the message area, add the text: Please add your summer sales figures. Thank you.

   h. On the Outlook window toolbar, click `Send`. The e-mail is sent to your classmate for collaboration.

   i. Close Widget Sales.

③ *COLLABORATE ON A WORKSHEET*

   a. Check your e-mail.

   b. Open the e-mail from your classmate. Note that the e-mail message asks you to review the attached document.

   c. Open the attachment. The workbook is displayed in Excel.

d. Open SUMMER SALES, which is an Excel data file for this text.

e. Select cells B4 through B8. The sales figures are selected.

f. On the toolbar, click the Copy button.

g. Use the taskbar to display the Widget Sales workbook.

h. Select cell E4.

i. On the toolbar, click the Paste button. The summer sales figures are added:

	A	B	C	D	E
1	Widget Corporation				
2	2006 Sales				
3					
4	Division	Fall	Winter	Spring	Summer
5	North	1,467	2,310	1,682	2,030
6	South	1,200	1,196	890	1,760
7	East	640	994	1,245	1,380
8	West	1,067	875	1,011	2,298
9					

j. On the Reviewing toolbar, click ↩ Reply with Changes… . After several seconds, an Outlook mail window is displayed.

k. On the Outlook toolbar, click ✉ Send . The document is e-mailed back to the sender.

l. Close the workbook.

m. Close SUMMER SALES.

④ REVIEW CHANGES

a. Check your e-mail.

b. Open the e-mail reply from your classmate. The e-mail message includes the reviewed document as an attachment.

c. Open the attachment. You will get a message about merging changes. Select Yes.

d. Point to one of the summer sales figures. Information about the modified cell contents are displayed.

e. Select Tools → Track Changes → Highlight Changes. A dialog box is displayed.

f. Clear the Track changes while editing. check box:

g. Select OK. The cells no longer display markers that indicate the contents have been modified.

⑤ SAVE THE MODIFIED WIDGET SALES, PRINT A COPY, AND CLOSE THE WORKBOOK

Adding a Picture

A picture, such as a business logo, can be added to a worksheet to give it recognition and a professional appearance. Images in digital format come from various sources, including scanned artwork, digital camera pictures, screen captures, and illustration software. Select Insert → Picture → From File to display the Insert Picture dialog box with a list of image files.

clip art

Clip art is an image file with a general-purpose picture created by an artist using illustration software. Select Insert → Picture → Clip Art to display the Clip Art task pane:

Copyright

Downloading images from the Internet may be copyright infringement unless a notice specifically states that an image is free for download.

---

keyword

Type a *keyword*, which is a descriptive word, in the Search for box and select Go to find all the clip art that have the keyword in their description. To narrow a search, use the options in the Search in list, which contains clip art collection names, and the Results should be list, which contains file formats. To place clip art into the document, click the arrow to the right of the image and select Insert from the menu.

Once in the worksheet, an image may need to be sized. Click a picture to select it and display handles:

A picture can be sized by dragging a corner handle

Point to a corner handle, which changes the pointer to a double-headed arrow shape, and then drag to size the picture.

Drag the center of an image (not a handle) to move the picture. The Cut, Copy, and Paste buttons on the toolbar can be used to create copies or move a selected picture. Press the Delete key to delete the selected picture. Click anywhere in the worksheet other than the picture to remove the handles.

Hyperlinks in a Worksheet

When a Web site address is typed into a cell, Excel automatically turns it into a blue, underlined hyperlink. For example, www.lpdatafiles.com typed into a cell is automatically formatted as a blue underlined label. A reader viewing the worksheet on screen can click once to follow the link or click and hold to select the cell. Pointing to the cell changes the pointer to ⁖. Clicking once displays the Web page in a browser window if there is Internet access.

Excel also recognizes an e-mail address and formats it as blue underlined characters. A reader viewing the worksheet on screen can click once to display a new e-mail message window.

The Insert Hyperlink dialog box contains options for inserting a hyperlink into a document. To use this dialog box, select Insert → Hyperlink or click the Insert Hyperlink button (⬚) on the toolbar. Select a type of link from the Link to list and then type a label in the Text to display box. For Web page links, type a URL in the Address box. For an e-mail address link, type an address in the E-mail address box. The label is placed in the active cell, but the URL will be followed when the reader clicks the label.

To remove the blue underline from text, right-click the link and then select Remove Hyperlink from the menu. The text remains, but is no longer a hyperlink.

Practice: Widget Invoice – part 1 of 2

You will create an invoice with a company logo and Web site address. Excel should already be started.

   ① *CREATE NEW A WORKBOOK*

   ② *ADD THE COMPANY LOGO*

      a. Select Insert → Picture → From File. A dialog box is displayed.

         1. Use the Look in list and contents box below to select WIDGET LOGO, which is an image data file for this text.

         2. Select Insert. The picture is displayed on the worksheet.

      b. Drag the logo so that it is near the upper-left corner of the worksheet, if needed.

   ③ *ADD A WEB SITE ADDRESS*

      a. Select cell A5, which should be just below the company logo. Size the logo by dragging a handle, if necessary, so that cell A5 is visible.

      b. In cell A5, type: www.lpdatafiles.com/widget.htm

c. Select cell B5. Note how the link in cell A5 is now blue and underlined:

	A	B	C	D
1				
2	Widget			
3	Corporation			
4				
5	www.lpdatafiles.com/widget.htm			
6				

④ **SAVE AND CLOSE THE WORKBOOK**

   a. **Save** the workbook naming it: Widget Invoice

   b. **Close** Widget Invoice.

Cell Borders, Patterns, and Color

TIP To apply a preformatted design to a worksheet, select Format → AutoFormat.

Cells can be formatted with borders, shading, and patterns. This type of formatting can make a spreadsheet easier to use and understand. For example, rows of similar information are easier to read when alternate rows are shaded and borders are included. Text can also have a font color, which can help titles stand out:

	A	B	C
1	Sales Summary		
2			
3	Region	Units Sold	
4	North	220	
5	South	504	
6	East	109	
7	West	323	
8			
9			

TIP Color should be used to emphasize or distinguish data. Too much color can make a worksheet confusing.

To format cell borders and patterns, select Format → Cells to display the dialog box. Click the Border tab to display options for changing borders. A preview in the center of the dialog box changes as options are selected. Select the Patterns tab for cell shading options. Select the Font tab for text color options. Buttons on the toolbar can also be used to change the formatting. Click the arrow in the Borders button (⊞▾), Fill Color button (🎨▾) or the Font Color button (**A**▾) to display a list of options or to copy just cell formatting to other cells, click the Format Painter button (🖌) on the toolbar, and then click another cell.

Conditional Formatting

Conditional formatting is used to help make spreadsheet data easier to evaluate. For example, if test scores over 90 are displayed in blue and test scores below 70 are red, the spreadsheet becomes visually informative.

To choose formats that are applied to a cell when a condition is met, select the cell and then select Format → Conditional Formatting, which displays a dialog box. Create a condition by clicking the arrows in the lists and selecting options and then typing a value or cell reference in the third box. Next, click Format and select the formats to be applied when the condition is met:

When the cell value is less than 10, the value is displayed in red

Select **Add** in the Conditional Formatting dialog box to add additional conditions. Up to three conditions can be added. To copy conditional formatting to other cells, click the Format Painter button ( ) on the toolbar, and then click another cell.

Practice: Grades – part 5 of 5

You will apply conditional formatting. Excel should already be started.

① *OPEN GRADES*

② *CHANGE CELL BORDERS AND PATTERNS*

   a. Select cells A1 through F10.

   b. Select Format → Cells. A dialog box is displayed.

   c. Select the Border tab. Click the Outline and Inside options in the Presets. Your dialog box should show a preview similar to:

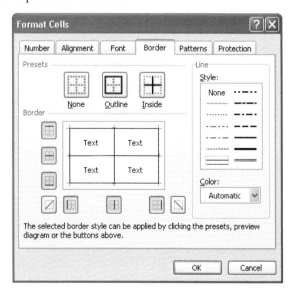

   d. Select OK. The selected cells have solid borders.

   e. Select cells A4 through F4.

   f. On the toolbar, click the arrow in the Fill Color button ( ). Click the light yellow color. The cells are shaded.

   g. Select cells A4 through F4, if they are not still selected.

   h. On the toolbar, click the Format Painter button ( ).

   i. Click cell A6.

   j. Use the Format Painter button to shade the data starting in cell A8.

③ **CREATE CONDITIONAL FORMATS**

a. Select cells B4 through E9.

b. Select Format → Conditonal Formatting. Create a condition as shown:

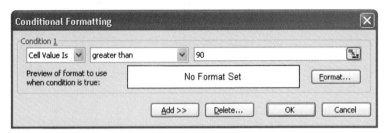

c. Select Format. Select the following Color format:

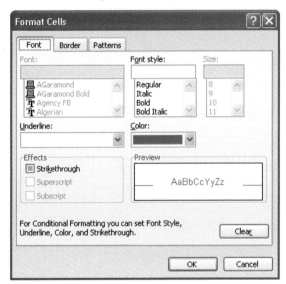

d. Select OK.

e. Select Add.

f. Create a second condition with red formatting for cell values below 70:

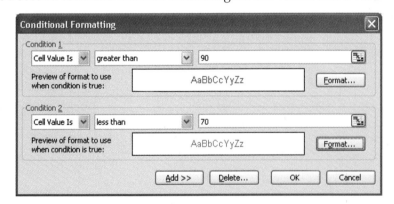

g. Select OK. The test scores are formatted.

④ **SAVE THE MODIFIED GRADES AND PRINT A COPY**

⑤ **CLOSE GRADES**

Templates

A *template* is a master spreadsheet that includes the basic elements for a particular type of spreadsheet. Templates are used again and again whenever a spreadsheet of that type is needed. For example, a spreadsheet can be used to produce an invoice. Invoices usually contain the same data (quantity, service, unit price, and total), with only the invoice number, date, and total changing for each new invoice. Instead of adding labels and formatting cells every time, a more efficient approach would be to create a template that contains the unchanging data and then use this template each time a new invoice is needed.

To create a template, enter data in a new spreadsheet and apply formatting. Select File → Save As to display a dialog box. Type a file name in the File name box and select Template in the Save as type list. To open a template, click the <u>On my computer</u> link in the New Workbook task pane, which displays the Templates dialog box. The new template appears in the General tab.

When a template is used, Excel creates a new, blank, untitled workbook that contains the same formatting and data as the template. This prevents accidentally saving over and changing the original template.

Formatting in Templates

Templates supplied with Excel make use of cell borders and pattern formatting to give templates a professional appearance. The templates dialog box separates templates into tabbed categories.

TIP Excel templates have the .xlt file name extension.

Practice: Widget Invoice – part 2 of 2

You will create a template and then create a new worksheet based on the template. Excel should already be started.

① *OPEN WIDGET INVOICE*

② *ENTER AND FORMAT DATA*

    a. Add labels as shown in the worksheet below.

    b. Bold labels as shown.

    c. Widen column A so that the "Customer Information" label is completely displayed in just cell A8.

    d. Format cell D8 to display a date in a format similar to 3/14/01.

    e. Format cells C14 through D19 to display currency with 2 decimal places.

    f. Right align the Date, Quantity, Unit Price, and Total labels, and widen column C:

	A	B	C	D	
1					
2	Widget				
3	Corporation				
4					
5	www.lpdatafiles.com/widget.htm				
6					
7					
8	Customer Information:		Date:		
9					
10					
11					
12					
13	Description	Quantity	Unit Price	Total	
14					

③ FORMAT CELLS

   a. Select cells A13 through D19.

   b. On the toolbar, click the arrow in the Borders button (▦▾). Click the option for creating borders on all sides of the cell.

   c. Select cells D14 through D19.

   d. On the toolbar, click the arrow in the Fill Color button (🖌▾). Click the light green color. The selected cells are shaded.

④ ADD FORMULAS AND FORMAT CELLS

   a. In cell C21, type Total Due: and then bold and right align the label.

   b. Copy cell D14 to cell D21. Cell D21 is now shaded with a solid border and contains currency formatting.

   c. In cell D14, enter the formula =B14*C14. $0.00 is displayed.

   d. In cell D21, enter the formula =D14+D15+D16+D17+D18+D19. $0.00 is displayed:

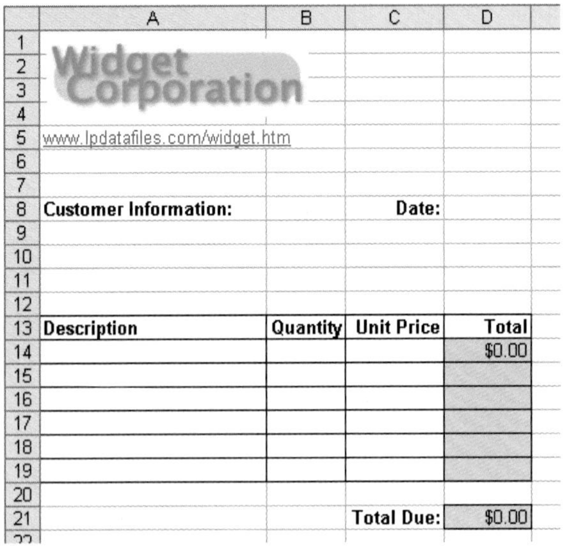

	A	B	C	D
1				
2	Widget			
3	Corporation			
4				
5	www.lpdatafiles.com/widget.htm			
6				
7				
8	Customer Information:		Date:	
9				
10				
11				
12				
13	Description	Quantity	Unit Price	Total
14				$0.00
15				
16				
17				
18				
19				
20				
21			Total Due:	$0.00
22				

⑤ SAVE THE TEMPLATE

   a. Select File → Save As. The Save As dialog box is displayed.

   b. The File name box should already display Widget Invoice. In the Save as type list, select Template. Note that the Save in list has changed to display the Templates folder:

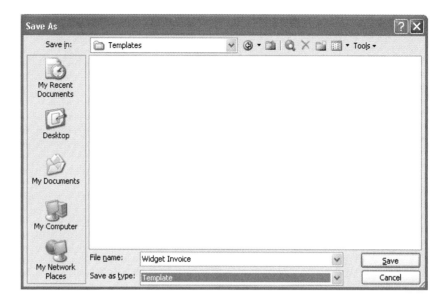

c. Select Save.

⑥ *CLOSE THE TEMPLATE*

⑦ *CREATE A NEW WORKSHEET USING THE TEMPLATE*

a. Select View ➔ Task Pane, if a task pane is not showing.

b. From the Other Task Panes list, select New Workbook:

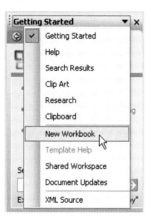

c. In the New Workbook task pane, click <u>On my computer</u>. The Templates dialog box is displayed.

   1. Select the General tab if those icons are not already displayed.

   2. Click the Widget Invoice icon and then select OK. A new workbook is displayed.

⑧ *COMPLETE AN INVOICE*

a. Add data into the invoice template so that the invoice appears similar to the following. Copy cell D14 to cell D15. The total for the second item is calculated and the Total Due is recalculated:

	A	B	C	D
1				
2	Widget			
3	Corporation			
4				
5	www.lpdatafiles.com/widget.htm			
6				
7				
8	Customer Information:		Date:	2/27/06
9	LVP			
10				
11				
12				
13	Description	Quantity	Unit Price	Total
14	Thingamajig	3	$12.50	$37.50
15	Doodad	7	$8.65	$60.55
16				
17				
18				
19				
20				
21			Total Due:	$98.05

⑨ *SAVE, PRINT, AND THEN CLOSE THE WORKBOOK*

  a. Select File ➡ Save. The Save As dialog box is displayed.

    1. In the File name box, type: LVP Invoice

    2. Use the Save in list and the contents box below it to select the appropriate location for the file to be saved.

    3. Select Save. The document is saved.

  b. Print the invoice and then close the workbook.

Creating an HTML File

HTML is the file format for documents viewed using a browser, such as documents on the Web. A workbook in HTML format is more versatile because Excel is not needed to view it, just a browser, such as Internet Explorer. Select File ➡ Save as Web Page to save a workbook in Web format. The Save As dialog box includes a Change Title button. Click this button

title   to give the Web page a descriptive *title*, which is text displayed in the title bar of the browser window.

Select File ➡ Web Page Preview to open a browser window from Excel and view the data as it will appear in a browser. Save a workbook as a Web page to create a copy of the file with the extension .htm. To view the file directly from a web browser, open a browser, such as Internet Explorer and select File ➡ Open.

Practice: Widget Order Form

You will create a new workbook and then save it as a Web page. The Web page document will then be viewed in a browser. This practice requires browser software. Internet access is not required.

① *CREATE A NEW WORKBOOK*

  In the worksheet, enter the following data, widening column A as necessary:

	A	B	C	D	E	F	G	
1	Widget Order Form							
2								
3	Item	Price	Quantity	Total				
4	Doodad	$8.65						
5	Thingamajig	$12.50						
6	Thingamabob	$11.95						
7								
8			Total:					
9								
10								
11	Please print this form and then fax completed form to Widget Sales at 555-1234.							
12								
13								

② FORMAT CELLS

a. Format the company name in cell A1 as 28 point and bold.

b. Bold the column labels in row 3 and the "Total:" label.

c. Right align the "Price," "Quantity," "Total," and "Total:" labels.

d. Format the "Please print this form…" label as italic.

e. Add borders to the order form:

	A	B	C	D	E	F	G	
1	**Widget Order Form**							
2								
3	**Item**	**Price**	**Quantity**	**Total**				
4	Doodad	$8.65						
5	Thingamajig	$12.50						
6	Thingamabob	$11.95						
7								
8			**Total:**					
9								
10								
11	*Please print this form and then fax completed form to Widget Sales at 555-1234.*							
12								

③ SAVE THE WORKBOOK

Save the workbook naming it: Widget Order Form

④ SAVE THE WORKBOOK AS HTML

a. Select File ➔ Save as Web Page. A dialog box is displayed.

b. Click Change Title. In the dialog box displayed, type a title and select OK:

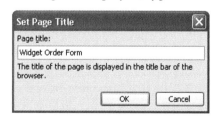

b. Select Save. The dialog box is removed.

⑤ PREVIEW THE HTML DOCUMENT IN A BROWSER

a. Select File ➔ Web Page Preview. A browser window displays the HTML document.

b. Expand the window, if necessary, to view the entire document. Note the title in the title bar.

c. Close the browser window.

⑥ CLOSE WIDGET ORDER FORM AND QUIT EXCEL

This chapter introduced the spreadsheet for storing and analyzing data. Microsoft Excel is the spreadsheet application in Microsoft Office. In Excel, spreadsheet files are called workbooks, and each workbook contains three worksheets. Worksheets are used to present data in an organized format. Before entering data, a spreadsheet plan is developed.

Worksheet cells can store three types of data: labels, values, and times/dates. To enter data into a cell, select that cell, type the data, and then click the Enter button. Press the Enter key, Tab key, or arrow key after typing data in a cell to enter the data and move to another cell. The width of a column is changed by dragging its right boundary. Cells can be formatted to display numeric data differently, and alignments, fonts, styles, and colors can be selected for a cell.

A worksheet should be previewed before printing by using the Print Preview command or the Print Preview button

Data can be duplicated using the Copy and Paste buttons on the toolbar. Data can be moved to a different location in the worksheet using the Cut and Paste buttons on the toolbar. Drag a cell's Fill handle to copy its contents to adjacent cells.

A range is a selection of two or more adjacent cells. A range is selected by dragging from one cell to another.

Formulas are mathematical statements used to calculate values. Formulas must begin with an equal sign (=) and may contain cell references. Excel uses an order of operations when evaluating a formula. Excel automatically checks formulas for errors and displays an error value if the formula is invalid.

Cell references can be entered into a formula by clicking the cell. This technique is called pointing. The formulas in a worksheet are displayed by pressing Ctrl+`.

Select the From File command to insert a picture from a file. Use the Clip Art task pane to add clip art. Click a picture in the task pane to place it in the worksheet and display handles for sizing.

A worksheet can be saved in HTML format, which allows the data to be viewed in a web browser.

An open workbook can be e-mailed by clicking the E-mail button. A workbook can also be e-mailed as an attachment. E-mailing attached workbooks allows for collaboration.

A template contains the basic elements for a particular type of workbook. Create a template by saving a workbook as type Template. To open a template, click On my computer in the New Workbook task pane.

A worksheet can include hyperlinks to a Web page or to an e-mail address. Pointing to a hyperlink, holding down the Ctrl key, and clicking displays the Web page or displays a new e-mail message window.

Active cell The cell displayed with a bold border. Also called the selected cell.

Adjacent cells Cells that are next to each other.

Boundary The bar separating the column letters at the top of the worksheet.

Cell The intersection of a row and column.

Cell reference The column letter and row number that identify a cell, such as B3.

Circular reference An error that occurs when a formula references the cell it is stored in.

Clip art A picture file with an image created by an artist using illustration software.

Column letter Letter at the top of the worksheet used to identify individual columns.

Conditional formatting Formatting that is applied to a cell when a specified condition is met.

Data Information stored in a spreadsheet. Categorized as either label, value, or time/date.

Date Data displayed as a calendar date.

Destination The upper-left cell of the range where data is to be pasted.

Duplicate data To make a copy of data and then place that copy at a different location in the worksheet or into a completely different document.

Excel The Microsoft Office spreadsheet application.

Fill handle The solid square in the lower-right corner of a selected cell that is dragged to copy the contents of a cell to adjacent cells.

Formula Mathematical statement used to calculate a value. A formula must always begin with an equal sign.

Formula bar Displays the active cell's contents. Located above the cells.

Getting Started task pane A task pane shown in the Excel window with options for creating and opening a workbook.

Gridlines Solid lines that mark off the rows and columns in a worksheet.

HTML The file format for documents viewed using a browser.

Insertion Point A blinking vertical line that indicates where the next character typed will be placed.

Keyword A descriptive word used to search for clip art.

Label Text stored in a cell that cannot be used in calculations.

Move data Delete data from a worksheet and then place that data at a different location in the worksheet of into a completely different document.

Name box Displays the cell reference of the active cell. Located near the top of the worksheet.

Order of operations The precedence Excel follows to evaluate a mathematical expression.

Pointing Clicking a cell to place its reference in a formula.

Range Selection of two or more cells.

Relative cell reference A cell reference that reflects the row or column it has been copied to.

Row number Number on the left side of the worksheet used to identify individual rows.

Selected cell *See* Active cell.

Sheet tab Used to display a worksheet.

Sheets *See* Worksheet.

Source Selected cells to be copied or moved.

Spreadsheet A computer application for storing and analyzing data.

Template A master spreadsheet that includes the basic elements for a particular type of spreadsheet.

Time Data displayed in a cell as a time (i.e., 12:30 PM).

Value Numeric data that is stored in a cell that can be used in calculations.

Workbook An Excel spreadsheet document.

Worksheet Sheets in an Excel workbook.

Accept or Reject Changes command Displays a dialog box prompting for which changes to review. Found in Tools → Track Changes.

Align Left button Formats the active cell as left aligned. Found on the toolbar.

Align Right button Formats the active cell as right aligned. Found on the toolbar.

Bold button Formats the active cell as bold. Found on the toolbar.

Borders button Used to format cell borders. Found on the toolbar.

Cancel button Restores the original contents of the active cell.

Cells command Displays a dialog box with formatting options. Found in the Format menu.

Center button Formats the active cell as center aligned. Found on the toolbar.

Clip Art command Displays a dialog box used to place a clip art image on the worksheet. Found in Insert → Picture.

Close Closes print preview. Found on the toolbar in the Print Preview window.

Conditional Formatting command Displays a dialog box used to specify conditional formatting criteria. Found in the Format menu.

Copy command Creates a duplicate of the selected cell(s) contents for pasting. Found in the Edit menu. The Copy button on the toolbar can be used instead of the command.

Currency Style button Applies the Accounting format to the active cell. Found on the toolbar.

Cut command Removes the selected cell(s) contents. Found in the Edit menu. The Cut button on the toolbar can be used instead of the command.

E-mail button Displays options for e-mailing the current worksheet. Found on the toolbar.

Enter button Enters data in the active cell. Found on the Formula bar.

Fill Color button Used to format cells with shading. Found on the toolbar.

Font box Displays a list of fonts to choose from. Found on the toolbar.

Font Color button Used to format the text color of selected cells. Found on the toolbar.

Font Size box Displays a list of font sizes to choose from. Found on the toolbar.

Format Auditing toolbar Contains advanced formula editing features. Displayed when formulas are showing.

Format Painter button Copies a cell format from one cell to another. Found on the toolbar.

From File command Displays a dialog box used to place a picture on the worksheet. Found in Insert → Picture.

Highlight Changes command Displays a dialog box with options for tracking changes. Found in Tools → Track Changes.

Hyperlink command Displays a dialog box used to insert a hyperlink into the active cell. Found in the Insert menu. The Insert Hyperlink button on the toolbar can be used instead of the command.

Italic button Formats the active cell as italic. Found on the toolbar.

Mail Recipient (as Attachment) command Displays an e-mail window with the workbook as an attached file. Found in File → Send To.

Mail Recipient (for Review) command Displays an e-mail window with the workbook as an attached shared file that will be tracked for changes. Found in File → Send To.

New button Displays options for e-mailing the current worksheet. Found on the toolbar.

Open in Microsoft Excel 11 command Starts Excel and opens the spreadsheet data from an e-mail in a workbook. Found in the menu displayed by right-clicking the spreadsheet data in an e-mail.

Page Setup command Displays a dialog box with options for printing gridlines and row and column headings and creating a header or footer. Found in the File menu.

Paste command Places the most recently copied or cut data into a worksheet starting at the selected cell. Found in the Edit menu. The Paste button on the toolbar can be used instead of the command.

Percent Style button Formats the active cell as percentage with no decimal places. Found on the toolbar.

Prints a copy of the worksheet. Found on the toolbar in the Print Preview window.

Print Preview command Displays a worksheet as it will appear when printed. Found in the File menu. The Print Preview button on the toolbar can be used instead of the command.

Remove Hyperlink **command** Removes the blue underline from text in a cell. Found in the menu displayed by right-clicking the cell containing a link.

Repeat **command** Repeats the last action. Found in the Edit menu. The Redo button on the toolbar can be used instead of the command.

Sends the open worksheet as an e-mail message back to the original sender. Found on the Reviewing toolbar.

Save As **command** Displays a dialog box used to save a workbook as a template. Found in the File menu.

Save as Web Page **command** Displays a dialog box used to save a worksheet in HTML format. Found in the File menu.

Sends the open worksheet as an e-mail message. Displayed after selecting the E-mail button.

Trace Error button Displayed by a cell with an error in the formula it stores.

Underline button Formats the contents of the active cell as underlined. Found on the toolbar.

Undo **command** Reverses the previous action. Found in the Edit menu. The Undo button on the toolbar can be used instead of the command.

Web Page Preview **command** Displays a workbook in a browser as it will appear in HTML format.

1. What is a spreadsheet?

2. a) What is a spreadsheet document called in Excel?
   b) How many worksheets does a new workbook contain?

3. a) How are individual columns identified on a worksheet?
   b) How are individual rows identified on a worksheet?
   c) What are scroll bars used for?

4. a) What is a cell?
   b) Give an example of a cell reference.
   c) What does the Name box display?
   d) What does the Formula bar display?

5. What are the three steps in the spreadsheet planning process?

6. After selecting a cell and typing data, what happens when you:
   a) click the Enter button?
   b) press the Enter key?
   c) press the Tab key?
   d) press the Esc key?

7. Is it possible to change the width of only a single cell? If so, how?

8. List two ways to change which cell is active.

9. If a cell contains the wrong data, how can it be corrected?

10. What is displayed when the Undo button arrow is clicked?

11. How many of each of the following types of data are stored in part 1 of the Grades worksheet created in the Practices?
    a) labels
    b) values
    c) dates
    d) times

12. Is the underline style a good choice for a label? What might the label be confused with?

13. How should the cell for each of the following data be formatted? Include the alignment and the numeric formats, if applicable.
    a) $12.50
    b) Quantity
    c) 1,200,450
    d) 23%
    e) 0.15
    f) $1,000

14. When does a cell display ####?

15. a) What is a range?
    b) List two ways to select the range B3 through C12.
    c) How is an entire column selected?
    d) What button selects the entire worksheet?

16. a) Give one reason why you think a worksheet should be previewed before printing?
    b) In print preview, how can the view be enlarged?

17. What options can be selected from the Page Setup dialog box to make a worksheet printout easier to read?

18. Briefly explain what a formula is and give two examples.

19. a) What is meant by order of operations?
    b) Which operation is performed first?
    c) Which operations are performed last?
    d) How can the order of operations within a formula be changed?

20. If 10/20 is entered into a cell, Excel considers it a label. How must the entry be changed so that 10 will be divided by 20?

21. What value would be calculated by Excel for each of the following formulas?
    a) =2+7*5+4
    b) =(2+7)*(5+4)
    c) =5+10/5
    d) =(5+10)/5
    e) =2^3+4

22. a) What is displayed in a cell if an invalid formula is entered?
    b) What button is displayed when a cell with an error value is selected?
    c) Where can a description of an invalid formula error be found?

23. In a formula, do cell references have to be typed in capital letters?

24. How can the formulas stored in the cells of a worksheet be displayed instead of the values they calculate?

25. What value would be calculated by Excel for each of the following formulas if cell C15 stores a value of 6 and cell D8 a value of 3?
    a) =C15*D8
    b) =C15+5+D8
    c) =C15*5+D8
    d) =C15*(5+D8)
    e) =C15/D8

26. What is usually the best method for entering cell references in a formula? Why?

27. What is a circular reference?

28. List one way to copy the values stored in cells A1, A2, and A3 to cells T1, T2, and T3.

29. List the steps required to move the contents of cell B4 into cell A9.

30. When pasting cell contents in the range G1 through H10, what cell needs to be selected before selecting the Paste command?

31. What key is pressed to remove the dashed border from the source cells once the cells have been pasted?

32. a) What is a relative cell reference?
    b) What are the contents of cells D22 and E22 after copying cell C22, which stores the formula =C5 + C6, into cells D22 and E22?

33. When worksheet data is needed in a Word document, would it be best to retype the data into the document or copy and paste the data from the worksheet? Why?

34. Is it possible to copy and paste a table of data from a Word document to an Excel worksheet? If so, how will the data be organized in the worksheet?

35. Give three examples of how collaboration might occur for a worksheet.

36. List three ways to e-mail worksheet content.

37. How is e-mail important to worksheet collaboration?

38. a) List two ways a picture can be added to a worksheet.
    b) Would a company logo likely be clip art? Explain.
    c) List the steps to size a clip art image.

39. List two ways to enter a Web site address in a cell.

40. When there are many rows of similar information, how can a worksheet be formatted so that the rows are easier to read?

41. Describe a situation where conditional formatting could be applied.

42. a) What is a template?
    b) Give two examples of worksheets that might be based on templates.

43. a) Explain why a worksheet would be saved in HTML format.
    b) What software is required to view a document for the Web?

True/False

44. Determine if each of the following are true or false. If false, explain why.
    a) A cell reference consists of a column letter only. *F*
    b) Selected cell and active cell mean the same thing. *T*
    c) The contents of the active cell are displayed in the Name box. *F → Formular Bar*
    d) The width of just a single cell can be changed. *F → Has to be entire column*
    e) A cell's alignment can be changed. *T*
    f) The Accounting and Currency formats are exactly the same. *F → Account Align $ on left.*
    g) Division is performed first in the order of operations. *F → Exponention First, then multiplication then Div.*
    h) Pointing when entering cell references helps to avoid typing errors. *T*
    i) Spreadsheet collaboration means to give someone else your worksheet for printing. *F → editing*
    j) A keyword can be typed to find a clip art image with that word in its description.

k) A hyperlink is added to a worksheet by applying the underline format to a label. F → By clicking Hyperlink Button or adding web address.

l) Conditional formatting applies to all cells on the worksheet. F → only when value is ~~so~~ true

m) If the Format Painter button is used to copy a conditional format to a cell, the conditional formatting will automatically be applied to the cell even if the condition is not true. F

n) A template should be created when a worksheet for a specific purpose is needed only once. F only when it is use often, again & again

Exercise 1 ———————————————————— Activity

A worksheet can be used to determine the time you spend on different activities during one week.

a) Create a new workbook.

b) Enter the following labels in row 1 starting in column A: Activity, Sun, Mon, Tue, Wed, Thu, Fri, Sat

c) Bold all the labels in row 1. Right align all the days of the week labels.

d) Change the width of columns B through H so they are just wide enough to display the labels entirely.

e) Starting in row 3, enter the appropriate label and number of hours you spend each day of the week on each of the following activities:

- school classes
- athletics
- extracurricular groups and clubs
- studying and doing homework
- eating
- sleeping
- watching television, listening to music, or relaxing
- talking on the phone
- doing chores
- working at a job

Change the width of column A to display all the labels and data entirely. Format all the hours to display 2 decimal places.

f) Save the workbook naming it Activity.

g) Most people's schedules do not account for all 24 hours in a day. In the row after the last activity, enter formulas that calculate the amount of unaccounted time in your schedule for each day. Include an appropriate label for the unaccounted time.

h) In cell I1, enter the label Total Hours and widen the column to entirely display the label. Enter formulas that calculate the total hours spent for the week on each activity. Format the total hours to display 2 decimal places.

i) In cell J1, enter the label Avg. Hours and widen the column to entirely display the label. Enter formulas that calculate the average number of hours spent per day on each activity for the week. Format the averages to display 2 decimal places.

j) Create a header that right aligns your name. Add gridlines and row and column headings.

k) Save the modified Activity and print a copy.

l) E-mail Activity to a classmate. In the message area, add the text: This is how I spend my time.

Exercise 2 Balance Sheet

A company uses a balance sheet to list assets (what they own), liabilities (what they owe), and stock-holder's equity (total assets minus total liabilities) as of a specific date.

a) Create a new workbook.

b) Enter the data and apply formatting as shown below. Add the NLG LOGO, which is an image data file for this text:

	A	B	C	D
1	**Northern Lights Gym**			
2				
3	Balance Sheet for 2006			
4				
5	*Assets:*			
6		Cash	$12,000	
7		Accounts Receivable	$15,000	
8		Gym Equipment	$45,000	
9		Office Computers	$98,990	
10		**Total Assets:**		
11				
12	*Liabilities:*			
13		Accounts Payable	$75,987	
14		Short-term Debt	$1,200	
15		**Total Liabilities:**		
16				
17				
18		**Total Stockholder's Equity:**		
19				
20				

c) Save the workbook naming it Balance Sheet.

d) In cell C10, enter a formula that uses cell references to calculate the total assets.

e) In cell C15, enter a formula that uses cell references to calculate the total liabilities.

f) In cell C18, enter a formula that uses cell references to calculate the stockholder's equity.

g) Format cells C10, C15, and C18 in a dark green font color with a bottom double border.

h) Create a header that right aligns your name and a footer that center aligns the current date. Add gridlines and row and column headings.

i) Save the modified Balance Sheet and print a copy.

j) Create an HTML document from the workbook with the title Northern Lights Gym Finances. When saving as a Web page, select Single File Web Page from the Save as type list in the Save As dialog box. This option will save the logo as well as the data in one Web page.

k) Preview the HTML file in a Web browser.

Exercise 3 ————————————————— Temp Conversion

The local university's Meteorology department wants to use a worksheet to convert Fahrenheit temperatures to the equivalent Celsius temperatures.

a) Create a new workbook.

b) Enter the data and apply formatting as shown below. In cell E3 enter the formula =5/9*(B3−32) to convert the Fahrenheit temperature stored in cell B3 to degrees Celsius:

	A	B	C	D	E
1	Temperature Conversion				
2					
3	Fahrenheit Temp:	20		Celsius Temp:	-6.66667
4					

c) Save the workbook naming it Temp Conversion.

d) Format cell E3 to display 0 decimal places.

e) Apply conditional formatting to cells B3 and E3 so that negative values will be displayed in a red font color.

f) Enter the following Fahrenheit temperatures in cell B3, one at a time: 0, 32, and 80. What Celsius temperature does each of these convert to?

g) In row 5, have the worksheet convert temperatures from a Celsius temperature entered in cell B5 to a Fahrenheit temperature displayed in cell E5. Use 26 for the Celsius temperature. Include appropriate labels. The formula needed for converting from degrees Celsius to Fahrenheit is =9/5*B5+32. Display the result with 0 decimal places. Change the column widths as necessary so that all the data is displayed entirely.

h) Enter the following Celsius temperatures in cell B5, one at a time: 0, 12, and –21. What Fahrenheit temperature does each of these convert to?

i) In cell D1, add a link to a Web site, such as www.weather.com, where users could access current temperature data.

j) Create a header that right aligns your name and a footer that center aligns the current date. Add gridlines and row and column headings.

k) Save the modified Temp Conversion and print a copy.

l) Display the formulas in the cells instead of values. Change the column widths as necessary so that the formulas are completely displayed. Print a copy.

Exercise 4 — Metric Conversions

Although the metric system (also called SI) is used throughout the world, the U.S. still widely depends on the English system of measurements.

a) Create a new workbook.

b) Enter the data and apply formatting as shown below:

	A	B	C	D	E
1	**Metric Conversions**				
2					
3	**English**		**Metric**		
4		cubic feet		cubic meters	
5		cubic yards		cubic meters	
6		feet		meters	
7		gallons		liters	
8		inches		centimeters	
9		miles		kilometers	
10		pounds		kilograms	
11		square feet		square meters	
12		square miles		square kilometers	
13		square yards		square meters	
14		yards		meters	
15					
16					

c) Save the workbook naming it Metric Conversions.

d) Use the information below to add the appropriate formulas that use cell references into cells C4 through C14:

cubic meters = 0.0283*cubic feet

cubic meters = 0.7646*cubic yards

meters = 0.3048*feet

meters = 0.9144*yards

liters = 3.7853*gallons

centimeters = 2.54*inches

kilometers = 1.6093*miles

kilograms = 0.3732*pounds

square meters = 0.0929*square feet

square kilometers = 2.59*square miles

square meters = 0.8361*square yards

e) Check your spreadsheet by entering 5 in cell A4. Cell C4 should display 0.1415 because it automatically calculates the metric equivalent of 5 cubic feet.

f) Enter the following measurements into cells A4 through A14. Your worksheet should look similar to:

	A	B	C	D	E
1	**Metric Conversions**				
2					
3	**English**		**Metric**		
4	5	cubic feet	0.1415	cubic meters	
5	10	cubic yards	7.646	cubic meters	
6	10	feet	3.048	meters	
7	1	gallons	3.7853	liters	
8	12	inches	30.48	centimeters	
9	2	miles	3.2186	kilometers	
10	25	pounds	9.33	kilograms	
11	40	square feet	3.716	square meters	
12	12	square miles	31.08	square kilometers	
13	10	square yards	8.361	square meters	
14	5	yards	4.572	meters	
15					
16					

g) Create a header that right aligns your name and a footer that center aligns the current date. Add gridlines and row and column headings.

h) Save the modified Metric Conversions and print a copy.

i) Display the formulas in the cells instead of values. Change the column widths as necessary so that the formulas are completely displayed. Print a copy.

Exercise 5 ———————————————————————Recipe

Estimate how much it will cost to make a recipe assuming all the ingredients need to be purchased.

a) Find a delicious recipe that requires eight or fewer ingredients.

b) Create a new workbook.

c) In cell A1, enter the title Calculating the Cost of a Recipe.

d) In cell A3, enter the name of the recipe.

e) In cell A5, enter the label Ingredient.

f) In cells B5, C5, and D5, enter the labels Store #1, Store #2, and Store #3.

g) Bold all column labels.

h) Starting in cell A6, enter the name of each ingredient required to make the recipe.

i) Use the Internet or newspapers to find the price of each ingredient at two different stores. Be sure the prices are for the same size container (but not necessarily the same brand name) of the ingredient.

j) Starting in cell B6, enter the corresponding ingredient prices.

k) Format the cells storing prices as currency with 2 decimal places.

l) Save the workbook naming it Recipe.

m) Create a header that right aligns your name and a footer that center aligns the text Recipe. Add gridlines and row and column headings.

n) Save the modified Recipe.

o) E-mail the worksheet to a classmate for collaboration. In the message area, add the text: Please compare prices at a third store and add the appropriate data.

p) Open the e-mail from your classmate and open the attachment. Review the document and shade the store that has the best overall prices.

q) Save the modified Recipe document and print a copy.

Exercise 6 ———————————— Expenses, Expenses Analyzed

When determining a budget, it is important to come up with realistic figures. One way to determine actual expenses is to keep careful track of all money spent for a period. Keeping track of expenses for one week can work in some cases, but when there are responsibilities such as loan payments and utility bills, expenses need to be tracked for at least one month. Tracking expenses can also help determine where too much money is being spent.

a) Create a new workbook.

b) Enter data and apply formatting as shown below:

	A	B	C	D
1	Expense Description	Amount	Transaction Type	
2				
3				

c) The worksheet should record how each expense was taken care of. For faster, less error-prone data entry, a cell can get data from a list. Select cell C2 and define a list of data:

    1. Select Data → Validation. A dialog box is displayed.

    2. In the Allow list, select List.

    3. In the Source box, type: Cash, Credit, Check

    4. Select OK. The cell displays an arrow button indicating data should be selected from a list.

    5. Copy cell C2 to cells C3 through C15.

d) Format cells B2 through B15 as currency with 2 decimal places.

e) Save the workbook naming it Expenses.

f) Save the receipts from every purchase made over the next week and be sure to record every check in your checkbook register.

g) Update the worksheet with the saved receipts and checkbook register. Each transaction should be on a separate row in chronological order. Select the transaction type (Cash, Credit, or Check) from the list.

h) Create a header that right aligns your name and a footer that center aligns the current date. Add gridlines and row and column headings.

i) Format the spreadsheet with borders and shade alternate rows.

j) Add a formula that sums the expenses.

k) Save the modified Expenses.

l) Create a new Word document. Write a paragraph that analyzes your spending. Describe your source of income. Is your spending for the period too high relative to your income for the same period? Is there one type of spending that could be reduced? Spending with credit can be more expensive than spending with cash because credit incurs interest charges. Are credit expenses too high?

m) Save the Word document naming it Expenses Analyzed.

n) Below the paragraph that analyzes your spending, place a copy of the data from the Expenses worksheet.

o) Save the modified Expenses Analyzed document and print a copy.

Exercise 7 ———————————————————— Personal Finances

Worksheets can be helpful with personal financial management.

a) Create a new workbook.

b) Enter data and apply formatting as shown below:

	A	B	C	D	E
1	Date	Description of Transaction	Payment (Debit)	Deposit (Credit)	
2					
3	1-Feb-2006	Opening Deposit		$200.00	
4	5-Feb-2006	Cell Phone Bill	$20.00		
5	8-Feb-2006	Paycheck		$100.00	
6	10-Feb-2006	Sally's Diner	$15.35		
7	11-Feb-2006	Coral Square Cinema	$6.75		
8	17-Feb-2006	Deposit		$25.00	
9	18-Feb-2006	Book Palace	$15.98		
10	19-Feb-2006	Full Belly	$10.50		
11	24-Feb-2006	Coral Square Mall	$5.75		
12	24-Feb-2006	Coral Gas	$15.00		
13	28-Feb-2006	Deposit		$100.00	
14					
15					

c) Save the workbook naming it Personal Finances.

d) In cell E1, enter the label Balance. Right align and bold the label if necessary.

e) In column E, enter formulas that use cell references to calculate the balance after each transaction. To calculate the balance, subtract the expense from the previous balance and add the income to the previous balance.

f) In cell B14, enter the label Total: and then right align and bold it. Enter formulas that calculate the total expenses and total income for the month.

g) Create a header with your name right aligned and a footer with the text Personal Finances center aligned. Add gridlines and row and column headings.

h) Save the modified Personal Finances and print a copy.

j) Display the formulas in the cells instead of values. Change the column widths as necessary so that the formulas are completely displayed. Print a copy.

Exercise 8 ———————————————————— Income Statement

An income statement lists a company's revenue (money they earn), expenses (money they pay out), and net income/loss (revenue minus expenses) for a specific time period. Fluffy Bakery is a small home business that wants to use a worksheet to produce an income statement.

    a) Create a new workbook.

    b) Enter data and apply formatting as shown below:

	A	B	C	D	E
1		Fluffy Bakery			
2		Income Statement			
3		for the years 2005-2007			
4					
5		2005	2006	2007	
6	Revenue:				
7	Cookie Sales	$15,500	$16,896	$17,864	
8	Cake Sales	$27,589	$26,298	$25,982	
9	Bread Sales	$24,980	$25,298	$25,398	
10	Total Revenues:				
11	Expenses:				
12	Advertising	$5,000	$4,500	$4,500	
13	Baking Supplies	$2,000	$1,000	$2,750	
14	Ingredients	$13,275	$15,298	$16,490	
15	Salaries	$30,000	$30,000	$35,000	
16	Utilities	$6,570	$7,250	$8,090	
17	Total Expenses:				
18	Net Income/(Loss):				
19					
20					

    c) Save the workbook naming it Income Statement.

    d) In row 10, enter formulas that calculate the total revenue for each year.

    e) In row 17, enter formulas that calculate the total expenses for each year.

    f) In row 18, enter formulas that use cell references to calculate the net income or loss for each year. The net income/loss is calculated by subtracting total expenses from total revenue. Format the values as currency with 0 decimal places, if necessary.

    g) Create a header that right aligns your name. Add gridlines and row and column headings.

    h) Save the modified Income Statement.

    i) Display the formulas in the cells instead of values. Change the column widths as necessary so that the formulas are completely displayed. Print a copy.

Exercise 9 ———————————————————— FRANKLIN TOURS

The FRANKLIN TOURS document contains a partial newsletter. The TOURS document and the TOUR PRICES workbook contain information for the newsletter. Open FRANKLIN TOURS, TOURS, and TOUR PRICES, which are data files for this text, and complete the following steps:

    a) Place a copy of all the text in the TOURS document into the FRANKLIN TOURS document in the blank paragraph at the end of the newsletter.

b) The data in cells A1 through B5 in the TOUR PRICES workbook needs to be added to the FRANKLIN TOURS newsletter. Place a copy of the data into the newsletter in the blank paragraph at the end of the newsletter.

c) In the FRANKLIN TOURS document, create a footer with your name right aligned.

d) Save the modified FRANKLIN TOURS and print a copy.

Exercise 10 ——————————————————————— Budget

A student wants to use a worksheet to create a personal budget for her fall semester in college.

a) Create a new workbook.

b) Enter data and apply formatting as shown below:

	A	B	C	D	E	F	G	H	I
1	**Personal Budget**								
2									
3		**Sep-06**		**Oct-06**		**Nov-06**		**Dec-06**	
4		Budgeted	*Actual*	Budgeted	*Actual*	Budgeted	*Actual*	Budgeted	*Actual*
5	**Income:**								
6	Loan	$7,000	$7,000	$0	$0	$0	$0	$0	$0
7	Job	$1,000	$925	$500	$465	$500	$485	$600	$725
8	Parents	$5,500	$5,500	$0	$0	$0	$0	$0	$0
9	*Total:*								
10	**Expenses:**								
11	Tuition	$6,000	$5,943	$0	$0	$0	$0	$0	$0
12	Room/Board	$5,500	$5,575	$0	$0	$0	$0	$0	$0
13	Books	$700	$635	$0	$45	$0	$0	$0	$0
14	Food	$300	$315	$300	$325	$300	$320	$250	$375
15	Entertainment	$150	$0	$50	$80	$50	$0	$100	$100
16	Clothes	$50	$0	$50	$80	$50	$0	$100	$100
17	*Total:*								
18									
19									

c) Save the workbook naming it Budget.

d) In cell B9, enter a formula that calculates the total budgeted income for September. Use the cell's fill handle to copy the formula to cells C9 through I9. In the Auto Fill Options button, select Fill Without Formatting.

e) In cell B17, enter a formula that calculates the total budgeted expenses for September. Use the cell's fill handle to copy the formula to cells C17 through I17. In the Auto Fill Options button, select Fill Without Formatting.

f) In cell A18, enter the label: Savings: Right align the label and format it as italic. Enter formulas that use cell references to calculate the savings for each month. Savings are calculated by subtracting the total expenses from the total income.

g) Use the Format Cells dialog box to format the data in row 18 as currency with negative numbers in red.

h) Create a header that right aligns your name. Add gridlines and row and column headings.

i) Save the modified Budget and print a copy.

j) Display the formulas in the cells instead of values. Change the column widths as necessary so that the formulas are completely displayed. Print a copy.

A mutual fund is a collection of stocks and/or bonds. A stock is a share of ownership in a company and a bond is a loan funded by investors. Mutual fund investors own shares that represent a portion of the mutual fund holdings. Mutual funds offer investment diversification because a single fund can consist of hundreds or even thousands of different stocks and/or bonds. Such diversification minimizes the effects of stocks performing poorly, but also dilutes the effects of stocks performing well. Important considerations for most mutual funds are:

- Mutual funds typically have a manager who buys and sells stocks and/or bonds.

- Mutual funds require fees to pay for management. These fees, called the expense ratio, reduce the return on investment.

- The majority of mutual funds do not perform as well as the market average.

Unlike most mutual funds, a stock index fund consists of only stocks from a particular index. An index is a defined subset of all stocks available on stock markets. A statement about how "the market" is doing is referring to the performance of the Dow or another index. Popular indexes include:

- **Dow Jones Industrial Average (DJIA or Dow)** A collection of 30 blue-chip stocks. Blue-chip stocks are widely held and are considered solid, reliable, and having sustained growth. Stocks include Microsoft, Intel, Coca-Cola, McDonald's, and American Express.

- **Standard & Poor's 500 (S&P 500)** A collection of the 500 largest company stocks. Stocks include Microsoft, Wal-Mart, and IBM.

- **Nasdaq 100** A collection of the 100 largest company stocks listed on the Nasdaq. Stocks include Microsoft, Intel, Dell, and Yahoo!.

- **Nasdaq Composite** A collection of all stocks listed on the Nasdaq.

- **Amex Composite** A collection of all stocks listed on the American Stock Exchange.

- **Russell 2000** A collection of 2,000 small-company stocks. Atari, Zale, and Fossil are stocks in the Russell 2000.

- **Wilshire 5000** Although the name seems to indicate a set of 5,000 stocks, the Wilshire index actually contains over 6,000 stocks. Sometimes referred to as the Total Stock Market Index because it includes the stock for nearly every U.S. corporation.

Because of its holdings, a stock index fund typically performs as well as the market average. This means stock index funds outperform most other mutual funds. Stock index funds also have very low expense ratios and are offered by many companies.

The first index fund was started in 1975 by the Vanguard Group. The Vanguard 500 Index Fund (VFINX) remains one of the most popular and outperforms the vast majority of other mutual funds. Other index funds include the Vanguard Total Stock Market Fund (VTSMX) and the Vanguard TSM VIPERS (VTI) which follow the Wilshire 5000 index.

a) Create a new workbook. Enter and format labels as shown. The current date should appear below the Price label:

	A	B	C	D
1	**Index Funds**			
2				
3	**Fund Name**	**Symbol**	**Price**	
4			2/6/2006	
5				

b) Add the three Vanguard fund names and their symbols to the worksheet.

c) Save the workbook naming it Index Funds.

d) Use a Web site such as finance.yahoo.com to get a price quote for each of the funds and then enter the information into column C.

e) Research and then choose three other index funds using the Internet, newspapers, or financial magazines. Search criteria for the Internet could include "Dow fund," "Nasdaq Composite fund," and "Russell 2000 fund." Add the three selected funds to the Index Funds spreadsheet.

f) Update the Index Funds spreadsheet on at least three different days to include new fund quotes.

Exercise 12 —————————— Mileage Log, April Mileage Log

Many jobs, such as sales and marketing positions, require employees to travel outside the office using their own vehicle. For this type of travel, employees are required to keep track of their mileage on a mileage log form and then submit the form for reimbursement based on a rate per kilometer or mile.

a) Create a new workbook.

b) Enter data and apply formatting similar to:

	A	B	C	D	E	F	G
1			Flat Technologies				
2			Monthly Mileage Log				
3		Employee Name:					
4		Submit Date:					
5							
6	Date	Description	From	To	Odometer		Mileage
7					Start	Finish	
8					0	0	0
9					0	0	0
10					0	0	0
11					0	0	0
12					0	0	0
13					0	0	0
14					0	0	0
15					0	0	0
16					0	0	0
17					0	0	0
18					0	0	0
19					0	0	0
20					0	0	0
21					0	0	0
22					0	0	0
23					0	0	0
24					0	0	0
25					0	0	0
26					Total Mileage		
27					Rate		
28					Reimbursement		

c) In cell G8, enter a formula to calculate the mileage from the starting point to the finish point. Format the cell to include a thousands separator. Use the cell's fill handle to copy the formula to cells G9 through G25. In the Auto Fill Options button, select Fill Without Formatting.

d) Enter a formula to calculate the total mileage.

e) Employees are reimbursed at a rate of $0.32 per mile. Type the rate in the appropriate cell and then enter a formula to calculate the total reimbursement. Format the cells appropriately.

f) Save the worksheet as a template naming it Mileage Log.

g) Close Mileage Log.

h) Create a new workbook based on the Mileage Log template.

i) Enter your name for the Employee Name and today's date for the Submit Date.

j) Starting in cell A8, enter the data:

Date	Description	From	To	Start	Finish
4/2/2006	Microsoft Seminar	Miami	Boca Raton	33,580	33,610
4/28/2006	Sales Call	Boca Raton	Palm Beach	34,800	34,830
4/28/2006	Sales Call	Palm Beach	Boca Raton	34,830	34,860

k) Create a header that right aligns your name.

l) Save the worksheet naming it April Mileage Log and print a copy.

m) E-mail the worksheet to a classmate. In the message area, add the text: Attached please find my monthly mileage log.

Exercise 13 —————— Travel Expenses, Chicago Travel Expenses

Many jobs require travel. When traveling for business, employees are required to fill out a travel expense form for any out-of-pocket expenses.

a) Create a new workbook.

b) Enter data and apply formatting similar to that shown below. Cells B9 through B16 are formatted for the Accounting currency style and 0 (zero) has been typed into each cell. Accounting style displays a dash in place of 0:

	A	B	C	D	E
1	Flat Technologies				
2					
3	Travel Expense Statement				
4	Employee Name:				
5	Employee Number:				
6	Date:				
7	Travel Destination:				
8	Travel Dates:				
9	Airfare	$ -			
10	Hotel	$ -			
11	Food	$ -			
12	Car rental	$ -			
13	Gas	$ -			
14	Entertainment	$ -			
15	Miscellaneous	$ -			
16	Total Expenses	$ -			
17					
18	Complete, attach all receipts, and submit to Human Resources.				
19					

c) Enter a formula to calculate the total expenses.

d) Save the worksheet as a template naming it Travel Expenses and then close Travel Expenses.

e) Create a new workbook based on the Travel Expenses template.

f) Enter your name for the Employee Name and today's date for the Date. Enter Chicago for the Travel Destination and enter 05/15/06 - 05/20/06 for the Travel Dates.

g) Use the Internet to research the cost of a five-day trip to Chicago. Include a car rental for the entire five days. Type the estimated amounts into the appropriate cells.

h) Create a header that right aligns your name. Add gridlines and row and column headings.

i) Save the worksheet naming it Chicago Travel Expenses and print a copy.

Exercise 14 ——————————————————————————— KEYPAD

The numeric keypad can make the entering of large amounts of numeric data more efficient. It also allows easy access to the mathematical operators +, -, *, and /. Most keyboards require pressing the Num Lock key on the numeric keypad before numbers can be entered.

Before beginning to enter data, the right hand should be placed lightly on the keypad with slightly curved fingers. The right index finger is placed on the number 4 key, the right middle finger is placed on the number 5 key, the right ring finger is placed on the number 6 key, and the right pinky finger is placed on the + key. The right thumb is placed over the 0 key. With the fingers placed as just described, this is called the home position. Open KEYPAD, which is an Excel data file for this text, and complete the following steps:

a) Data entry into a range of cells can be made easier by selecting the range before entering the data. In a selected range, pressing Enter makes the next cell in the range active. When the last cell in a column is reached, pressing Enter makes the cell at the top of the next column in the range active. Select cells A1 through G6 and then place the right hand on the keypad in the home position as described above.

b) Enter the following numbers starting in cell A1, pressing the Enter key with the right pinky after each number. Do not look at the right hand while entering data, refer only to the picture of the keypad above. Note that the data entered will not be entered as a formula because the data does not begin with an equal sign (=).

	A	B	C	D	E	F	G	H
1	444	555	666	405	444	4++	55+	
2	445	446	444	44+	445	5+5	445	
3	455	466	400	4++	555	6+5	554	
4	555	545	565	566	666	5+0	505	
5	666	646	656	606	506	0+4	6+6	
6	604	404	505	406	405	6++	0+0	
7								

c) Repeat part (b) until the characters can be typed without referring to the keypad image.

d) The number 7 is typed using the index finger of the right hand, the number 8 is typed using the middle finger of the right hand, the number 9 is typed using the ring finger of the right hand and the - is typed using the pinky finger of the right hand. Select cells A8 through G13 and enter the following numbers in the same manner as part (b):

	A	B	C	D	E	F	G	H
7								
8	777	888	999	77-	888	999	9--	
9	778	779	777	778	779	888	778	
10	788	7799	898	788	799	787	878	
11	888	878	989	878	878	989	9--	
12	999	979	787	88-	979	7--	789	
13	797	777	888	-88	797	8--	987	
14								

e) Repeat part (d) until the characters can be typed without referring to the keypad image.

f) The number 1 is typed using the index finger of the right hand, the number 2 is typed using the middle finger of the right hand, the number 3 and the . key are typed using the ring finger of the right hand. Select cells A15 through G20 and enter the following numbers in the same manner as parts (b) and (d):

	A	B	C	D	E	F	G	H
14								
15	111	212	363	171	252	112	1.2	
16	121	222	282	147	414	113	1.3	
17	131	213	111	258	222	242	2.3	
18	222	222	222	369	115	282	2.1	
19	223	252	333	216	114	273	3.2	
20	221	141	282	246	116	198	2.1	
21								

g) Repeat part (f) until the characters can be typed without referring to the keypad image.

h) The / key is typed using the middle finger of the right hand, the * key is typed using the ring finger of the right hand, and the + key is typed using the pinky finger of the right hand. Select cells A22 through G27 and enter the following numbers in the same manner as parts (b), (d), and (f):

	A	B	C	D	E	F	G	H
21								
22	4/5	4*5	4*5	6/4	1*3	-7*3	3+3	
23	5/5	5*5	5*6	5/5	5+6+9+3	-1*2	5+5	
24	1*4	2-6	6+4	4*7	2+6	5+5+4	4*8	
25	4*5	3+5	2+6	3+5	-4+8	1*1.5	3+2+5	
26	4+5	3/3	3/3	5.6*1.3	5+3	4+6/1	4.5*4+1	
27	0.5*1.3	4-5	0.6*1.08	3/6	1+1	5*8-2.5	2+9	
28								

i) Repeat part (h) until the characters can be typed without referring to the keypad image.

j) Save and close the modified workbook.

Chapter 8

Working with Functions and Organizing Data

This chapter discusses how to use a worksheet to answer "What If?" questions. Functions, amortization tables, and multiple sheets in a workbook are also discussed. *Cost of Money/time*

Asking What If?

A worksheet is often used to answer "What If?" questions. A *What If question* asks how a value or set of values impacts results. For example, the worksheet on the left shows the profit from a fundraiser if 200 people attend. On the right, a different scenario shows the profit if 300 people attend:

	A	B
1	**Charity Fundraiser**	
2		
3	**Attendance:**	200
4	**Ticket Price:**	$10.00
5		
6	**Income:**	
7	Ticket Revenue	$2,000.00
8		
9	**Expenses:**	
10	Auditorium Rental	$350.00
11	Printing Costs	$175.00
12	Equipment Rentals	$500.00
13	Advertising Costs	$200.00
14		
15	**Profit**	$975.00

	A	B
1	**Charity Fundraiser**	
2		
3	**Attendance:**	300
4	**Ticket Price:**	$10.00
5		
6	**Income:**	
7	Ticket Revenue	$3,000.00
8		
9	**Expenses:**	
10	Auditorium Rental	$350.00
11	Printing Costs	$175.00
12	Equipment Rentals	$500.00
13	Advertising Costs	$200.00
14		
15	**Profit**	$1,975.00

Selling an additional 100 tickets has a positive impact on the profits, with an increase of $1,000.

A worksheet that includes related data and formulas for analyzing the data is called a *spreadsheet model*. The Charity Fundraiser worksheet above is a spreadsheet model. Businesses often ask "What If" questions of their spreadsheet models in order to make predictions. This process is sometimes referred to as a *what-if analysis*.

What If Scenarios

A what-if analysis can be conducted in Excel using scenarios. Scenarios are used to define different data sets within the same workbook. For example, a worksheet could be created that projects a company's profit for the year. Since many factors can affect a company's profit, worst case and best case scenarios could be defined and analyzed.

Select **Tools → Scenarios** to display a dialog box that can be used to define scenarios.

Practice: FUNDRAISER

You will start Microsoft Excel and ask "What If" questions of a spreadsheet model.

① *OPEN FUNDRAISER*

    a. Start Excel.

    b. Open FUNDRAISER, which is an Excel data file for this text. The FUNDRAISER workbook contains the projected income and expenses involved in producing a charity event.

② *ANSWER WHAT IF QUESTIONS*

    A last minute problem has required that the fundraiser be moved to a different auditorium. The organizers want to know how the profit will be affected.

    a. The Auditorium Rental expense will increase from $350.00 to $500.00. Change the Auditorium Rental expense to $500.00 and note how the profit is affected.

    b. The new auditorium only seats 150. Change the Attendance to 150 and note how the profit is affected.

    c. The organizers have set a goal to raise a minimum profit of $625.00. Due to the increased Auditorium Rental expense and limited seating, they are forced to raise the ticket price. Change the ticket price until the minimum profit is met.

③ *ADD A FOOTER*

    Create a footer that center aligns the date and right aligns your name.

④ *SAVE, PRINT, AND THEN CLOSE THE MODIFIED FUNDRAISER*

Using Functions to Perform Calculations

arguments

    Excel contains built-in functions that can be included in a formula to perform common calculations. A *function* performs a calculation that results in a single value. A function requires data, called *arguments*, to perform its calculation. The arguments of a function are enclosed in parentheses after the function name and are usually cell references.

SUM

    The *SUM function* adds the value of the cells in the range. For example, to add the values in cells G1, G2, and G3, use the formula:

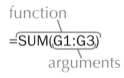

function

=SUM(G1:G3)

arguments

Function Names

Function names can be typed in uppercase or lowercase letters. However, Excel automatically converts a function to uppercase letters when entered.

Note that a colon (:) is used to separate the first cell reference and the last cell reference in the range. Nonadjacent cells can also be used as arguments in a SUM function by separating the arguments with a comma (,). For example, to add the values stored in cells A1, B5, and E7, use the formula:

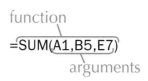

function

=SUM(A1,B5,E7)

arguments

As a function is typed, an argument tooltip is displayed illustrating the structure, or syntax, of the function:

$12.00
$3.75
$8.33
=sum(
SUM(**number1**, [number2], ...)

Pointing is the best method for entering a cell range into a function because typing errors are avoided. After typing the opening parenthesis for the function, drag from the first cell in the range to the last:

$12.00
$3.75
$8.33
=sum(C4:C6|
SUM(**number1**, [number2], ...)

Function Categories

Functions can be divided into categories. For example, the SUM function is considered a Math and Trigonometric function and the AVERAGE, MAX, and MIN functions are considered Statistical functions.

Press Enter to complete the formula. Excel automatically adds the closing parenthesis. The value produced from the calculation is automatically formatted with the same format as the argument cells.

Other commonly used functions include:

- The **AVERAGE function** adds the values of the cells in the range and then divides the result by the number of cells in the range. For example, =AVERAGE(E10:E15) sums the values in cells E10, E11, E12, E13, E14, and E15 and then divides the total by 6.

- The **MAX function** determines the maximum value in the range of cells. For example, =MAX(B2:B26) displays the maximum (largest) of all the values in the range B2 through B26.

The COUNT Function

The COUNT function determines the number of cells that contain values. For example, =COUNT(C1:C8) displays the number of cells in the range C1 through C8 that contain values.

- The **MIN function** determines the minimum value in the range of cells. For example, =MIN(C18:F18) displays the minimum (smallest) of all the values in the range C18 through F18.

Note that the SUM, AVERAGE, MIN, and MAX functions ignore cells that contain text or are empty when their cell references are included as arguments.

Using Absolute Cell References in Formulas

As discussed in Chapter 7, relative cell references automatically change when copied. However, there are situations when a cell reference should remain the same when copied. A cell reference that does not change when copied is called an *absolute cell reference*. An absolute cell reference contains a dollar sign in front of both the column letter and row number, such as $A$1.

In the worksheet below, shipping charges are calculated by multiplying the item's weight by a shipping cost per kg, which is stored in cell B4. The cell reference, B4, is entered into the formula as an absolute cell reference because it should not change when copied:

C7	▼	f_x =B7*$B$4		
	A	B	C	D
1	The Fresh Fruit Company			
2	Shipping Rates			
3				
4	Shipping per kg:	$1.75		
5				
6	Item	Weight (kg)	Shipping	
7	Crate of Oranges	4	$7.00	
8	Crate of Grapefruit	5		
9	Assorted Fruit Crate	8		
10	Seasonal Fruit Basket	7		
11				

The formula in cell C7 contains a relative cell reference and an absolute cell reference

Mixed Cell Reference

A mixed cell reference is a combination of a relative and an absolute cell reference. For example, $A1 is a reference where the column is absolute and the row is relative.

When the formula in cell C7 is copied to cell C8, the formula will change to =B8*$B$4.

Practice: Mileage Log

You will use formulas that contain functions and absolute cell references. Excel should already be started.

① **CREATE A NEW WORKBOOK**

Enter and format data similar to that shown in the worksheet below:

	A	B	C	D
1	Employee Mileage Expenses			
2				
3	Rate:	$0.34		
4				
5	Date	Miles	Expense	
6	4/5/2006	120		
7	5/23/2006	125		
8	5/24/2006	32		
9	5/30/2006	232		
10		Total		
11				

② **ENTER A FORMULA WITH AN ABSOLUTE CELL REFERENCE**

a. In cell C6, type = and then click cell B6. Type * and then click cell B3. Press the F4 key. Pressing F4 places a dollar sign in front of both the column letter and the row number. The formula bar displays =B6*$B$3

b. Press Enter. $40.80 is displayed in cell C6.

③ **COPY THE FORMULA**

a. In cell C6, drag the Fill handle to cell C9. The formula is copied to the cells with the relative cell reference automatically changing and the absolute cell reference staying the same.

b. Select cell C9 and then view the formula on the Formula bar to see the absolute reference.

④ *CALCULATE THE TOTAL EXPENSES*

a. In cell B10, enter the label Total and bold and right align the label.

b. In cell C10, type =SUM(and then drag the pointer from cell C6 to cell C9:

	A	B	C	D	E
1	Employee Mileage Expenses				
2					
3	Rate:	$0.34			
4					
5	Date	Miles	Expense		
6	4/5/2006	120	$40.80		
7	5/23/2006	125	$42.50		
8	5/24/2006	32	$10.88		
9	5/30/2006	232	$78.88		
10		Total	=SUM(C6:C9		
11			SUM(**number1**, [number2], …)		

c. Press Enter to complete the formula. Excel automatically adds a right parenthesis. The expense total is displayed in cell C10 and is automatically formatted with the same format as the argument cells.

⑤ *SAVE THE WORKBOOK AND PRINT A COPY*

a. Add a footer that right aligns your name and add gridlines and row and column headings.

b. Save the workbook naming it Mileage Log and print a copy.

c. Close Mileage Log.

Inserting a Function into a Formula

TIP Press Shift+F3 to display the Insert Function dialog box.

Instead of typing the name of a function into a formula, click the Insert Function button (ƒₓ) on the Formula bar to display the Insert Function dialog box, which places an equal sign (=) in the cell and displays a list of functions that can be inserted into a formula. Select an option in the Or select a category list to limit the functions that are displayed:

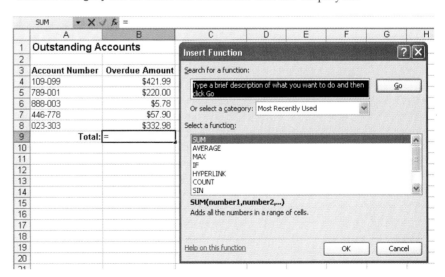

Select a function in the Select a function list and then OK to display the Function Arguments dialog box for the function. For example, select SUM

TIP Drag the title bar of the Functions Argument dialog box to move the dialog box and view the cells behind it.

and then select OK to display the Function Arguments dialog box for the SUM function:

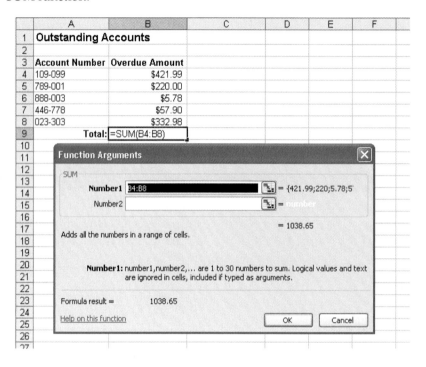

A range of cells is automatically entered in the Number1 box based on the location of the active cell. Excel assumes the range of cells is to the right or above the active cell. Type in the Number1 box or point to cells on the work-sheet to change the cell range if necessary. Select OK to remove the Function Arguments dialog box and display the formula result in the cell.

The AutoSum button (Σ ▾) can also be used to create a formula with the SUM function. The range placed in the SUM function is the series of cells to the right or above the active cell. This range should be double-checked since Excel guesses the range. Press the Enter key to enter the formula. Click the arrow in the AutoSum button to display a list of other functions, such as Average, Min, and Max.

Functions List

When an equal sign is typed in a cell, the Functions list appears on the Formula bar:

Select a function name from the list to display the Function Arguments dialog box for the selected function. Select **More Functions** to display the Insert Function dialog box.

Common Error Values

As discussed in Chapter 7, Excel automatically checks a formula for errors when it is entered into a cell. A cell with an invalid formula displays an error value and a green triangle in the upper-left corner of the cell. Common error values include:

#DIV/0 The formula is trying to divide by zero.

#REF The formula contains a reference that is not valid.

#NUM A numeric value is invalid, such as a value that is too large or too small.

#VALUE The formula is using the wrong type of argument, such as a label instead of a value.

The result of the formula is too wide to fit in the column or the result is a negative time or date value. If the result should fit in the column, check the formula for errors.

To correct a formula and remove the error value, select the cell with the error to display the Trace Error button (⟡). Click this button to display the error and a list of options.

Some formulas may produce a result, but also display a green triangle in the cell which indicates a possible formula error. Common formula errors include:

- **Formula Omits Adjacent Cells**   The formula includes a range of values and the range does not include a value in an adjacent cell. For example, the formula =SUM(A2:25) entered in cell A26, may produce this type of error if cell A1 contains a column label that is a value, such as a date.

- **Inconsistent Formula in Region**   The formula does not match the pattern of formulas near it.

To remove the green triangle, select the cell to display the Trace Error button (⟡). Click this button to display the error and a list of options. If the formula does not contain an error, select the Ignore Error option.

Practice: MILEAGE SUMMARY

You will insert functions into formulas. Excel should already be started.

① *OPEN MILEAGE SUMMARY*

Open MILEAGE SUMMARY, which is an Excel data file for this text. The worksheet summarizes a mileage log by month.

② *DETERMINE THE TOTAL MILEAGE AND REIMBURSEMENT*

a. Select cell B18 and click the Insert Function button (𝑓ₓ) on the Formula bar. The Insert Function dialog box is displayed:

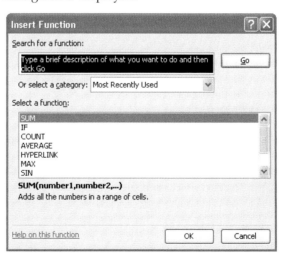

1. In the Select a function list, select SUM and then select OK. The Function Arguments dialog box is displayed:

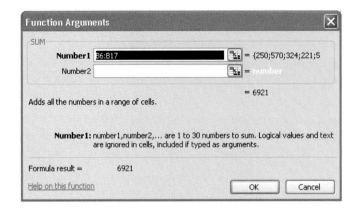

2. The range B6:B17 is automatically entered in the **Number1** box and the Formula result 6921 is displayed. Select **OK** to accept the range entered by Excel. The total mileage is displayed in cell B18.

b. Copy the formula in cell B18 to cell C18. The total reimbursement is displayed.

③ *DETERMINE THE AVERAGE MONTHLY MILEAGE AND REIMBURSEMENT*

a. Select cell B19 and click the Insert Function button (𝑓ₓ) on the Formula bar. The Insert Function dialog box is displayed.

1. In the **Select a function** list, select AVERAGE and then select **OK**. The Function Arguments dialog box is displayed. Note that the range B6:B18 in the **Number1** box is not the correct range.

2. In the **Number1** box, change the range to: B6:B17

3. Select **OK**. The average monthly mileage is displayed in cell B19.

b. Copy the formula in cell B19 to cell C19.

④ *DETERMINE THE MINIMUM MONTHLY MILEAGE AND REIMBURSEMENT*

a. Select cell B20 and click the arrow in the AutoSum button (Σ ▾) on the toolbar. A menu is displayed.

b. Select Min. A formula with the MIN function is displayed in cell B20. Note that the range B6:B19 in the formula is not the correct range.

c. On the Formula bar, change the range to B6:B17 and press Enter.

d. Copy the formula in cell B20 to cell C20.

⑤ *DETERMINE THE MAXIMUM MONTHLY MILEAGE AND REIMBURSEMENT*

a. Select cell B21 and click the arrow in the AutoSum button (Σ ▾) on the toolbar. A menu is displayed.

b. Select Max. A formula with the MAX function is displayed in cell B21. Note that the range B6:B20 in the formula is not the correct range.

c. On the Formula bar, change the range to B6:B17 and press Enter.

d. Copy the formula in cell B21 to cell C21.

e. Format cells C18 through C21 as currency with 2 decimal places.

⑥ *ADD A FOOTER*

Add a footer that right aligns your name.

⑦ *SAVE, PRINT, AND THEN CLOSE THE MODIFIED MILEAGE SUMMARY*

The ROUND Function

The *ROUND function* changes a value by rounding it to a specific number of decimal places:

value to be rounded

$$=ROUND(C16,1)$$

decimal places

If the value stored in C16 is 42.851, the rounded result is 42.9.

Rounding is different than formatting in that the ROUND function changes the value stored in a cell and formatting only changes the way data is displayed. Excel follows certain rules when rounding numbers. A number with a decimal portion greater than or equal to 0.5 is rounded up and a number with a decimal portion less than 0.5 is rounded down.

To round a value to the nearest whole number, a 0 is used to indicate no decimal places, as in =ROUND(AVERAGE(B3:B8), 0). A negative number as the second argument of the ROUND function rounds a value to the nearest 10s, 100s, and so forth. For example, =ROUND(72.86, -1) displays 70 and =ROUND(72.866, -2) displays 100.

ROUNDDOWN and ROUNDUP Functions

The ROUNDDOWN and ROUNDUP functions perform the same function as the ROUND function but always rounds a number down or up, respectively.

Practice: HOTEL OCCUPANCY — part 1 of 3

You will calculate the average daily rate charged by a hotel for its rooms and use the ROUND function. Excel should already be started.

1. **OPEN HOTEL OCCUPANCY**

   Open HOTEL OCCUPANCY, which is an Excel data file for this text. The worksheet lists the hotel rooms occupied on a particular date and the daily rate.

2. **DETERMINE THE AVERAGE DAILY RATE**

   a. In cell A24, enter the label Average Daily Rate and bold and right align the label.

   b. In cell B24, enter =AVERAGE(B4:B23). The average rate 149.8265 is displayed.

3. **ROUND THE AVERAGE DAILY RATE TO 2 DECIMAL PLACES**

   a. Select cell B24.

   b. On the Formula bar, click between the equal sign and the word AVERAGE and type: ROUND(

   c. On the Formula bar, click at the end of the formula and type ,2) to complete the formula: =ROUND(AVERAGE(B4:B23),2)

   d. Click the Enter button. The average is now rounded to 2 decimal places: 149.83

4. **FORMAT RATES**

   Format cells B4 to B24 as currency with 2 decimal places.

5. **SAVE THE MODIFIED HOTEL OCCUPANCY**

   a. Add a footer that right aligns your name.

   b. Save the modified HOTEL OCCUPANCY.

Sorting Data

ascending, descending

alphabetical, chronological

Arranging data in a specified order is called *sorting*. In Excel, rows can be sorted in either *ascending* (low to high) or *descending* (high to low) order based on the data in a specified column. Ascending order is also called *alphabetical* order when the data is text and *chronological* order when the data is times or dates.

To sort data, select a range and then click the Sort Ascending button (⊞) on the toolbar. The data will be placed in alphabetic order based on the values displayed in the first column of selected data. To sort the data in descending order, click the Sort Descending button (⊞) after selecting a range.

key sort column

The Sort Ascending and Sort Descending buttons use the first selected column as the key sort column. The *key sort column* is the column that contains the values that a sort is based on. The Sort dialog box contains options designating a different column as the key sort column. To use this dialog box, select Data ➜ Sort. Select a column label from the Sort by list and select the method of sort, such as Descending. The Then by area can be used to specify a column and order for rows that have the same data in the key sort column.

Inserting and Deleting Rows and Columns

Rows and columns can be inserted between data in a worksheet. Right-click the row number or column letter where the new row or column is to appear and then select Insert from the menu to add a row or column.

Inserted rows and columns contain no data. However, cells in the new row or column have the same formatting as the cells above or to the left of them, respectively. Click the Insert Options button (⊞ ▾) that is displayed when a new row or column is inserted to change the formatting.

To delete a row or column, right-click the row number or column letter and select Delete from the menu.

When cells are inserted or deleted, Excel automatically changes the relative cell references in any affected formulas. For example, if row 3 is deleted, the formula =SUM(C1:C10) changes to =SUM(C1:C9). If a row is inserted between rows 1 and 10, the formula becomes =SUM(C1:C11).

Find and Replace

Select Edit ➜ Find to display a dialog box used to search a worksheet for data, cell references, and formulas. Select Edit ➜ Replace to search for data and replace it with other data.

For a more specific search, options such as Match case and Match entire cell contents can be selected. Match case selects textual data with the same capitalization as the search data.

TIP Select Edit ➜ Undo or click the Undo button on the toolbar to restore a deleted row or column.

You will sort data. Excel should already be started with the HOTEL OCCUPANCY workbook displayed from the last practice.

① *SORT THE ROOM RATE DATA*

    a. Select cells A4 through B23 to select all the room numbers and their corresponding rates, which is the data to be sorted.

    b. On the toolbar, click the Sort Descending button (⚏). The data is sorted in descending order by room number.

    c. On the toolbar, click the Sort Ascending button (⚏). The data is sorted in ascending order by room number.

② *CHANGE THE KEY SORT COLUMN*

    a. Select cells A4 to B23, if they are not already selected.

    b. Select Data → Sort. A dialog box is displayed.

    c. In the Sort by list, select Rate and select Ascending:

    d. Select OK. The data is sorted in ascending order by Rate.

③ *INSERT A ROW*

    a. Right-click the row number 9. A menu is displayed.

    b. Select Insert. A row is inserted and the data that was in row 9 and all the rows below it move down to accommodate the newly inserted row.

    c. Select cell A9 and type: 420

    d. Select cell B9 and type: 110

④ *SAVE THE MODIFIED HOTEL OCCUPANCY*

⑤ *CLOSE HOTEL OCCUPANCY*

The IF Function

The *IF function* is used to make a decision based on a comparison. If the comparison is true, one value is displayed in the cell; if the comparison is false, a second value is displayed. The IF function has three arguments and takes the form:

=IF(<comparison>, <value if true>, <value if false>)

For example, the formula

=IF(C4<E7, 10, 20)

displays a 10 if the value in C4 is less than the value in E7. If the value in C4 is greater than or equal to the value in E7, 20 is displayed.

The comparison argument of the IF function can contain one of the following *relational operators*, which are used to compare two values:

> = equal to
>
> < less than
>
> > greater than
>
> <= less than or equal to
>
> >= greater than or equal to
>
> <> not equal to

The arguments of an IF function can contain values, cell references, or calculations as shown in the following formulas:

=IF(N1<=25, 50, 100)

=IF(B2<K25, 0, B2*15%)

=IF(C9>MIN(C2:C7), C11, C14)

=IF(D22<>F25, 0, SUM(E1:E10))

Commas

Do not include commas as thousands separators when entering a large number in the comparison argument of the IF function. This causes an error because Excel expects commas to separate arguments.

Nested Functions

A nested function is created when a function is used as one of the arguments of another function. For example, =IF(SUM(A1:A10)>10,10,0) uses a nested SUM function.

Printing a Large Worksheet

A worksheet that has many columns of data is often too wide to print on a single sheet of paper. When this happens, Excel prints the worksheet on consecutive sheets starting from the leftmost column and proceeding to the right. However, changing the print orientation or the margins before printing can help fit the worksheet on fewer sheets of paper.

print orientation

Select File → Page Setup to display the Page Setup dialog box for changing the print orientation. Select the Page tab and then click Landscape to print the worksheet across the widest part of the page in *landscape orientation*. This allows more columns and fewer rows to fit on a page. *Portrait orientation* is the default and allows more rows to be printed on a page.

decreasing margins

Options in the Margins tab in the Page Setup dialog box are used to change the margins in order to fit more rows and columns on the page. Decreasing the Top and Bottom margins may allow more rows to fit on a page, and decreasing the Left and Right margins may allow more columns to fit on a page.

inserting page breaks

Page breaks control worksheet pagination. Select Insert ➜ Page Break to insert a page break before the currently selected row or column. If a single cell is selected before selecting the command, the page break is created above and to the left of that cell. A page break is indicated on the screen by a dashed line, and the effects of page breaks can be seen by previewing the worksheet. To remove a page break, select a cell in the row or column after the page break and then select Insert ➜ Remove Page Break.

TIP Preview a worksheet before printing to see if it is necessary to change the orientation, margins, or page breaks.

row and column headings

Row and column headings should be added to all printed pages to make the printout easier to read. Select File ➜ Page Setup to display the Page Setup dialog box. Select the Sheet tab and select the row and column headings check box.

printing part of a worksheet

Instead of printing an entire worksheet, part of a worksheet is printed by setting the print area. Select the range to be printed and then select File ➜ Print Area ➜ Set Print Area to set the print area. Once the print area is set, only those cells will be displayed in print preview and included in a printout. Select File ➜ Print Area ➜ Clear Print Area to clear the set print area.

Practice: PAYROLL – part 1 of 3

You will insert columns, enter formulas to calculate a company's payroll, and change the print orientation. Excel should already be started.

① *OPEN PAYROLL*

Open PAYROLL, which is an Excel data file for this text.

② *CALCULATE GROSS PAY*

Gross pay is the amount earned before any deductions and is calculated by multiplying the hours worked by the employee's rate per hour.

a. In cell E7, enter the formula: =D7*C7

b. Select cell E7 and drag the Fill handle to cell E23.

③ *CALCULATE SOCIAL SECURITY*

Social security tax is calculated by multiplying the gross pay by the social security rate, which is stored in cell B3.

a. In cell F7, enter the formula: =E7*$B$3

b. Select cell F7 and drag the Fill handle to cell F23.

c. Change the Social Security Rate to 6.0%. Excel automatically recalculates all the values in column F.

④ *CALCULATE TAXES AND NET PAY*

Taxes are calculated by multiplying the gross pay, which is stored in cell E7, by 15%.

a. In cell G7, enter the formula =E7*15%.

Net pay is the amount that the employee receives after deductions and is calculated by subtracting social security and taxes from the gross pay.

b. In cell H7, enter the formula: =E7-F7-G7

c. Select cells G7 and H7 and then drag the Fill handle to cells G23 and H23.

⑤ INSERT A COLUMN FOR THE OVERTIME HOURS

Overtime hours are hours that are worked beyond the typical work week. Often employees are paid for overtime hours at a higher hourly rate.

a. Right-click the column letter E. A menu is displayed.

b. Select Insert. A new column is inserted. Ignore the Insert Options button.

c. In cell E5, enter the label Overtime Hours. Note that the label is automatically formatted, but not entirely displayed.

d. Select cell E5 and then select Format → Cells. A dialog box is displayed.

    1. Select the Alignment tab.

    2. Select the Wrap text check box.

    3. Select OK. The label "Overtime Hours" is displayed on two lines in the cell.

e. Widen column E just enough to fit the entire word Overtime on one line and Hours below it:

	A	B	C	D	E	F
1	Payroll					
2						
3	Soc. Sec. Rate:	6.0%				
4						
5	Last Name	First Initial	Rate/Hr	Hours	Overtime Hours	Gross
6						

⑥ ENTER A FORMULA TO CALCULATE OVERTIME HOURS

An IF function is used to check to see if the Hours value stored in cell D7 is greater than 40, which is the number of hours in a work week. If the value is greater than 40, overtime hours are calculated and displayed in the cell. If not, zero is displayed. Overtime hours are calculated by subtracting 40 from the number of Hours, which is stored in cell D7.

a. In cell E7, enter the formula: =IF(D7>40, D7–40, 0). An argument tooltip is displayed as the formula is being typed. Since the Hours value is less than 40, 0.0 is displayed.

b. In cell E7, drag the Fill handle to cell E23.

⑦ INSERT A COLUMN FOR THE OVERTIME PAY

a. Right-click the column letter F. A menu is displayed.

b. Select Insert. A column is inserted and the Insert Options button is displayed.

c. Click the Insert Options button (⬚▾) and select Format Same As Right. Column G formatting is applied to column F.

d. In cell F5, enter the label Overtime Pay.

e. Select cell E5, click the Format Painter button (⬚) and then click cell F5. The wrap text format is copied to cell F5.

⑧ ENTER A FORMULA TO CALCULATE OVERTIME PAY

Overtime pay is calculated by multiplying the overtime hours by the overtime rate, which is the hourly rate multiplied by 1.5.

a. In cell F7, enter the formula: =E7*(C7 *1.5)

b. In cell F7, drag the Fill handle to cell F23.

⑨ ENTER A NEW GROSS PAY FORMULA

a. The Gross Pay formula needs to be modified to add the Overtime Pay. Modify the formula in cell G7 to =(D7*C7)+F7. Because the value in cell F7 is 0, the gross pay does not change.

b. In cell G7, drag the Fill handle to cell G23.

Check — Your worksheet should look similar to:

	A	B	C	D	E	F	G	H	I	J
1	Payroll									
2										
3	Soc. Sec. Rate:	6.0%								
4										
5	Last Name	First Initial	Rate/Hr	Hours	Overtime Hours	Overtime Pay	Gross Pay	Soc. Sec.	Taxes	Net Pay
6										
7	Alban	B.	$7.50	30.0	0.0	$0.00	$225.00	$13.50	$33.75	$177.75
8	Angulo	M.	$8.00	29.5	0.0	$0.00	$236.00	$14.16	$35.40	$186.44
9	Balto	Y.	$8.00	29.0	0.0	$0.00	$232.00	$13.92	$34.80	$183.28
10	Cruz	S.	$7.75	13.0	0.0	$0.00	$100.75	$6.05	$15.11	$79.59
11	Del Vecchio	E.	$9.00	43.5	3.5	$47.25	$438.75	$26.33	$65.81	$346.61
12	Eklund	E.	$9.50	31.0	0.0	$0.00	$294.50	$17.67	$44.18	$232.66
13	Esposito	S.	$11.75	43.5	3.5	$61.69	$572.81	$34.37	$85.92	$452.52
14	Hirsch	I.	$9.50	18.0	0.0	$0.00	$171.00	$10.26	$25.65	$135.09
15	Juarez	V.	$7.75	21.0	0.0	$0.00	$162.75	$9.77	$24.41	$128.57
16	Karas	A.	$8.00	15.0	0.0	$0.00	$120.00	$7.20	$18.00	$94.80
17	Keller-Sakis	G.	$8.50	20.0	0.0	$0.00	$170.00	$10.20	$25.50	$134.30
18	Lopez	R.	$9.00	17.0	0.0	$0.00	$153.00	$9.18	$22.95	$120.87
19	Parker	L.	$10.75	29.0	0.0	$0.00	$311.75	$18.71	$46.76	$246.28
20	Quinn	P.	$11.75	41.0	1.0	$17.63	$499.38	$29.96	$74.91	$394.51
21	Ramis	C.	$8.00	18.0	0.0	$0.00	$144.00	$8.64	$21.60	$113.76
22	Rappaport	L.	$7.75	18.0	0.0	$0.00	$139.50	$8.37	$20.93	$110.21
23	Rosen	R.	$9.50	10.0	0.0	$0.00	$95.00	$5.70	$14.25	$75.05

⑩ CHANGE PRINT ORIENTATION AND PRINT THE WORKSHEET

a. Select File ➜ Print Preview. The worksheet is displayed in the print preview.

b. On the Print Preview toolbar, click [Next]. In portrait orientation, the worksheet is displayed on two pages.

c. Select [Setup...]. A dialog box is displayed.

   1. Select the Page tab.

   2. Select Landscape.

   3. Select the Header/Footer tab.

   4. Create a header that center aligns the date and right aligns your name.

   5. Select OK. Note that in landscape orientation the worksheet is displayed on one page.

d. Select [Print...] and then OK to print a copy of the worksheet

e. Save the modified PAYROLL workbook.

⑪ CLOSE PAYROLL

Using Text in the IF Function

Text used in the IF function must have quotation marks around it. For example, the formula:

=IF(B3>=70, "Plenty", "Reorder")

displays Plenty if the value in cell B3 is greater than or equal to 70. Otherwise, Reorder is displayed. Quotation marks must surround text in a function. Cell references of a cell storing a label can also be used in the IF function. For example, if Plenty is stored in cell E1 and Reorder in cell E2, then the formula =IF(B3>=70, E1, E2) produces the same result as the formula shown above.

To check to see if a cell's contents are empty, two adjacent quotation marks can be used. For example, =IF(B20="", "Yes", "No") displays Yes if the cell contents are empty and No if there is data in the cell. Two adjacent quotation marks can also be used to display nothing in a cell. For example, =IF(B3>=70, "", "Reorder") displays a blank cell if the value in cell B3 is greater than or equal to 70, otherwise Reorder is displayed.

Text can also be used in the comparison part of the IF function. When compared, the alphabetical order of the text is determined. For example, the following formula displays True because apple comes before orange alphabetically:

=IF("apple"<"orange", "True", "False")

Cells that store labels can also be compared. If apple is stored in cell B3 and orange is stored in cell B5, the formula =IF(B3<B5, B3, B5) displays apple.

> ### The COUNTIF Function
>
> The COUNTIF function is used to calculate how many cells meet a certain condition. For example, the formula =COUNTIF(D1:D50, "Reorder") determines how many cells in the range D1 through D50 contain the label Reorder.

Practice: HOTEL OCCUPANCY — part 3 of 3

You will add a formula that contains an IF function to determine the type of room that was rented. Excel should already be started.

① *OPEN HOTEL OCCUPANCY*

② *INSERT A COLUMN*
   a. Right-click the column letter B. A menu is displayed.
   b. Select Insert. A column is inserted and the Rate column moves to the right to accommodate the newly inserted column. Ignore the Insert Options button.
   c. Select cell B3, type the label Room Type and center align the label.

③ *ENTER FORMULAS TO DETERMINE THE TYPE OF ROOM RENTED*

   If the room rate is greater than or equal to $179.00, the room is considered a suite. If the room rate is less than $179.00, the room is considered a standard room.

   a. In cell B4, enter the formula =IF(C4>=179, "Suite", "Standard")
   b. Select cell B4, drag the Fill handle to cell B24, and center align the labels.
   c. Move the "Average Daily Rate" label from cell A25 to cell B25.

④ *SAVE, PRINT, AND THEN CLOSE THE MODIFIED HOTEL OCCUPANCY*

Amortization Tables and the PMT Function

 *installment loan*

 principal

A useful application of a worksheet is an amortization table. *Amortization* is a method for computing equal periodic payments for an *installment loan*. Car loans and mortgages are often installment loans. Each installment, or payment, is the same and consists of two parts: a portion to pay interest due on the principal for that period and the remainder which reduces the principal. The *principal* is the amount of money owed and it decreases with each payment made.

An *amortization table* displays the interest and principal amounts for each payment of an installment loan. For example, the monthly payment on a 30 year loan of $100,000 borrowed at 6% interest (0.5% per month) is $599.55. In the first payment, $500.00 pays the interest due (0.5% x $100,000) and $99.55 goes to reduce principal ($599.55 – $500.00). In the next payment, $499.50 pays the interest due and $100.05 goes to reduce principal. As payments are made, the interest due decreases because there is less principal to charge interest on. In the final payment, $2.98 pays the interest due and $596.57 pays off the principal.

The PMT function is used to calculate the equal periodic payment for an installment loan. The PMT function takes the form:

=PMT(<rate>, <term>, <principal>)

<rate> is the interest rate per period, <term> is the total number of payments to be made, and <principal> is the amount borrowed. For example, the PMT function would be used to determine the monthly payment on a mortgage. The formula below calculates the monthly payments on a 30-year, $100,000 loan with an annual interest rate of 6%:

=PMT(6%/12, 360, –100000)

Since the payments are made monthly, the interest rate must also be computed monthly by dividing the annual interest rate of 6% by 12. The number of payments is 360, 30 years x 12 months. The principal is negative because it is the amount borrowed and it does not include a dollar sign or commas. This formula computes the monthly payment as $599.55.

Practice: LOAN

You will complete an amortization table. Excel should be started if it is not already displayed.

① *OPEN LOAN*

Open LOAN, which is an Excel data file for this text. The displayed worksheet is a partially completed amortization table.

② *ENTER THE LOAN'S INFORMATION*

In order to purchase a house, a loan called a mortgage is usually obtained.

a. In cell B3, enter the yearly interest rate: 7%

b. In cell B4, enter the number of payments: 360 (30 years x 12 monthly payments)

c. In cell B5, enter the principal: $200,000

③ CALCULATE THE MONTHLY PAYMENT

In cell B7, enter the formula: =PMT(B3/12, B4, –B5)

The division by 12 is needed to convert the yearly interest rate in cell B3 to a monthly value. $1,330.60 is displayed.

④ CALCULATE TOTAL PAID AND TOTAL INTEREST

a. In cell B9, enter the formula: =B4*B7

This formula computes the total paid for the loan, $479,017.80, including principal and interest.

b. In cell B10, enter the formula: =B9–B5. The total interest paid over the 30 years, $279,017.80 is displayed:

	A	B
1	Loan Amortization Table	
2		
3	Interest rate =	7%
4	Number of payments =	360
5	Principal =	$200,000.00
6		
7	Monthly payment =	$1,330.60
8		
9	Total paid =	$479,017.80
10	Total interest =	$279,017.80

⑤ ENTER THE FIRST PAYMENT DATA

a. In cell A13, enter: 1

b. In cell B13, enter: =B5

c. In cell C13, enter the formula: =B13*($B$3/12)

This formula calculates one month's interest on the loan. $1,166.67, which is 1% (7%/12) of the principal, is displayed. The cell reference B3 is an absolute cell reference because the interest rate will be the same for each payment.

d. In cell D13, enter the formula: =IF(C13<0.01, 0, $B$7–C13)

This formula calculates the amount of the payment which is applied to the principal, $163.94. If the value in cell C13 is less than 0.01 (less than a penny), then 0 is displayed. An IF function is used to avoid problems due to rounding.

e. In cell E13, enter the formula: =B13–D13. The new principal owed is displayed.

⑥ ENTER FORMULAS FOR THE SECOND PAYMENT

a. In cell A14, enter the formula: =A13+1

b. In cell B14, enter: =E13

c. Copy the formulas in cells C13 through E13 to cells C14 through E14:

	A	B	C	D	E
1	Loan Amortization Table				
2					
3	Interest rate =	7%			
4	Number of payments =	360			
5	Principal =	$200,000.00			
6					
7	Monthly payment =	$1,330.60			
8					
9	Total paid =	$479,017.80			
10	Total interest =	$279,017.80			
11					
12	Payment	Principal	Pay to Interest	Pay to Principal	Principal Owed
13	1	$200,000.00	$1,166.67	$163.94	$199,836.06
14	2	$199,836.06	$1,165.71	$164.89	$199,671.17

⑦ COMPLETE THE TABLE

Copy the formulas in cells A14 through E14 into cells A15 through E372. The principal owed is $0.00 in cell E372, which indicates the loan has been paid in full.

⑧ ADD A HEADER AND FOOTER AND PRINT A PORTION OF THE WORKSHEET

a. Create a header that center aligns the date and right aligns your name.

b. Select cells A1 through E15.

c. Select File → Print Area → Set Print Area. Note the dashed lines around the cells indicating the print area.

d. Click anywhere to remove the selection.

e. Print preview the worksheet. Note that only the cells designated as the print area are displayed.

f. Save the modified LOAN and then print the worksheet.

g. Select File → Print Area → Clear Print Area. The print area is now set to the entire worksheet.

⑨ CREATE AN AUTO LOAN MODEL

a. In cell B3, enter: 10%

b. The car loan is a 5 year loan; therefore, the number of monthly payments will be 5 x 12. In cell B4, enter: 60

c. In cell B5, enter: $12,000

d. Scroll down to row 72 which contains the last payment. The worksheet can easily model loans with less than 360 payments.

e. Save the modified LOAN.

⑩ ENTER YOUR OWN VALUES INTO THE LOAN WORKSHEET

a. Create different loan scenarios by changing the rate, term, and principal of the LOAN worksheet to any values you like. Change the number of payments to see how that affects the interest paid.

b. Select File → Close. Click No in the dialog box when prompted to save the file. The only change that is not saved is the experimenting with values in step 10 (a).

Using Multiple Sheets

> ### Sheet Tab Color
>
> The sheet tab color can be changed to color-code related sheets. To change the sheet tab color, right-click the tab and select Tab Color from the menu. A tab color can then be selected from the Format Tab Color dialog box.

Multiple sheets within a workbook can be used to organize, store, and link related information. For example, a workbook could contain a sheet for the 2004 Sales data, a sheet for the 2005 Sales data, and a sheet for the 2006 Forecast:

Click the appropriate tab at the bottom of the Excel window to make a sheet active. In the workbook shown above, 2004 Sales is the active sheet. Sheets in the worksheet shown have been renamed. By default, sheets are named Sheet1, Sheet2, and Sheet3. To rename a sheet, double-click the sheet tab, type a new sheet name, and then press Enter.

The number of worksheets in a workbook can be changed. To insert a new sheet in front of the active sheet, select Insert → Worksheet. To delete a worksheet, right-click the sheet and select Delete from the menu. Sheet order can be changed by dragging a sheet tab to a new location within the sheet tabs.

Headers, footers, and orientation can be specified for each sheet. For example, Sheet1 can be set up to print in portrait orientation and Sheet2 in landscape orientation. The Page Setup dialog box is used to select options for the active sheet.

printing sheets

The Print dialog box is used to specify which sheets are printed. Select Active sheet(s) and then OK or click the Print button on the toolbar to print only the active sheet. Select Entire workbook to print all the sheets in the workbook.

> ### Scrolling Sheets
>
> Use the tab scrollling buttons to access sheets in a workbook that are not displayed:
>
> |◄ ◄ ► ►|

Copying and Moving Data Between Sheets

Data can copied and moved between sheets. The Cut (✂), Copy (📋), and Paste (📋▾) commands from the Edit menu are used to move and duplicate data.

1. Select the *source*, which is the cell or range to be copied.

2. Select Cut or Copy. The source displays a moving dashed border.

3. Click the sheet tab of the worksheet that is to receive the copied data.

4. Select the *destination*, which is the upper-left cell of the range where the data is to be pasted.

5. Select Paste. The data as well as the source formatting is pasted and the Paste Options button (📋) is displayed. Any pre-existing cell contents are replaced with the pasted data. Press the Esc key to remove the dashed border.

By default, pasted data is *static*, which means it does not change when the source data changes. To link pasted data to the source data, click the Paste Options button (📋) and select Link Cells:

> ### Column Widths
>
> When data is copied between sheets, it is possible to retain the column width of the source data. Click the Paste Options button and select Keep Source Columns Widths.

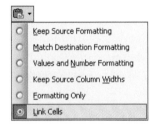

*Linked cell*s contain a reference to the original data and will automatically update if the source data changes.

Practice: CAR SALES

You will reference data between three sheets in a workbook. Excel should be already be started.

① *OPEN CAR SALES*

Open CAR SALES, which is an Excel data file for this text. This workbook contains data in three sheets: New Car Sales, Sheet2, and Used Car Sales. The Total Sales column in the New Car Sales sheet contains formulas.

② *VIEW THE DIFFERENT SHEETS IN THE WORKBOOK*

a. Click the Sheet2 tab. The second sheet in the workbook is displayed.

b. Click the Used Car Sales tab. The third sheet in the workbook is displayed.

③ *CHANGE THE ORDER OF THE SHEETS*

Drag the Used Car Sales tab to the left until a solid triangle is shown to the left of the Sheet2 tab:

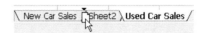

The sheet order is changed.

④ *RENAME SHEET2*

a. Double-click the Sheet2 tab.

b. Type Total Sales and then press Enter.

⑤ *LINK LABELS TO THE TOTAL SALES SHEET*

a. Display the New Car Sales sheet.

b. Select cells A4 through A12.

c. Select Edit → Copy.

d. Display the Total Sales sheet.

e. Select cell A4.

f. Select Edit → Paste. The Paste Options button (📋) is displayed.

g. Click the Paste Options button. A list of options is displayed.

h. Select Link Cells.

i. Click cell A4. Note that ='New Car Sales'!A4 is displayed on the Formula bar.

j. Display the New Car Sales sheet and then press Esc. The moving dashed line is removed.

k. In the New Car Sales sheet, copy cell E3 and then paste a copy into cell B3 in the Total Sales sheet. Link the data.

l. In the Used Car Sales sheet, copy cells A4 through A14 and then paste a copy into cells A13 through A23 in the Total Sales sheet. Link the data.

Check — The Total Sales sheet should look similar to:

	A	B	C	D
1	**Total Car Sales**			
2				
3		**Total Sales**		
4	Cherisma			
5	Sun			
6	Washington			
7	Alfred			
8	Delva			
9	Heydt			
10	Tullos			
11	Zappa			
12	Bass			
13	King			
14	Zelaya			
15	Antonie			
16	Hinton			
17	Bunnis			
18	Nudelman			
19	Dixon			
20	Bradley			
21	Lamons			
22	Fleuridor			
23	Dearborn			
24				
25				

⑥ MODIFY LABELS

a. Display the New Car Sales sheet.

b. Select cell A12.

c. Edit the cell contents so that the name is: Base

d. Display the Total Sales sheet. In cell A12 the cell contents have been automatically updated because the cell was linked to cell A12 in the New Car Sales sheet.

⑦ TOTAL THE SALES FOR ALL EMPLOYEES

a. Select cell B4 and type an equal sign (=).

b. Display the New Car Sales sheet. Note that ='New Car Sales'! is displayed in the Formula bar.

c. Click cell E4. The Formula bar now displays ='New Car Sales'!E4.

d. Click the Enter button. The Total Sales sheet is displayed and cell B4 displays $157,774.

e. Select cell B4 and drag the Fill handle to cell B12.

f. Select cell B13 and type an equal sign (=).

g. Display the Used Car Sales sheet and click cell E4 and press Enter. The Total Sales sheet is displayed and cell B13 displays $280,883.

h. Select cell B13 and drag the Fill handle to cell B23.

i. In cell A24, enter the label Total and format the label as right align and bold.

j. In cell B24, enter a formula to calculate the total sales for all employees.

⑧ MODIFY SALES DATA

a. In the New Car Sales sheet, select cell D4 and change the value to 143,000. The total sales in cell E4 automatically recalculates.

b. Display the Total Sales sheet. Note the total sales for Cherisma automatically updated in cell B4.

⑨ SET PRINT OPTIONS

    a. Display the Total Sales sheet, then select File ➤ Page Setup. A dialog box is displayed.

        1. Select the Sheet tab if those options are not already displayed.

        2. Select the Gridlines check box.

        3. Select the Row and column headings check box.

        4. Select the Header/Footer tab and then use the Header list to create a header with the sheet name.

        5. Create a footer that right aligns your name.

        6. Select OK.

    b. For the New Car Sales and Used Car Sales sheets, create a header that center aligns the sheet name and a footer that right aligns your name.

⑩ SAVE, PRINT, AND THEN CLOSE THE MODIFIED CAR SALES

    a. Save the modified CAR SALES.

    b. Select File ➤ Print. A dialog box is displayed.

    c. In the Print what section of the dialog box, select Entire workbook:

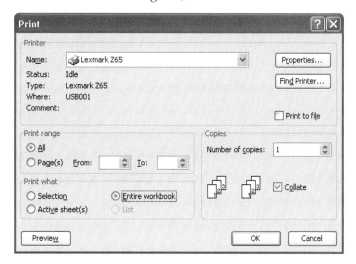

    d. Select OK. All three sheets in the workbook are printed. Note that only the Total Sales sheet contains gridlines and row and column headings.

    e. Close CAR SALES.

Chapter Summary

This chapter explained how worksheets can be used to answer "What If?" questions. A What If question asks how changing data will impact results.

Excel contains built-in functions used to perform common calculations. Functions include SUM, AVERAGE, MIN, MAX, and ROUND. The Insert Function dialog box is used to insert a function name into a formula. Absolute cell references are used in formulas so that the cell reference does not change when copied. An invalid formula displays an error value and the Trace Error button, which is clicked to display the error and a list of options.

Excel data can be sorted in ascending or descending order. Rows and columns can be inserted between data in a worksheet.

The IF function is used to make a decision based on a comparison. The arguments of an IF function can contain values, cell references, calculations, or text.

The print orientation and margins can be changed to help fit the worksheet on a single printed page. Page breaks control how a worksheet is divided into pages. Part of a worksheet is printed by setting a print area.

Multiple sheets within a workbook are used to organize, store, and link related information.

Absolute Cell Reference A cell reference that does not change when copied because a dollar sign has been placed in front of both the column letter and row number, such as $A$5.

Alphabetical Order of sorted text in ascending order from A to Z.

Amortization A method for computing equal periodic payments for an installment loan.

Amortization table Displays the interest and principal amounts for each payment of an installment loan.

Arguments The data required by a function.

Ascending Increasing in value from low to high, such as alphabetical order.

AVERAGE Function that adds the values in a range of cells and then divides the result by the number of cells in the range.

Chronological Order of sorted times or dates in ascending order.

Descending Decreasing in value from high to low.

Function Performs a calculation that results in a single value.

IF function Function that is used to make a decision based on a comparison.

Installment loan Loan that is repaid in a series of periodic payments.

Key sort column The column that contains the values that a sort is based on.

Landscape orientation A print orientation that prints a worksheet across the widest part of the page.

Linked Data that is connected to the source cell and will automatically update if the source cell is changed.

MAX Function that displays the largest value in a range of cells.

MIN Function that displays the smallest value in a range of cells.

PMT Function that calculates the periodic payment for an installment loan.

Portrait orientation The default print orientation that allows more rows to be printed on a page.

Principal The amount of money owed on a loan.

Relational operators Used to compare two values. Operators include =, <, >, <=, >=, <>.

ROUND function Changes a value by rounding it to a specific number of decimal places.

Sorting Arranging rows of data in a specified order.

Spreadsheet model A worksheet containing data relating to a particular situation.

Static Copied data that is not connected to the source data.

SUM Function that adds the values in a range of cells.

What-if analysis The process of making decisions using a spreadsheet model.

What If question A question that is answered using a worksheet model.

Excel Commands and Buttons

Σ ▾ AutoSum button Creates a formula with the SUM function. The AutoSum button arrow displays a list of other functions that can be used in formulas. Found on the toolbar.

Clear Print Area command Clears a set print area. Found in File → Print Area.

Delete command Removes a sheet from the workbook. Found in the menu displayed by right-clicking a sheet tab.

Insert command Inserts a row or column. Found in the menu displayed by right-clicking a row number or column letter.

ƒx Insert Function button Displays a dialog box used to insert a function into a formula. Found on the toolbar.

◆ ▾ Insert Options button Displayed when a new row or column is inserted.

Page Break command Inserts a page break before the currently selected row or column. Found in the Insert menu.

Page Setup command Displays a dialog box with options for printing gridlines and row and column headings and creating a header or footer. Found in the File menu.

⬚ Paste Options button Displayed when contents of the Clipboard are placed in cells. Used to link cells between sheets.

Remove Page Break command Removes a page break. Found in the Insert menu.

Set Print Area command Designates a specific range of cells to be printed. Found in File → Print Area.

⬚↓ Sort Ascending button Places selected rows of data in order from low to high based on the column that was selected first. Found on the toolbar.

Sort command Displays a dialog box used to sort data. Found in the Data menu.

⬚↓ Sort Descending button Places selected rows of data in order from high to low based on the column that was selected first. Found on the toolbar.

◈ Trace Error button Displays a list of options for correcting an error. Displayed when clicking a cell that contains an error.

Worksheet command Inserts a new sheet in front of the active sheet. Found in the Insert menu.

1. a) What does a "What If?" question ask?
   b) What is a spreadsheet model?

2. List two other "What If?" questions that can be answered using the Charity Fundraiser workbook.

3. a) What is a function?
   b) What does a function require to perform a calculation?

4. Using functions, write a formula to calculate:
   a) the sum of the values stored in cells B4, B5, B6, and B7.
   b) the sum of the values stored in cells B4, C4, D4, and E4.
   c) the average of the values stored in the column of cells D7 through D35.
   d) the average of the values stored in the row of cells F3 through J3.
   e) the maximum value stored in the range of cells D4 through Y5.
   f) the minimum value stored in the range of cells C1 through C9.

5. What is the difference between a relative cell reference and an absolute cell reference?

6. List the steps required to create a formula in cell G5 that multiplies the value in cell F5 with the value in cell B1 so that when the formula is copied, the cell reference to B1 remains constant.

7. List two advantages of using the Insert Function dialog box to insert the name of a function in a formula instead of typing the formula.

8. Why is it important to check the range placed in the SUM function when using the AutoSum button?

9. Describe two common error values.

10. a) Describe two common formula errors.
    b) List the steps required to remove the green triangle from a cell that displays a result and the formula does not contain an error.

11. Using functions, write a formula to calculate:
    a) the sum of the values in cells C5, C6, C7, C8, and C9 rounded to 2 decimal places.
    b) the sum of the values in cells B5, C5, D5, and E5 rounded to the nearest integer.
    c) the average of the values in cells A1, A2, A3, B1, B2, and B3 rounded to 1 decimal place.

12. a) List the steps required to sort the data in a workbook in descending order based on the data in column C.
    b) What is the key sort column?

13. List the step required to insert a column between column A and column B.

14. List the step required to delete row 8.

15. a) What formatting does a newly inserted row contain?
    b) What formatting does a newly inserted column contain?

16. The formula =SUM(C3:C22) is used to sum the values in cells C3 through C22.
    a) If a row is inserted directly above row 20, what must be done in order to include the new cell in the sum?
    b) If a row is inserted directly above row 24, what must be done to include the new cell in the sum?
    c) If row 20 is deleted, what must be done to the formula so that the deleted cell is no longer in the range?

17. What will be displayed by the following formulas if cell D4 stores a value of 30 and cell E7 stores a value of −12?
    a) =IF(D4<=E7, 10, 20)
    b) =IF(E7*D4<-5, E7, D4)
    c) =IF(D4−42=E7, D4*2, E7*3)

18. Using functions, write a formula to:
    a) display 50 if the value stored in D20 equals the value in C70, or 25 if they are not equal.
    b) display the value in B40 if the sum of the range of cells C20 to C30 exceeds 1000, otherwise display a 0.
    c) display the value of R20*10 if R20 is less than 30, otherwise display the value in R20.

19 a) List the steps required to print a worksheet across the widest part of the paper.
    b) What can be decreased in order to fit more rows and columns on a printout?
    c) What can be used to control how a worksheet is divided into pages?
    d) List the steps required to print only the values displayed in the cell range A3:D17.
    e) List the steps required to print the entire worksheet after a print area was previously set.

20. Write formulas using the IF function for each of the following:
    a) if B3 is less than or equal to C12 display Low; if greater than, display High.
    b) if A5 is equal to Z47 display Jonathan; if not equal to, display Judith.
    c) if cell C6 is empty, display the contents of cell D3, otherwise display New Student.

21. Briefly explain what an amortization table is and the terminology associated with it.

22. a) How much interest is paid in the first month of a loan of $5,000 borrowed for 5 years at 12% per year interest?
    b) Write the PMT function used to calculate the monthly payments on the above loan.

23. a) How is a sheet made active?
    b) List the steps required to rename Sheet1 to Jan Sales.
    c) Can a workbook contain more than three sheets?
    d) List the step required to insert a new worksheet.
    e) How is the sheet order changed?

24. List the step required to print all the sheets in a workbook at one time.

25. List the steps required to print Sheet1 in landscape orientation and Sheet2 in portrait orientation.

26. List the steps required to copy or move data between sheets in a workbook.

27. List the steps required to reference cell B5 on Sheet1 and multiply its value by 3.6 in a formula stored in cell C4 on Sheet2.

28. a) What is the difference between pasting data and linking data?
    b) List the steps required to link cell A25 on Sheet2 to cell A20 on Sheet1.

True/False

29. Determine if each of the following are true or false. If false, explain why.
    a) The SUM function ignores cells that contain text when their cell references are included as arguments. T
    b) An absolute cell reference changes when copied. F
    c) The range placed in the SUM function when the AutoSum button is clicked is always correct. F
    d) A #### error value indicates the formula is trying to divide by zero. F
    e) When a formula produces a result and a green triangle in the cell, this indicates a correct formula. F
    f) There is no difference between formatting and rounding. F
    g) The key sort column can be any column with data on the worksheet. T
    h) When cells are inserted, Excel automatically changes the cell references in any affected formulas. T
    i) The arguments of an IF function can only contain values. T
    j) The location of page breaks in a worksheet can be changed. T
    k) Clearing a print area sets the entire worksheet as the print area. T
    l) The principal of a loan decreases each time a payment is made. Interest
    m) Sheet1 can print a different header than Sheet2. T
    n) Pasted data will automatically update if the source cell is changed. F

Exercise 1 ——————————————————————————Dive Log

Researchers of a coral reef study want to use a worksheet to computerize their scuba diving log.

a) Create a new workbook.

b) Enter the data and apply formatting as shown below:

	A	B	C	D	E
1	Date	Depth (m)	Duration (min)	Water Temp (Celsius)	Visibility (m)
2					
3	5/8/2006	10	60	26	10
4	5/10/2006	18	45	25	12
5	5/11/2006	13	50	27	9
6	5/13/2006	27	15	23	10
7	5/14/2006	11	53	28	11

c) Save the workbook naming it Dive Log.

d) In cell A8, enter the label Average and then format the label as right align and italic. Enter formulas that use a function to average the depth and duration of all five dives.

e) Modify the average depth and duration formulas to use a function to round the results to 0 decimal places.

f) Two dives were not recorded. Insert the new data shown below into the worksheet so that the dates remain in chronological order:

Date	Depth (m)	Duration (min)	Water Temp (Celsius)	Visibility (m)
5/9/2006	15	45	28	11
5/12/2006	20	40	24	9

g) In rows 11 and 12, enter formulas that use functions to calculate:

   • the maximum depth of the dives and the maximum duration of the dives
   • the minimum depth of the dives and the minimum duration of the dives

   Include appropriate labels and proper formatting.

h) Create a header that right aligns your name and a footer that center aligns the date. Add gridlines and row and column headings.

i) Save the modified Dive Log and print a copy.

j) Display the formulas in the cells instead of values. Change the column widths as necessary so that the formulas are completely displayed. Print a copy.

The owner of Pizza Palace wants to use a worksheet to keep track of expenses.

a) Create a new workbook.

b) Enter the data and apply formatting as shown below:

	A	B	C	D
1	Pizza Palace			
2	Expenses per Pizza			
3				
4	Ingredients	Everything	Vegetarian	Cheese
5				
6	Dough	$1.25	$1.25	$1.25
7	Cheese	$1.50	$1.50	$1.50
8	Sauce	$0.50	$0.50	$0.50
9	Pepperoni	$0.75	$0.00	$0.00
10	Sausage	$1.00	$0.00	$0.00
11	Onion	$0.15	$0.15	$0.00
12	Mushroom	$0.35	$0.35	$0.00
13	Green Pepper	$0.40	$0.40	$0.00
14				

c) Save the workbook naming it Pizza Palace.

d) In cell A14, enter the label Cost of Pizza and then format the label as right align and italic. Enter formulas that use a function to calculate the total cost of each pizza type.

e) Pepperoni pizza needs to be added to the worksheet between the Vegetarian and Cheese pizza columns. Enter an appropriate column heading and values for the pepperoni pizza. Copy the cost of pizza formula for the pepperoni pizza into cell D14.

f) The menu price for each pizza needs to be added to the worksheet in row 15. When the cost of pizza is less than or equal to $4.00 the price is one and a half (1.5) times the cost, and it is two (2) times the cost when it is greater than $4.00. Enter formulas that use a function and cell references to calculate the menu price of the pizzas. Include an appropriate label and proper formatting.

g) In cell A16, enter the label Profit and then format the label as right align and italic. Enter formulas that calculate the profit from each pizza type by subtracting the total cost of each type of pizza from the menu price.

h) Change the price of Cheese from $1.50 to $2.00 for each pizza type and change the price of Dough from $1.25 to $1.50. How does this affect the profit?

i) Create a header that right aligns your name and a footer that center aligns the date. Add gridlines and row and column headings.

j) Save the modified Pizza Palace and print a copy.

k) Display the formulas in the cells instead of values. Change the column widths as necessary so that the formulas are completely displayed. Print a copy.

Exercise 3 ——————————————————————— SCHOOL LOAN

The SCHOOL LOAN workbook contains a loan amortization table. Open SCHOOL LOAN, which is an Excel data file for this text, and answer the following What If? questions:

a) The tuition and room/board fees for one year at the state university are $10,250. The loan options are:

- 6% interest for a three year loan
- 7% interest for a five year loan
- 8% interest for a ten year loan

In cells B3, B4, and B5, enter the appropriate data for the three-year loan at 6%.

b) In cell B7, enter a formula that uses the PMT function with cell references to calculate the periodic payment for the three year loan option.

c) In cells B9 and B10, enter formulas that calculate the total amount paid and the total interest paid.

d) In cells C3, C4, and C5, enter the appropriate data for the three year loan option and calculate the monthly payment, total amount paid, and total interest paid.

e) In cells D3, D4, and D5, enter the appropriate data for the ten year loan option and calculate the monthly payment, total amount paid, and total interest paid.

f) Create a header that right aligns your name and a footer that center aligns the date.

g) Save the modified SCHOOL LOAN and print a copy.

h) Display the formulas in the cells instead of values. Change the column widths as necessary so that the formulas are completely displayed. Print a copy.

Exercise 4 ——————————————————————— Car Loan

A loan amortization table can be used for any kind of loan, including car loans. Amortization tables can also be combined with What If? questions to help make decisions when purchasing a new car.

a) Create a new workbook.

b) Enter the data and apply formatting as shown below:

	A	B	C	D	E
1	New Car Loan Amortization Table				
2					
3		3 Year Loan	3 Year Loan	5 Year Loan	5 Year Loan
4					
5	Interest rate =	7%	10%	7%	10%
6	Number of payments =	36	36	60	60
7	Principal =				
8					
9	Monthly payment =				
10					
11	Total paid =				
12	Total interest =				
13					
14					

c) Save the workbook naming it Car Loan.

d) Using the Internet or a newspaper, find an advertisement for a new car.

e) Enter the price of the car in the ad as the principal of the car loan in row 7 of the worksheet.

f) In row 9, enter formulas that use the PMT function with cell references to calculate the periodic payment for the different loan interest rates and payment periods.

g) In row 11, enter formulas that use cell references to calculate the total amount paid (number of payments multiplied by the monthly payment).

h) In row 12, enter formulas that use cell references to calculate the total interest paid (total amount paid minus the principal).

i) Create a header that right aligns your name and a footer that center aligns the date. Add gridlines and row and column headings.

j) Save the modified Car Loan and print a copy.

k) Display the formulas in the cells instead of values. Change the column widths as necessary so that the formulas are completely displayed. Print a copy.

Exercise 5 ———————————————————— Credit

A cash advance is borrowing money with a credit card. This is usually an expensive method of borrowing money and is best used for only short periods of time or not at all. Banks typically loan money at rates between 5% and 15%. Cash advances are based on the credit card APR (annual percentage rate), which is typically 15% or higher.

a) Create a new workbook that stores the amount of money to borrow, the number of months to pay back the borrowed money, and the annual interest rate. Include labels and format cells appropriately.

b) To compare the cost of borrowing, include columns for annual interest rates ranging from 5% to 25% in increments of 5%.

c) Add formulas that calculate the monthly payment, total amount paid, and total interest paid for each of the different interest rates.

d) Create new scenarios by changing the amount borrowed and the length of time.

e) Create a header that right aligns your name and a footer that center aligns the date. Add gridlines and row and column headings.

f) Save the workbook naming it Credit and print a copy.

Exercise 6 ——————Stock Categories, Diversified Stock Portfolio, Investor Proposal, Portfolio Analysis

An educated investment in the stock market has historically provided the highest rate of return on a long-term investment compared to other investment options, such as a savings account. Stocks give an investor a portion, or *share*, of ownership in publicly held companies. Stocks can provide income as well as a long-term investment, and are categorized as:

- **Income stocks** pay dividends that provide income. *Dividends* are money paid annually to investors and are calculated by multiplying a stock's dividend (the DIV amount on a stock table) by the number of shares owned.

- **Blue-chip stocks** are companies that are considered solid, reliable, and having sustained growth. They provide consistent, reliable growth with regular, but small dividends.

- **Growth stocks** are shares of young, entrepreneurial companies that are experiencing a fast rate of growth. Growth stocks show considerable rise in stock price over a period of several months or years. These stocks normally do not pay dividends. Although sometimes riskier than other types of stock, growth stocks offer more potential for appreciation.

- **Cyclical stocks** are shares of companies that are affected by economic trends. The price of these stocks tend to go down in a recession and up during economic booms.

- **Defensive stocks (non-cyclical)** are shares of companies that are considered recession-resistant. These companies often provide staples, which will be purchased regardless of how the economy is doing. These stocks are least affected by economic cycles and typically maintain their value regardless of the economic outlook.

a) Ask a parent or another adult for input on how the stock from companies they know would be categorized. Discuss at least ten different companies.

Use Word to create a memo to your teacher regarding the information gathered from the adult you met with. Include the name of the adult you met with in the subject line. List the companies discussed and briefly explain how each was categorized and why. Save the memo naming it Stock Categories.

b) The stock market is sometimes referred to as being either a "bull market" or a "bear market." A *bull market* is when stocks are considered to be generally rising in value. In a *bear market*, stocks are considered to be generally falling in price. When building a stock portfolio, different types of stock should be added. Having a mix of income, blue-chip, and defensive stocks along with growth and cyclical stocks will diversify a portfolio and may help the overall performance of the portfolio during a bear market. *Portfolio* refers to a set of investments owned by an individual.

A company's Web site typically includes a link called "Company" or "Investor Information" that provides the information you will need. Be sure to also check the bottom navigation bar for links to investor information. Many sites can also be searched for investor information.

Create a workbook named Diversified Stock Portfolio to keep track of an investment of 100 shares from ten different companies. Include the company name and the stock symbol (called the *ticker symbol*). Be sure to create a diversified portfolio.

c) Use Word to create a memo to an investor that includes the Diversified Stock Portfolio spreadsheet data. Briefly explain to the investor why you feel the selected stocks create a diversified portfolio. In a separate paragraph, explain why the income, blue-chip, and defensive stocks hedge against a downturn in the portfolio value during a bear market. Save the document naming it Investor Proposal and then print a copy.

d) One investment strategy for choosing stocks is *fundamental analysis*, which uses actual company data to determine the value of a stock and its potential for growth. A company's annual report provides data about its financial situation and all traded companies are required to make it publicly available. The *annual report* includes a balance sheet, which shows assets, liabilities, and net worth for the past year. *Net worth* is also called the stockholder's equity. The figures in the balance sheet can be used to calculate:

- **Current Ratio** Also called Working Capital Ratio. Current Ratio is assets divided by liabilities. This measure determines if a company can meet financial obligations. A value between 1.2 and 2.0 is considered good. Less than 1 means assets cannot cover liabilities. A value greater than 2 means the company may not be reinvesting excess cash or has too much inventory.

- **Quick Ratio** Also called the Acid Test Ratio. Quick Ratio is assets minus inventories divided by liabilities. This measure determines if a company can meet short-term liability, such as employee salaries. A value greater than 1 is considered good.

Fundamental analysis also includes considering the P/E, which is listed for each stock in a newspaper stock table or by viewing a stock quote on the Internet:

- **P/E** Price to Earnings ratio. P/E is stock price divided by the trailing EPS. *Trailing EPS* is a company's earnings for the last four quarters divided by the number of shares outstanding. P/E can indicate the profitability of a company and is used to value a stock. The P/E is generally between 15 and 25. A lower P/E can mean a stock may be undervalued. However, a single P/E should not be used to value a stock. One way to use the P/E is to compare P/E ratios among companies in the same industry. Values for P/E ratios by industry can be found on the Internet.

Modify the Diversified Stock Portfolio workbook to include a new worksheet named Analysis. Add each of the stocks from Sheet1, grouped by industry where possible. For each stock, create formulas that calculate the Current Ratio and Quick Ratio. Use the Internet to find each company's annual report. Annual reports are usually PDF documents within an Investor link at a company Web site. Look for the Balance Sheet within the report, and then look for total current assets and total current liabilities for calculating the Current Ratio and Quick Ratio. For each stock, list its P/E, which can be found in the annual report or through a stock quote on the Internet.

e) Use Word to create a letter to an investor that includes the data from the Analysis sheet in the Diversified Stock Portfolio workbook. Explain to the investor what the ratios mean for each stock. Where possible compare the stock P/E ratios. In a separate paragraph, make recommendations to the investor about which stocks to keep and which to sell for a portfolio that represents a long-term investment. Save the document naming it Portfolio Analysis and then print a copy.

Exercise 7 ———————————————Club Treasurer

The role of a *club treasurer* is to manage the finances of a club or organization. One task of the treasurer is to keep a record of all credit card transactions to compare with bank statements which are usually received at the end of the month. Computer-related issues, such as identity theft and online credit card fraud, have increased the importance of tracking all credit card transactions.

    a) Create a new workbook.

    b) Enter the data and apply formatting as shown below:

	A	B	C	D	E	F
1	Credit Card Transactions					
2	Date	Description of Transaction	Debit	Credit	Balance	
3	1/1/2006	Outstanding Balance			$1,200.50	
4	1/1/2006	Office Chair	$145.00			
5	1/2/2006	Interest/Service Charges	$15.16			
6	1/2/2006	December Payment		$45.00		
7	1/5/2006	Van Rental	$212.00			
8	1/7/2006	Holiday Inn Express	$445.00			
9	1/9/2006	Refreshments for September Meeting	$124.50			
10	1/29/2006	Interest/Service Charges	$45.50			
11	1/29/2006	January Payment		$500.00		
12						
13						

    c) Save the workbook naming it Club Treasurer.

    d) In column E, enter formulas that use cell references to calculate the balance after each transaction. To calculate the balance, subtract the debits from the previous balance and add the credits to previous balance.

    e) Create a header that right aligns your name and a footer that center aligns the text Club Treasurer.

    f) Save the modified Club Treasurer and print a copy.

    g) Display the formulas in the cells instead of the values. Change the column width as necessary so that the formulas are completely display. Print a copy.

Exercise 8 ———————————————Depreciation Calculator

Businesses must keep track of their assets in order to portray a realistic net worth. Assets are material items with considerable value, such as computers, machinery, and vehicles. Because assets lose value over time, a business must depreciate assets in order to determine net worth. For example, suppose the assets of a small advertising agency include a new computer. The computer was purchased for $4,000 (the cost). It is expected to meet the company's needs for 3 years (the total life). After 3 years, the agency expects to trade it in for $350 (the salvage value). When the agency purchased the computer, it used cash ($4,000) for the purchase. If the business subtracts the cash spent when the asset is acquired, the net worth for that year will go down by $4,000. However, the computer will be useful for three years. Therefore, the business should determine the depreciation per year for the computer and then subtract that value from the net worth to portray a realistic net worth.

The SLN() function uses the straight-line depreciation method to return the depreciation per period for an item.

    a) Create a new workbook.

    b) Label cells for the initial cost of an item, the salvage value of the item at the end of its useful life, and the total life of the item.

c) Save the workbook naming it Depreciation Calculator.

d) The SLN() function returns the depreciation of an asset for a single period. The SLN() function takes the form:

SLN(*cost, salvage, life*)

The cost is the initial cost of the asset, salvage is the salvage value of the asset at the end of its useful life, and life is the expected period of usefulness for the asset. The life determines the period of depreciation. If life is in months, then SLN() returns the depreciation per month. If life is in years, then SLN() returns depreciation per year.

Label a cell SLN Value and then create a formula that includes the SLN() function to determine the depreciation per year for an item. In the example above, an item that costs $4,000 with a life of 3 years and worth $350 when salvaged will have a depreciation of $1,216.67 per year.

e) Create a header that right aligns your name and a footer that center aligns the file name. Add gridlines and row and column headings.

f) Save and then print the modified Depreciation Calculator with $3,500 entered for the cost of an item, 4 years for the life of the item, and $25 for the salvage value of the item.

g) Display the formulas in the cells instead of the values. Change the column widths as necessary so that the formulas are completely displayed. Print a copy.

Exercise 9 ———————————————— Remodeling Costs

Planning a remodeling project usually starts with an estimation of costs that will be incurred. Choose a room to remodel and then create a worksheet to keep track of remodelling costs.

a) Create a new workbook.

b) Enter the data and apply formatting as shown below:

	A	B	C
1	**Remodeling Costs Worksheet**		
2			
3	Items	Cost	
4		Estimated	Actual
5			
6			
7			
8			
9			
10	Subtotal		
11	Taxes		
12	Total		

c) Save the workbook naming it Remodeling Costs.

d) In the Items column, list all the items required to complete the remodelling project. More rows may need to be added.

e) In the Estimated column, estimate and enter the costs associated with each item.

f) In the Estimated column, enter a formula that uses a function to calculate the Subtotal.

g) In the Estimated column, enter a formula to calculate the Taxes based on the appropriate tax rate.

h) In the Estimated column, enter a formula to calculate the Total costs.

i) Use the Internet or catalogs to research the actual cost associated with each item. Enter the costs in the Actual column.

j) Enter formulas to calculate the Subtotal, Taxes, and Total of the Actual column.

k) Format columns B and C as currency with 2 decimal places.

l) Create a header that right aligns your name and a footer that center aligns the text Remodeling Costs. Add gridlines and row and column headings.

m) Save the modified Remodeling Costs and print a copy.

n) Display the formulas in the cells instead of values. Change the column widths as necessary so that the formulas are completely displayed. Print a copy.

Exercise 10 ——————————————————Coral Employees

The accountant for Coral county has decided to use a worksheet for the city hall payroll.

a) Create a new workbook.

b) Enter the data and apply formatting as shown below:

	A	B	C	D
1	Coral County Employees			
2				
3	First Name	Last Name	Salary	
4	Sang	Cho	$42,000	
5	Jill	Grossman	$25,500	
6	Jason	Jones	$26,000	
7	Christa	Smith	$28,900	
8	Tanya	White	$32,000	
9				
10				

c) Save the workbook naming it Coral Employees.

d) Employees are paid weekly. In cell D3, enter the label Weekly Pay and format it appropriately. Enter formulas that use cell references to calculate the weekly pay for each employee. Weekly pay is calculated by dividing the annual salary by 52 (the number of weeks in a year).

e) In cell B9, enter the label Average and then right align the label and format it as italic. In cells C9 and D9, enter formulas that use a function to calculate the average salary and average weekly pay for the employees. Format the average weekly pay as currency with 2 decimal places.

f) Modify the weekly pay formulas to use a function to round the weekly pay amounts in column D to 0 decimal places (do not round the average weekly pay formula). The average weekly pay also changes because the numbers have been rounded.

g) Coral County has hired two more employees. Insert the new data shown below into the worksheet so that the employee names remain in alphabetical order by last name:

First Name	Last Name	Salary
Dedra	Roberts	$42,000
Philip	Jorge	$28,000

Copy the weekly pay formula for the new employees into the appropriate cells.

h) Tax deductions are calculated by multiplying 15% by the weekly pay when the salary is less than $30,000, and 28% by the weekly pay when the salary is equal to or higher than $30,000. In column E, enter the label Taxes and then enter formulas that use a function and cell references to calculate the taxes. Right align the label and format the values as currency with 2 decimals.

i) Social security deductions also need to be calculated. Insert two blank rows at the top of the worksheet. In cell A1, enter the label Soc. Sec. Rate:. In cell C1, enter the value 6%. In cell F5, enter the label Soc. Sec., right align it, and then enter formulas that use absolute and relative cell references to calculate social security of each employee by multiplying the rate by the weekly pay.

j) Net pay is computed by making the necessary deductions from the weekly pay. In column G, enter the label Net Pay, right align it, and then enter formulas that use cell references to deduct the taxes and social security from the weekly pay of each employee to get the net pay.

k) The employees of Coral County receive yearly bonuses based on the position they hold. Cho, Roberts, and White are managers. The rest of the employees are assistants. Insert a column after the salary column, and enter the label Position. Enter the appropriate position for each person, either Manager or Assistant and center align the entire column.

l) Every year, managers receive a bonus of 20% of their weekly pay and assistants receive a bonus of 10% of their weekly pay. In column I, enter the label Bonus, right align it, and enter formulas that use a function and cell references to calculate the bonus amounts for each employee.

m) Format all the data appropriately. Change the column widths so that all the data is displayed entirely and fits on one page.

n) Create a header that right aligns your name. Add gridlines and row and column headings.

o) Save the modified Coral Employees and print a copy.

p) Display the formulas in the cells instead of values. Change the column widths as necessary so that the formulas are completely displayed. Print a copy.

Exercise 11 —————————————————— Theater Attendance

A local theater wants to use a worksheet to keep track of the attendance for their performances for the last two years.

a) Create a new workbook.

b) Enter the data and apply formatting as shown below:

	A	B	C	D
1		Students	Adults	Senior Citizens
2				
3	Romeo and Juliet	356	125	89
4	Othello	259	98	175
5	Bus Stop	289	125	112

c) Save the workbook naming it Theater Attendance.

d) Rename Sheet1 to 2005 Attendance and rename Sheet2 to 2006 Attendance.

e) Copy all the labels from the 2005 Attendance sheet into the 2006 Attendance sheet, pasting them into the same cell locations. Change the column widths as necessary so that all the data is displayed entirely.

f) Enter the attendance for 2006 into the 2006 Attendance sheet:

	A	B	C	D
1		Students	Adults	Senior Citizens
2				
3	Romeo and Juliet	389	255	110
4	Othello	188	145	175
5	Bus Stop	97	112	99

g) Rename Sheet3 to Total Attendance and copy all the labels from the 2006 Attendance sheet into the Total Attendance sheet, pasting them into the same cell locations. Change the column widths as necessary so that all the data is displayed entirely.

h) In the Total Attendance sheet, enter formulas that use cell references to the first two sheets to calculate:

- the total number of students, adults, and senior citizens attending Romeo and Juliet

- the total number of students, adults, and senior citizens attending Othello

- the total number of students, adults, and senior citizens attending Bus Stop

i) Create a header on each sheet that right aligns your name and a footer that center aligns the sheet name. Add gridlines and row and column headings to each sheet.

j) Save the modified Theater Attendance and print a copy of the entire workbook.

k) In the Total Attendance sheet, display the formulas in the cells instead of values. Change the column widths as necessary so that the formulas are completely displayed. Print a copy.

Exercise 12 ——————— Estimated Candle Sales, CANDLE MEMO

The CANDLE MEMO document contains sales figures which can be copied into a new workbook to ask What If? questions. Open CANDLE MEMO, which is a Word data file for this text, and complete the following steps:

a) Create a new workbook.

b) Place a copy of the entire table containing the sales figures from the CANDLE MEMO document in the new workbook starting in cell A1.

c) Change the font of the copied data to Arial 10 point, bold the labels in row 1, and right align the October, November, and December labels. Size columns as necessary so that all the data is displayed entirely.

d) Save the workbook naming it Estimated Candle Sales.

e) In cell A8, enter the label Total and format the label as bold and right align it. In row 8, enter formulas that use a function to total the sales for each month.

f) In cell E1, enter the label Q4 Total. In column E, enter formulas that use a function to total the fourth quarter sales for each item. Fourth quarter sales are calculated by summing the October, November, and December sales.

g) Insert a row at the top of the workbook. In cell F1, enter the label Expected Quarter 1 Sales and format the label as bold.

h) In cell F2, enter the label 3% Increase and in cell G2 enter the label 8% Increase.

i) The sales manager wants to know the expected sales for the first quarter of next year if the first quarter sales increase 3% from the fourth quarter totals. In column F, enter formulas that use cell references to calculate the expected first quarter sales for each item if there is a 3% sales increase.

j) The sales manager wants to know the expected sales for the first quarter of next year if the first quarter sales increase 8% from the fourth quarter totals. In column G, enter formulas that use cell references to calculate the expected first quarter sales for each item if there is an 8% sales increase.

k) Format the values in columns F and G as currency with 0 decimal places. Size the columns as necessary so that all the data is displayed entirely.

l) In cell A11, insert a hyperlink to the CANDLE MEMO document.

m) Create a header that right aligns your name.

n) Save the modified Estimated Candle Sales and print a copy in landscape orientation with gridlines and row and column headings.

Exercise 13 ——————————— Automobile Lease, Buy vs Lease

Many automobile dealers offer the option of leasing rather than purchasing an automobile. When leased, a car is owned by the agency holding the lease and the user pays a monthly fee for the use of the car. Most leases are set for a fixed time, for example four years, and a maximum number of miles the car may be driven, usually in the range of 12,000 to 15,000 miles per year. If the car is driven in excess of this limit an additional fee per mile is charged. At the end of the lease the car must be returned to the lease holder.

The leasing price is usually determined by taking the purchase price of the car minus the estimated value of the car at the end of the lease and then adding an interest charge. The advantage of a lease is that a low or no down payment is usually required, but the disadvantage is that it is usually more expensive to lease than to own a car. Owning is almost always better if you plan to keep the car for an extended period of time, well over the four year lease time. It is important to realize that when you purchase an automobile you own it—the car is yours, and may be sold by you at any time. When you lease a car you are in effect renting it.

a) Develop a plan for a worksheet that compares the cost of leasing versus purchasing an automobile.

b) Use the Internet, newspapers, or local automobile dealer to research the cost associated with buying and with leasing a particular automobile.

c) Create a new workbook and enter the appropriate data, formulas, and formatting.

d) Save the workbook naming it Automobile Lease.

e) Use Word to create a document named Buy vs Lease that briefly describes the automobile and explains whether leasing or buying would be a better decision. Include the data from the Automobile Lease workbook to support the decision.

f) Save and then print the Buy vs Lease document.

A swim team wants to use a worksheet to keep track of the last swim meet's results.

a) Create a new workbook.

b) Enter the data and apply formatting as shown below. Use the Format Cells dialog box to format the swim times. Select the Number tab, select Time from the Category list and then a format similar to 30:55.2 in the Type list:

	A	B	C	D	E
1	Swimming Event	Floyd	Abby	Eric	Katina
2					
3	100 M Freestyle	01:39.0	01:41.0	01:39.8	01:43.2
4	100 M Breaststroke	01:02.6	01:05.6	01:04.8	01:07.3
5	100 M Freestyle	00:51.9	01:05.6	00:53.8	01:07.3
6	100 M Backstroke	01:05.6	01:10.8	01:06.8	01:12.8
7	200 M Individual Medley	01:49.9	01:53.3	01:50.3	01:56.9
8	400 M Medley Relay	03:30.2	03:40.3	03:28.3	03:40.8

c) Save the workbook naming it Swim Meet.

d) In cell F1, enter the label Avg. Time. Enter formulas that use a function to calculate the average time of each swimming event.

e) Pats's scores need to be added to the worksheet. The following are the times for Pat: 1:45.55, 1:12.07, 1:45.19, 1:02.00, 1:45.57, and 3:45.10. Insert a column between columns E and F, and then enter the values and an appropriate column heading.

f) In the next available columns, enter formulas that use functions to calculate the fastest time and slowest time for each event (remember the fastest time in swimming is the lowest time). Include appropriate column headings and right align the labels. Change the column widths so that all the data is displayed entirely, if necessary.

g) Create a header that right aligns your name and a footer that center aligns the text September 10 Swim Meet. Add gridlines and row and column headings.

h) Save the modified Swim Meet and print a copy in landscape orientation.

i) Display the formulas in the cells instead of values. Change the column widths as necessary so that the formulas are completely displayed. Print a copy.

The DANCE workbook contains income and expenses information for a dance. The dance coordinator wants to know how much profit the dance will make depending on the number of people attending. Open DANCE, which is an Excel data file for this text, and complete the following steps:

a) In row 4, enter a formula that uses cell references to calculate expected income from tickets when 50 people attend the dance.

b) In row 5, enter a formula that uses cell references to calculate expected income from food when 50 people attend the dance.

c) In row 6, enter a formula that uses cell references to calculate expected income from beverages when 50 people attend the dance.

d) In row 8, enter formulas that calculate the ticket printing expense when 50 people attend the dance.

e) In row 9, enter a formula that uses cell references to calculate the food expense when 50 people attend the dance.

f) In row 10, enter a formula that uses cell references to calculate the beverages expense when 50 people attend the dance.

g) In row 11, enter formulas to calculate the profit (total income less total expenses).

h) The scenarios feature of Excel allows different data sets to be defined and used within the same worksheet. Scenarios can be used to determine the affect of a different number of people attending the dance. Add two scenarios to the spreadsheet by following the steps:

   1. Select Tools ➙ Scenarios to display the Scenario Manager dialog box.
   2. Select Add to display the Add Scenario dialog box.
   3. Type 100 People in the Scenario name box.
   4. Type C2 in the Changing cells box and select OK. The Scenario Values dialog box is displayed.
   5. In the Scenario Values dialog box, type the value 100 in the $C$2 box and select OK. The Scenario Manager dialog box is displayed.
   6. In the Scenario Manager dialog box, select Show. The value in cell C2 changes to 100 and the formulas automatically recalculate.

i) Add a scenario for 200 people attending.

j) Create a header that right aligns your name and a footer that center aligns text Dance. Add gridlines and row and column headings.

k) Save the modified DANCE and print a copy.

Chapter 9

Creating Charts

Charts are used to display worksheet data. Chart types and creating charts are explained in this chapter. Inserting charts into a Word document is also discussed.

Charts

A *chart* is a visual representation of worksheet data. A chart can enhance and simplify the understanding of numerical data in a worksheet because the relationship between data is illustrated:

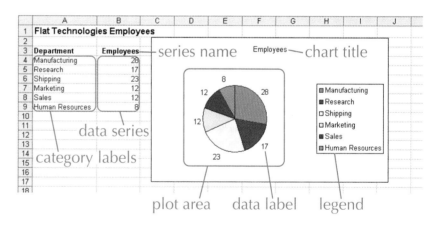

data series
series names
categories
category labels

A chart is based on a range of related data. For example, cells A3 through B9 are used in the pie chart. The column with numerical data is the *data series*. The label for the data series is called the *series name*. Within a series, data is divided into *categories*. Text in cells adjacent to the data series are the *category labels*. Note that the data in cell A3 is ignored because it is to the left of the series name.

Charts contain different objects depending on the type of chart. In the pie chart shown:

TIP The chart symbol that represents a single data point, such as a pie slice, is called a data marker.

- A **chart title** describes what is charted. Excel automatically uses the series name, if one exists.

- The **legend** corresponds to category labels.

- **Data labels** identify each value in the data series.

- The **plot area** is the part of the chart that displays data.

Chart Location

To view the data in the worksheet and its associated chart at the same time, place the chart as an object in the sheet. Place a chart that is large and complex as a new sheet.

To change where an existing chart is displayed, right-click a chart and select **Location** from the displayed menu.

In Excel, a chart can be placed as an object in a worksheet as shown on the previous page or as a separate sheet in a workbook:

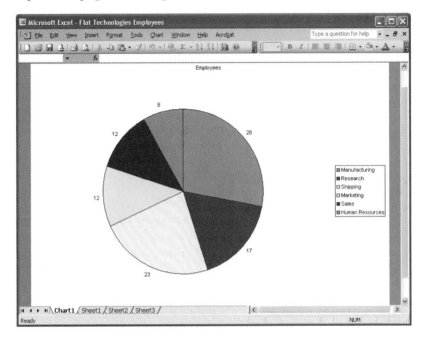

A pie chart in its own sheet

A chart is linked to the data range. Therefore, if a value or label in the data range is changed, the chart automatically updates.

Creating Pie Charts

slice

Pie charts are best for charting data that is a percentage of a whole. A pie chart can include only one series of data. Each value from the series is represented as a *slice*. The size of a slice varies with its percentage of the series total. For example, the chart below illustrates that Groceries account for 41% of the total sales. Note that data labels can display the percentage for each slice:

Exploded Pie

Drag a slice of a pie chart with the mouse to create an exploded pie chart.

	A	B	C	D	E	F	G
1	Department Store Sales Summary						
2							
3	Department	Clothing	Toys	Groceries	Hardware		
4	Sales	$539,887	$123,988	$670,030	$320,000		
5							

one series

Sales

19% 33% 7% 41%

■ Clothing
■ Toys
□ Groceries
□ Hardware

data range

To create a pie chart, first select the *data range*, which is the portion of the worksheet to be charted. For the chart on the previous page, cells A3 through E4 are the data range. Next, click the Chart Wizard button (📊) on the toolbar to start the Chart Wizard. The *Chart Wizard* displays a series of dialog boxes used to specify how the data is to be charted. Options in the Chart Wizard dialog boxes include:

Chart Wizard

- chart sub-types, such as exploded pie and 3-D pie

- series name changes

- title changes

- legend placement

- data labels that show series name, category name, value, percentage, as well as a legend key

- embedded or new sheet for the chart location

Practice: CONTINENTS – part 1 of 2

You will create a pie chart using the Chart Wizard.

① **OPEN CONTINENTS**

a. Start Excel.

b. Open CONTINENTS, which is an Excel data file for this text. The CONTINENTS workbook contains the approximate area of the seven continents of the world in square kilometers.

② **CREATE A PIE CHART**

a. Select cells A3 through B10. The data range for the chart is selected:

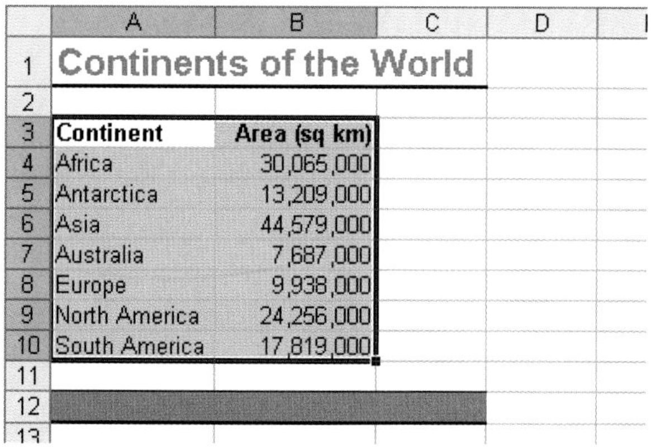

	A	B	C	D	
1	**Continents of the World**				
2					
3	**Continent**	**Area (sq km)**			
4	Africa	30,065,000			
5	Antarctica	13,209,000			
6	Asia	44,579,000			
7	Australia	7,687,000			
8	Europe	9,938,000			
9	North America	24,256,000			
10	South America	17,819,000			
11					
12					
13					

b. On the toolbar, click the Chart Wizard button (📊). The first Chart Wizard dialog box is displayed.

c. In the Chart type list, click Pie:

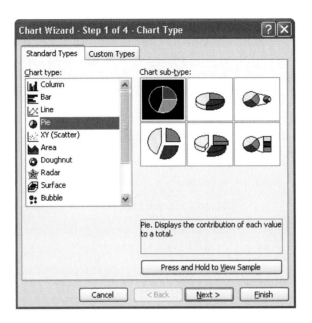

d. Select Next. The second Chart Wizard dialog box is displayed. Verify that the correct range =Sheet1!$A$3:$B$10 is displayed in the Data range box and that Columns is selected to indicate the worksheet data is in a column format:

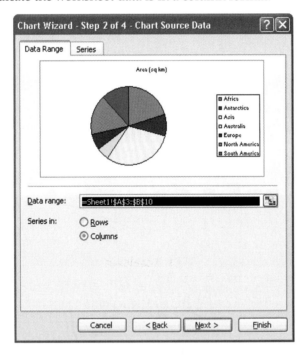

e. Select Next. The third Chart Wizard dialog box is displayed. Modify the Chart title to read: Area of Continent (sq km)

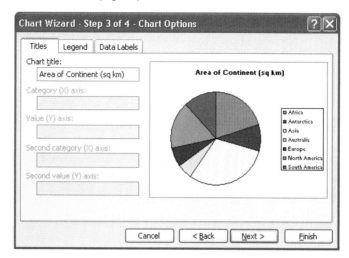

f. Select the Data Labels tab to display those options. Select the Percentage check box. The pie chart example now displays percentages next to each slice:

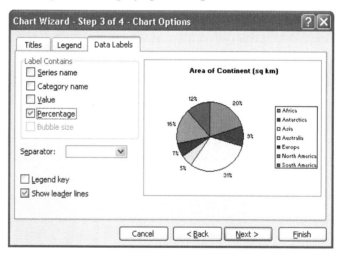

g. Select Next. The fourth Chart Wizard dialog box is displayed. Select the As object in option if it is not already selected:

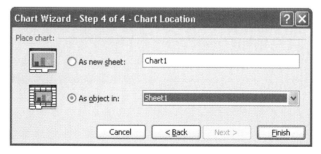

h. Select Finish to display the pie chart as an embedded object in the worksheet. The series label, category labels, and data series are outlined in color and the Chart toolbar is displayed. If necessary, move the Chart toolbar by dragging its title bar.

Check — The chart should look similar to:

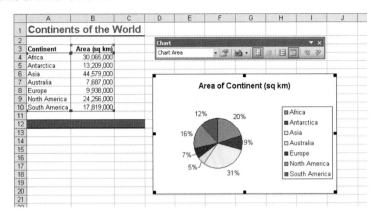

(3) CHANGE A VALUE IN THE WORKSHEET

a. What is the size of the Africa slice in the pie chart?

b. A mistake was made when recording the area of Africa. Type the correct value of 30,330,000 in cell B4. The chart adjusts to reflect the modified value.

(4) SAVE THE MODIFIED CONTINENTS

Moving, Sizing, and Deleting Charts

Chart Area

The *Chart Area* is the blank portion of a chart. Clicking the Chart Area selects a chart. When selected, a chart is displays handles, and the corresponding data series and labels are outlined in color on the worksheet. The Chart toolbar is also displayed:

TIP If the Chart toolbar is not displayed, select View → Toolbars → Chart.

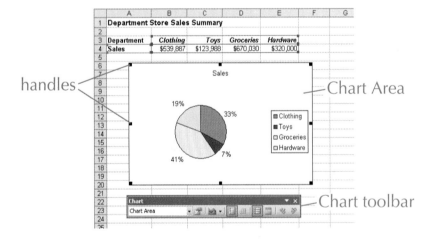

moving a chart

When a chart is placed as an object on a worksheet, it may need to be moved to display data stored in cells behind the chart. Drag the Chart Area to move a chart.

sizing a chart

A chart may also need to be sized. Drag a corner handle of a selected chart to size the chart proportionately:

Sizing a Chart

Hold down the Ctrl key while dragging to keep the center of the chart stationary while sizing.

Hold down the Shift key while dragging to keep the aspect ratio of the chart.

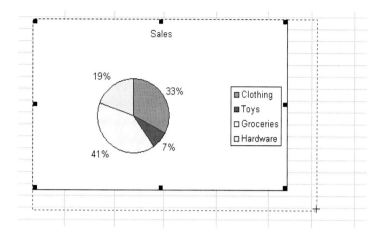

Select Edit ➡ Cut or press the Delete key to delete a selected chart.

Printing a Chart

object in a worksheet

A chart that is an object in a worksheet is printed when the worksheet is printed. Select File ➡ Print Preview to determine if the chart will fit completely on a page before printing. Sizing or moving a chart may be necessary to fit it on a single sheet of paper. Changing the orientation to landscape or changing the margins may also help fit a worksheet with a chart onto a single sheet of paper. Select File ➡ Print to print the active worksheet.

To print only the chart on a single sheet of paper in landscape orientation, select the chart before printing. A chart printed in this manner will not contain the worksheet header or footer. To add a header or footer to the chart, select File ➡ Page Setup to display the Page Setup dialog box. Select the Header/Footer tab and then select an option from the Header and Footer lists. If additional information is needed in the header and footer, select the Custom Header or Custom Footer button.

a chart in its own sheet

To print a chart that is in its own sheet, display the chart sheet and then select File ➡ Print or click the Print button on the toolbar. A header and footer can be added to a chart sheet the same way it is added to a worksheet.

Practice: CONTINENTS – part 2 of 2

You will size, move, and print the pie chart and data stored in the CONTINENTS workbook. Excel should already be started with the CONTINENTS workbook displayed from the last practice.

① *SIZE AND MOVE THE CHART*

    a. If the chart is not selected, click the Chart Area. Handles are displayed.

    b. Move the pointer over the handle in the bottom-right corner of the chart. The pointer changes to a double-headed arrow shape.

    c. Drag the handle down and to the right a little. The chart is larger.

d. Move the pointer into the Chart Area until a ScreenTip is displayed:

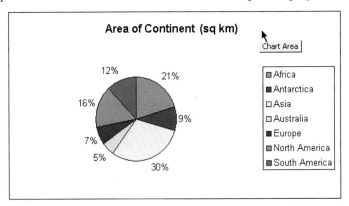

e. Drag the chart so that it is below the worksheet data.

② *SAVE, PRINT, AND THEN CLOSE THE MODIFIED CONTINENTS*

a. Select the chart if it is not already selected.

b. Select File ➤ Print Preview. Only the chart is displayed in the Print Preview window.

c. Select [Close] to return to Normal view.

d. Click a cell in the worksheet to remove the chart handles.

e. Select File ➤ Print Preview.

f. Select [Setup...]. A dialog box is displayed.

   1. Select the Header/Footer tab.

   2. Create a header that center aligns the date and right aligns your name.

   3. Select OK.

g. Select [Print...] to display the Print dialog box. Select OK to print a copy of the worksheet with the chart.

h. Save the modified CONTINENTS workbook.

i. Close CONTINENTS.

Copying a Chart Object into a Word Document

Charts are often included in reports and other business documents to support and simplify the understanding of the text. To copy and paste a selected Excel chart to a Word document, click the Copy button (⧉) on the Excel toolbar, display the Word document, place the insertion point where the chart is to appear, and then click the Paste button (⧉▾) on the Word toolbar. A picture of the chart is copied from Excel and pasted into the Word document:

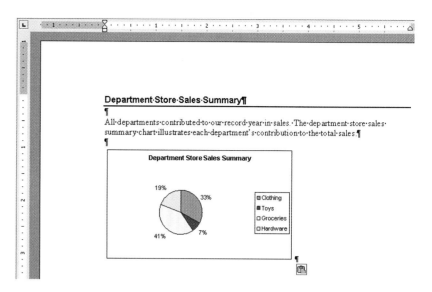

Click the Paste Options button (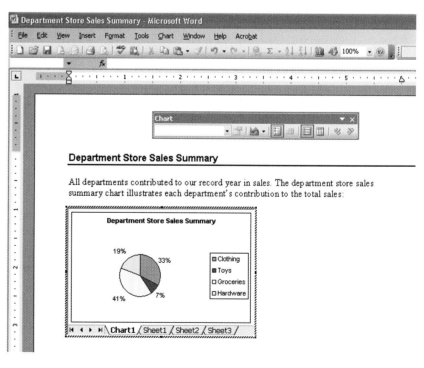) to display a list of options for the pasted data. Select Excel Chart to embed the chart, or select Link to Excel Chart to have the Word document chart update automatically whenever the chart is updated in Excel. A linked chart can be opened from Word. Double-click the linked object to start Excel and display the workbook containing the chart.

embedding a chart
linking a chart

static

An embedded chart is *static*, which means the chart will not automatically change if the worksheet does. To edit an embedded chart, double-click the embedded object to display the Excel Chart menu, Formula bar, Chart toolbar, and workbook:

TIP In Word, an embedded chart is displayed in a separate chart sheet when it is double-clicked.

Creating Bar and Line Charts

Bar charts are useful for comparing the differences between values. A bar chart can include several series of data, with each bar representing a value. Excel can create bar charts with either vertical bars or horizontal bars. In Excel, a horizontal bar chart is called a bar chart and a vertical bar chart is called a *column chart*:

column chart

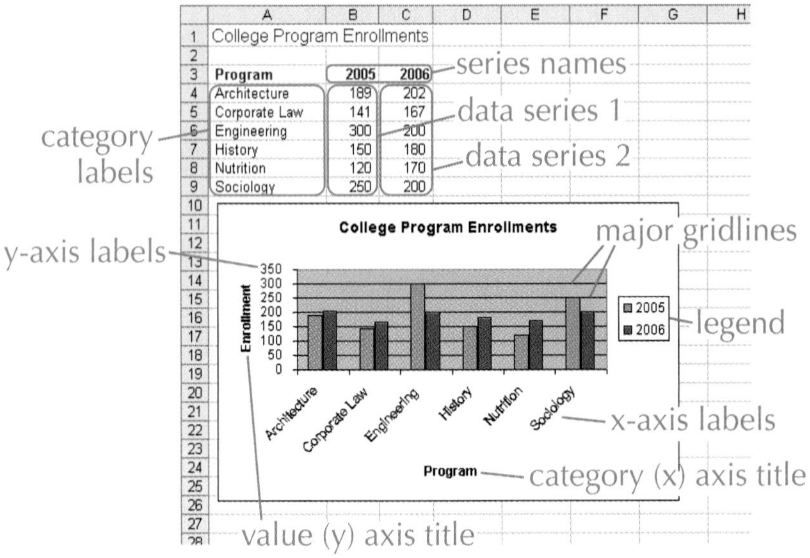

Non-Adjacent Cells

If the chart data range contains non-adjacent cells, hold down the Ctrl key while selecting the data range.

Bar charts contain the following objects:

- A **chart title** describes what is charted and axes titles describe the data. These titles are not automatically selected by Excel.

- The **legend** corresponds to the series names.

- The **value** or **y-axis** is vertical and contains values.

- The **category** or **x-axis** is horizontal and contains category labels.

- The **x-axis labels** corresponds to the category labels.

- The **y-axis labels** are calculated by Excel based on the maximum value in the data.

- **Major gridlines** mark the major intervals on an axis.

A *line chart* can include several series of data with each line representing a series. Each value in a series is a point on the line. Line charts are therefore useful for displaying the differences of data over time. Line charts contain similar objects to bar charts:

TIP Most chart types have two axes. Pie charts do not have axes.

Scaling the Y-Axis

The maximum and minimum values of the y-axis can be changed. Select the axis and then select Format → Selected Axis to display the Format Axis dialog box. Minimum and maximum axis values can then be specified in the Scale tab.

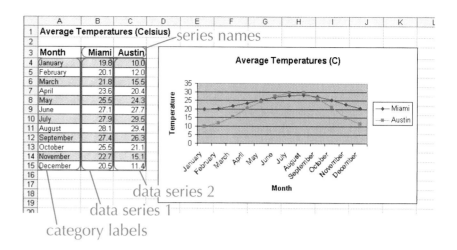

series names

data series 2

data series 1

category labels

If category labels are values, rather than text, select the Series tab in the second Chart Wizard box to define the column of data as Category (X) axis labels.

Practice: TEMPERATURE – part 1 of 2

You will create a bar chart and a line chart. Excel should already be started.

① *OPEN TEMPERATURE*

Open TEMPERATURE, which is an Excel data file for this text. The TEMPERATURE workbook contains the average monthly temperature of two cities.

② *CREATE A LINE CHART*

a. Select cells A3 through C15. The data range is selected:

	A	B	C	D	E
1	Average Temperatures (Celsius)				
2					
3	Month	Miami	Austin		
4	January	19.8	10.0		
5	February	20.1	12.0		
6	March	21.8	15.5		
7	April	23.6	20.4		
8	May	25.5	24.3		
9	June	27.1	27.7		
10	July	27.9	29.5		
11	August	28.1	29.4		
12	September	27.4	26.3		
13	October	25.5	21.1		
14	November	22.7	15.1		
15	December	20.5	11.4		
16					

b. On the toolbar, click the Chart Wizard button ( ). The first Chart Wizard dialog box is displayed.

c. In the dialog box, select the options as shown:

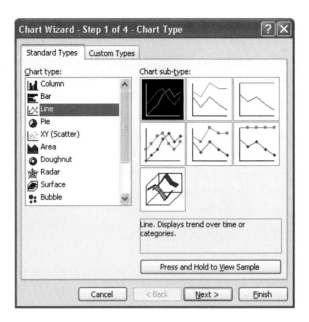

d. Select Next. The second Chart Wizard dialog box is displayed. Verify that the correct range =Sheet1!$A$3:$C$15 is displayed in the **Data range** box. Verify that **Columns** is selected since the data is organized in a column format:

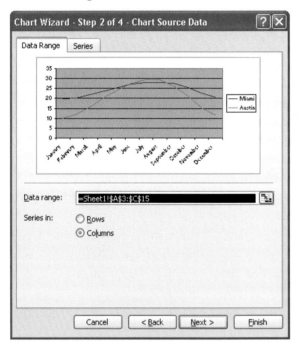

Chapter 9

e. Select Next. The third Chart Wizard dialog box is displayed. Select the Titles tab if it is not already displayed and type the three titles:

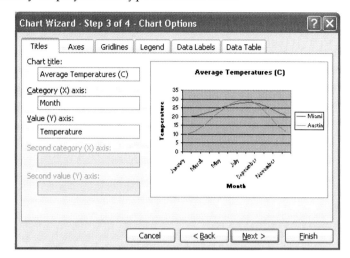

f. Select the Legend tab to display those options. Select Bottom:

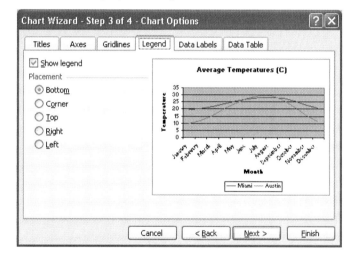

g. Select Next. The fourth Chart Wizard dialog box is displayed. Select As new sheet.

h. Select Finish. The sheet is displayed in a new sheet named Chart1 and the worksheet data remains on Sheet1:

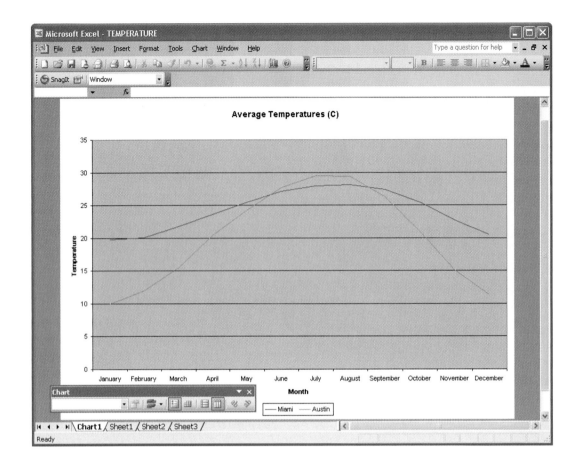

③ **SAVE THE MODIFIED TEMPERATURE**

④ **CREATE A BAR CHART**

    a. Select the Sheet1 tab.

    b. Click an empty cell to remove the selection.

    c. Select cells A5 through C6. The data range is selected:

	A	B	C	D	E
1	**Average Temperatures (Celsius)**				
2					
3	**Month**	**Miami**	**Austin**		
4	January	19.8	10.0		
5	February	20.1	12.0		
6	March	21.8	15.5		
7	April	23.6	20.4		
8	May	25.5	24.3		
9	June	27.1	27.7		
10	July	27.9	29.5		
11	August	28.1	29.4		
12	September	27.4	26.3		
13	October	25.5	21.1		
14	November	22.7	15.1		
15	December	20.5	11.4		
16					

    d. On the toolbar, click the Chart Wizard button (). The first Chart Wizard dialog box is displayed.

    e. In the Chart type list, click Column, if it is not already selected:

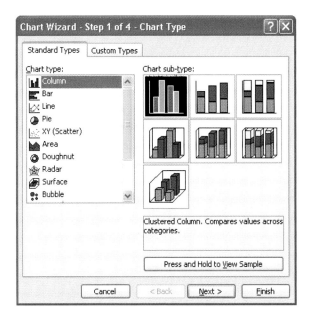

f. Select Next. The second Chart Wizard dialog box is displayed. Verify that the correct range =Sheet1!$A$5:$C$6 is displayed in the **Data range** box and that Rows is selected. Note that the x-axis labels are incorrect:

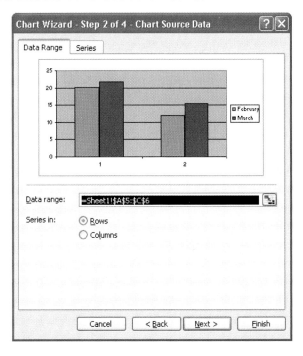

g. Select the Series tab to display those options. Click the Category (X) axis labels box to place the insertion point:

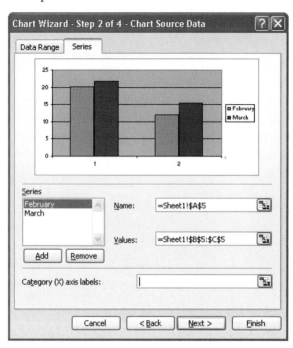

On the worksheet, select cells B3 through C3 to add category (X) axis labels to the chart:

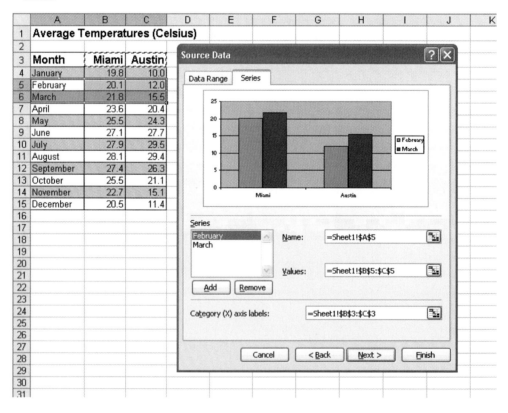

h. Select Next. The third Chart Wizard dialog box is displayed. Select the Titles tab and type the three titles:

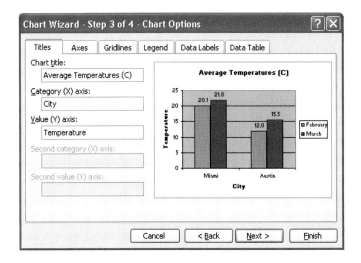

i. Select the Data Labels tab to display those options. Select Value to add data labels to the chart:

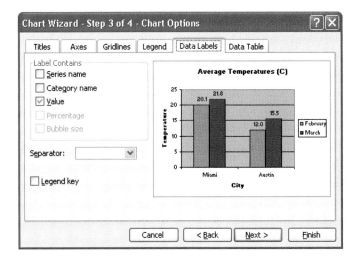

j. Select Next. The fourth Chart Wizard dialog box is displayed. Select As object in.

k. Select Finish. The sheet is displayed as an object in Sheet1.

l. Move the chart below the data.

⑤ *SAVE THE MODIFIED TEMPERATURE*

⑥ *OPEN TRAVEL*

Open TRAVEL, which is a Word data file for this text. Read through the unfinished document.

⑦ *COPY DATA TO THE CLIPBOARD*

a. Use the taskbar to display the TEMPERATURE workbook.

b. Select the chart on Sheet1.

c. On the toolbar, click the Copy button. The data is copied to the Clipboard.

⑧ *PASTE DATA*

a. Use the taskbar to display the TRAVEL document.

b. Place the insertion point in the second blank paragraph after the text that reads "…average temperatures are:"

c. On the toolbar, click the Paste button. A picture of the chart is pasted. The document looks similar to:

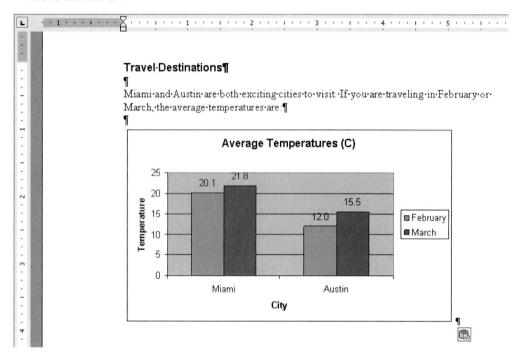

⑨ *CREATE A HEADER*

Create a header with the date and your name and center align all the header text.

⑩ *SAVE THE MODIFIED TRAVEL DOCUMENT AND PRINT A COPY*

⑪ *CLOSE TRAVEL AND QUIT WORD*

Modifying a Chart

A chart can be modified using the Chart Wizard. To redisplay the Chart Wizard, select the chart and click the Chart Wizard button (▦) on the toolbar. Click the Next and Previous buttons to display the options needed to modify the chart. After making changes, select Finish to update the chart.

The Chart toolbar can also be used to modify a chart. When a chart is selected, Chart Area is displayed in the Chart Objects list:

▨▾ Click the Chart Type button to change the chart type.

▤ Click the Legend button to display or remove the legend.

▤ ▥ Click the By Column or By Row button to indicate how the charted data is organized in the worksheet.

positioning chart objects   In the Chart Area, position the chart title, axis titles, data labels, and legend by dragging the objects.

The Chart Menu

When a chart is selected, the Excel Data menu changes to the Chart menu. Commands in the Chart menu can be used to modify a chart.

TIP Select View → Toolbars → Chart to display the Chart toolbar.

Data and labels can be added to an existing chart. To add an adjacent data series to a selected chart, drag one of the handles of the outlined original data to include the new series. To add an adjacent label, drag one of the handles of the outlined labels.

To add a non-adjacent data series and corresponding label to a selected chart, select Chart → Add Data to display the Add Data dialog box and then type or select the data range of the new data series and corresponding label. If the labels are not adjacent to the series of data they are describing, select Chart → Source Data and then select the Series tab to display those options. Click the Category (X) axis labels box to place the insertion point and then select the appropriate cells on the worksheet.

Adding a Data Series

The Copy and Paste commands can be used to add a non-adjacent data series and label to a chart. Select the data series and label, select Copy and then select the chart and select Paste.

Formatting a Chart

The appearance of a chart can be enhanced with formatting. For example, the chart below has been formatted so that the axes labels are on an angle, the data label color is white, and the chart type is 3-D Column:

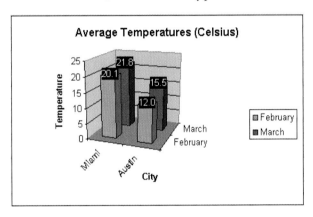

If a chart is to be used in a report or other document, select formatting that will compliment the formatting used in the document or the report. Many businesses and companies have a protocol that specifies a particular color scheme, fonts, and logos that should be used in all business or company documents.

Double-click any object in a chart to display a Format dialog box. For example, double-click the legend to display the Format Legend dialog box:

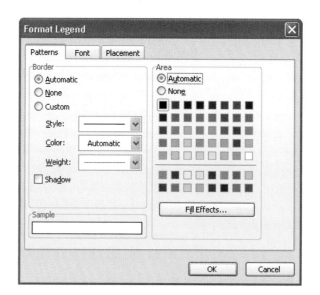

Patterns, fonts, and placement of the legend can be changed

The Chart toolbar can also be used to format a chart. Select an object from the Charts Object list:

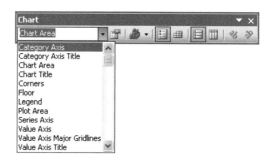

and then select the Format button (![]) to display the appropriate Format dialog box.

Other formatting options on the Chart toolbar include the Angle Clockwise button (![]) and the Angle Counterclockwise button (![]), which allow titles and axes labels to be displayed on an angle.

Practice: TEMPERATURE – part 2 of 2

You will modify and format a chart. Excel should already be started with the TEMPERATURE workbook displayed from the last practice.

① *RENAME SHEETS*

    a. Rename Sheet1: City Temperatures

    b. Rename Chart1: 12-Month Comparison

    c. Select the City Temperatures sheet.

a. Select the column chart.

b. On the toolbar, click the Chart Wizard button (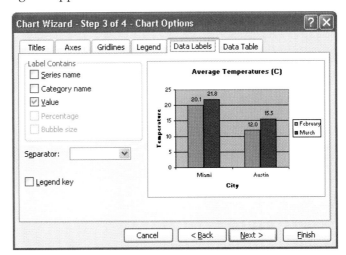). Click Next until the third Chart Wizard dialog box appears. Click the Data Labels tab:

c. Clear the Value check box. Data labels are removed from the chart.

d. Select Finish.

③ ADD DATA TO THE WORKSHEET

a. Enter the following label and data into column D:

	A	B	C	D	E
1	Average Temperatures (Celsius)				
2					
3	**Month**	**Miami**	**Austin**	Los Angeles	
4	January	19.8	10.0	13.4	
5	February	20.1	12.0	13.6	
6	March	21.8	15.5	14.1	
7	April	23.6	20.4	15.2	
8	May	25.5	24.3	16.4	
9	June	27.1	27.7	17.7	
10	July	27.9	29.5	19.5	
11	August	28.1	29.4	20.4	
12	September	27.4	26.3	20	
13	October	25.5	21.1	18.5	
14	November	22.7	15.1	15.7	
15	December	20.5	11.4	13.5	
16					

b. Select cells C3 through C15.

c. On the toolbar, click the Format Painter button ().

d. Click cell D3. Formatting is applied to the data.

e. Widen column D until the label is displayed entirely.

④ ADD A DATA SERIES TO THE COLUMN CHART

a. Select the column chart. The data series and labels and associated with the chart are outlined in color.

b. Drag the bottom handle in cell C6 to cell D6. The Los Angeles average temperatures for February and March and x-axis label are added to the chart:

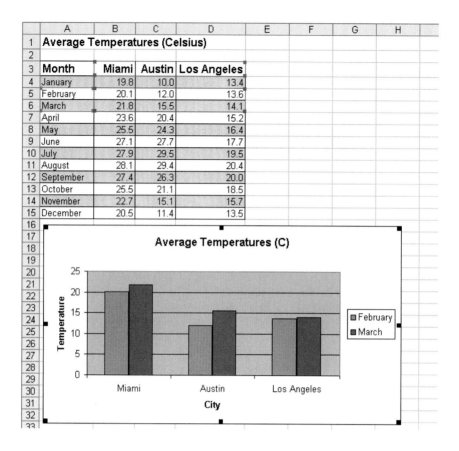

⑤ MODIFY THE CHART

a. Select View → Toolbars → Chart to display the Chart toolbar if it is not already displayed.

b. On the Chart toolbar, click the Legend button (📋). The legend is removed. Click the Legend button again. The legend is redisplayed.

c. On the Chart toolbar, click the arrow in the Chart Type button and select the 3-D Column Chart button:

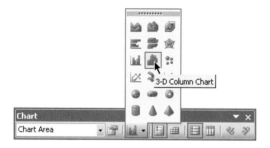

⑥ FORMAT THE CHART

a. Select the x-axis.

b. On the Chart toolbar, click the Angle Counterclockwise button (🖉). The x-axis labels are displayed on an angle.

c. Drag the x-axis title, City to an appropriate location to the right of the labels. The chart should look similar to:

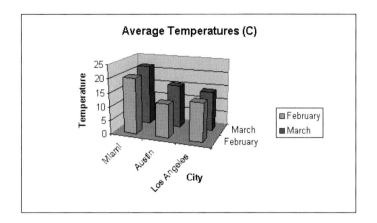

d. Double-click the chart title. The Format Chart Title dialog box is displayed. Select the Font tab to display those options.

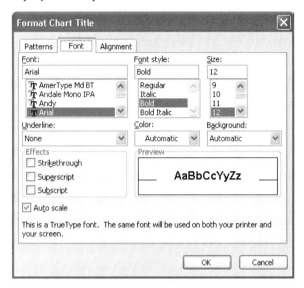

e. Select a different font, size, and color of your choice for the chart title.

f. Repeat steps (d) and (e) to change the font for both the axis titles and the legend.

g. Double-click the bar that represents the February average temperature in Miami. The Format Data Series dialog box is displayed. Select the Patterns tab if it is not already selected:

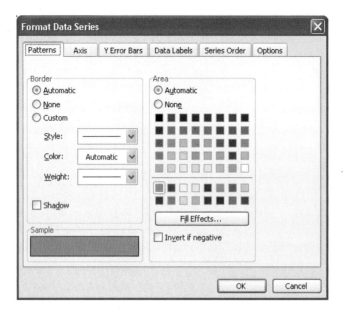

h. The current bar color of the February data series is selected in the Area section. Select a different color for the February data series bars and then select OK. The color of the February bars changes to the selected color.

i. Repeat steps (g) and (h) to change the color of the March data series bars.

⑦ *SAVE THE MODIFIED TEMPERATURE*

⑧ *PRINT TWO WORKSHEETS*

Print a copy of the 12-Month Comparison and City Temperatures sheets.

⑨ *CLOSE TEMPERATURE AND QUIT EXCEL*

Chart Types

Column, bar, line, and pie are common types of charts. Excel allows various other types of charts to be created:

- An **XY (Scatter) chart** compares pairs of values.

- An **Area chart** shows the trend of values over time.

- A **Doughnut chart** is similar to a pie chart, but can contain more than one data series.

- A **Radar chart** shows changes in values relative to a center point.

- A **Surface chart** shows trends in values.

- A **Bubble chart** compares sets of three values.

- A **Stock chart** displays stock prices.

- **Cylinder**, **Cone**, and **Pyramid** charts are used to add a different chart symbol to bar and column charts.

Each chart type also has several sub-types that can be selected after selecting the chart type. For example, the Area chart type has six subtypes:

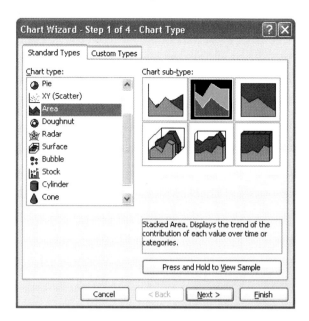

Click the Press and Hold to View Sample button to view selected data in the selected chart sub-type.

Chapter Summary

A chart is a visual representation of worksheet data. Pie charts show the percentage relationship between different parts of a whole quantity, bar charts compare different values, and line charts track data over time. In Excel a vertical bar chart is called a column chart. A chart can be created using the Chart Wizard.

Before it can be moved, sized, or deleted, click the Chart Area to select an existing chart. A chart should be previewed before it is printed to determine if the chart will fit completely on a page. The entire worksheet and any charts it contains can be printed by selecting the Print command. A chart can be printed by itself on a single sheet of paper by first selecting the chart.

Charts are often included in reports and other business documents to support and simplify the understanding of the text. The Copy and Paste buttons can be used to copy an Excel chart to a Word document.

A chart can be modified using the Chart Wizard. The Chart toolbar can also be used to modify a chart. Data in adjacent and non-adjacent data can be added to an existing chart.

Double-clicking any object in a chart displays a Format dialog box where options can be selected to change the appearance of the chart.

Vocabulary

Bar chart   Data graphed as a series of bars.

Category   The division of data within a series.

Category axis   The horizontal axis that contains category labels.

Category labels   Text in cells adjacent to the data series that are displayed on the x-axis.

Chart   A visual representation of worksheet data.

Chart Area   The blank portion of a chart.

Chart title   Describes what is charted.

Chart Wizard   Displays dialog boxes where the user can select options to create a chart.

Column chart   Data graphed as a series of vertical bars.

Data labels   Labels that identify each value in the data series.

Data range   The portion of the worksheet data to be charted.

Data series   A set of related numerical data to be plotted on a chart.

Legend   Corresponds to the category labels in a pie chart and series names in other chart types.

Line chart   Data graphed using a continuous line.

Major gridlines   Gridlines that mark the major intervals on an axis.

Pie chart   Data graphed as slices of a circular pie.

Plot area   The part of the chart that displays data.

Series name   The label that identifies the data series.

Slice   Part of a pie chart that represents each value from the series.

Static   Pasted data that will not automatically change if the source worksheet does.

Value axis   The vertical axis that contains values.

X-axis   *See* Category axis.

X-axis label   Category labels displayed on the x-axis of a chart.

Y-axis   *See* Value axis.

Y-axis labels   Labels calculated by Excel based on the maximum value in the data and displayed on the y-axis of a chart.

Add Data **command**   Displays a dialog box where a non-adjacent data series and corresponding label can be added to an existing chart. Found in the Chart menu.

Angle Clockwise button   Displays a selected title or axis label on a clockwise angle. Found on the Chart toolbar.

Angle Counterclockwise button   Displays a selected title or axis label on a counter-clockwise angle. Found on the Chart toolbar.

By Column button   Indicates the charted data is organized in columns on the worksheet. Found on the Chart toolbar.

By Row button   Indicates the charted data is organized in rows on the worksheet. Found on the Chart toolbar.

Chart **command**   Displays the Chart toolbar. Found in View → Toolbars.

Chart Type button   Displays options for changing the chart type. Found on the Chart toolbar.

Chart Wizard button   Displays the Chart Wizard dialog box used to create or modify a chart. Found on the toolbar.

Copy button   Places the selected chart on the Clipboard. Found on the toolbar.

Cut **command**   Deletes a selected chart. Found in the Edit menu. The Delete key can be used instead of the command.

Format button   Displays a Format dialog box used to format a chart. Found on the Chart toolbar.

Legend button   Displays or removes the legend. Found on the Chart toolbar.

Page Setup **command**   Displays a dialog box with page options for the active sheet. Found in the File menu.

Print **command**   Displays a dialog box used to print the active worksheet or chart. Found in the File menu. The Print button on the toolbar can be used instead of the command.

Print Preview **command**   Displays the worksheet or chart as it will appear when printed. Found in the File menu.

Source Data **command**   Displays a dialog box used to add labels to non-adjacent data in a chart. Found in the Format menu.

1. a) What is a chart?
    b) Explain how charts can simplify the understanding of numeric data.

2. a) What is a data series?
    b) How will a chart be affected if a value in a data range is changed on the worksheet?
    c) What does a legend correspond to?
    d) What are categories?
    e) How many categories are in the data charted on the first page of this chapter?
    f) What is the plot area?

3. List the two locations a chart can be placed.

4. a) How many series of data can a pie chart include?
    b) What does a pie chart use to represent values?
    c) What is the first step in creating a pie chart?
    d) What does the Chart Wizard display?

5. What are three kinds of information that can be displayed in a data label?

6. a) What is the Chart Area?
    b) What happens to the corresponding data series and labels when a chart is selected?
    c) How is a chart moved on a worksheet?
    d) List the step required to size a chart proportionately.
    e) Why should a corner handle be used to size a chart?

7. a) List the step required to print a chart that is stored on the same sheet as the charted data.
    b) List the steps required to print a chart that is stored on the same sheet as the charted data so that only the chart is printed.

8. Why would a chart be included in a report?

9. a) What is the difference between embedding a chart and linking a chart.
    b) Describe a situation where it would be advantageous to link a chart in a Word document to the Excel source chart.

10. What type of chart (bar, line, or pie) is best suited to display:
    a) a student's GPA over four years.
    b) the percentage each department spent of a company's total budget.
    c) the number of full-time, part-time, and temporary employees in a company.
    d) the number of books sold each day for a month at the college bookstore.

11. In Excel, what is a vertical bar chart called?

12. a) What does the x-axis show?
    b) Is the x-axis vertical or horizontal?
    c) What does the y-axis show?
    d) Is the y-axis vertical or horizontal?

13. List the step required to modify a chart's title.

14. List the steps required to modify a chart to include an additional nonadjacent series of data.

True/False

15. Determine if each of the following are true or false. If false, explain why.
    a) If a value in a data series changes, the corresponding chart will automatically update.
    b) Pie charts are best for showing differences of data over time.
    c) The data range for a chart always includes all the data on the worksheet.
    d) A chart that appears as an embedded object will print on a single sheet of paper in landscape orientation if the chart is selected before selecting the Print command.
    e) An Excel chart that is an object in a Word document can be edited in Word using Excel commands.
    f) Bar charts are useful for comparing the differences between values.
    g) Pie charts have axes.
    h) A chart in a report should contain formatting that compliments the report.
    i) Commands in the Excel Format menu never change.
    j) Each chart type has sub-types.

Exercise 1 ——— Education Expenses, College Cost Comparison

Selecting an appropriate college or university requires comparing many factors, such as cost. Expenses involved in the cost of college and university typically include:

- tuition
- course fees
- books
- travel
- room/rent
- meal plan/groceries
- entertainment
- parking permit

Create a report that compares the cost of attending three different colleges or universities by completing the following steps:

a) Create a new workbook.

b) Enter data and apply formatting similar to:

	A	B	C	D
1	The Cost of a Year of College/University			
2				
3	Expenses			
4	Tuition			
5	Course Fees			
6	Books			
7	Travel			
8	Room/Rent			
9	Meal Plan/Groceries			
10	Entertainment			
11	Parking Permit			
12	Total Cost			
13				
14				

c) Save the workbook naming it Education Expenses.

d) Research three colleges or universities that offer similar programs in an area that you are interested in studying. For each college or university, research and estimate the costs associated with each of the expense categories. Enter the data in the appropriate cells. A value of 0 can be used if the cost is not applicable. Note that additional expense categories can be added if applicable.

e) In cells B3 through D3, enter the names of the three selected colleges or universities and bold and right-align the labels.

f) Enter an appropriate formula to calculate the total cost of a year at each of the colleges or universities.

g) Format the expense values as currency with 2 decimal places.

h) Produce a column chart on the active sheet that displays the total cost for all three colleges or universities. Include an appropriate title, legend, and axes labels.

i) Save the modified Education Expenses.

j) Create a new Word document, type Calculating the Cost of College or University and press Enter twice.

k) Type a paragraph explaining which program was selected and what three schools will be compared.

l) In a new paragraph, type The chart below illustrates the difference in total cost: and press Enter.

m) Copy the column chart to the Word document in the blank paragraph you just typed.

n) Size the chart appropriately.

o) Type a concluding paragraph which indicates which school would be the best choice and why.

p) Create a footer with your name and right align the footer text.

q) Save the Word document naming it College Cost Comparison and print a copy.

Exercise 2 ——————————— AQUARIUM, Nitrogen Cycle

The AQUARIUM worksheet contains data that tracks the Nitrogen cycle. The Nitrogen cycle is the biological process that converts ammonia, created by fish waste products, into other relatively harmless nitrogen compounds. Open AQUARIUM, which is an Excel data file for this text, and complete the following steps:

a) Produce a line chart on a new sheet that displays the ammonia, nitrite, and nitrate levels for each day since set-up. Include the title, legend, and axes labels as shown below:

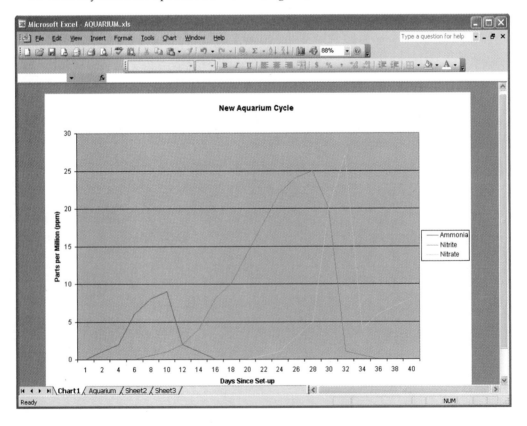

b) Save the modified AQUARIUM.

c) Research the Nitrogen cycle for an aquarium using the Internet or books.

d) Create a new Word document. Summarize your research on the Nitrogen cycle. Use the AQUARIUM line chart to enhance the summary.

e) Create a footer with your name and right align the footer text.

f) Save the Word document naming it Nitrogen Cycle and print a copy.

Exercise 3 ———————————————————————— Population

The U.S. Census Bureau carries out a census every ten years. According to the first census in 1790, there were 3,900,000 people in the United States. The most recent census in 2000 counted 281,421,906 people in the United States. Census data also indicates how many people live in a specific city.

a) Create a new workbook.

b) Enter data and apply formatting similar to:

	A	B	C	D
1	Population Statistics			
2				
3	City	State	Population	
4	Albuquerque	New Mexico	448,607	
5	Houston	Texas	1,953,631	
6	Miami	Florida	362,470	
7	Phoenix	Arizona	1,321,045	
8	New York	New York	8,008,278	
9	Los Angeles	California	3,694,820	
10	Seattle	Washington	563,374	
11	Wichita	Kansas	344,284	
12	Philadelphia	Pennsylvania	1,517,550	
13				
14				

c) Sort the data in descending order by population.

d) Produce a bar chart on the active sheet that compares the population of the four cities in the list with the highest population. Include an appropriate title, legend, and axes labels.

e) Create a header that right aligns your name and a footer that center aligns the date on the worksheet. Add gridlines and row and column headings.

f) Print preview and move and size the chart so that the chart and data fit on one page.

g) Save the workbook naming it Population and print a copy.

Some of the largest countries by land area include Russia, China, Canada, Brazil, Australia, and the United States. A large land area does not necessarily equate to a large population. Compare the land area and population of these countries by completing the following steps:

a) Create a new workbook.

b) Enter data and apply formatting similar to:

	A	B	C	D
1	**Country Statistics**			
2				
3	**Country**	**Area (sq km)**	**Population**	
4	China	9,596,960	1,286,975,468	
5	United States	9,629,091	290,342,554	
6	Brazil	8,511,965	182,032,604	
7	Russia	17,075,200	144,526,278	
8	Canada	9,976,140	32,207,113	
9	Australia	7,686,850	19,731,984	
10				
11				

c) Sort the worksheet so that the countries and their corresponding data is listed in descending order by area.

d) Produce a column chart on the active sheet that displays the area of each country. Include the title, legend, and axes labels as shown below:

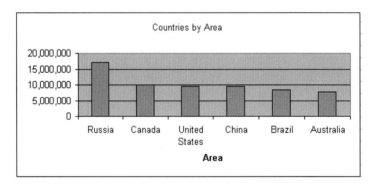

e) Manually scale the y-axis to have a minimum value of 5,000,000.

f) Save the workbook naming it Country Statistics.

g) Sort the worksheet so that the countries and their corresponding data is listed in descending order by population.

h) Produce a 3-D column chart on its own sheet that displays the population of each country:

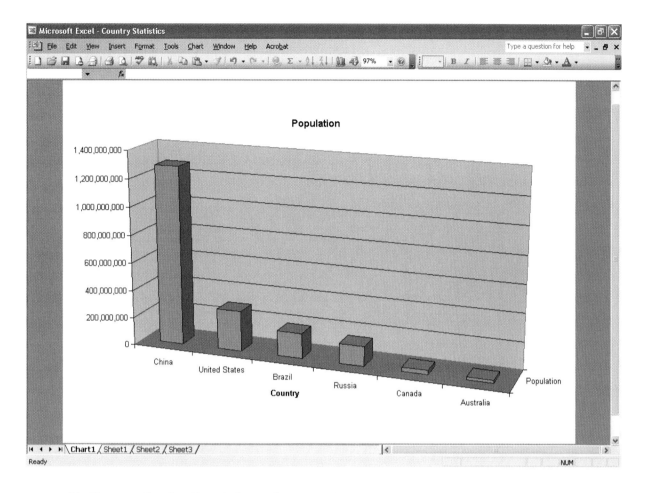

h) Rename **Chart1** to Population and rename **Sheet1** to Area.

i) Create a header that right aligns your name on the **Population** and **Area** sheets.

j) Print preview the **Area** sheet and then move the chart so that the chart and data fit on one page in landscape orientation.

k) Print a copy of the **Area** and **Population** sheets.

Exercise 5 ———————————————————————Enrollment

Learn Now Computer Training provides software training. They have four training sites located in the east, west, north, and south ends of a city. They provide Windows, Word, Access, Excel, and PowerPoint training classes.

a) Create a new workbook.

b) Enter data and apply formatting similar to:

	A	B	C	D	E	F
1	**Learn Now Computer Training**					
2	**Course**	**East Site**	**West Site**	**North Site**	**South Site**	**Course Enrollment**
3	Windows	8	10	6	12	
4	Word	25	30	40	35	
5	Access	12	10	8	6	
6	Excel	20	30	35	25	
7	PowerPoint	40	42	20	12	
8	**Site Enrollment**					
9						

c) Save the workbook naming it Enrollment.

d) In cell F3, enter a formula that uses a function to calculate the course enrollment. Copy the formula to the appropriate cells.

e) In cell B8, enter a formula that uses a function to calculate the site enrollment. Copy the formula to the appropriate cells.

f) Create a header that right aligns your name.

g) Produce a column chart on a new sheet named Enrollment that displays the number of students enrolled in each course at each site. Include the title, legend, and axes labels as shown below. Hint: The chart sheet can be renamed in the fourth Chart Wizard dialog box.

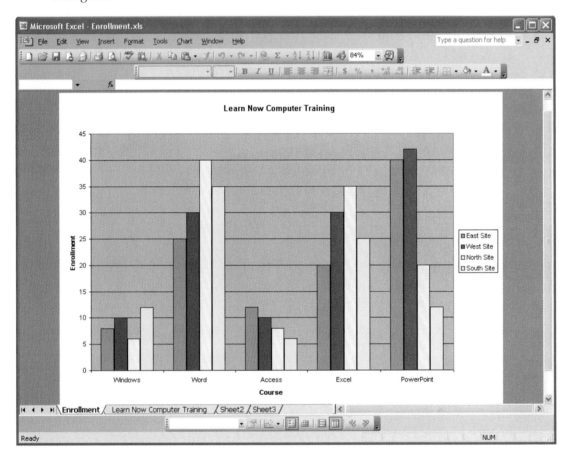

h) Rename Sheet1 to Learn Now Computer Training.

i) Create a header on the Enrollment sheet that right aligns your name.

j) Print a copy of the Enrollment and Learn Now Computer Training sheets.

Exercise 6 ———————————— BREAK EVEN, Break Even Point

In business, the break even point is when the sales revenue (money earned) equals the expenses (money paid out). A line chart can be used to determine the break even point. Open BREAK EVEN, which is an Excel data file for this text, and complete the following steps:

a) Produce a line chart on the active sheet that displays the revenues and expenses per units sold. Include the title, legend, and axes labels as shown below:

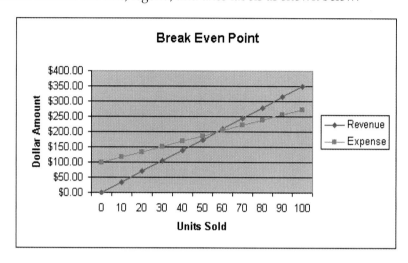

b) Save the modified BREAK EVEN.

c) Create a new Word document. Write a paragraph that defines what a break even point is. Below the definition, place a copy of the line chart from the BREAK EVEN workbook. Write another paragraph that interprets the chart data by determining where the break even point occurs and what it means.

d) Create a footer with your name and right align the footer text.

e) Save the Word document naming it Break Even Point and print a copy.

Exercise 7 ———————————— Stock Exchanges, Portfolio Update

A company can choose to "go public" to raise capital (money) for operations, expansion, and so on. Publicly held companies are listed on a stock exchange where a portion, or *share*, of ownership can be purchased by individuals. The price of a share of stock varies depending on supply and demand within the market. Sellers compete with other sellers for the highest price, while buyers compete with other buyers for the lowest share price. The stock price of an established company showing sustained growth is typically higher than the stock price of a younger company with no track record for profits.

There are many stock exchanges, with the AMEX, NYSE, and Nasdaq being the three largest auction markets in the world. Nearly every leading U.S. corporation as well as hundreds of non-U.S. corporations are listed on either the NYSE, the AMEX, or Nasdaq. The *New York Stock Exchange* (NYSE) and the *American Stock Exchange* (AMEX or ASE) have centralized trading floors where stocks are bought and sold. The *National Association of Securities Dealers Automatic Quotation System* (Nasdaq) is an electronic stock market with a subscriber network connecting more than 11,000 traders in more than 83 countries.

a) An educated investment in the stock market has historically provided the highest rate of return on a long-term investment compared to other investment options, such as a savings account. Choose seven companies that interest you and then use the Internet to determine the stock exchange listing for each company (NYSE, AMEX, or Nasdaq) and each company's symbol (called the ticker symbol) on the exchange. A company's Web site typically includes a link called "Company" or "Investor Information" that provides the information you need. Be sure to also check the bottom navigation bar for links to investor information. Many sites can also be searched for investor information.

Create a spreadsheet named Stock Exchanges and in separate rows add the company name, ticker symbol, and stock exchange (NYSE, AMEX, or Nasdaq) for the seven companies you chose.

b) Stock information can be found on a stock exchange's Web site, some corporate Web sites, and in many newspapers. Newspapers print stock tables with the last price paid for a stock on the previous day, as well as other information. Stock tables have a format similar to:

	A	B	C	D	E	F	G	H	I
1	52 Weeks								
2	HI-LO	SYM	DIV	VOL	YLD	PE	HI-LO	CLOSE	NET CHG
3	22.55 - 30.00	MSFT	0.16	59,852,304	5	32.29	26.20 - 26.60	26.37	0.02

- **52 Week Hi-Lo** is the highest and lowest prices at which the stock sold in the past year.

- **SYM** is the company stock symbol, which is the abbreviated name of the company issuing the stock. For example, MSFT is the stock symbol for Microsoft.

- **DIV** is the annual dividend paid per share to the stockholders.

- **VOL** is the volume of shares traded during the trading day.

- **YLD** is the dividend yield, which is the return on invested capital.

- **P/E** is the price to earnings ratio, which compares the price per share to the earnings per share.

- **HI-LO** is the highest and lowest price during the last trading day.

- **CLOSE** is the last price a trade was made at during the trading day.

- **NET CHG** is the difference between the closing price for the previous day and the current day in a dollar value.

Web sites contain stock data that is real-time or delayed by just minutes. When using a Web site to check stock prices, it is important to remember that the price shown is usually the price the stock is being currently traded at, not the final price for the day. Look for a previous day's close price to determine a stock's last price. The www.nyse.com, www.amex.com, and www.nasdaq.com sites each have a Quote lookup on the home page for entering a ticker symbol to receive stock information.

On at least five different days, update the Stock Exchange spreadsheet to include each stocks' closing price for that day.

c) Create a line chart that shows the change over time for each stock.

d) If you had purchased 50 shares of each of the seven stocks, would your investment have been a wise one? *Portfolio* refers to a set of investments owned by an individual. Add a new worksheet named Portfolio to the Stock Exchange workbook and enter data that shows how the value of 50 shares of each stock changed over the investment period (the five days the spreadsheet was updated). Include formulas that show the dollar amount of the initial investment for each stock and the dollar amount of the investment after each update.

e) On the Portfolio sheet, create a bar chart that shows the initial and final value of the 50 shares of each stock.

f) Use Word to create a letter named Portfolio Update that includes the bar chart showing investment losses and gains. Explain to the investor why you think each of the stocks either lost or gained value over the time of the investment.

Exercise 8 — Stock Indexes

Stocks are tradable financial instruments that give an investor a portion, or share, of ownership in a publicly held company. There are thousands of stocks available because nearly every leading U.S. corporation as well as hundreds of non-U.S. corporations are listed on either the AMEX, the NYSE, or Nasdaq stock markets. Within the set of all stocks, subsets called *indexes* have been defined. An index is tracked to gauge the movement of the stock market as a whole. For example, the oldest index is the Dow Jones Industrial Average (DJIA or Dow), which tracks 30 blue-chip stocks. The *performance* of an index is the average of the gains or losses of the stocks in the index. A statement about how "the market" is doing is usually referring to the performance of the Dow. In addition to the Dow, there are several other indexes that are also used to measure the market:

- **Dow Jones Industrial Average (DJIA or Dow)**   A set of 30 blue-chip stocks. Blue-chip stocks are widely held and are considered solid, reliable, and having sustained growth. Stocks include Microsoft (MSFT), Intel (INTC), Coca-Cola (COKE), McDonald's (MCD), and American Express (AXP).

- **Standard & Poor's 500 (S&P 500)**   A set of the 500 largest company stocks. Stocks include Microsoft (MSFT), Wal-Mart (WMT), and IBM (IBM).

- **Nasdaq 100**   The set of the 100 largest company stocks listed on the Nasdaq. Stocks include Microsoft (MSFT), Intel (INTC), Dell (DELL), and Yahoo! (YHOO).

- **Nasdaq Composite**   The set of all stocks listed on the Nasdaq.

- **Amex Composite**   The set of all stocks listed on the American Stock Exchange.

- **Russell 2000**   A set of 2,000 small-company stocks. Atari (ATAR), Zale (ZLC), and Fossil (FOSL) are stocks in the Russell 2000.

- **Wilshire 5000**   Although the name seems to indicate a set of 5,000 stocks, the Wilshire index actually contains over 6,000 stocks and is sometimes referred to as the Total Stock Market Index.

a) The www.nyse.com and www.nasdaq.com sites each have links to index information on their home pages, as well as a quote lookup for individual stocks. Newspapers also publish stock and index performance information. Each of the indexes have corresponding Web sites, with most sites providing a list of stocks in the index.

Create a spreadsheet named Stock Indexes that includes each of the indexes and three stocks from each index. The stock data should include the company name, ticker symbol, and index that tracks the stock. Add data for the last closing price for each of the stocks and the closing value for each of the indexes.

b) Expand the Stock Indexes spreadsheet by adding closing stock prices and index values for at least five different days. Be sure to include dates.

c) How does individual stock performance compare to the overall performance of the index that tracks the stock? Chart the data to show this information.

Exercise 9 ———————————————— Local Temperatures

Plan a worksheet that stores the average temperature for each month in your city or local area.

a) Research monthly average temperature data for your local area using the Internet or newspapers.

b) Create a new workbook.

c) Enter the researched data and apply appropriate formatting.

d) Create a line chart on the active sheet that illustrates the differences in the average monthly temperatures over a year. Include an appropriate title, legend, axes labels and formatting.

e) Print preview and move and size the chart so that the chart and data fit on one page in landscape orientation.

f) Create a header that right aligns your name.

g) Save the workbook naming it Local Temperatures and print a copy with gridlines and row and column headings.

Exercise 10 ———————————————— Driving Distances

Plan a worksheet that stores the driving distance from your city or local area to six cities you would like to visit.

a) Research the driving distance from your city or local area to six cities using the Internet or an atlas.

b) Create a new workbook.

c) Enter the researched data and apply appropriate formatting.

d) Decide what type of chart would best illustrate the data and create a chart on the active sheet that illustrates the distance between your city or local area and the six cities. Include an appropriate title, legend, axes labels, and formatting.

e) Print preview and move and size the chart so that the chart and data fit on one page in landscape orientation.

f) Create a header that right aligns your name.

g) Save the workbook naming it Driving Distances and print a copy with gridlines and row and column headings.

Exercise 11 ⟳ ——————————————————————— Pizza Palace

The owner of Pizza Palace wants the data charted for the Pizza Palace worksheet created in Chapter 8, Exercise 2. Open Pizza Palace and complete the following steps:

    a) Produce a pie chart on the active sheet that displays the ingredients and the percentage of their costs for the Everything pizza. Include and format the title, legend, and data labels as shown below:

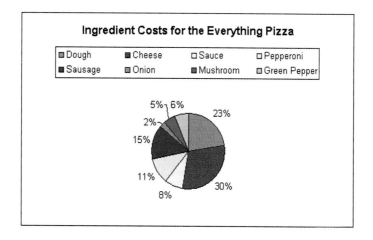

    b) Print preview and move the chart so that the chart and data fit on one page in landscape orientation.

    c) Save the modified Pizza Palace and print a copy.

Exercise 12 ⟳ ——————————————————————— Car Loan

The monthly payments calculated for a three year loan at two different interest rates in the Car Loan workbook created in Chapter 8, Exercise 4 can be compared in a column chart. Open Car Loan and complete the following steps:

    a) Produce a column chart on the active sheet that displays the monthly payment for a three year loan at 7% interest and at 10% interest. Include an appropriate title, legend, data labels, and formatting.

    b) Research the current rate for a 3 year car loan using the Internet or by contacting a local bank or financial institution. Change the 7% interest rate in cell B5 to the current rate.

    c) Print preview and move the chart so that the chart and data fit on one page.

    d) Save the modified Car Loan and print a copy.

Exercise 13 ↻ ———————————— Automobile Lease, Buy vs Lease

The Automobile Lease workbook created in Chapter 8, Exercise 13 compares the cost of leasing versus purchasing an automobile. The comparison can be illustrated in a column chart. Open Automobile Lease and complete the following steps:

   a) Create a column chart on the active sheet that displays the cost of leasing versus the cost of purchasing an automobile. Include an appropriate title, legend, data labels, and formatting.

   b) Open the Buy vs Lease Word document, which was created in Chapter 8, Exercise 13.

   c) Use the chart to enhance the report by copying the column chart to the Word document and making any appropriate edits to the text.

   d) Save and then print the Word document.

Exercise 14 ———————————————— KITCHEN RENOVATIONS

A renovation project should start with a budget that estimates all the expenses involved in undertaking a project. The KITCHEN RENOVATIONS workbook contains a list of estimated and actual costs for a kitchen renovation project. The home owner wants the data charted to compare the estimated and actual costs. Open KITCHEN RENOVATIONS, which is an Excel data file for this text, and complete the following steps:

   a) Produce a column chart on a new sheet named Costs that displays the estimated and actual expenses for the project. Include and format the titles and legend as shown:

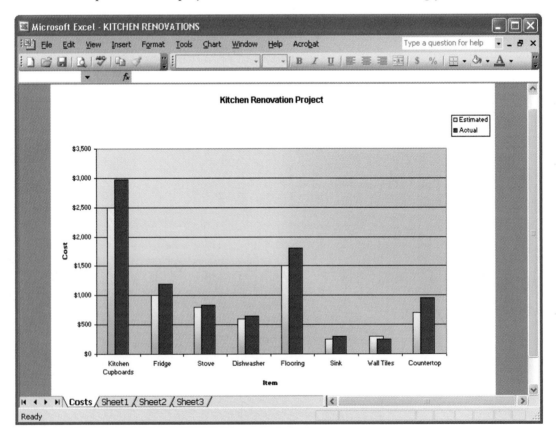

b) On the Chart toolbar, select Plot Area in the Chart Objects list and then select the Format Plot Area button. In the Format Plot Area dialog box, select the Fill Effects button and then select the Gradient tab. Experiment and then select gradient fill options to change the appearance of the plot area.

c) Double-click the first bar on the chart that represents an estimated cost to display the Format Data Series dialog box. Select the Options tab and then change the Overlap to 50. The estimated cost bars appear to move behind the actual costs bars. Select the Patterns tab and then select the Fill Effects button. Select a pattern or texture to change the appearance of the estimated bars.

d) Create a header on the Costs sheet with your name right aligned.

e) Save the modified KITCHEN RENOVATIONS and print a copy of the Costs sheet.

Exercise 15 ———————————————————— Chart Types

Excel allows many different types of charts to be created. For example, a stock chart, such as the Hi-Lo-Close chart illustrates the high, low, and close price of a stock over a period of time:

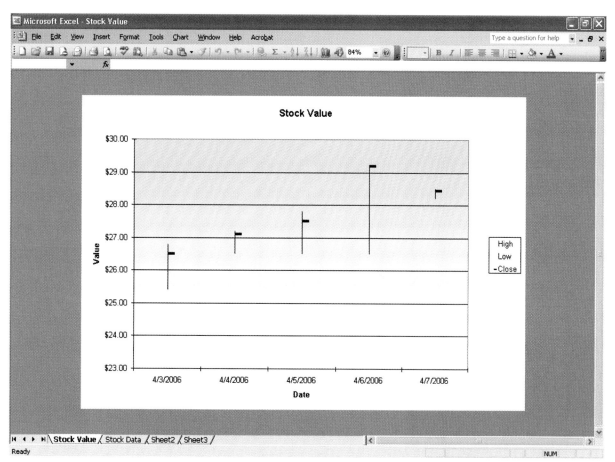

The data for the Hi-Lo-Close chart should be organized similar to:

	A	B	C	D
1	Date	High	Low	Close
2	3-Apr	$26.80	$25.40	$26.50
3	4-Apr	$27.20	$26.50	$27.10
4	5-Apr	$27.80	$26.50	$27.50
5	6-Apr	$29.20	$26.50	$29.20
6	7-Apr	$28.50	$28.20	$28.45

a) Create a new workbook.

b) Use the three sheets in the workbook to enter data that can be charted using chart types other than pie, line, and bar charts. Create the corresponding chart on the active sheet. Research chart types using the Excel help features before starting.

c) Create a header that right aligns your name and a footer that center aligns the sheet name on all three sheets. Add gridlines and row and column headings.

d) Save the workbook naming it Chart Types.

e) Print a copy of the entire workbook.

Chapter 10

Advanced Spreadsheet Techniques

This chapter introduces the CHOOSE and VLOOKUP functions. Creating hyperlinks within a workbook, data forms, data validation, lists, and macros are also discussed.

The CHOOSE Function

The *CHOOSE function* is a lookup function that is used to return a value from a list of values. The CHOOSE function takes the form:

=CHOOSE(<choice>, <option$_1$>, <option$_2$>, ..., <option$_N$>)

<choice> is a number between 1 and 29 or a formula or reference to a cell containing a number between 1 and 29.

<option$_1$>, <option$_2$>, ... store the possible values to return.

CHOOSE returns the value in the list of arguments that corresponds to <choice>. If <choice> is 1, CHOOSE returns <option$_1$>; if <choice> is 2, then <option$_2$> is returned, and so on. For example, the worksheet below is used to determine an employee's bonus based on the performance rating score the employee received:

C4		▼	*fx* =CHOOSE(B4, 2500, 2000, 1500, 1000)		
	A	B	C	D	E
1	**Employee Performance Rating**				
2					
3	Employee	Rating	Bonus		
4	Boston, J.	2	$2,000		
5	Carrier, T.	3	$1,500		
6	Perez, A.	1	$2,500		
7	Williams, B.	4	$1,000		

Cell C4 displays 2000 (<option$_2$>) because the value <choice> in cell B4 is 2

Only the integer portion of <choice> is used to determine which value to return. For example, in the worksheet above, if cell B4 stored 1.6, 2500 would be displayed because only the integer portion of the value, 1, is used. If <choice> is less than 1 or greater than N, #VALUE! is displayed, indicating a corresponding value is not available.

The options (<option₁>, <option₂>, ...) in the CHOOSE function can also include formulas, cell references, and text. For example, the formula in cell D4 uses a CHOOSE function to return text:

	D4	▼	ƒ	=CHOOSE(B4, "Outstanding", "Excellent", "Good", "Satisfactory")		
	A	B	C	D	E	F	G
1	**Employee Performance Rating**						
2							
3	Employee	Rating	Bonus	Comments			
4	Boston, J.	2	$2,000	Excellent			
5	Carrier, T.	3	$1,500	Good			
6	Perez, A.	1	$2,500	Outstanding			
7	Williams, B.	4	$1,000	Satisfactory			
8							

Practice: EMPLOYEE DISCOUNT PROGRAM

You will use the CHOOSE function to calculate the discount an employee receives when purchasing company merchandise.

① **OPEN EMPLOYEE DISCOUNT PROGRAM**

a. Start Excel.

b. Open EMPLOYEE DISCOUNT PROGRAM, which is an Excel data file for this text. The EMPLOYEE DISCOUNT PROGRAM workbook contains a list of employees and their level ranking within the company:

	A	B	C
1	**Employee Discount Program**		
2			
3	Employee	Level	Discount
4	Andrews, P.	4	
5	Barnes, J.	3	
6	Briglio, K.	1.5	
7	Carswell, I.	0	
8	King, P.	4	
9	Rowlinson, B.	4	
10	Smith, A.	2	
11	Thomas, M.	2	
12	Tucci, M.	1	
13	Young, H.	1	

② **ENTER FORMULAS TO CALCULATE THE DISCOUNT**

Each of the levels corresponds to the percentage discount an employee receives on company merchandise:

Level	Percentage
1	10%
2	15%
3	20%
4	25%

a. In cell C4, enter the formula: =CHOOSE(B4, 10%, 15%, 20%, 25%)

The CHOOSE function first looks in cell B4 to determine the value of <choice>. Because the value in cell B4 is 4, this corresponds to <option₄> and Excel displays 0.25, which is the decimal equivalent of 25%.

b. Copy the formula in cell C4 to cells C5 through C13:

	A	B	C	D
1	Employee Discount Program			
2				
3	Employee	Level	Discount	
4	Andrews, P.	4	0.25	
5	Barnes, J.	3	0.2	
6	Briglio, K.	1.5	0.1	
7	Carswell, I.	0	#VALUE!	
8	King, P.	4	0.25	
9	Rowlinson, B.	4	0.25	
10	Smith, A.	2	0.15	
11	Thomas, M.	2	0.15	
12	Tucci, M.	1	0.1	
13	Young, H.	1	0.1	
14				
15				

③ *FORMAT THE DISCOUNT RATES AND EXAMINE RESULTS*

a. Format cells C4 through C13 as percentage with 0 decimal places:

	A	B	C
1	Employee Discount Program		
2			
3	Employee	Level	Discount
4	Andrews, P.	4	25%
5	Barnes, J.	3	20%
6	Briglio, K.	1.5	10%
7	Carswell, I.	0	#VALUE!
8	King, P.	4	25%
9	Rowlinson, B.	4	25%
10	Smith, A.	2	15%
11	Thomas, M.	2	15%
12	Tucci, M.	1	10%
13	Young, H.	1	10%

b. Note that the employee in row 6 has a ranking of 1.5 and receives a discount of 10%. Why does this employee receive the same discount as level 1 employees?

c. Why is #VALUE! displayed in cell C7?

d. Change the value in cell B7 to 2.

④ *SAVE, PRINT, AND CLOSE THE MODIFIED EMPLOYEE DISCOUNT PROGRAM*

a. Add a footer that right aligns your name.

b. Save the modified EMPLOYEE DISCOUNT PROGRAM.

c. Print a copy.

d. Close EMPLOYEE DISCOUNT PROGRAM.

Naming a Cell or Range

Complicated and repetitive formulas can use named cells or cell ranges to simplify a formula, save time, and prevent data entry errors. To name a cell or range of cells, select the cell(s) and then type a descriptive name in the Name box. For example, in the worksheet on the next page, the selected range is named Test1:

Name box ———

	A	B	C	D	E	F
		Test1 ▾	*fx* 85			
1	Name	Test 1	Test 2	Test 3	Test 4	
2		9/4/06	9/14/06	9/20/06	10/9/06	
3						
4	Garcia, E.	85	73	88	95	
5	Neave, C.	92	88	85	91	
6	Jones, D.	72	81	67	72	
7	McCallister, T.	87	92	85	93	
8	Smith, L.	94	91	93	84	
9	Bell, M.	70	74	80	83	
10						
11						

Rules for Naming

When naming a cell or range of cells, all names must begin with a letter, backslash (\), or an underscore. Single letters and names that are similar to cell references should not be used.

HLOOKUP Function

The HLOOKUP function is very similar to the VLOOKUP function in that both functions return a value from a table of values stored in a worksheet.

To use a VLOOKUP function, the values in the lookup table must be organized vertically in columns and to use an HLOOKUP function the values in the lookup table must be organized horizontally in rows.

The named range can then be used in formulas. For example, the formula =AVERAGE(Test1) would calculate the average of the test scores in cells B4 through B9. A named range is an absolute reference.

To select a named range, click the Name box arrow and then click the name. To delete a range name, select Insert → Name → Define to display the Define Name dialog box. Select the named range and then select Delete. To modify a range name, a new named range must be created and then the old one deleted.

VLOOKUP Function

The *VLOOKUP function* is a lookup function that is used to return a value from a table of values stored in the worksheet. The VLOOKUP function takes the form:

=VLOOKUP(<value>, <range>, <column>)

<value> is a number to be looked up in a table of values.

<range> is the cell range where the VLOOKUP table is stored.

VLOOKUP finds the largest number in the first column of <range> which is less than or equal to <value>, and then returns the value stored in the same row in column <column> of the VLOOKUP table. The value of <column> is usually 2 to indicate that the second column in the VLOOKUP table stores the value to be returned.

For example, the worksheet below determines the shipping cost based on the amount of the order, with orders over $1,000 receiving free shipping:

	A	B	C	D	E	F
	C4 ▾		*fx* =VLOOKUP(B4, $D$11:$E$15, 2)			
1	**Boca Distributing**					
2						
3	Customer	Amount	Shipping			
4	Express Stop	$245.25	$12.50			
5	West Lake Produce	$230.50	$12.50			
6	The Moving Company	$459.80	$25.00			
7	Hospital Food Services	$1,250.67	$0.00			
8	Office Supply	$678.93	$40.00			
9						
10				Shipping Fees		
11				$0.00	$12.50	
12				$250.00	$25.00	
13				$500.00	$40.00	
14				$750.00	$60.00	
15				$1,000.00	$0.00	
16						

With the formula =VLOOKUP(B4, $D$11:$E$15, 2) in cell C4:

1. Excel looks in cell B4 for the lookup value, which is $245.25.

2. Excel then looks in the first column of the VLOOKUP table for the largest value which is less than or equal to $245.25, in this case $0.00 (stored in D11).

3. The corresponding value in the second column of the table, in this case $12.50, is then displayed in cell C4.

In a similar manner, the function displays $0.00 in cell C7 because cell D15 stores the largest value in the VLOOKUP table which is less than or equal to $1,250.67 (the value stored in cell B7).

The values in the first column of a VLOOKUP table must be in ascending order for VLOOKUP to work correctly. If <value> is less than the first value stored in the VLOOKUP table, #N/A! is displayed. For this reason, the first value stored in the VLOOKUP table must be less than or equal to any value that will be looked up.

In the VLOOKUP function, absolute references are used for the VLOOKUP table range so that the range does not change when the formula containing the VLOOKUP function is copied.

named range   The range that defines the VLOOKUP table can be named to simplify the formula containing the function. For example, in the worksheet below, the table range D11 through E15 has been named Shipping and the VLOOKUP function modified accordingly:

	C4	▾	*fx* =VLOOKUP(B4, Shipping, 2)			
	A	B	C	D	E	F
1	**Boca Distributing**					
2						
3	*Customer*	*Amount*	*Shipping*			
4	Express Stop	$245.25	$12.50			
5	West Lake Produce	$230.50	$12.50			
6	The Moving Company	$459.80	$25.00			
7	Hospital Food Services	$1,250.67	$0.00			
8	Office Supply	$678.93	$40.00			
9						
10				*Shipping Fees*		
11				$0.00	$12.50	
12				$250.00	$25.00	
13				$500.00	$40.00	
14				$750.00	$60.00	
15				$1,000.00	$0.00	
16						

displaying text   The VLOOKUP function will display text if labels are stored in the VLOOKUP table. For example, the worksheet on the next page uses a VLOOKUP function to return a diagnosis label:

	C2	▼	f_x =VLOOKUP(B2, $B$8:$C$11, 2)		
	A	B	C	D	E
1	Patient #	Blood Pressure	Diagnosis		
2	09-98-677	130	High Normal		
3	08-54-211	128	Normal		
4	09-06-777	150	High		
5	02-11-459	129	Normal		
6					
7		Systolic Blood Pressure Table			
8		0	Error		
9		60	Normal		
10		130	High Normal		
11		140	High		
12					
13					

Hiding Columns

An entire column can be temporarily hidden on a worksheet. To hide a column, right-click a column label and select Hide from the menu. To unhide a column, select the column headings on both sides of the hidden column, right-click, and select Unhide from the menu.

TIP Freezing cells does not affect how the worksheet is printed, only how the data is viewed on the screen.

Splitting Panes

A worksheet can be split into two panes so that the two areas can be viewed and scrolled at the same time. Select the cell one row below and a column to the right of the area to split and then select Window → Split. Select Window → Remove Split to remove split panes.

TIP The wheel on a mouse can be rolled to scroll a large worksheet quickly. The wheel can also be used to zoom. Press the Ctrl key and roll the wheel backward and forward to zoom out and in, respectively.

Freezing Cells

One difficulty encountered when working with a large worksheet is that rows and columns that contain descriptive labels may scroll off the screen. This makes it difficult to determine which columns or rows the displayed cells are in. One way to solve this problem is to freeze selected rows and columns in place so they will not scroll when the rest of the worksheet is scrolled.

Select Window → Freeze Panes to designate every row above the active cell and every column to the left of the active cell as frozen. For example, select cell B6 and then select Window → Freeze Panes to freeze the cells in column A and rows 1 through 5 from scrolling:

	A	B	C	D	E	F	G	H	I	J
1	The Garden Store									
2										
3	2006 Sales									
4										
5	Product	Jan	Feb	Mar	Apr	May	Jun	Jul	Aug	Sep
6	Pots and Planters	$320	$540	$2,056	$1,120	$1,980	$6,500	$7,000	$8,450	$4,220
7	Stepping Stones	$125	$125	$289	$2,560	$5,026	$6,502	$3,737	$4,588	$5,030
8	Lanterns	$250	$250	$389	$1,890	$2,888	$5,508	$3,500	$4,690	$1,250
9	Fountains	$125	$1,200	$2,560	$8,500	$5,800	$5,860	$7,500	$5,094	$4,600
10	Lawn & Patio Furniture	$800	$1,600	$2,562	$4,585	$7,856	$8,489	$19,887	$25,004	$12,980
11	Chimes and Bells	$810	$982	$1,012	$1,885	$4,500	$6,400	$6,989	$5,400	$2,900
12	Gas Barbeques	$1,950	$2,560	$3,200	$6,692	$8,500	$9,072	$9,000	$5,923	$7,618
13	Arbors and Trellises	$2,536	$4,100	$6,328	$3,807	$7,850	$1,649	$5,253	$3,934	$4,261
14	Sundials	$3,104	$2,467	$5,349	$7,142	$9,305	$2,712	$4,629	$3,961	$1,250
15	Bird Baths	$5,442	$2,783	$1,642	$1,582	$2,456	$5,584	$9,140	$7,915	$2,343
16	Statues	$7,815	$8,626	$6,020	$5,200	$9,107	$7,728	$5,055	$1,775	$2,211

Frozen cells are displayed with a solid border

When scrolling vertically, frozen columns remain on the screen. Frozen rows remain on the screen when scrolling horizontally. Select Window → Unfreeze Panes to unfreeze all frozen cells.

Hyperlinks to a Workbook Location

TIP Select the ScreenTip button in the Insert Hyperlink dialog box to add a ScreenTip to a hyperlink.

Hyperlinks to workbook locations can help users move within a workbook. The Insert Hyperlink dialog box contains options for inserting a hyperlink to a workbook location. To use this dialog box, select Insert → Hyperlink or click the Insert Hyperlink button ( ) on the toolbar. Select Place in This Document to display those options. Replace the existing cell reference with a label in the Text to display box. The label will be placed in the active cell as blue underlined text. Type the hyperlink destination in the Type the cell reference box.

removing a hyperlink

To remove the blue underline from the label, right-click the link and then select Remove Hyperlink from the menu. The text remains, but is no longer a hyperlink.

Practice: PAYROLL – part 2 of 3

You will modify PAYROLL to include a VLOOKUP function that determines the tax rate. Cells will also be frozen to keep the employee names and column titles on the screen. Excel should already be started.

① *OPEN PAYROLL*

Open PAYROLL, which is an Excel data file last modified in Chapter 8.

② *FREEZE TITLES*

   a. Select cell C6. Be sure that cell A1 is displayed on the screen as well.

   b. Select Window → Freeze Panes. The frozen cells are indicated by solid borders:

	A	B	C	D	E	F	G	H	I	J	K
1	Payroll										
2											
3	Soc. Sec. Rate:	6.0%									
4											
5	Last Name	First Initial	Rate/Hr	Hours	Overtime Hours	Overtime Pay	Gross Pay	Soc. Sec.	Taxes	Net Pay	
6											
7	Alban	B.	$7.50	30.0	0.0	$0.00	$225.00	$13.50	$33.75	$177.75	
8	Angulo	M.	$8.00	29.5	0.0	$0.00	$236.00	$14.16	$35.40	$186.44	
9	Balto	Y.	$8.00	29.0	0.0	$0.00	$232.00	$13.92	$34.80	$183.28	
10	Cruz	S.	$7.75	13.0	0.0	$0.00	$100.75	$6.05	$15.11	$79.59	
11	Del Vecchio	F.	$9.00	42.5	2.5	$47.25	$439.75	$26.39	$65.81	$346.61	

   c. Click the right scroll arrow several times to scroll horizontally until column L is displayed beside column B. Note that columns A and B remain displayed while other columns are scrolled off the screen.

   d. Click the down scroll arrow until row 45 is displayed in the window. Note that rows 1 through 5 remain on the screen.

   e. Press Ctrl+Home to return to cell C6.

③ *ADD A VLOOKUP TABLE TO THE WORKSHEET*

The following tax rates will be used in calculating taxes:

Salary	Tax Rate
under $101	0%
$101 – $524	15%
$525 – $1,124	28%
$1,125 and above	31%

a. In cell J26, enter the label Tax Rate Table and bold the label.

b. Enter the following values into the indicated cells to create the VLOOKUP tax table:

In cell	J27	enter	$0	In cell	K27	enter	0%
	J28		$101		K28		15%
	J29		$525		K29		28%
	J30		$1,125		K30		31%

④ *NAME THE TABLE RANGE*

a. Select cell J27 through K30.

b. Click in the Name box. Type Rate and press the Enter key:

⑤ *CALCULATE TAXES USING THE VLOOKUP FUNCTION*

In the PAYROLL worksheet, taxes are currently calculated by applying a 15% tax rate to all employees. Typically tax rates are based on gross pay, therefore the existing formula will be modified to include a VLOOKUP function to retrieve the appropriate tax rate.

a. In cell I7, replace the existing formula with: =G7*VLOOKUP(G7, Rate, 2)

The gross pay stored in cell G7 is $225.00, which is multiplied by 15% to compute the tax deduction of $33.75.

b. Copy the formula in cell I7 to cells I8 through I23.

c. Click any cell to remove the selection. The worksheet should look similar to:

	A	B	C	D	E	F	G	H	I	J	K	L
1	Payroll											
2												
3	Soc. Sec. Rate:	6.0%										
4												
5	Last Name	First Initial	Rate/Hr	Hours	Overtime Hours	Overtime Pay	Gross Pay	Soc. Sec.	Taxes	Net Pay		
6												
7	Alban	B.	$7.50	30.0	0.0	$0.00	$225.00	$13.50	$33.75	$177.75		
8	Angulo	M.	$8.00	29.5	0.0	$0.00	$236.00	$14.16	$35.40	$186.44		
9	Balto	Y.	$8.00	29.0	0.0	$0.00	$232.00	$13.92	$34.80	$183.28		
10	Cruz	S.	$7.75	13.0	0.0	$0.00	$100.75	$6.05	$0.00	$94.71		
11	Del Vecchio	E.	$9.00	43.5	3.5	$47.25	$438.75	$26.33	$65.81	$346.61		
12	Eklund	E.	$9.50	31.0	0.0	$0.00	$294.50	$17.67	$44.18	$232.66		
13	Esposito	S.	$11.75	43.5	3.5	$61.69	$572.81	$34.37	$160.39	$378.06		
14	Hirsch	I.	$9.50	18.0	0.0	$0.00	$171.00	$10.26	$25.65	$135.09		
15	Juarez	V.	$7.75	21.0	0.0	$0.00	$162.75	$9.77	$24.41	$128.57		
16	Karas	A.	$8.00	15.0	0.0	$0.00	$120.00	$7.20	$18.00	$94.80		
17	Keller-Sakis	G.	$8.50	20.0	0.0	$0.00	$170.00	$10.20	$25.50	$134.30		
18	Lopez	R.	$9.00	17.0	0.0	$0.00	$153.00	$9.18	$22.95	$120.87		
19	Parker	L.	$10.75	29.0	0.0	$0.00	$311.75	$18.71	$46.76	$246.28		
20	Quinn	P.	$11.75	41.0	1.0	$17.63	$499.38	$29.96	$74.91	$394.51		
21	Ramis	C.	$8.00	18.0	0.0	$0.00	$144.00	$8.64	$21.60	$113.76		
22	Rappaport	L.	$7.75	18.0	0.0	$0.00	$139.50	$8.37	$20.93	$110.21		
23	Rosen	R.	$9.50	10.0	0.0	$0.00	$95.00	$5.70	$0.00	$89.30		
24												
25												
26										Tax Rate Table		
27										$0	0%	
28										$101	15%	
29										$525	28%	
30										$1,125	31%	
31												

⑥ ADD A HYPERLINK TO A WORKBOOK LOCATION

   a. Select cell I5.

   b. On the toolbar, click the Insert Hyperlink button (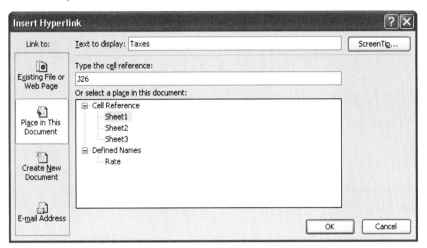). The Insert Hyperlink dialog box is displayed.

   c. Select Place in This Document to display those options. In the Text to display box, verify the label is Taxes. In the Type the cell reference box, replace the existing cell reference with J26:

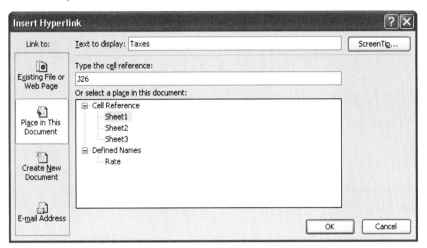

   d. Select OK. The column label is a hyperlink.

⑦ DISPLAY THE TAX RATE TABLE

   a. Select cell A1 to make it the active cell.

   b. Click the hyperlink in cell I5. The active cell is moved to the hyperlink destination, cell J26.

⑧ SAVE AND PRINT THE MODIFIED PAYROLL

Embedding and Linking Objects

static data

When Copy and Paste are used to copy data between the Word and Excel applications, the pasted data is *static*, which means it does not change when the source data changes. The Paste Special dialog box in both applications can be used to embed or link objects. An *embedded object* keeps the features of the application it was created in. A *linked object* automatically updates when the source data is updated.

To create an embedded or linked object in Word or Excel:

1. Select the data.

2. Click the Copy button (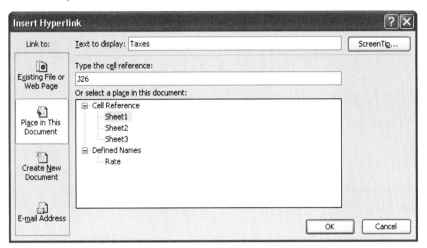).

3. Display the destination document or workbook.

4. Select Edit → Paste Special. A dialog box is displayed.

5. Select the type of object to be pasted and then select OK. To create a linked object, select Paste link before selecting OK.

Word data is pasted in Excel as a floating object that can be positioned by dragging. Excel data is pasted in Word as an inline object that can be positioned using paragraph alignments, indents, and tabs.

Double-click an embedded object to edit and update it using the source application's features. Double-click a linked object to open the source application and display the source document or workbook.

Practice: PAYROLL – part 3 of 3

You will use data in the PAYROLL worksheet to create embedded and linked objects. Excel should already be started with the PAYROLL worksheet displayed from the last practice.

① *UNFREEZE TITLES*

Select Window → Unfreeze Panes. The solid borders are removed from the worksheet.

② *COPY DATA*

a. Select cells A5 through J23.

b. On the toolbar, click the Copy button. The data is copied to the Clipboard.

③ *CREATE A LINKED OBJECT*

a. Open PAYROLL MEMO, which is a Word data file for this text.

b. Place the insertion point in the second blank paragraph after the text that reads "The company payroll for the week of April 3 is summarized below:"

c. Select Edit → Paste Special. The Paste Special dialog box is displayed. Select Microsoft Office Excel Worksheet Object and Paste link:

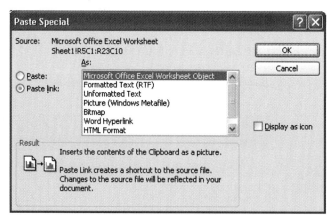

d. Select OK. The worksheet data is pasted as a linked object:

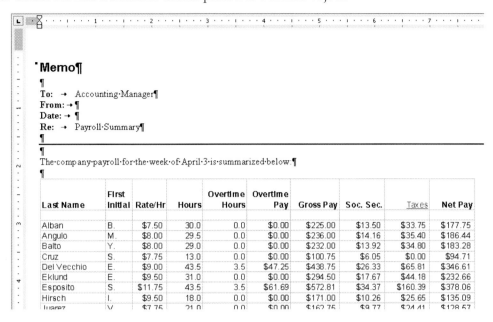

Memo¶
¶
To: →   Accounting·Manager¶
From: →¶
Date: →¶
Re: →   Payroll·Summary¶
¶
¶
The·company·payroll·for·the·week·of·April·3·is·summarized·below:¶
¶

Last Name	First Initial	Rate/Hr	Hours	Overtime Hours	Overtime Pay	Gross Pay	Soc. Sec.	Taxes	Net Pay
Alban	B.	$7.50	30.0	0.0	$0.00	$225.00	$13.50	$33.75	$177.75
Angulo	M.	$8.00	29.5	0.0	$0.00	$236.00	$14.16	$35.40	$186.44
Balto	Y.	$8.00	29.0	0.0	$0.00	$232.00	$13.92	$34.80	$183.28
Cruz	S.	$7.75	13.0	0.0	$0.00	$100.75	$6.05	$0.00	$94.71
Del Vecchio	E.	$9.00	43.5	3.5	$47.25	$438.75	$26.33	$65.81	$346.61
Eklund	E.	$9.50	31.0	0.0	$0.00	$294.50	$17.67	$44.18	$232.66
Esposito	S.	$11.75	43.5	3.5	$61.69	$572.81	$34.37	$160.39	$378.06
Hirsch	I.	$9.50	18.0	0.0	$0.00	$171.00	$10.26	$25.65	$135.09
Juarez	V.	$7.75	21.0	0.0	$0.00	$162.75	$9.77	$24.41	$128.57

e. In the From: line, type your name.

f. In the Date: line, type today's date.

g. What is the hourly rate for the employee B. Alban?

④ **UPDATE THE PAYROLL WORKSHEET**

a. Use the taskbar to display the PAYROLL workbook.

b. A data entry error was made when B. Alban's rate was entered. Modify the rate in cell C7 to $17.50. The formulas adjust to reflect the new rate.

c. Save the modified PAYROLL.

d. Use the taskbar to display the PAYROLL MEMO document. The linked object automatically reflects the changes in the source workbook. If your data has not updated, right-click the linked object and select Update Link from the menu.

⑤ *SAVE THE MODIFIED PAYROLL MEMO AND PRINT A COPY*

⑥ *CLOSE PAYROLL MEMO AND QUIT WORD*

⑦ *CLOSE PAYROLL*

Using Dates and Times in Formulas

Date and Time Functions

The =TODAY() function displays the current date.

The =NOW() function displays the current date and time. The time displayed by the NOW() function can be updated at any time by pressing the F9 key.

Excel stores dates as sequential serial values. For example, January 1, 1900 is represented by the serial value 1 and January 1, 2006 is represented by the serial value 38718 because it is 38,718 days after January 1, 1900. To view the serial value of an existing date, format the date as General.

Because dates are stored as sequential serial values, they can be used in formulas. For example, the worksheet on the next page determines when the next maintenance check is due by adding 180 days (approximately 6 months) to the date of the last check:

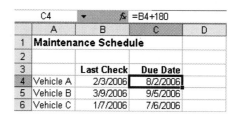

Time can also be used in calculations. For example, the worksheet below determines the duration it took to complete a task by subtracting the start time from the end time:

The result of a time calculation needs to be formatted as a 24-hour Time format, such as 13:30.

Protecting Worksheets and Workbooks from Changes

There are instances when the data in a worksheet or workbook should not be changed. The Protect Sheet dialog box contains options for protecting the contents of the active sheet. To use this dialog box, select Tools → Protection → Protect Sheet:

TIP To keep certain cells unprotected, select the cells, and then select Format → Cells to display the Format Cells dialog box. Select the Protection tab and then clear the Locked check box. This step has to be completed before protecting a sheet.

Specific tasks can be allowed even if a worksheet is protected. For example, select the Format cells check box to allow users to change the cell format, but not the values in the cell. Select OK to protect all the cells on the active worksheet. Select Tools → Protection → Unprotect Sheet to unprotect the sheet. If a password was typed in the Password to unprotect sheet box, the password will be needed to unprotect the sheet.

The Protect Workbook dialog box contains options for protecting the contents of the entire workbook. To use this dialog box, select Tools → Protection → Protect Workbook:

Select the **Structure** check box to prevent sheets from being deleted, moved, renamed, or inserted. Select the **Windows** check box to prevent the window from being moved, sized, or closed. Select Tools → Protection → Unprotect Workbook to unprotect the workbook. If the workbook was password protected, the password will be needed.

Practice: Project Timeline

You will determine the project dates and the length of a workday using dates and times in calculations. You will also protect the worksheet from changes.

① *CREATE A NEW WORKBOOK*

    a. In a new workbook, enter the following data and format it as shown:

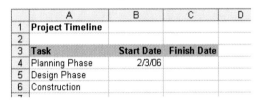

	A	B	C	D
1	**Project Timeline**			
2				
3	**Task**	**Start Date**	**Finish Date**	
4	Planning Phase	2/3/06		
5	Design Phase			
6	Construction			

    b. Save the workbook naming it: Project Timeline

② *CALCULATE DATES*

    a. Two weeks (14 days) are required for the Planning Phase of the project. In cell C4, enter the formula =B4+14.

    b. What is the finish date for the Planning Phase of the project?

    c. The Design Phase will be started three days after the Planning Phase is finished. In cell B5, enter the formula =C4+3.

    d. What is the start date for the Design Phase of the project?

    e. The Design Phase will take 4 weeks (28 days) to complete. In cell C5, enter the formula =C4+28.

    f. What is the finish date of the Design Phase?

    g. The Construction will start one day after the Design Phase is finished and will take 6 months (180 days) to complete. In cells B6 and B7, enter formulas to calculate the start and finish date for the Construction.

③ *ADD TIME CALCULATIONS*

   a. Add a work schedule for the project teams. Starting in cell A8, enter the following data and format it as shown:

	A	B	C	D	E
1	**Project Timeline**				
2					
3	**Task**	**Start Date**	**Finish Date**		
4	Planning Phase	2/3/06	2/17/06		
5	Design Phase	2/20/06	3/17/06		
6	Construction	3/18/06	9/14/06		
7					
8	**Work Schedule**	**Start Time**	**End Time**	**Hours**	
9	Planning Team	9:30 AM	4:30 PM		
10	Design Team	12:30 PM	7:30 PM		
11	Construction Team	7:00 AM	5:00 PM		
12					

   b. Select cells D9 through D11 and format the cells as Time, similar to 13:30.

   c. In cell D9, calculate how many hours the Planning Team will work during the day by entering the formula =C9-B9.

   d. Copy the formula in cell D9 to cells D10 and D11.

   e. Which team works the longest hours during the day?

④ *PROTECT THE WORKSHEET*

   a. The project manager wants to be sure the dates and times are not altered in the worksheet. Select Tools → Protection → Protect Sheet. The Protect Sheet dialog box is displayed.

   b. In the Password to unprotect sheet box, type lock and select the options as shown:

   c. Select OK. The Confirm Password dialog box is displayed:

d. Type password lock in the Reenter password to proceed box. Why would it be a good idea to write down the password in a secret location at this point?

e. Select OK.

f. Select cell A2. Try to type your name. A warning dialog box is displayed because the sheet is protected. Select OK to remove the warning dialog box.

⑤ *UNPROTECT THE SHEET*

a. Select Tools → Protection → Unprotect Sheet. A dialog box is displayed:

b. Type lock in the Password box and select OK.

c. Select cell A2. Type your first and last name. You are able to enter your name because the protection has been removed from the worksheet.

⑥ *SAVE, PRINT, AND THEN CLOSE THE MODIFIED PROJECT TIMELINE*

Data Validation

Data entry criteria can be specified for a cell or range of cells to avoid data entry errors. To create data entry criteria, select a range of cells and then select Data → Validation, which displays a dialog box:

The type of data to allow, such as Whole numbers or Decimals is selected in the Allow list. A specific range of numbers can then be specified in the Data list. To prompt the user with a message about the type of data to enter, select the Input Message tab and then type the message in the Input message box. Cells with validation criteria will display an error message if a user enters invalid data.

To remove data validation criteria, select the affected cells, select Data → Validation and then select Clear All.

Data Forms

A data form can be generated from a range of data in order to simplify data entry. For example, the data form below was created based on the column labels in row 1:

TIP The title bar of a data form contains the name of the worksheet.

To create a data form, type column labels and then select the cell in the next row. Select Data → Form to display a form. If a warning dialog box is displayed, select OK. Type the entry for the first row, pressing the Tab key to move between entry boxes. Select New to add data for the next row. Select Close when data entry is complete.

Creating Lists

TIP An Excel list is similar to a flat file database.

An *Excel list* is a range of related data that can be sorted and filtered. The list must be data that is organized into rows and columns, with column labels in the first row. To create a list, select the cells containing the data for the list and then select Data → List → Create List: The list is marked with a thick border and a ✳ marks the row where additional data can be entered:

	A	B	C	D	E
1	ID	First Name	Last Name	Department	
2	990	Michael	Edwards	Sales	
3	245	Sarah	Quinn	Marketing	
4	238	Allan	Ramirez	Marketing	
5	456	Jenny	Evans	Events	
6	722	Emily	Smith	Sales	
7	212	Darren	Graham	Security	
8	✳				
9					

Building Lists

When entering the data for a list, the top row should contain labels, each column label has to be unique, and the list cannot contain blank rows or columns.

Each column label includes an arrow for displaying sort commands and filter criteria:

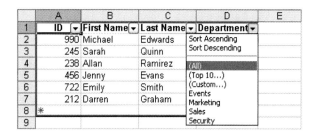

- Select Sort Ascending or Sort Descending to sort the rows in the list based on the data in the selected column.

filter
- A *filter* displays only the rows that meet specific criteria, which is selected from a column label list. For example, select Marketing from the Department list above to display only the rows that have Marketing in the Department column. To further narrow a filter, select criteria from one of the other column lists. Select (All) to remove filter criteria.

Practice: ART STUDIO STUDENTS

You will create a data form to enter a list of art studio students. You will also specify what type of data can be entered into a column.

① *OPEN ART STUDIO STUDENTS*

Open ART STUDIO STUDENTS, which is an Excel data file for this text.

② *SET DATA VALIDATION CRITERIA*

a. Select cells A4 through A12.

b. The ID column will contain a number for each student at the Art Studio. The numbers will be between 1 and 75. Select Data → Validation. A dialog box is displayed. Select data validation options as shown:

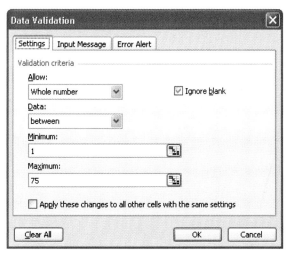

c. Select OK. The data validation criteria is applied to cells A4 through A12.

d. In cell A4, type 789 and press Enter. An error message is displayed indicating the value entered is not valid. Select Cancel.

③ *CREATE A DATA FORM*

   a. Select cell A4 if it is not already selected.

   b. Select Data → Form. A warning dialog box is displayed.

   c. Select OK. A data form is displayed:

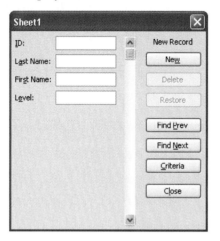

   d. Use the data form to enter the following student information, pressing the Tab key to move between entry boxes. Click New before entering the data for the next student.

ID	Last Name	First Name	Level
32	Rodriguez	Miguel	Beginner
34	Baron	Simon	Intermediate
22	Russell	Kayla	Intermediate
1	Marshall	Renee	Advanced
7	Jones	Henry	Advanced
18	Quinn	Martin	Beginner
12	Ianni	Michelle	Beginner
5	Torres	Marcia	Intermediate
8	Manchester	Madeline	Intermediate
37	Williams	Bill	Advanced
52	Dodds	Terry	Beginner
44	Martinez	Antonio	Beginner

   e. Select Close.

Check – Your worksheet should look similar to:

	A	B	C	D	E
1	Art Studio Students				
2					
3	ID	Last Name	First Name	Level	
4	32	Rodriguez	Miguel	Beginner	
5	34	Baron	Simon	Intermediate	
6	22	Russell	Kayla	Intermediate	
7	1	Marshall	Renee	Advanced	
8	7	Jones	Henry	Advanced	
9	18	Quinn	Martin	Beginner	
10	12	Ianni	Michelle	Beginner	
11	5	Torres	Marcia	Intermediate	
12	8	Manchester	Madeline	Intermediate	
13	37	Williams	Bill	Advanced	
14	52	Dodds	Terry	Beginner	
15	44	Martinez	Antonio	Beginner	
16					

④ **CREATE A LIST**

a. Select cells A3 through D15.

b. Select Data ➜ List ➜ Create List. The Create List dialog box is displayed:

c. Select OK. Each column label contains an arrow and the List toolbar is displayed.

d. Click any cell to remove the selection.

e. Click the ID list and select Sort Ascending. The list is sorted in ascending order by ID.

f. Click the Last Name list and select Sort Descending. The list is resorted in descending order by Last Name.

g. Select the Level list and then select Beginner to apply a filter. Just the rows where Level contains Beginner are displayed:

	A	B	C	D	E
1	Art Studio Students				
2					
3	ID	Last Name	First Name	Level	
7	32	Rodriguez	Miguel	Beginner	
8	18	Quinn	Martin	Beginner	
9	44	Martinez	Antonio	Beginner	
13	12	Ianni	Michelle	Beginner	
14	52	Dodds	Terry	Beginner	
16					

h. Select the Level list and then select (All) to redisplay all the rows in the list.

⑤ **SAVE AND PRINT THE MODIFIED ART STUDIO STUDENTS**

a. Create a header with your name right-aligned.

b. Save the modified ART STUDIO STUDENTS.

c. Print a copy.

d. Close ART STUDIO STUDENTS.

Macros

When creating or modifying a worksheet, a series of steps may need to be repeated. Macros can be created to perform repetitive tasks. A *macro* is a series of recorded commands and actions that perform a specific task.

The Record Macro dialog box is used to create a macro. Select Tools → Macro → Record New Macro to display the dialog box:

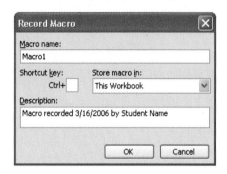

Type a descriptive name for the macro in the Macro name box. A macro name cannot contain spaces. A macro is played or started by pressing a shortcut key. Type a letter in the Ctrl+ box to create the shortcut key for the macro. Select This Workbook in the Store macro in box to store the macro in the active workbook. Type a description of the macro in the Description box. Select OK to begin recording the macro. The status bar displays Recording and the Stop Recording toolbar is displayed:

running a macro   Perform the sequence of steps to be recorded in the macro. Click the Stop Recording button on the Stop Recording toolbar to end the recording. Press the assigned shortcut key to run the macro.

editing and deleting macros   Select Tools → Macro → Macros to display the Macro dialog box to edit and delete macros.

Practice: Company Name

You will create a macro to insert a company name and address.

① **CREATE A NEW WORKBOOK**

② **CREATE A MACRO**

The company Flat Technologies Incorporated, places its name and contact information in the upper-right corner of each worksheet. Instead of having to type this information repetitively, a macro will be created.

a. Select Tools → Macro → Record New Macro. The Record Macro dialog box is displayed. Enter the options as shown, replacing Student Name with your name:

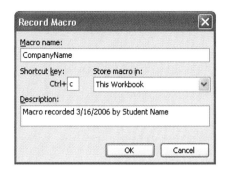

b. Select **OK**. Recording is displayed in the status bar and the Stop Recording toolbar is displayed.

c. In cell A1, type Flat Technologies Incorporated and format it as bold.

d. In cell A2, type 67 South West Drive Suite 501 and format it as italic.

e. In cell A3, type Delray Beach, FL 33445 and format it as italic.

f. In cell A4, type 561.555.3343 and format it as bold and italic.

g. On the Stop Recording toolbar, click the Stop Recording button (▣).

③ *TEST THE MACRO*

a. Display **Sheet2** in the workbook and select cell A1.

b. Press Ctrl+c, which is the shortcut key for the macro. The company name and address is displayed.

c. Display **Sheet 3**, select cell A1 and press Ctrl+c.

④ *EXPERIMENT WITH MACROS*

Create a macro for a task you do repetitively.

⑤ *DELETE MACROS*

a. Select **Tools → Macro → Macros**. The Macro dialog box is displayed.

b. Select CompanyName in the Macro name box and then select **Delete**. A warning dialog box is displayed. Select Yes.

c. Repeat steps (a) and (b) to delete macros created in step 4.

⑥ *CLOSE THE WORKBOOK*

Close the workbook without saving.

⑦ *QUIT EXCEL*

The CHOOSE function returns one value from a list of many. The VLOOKUP function returns values from a table that is stored in a range of cells. When given a numeric expression and the cell range where values are stored, VLOOKUP finds the largest number in the VLOOKUP table which is less than or equal to the numeric expression. It then returns the value stored in the specified column of the table. The range that defines the VLOOKUP table can also be specified as a named range. Both the CHOOSE and VLOOKUP functions can be used to display text.

The Name box can be used to name a cell or range of cells. The named range can then be used in formulas.

In a large worksheet, the Freeze Panes command is used to keep rows and columns containing labels from scrolling off the screen. Hyperlinks to a workbook location can help users move within a workbook.

The Paste Special dialog box in Word and Excel can be used to create embedded or linked objects. An embedded object keeps the features of the application it was created in. A linked object automatically updates when the source data is updated.

Dates and times can be used in formulas. In Excel, dates are stored as sequential serial values.

Worksheets and workbooks can be protected from changes. Data entry criteria can be specified for certain cells to avoid data entry errors. A data form can be generated for adjacent labels in order to simplify data entry.

In Excel, information in a worksheet can be defined as a list and then managed independently from the other data on the worksheet. Lists can be sorted and filtered.

Macros can be created to help perform repetitive tasks. A macro is run by pressing a designated shortcut key.

CHOOSE   A lookup function that returns a value from a list of many values.

Embedded object An object that keeps the features of the application it was created in.

Excel list   Range of related data that can be sorted and filtered.

Filter   The process of displaying only the rows in a list that meet specific criteria.

Linked object An object that automatically updates when the source data is updated.

Macro A series of recorded commands and actions that perform a specific task.

Static Pasted data that is not connected to the source file or to the source application.

VLOOKUP A lookup function used to return a value from a table of values stored in the worksheet.

Create List command Creates a list from the data in selected cells. Found in Data → List.

Define command Displays a dialog box used to delete named cell or range. Found in Insert → Name.

Form command Display a data form based on the column labels in the row above the active cell. Found in the Data menu.

Freeze Panes command Designates every row above the active cell and every column to the left of the active cell as frozen. Found in the Window menu.

Hyperlink command Displays a dialog box used to insert a hyperlink into the active cell. Found in the Insert menu. The Insert Hyperlink button on the toolbar can be used instead of the command.

Macros command Displays a dialog box used to edit and delete macros. Found in Tools → Macro.

Paste Special command Displays a dialog box used to embed and link objects. Found in the Edit menu.

Protect Sheet command Displays a dialog box used to protect the contents of the active sheet. Found in Tools → Protection.

Protect Workbook command Displays a dialog box used to protect the contents of the entire workbook. Found in Tools → Protection.

Record New Macro command Displays a dialog box used to create a macro. Found in Tools → Macro.

Remove Hyperlink command Removes the blue underline from text in a cell. Found in the menu displayed by right-clicking the cell containing a link.

Unfreeze Panes command Unfreezes all the frozen cells on a worksheet. Found in the Window menu.

Unprotect Sheet command Removes protection from a sheet. Found in Tools → Protection.

Unprotect Workbook command Removes protection from a workbook. Found in Tools → Protection.

Validation command Displays a dialog box used to specify data entry criteria for a cell or range of cells. Found in the Data menu.

1. Describe three situations in which the CHOOSE function could be used.

2. Write a CHOOSE function that displays 100 if cell B20 contains a value of 1, 500 if a 2, 900 if a 3, and 1200 if a 4.

3. Write a CHOOSE function that displays the word Excellent if cell B20 contains a value of 1, Good if a 2, Fair if a 3, and Poor if a 4.

4. a) List the steps required to name a range using the Name box.
   b) Does a named range change when it is copied as part of a formula?

5. Describe three situations in which a VLOOKUP table could be used.

6. The Widget Company uses the following discount rates when large numbers of widgets are ordered:

Number of Widgets	Discount
100 - 149	10%
150 - 999	20%
1000 - 1999	30%
2000 and above	70%

   a) Convert this into a VLOOKUP table and make a sketch of the table.
   b) Write a formula that uses the VLOOKUP function to display the proper discount percent if cell C12 stores the number of widgets and cells A1 through B5 store the VLOOKUP table created in part (a).

7. What cell should be selected to freeze the cells in column A and rows 1 through 4 before selecting the Freeze Panes command?

8. List the steps required to insert a hyperlink in cell B7 that links to cell K38.

9. Explain the difference between linked and embedded objects.

10. a) How are dates stored in Excel?
    b) List the step required to view the serial value of an existing date.

11. a) Describe a situation where worksheet data should be protected.
    b) Why would a password be added when protecting a worksheet?
    c) What two types of protection can be applied to a workbook? Explain each.

12. Why would data validation criteria be used?

13. A form should be used to more efficiently enter several rows of data. Explain this statement.

14. a) List the steps required to create a list.
    b) What is added to each column label in a list?
    c) Describe a situation where a filter could be used.

15. a) What is a macro?
    b) List the steps required to create a macro to enter the label Date, format the label in a blue font color, and right align it.
    c) List the steps required to delete a macro.

True/False

16. Determine if each of the following are true or false. If false, explain why.
    a) The <choice> argument in a CHOOSE function has to be a number between 1 and 99.
    b) The name given to a cell or range of cells can contain spaces.
    c) The values in the first column of a VLOOKUP table must be in descending order to work correctly.
    d) The range that defines the VLOOKUP table can be specified as a named range.
    e) Frozen rows remain on the screen when scrolling vertically.
    f) A password is required to unfreeze cells.
    g) A hyperlink in a cell always opens a Web browser when clicked.
    h) Word data is pasted in Excel as an inline object.
    i) The result of a time calculation needs to be formatted using a 24-hour Time format.
    j) A protected worksheet can never be changed.
    k) More than one filter can be applied to the same list.

Exercise 1 ——————————————————— FLORIDA FLIGHTS

A small commuter airline wants to use a worksheet to calculate revenue (money they collect). Open FLORIDA FLIGHTS, which is an Excel data file for this text, and complete the following steps:

a) Revenue is based on the number of tickets purchased and the type of ticket. Column B contains the type of ticket: 1 for coach, and 2 for first class. The price for tickets will be determined by the following scale:

Ticket Type	Ticket Price
1	$99
2	$150

b) Revenue is calculated by multiplying the ticket price by the number of tickets purchased. In column D, enter the label Revenue and bold and right align it. Enter formulas that use the CHOOSE function to calculate and display the revenue earned for each route.

c) Format the revenue as currency with 0 decimal places. Change the column width as necessary so that all the data is displayed entirely.

d) Create a header that right aligns your name. Add gridlines and row and column headings.

e) Save the modified FLORIDA FLIGHTS and print a copy.

f) Display the formulas in the cells instead of values. Change the column widths as necessary so that the formulas are completely displayed. Print a copy.

Exercise 2 ——————————————————— Used Books

A university bookstore buys used textbooks based on their condition. A student wants to use a worksheet to determine how much the bookstore will pay for last semester's books.

a) Create a new workbook.

b) Enter the data and apply formatting as shown below.

	A	B	C	D
1	Book Title	Original Price	Condition	
2				
3	Introduction to Digital Logic Design	$75.80	1	
4	A Guide to Computing Fundamentals	$125.25	1	
5	College Physics	$32.50	3	
6	Fiction Writing Basics	$15.45	2	
7				
8				

c) Save the workbook naming it Used Books.

d) The bookstore buys used textbooks at a percentage of the original price based on the condition of the book:

Condition	Percentage
1	40%
2	20%
3	10%

The used price is calculated by multiplying the original price by the appropriate percentage. In column D, enter the label Used Price. Enter formulas that use the CHOOSE function to calculate and display the used price for each book.

e) Bold and right align the label in cell D1. Format the values in column D as currency with 2 decimal places.

f) The student has decided that if the used price is over $20, it would be best to sell the book, otherwise it is best to donate the book to the library. In column E, enter the label What To Do. Enter formulas that use a function to display Sell for the books that will be sold or Donate for books that will be donated to the library.

g) Center align all the data in column E. Change the column widths as necessary so that all the data is displayed entirely.

h) Create a header that right aligns your name. Add gridlines and row and column headings.

i) Save the modified Used Books and print a copy.

j) Display the formulas in the cells instead of values. Change the column widths as necessary so that the formulas are completely displayed. Print a copy.

Exercise 3 —————————————————————— Target Zone

A gym wants to use a worksheet to determine the target heart rate zone for its members.

a) Create a new workbook.

b) Enter the data and apply formatting as shown below.

	A	B	C
1	**Gym Member**	**Age**	
2			
3	Brian	25	
4	Christine	20	
5	Stephanie	32	
6	Marchello	44	
7			
8			

c) Save the workbook naming it Target Zone.

d) The target heart rate is based on a person's age. In cell A8, enter the label Target Heart Rate Table and bold it. Starting in cell A9, create a VLOOKUP table based on the following criteria:

Age	Target Zone
20 – 24	100 to 150
25 – 29	98 to 146
30 – 34	95 to 142
35 – 39	93 to 138
40 – 44	90 to 135
45 – 49	88 to 131
50 – 54	85 to 127
55 – 59	83 to 123
60 – 64	80 to 120
65 – 69	78 to 116
70 and older	75 to 113

e) Name the table range Zone.

f) In column C, enter the label Target Zone and format the label as bold. Enter formulas that use the VLOOKUP function to display the target zone for each gym member.

g) Center align all the data in column C. Change the column width as necessary so that all the data is displayed entirely.

h) Create a header that right aligns your name. Add gridlines and row and column headings.

i) Save the modified Target Zone and print a copy.

j) Display the formulas in the cells instead of values. Change the column widths as necessary so that the formulas are completely displayed. Print a copy.

Exercise 4 ———————————————————— MUSIC SALE

The MUSIC SALE workbook contains an inventory of used musical instruments. Open MUSIC SALE, which is an Excel data file for this text, and complete the following steps:

a) Sort the worksheet so that the instruments and their corresponding information are in alphabetical order.

b) The selling price is a percentage of the original price based on the condition of the instrument:

Condition	Percentage
1	60%
2	50%
3	40%
4	30%
5	20%

The selling price is calculated by multiplying the original price by the appropriate percentage. In column D, enter the label Selling Price and bold and right align it. Enter formulas that use the CHOOSE function to calculate and display the selling price for each instrument. Format the values as currency with 2 decimal places.

c) Each instrument will either be sold, donated, or thrown away based on the selling price. In cell A12, enter the label What To Do Table. Starting in cell A13, create a VLOOKUP table based on the following criteria:

Sale Price	What to Do?
under $100	Throw Away
$100 – $499	Donate
$500 and above	Sell

d) Name the table range Action.

e) In column E, enter the label What To Do and format the label as bold. Enter formulas that use the VLOOKUP function to display what to do with each instrument.

f) Center align all the data in column E. Change the column widths as necessary so that all the data is displayed entirely.

g) Create a header that right aligns your name.

h) Save the modified MUSIC SALE and print a copy.

i) Display the formulas in the cells instead of values. Change the column widths as necessary so that the formulas are completely displayed. Print a copy.

Exercise 5 ⟳ ——————————————————— AQUARIUM

The AQUARIUM workbook modified in Chapter 9, Exercise 2 can be modified to evaluate the toxicity of the water to marine animals. Open AQUARIUM and complete the following steps:

a) The toxicity of water in a marine aquarium is based on the nitrite levels. On Sheet1, in cell B27, enter the label Nitrite Table and bold it. Starting in cell B28, create a VLOOKUP table based on the following criteria:

ppm	Result
under 0.25	safe
0.25 – 0.49	OK
0.5 – 0.99	unsafe
1 – 1.99	very unsafe
2 – 3.99	toxic
4 and above	very toxic

b) Name the table range Result.

c) In column E, enter the label Water is:. Enter formulas that use the VLOOKUP function to display the toxicity of the water. Center align all the data in column E.

d) Format all the data appropriately.

e) Create a header that right aligns your name.

f) Save the modified AQUARIUM and print a copy.

g) Display the formulas in the cells instead of values. Change the column widths as necessary so that the formulas are completely displayed. Print a copy.

Exercise 6 ———————————————— BOOKSTORE PAYROLL

The BOOKSTORE PAYROLL workbook contains the monthly payroll information for a bookstore's employees. Open BOOKSTORE PAYROLL, which is an Excel data file for this text, and complete the following steps:

a) Add data validation criteria to cells C6 through C11 so that only whole numbers between 1 and 15 can be entered.

b) Create a data form to enter Employee, Monthly Gross Pay, and Dependents data.

c) Enter the following data using the data form:

Diez, G.	$1,250.00	3
Roberts, D.	$1,475.00	1
Martin, P.	$1,650.00	1
Jorge, P.	$1,250.00	2
Romani, D.	$2,050.00	3
Berry, H.	$1,475.00	2

d) The taxes for each employee need to be calculated. Tax deductions are based on the number of dependents each employee has:

Dependents	Percentage
1	8%
2	7%
3	6%

Taxes are calculated by multiplying the monthly gross pay by the appropriate percentage. In column D, enter the label Taxes and right align and bold the label. Enter formulas that use the CHOOSE function to calculate and display the tax for each employee.

e) Social security is calculated by multiplying the social security rate in cell B3 by the monthly gross pay. In column E, enter the label Soc. Sec.. Enter formulas that use absolute and relative cell references to calculate the social security deductions.

f) The net pay for each employee is calculated by making the necessary deductions from the monthly gross pay. In column F, enter the label Net Pay. Enter formulas that use cell references to deduct the taxes and social security from the gross pay of each employee to get the net pay.

g) Select cells A5 through F11 and create a list.

h) Sort the list in ascending order by Employee.

i) Filter the list to display employees with 2 dependents.

j) Display all rows in the list.

k) Create a header that right aligns your name.

l) Save the modified BOOKSTORE PAYROLL and print a copy.

m) Display the formulas in the cells instead of values. Change the column widths as necessary so that the formulas are completely displayed. Print a copy.

Exercise 7 ———————————————————— FLOWER STORE

The FLOWER STORE workbook contains the items sold at a discount flower retailer. Open FLOWER STORE, which is an Excel data file for this text, and complete the following steps:

a) Add data validation criteria to cells B4 through B11 so that only decimal numbers between 20 and 99.99 can be entered.

b) Create a data form to enter Flower Arrangement, Cost, and Discount Code data.

c) Enter the following data using the data form:

Red and White Carnations	$24.00	1
Daisies and Carnations	$24.00	4
Multicolor Tulips	$26.00	2
Daisies and Yellow Roses	$27.50	2
Yellow Roses	$39.00	2
Red Roses	$39.00	1
White Roses	$39.00	3
Exotic Flowers	$46.00	4

d) The selling price of the flower arrangements are based on a percentage markup. In cell B13, enter the label Markup Table and bold it. Starting in cell A14, create a VLOOKUP table based on the following criteria:

Cost	Markup
$25 and under	35%
from $26 to $45	45%
$46 and above	35%

e) Name the table range Markup.

f) Insert a column between columns B and C, and enter the label Selling Price. The selling price is calculated by multiplying the cost by the markup percentage and then adding that total to the cost. Enter formulas in the new column that use the VLOOKUP function to display the selling price.

g) Frequent buyers receive discounts that vary depending on the flower. Column D contains the discount codes 1 through 4. The discount on the selling price is determined by the following percentages:

Discount Code	Percentage
1	20%
2	15%
3	10%
4	5%

The discount price is calculated by multiplying the selling price by the appropriate percentage and then subtracting all of that from the selling price. In column E, enter the label Discount Price. Enter formulas that use the CHOOSE function and cell references to calculate and display the discounted selling price for each item.

h) Format all the data appropriately. Change the column widths as necessary so that all the data is displayed entirely.

i) Select cells A3 through E11 and create a list.

j) Sort the list in ascending order by Selling Price.

k) Filter the list to display arrangements with a Discount Code of 2.

l) Display all rows in the list.

m) Create a header that right aligns your name. Add gridlines and row and column headings.

n) Save the modified FLOWER STORE and print a copy.

o) Display the formulas in the cells instead of values. Change the column widths as necessary so that the formulas are completely displayed. Print a copy.

Exercise 8 ——————————————————————Warranties

Most home electronic equipment is covered by a warranty. A worksheet can be used to keep track of warranty expiration dates.

a) Create a new workbook.

b) Enter the data and apply formatting as shown below.

	A	B	C
1	Warranties		
2			
3	Item	Purchase Date	Expiration Date
4	DVD Player	3/5/2004	
5	TV	2/1/2003	
6	Car	7/8/2005	
7	Truck	9/23/2003	
8	Computer	12/12/2005	
9			

c) The DVD player, TV, and computer have 90-day warranties. Enter a formula to calculate the warranty expiration date for this equipment.

d) The car and truck were previously owned and have 2.5 year warranties. Enter a formula to calculate the warranty expiration date of the car and truck.

e) Protect the worksheet.

f) Create a header that right aligns your name. Add gridlines and row and column headings.

g) Save the workbook naming it Warranties and print a copy.

Exercise 9 —————————————————Contest, SERVICE HOURS

A university is holding a community service contest. The college (College of Business, College of Nursing, and so on) whose students perform the most community service hours receives ten new computers. The SERVICE HOURS workbook contains the number of community service hours completed so far. Open SERVICE HOURS, which is an Excel data file for this text, and complete the following steps:

a) In a new Word document create a one page document that promotes the contest. The document should include a short description of the contest and a paragraph about why community service is important. It should also include the deadline, which is the end of the semester. The document will be e-mailed to each college.

b) Save the document naming it Contest.

c) Insert two blank lines after the last line of text in the document and enter the following sentence:

    To date, students have performed the following community service hours:

d) The document needs to display the number of community service hours completed for each college. Using all the data in the SERVICE HOURS workbook, insert a linked object into the Contest document after the sentence you just entered. There should be a single blank line between the linked object and the last paragraph.

e) In the Contest document, create a header with your name right aligned.

f) The undergraduate students in the College of Business have just completed a total of 650 hours of community service. Edit the workbook appropriately.

g) Save the modified Contest and print a copy.

Exercise 10 ——————————————————Decibels

When quantities can vary over very large or very small ranges, it is sometimes convenient to take their logarithms in order to get a more manageable set of numbers. The measure of the loudness of sound is one example. A sound has a value of one unit if so faint that it is barely audible. All other sounds are multiples of the sound of value 1 unit. The table below lists some common sounds and their intensities:

Type of Sound	Intensity of Sound (Units)
barely audible	1
rustle of leaves	10
whisper	100
quiet conversation	1000
ordinary conversation	10 000 – 100 000
ordinary traffic	1 000 000 – 10 000 000
heavy traffic	100 000 000 – 1 000 000 000
jack hammer	10 000 000 000 – 100 000 000 000
amplified rock music	1 000 000 000 000
jet plane (20 miles away)	10 000 000 000 000 – 100 000 000 000 000

As the table conveys, stating the numerical intensity of some common sounds can be cumbersome. Logarithms are used to make the numbers more manageable. The intensity of sound is stated in decibels, which are calculated according to the formula:

$$\text{decibels(db)} = 10 \log_{10} L$$

where *L* is the loudness of the sound.

a) Create a new workbook.

b) Enter data that includes the table above. Below the table create a decibels calculator that converts the number (sound units) typed in a cell labeled Sound to the corresponding decibels, displayed in another appropriately labeled cell.

c) Create a header that right aligns your name. Add gridlines and row and column headings.

d) Save the workbook naming it Decibels and print a copy with 10000 entered into the Sound cell.

Chapter 11

Using a Relational Database

Access is the Microsoft Office database application. This chapter introduces Access for storing and organizing data in a relational database management system.

What is a Database?

A *database* is a computer application for storing, organizing, and analyzing related data. It is used in many different ways, for inventory control, sales order entry, and maintaining information about a collection. The Microsoft Access 2003 window with an open database looks similar to:

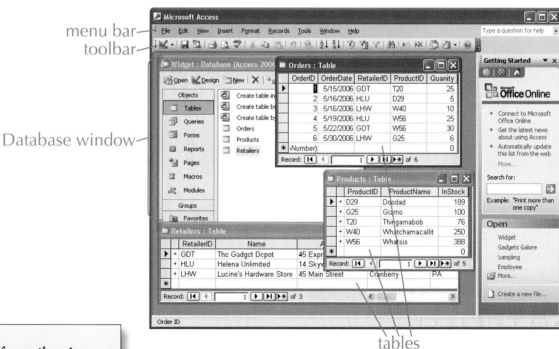

The Access window includes tools for working with a database:

- The **Database window** displays the file name of the current database. A database must be given a descriptive name at the time it is created.

- Select commands from menus in the **menu bar**.

Information Age

Our present time is referred to as the "Information Age" because the computer's fast retrieval and large storage capabilities enable us to store and manipulate vast amounts of information.

- Click a button on the **toolbar** to perform an action. Click the New button (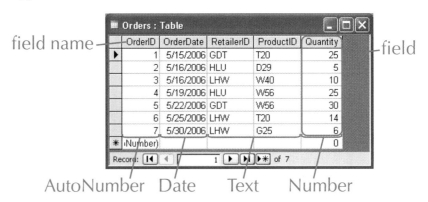) to display the New File task pane and then click the Blank database link to display the File New Database dialog box.

- Links for opening a database or creating a new database are in the **Getting Started task pane**. Click the arrow in the **Other Task Panes list** to select a different task pane to display. Click the Create a new file link for the New File task pane.

Access is a *relational database management system* (RDBMS). An RDBMS stores related data in *tables*, which are organized into columns and rows. In each table, columns are uniquely named according to the data they contain, and no two rows of data are the same. By dividing data into tables, there is less redundancy in data storage. The only repeated data between tables are the columns that create a relationship. For example, the relationship between the Products table and Orders table is the product ID data.

Database Fields

The columns in a table are called *fields*. A field is defined by its name, type, size, and format:

A well-designed database has fields that store one piece of data only. For example, a field named FullName that stores both a first and last name is considered poor design because it limits the sorting and searching capabilities of the database. A better design would include FirstName and LastName fields to separate name data.

field name

A field has a *name* that should be descriptive of its contents. Use the following guidelines when choosing field names:

- **Make field names unique**. Duplicate field names cannot be used to represent similar data. For example, a sales ID and a customer ID cannot be represented by two fields that are both named ID. Instead, SalesID and CustomerID could be used as field names.

- **Choose the shortest possible name that accurately describes the contents of the field**. In Access, field names may be up to 64 characters. When multiple words are used for a field name, each word should begin with an uppercase letter. As a matter of good design, the field name should not contain spaces. For example, ItemName is a field name that contains multiple words but no spaces.

Flat-File Database

A spreadsheet is sometimes referred to as a flat-file database because data is organized into rows and columns, but only one "table" exists for each spreadsheet file.

TIP Fields and columns are also called table attributes.

TIP Databases store many types of data. Data can be text, numbers, and links to photos, graphics, sound files, e-mail addresses, and Web sites.

- **Use complete words instead of numbers or abbreviations**. For example, FirstName is better than 1stName, or FName. Some users may not understand abbreviations.

- **Avoid special characters**. For example, #1Name, ?Name, and *Name, are poor choices for field names. Some special characters are not permitted.

field type

Fields are classified by the *type* of data they store:

- **Text fields** store characters (letters, symbols, words, a combination of letters and numbers) and numbers that do not require calculations, such as telephone numbers and Zip codes.

- **Number fields** store only numeric values.

- **Date/Time fields** store dates or times.

- **Currency fields** store dollar amounts.

- **Memo fields** store several lines of text.

- **Yes/No fields** are either selected or not selected to represent yes/no, true/false, or on/off.

- **Hyperlink fields** store links to files, e-mail addresses, and Web site addresses.

- **AutoNumber fields** automatically store a numeric value that is one greater than that in the last record added. AutoNumber fields will automatically contain unique values.

- **Lookup fields** store data retrieved from a field in another table.

Relationships

Access automatically defines relationships between tables when a lookup field is created. Relationships are discussed in Chapter 12.

field size

The *size* of a field is the number of characters or the type of number it can store. Text fields can store up to 255 characters. The size of a number field is defined by the type of value it stores. For fields that store a number with a decimal portion, the field size *Single* is used. Fields that store only whole numbers use the *Long Integer* field size. A size cannot be defined for date/time, currency, and hyperlink fields.

field format

The *format* of a field is how the data is displayed. Text, memo, and hyperlink fields usually have no format. Numeric field formats include:

- **General Number** is the default and displays a number as typed.

- **Fixed** displays a value to a specified number of decimal places.

- **Percent** multiplies the value entered by 100 and displays it with a percent (%) sign.

- **Standard** displays the value with a thousands separator, usually a comma.

Date/time field formats include:

- **Long** (e.g., Saturday, June 24, 2006 or 10:12:30 AM)

- **Medium** (e.g., 24-June-06 or 10:12 AM)

- **Short** (e.g., 6/24/06 or 10:12)

Decimal places can be set as appropriate for numeric field types. A number field with the long integer field size should have the number of decimal places set to 0. A number greater than 0 results in the long integer data value being rounded.

The Primary Key

record

The rows in a table are called *records*:

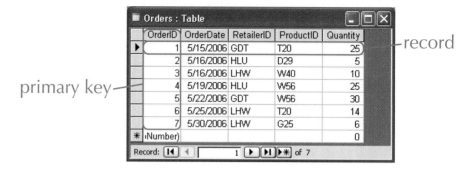

primary key

record

A table with meaningful data contains only unique records. To ensure that no two records in a table are the same, one field in each table must be designated the *primary key*. The primary key column cannot contain duplicate entries. Fields such as SocialSecurityNumber, ProductID, and SerialNumber make good primary key fields. The primary key may also be a combination of fields designated to have a unique combination of entries.

TIP If a duplicate value is entered into a primary key field, Access displays a warning dialog box.

Developing a Database Schema

A *database schema* is a description of the data and the organization of the data in a relational database. Developing a schema can be a complex project and is often handled by individuals with specialized education in database systems and database theory. However, as an introduction, below is a three-step approach for developing a schema for a simple database:

1. Determine what information should be included in the database. This decision requires considering the purpose of the database.

   For example, Widget Corporation is a wholesaler of various products and needs a database to keep track of inventory, retailers, and orders. Therefore, information such as product names, retailer names, order information, and so on should be included in its database.

2. Divide information into related groups and then give each group a descriptive name. Information should be grouped so that there is little or no data redundancy. Each of the groups should be related by one piece of information, which will require data duplication. Duplicate data is not the same as data redundancy.

   For example, the Widget database should contain product information (product ID, product name, number in stock), retailer information (retailer ID, retailer name and address information, contact information), and order information (order ID, date, retailer ID, product ID, and quantity). Appropriate names for each group are Products, Retailers, and Orders, respectively.

Normalizing a Database

Database design, or schema design, involves normalization theory, which when implemented reduces data redundancy by separating data into tables. Most designers try to achieve First, Second, and Third Normal Form, also called Boyce-Codd Normal Form (BCNF). There are many books about normalizing a database and database theory.

Metadata

Data that describes other data is called metadata. A database schema contains metadata because it describes the data in a database.

3. Describe the fields and determine the primary key for each table. Determine appropriate field names, types, sizes, and formats, if any. Determine also which field should be the primary key for each table.

For example, the field names and primary key for the Products table are:

ProductID	text field, 3 characters (primary key)
ProductName	text field, 20 characters
InStock	number field, long integer, fixed, 0 decimal places

Practice: Widget – part 1 of 12

You will use pencil and paper to complete a database schema for the Widget database. Part of the schema was developed in the previous section.

① DEFINE FIELDS FOR THE ORDERS TABLE

The Orders table should contain an order ID (a unique number automatically generated), date order was placed (similar to 6/24/06), retailer ID (a maximum three-letter abbreviation), product ID (a three-letter abbreviation), and quantity ordered.

a. Write appropriate field names for the Orders table information and next to each field name write down its type, size (keep in mind that date/time fields do not have a size), and field format, if any (keep in mind that text fields do not have a format).

b. Determine the primary key for the Orders table, which is the field that will have a unique value for each record. Write "primary key" next to this field.

Check – Your Orders table design should look similar to:

OrderID	AutoNumber field (primary key)
Date	date field, short form
RetailerID	text field, maximum 3 characters
ProductID	text field, 3 characters
Quantity	number, long integer, fixed format, 0 decimal places

② DEFINE FIELDS FOR THE RETAILERS TABLE

The Retailers table should contain a retailer ID (a maximum three-letter abbreviation), retailer name and complete address information (street address, city, state or province, zip or postal code), contact information (first and last name of contact, telephone and fax number, and e-mail address). Define the fields, including the primary key, for the Retailers table.

Creating Tables and Fields

Access displays the Database window for an open database. The Database window contains the tools for creating objects for a database. To create a new table, click [▢ Tables] in the **Objects** list and then double-click the Create table in Design view icon. A new, empty table is displayed. Create fields for the table by adding one field definition per row. A field is being added to the table below:

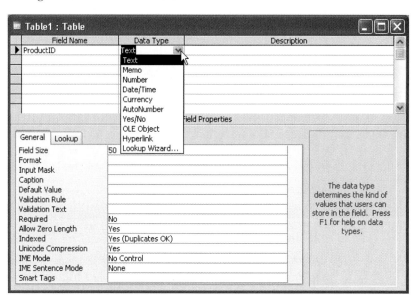

Use the following steps to define a field:

1. Type the field name in the first empty **Field Name** box. Press Tab to move to the next column in the row.

2. Select the field type from the corresponding **Data Type** box. For a lookup field, select Lookup Wizard to display a series of dialog boxes for defining where data is to come from.

3. Type a description of the data the field will store in the corresponding **Description** box.

4. Type the field size in the corresponding **Field Size** box of the **General** options at the bottom of the Table design window. For a text field, the size is the greatest number of characters allowed. For a number field, either Long Integer or Single should be selected. Date/time and currency fields do not have a field size.

5. Select a field format in the **Format** box of the **General** options at the bottom of the Table design window. Text and memo fields do not have a format.

6. Type the number of decimal places for numeric data in the **Decimal Places** box of the **General** options at the bottom of the Table design window.

To complete a table, designate a primary key. Click the Primary Key button (▯) on the toolbar or select Edit → **Primary Key** to designate the active field as the primary key. Click anywhere in a field definition row to make a field active.

TIP Field types can be selected quickly by typing the first letter of the type name.

Required option	The primary key field should require an entry to ensure that each record is unique. Click the Required option of the General options at the bottom of the Table design window, and then select Yes.
multiple-field primary key	If the combination of data in two fields is required to make every record in a table unique, then both fields together should be designated the primary key. To select multiple fields, click the gray box to the left of the first field, hold down the Ctrl key, and then click the gray box to the left of the second field. Next, click the Primary Key button (🔑) on the toolbar to create a multiple-field primary key.

TIP A multiple-field primary key is also called a composite key.

Practice: Widget – part 2 of 12

You will create the Widget relational database and its tables.

① *START ACCESS*

    a. Ask your instructor for the appropriate steps to start Microsoft Access 2003.

    b. Look at the Access window. Note the title bar, menu bar, toolbar, and Getting Started task pane.

② *CREATE A NEW DATABASE*

    a. On the toolbar, click the New button (🗋). The New File task pane is displayed.

    b. In the New File task pane, click <u>Blank database</u>. The File New Database dialog box is displayed.

        1. Use the Save in list and the contents box below it to select the appropriate location for the database file to be saved.

        2. In the File name box, replace existing text with Widget and then select Create. The Widget : Database window is displayed.

③ *CREATE A NEW TABLE*

    a. In the Widget : Database window, click ▢ Tables if it is not already selected.

    b. Double-click the Create table in Design view icon. A new table is displayed in Design view.

④ *CREATE THE FIELDS FOR THE PRODUCTS TABLE*

    a. In the first Field Name box, type: ProductID

    b. Press the Tab key to select the Data Type box. Text is the default type, which is appropriate for this field.

    c. Press Tab to move to the Description box. Type: Three character product ID

    d. In the General options, change the Field Size to 3, which is the maximum number of characters allowed for an entry in this field.

    e. In the next Field Name box, create a field named ProductName, of type Text, with the description Name of product, and a Field Size of 20.

    f. In the third Field Name box, create a field named InStock, of type Number, with the description Units remaining in stock, a Field Size of Long Integer, a Format of Fixed, and Decimal Places set to 0.

Check – Your table should look similar to:

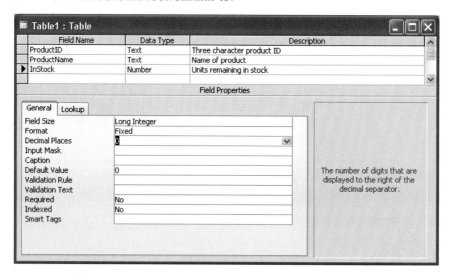

⑤ **SELECT THE PRIMARY KEY FOR THE TABLE**

The ProductID field is the primary key for this table because each ID is unique.

a. Click anywhere in the ProductID field definition row to make the field active.

b. On the toolbar, click the Primary Key button (🔑). A 🔑 symbol is displayed next to the ProductID field indicating that it is now the primary key for the table:

c. In the General options, click the Required box and then select Yes from the list.

⑥ **SAVE THE TABLE**

a. Select File → Save. A dialog box is displayed.

    1. In the Table Name box, type: Products

    2. Select OK. The Products table is saved with the database.

b. Close the table. Products appears as a table name in the Database window.

⑦ **CREATE THE RETAILERS TABLE**

a. Double-click the Create table in Design view icon. A new table is displayed in Design view.

b. Create fields for the Retailers table using the information below. Enter appropriate descriptions for each of the fields.

RetailerID	Text field, 3 characters
Name	Text field, 50 characters
Address	Text field, 50 characters
City	Text field, 25 characters
StateOrProvince	Text field, 2 characters
ZipOrPostalCode	Text field, 10 characters
ContactFirstName	Text field, 20 characters
ContactLastName	Text field, 25 characters
ContactEmail	Hyperlink field
TelephoneNumber	Text field, 20 characters
FaxNumber	Text field, 20 characters

c. Make RetailerID the primary key.

d. In the General options, select Yes in the Required box for the RetailerID field:

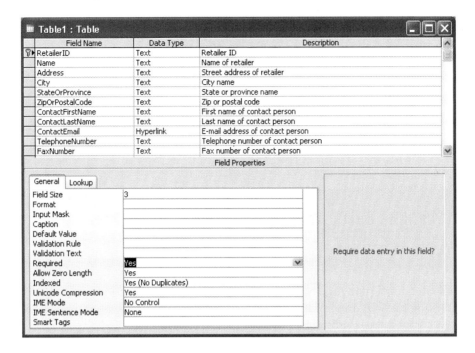

e. Save the table naming it: Retailers

f. Close the Retailers table.

⑧ **CREATE THE ORDERS TABLE**

a. Create a new table in Design view.

b. Create a field named OrderID, of **Data Type** Autonumber, with the description Order ID, and **Field Size** Long Integer. Make this field the primary key.

c. In the next **Field Name** box, create a field named Date, of type Date/Time, with the description Date order was placed, and a **Format** of Short Date.

d. In the third **Field Name** box, create a field named RetailerID, of type Text, with the description Retailer ID, and **Field Size** 3.

e. In the fourth **Field Name** box, create a field named ProductID, of type Text, with the description Product ID, and **Field Size** 3.

f. In the fifth **Field Name** box, create a field named Quantity, of type Number, with the description Number of units ordered, **Field Size** Long Integer, a **Format** of Fixed, and **Decimal Places** set to 0.

g. Save the table naming it: Orders

Check – Your table should look similar to that shown on the next page:

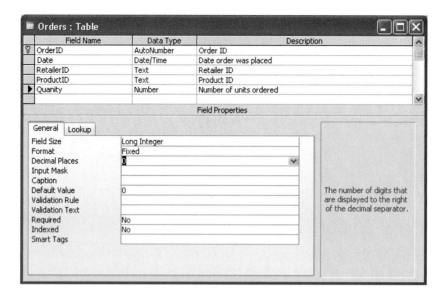

⑨ CREATE TWO LOOKUP FIELDS

The RetailerID and ProductID fields should be lookup fields because only data for existing retailers and products should be entered. Lookup fields store only existing data from a specified field in another table.

a. In the RetailerID field, click the Data Type arrow and select Lookup Wizard. A dialog box is displayed. The first option should already be selected:

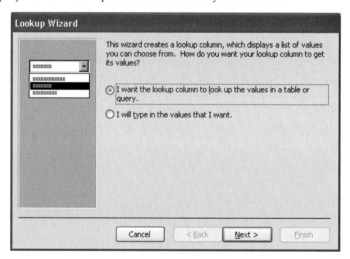

b. Select Next. The second Lookup Wizard dialog box is displayed.

c. Select Table: Retailers:

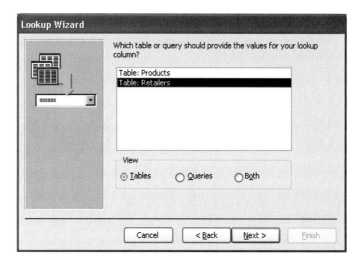

d. Select Next. The third Lookup Wizard dialog box is displayed.

e. With RetailerID selected in the Available Fields list, click $\boxed{>}$ to move the field name to the Selected Fields list:

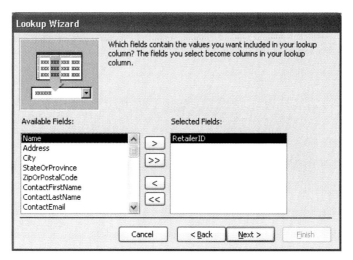

f. Select Next. The fourth Lookup Wizard dialog box is displayed.

g. In the first sort list, select RetailerID:

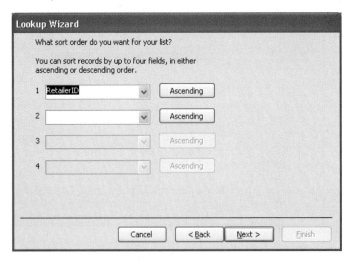

h. Select Next. The fifth Lookup Wizard dialog box is displayed:

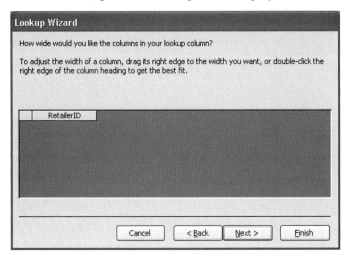

i. Select Next to accept the default size and display the last Lookup Wizard dialog box:

j. Select Finish to accept the default label name. A warning dialog box is displayed.

k. Select Yes.

l. In the ProductID field, click the **Data Type** arrow and select Lookup Wizard. Use the Lookup Wizard to create a field that looks up values in the ProductID field of the Product table. Select **Yes** to any warning dialog boxes that may be displayed.

m. Close the Orders table.

Creating and Using Forms

A *form* is a database object that displays a window with a single record in a database. A single piece of data for a field is called an *entry*. An entry box is displayed for each field in the form:

The Products form is in the *columnar form style*, which lists one field below the other in a column.

A form is based on the fields in a database. To create a new form, click [🔲 Forms] in the **Objects** list in the Database window and then double-click the Create form by using wizard icon. The Form Wizard displays dialog boxes for selecting the fields, layout, and style of a new form.

record controls To open an existing form, click [🔲 Forms] in the Database window and then double-click the form's icon. *Record controls* are displayed at the bottom of a form and are used to display a specific record:

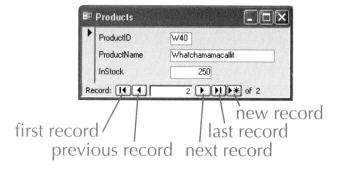

Record controls are dimmed if they cannot be used at the current time. If a table contains no data, then its corresponding form will display an empty record. Number fields automatically display a 0 until they are replaced by another value. AutoNumber field values are not displayed until another field of the record contains data. Lookup fields contain an arrow for selecting an entry.

Adding Records

TIP Adding records to a data-base is called populating the database.

When adding records to a database, it is usually best to use a form. A form displays all the fields for one record without needing to scroll, and because only one record at a time is displayed, data entry is less error-prone.

To add a new record, click the ▶✱ record control at the bottom of a form and then type the data for the new record. Click an entry box to place the insertion point in that box. For faster data entry, keep hands on the keyboard by pressing the Enter key or Tab key to move from entry box to entry box. Press Shift+Tab to move to the previous entry box in the form. When the insertion point is in the last entry box of the form, press Enter or Tab to display the next record, if there is one, or a blank record otherwise.

hyperlink fields

To enter data into a hyperlink field, select its entry box and then click the Insert Hyperlink button (🔗) on the toolbar to display a dialog box with options for specifying a link to a Web page, a file, or an e-mail address. Type the Web site URL in the Address box to create an entry that is a hyperlink to a Web site. Use the Look in box and contents box below it to specify a link to a file. Click E-mail Address to display options for specifying an e-mail address. To modify a hyperlink entry, use the Tab key to select the entry and then click the Insert Hyperlink button.

TIP Click Browsed Pages in the Insert Hyperlink dialog box to display a list of recently visited Web pages.

lookup fields

A form with lookup fields is not automatically changed to include new records. If records are added to a table with lookup fields, then a new form must be created.

As a reminder of what data a field should contain, the status bar at the bottom of the Access window displays the description of the selected field. The field description is the text that was typed in the Description box in table Design view.

Practice: Widget – part 3 of 12

You will create and then use forms to add records to the Widget database. Records will be viewed in Datasheet view. Access should already be started with the Widget Database window displayed.

① *CREATE A NEW FORM*

    a. In the Widget : Database window, click ⊞ Forms .

    b. Double-click the Create form by using wizard icon. A dialog box is displayed.

    c. In the Tables/Queries list, select Table: Retailers, and then click >> to move all the fields to the Selected Fields list:

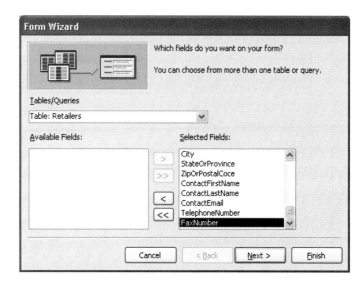

d. Select Next. In the form layout options, select Columnar, if it is not already selected:

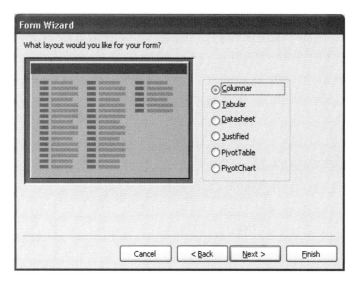

e. Select Next. In the form style options, select Standard if it is not already selected:

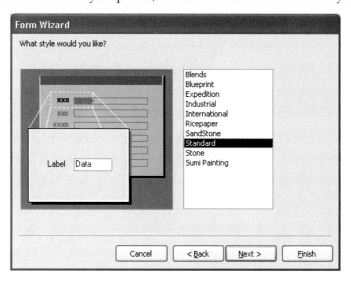

f. Select Next. In the What title do you want for your form? box, type Retailers if it not already displayed and then select Open the form to view or enter information. if it is not already selected:

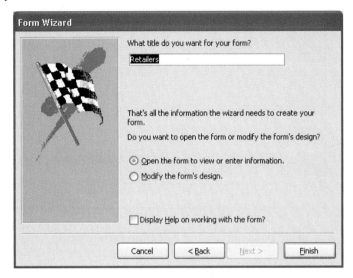

g. Select Finish. The Retailers form is displayed. Records have not yet been entered, so a blank form is displayed.

② *ADD A RECORD USING A FORM*

a. Move the insertion point to the RetailerID entry box if it is not already there. The Status bar at the bottom of the Access window displays the field description.

b. Type LHW and then press Enter. The next field entry box is active.

c. Continue entering data until your form looks like the following:

d. Click the ContactEmail entry box.

e. On the toolbar, click the Insert Hyperlink button (🖼). A dialog box is displayed.

f. In the Link to list, click E-mail Address and then complete the E-mail address box as shown. There is no need to type mailto: in front of the address because Access automatically adds it as the address is typed:

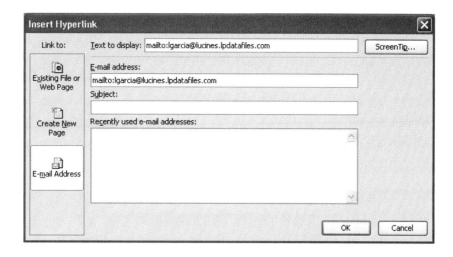

g. Select OK. A hyperlink is displayed in the entry box.

h. Press Tab. Type (278) 555-1445 for the TelephoneNumber.

i. Press Tab. Type (278) 555-1446 for the FaxNumber.

j. Press Tab. A new blank record is displayed. The record controls indicate that record 2 is displayed.

③ ADD TWO MORE RECORDS

Enter the next two records:

GDT; The Gagdet Depot; 45 Expressway Blvd.; Saulte Ste. Marie; ON; P6A 5L3; Ann; Marchand; amarchand@gd.lpdatafiles.com; (759) 555-2554; (759) 555-2556

HLU; Helena Unlimited; 14 Skyway Drive; Pepperville; NV; 89825; Marcus; Trent; mtrent@helena.lpdatafiles.com; (456) 555-7788; (456) 555-9087

④ VIEW THE RECORDS OF THE RETAILERS TABLE

a. In the record controls, click [◄] to view the first record in the table.

b. Click [►] to view the next record in the table.

c. Click [►|] to view the last record in the table.

d. Close the form. The Widget : Database window displays the Retailers form object.

e. In the Widget : Database window, click [☐ Tables]. Table names are displayed.

f. Double-click the Retailers icon. The Retailers table is displayed in Datasheet view. Note the retailer records.

g. Close the Retailers : Table window.

⑤ CREATE A FORM FOR THE PRODUCTS TABLE AND ADD PRODUCT RECORDS

a. Use the Form Wizard to create a Products form using all the fields from the Products table, in the columnar layout, standard style. Name the form Products.

b. Add the following five products records:

G25; Gizmo; 100

W40; Whatchamacallit; 250

W56; Whatsis; 388

T20; Thingamajig; 76

D29; Doodad; 189

c. Close the Products form.

a. Use the Form Wizard to create an Orders form using all the fields from the Orders table in the columnar layout, standard style. Name the form Orders.

b. The new form is displayed with (AutoNumber) selected in the OrderID field. Press the Enter key. The Date entry box is selected.

c. In the Date entry box, type 5/15/06. The OrderID value changes to a 1 because this is the first record entered.

d. In the RetailerID entry box, click the arrow. Note the IDs are those from Retailer records entered previously. Select GDT.

e. Complete the first record so that your form looks like:

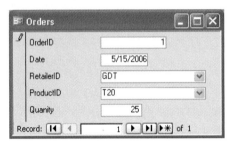

f. Add the remaining six order records. Remember to skip the OrderID entry box when entering records:

5/16/06; HLU; D29; 5

5/16/06; LHW; W40; 10

5/19/06; HLU; W56; 25

5/22/06; GDT; W56; 30

5/25/06; LHW; T20; 14

5/30/06; LHW; G25; 6

g. Close the Orders form.

Datasheet View

Datasheet view displays all the records for a table at once. To open a table in Datasheet view, click [☐ Tables] in the Objects list in the Database window and then double-click a table's icon. For example, the Products table in Datasheet view looks similar to:

The asterisk (*) that appears to the left of the row below the last record indicates where a new record will appear. It is not a blank record and it cannot be deleted or removed. The gray box to the left of each record is a record selector. Click a record selector to make a record active. The first record in the datasheet above is the active record.

The columns in Datasheet view may not entirely display field names and data. To change the width of a column, point to the *boundary*, the bar separating the column names at the top of the datasheet, until the pointer changes to ✛. Drag the boundary to the right to increase the width of the column, and drag it to the left to decrease the width.

The order in which the fields appear in a table can be changed by dragging a selected field to a new location. Select a field by pointing to the field name until the pointer changes to ↓ and then click once. Next drag the selected field to the new position. A heavy dark line indicates where the field will be moved.

After formatting Datasheet view, the table must be saved to retain the new layout.

Sorting Records

Placing records in a specified order is called *sorting*. In Access, records can be sorted in either ascending or descending order based on the data in a specified field. *Ascending order* places records from lowest to highest and is also called *alphabetical order* when a sort is based on a text field and *chronological order* when a sort is based on a date/time field. *Descending order* places records from highest to lowest.

Click the Sort Ascending (🔼) or Sort Descending (🔽) button on the toolbar to sort records. Clicking a sort button orders records in a table based on the data in the active field. For example, to place the records in the Widget Products table in alphabetical order by ProductName, click one of the ProductName entries and then click the Sort Ascending button.

Sorting the records of a table does not affect the order of the records in a form. The records in a form are ordered by clicking a field entry box and then clicking the appropriate sort button on the toolbar.

Previewing and Printing Records

A table or form should be previewed before printing. Select File → Print Preview or click the Print Preview button (🔍) on the toolbar to display the Print Preview window. Once in print preview, the document can be viewed in different ways:

- Click the **scroll arrows** in the bottom-left of the window to display the previous or next page.

- Click the **Zoom button** (🔍) on the toolbar to magnify the view. Click again to display the entire page.

Click the Print button (🖨) on the toolbar to print a copy of the table of form using the default printer settings. Click Close on the toolbar or press the Esc key to close print preview.

A table that has many columns is often too wide to print on a single sheet of paper. When this happens, Access prints the table on consecutive sheets starting from the leftmost field and proceeding to the right. If the table is too long to fit on a single sheet, rows are printed on consecutive sheets starting from the first record and proceeding to the last. However, changing the print orientation or the margins before printing can help fit the table on fewer sheets of paper.

print orientation

Select File → Page Setup to display a dialog box with page and margin options. Select the Page tab and then click Landscape to print the datasheet across the widest part of the page in *landscape orientation*. This allows more columns, but fewer rows to fit on a page. *Portrait orientation* is the default and allows more rows to be printed on a page. Select the Margins tab and decrease the margins to allow more columns and rows to fit on a page.

printing specific records

The Selected Record(s) option in the Print dialog box is used to indicate that only the active record should be printed. In a table, multiple records can be selected for printing by pressing and holding the Shift key and then clicking the record selector boxes to the left of the records to print. In a form, only the displayed record will be printed.

Practice: Widget – part 4 of 12

You will format and print tables in the Widget database. The Orders form will also be printed. Access should already be started with the Widget Database window displayed.

① *PREVIEW AND THEN PRINT THE RETAILERS RECORDS*

a. In the Widget : Database window, click ▣ Forms . The Orders, Products, and Retailers form names are listed.

b. Open the Retailers form.

c. Select File → Print Preview. The Print Preview window is displayed. Records are displayed one after another. Click the Zoom button (🔍) on the toolbar for a larger view

d. On the toolbar, click the Print button (🖨). The records are printed.

e. Close the Retailers print preview.

② *DISPLAY THE RETAILERS TABLE IN DATASHEET VIEW*

a. In the Widget : Database window, click ▦ Tables . The Orders, Products, and Retailers table names are listed.

b. Double-click the Retailers icon. The Retailers table is displayed in Datasheet view.

③ *CHANGE THE WIDTH OF COLUMNS*

a. Point to the boundary between the RetailerID and Name fields. The pointer changes to ✛.

b. Double-click the boundary. The column narrows so that it is just wide enough to display the field name and field data.

c. Double-click the boundary to the right of the Name field. The Name field column expands so that it is just wide enough to display the field name and field data entirely.

d. Continue to double-click column boundaries until all the columns are sized to display field names and field data entirely.

Check – Your Retailers table should look similar to:

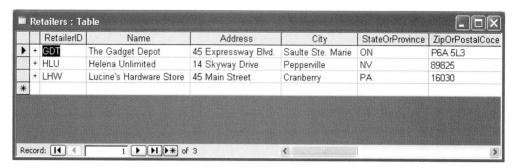

e. Save and close the Retailers table.

④ FORMAT AND PRINT THE PRODUCTS TABLE

a. Open the Products table in Datasheet view.

b. Double-click each field's right boundary. The columns are sized appropriately.

c. Save the modified Products table.

d. Print and then close the Products table.

⑤ FORMAT THE ORDERS TABLE

a. Open the Orders table in Datasheet view.

b. Double-click each field's right boundary. The columns are sized appropriately.

⑥ SORT THE ORDERS TABLE

a. Click an entry in the RetailerID field. The RetailerID field is active.

b. On the toolbar, click the Sort Ascending button (⊞). The records are sorted in alphabetical order by retailer ID.

c. Save, print, and then close the table.

⑦ SORT AND THEN PRINT THE ORDERS RECORDS

a. In the Widget : Database window, click ⊞ Forms .

b. Double-click the Orders form icon. The Orders form is displayed.

c. Click the RetailerID entry box. The RetailerID field is active.

d. On the toolbar, click the Sort Descending button (⊞).

e. Use the record controls at the bottom of the form to scroll through the records. Note that the records are in reverse alphabetical order by RetailerID.

f. Select File → Print Preview. The Print Preview window is displayed. Zoom in, if necessary, for a larger view.

g. On the toolbar, click the Print button (⊞). The records are printed one after the other in a column.

h. Close the Orders print preview window.

Modifying a Table

TIP Access automatically and periodically saves changes to a database.

A table can be modified by adding a new field, changing a field name, or deleting a field. Modifications should be done only after carefully considering and reviewing the original database schema.

A table can be modified in Design view. To switch a displayed table in Datasheet view to Design view, click the View button ( ) on the toolbar. To open a table in Design view, click [Tables] in the Database window, select a table icon, and then click [Design] on the Database window toolbar.

adding a field
renaming a field

A new field is added the same way as one is added when the table was created. To rename a field, place the insertion point in a Field Name box, edit the existing text, and then press Enter.

deleting a field

To delete a field, right-click a field name and then select Delete Rows from the menu. A warning dialog box is displayed. Select Yes to remove the field and any data in that field from every record in the table. Select No to retain the field.

creating a new form

A form is not automatically changed to match table modifications. To include table changes in a corresponding form, delete the original form and create a new one using the Form Wizard. A form is a "window" to a table of data. Deleting a form does not remove any records from the database.

Modifying a Form

Creating a Form in Design View

To create a form in Design view, with form objects selected, click [New] on the Database window toolbar to display the New Form dialog box. In this dialog box, select Design View and then select a table from the list. Add fields to the form by dragging them from the displayed field list.

A form is modified in Design view. In this view, fields can be moved to any location on the form, images can be added, and fonts and colors can be customized.

To switch a displayed form to Design view, click the View button ( ) on the toolbar. To open a form in Design view, click [Forms] in the Database window, select a form icon, and then click [Design] on the Database window toolbar. For example, the Orders form is shown in Design view. A field and its corresponding field box object are selected:

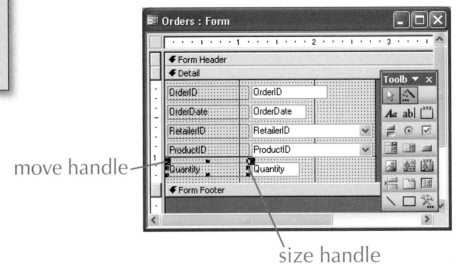

move handle

size handle

Click a field to select both the field name object and the field box object. Drag a move handle to relocate an object. Drag the center of an object to relocate a field name and its field box at the same time. Move objects as a group to maintain the current spacing. To select a group of objects, press and hold the Shift key and then click the objects to select them. Click outside an object to remove the selection from all objects. Drag a size handle to change the object size.

The Toolbox is automatically displayed when a form is in Design view. Controls in the Toolbox are used to add labels, images, and other objects to the form. To add a label, click the Label control (*Aa*) in the Toolbox. Next, click the form to place the insertion point. Type text and then press Enter. Images are added with the Image control (▨), also in the toolbox. Click the Image control and then click the form, which displays a dialog box for selecting the location of the image file.

adding an image

changing the form size

When modifying a form, size the Detail section to provide more or less room for objects by dragging the black line separating the Detail section from the dark gray area. If a Form Footer is displayed, drag just above the footer object to size the Detail section.

formatting

When a form is displayed in Design view, the Formatting toolbar is displayed in the Access window:

Formatting can be applied to any selected object. Buttons include the Fill/Back Color (▨▾), Font/Fore Color (**A**▾), Line/Border Color (▨▾)., and Line/Border Width (▭▾). Change the background color of the form by clicking an empty portion of the Detail section and then selecting a color from the Fill/Back Color button (▨▾) on the toolbar.

Updating and Deleting Records

The information in a database usually requires frequent changes. These changes include modifying existing records and deleting outdated records.

Modifying a record is called *updating*. Click the record controls at the bottom of a form until the appropriate record is displayed. Next, double-click the entry to be changed and then type to replace the existing data. Click once in a field entry box to place the insertion point so that existing data can be edited. To modify a hyperlink entry, use the Tab key to select the entry and then click the Insert Hyperlink button (▨) on the toolbar.

To delete the active record, click the Delete Record button (▶X) on the toolbar. Access displays a warning dialog box before a record is deleted. Select Yes to remove the active record. Select No to retain the record.

A form with lookup fields is not automatically changed to match modifications to records. If updates or deletions affect a table with lookup fields, then a new form must be created.

You will update a record and modify the Orders table and the Orders form of the Widget database. Access should already be started with the Widget Database window displayed.

① **UPDATE A PRODUCT RECORD**

   a. Display the Products form.

   b. Scroll to the record with ProductID T20.

   c. Change the product name to: Thingamabob

   d. Close the Products form.

② **DISPLAY THE ORDERS TABLE IN DESIGN VIEW**

   a. In the Widget : Database window, click ▢ Tables .

   b. Click Orders to select it.

   c. On the Widget : Database window toolbar, click ▨Design . The Orders table is displayed in Design view.

③ **EDIT THE DATE FIELD**

   a. Edit the Date field name so that it now reads OrderDate.

   b. Select File ➝ Save. The modified Orders table is saved.

   c. On the toolbar, click the View button (▥ ▾). The Orders table is displayed in Datasheet view. Note the OrderDate field in place of the Date field.

   d. Close the Orders table.

④ **CREATE A NEW ORDERS FORM**

   a. In the Widget : Database window, click ▦ Forms .

   b. Open the Orders form. Note the Date field has not been updated to OrderDate.

   c. Close the Orders form.

   d. To easily modify the Orders form to include the modified field, create a new form. With the Orders form name selected, press the Delete key. A warning dialog box is displayed.

   e. Select Yes. The Orders form is removed from the database.

   f. Double-click the Create form by using wizard icon. A dialog box is displayed.

   g. Use the Form Wizard to create a form using all the fields from the Orders table, in the columnar layout, standard style. Name the form Orders. The new Orders form is displayed with the modified field name.

⑤ **MODIFY THE ORDERS FORM IN DESIGN VIEW**

   a. On the toolbar, click the View button (▨ ▾). The Orders form is displayed in Design view. Size the window so that all the fields are displayed.

   b. Click the OrderID field name to select it.

   c. Drag the OrderID field name size handle so that the field name does not take up so much space:

d. Size the remaining field names and field boxes:

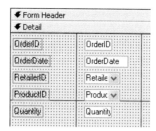

e. Click in the Detail section. The Detail bar is solid black and there are no fields selected.

f. On the toolbar, click the arrow in the Fill/Back Color button () and then select the white color. The background of the form changes to white.

g. Click the OrderID field box. Press and hold the Shift key and click the remaining field boxes:

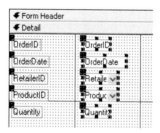

h. On the toolbar, click the arrow in the Line/Border Color button () and then select a very dark blue color. Click anywhere to remove the selection and see that the borders of the field boxes are changed.

i. Point to just above the Form Footer, the pointer changes to a double-headed arrow. Drag the Detail section down so that the form is about a half inch taller. Use the ruler on the left of the window as a guide. You may need to make the Design window larger before starting to size the Detail section:

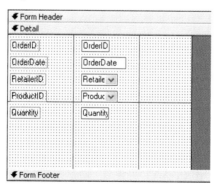

j. Use the move handles on the field boxes to move them closer to their field names. Rearrange the fields by dragging the center of a field. Leave about 1 inch of blank space above the fields. Use the ruler as a guide:

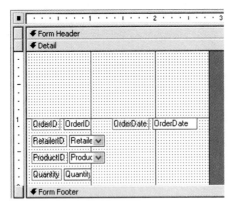

k. In the toolbox, click the Image control () and then click in the area above the fields. The Insert Picture dialog box is displayed.

    1. Use the Look in list and the contents box below to select WIDGET LOGO, which is an image data file for this text.

    2. Select OK. The Widget logo is placed on the form.

l. Drag the Widget logo, if necessary, so that your form looks similar to:

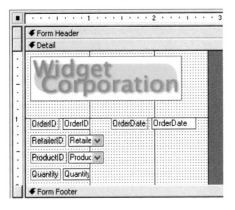

m. On the toolbar, click the View button (). The form is displayed. Resize the window appropriately and then save the form.

    Check – The Orders form should look similar to:

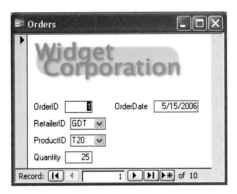

⑥ *CLOSE THE FORM*

Copy and Paste

Selecting Entries

In a datasheet, select a field entry by placing the pointer just to the left of the data until the pointer changes to ✛ and then click. Adjacent data can then be selected by dragging.

Selecting Records

In Datasheet view, select an entire record by clicking its record selector. Select multiple records by dragging a record selector.

Businesses often present database information in letters, annual reports, and other documents. Rather than retype entries and records, which could introduce typing errors, data should be copied and pasted directly into the document from the database. To copy and paste selected entries from a table to a Word document, click the Copy button (🖻) on the Access toolbar, display the Word document, place the insertion point where the data is to appear, and then click the Paste button (🖻▾) on the Word toolbar.

Data copied from Access is pasted as a table into a Word document:

Click the Paste Options button (🖻▾) to display a list of formatting options for the pasted data. Select Match Destination Formatting to format the data in the default Word table style with solid borders and Times New Roman font.

To copy database entries to a spreadsheet, select entries in a table, click the Copy button on the Access toolbar, display the Excel spreadsheet, select the cell to receive the data, and then click the Paste button on the Excel toolbar. The data is pasted starting in the selected cell.

Data for a new record often comes from another document, such as an e-mail message or an electronic form. When possible, use the Copy (🖻) and Paste (🖻) commands to copy data to database entry boxes to avoid typographical errors.

Practice: Widget – part 6 of 12

You will copy and paste data between Access and Word. Access should already be started with the Widget Database window displayed.

  ① **OPEN PRODUCTION MEMO**

    a. Start Word.

    b. Open PRODUCTION MEMO, which is a Word data file for this text. Read through the unfinished memo.

  ② **COPY DATA TO THE CLIPBOARD**

    a. Use the taskbar to display the Widget database.

    b. Display the Products table in Datasheet view.

c. Select the product name and stock data:

d. On the toolbar, click the Copy button (⬚). The data is copied to the Clipboard.

③ **PASTE DATA**

a. Use the taskbar to display the PRODUCTION MEMO document.

b. Place the insertion point in the second blank paragraph after the text that reads "…will need to work overtime:"

c. On the toolbar, click the Paste button. The data is pasted.

d. Click the Paste Options button (⬚ ▾) and select Match Destination Formatting. The memo looks similar to:

④ **COMPLETE THE MEMO**

a. In the FROM: line, type your name.

b. In the DATE: line, type today's date.

c. Save the modified PRODUCTION MEMO and then print a copy.

d. Close PRODUCTION MEMO.

⑤ **ADD A NEW RETAILER RECORD**

a. Open NEW RETAILER, which is a Word data file for this text. Read through the letter.

b. Use the taskbar to display the Widget database.

c. Display the Retailers form.

d. Click ▶✳ to display a new record.

e. In the RetailerID entry box, type: ASI

f. Use the taskbar to display the NEW RETAILER letter.

g. Select the company name that appears at the beginning of the letter and then click the Copy button on the toolbar. The data is copied to the Clipboard.

h. Display the Retailers form in the Widget database.

i. Select the Name entry box and then click the Paste button on the toolbar. The company name is pasted into the Name field.

j. Continue to switch between the letter and the database and copy and paste the appropriate data to complete the record.

k. Close the Retailers form.

⑥ *CREATE A NEW ORDERS FORM*

Adding a new retailer record requires that a new Orders form be created because the RetailerID lookup field is not automatically modified to contain the new ID.

a. In the Widget : Database window, click ▣ Forms , if it is not already selected.

b. Double-click the Create form by using wizard icon. A dialog box is displayed.

c. Use the Form Wizard to create a form using all the fields from the Orders table in the columnar layout, standard style. Name the form Orders.

d. A dialog box warns that the existing form will be replaced. Select Yes.

⑦ *ADD THREE NEW ORDER RECORDS*

a. At the bottom of the Orders form, click ▶✳ to display a new record.

b. Starting in the OrderDate field, type entries for the new record:

5/31/06; ASI; G25; 10

5/31/06; ASI; D29; 50

5/31/06; ASI; W56; 75

c. Close the form.

Creating an HTML File

Dynamic HTML

Dynamic HTML, also called server-generated HTML, connects the user to a database so that current data, also called live data, can be retrieved. The database must be on a server where the data can be shared.

HTML is the file format for documents viewed using a browser, such as documents on the Web. Select File ➙ Export to create an HTML document from table data, which displays the Export Table dialog box. Select HTML Documents in the Save as type list and then select Export. The HTML document can be viewed by anyone with a browser, such as Internet Explorer.

Data exported to HTML format is *static data*, which means it does not change. Therefore, whenever data in a table changes, the table must be exported again if the HTML document is to include the changes.

Exporting table data to HTML format creates an HTML file that can be published to the Web for viewing by many users. To send an HTML document to a limited number of viewers, select the data and then select File ➙ Send to ➙ Mail Recipient (as Attachment). A dialog box is displayed. Select HTML in the displayed dialog box and then OK. Another dialog box is displayed. Select OK to display an e-mail window with the HTML document attached and ready for sending.

Practice: Products.html

You will export a table as a Web page. The Web page document will then be viewed in a browser. This practice requires browser software. Internet access is not required. Access should already be started with the Widget Database window displayed.

① *EXPORT THE PRODUCTS TABLE*

    a. Close any open tables and forms.

    b. In the Database window, click [🔲 Tables].

    c. Click Products to select it.

    d. Select File → Export. The Export Table dialog box is displayed.

    e. Use the Save in list and the contents box below it to navigate to the same folder that stores the Widget database.

    f. In the Save as type list, select HTML Documents. Products is displayed in the File name box.

    g. Select Export. An HTML file is created.

② *VIEW THE HTML DOCUMENT*

    a. Ask your instructor for the appropriate steps to start Internet Explorer or another browser application.

    b. Select File → Open. A dialog box is displayed.

    c. Browse to the location of Products.html and then open the file.

    d. The HTML document is displayed.

    e. Quit Internet Explorer.

③ *CLOSE WIDGET AND QUIT ACCESS*

Chapter Summary

A database is a computer application for storing, organizing, and analyzing related data. Access is the Microsoft relational database management system for creating databases.

A relational database is organized into tables that contain fields and records. A field is defined by its name, type, size, and format. A record is data for a set of fields. A table must have a primary key, which is a field designated to contain unique data. The primary key of a table may also be a combination of fields designated to have a unique combination of entries. A database should be created based on a schema.

Fields for a table are created when a new table is displayed in Design view. In Datasheet view, the column width of a table is changed by dragging the right boundary of a column. A selected column is moved by dragging it to a new position.

A form is based on the fields of a table, and is used for entering and viewing records. A form is easily created using the Form Wizard and can be modified in Design view. The record controls at the bottom of a form are used for displaying a specific record in a table. A record is added to a database by typing data into a blank form. Changing the entries in an existing record is called updating. Records are deleted using the Delete Record button on the toolbar.

Records can be sorted in ascending or descending order using the Sort buttons on the toolbar.

A table displayed in Datasheet view can be printed in landscape orientation to allow more columns on a sheet of paper. Selecting Print when a form is displayed prints the records one right after the other in a column.

Data can be copied and pasted between Access, Word, and Excel. An Access table can be exported as an HTML file for viewing in a browser. When table data is sent as an e-mail, Access first converts the data to HTML before attaching the data as a file to an e-mail.

Access The Microsoft Office database application.

Alphabetical order *See* Ascending order.

Ascending order In order from lowest to highest. Also called alphabetical order when a sort is based on a text field and chronological when a sort is based on a date field.

AutoNumber field A field that automatically stores a numeric value that is one greater than that in the last record added.

Boundary The bar separating the field names at the top of a datasheet.

Chronological order *See* Ascending order.

Columnar form A form that displays a record with one field below the other in a column.

Currency field A field that stores dollar amounts.

Database A computer application for storing, organizing, and analyzing related data.

Database schema A description of the data and the organization of the data in a relational database.

Datasheet view The view used for displaying all the records for a database at once.

Date/Time field A field that stores a date or time.

Descending order In order from highest to lowest.

Design view The table view that shows the field definitions for a table.

Entry A single piece of data for a field.

Field A column in a table.

Fixed A field format that displays a value to a specified number of decimal places.

Form A database object that displays a window with a single record in a database. Used for entering and viewing records.

Format The way in which data in a field is displayed.

General number A field format that displays a number exactly as entered.

HTML File format for documents viewed with a browser.

Hyperlink field A field that stores a link to a file, e-mail address, or Web site address.

Landscape orientation A print setting that uses the widest part of the paper to print across.

Long form A date/time format that displays data in a form similar to Friday, May 5, 2006 or 10:12:30 AM.

Long integer A field size that indicates a whole number.

Lookup field A field that stores data retrieved from a field in another table.

Medium form A date/time format that displays data in a form similar to 24-June-06 or 10:12 AM.

Memo field A field that stores many lines of text.

Number field A field that stores only numeric values.

Percent A field format that multiplies the value entered by 100 and displays it with a percent sign.

Portrait orientation A print setting that uses the narrowest part of the paper to print across.

Primary key A field in a table that is designated to contain unique data.

RDBMS (Relational database management system) A database in which data is stored in related tables.

Record A row in a table.

Record controls Used for displaying a specific record in a form. Located at the bottom of a form.

Required option Used to ensure that a field contains an entry. Located in the General options at the bottom of a table in Design view.

Short form A date/time format that displays data in a form similar to 6/24/06 or 10:12.

Single A field size that indicates a number with a decimal portion.

Size The number of characters or the type of number a field can store.

Sorting Placing records in a specified order.

Standard   A field format that displays a number with a thousands separator, usually a comma.

Static data   Data that does not change.

Table   A database object that stores related data organized into rows and columns.

Text field   A field that stores characters (letters, symbols, words, a combination of letters and numbers) and numbers that do not require calculations.

Type   Field classification based on the data stored.

Updating   Modifying a record.

Yes/No field   A field that is either selected or not selected to represent yes/no, true/false, or on/off.

Close Clicked to close the Print Preview window. Found on the toolbar. The Esc key can be used instead of the button.

Copy **command** Creates a duplicate of the selected data for pasting. Found in the Edit menu. The Copy button on the toolbar can be used instead of the command.

Delete Record button Clicked to delete the active record. Found on the toolbar.

Delete Rows **command** Deletes a field. Found in the menu displayed when a field name is right-clicked.

Design Displays a table in Design view. Found on the Database window toolbar.

E-mail (as Attachment) **command** Displays an e-mail window with the table data attached as an HTML file. Found in the File menu.

Export **command** Generates an HTML document from a table. Found in the File menu.

Fill/Back Color button Formats a selected object in form Design view with the selected color. Found on the toolbar.

Forms Displays the form objects. Found in the Database window.

Font/Fore Color button Formats the font or fore color of a selected object in form Design view with the selected color. Found on the toolbar.

Image control Clicked to add an image to a form in Design view. Found in the Toolbox.

Insert Hyperlink button Displays a dialog box for specifying a link to a file, a Web page, or an e-mail address. Found on the toolbar.

Label control Clicked to add text to a form in Design view. Found in the Toolbox.

Line/Border Color button Formats the outline of a selected object in form Design view with the selected color. Found on the toolbar.

Line/Border Width button Formats the outline of a selected object in form Design view with the selected width. Found on the toolbar.

New button Displays the New File task pane. Found on the toolbar.

Page Setup **command** Displays a dialog box where margins and page orientation can be changed. Found in the File menu.

Paste **command** Places the most recently copied data into a database entry field. Found in the Edit menu. The Paste button on the toolbar can be used instead of the command.

Primary Key **command** Designates the active field as the primary key. Found in the Edit menu. The Primary Key button on the toolbar can be used instead of the command.

Print button Prints a copy of the table or form using the default printer settings. Found on the toolbar.

Print Preview **command** Displays a table or form in print preview. Found in the File menu. The Print Preview button on the toolbar can be used instead of the command.

Sort Ascending button Orders records from low to high based on the data in the active field. Found on the toolbar.

Sort Descending button Orders records from high to low based on the data in the active field. Found on the toolbar.

Tables Displays the table objects. Found in the Database window.

View button Switches a displayed table between Design view and Datasheet view. Found on the toolbar.

Zoom button Magnifies a print preview. Found on the toolbar.

1. a) What is a database used for?
   b) How does an RDBMS store data?
   c) What is one benefit of dividing data into tables?

2. a) What is a field?
   b) Explain why a field that stores more than one piece of data is considered poor design.

3. List four guidelines that should be followed when choosing field names.

4. List nine types of data that can be stored in a field.

5. a) What does the size of a field indicate?
   b) What field size should be used when a field will store numbers with a decimal portion?
   c) What field size should be used when a field will store whole numbers?

6. a) What does the format of a field determine?
   b) List four numeric field formats.
   c) List three date/time field formats.
   d) Do text fields have a field format?

7. For each of the field names below, list the most appropriate data type (Text, Number, Date/Time, Currency, Memo, Yes/No, Hyperlink, and AutoNumber). Use each type only once:
   a) RetailPrice
   b) OrderDate
   c) FirstName
   d) ProductDescription
   e) EMailAddress
   f) RecordID
   g) DeliveryTime
   h) PeanutAllergy
   i) Quantity

8. a) What is a record?
   b) Should a table contain duplicate records? Explain.
   c) What is used in a table to ensure that records are unique?

9. a) What is a database schema?
   b) Explain the considerations for dividing data into related groups.

10. a) What must be done to designate a primary key?
    b) What is the Required option in the Design view window used for?
    c) List the steps required to make two fields the primary key of a table.

11. a) What is a form?
    b) What does a form look like when the fields are organized in columnar style?

12. a) Where are the record controls located?
    b) What are the record controls used for?

13. How does a form make entering records less error-prone?

14. a) What is Datasheet view?
    b) What is the boundary in a datasheet?
    c) List one way to change a column's width.
    d) List the steps required to change the order of fields.

15. a) What is sorting?
    b) Explain the difference between ascending and descending order.

16. a) Why should a table or form be previewed before printing?
    b) How can more columns be printed on a sheet of paper?
    c) What option is used to print only the selected records?

17. Give two reasons for modifying a form in Design view.

18. List three buttons on the toolbar that are used for formatting a form in Design view and explain their purpose.

19. Give three examples of poor background/foreground color combinations for a form. Explain why these combinations could affect usability.

20. List the formatting considerations for a form that will be used by someone who is visually impaired, but can read text at 30 point in a color that contrasts well against the background. Be specific.

21. Explain the similarities between a database table and a worksheet.

22. Can database data be copied to a worksheet? Explain.

23. a) What is one advantage of exporting a table to an HTML file?
    b) What is one disadvantage of exporting a table to an HTML file?

24. When data in a table changes, what must be done to update the corresponding HTML file?

25. What format is table data in when e-mailed?

True/False

26. Determine if each of the following are true or false. If false, explain why.
    a) The data in a table must all be the same type.
    b) Each table in a database should be related to another table by one field.
    c) Entering 3 in a field formatted as percent displays 30% in the entry box.
    d) The primary key in a database is used to prevent duplicate records in a table.
    e) A LastName field is a good candidate for a primary key field.
    f) It is not possible to have a multiple-field primary key.
    g) Lookup fields allow for any type of data.
    h) A hyperlink field allows only e-mail entries.
    i) Datasheet view displays one record at a time.
    j) A form is automatically updated when changes are made to the corresponding table.
    k) A form cannot include an image.
    l) It is not possible to copy text from a Word document and paste it as an entry in a database form.
    m) A table exported as HTML creates a document with static data.

Exercise 1 ————————————————————————Museum Exhibits

Sunport Science Museum wants to use a relational database to store exhibit information.

a) Create a relational database naming it Museum Exhibits.

b) Create an Exhibits table for storing exhibits information:

Field Name	Data Type	Description	Size	Format
ExhibitID 🔑	Text	ID of permanent exhibit	4	
Name	Text	Name of exhibit	30	
Department	Text	Department exhibit is in	30	
Updated	Date/Time	Date exhibit was last updated		Short Date

c) Create an Attendance table for storing attendance data for years 2004 through 2006:

Field Name	Data Type	Description	Size	Format	Decimals
ExhibitID 🔑	Text	ID of permanent exhibit	4		
Year 🔑	Text	Year of attendance	4		
Attendance	Number	Number of people	Long Integer	Standard	0

The ExhibitID and Year fields are a multiple-field primary key because there can be only one record for a specific exhibit in a specific year.

d) Modify the Attendance table so that the ExhibitID field is a lookup field that looks up values in the ExhibitID field of the Exhibits table.

e) Create an Exhibits form and enter the following eight records:

LWL1; Minerals and Rocks; Land We Live On; 1/5/06

LWL2; Earth's Interior; Land We Live On; 3/6/05

LWL3; Atmosphere and Weather; Land We Live On; 5/3/04

SWD1; Oceans; Secrets of Water Depths; 5/3/05

SWD2; Fresh Water; Secrets of Water Depths; 7/12/06

SWD3; Lakes, Rivers & Streams; Secrets of Water Depths; 1/1/03

WDH2; Earthquakes & Hurricanes; Why Does That Happen; 2/7/04

WDH3; Volcanoes; Why Does That Happen; 11/23/04

f) Create an Attendance form and enter the following 27 records:

LWL1; 2004; 1,560	LWL1; 2005; 1,540	LWL1; 2006; 1,494
LWL2; 2004; 1,298	LWL2; 2005; 1,600	LWL2; 2006; 1,678
LWL3; 2004; 1,364	LWL3; 2005; 1,467	LWL3; 2006; 1,645
SWD1; 2004; 1,254	SWD1; 2005; 1,374	SWD1; 2006; 1,575
SWD2; 2004; 1,156	SWD2; 2005; 1,245	SWD2; 2006; 1,312
SWD3; 2004; 1,324	SWD3; 2005; 1,437	SWD3; 2006; 1,545
WDH1; 2004; 1,256	WDH1; 2005; 1,345	WDH1; 2006; 1,512
WDH2; 2004; 1,224	WDH2; 2005; 1,435	WDH2; 2006; 1,442
WDH3; 2004; 1,381	WDH3; 2005; 1,483	WDH3; 2006; 1,547

g) Format the Exhibits and Attendance tables in Datasheet view appropriately.

h) Print preview and then print both tables using the appropriate orientation.

Exercise 2 ———————————————— Library

The local library wants to use a relational database to store information on its books.

a) Create a relational database naming it Library.

b) Create an Authors table for storing author data:

Field Name	Data Type	Description	Size	Format
AuthorID 🔑	Text	ID of author	4	
FirstName	Text	First name of author	15	
LastName	Text	Last name of author	30	
Birth	Date/Time	Date of birth		Short Date
Death	Date/Time	Date of death		Short Date

c) Create a Books table for storing books data:

Field Name	Data Type	Description	Size
ISBN 🔑	Text	International Standard Book Number	13
Title	Text	Title of book	50
Type	Text	Type of book	10
AuthorID	Text	ID of author	4

d) Modify the Books table so that the AuthorID field is a lookup field that looks up values in the AuthorID field of the Authors table.

e) Create an Authors form and enter the following six records:

CB12; Carrie; Brennan; 6/12/1909; 12/3/1996

KW23; Karen; Willamson; 10/23/1974

MS12; Monica; Saliguero; 10/12/1912; 3/16/1990

SZ04; Slim; Zhorbyzki; 2/4/1959; 11/11/1993

TB22; Tomica; Broswell; 7/22/1921; 9/6/1992

ZT19; Zachery; Toening; 3/19/1923; 6/20/1989

f) Create a Books form and enter the following 12 records:

1-879233-01-0; My Wedding - Your Wedding; Family; KW23

1-879233-39-8; All The Presidents' Wives; History; CB12

1-879233-42-8; The Complete College Guide; Reference; TB22

1-879233-44-4; Appeasement In The Republic; History; CB12

1-879233-51-7; Build Your Muscles; Health; SZ04

1-879233-56-8; The Orange Tide; Drama; KW23

1-879233-57-6; Effective Management Skills; Business; MS12

1-879233-59-0; The Dog Wore a Red Coat; Mystery; ZT19

1-879233-62-2; Asian Alliances; History; CB12

1-879233-82-7; Healthy Eating; Health; SZ04

1-879233-84-3; Reading the Butler's Writing; Mystery; ZT19

1-879233-92-4; The Gold Necklace; Mystery; ZT19

g) Format the Books and Authors tables in Datasheet view appropriately.

h) Print preview and then print both tables using the appropriate orientation.

Exercise 3 — Pizza Payroll

The owner of Pizza Palace wants to use a relational database to store information on the company's employees and payroll.

a) Create a relational database naming it Pizza Payroll.

b) Create an Employees table for storing employee data:

Field Name	Data Type	Description	Size
EmployeeID 🔑	Text	ID of employee	2
FirstName	Text	First name of employee	15
LastName	Text	Last name of employee	30
Address	Text	Street address of employee	50
City	Text	City employee lives in	15
State	Text	State employee lives in	2
Zip	Text	Zip code of employee	10
Phone	Text	Phone number of employee	14

c) Create a Payroll table for storing payroll data:

Field Name	Data Type	Description	Size	Format	Decimals
EmployeeID 🔑	Text	ID of employee	2		
Date 🔑	Date/Time	Date of paycheck		Short Date	
GrossPay	Currency	Employee's gross pay			2
Taxes	Currency	Tax deductions			2

The EmployeeID and Date fields are a multiple-field primary key because there can be only one record for a specific employee on a specific date.

d) Modify the Payroll table so that the EmployeeID field is a lookup field that looks up values in the EmployeeID field of the Employees table.

e) Create an Employees form and enter the following five records:

EI; Edna; Incahatoe; 254 20th St.; Armine; CT; 19154-7901; (332) 555-1765

JF; Jess; Frank; 101 Red Villa Circle; Armine; CT; 19154-7901; (332) 555-2792

RD; Rita; DiPasquale; 5672 56th Ct.; Weidner; CT; 19165-3342; (332) 555-0276

TW; Thomas; Warner; 11 Roni Dr.; Weidner; CT; 19165-3342; (332) 555-2665

WF; Wimberly; Franco; 86 Luther Ct.; Weidner; CT; 19165-9088; (332) 555-1711

f) Create a Payroll form and enter the following 10 records:

EI; 3/13/06; 244; 36.60   RD; 3/13/06; 180; 27

EI; 3/20/06; 254; 38.10   TW; 3/6/06; 210.24; 31.53

JF; 3/20/06; 191.67; 28.75   TW; 3/13/06; 225.64; 33.84

JF; 3/27/06; 210.75; 31.50   WF; 3/13/06; 187.82; 28.17

RD; 3/6/06; 175; 26.25   WF; 3/20/06; 195.25; 29.28

g) Appropriately modify the Employees and Payroll forms to include the PIZZA PALACE LOGO, which is an image data file for this text.

h) Print the first record only in the Payroll form.

i) Format the Employees and Payroll tables in Datasheet view appropriately.

j) Print preview and then print both tables using the appropriate orientation.

Exercise 4 ———————————————— Boat Storage

Sunport Boat Storage wants to use a relational database to store information on its business.

a) Create a relational database naming it Boat Storage.

b) Create an Employees table for storing employee data:

Field Name	Data Type	Description	Size
EmployeeID 🗝	Text	ID of employee	4
FirstName	Text	First name of employee	15
LastName	Text	Last name of employee	30
Address	Text	Street address of employee	50
City	Text	City employee lives in	15
State	Text	State employee lives in	2
Zip	Text	Zip code of employee	10
Phone	Text	Phone number of employee	14

c) Create a Boat Owners table for storing boat owner data:

Field Name	Data Type	Description	Size
OwnerID 🗝	AutoNumber	ID of owner of a boat	Long Integer
FirstName	Text	First name of owner	15
LastName	Text	Last name of owner	30
Address	Text	Street address of owner	50
City	Text	City owner lives in	15
State	Text	State owner lives in	2
Zip	Text	Zip code of owner	10
Phone	Text	Phone number of owner	14

d) Create a Boats table for storing boat data:

Field Name	Data Type	Description	Size	Decimals
Boat 🗝	Text	Name of boat	30	
SlotNumber	Number	Slot boat is stored	Long Integer	
EmployeeID	Text	Employee in charge of boat	4	
Fee	Currency	Monthly maintenance fee		0
OwnerID	Number	ID of boat's owner	Long Integer	

e) Modify the Boats table so that the EmployeeID field is a lookup field that looks up values in the EmployeeID field of the Employees table.

f) Modify the Boats table so that the OwnerID field is a lookup field that looks up values in the OwnerID field of the Boat Owners table.

g) Create an Employees form and enter the following five records:

DK86; Denita; Kilcullen; 86 Hampshire Road; Cody; WA; 12232-1207; (617) 555-1229

HW28; Hillary; Walker; 1221 Rockledge Ave.; Cody; WA; 12232-1209; (617) 555-9800

NG12; Nate; Gervin; NE 66th Plaza; Rostock; WA; 12241; (617) 555-9462

SM23; Sherman; MacGragor; 2334 12th Ave.; Cody; WA; 12232-1207; (617) 555-0993

YA12; Yvette; Archibald; 13 Cypress Creed Rd.; Rostock; WA; 12241; (617) 555-7822

h) Create a Boats form and enter the following 10 records:

Donned Upon You; 10; NG12; 70; 6   SteadyAsSheGoes; 13; DK86; 60; 5

Jenny; 5; YA12; 62; 4   The Sugar Queen; 12; NG12; 45; 4

Just Desserts; 4; SM23; 50; 3   Tidal Wave; 17; SM23; 55; 2

Monkey Business; 3; HW28; 86; 2   UR Behind Me; 9; DK86; 65; 5

Shooting Star; 16; HW28; 77; 1   Viking 5; 2; SM23; 55; 1

i) Create a Boat Owners form named for the Boat Owners table and enter the following six records:

Rachell; Gundarssohn; 1671 Westchester Ave.; Poliney; WA; 12245; (232) 555-0912

Pamela; Hogart; 12 Street; Monterey; WA; 12259-4761; (232) 555-7021

Dermont; Voss; 1087 67th Terrace; Monterey; WA; 12259-4761; (232) 555-9000

Zane; McCaffrey; 689 King Blvd.; Poliney; WA; 12245-3309; (232) 555-7492

Bethany; Mulberry; 8625 West View Drive Apt. 9; Rostock; WA; 12241; (617) 555-6524

Damon; Deitrich; 4567 Sandalwood Ave.; Poliney; WA; 12245; (232) 555-2651

j) Format the Employees, Boats, and Boat Owners tables in Datasheet view appropriately.

k) Print preview and then print all the tables using the appropriate orientation.

Exercise 5 — Messages

A relational database can be used to allow an office manager to efficiently keep track of phone messages, visitors, and packages.

a) Create a relational database naming it Messages.

b) Create an Employees table for storing employee data:

Field Name	Data Type	Description	Size
EmployeeID 🔑	Text	ID of employee	5
FirstName	Text	First name of employee	15
LastName	Text	Last name of employee	30
Department	Text	Department employee works in	50
Extension	Text	Phone extension	4
Email	Hyperlink	E-mail address	

c) Create a Messages table for storing messages:

Field Name	Data Type	Description	Size	Format
MessageID 🔑	Autonumber	Automatically generated message ID	Long Integer	
EmployeeID	Text	ID of employee to receive message	5	
Date	Date/Time	Date of message		Short Date
Time	Date/Time	Time of message		Medium Time
CallerFirstName	Text	First name of caller	15	
CallerLastName	Text	Last name of caller	30	
CompanyName	Text	Company caller is representing	30	
PhoneNumber	Text	Telephone number of caller	30	
Message	Memo	Message from caller		
Urgent	Yes/No	Message requires immediate attention		
PleaseCall	Yes/No	Caller requests a call back		
StoppedBy	Yes/No	Visitor stopped by		
Package	Yes/No	Package delivered to front desk		

d) Modify the Messages table so that the EmployeeID field is a lookup field that looks up values in the EmployeeID field of the Employees table.

e) Create an Employees form and enter the following four records:

TJ122; Trey; Jones; IT; 122; tj@lpdatafiles.com

MB234; Michelle; Brooks; Human Resources; 234; mb@lpdatafiles.com

GM319; Gretchen; Milnap; Distribution; 319; gm@lpdatafiles.com

AB235; Alfonse; Burrows; Human Resources; 235; ab@lpdatafiles.com

f) Create a Messages form and enter the following eight records. Fields that should be left empty are indicated with *blank* for their entry:

MB234; 4/20/06; 10:15 AM; Olivia; Chornesky; *blank*; *blank*; Left her resume for your review; *blank*; *blank*; selected; selected

TJ122; 4/20/06; 12:39 PM; Gretchen; Milnap; *blank*; ext. 319; Bill of ladings are not printing correctly; selected; selected; *blank*; *blank*

AB235; 4/20/06; 2:20 PM; Gerald; Washburn; Office Fulfillment Services; (238) 555-9076; Cannot attend meeting; *blank*; selected; *blank*; *blank*

TJ122; 4/20/06; 4:12 PM; *blank*; *blank*; Downtown Delivery Services; *blank*; *blank*; *blank*; *blank*; *blank*; selected

GM319; 4/21/06; 8:40 AM; William; Marshall; Marshall Packaging; (376) 555-8877; *blank*; *blank*; selected; *blank*; *blank*

AB235; 4/21/06; 3:15 PM; *blank*; *blank*; Downtown Delivery Services; *blank*; *blank*; *blank*; *blank*; *blank*; selected

MB234; 4/22/06; 9:20 AM; Olivia; Chornesky; *blank*; (376) 555-2122; Would like to schedule an interview; *blank*; selected; *blank*; *blank*

TJ122; 4/23/06; 12:15 PM; *blank*; *blank*; Downtown Delivery Services; *blank*; *blank*; *blank*; *blank*; *blank*; selected

g) Modify the Messages form to look similar to that shown on the next page. You will need to use the Rectangle control in the Toolbox and the Line/Border Width button on the toolbar:

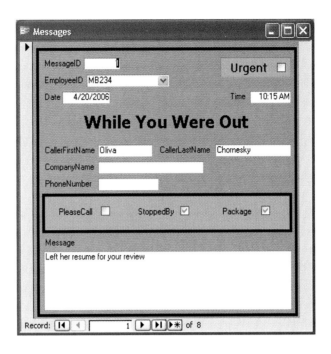

h) Display the record for GM319 in the Messages form. Print just the message for Gretchen Milnap.

i) Format the Employees and Messages tables in Datasheet view appropriately.

j) Print preview and then print both tables using the appropriate orientation.

Exercise 6 ——————————————————— Media Collection

Photos and movies are often in digital format. There are many software applications available for organizing media. These applications usually use a database to index media for easier retrieval. Use Access to organize your media collection.

a) Create a relational database naming it Media Collection.

b) Create a Media table for storing photo data:

Field Name	Data Type	Description	Size	Format
MediaLink 🔑	Hyperlink	File name with full path to file		
MediaType	Text	Type of media	10	
PhotographerID	Number	Photographer ID	4	
Title	Text	Title for photo or movie	15	
Event	Text	Event recorded	20	
Location	Text	Location recorded	30	
Date	Date/Time	Date of photo or movie		Long Date
Time	Date/Time	Time of photo or movie		Medium Time
Description	Memo	Description of recording		

c) Create a Photographers table for storing photographer information:

Field Name	Data Type	Description	Size
PhotographerID 🔑	Autonumber	Automatically generated ID	
FirstName	Text	First name of photographer	15
LastName	Text	Last name of photographer	20
EquipmentUsed	Memo	Camera, lighting, etc.	

d) Create a Media form and enter the following five records. Note that you will need to navigate to the location of the files, which are JPG and AVI data files for this text, when creating the hyperlink entries:

link to PUFFIN.JPG; Photo; 1; Single Puffin; Alaska trip; Alaska Sealife Center; 8/21/06; 10:00 AM; puffin perched on a rock, puffin, bird

link to BEAR1.JPG; Photo; 1; Bear in Water; Alaska trip; Alaska Sealife Center; 8/21/06; 10:20 AM; bear looking for fish in water, bear, mammal

link to BEAR2.JPG; Photo; 1; Bear with Fish; Alaska trip; Alaska Sealife Center; 8/21/06; 10:30 AM; bear with fish in mouth, bear, salmon, fish, mammal

link to CHICKS.AVI; Movie; 1; Baby Chicks; Montana trip; Local Petting Zoo; 6/12/06; 11:15 AM; baby chicks cheeping, chicken, bird

link to CRABS.AVI; Movie; 1; My Hermit Crabs; *blank*; Home; 10/11/06; 1:00 PM; hermit crabs racing, hermit crabs, animal

e) Create a Photographers form and enter a record for yourself.

f) Format the Media and Photographers tables in Datasheet view appropriately.

g) Print preview and then print both tables using the appropriate orientation.

Exercise 7 —————————————————————————Coral Research

The researchers who created the coral reef study proposal you edited in previous chapters want to create a relational database to store their research findings.

a) Create a relational database naming it Coral Research.

b) Create a Coral Sites table for storing coral data:

Field Name	Data Type	Description	Size
SiteID 🔑	AutoNumber	ID of site location	Long Integer
CoralName	Text	Name of coral	20
Color	Text	Main color of coral	15
Description	Text	Identifying features	30

c) Create a Growth Research table for storing growth data:

Field Name	Data Type	Description	Size	Format	Decimals
Date 🔑	Date/Time	Date of observation		Short Date	
SiteID 🔑	Number	Location of the coral	Long Integer		0
Time	Date/Time	Time of observation		Medium Time	
Size	Number	Coral size in meters	Single		3

The Date and SiteID fields are a multiple-field primary key because there can only be one record for a specific site on a specific date.

d) Create a Coral Sites form and enter the following five records:

Knobby Brain Coral; tan; hemispherical heads

Scroll Coral; light gray; rounded, thin blades

Slimy Sea Plume; violet; feather-like

Venus Sea Fan; lavender; network of branches

Yellow Sea Whip; bright yellow; branched colonies

e) Create a Growth Research form and enter the following six records:

5/8/05; 1; 6:10 AM; 0.8378	6/2/05; 4; 6:35 AM; 1.387
5/12/05; 2; 8:15 AM; 0.2045	5/11/06; 2; 8:15 AM; 0.205
5/25/05; 3; 7:25 AM; 0.144	6/4/06; 4; 6:35 AM; 1.389

f) Format the Coral Sites and Growth Research tables in Datasheet view appropriately.

g) Print preview and then print both tables using the appropriate orientation.

Exercise 8 ———————————————— Community Service

A local school needs a database to track community service hours performed by their students.

a) Create a relational database naming it Community Service.

b) Create a Students table for storing student data:

Field Name	Data Type	Description	Size
StudentID 🔑	Text	ID of student	4
FirstName	Text	First name of student	15
LastName	Text	Last name of student	30

c) Create an Organizations table for community service organization data:

Field Name	Data Type	Description	Size
OrganizationName 🔑	Text	Name of organization	50
ContactFirstName	Text	First name of contact person	20
ContactLastName	Text	Last name of contact person	30
ServicesProvided	Memo	List of services provided	

d) Create a Volunteer Hours table for storing data about student volunteer hours:

Field Name	Data Type	Description	Size	Format
ServiceHoursID 🔑	AutoNumber	Automatically generated ID	Long Integer	
StudentID	Text	ID of student	4	
OrganizationName	Text	Name of Organization	50	
Date	Date/Time	Date of hours worked		Short Date
Hours	Number	Number of hours worked	Single	Fixed, 2 Decimals

e) Modify the Volunteer Hours table so that the StudentID field is a lookup field that looks up values in the StudentID field of the Students table.

f) Modify the Volunteer Hours table so that the OrganizationName field is a lookup field that looks up values in the OrganizationName field of the Organizations table.

g) Create a Students form and enter the following ten records:

MJ07; Miranda; Jackson	ES08; Eric; Shakur
VS07; Victor; Shappiro	ND07; Neil; Daniels
SK06; Seth; Koppel	SR08; Shannon; Ross
TI08; Tanesha; Iglesias	LP06; Laura; Patrick
SS06; Simone; Shapelle	RS08; Robbie; Stemme

h) Create an Organizations form and enter the following three records:

City Soup Kitchen; Maria; Vuarez; free meals, free beverages between meals

Literacy for the Little; Mac; Friedel; mentoring for young readers, provides free books to children from donations, monthly storytime at public library

Sandy Beaches; Lee; Graff; beach cleanup, beach restoration, education programs about sea life

i) Create a Volunteer Hours form and enter the following 12 records:

ND07; City Soup Kitchen; 9/9/06; 1.5

TI08; Literacy for the Little; 9/9/06; 2.25

MJ07; Literacy for the Little; 9/9/06; 2

SK06; Sandy Beaches; 9/9/06; 3

VS07; Sandy Beaches; 9/9/06; 3

SS06; City Soup Kitchen; 9/10/06; 2

ES08; City Soup Kitchen; 9/10/06; 2.5

LP06; Literacy for the Little; 9/16/06; 3.5

RS08; City Soup Kitchen; 9/16/06; 1.5

ES08; Sandy Beaches; 9/17/06; 1.5

LP06; City Soup Kitchen; 9/17/06; 2.25

VS07; Literacy for the Little; 9/17/06; 3

j) Format the Students, Organizations, and Volunteer Hours tables in Datasheet view appropriately.

k) Print preview and then print all the tables using the appropriate orientation.

Exercise 9 ———————————————————————— Summer Camp

A summer camp facility needs a database to coordinate counselors, cabins, activities, and campers.

a) Create a relational database naming it Summer Camp.

b) Create a Counselors table for storing couselor information:

Field Name	Data Type	Description	Size
CounselorID 🔑	Text	ID of counselor	4
FirstName	Text	First name of counselor	15
LastName	Text	Last name of counselor	30

c) Create a Cabins table for storing cabin assignment data:

Field Name	Data Type	Description	Size
CabinName 🔑	Text	Name of cabin	30
CounselorID	Text	ID of counselor assigned to cabin	4
NumberOfBunks	Number	Camper capacity of cabin	Long Integer

d) Create an Activities table storing activity information:

Field Name	Data Type	Description	Size
ActivityName 🔑	Text	Name of activity	20
CounselorID	Text	ID of counselor running activity	20
Location	Text	Location of activity	20
MinimumAge	Number	Required minimum age	Long Integer

e) Modify the Activities table so that the CounselorID field is a lookup field that looks up values in the CounselorID field of the Counselors table.

f) Create a Campers table storing camper data:

Field Name	Data Type	Description	Size
CamperID 🔑	Text	ID of camper	4
FirstName	Text	First name of camper	20
LastName	Text	Last name of camper	30
Age	Number	Age of camper	Long Integer
CabinName	Text	Cabin assignment	30

g) Modify the Campers table so that the CabinName field is a lookup field that looks up values in the CabinName field of the Cabins table.

h) Create a Schedules table for storing activitiy schedules:

Field Name	Data Type	Description	Size
CamperID 🔑	Number	Camper ID	Long Integer
Day 🔑	Number	Activity day	Long Integer
ActivityName	Text	Name of activity	20

The CamperID and Day fields are a multiple-field primary key because there can only be one record for a camper on a specific day.

i) Modify the Schedules table so that the CamperID field is a lookup field that looks up values in the CamperID field of the Campers table.

j) Modify the Schedules table so that the Day field is a lookup field that uses values from a list. In the first Lookup Wizard dialog box, select the I will type in the values that I want. In the next Loopkup Wizard dialog box, in the Col1 box, type the value 1, press Tab and type 2, and then press Tab again and type 3. Your dialog box should look similar to:

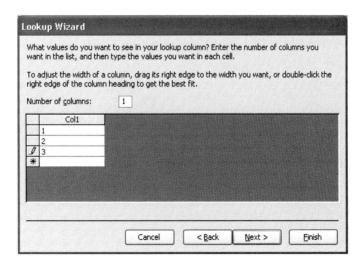

k) Modify the Schedules table so that the ActivityName field is a lookup field that looks up values in the ActivityName field of the Activities table.

l) Create a Counselors form and enter the following four records:

   TG01; Terry; Gray

   SP01; Sandra; Patel

   JN01; Jessie; Neel

   LW01; Leon; Washington

m) Create a Cabins form and enter the following four records:

   Egret; TG01; 8

   Alligator; SP01; 6

   Panther; JN01; 8

   Heron; LW01; 6

n) Create an Activities form and enter the following five records:

   Beading; SP01; Dining Hall; 8

   Canoeing; LW01; Lake; 10

   Pottery; JN01; Dining Hall; 8

   Rafting; TG01; Lake; 9

   Scavenger Hunt; Pavilion; SP01; 10

o) Create a Campers form and enter the following twenty records:

   AD08; Anthony; Davis; 8; Heron   JC10; Jayne; Clarke; 10; Egret

   AB09; Ann; Bennett; 9; Panther   JG10; Julian; Gray; 10; Alligator

   CH09; Carlos; Hernandez; 9; Heron   JL09; James; Lewis; 9; Alligator

   CR10; Christopher; Reed; 10; Alligator   KN09; Karl; Neldon; 9; Alligator

   DC10; Debi; Coleman; 10; Panther   LP09; Laura; Parker; 9; Egret

   DR11; Daniel; Ross; 11; Alligator   MC10; Marc; Cox; 10; Heron

   EC10; Evie; Cho; 10; Heron   MC11; Marguerite; Calo; 11; Egret

   FP11; Francisco; Perez; 11; Heron   MR08; Martha; Ramirez; 8; Panther

   IH10; Ivan; Hale; 10; Alligator   MT10; Mary; Thompson; 10; Egret

   JB08; Jodi; Butler; 8; Egret   SM11; Sharon; Martin; 11; Panther

p) Create a Schedules form and enter the following 60 records. Three records will be entered for each camper:

Camper	Day 1	Day 2	Day 3
AB09	Beading	Beading	Beading
AD08	Pottery	Beading	Pottery
CH09	Rafting	Rafting	Pottery
CR10	Rafting	Canoeing	Scavenger Hunt
DC10	Scavenger Hunt	Rafting	Canoeing
DR11	Canoeing	Beading	Scavenger Hunt

EC10	Scavenger Hunt	Beading	Canoeing
FP11	Canoeing	Rafting	Scavenger Hunt
IH10	Canoeing	Rafting	Scavenger Hunt
JB08	Beading	Beading	Pottery
JC10	Canoeing	Beading	Pottery
JG10	Pottery	Rafting	Canoeing
JL09	Rafting	Pottery	Scavenger Hunt
KN09	Rafting	Pottery	Rafting
LP09	Pottery	Beading	Beading
MC10	Rafting	Canoeing	Scavenger Hunt
MC11	Canoeing	Pottery	Scavenger Hunt
MR08	Pottery	Pottery	Pottery
MT10	Canoeing	Beading	Pottery
SM11	Canoeing	Beading	Scavenger Hunt

q) Format the Counselors, Cabins, Activities, Campers, and Schedules tables in Datasheet view appropriately.

r) Print preview and then print all the tables using the appropriate orientation.

Exercise 10 ——————————————————————— Travel Agency

The Hot Spot travel agency wants to use a relational database to store travel bookings.

a) Create a relational database naming it Travel Agency.

b) Create a Clients table for storing client data:

Field Name	Data Type	Description	Size
ClientID 🔑	Text	ID of client	2
FirstName	Text	First name of client	15
LastName	Text	Last name of client	30
Address	Text	Street address of client	50
City	Text	City client lives in	15
State	Text	State client lives in	2
Zip	Text	Zip code of client	10
Phone	Text	Phone number of client	14

c) Create a Vacations table for storing vacation packages data:

Field Name	Data Type	Description	Size	Decimals
Package 🔑	Text	Name of vacation package	20	
Cost	Currency	Cost of vacation		0
Nights	Number	Number of nights	Long Integer	0
Location	Text	State/Country of vacation	30	
Type	Text	Type of vacation	15	

d) Create a Booked Vacations table for storing information about purchased packages:

Field Name	Data Type	Description	Size	Format
ClientID 🔑	Text	ID of client	2	
Date 🔑	Date/Time	Vacation start date		Short Date
Package	Text	Name of vacation package	20	

The ClientID and Date fields are a multiple-field primary key because there can only be one record for a specific client for a package.

e) Modify the Booked Vacations table so that the ClientID field is a lookup field that looks up values in the ClientID field of the Clients table.

f) Modify the Booked Vacations table so that the Package field is a lookup field that looks up values in the Package field of the Vacations table.

g) Create a Clients form and enter the following six records:

DM; Diane; Mason; 8 Westchester Place; Bedrock; IL; 56224-9987; (445) 555-1552

GM; Gail; Mintzer; 8891 SW 63rd Circle; Wilbraham; IL; 76209-0324; (298) 555-7392

HQ; Harvey; Quay; 33 Buren Blvd. Apt. 452; Wilbraham; IL; 76209-0324; (298) 555-7782

JU; Juan; Ulloa; 352 Eagle Trace Blvd.; Bedrock; IL; 56224-9987; (445) 555-0287

RP; Richard; Pompeneur; 240 Keisha St.; Bedrock; IL; 56224-9988; (445) 555-0208

SV; Sandy; Vanderhorn; 12 343rd Terrace; Wilbraham; IL; 56624-9988; (445) 555-8927

h) Create a Vacations form and enter the following seven records:

Beach Fun; 475; 7; Bahamas; Relaxing

City Dude; 725; 5; Texas; Adventure

French Getaway; 1,525; 7; France; Sightseeing

HighRiser Crusade; 823; 8; New York; Sightseeing

Honolulu Hideaway; 950; 3; Hawaii; Relaxing

Mountain Explorer; 420; 3; Vermont; Ski

Summit Skiing; 1,250; 5; Switzerland; Ski

i) Create a Booked Vacations form and enter the following nine records:

DM; 4/21/06; HighRiser Crusade   JU; 5/20/06; Beach Fun

GM; 1/5/06; Honolulu Hideaway   JU; 12/13/06; Summit Skiing

GM; 11/4/06; HighRiser Crusade   RP; 11/23/06; Mountain Explorer

HQ; 2/16/06; Mountain Explorer   SV; 10/18/06; City Dude

JU; 12/8/05; French Getaway

j) Format the Clients, Vacations, and Booked Vacations tables in Datasheet view appropriately.

k) Print preview and then print all the tables using the appropriate orientation.

Exercise 11 VIDEO STORE

The VIDEO STORE relational database contains information on a video store's members, videos, and rentals. Open VIDEO STORE, which is an Access data file for this text, and complete the following steps:

a) The Name field of the Movies table should be called Title. Modify the table appropriately in Design view.

b) The Members table should also include the Address, City, State, and Zip fields for each member. Add the appropriate text fields to the Members table.

c) Update the Members form appropriately and enter the following ten records:

   CS; 654 First St.; Sunport; FL; 33654-7786   JS-2; 285 Boca Lane; Medusa; FL; 33656

   JF; 274 Boca Lane; Medusa; FL; 33656   LP; 655 First St.; Sunport; FL; 33654-7786

   JH; 9876 Dolphin St.; Medusa; FL; 33656   NL; 983 Jefferson Ave.; Medusa; FL; 33656

   JM; 985 Jefferson Ave.; Medusa; FL; 33656   RG; 9821 Dolphin St.; Medusa; FL; 33656

   JS; 9898 Dolphin St.; Medusa; FL; 33656   RG-2; 987 First St.; Sunport; FL; 33654-7786

d) Add a record for yourself to the Members table.

e) Format the Members table in Datasheet view appropriately.

f) Sort the Members table by LastName in ascending order.

g) Save the modified table.

h) Print preview and then print the Members table using the appropriate orientation.

Exercise 12 INVENTIONS

The INVENTIONS relational database contains information on inventions and inventors. Open INVENTIONS, which is an Access data file for this text, and complete the following steps:

a) In the Inventors table, rename the Country field BirthCountry. Update the Inventors form appropriately.

b) Delete the Cash Register record from the Inventions table.

c) Sort the Inventions table in ascending order by Inventor.

d) Preview and then print the Inventions table using the appropriate orientation.

e) Sort the Inventors table in ascending order by the year born.

f) Print preview and then print the Inventors table using the appropriate orientation.

Chapter 12

Relational Database Techniques

Q ueries are explained in this chapter. Select queries for viewing and analyzing data from multiple tables, parameter queries for getting user input, and update queries for changing multiple records at once are explained. Using queries to generate mail-merge documents in Word is also discussed.

Table Relationships

In a relational database, two tables are *related* when a field in one table corresponds to a field in another table. Every table in a relational database is related to at least one other table in the database. To view and analyze data from multiple tables, table relationships must first be defined.

TIP The field defining a relationship between two tables must have the same data type, but they are not required to have the same field name in each table.

To view table relationships, click the Relationships button (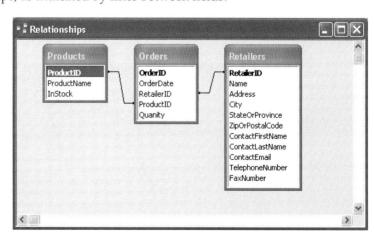) on the toolbar or select Tools → Relationships. The Relationships window appears. The Show Table dialog box is also displayed if relationships have not yet been defined. A database with lookup fields will already have one or more relationships defined because Access automatically defines a relationship between the table containing the lookup field and the table containing the data used by the lookup field. The Widget database has defined relationships, as indicated by lines between fields:

TIP Select Relationships → Show Table to display a dialog box for adding tables to the Relationships window.

TIP To delete a relationship, click a line that connects two tables and press the Delete key.

creating a relationship

Define a relationship by dragging a field from one table to a related field in another table. A dialog box is displayed after the field has been dragged into another table. Verify the related fields in the dialog box and then select Create to define a relationship.

Using Subdatasheets

TIP Select commands in the Subdatasheet menu to expand or collapse all subdatasheets.

Datasheet view includes subdatasheets when relationships have been defined for a database. A *subdatasheet* shows the records from another table that are related to the current record. A + is displayed next to each record in Datasheet view when subdatasheets are available. Click + to expand the subdatasheet for a record:

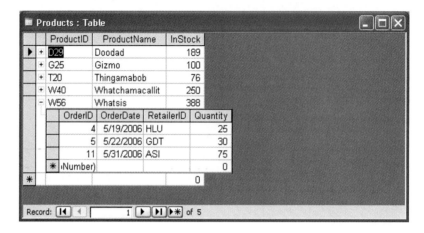

The subdatasheet shows the Whatsis orders because the Products table is directly related to the Orders table. A + changes to − when a subdatasheet is displayed. Click − to remove the subdatasheet.

Practice: Widget – part 7 of 12

You will define a relationship in the Widget database and view subdatasheets.

① *OPEN WIDGET*

    a. Start Access.

    b. Open Widget, which is an Access database that was last modified in Chapter 11.

② *VERIFY RELATIONSHIPS*

On the toolbar, click the Relationships button (⊞). The Relationships window displays lines connecting one table to another. The relationships for the three tables were defined when the lookup fields were created:

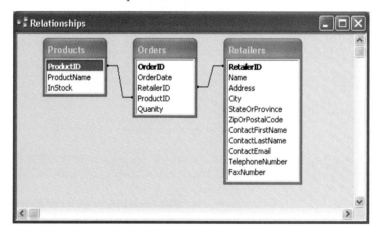

③ *CLOSE THE RELATIONSHIPS WINDOW*

④ *VIEW A SUBDATASHEET*

   a. Display the Products table. Note that each record displays a +.

   b. Next to ProductID D29, click +. A subdatasheet expands with sales for this item.

   c. Next to ProductID T20, click +. Another subdatasheet expands.

   d. Next to each subdatasheet, click − to close the subdatasheets.

   e. Close the Products table.

The Select Query

TIP Data retreived for a select query is called a recordset.

A *select query* retrieves, or "selects," data that matches specified criteria. A select query can include any number of fields from related tables in a database. The results are displayed in a Select Query datasheet. For example, the following query selects the product name (from the Products table), the retailer name (from the Retailers table) and the quantities ordered (from the Orders table) where product name is Gizmo:

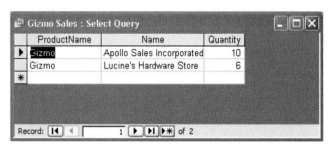

Add Only Required Tables

Only tables required for the query criteria should be added to the Select Query window. Tables that are not used may generate duplicate records in the query datasheet.

To create a select query, click [🗐 Queries] in the Objects list in the Database window and then double-click the Create query in Design view icon. A new, empty query is displayed in Design view. The Show Table dialog box is also displayed. Add tables to the Select Query window, drag fields into the design grid, and specify criteria and a sort order, if any. Design view for the datasheet above looks similar to:

TIP Double-click a field name in the Select Query window to add it to the next empty column in the design grid.

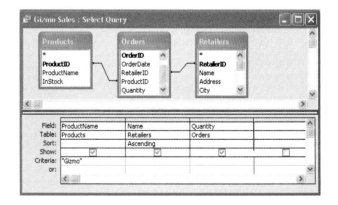

TIP Do not include $ and commas in numeric criteria.

sorting records Select either Ascending or Descending from a Sort list to display the records in a Select Query datasheet in order by the data in that field.

running a query After defining the select query, click the Run button (［❗］) or the View button (［▦ ▾］) on the toolbar, to display the datasheet.

To run an existing select query, click [🗐 Queries] in the Database window and then double-click the query name.

You will create a select query for the Widget database. Access should already be started with the Widget Database window displayed.

① **ADD TABLES TO THE SELECT QUERY WINDOW**

a. In the Widget : Database window, click ⊞ Queries .

b. Double-click the Create query in Design view icon. The Select Query window is displayed with the Show Table dialog box on top:

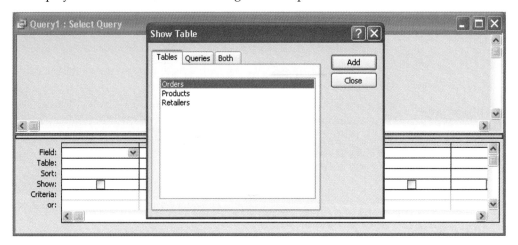

c. Click Orders if it is not already selected and then select Add. The Orders table is added to the Select Query.

d. Add the Products table to the Select Query.

e. Add the Retailers table to the Select Query.

f. Select Close. The Show Table dialog box is removed.

② **ADD FIELDS TO THE DESIGN GRID**

a. Drag the Name field from the Retailers table to the first Field box in the design grid.

b. In the Products table, double-click the ProductName field. The ProductName field is added to the second Field box.

c. Add the Quantity field from the Orders table to the third Field box. The design grid should look similar to:

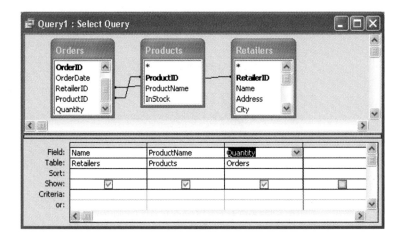

③ *SPECIFY CRITERIA AND A SORT ORDER*

a. In the ProductName Criteria box, type: Gizmo

b. Click in the first Sort box. Click the arrow to display a list and then select Ascending:

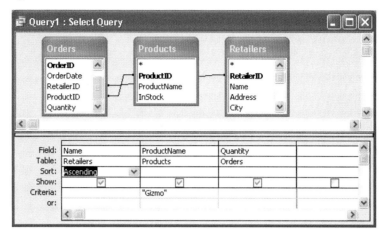

④ *RUN THE SELECT QUERY*

a. On the toolbar, click the Run button (!). The database is queried and the results shown in a datasheet. Two records are displayed:

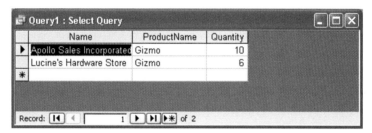

b. Select File ➜ Save. A dialog box is displayed. In the Query Name box, type: Gizmo Sales

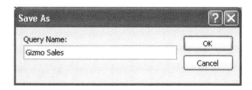

c. Select OK. The query is saved.

d. Select File ➜ Print. A dialog box is displayed.

   1. Select OK. The datasheet is printed.

e. Close the Select Query datasheet.

Modifying and Deleting a Select Query

Symbols in Criteria

Access automatically encloses text criteria with quotation marks ("") and dates with #.

A query can be modified by adding or removing fields, changing a sort order, or changing the order of fields in the design grid. Save the modified query to permanently save changes to the existing query or select File → Save As to create a new query. For example, a Gizmo Sales query could be modified to query for Whatsis sales. Select Save As to save the modified query with the name Whatsis Sales. The Gizmo Sales query remains in the database and the Whatsis Sales query is added.

A select query is modified in Design view. To switch a displayed query in Datasheet view to Design view, click the View button ( ) on the toolbar. To open a query in Design view, click Queries in the Database window, select a query icon, and then click Design on the Database window toolbar.

TIP Removing a table from the Design window removes its fields from the design grid.

To add a field to the design grid, drag the field from a table in the Select Query window to the column in the design grid where the field should appear. Existing fields will move to the right. For example, to place a LastName field between FirstName and RetailerID fields already in the design grid, drag the LastName field to the RetailerID field. RetailerID automatically moves to the right to make room for the new field. If the Select Query window does not contain the table needed to add a new field, click the Show Table button ( ) on the toolbar or select Query → Show Table.

deleting a field

column selector

Delete a column from the design grid by selecting it and then pressing the Delete key. The gray box at the top of a field in the design grid is called the *column selector*. Click a column selector to select a field. After removing fields, if a table is no longer needed in the Design window, click the table to select it and then press the Delete key.

To change the order of fields in the design grid, select the column containing the field to be moved and then drag the column selector to a new position.

deleting a query

Delete a query by selecting its name in the Database window and then pressing the Delete key. Access displays a warning dialog box, where selecting Yes permanently removes the query.

Practice: Widget – part 9 of 12

You will create a new query for the Widget database based on an existing query. Access should already be started with the Widget Database window displayed.

① *DISPLAY THE GIZMO SALES QUERY IN DESIGN VIEW*

    a. In the Widget : Database window, click Queries .

    b. Click Gizmo Sales to select it.

    c. On the Widget : Database window toolbar, click Design . The Gizmo Sales query is displayed in Design view.

② *CREATE A WHATSIS SALES SELECT QUERY*

    a. Change the ProductName criteria to: Whatsis

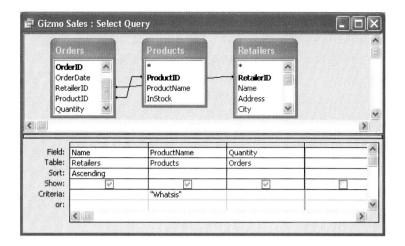

b. On the toolbar, click the Run button (!). The database is queried and the Whatsis sales records are displayed.

c. Select File ➡ Save As. A dialog box is displayed. Type Whatsis Sales as the new query name:

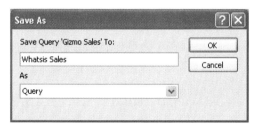

d. Select OK. A new query is created.

e. Print and then close the query datasheet. Both queries are listed in the Database window.

Range Queries

A select query with criteria that matches a range of values is called a *range query*. For example, the following query selects the product name (from the Products table) and the order date (from the Orders table) where order date is after 5/16/06:

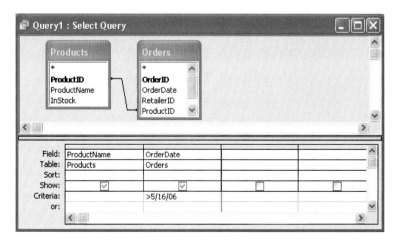

relational operator One of the following *relational operators* are used to specify criteria in a range query:

< less than
> greater than
<= less than or equal to
>= greater than or equal to
<> not equal to

When a range query compares text, alphabetical order is used to determine which data matches the criteria. For example, to query for customers with last names that come before the letter M, use the criteria <M in the LastName field.

Practice: Widget – part 10 of 12

You will create a range query for the Widget database. Access should already be started with the Widget Database window displayed.

① *CREATE A SALES AFTER 5/16/06 SELECT QUERY*

    a. In the Widget : Database window, click ⬚ Queries.

    b. Double-click the Create query in Design view icon. The Select Query window is displayed with the Show Table dialog box on top.

    c. Add the Orders table and the Products table and then close the dialog box.

    d. Add the OrderDate field and the ProductName field to the design grid.

    e. In the OrderDate Criteria box, type: >5/16/06

    f. In the OrderDate Sort list, select Ascending:

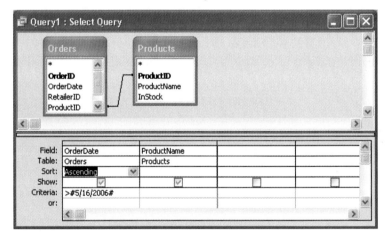

a. Run the query. The database is queried and the results shown in a datasheet:

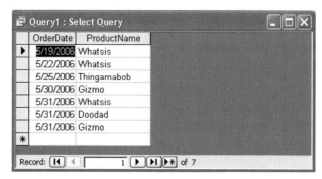

b. Save the query naming it: Sales after 5/16/06
c. Close the Select Query datasheet.

Complex Queries

A select query with multiple criteria is called a *complex query*. For example, the following query selects the product name (from the Products table) and the order date (from the Orders table) where product name is Gizmo AND order date is after 5/16/06:

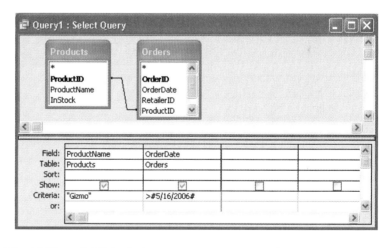

Boolean Expression

A Boolean expression uses relational or logical operators and evaluates to either true or false.

AND OR The AND and OR *logical operators* create a complex query:

AND requires data to match both criteria
OR requires data to match one criteria

In the query above, the AND operator is implied because the criteria is specified in the same row. A complex query with both criteria in the same field requires the AND operator to be typed. For example, the following query selects the product name (from the Products table) and the order date (from the Orders table) where order date is after 5/15/06 AND order date is before 5/30/06:

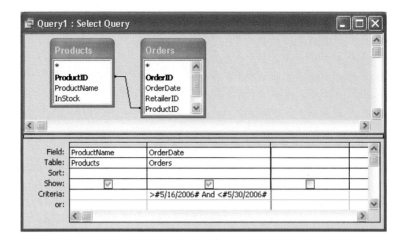

TIP Drag the bottom of the Select Query window to display more **Criteria** rows.

Complex queries using OR are created by using the **or** row of the design grid. For example, the following query selects the product name (from the Products table), the order date (from the Orders table), and the quantity (from the Orders table) where product name is Gizmo OR product name is Doodad:

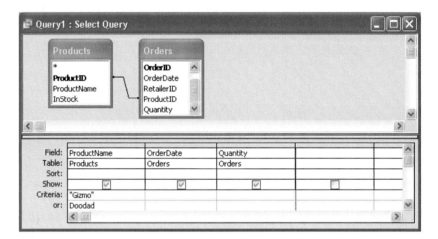

Complex queries can use multiple logical operators to create an expression. For example, the following query selects the product name (from the Products table), the order date (from the Orders table), and the quantity (from the Orders table) where product name is Gizmo AND order date is after 5/15/06 OR product name is Doodad AND order date is after 5/15/06:

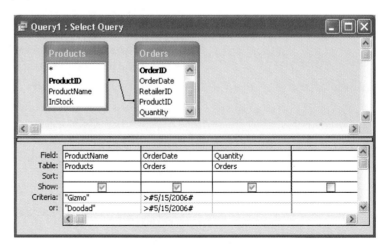

You will create complex queries for the Widget database. Access should already be started with the Widget Database window displayed.

① *DISPLAY THINGAMABOB AND WHATSIS SALES*

   a. In the Widget : Database window, click [🗗 Queries].

   b. Double-click the Create query in Design view icon. The Select Query window is displayed with the Show Table dialog box on top.

   c. Add the Orders table and the Products table and then close the dialog box.

   d. Add the OrderDate field, ProductName field, and Quantity field to the design grid.

   e. In the OrderDate Sort list, select Ascending.

   f. In the ProductName **Criteria** box, type: Thingamabob

   g. In the ProductName **or** row, type: Whatsis

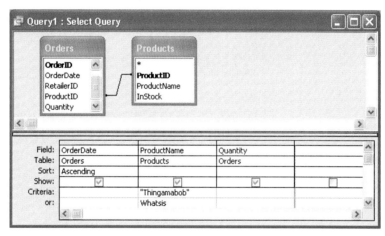

   h. Run the query. The database is queried and the results shown in a datasheet:

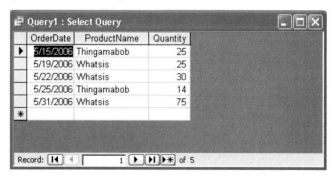

   i. Save the query naming it: Thingamabob and Whatsis Sales after 5/16/06

   j. Close the Select Query datasheet.

② *DISPLAY ORDERS FOR QUANTITIES BETWEEN 5 AND 25*

   a. Create a new select query in Design view.

   b. Add the Orders table and the Products table and then close the Show Table dialog box.

   c. Add the ProductName and Quantity fields to the design grid.

d. In the Quantity Criteria box, type: >5 AND <25

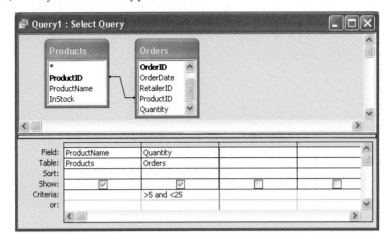

e. Run the query. The database is queried and the results shown in a datasheet:

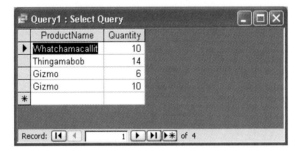

f. Save the query naming it: Sales between 5 and 25

g. Close the Select Query datasheet.

③ *CLOSE WIDGET*

Using Wildcards

A *wildcard* is a character that matches any one or more characters. The asterisk (*) and question mark (?) are two wildcards. The * wildcard matches any number of characters or no characters at all. For example, What* matches What, Whatsis, and Whatchamacallit.

The ? wildcard matches any one character or no character at all. For example, Ann? matches Ann, Anne, and Anna, but not Annette.

LIKE   Wildcards can be used to specify select query criteria. When wildcards are needed, use the LIKE operator to specify criteria. For example, the following query selects the product name (from the Products table) and the order date (from the Orders table) where product name is LIKE W*:

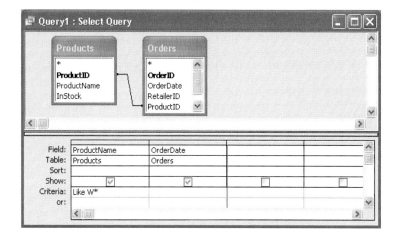

When run, the query displays the datasheet:

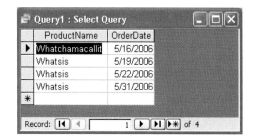

Practice: GADGET DEPOT – part 1 of 9

You will create a query that uses wildcards for the GADGET DEPOT database. Access should already be started.

① *DEFINE RELATIONSHIPS*

a. Open GADGET DEPOT, an Access data file for this text.

b. On the toolbar, click the Relationships button (![button]). The Relationships window is displayed with the Show Table dialog box. (Click the Show Table button (![button]) on the toolbar if the dialog box is not displayed.)

c. Add the Departments and Products tables to the window and then close the dialog box.

d. The two tables are related by the Name field in the Departments table and the Department field in the Products table. Drag the Name field from the Departments table to the Department field of the Products table:

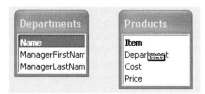

A dialog box is displayed:

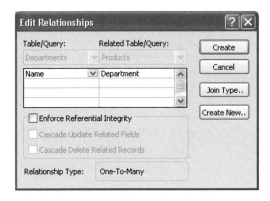

Select **Create**. (If your dialog box looks different, select **Cancel** and try creating the relating the tables again.) A line connects the related fields:

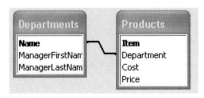

   e. Select File ➡ Save. The relationships are saved.

   f. Close the Relationships window.

② *QUERY FOR BRUSH PRODUCTS*

   a. Create a select query in Design view.

   b. Add the Departments table and the Products table.

   c. Add the Name field and Item field to the design grid.

   d. In the Name Sort list, select Ascending.

   e. In the Item **Criteria** box, type: *brush*

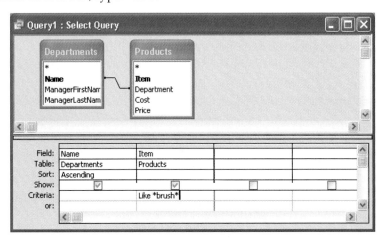

   f. Run the query. The database is queried and the results shown in a datasheet:

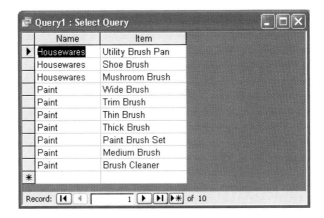

g. Save the query naming it Brush Items and then close the Select Query datasheet.

Using Fields in Query Criteria

A select query can specify another field in the database in the criteria. For example, The Gadget Depot uses their database to store prices. A select query could be used to display products with a 200% markup (a 200% markup equals three times the cost). For example, the following query selects the item (from the Products table) where price (from the Products table) is at least three times the cost (from the Products table):

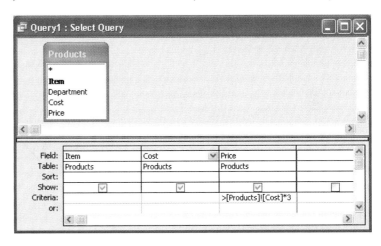

Operator Symbols

The * indicates multiplication, / indicates division, and ^ indicates exponentiation. Parentheses are used to change the order of operations.

Use the format [Table Name]![Field Name] to refer to a field. If a field name is unique to the database, then the table name is not needed in the reference. However, the table must be in the query window. When run, the select query displays the datasheet:

TIP Field references are not case sensitive. For example, [Products]![Cost] is the same as [products]![cost]. However, spaces generate an error, as in [Products] ! [Cost]

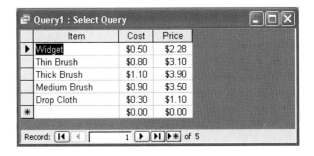

You will create a query that uses a field. Access should already be started and the GADGET DEPOT Database window displayed.

① *QUERY FOR PRODUCTS WITH A MARKUP OVER 100%*

    a. Create a select query in Design view.

    b. Add the Products table.

    c. Add the Item, Cost, and Price fields to the design grid.

    d. In the Item Sort list, select Ascending.

    e. In the Price Criteria box, type: >[Products]![Cost]*2

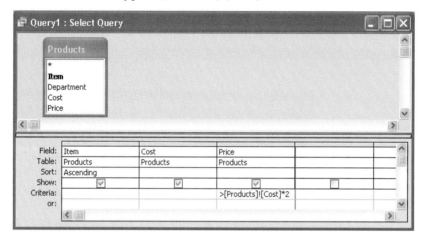

    f. Run the query. The database is queried and the results shown in a datasheet:

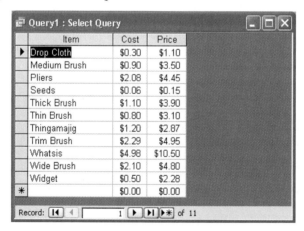

    g. Save the query naming it: 100% Markup

    h. Close the Select Query datasheet.

    i. Close the GADGET DEPOT database.

Mail Merge - Form Letters

form letter

In Word, the Mail Merge Wizard can be used to integrate data stored in an Access database with a document. *Mail merge* is commonly used to create personalized form letters. A *form letter* is a Word document with *merge fields*, which are placeholders for data from an Access table or query. For example, a business can create a letter to their customers that is personalized by merging customer name and address data from an Access table in the company database.

Use the Mail Merge task pane in Word to create a mail merge form letter. To display the task pane, select Tools → Letters and Mailings → Mail Merge or select Mail Merge from the Other Task Panes list:

Starting Mail Merge from Access

In the Database window, select the query or table that is needed for the mail merge document. Next, click the arrow in the OfficeLinks button (⊞▾) on the toolbar and select Merge It with Microsoft Offfice.

The bottom of the Mail Merge task pane indicates that there are six mail merge steps that need to be completed. The six steps are:

1. Select the document type. A description is displayed in the task pane.

2. Select the starting document. The current document can be used or an existing mail-merge document can be modified.

3. Select the recipients. Names, addresses, and other data can come directly from an Access database table or query.

   Click the <u>Browse</u> link to display the Select Data Source dialog box where the Access database is selected. A dialog box lists the tables and queries in the database. After selecting the appropriate table or query, the Mail Merge Recipients dialog box is displayed. Click the check boxes of recipients to be removed, if any.

4. Type the letter. Type the text that will appear in every letter and insert merge fields where appropriate. To insert a merge field at the insertion point, click the <u>More Items</u> link to display the Insert Merge Field dialog box, which contains a list of the fields from the selected table or query. Close the dialog box after inserting a field. Merge fields can then be formatted just like any other text.

5. Preview the merged letter. The letter for the first recipient is displayed in the Word window. The Mail Merge task pane contains options for previewing other letters and editing the recipient list.

6. Print the form letters. The Mail Merge task pane contains options for printing and editing the form letters.

Practice: June Sale

You will create a mail merge letter using data from the Widget database. Access should already be started.

① **CREATE A SELECT QUERY**

  a. Open the Widget database.

  b. Create a select query in Design view.

  c. Add the Orders, Products, and Retailers tables.

  d. Add the ProductID, ProductName, ContactFirstName, ContactLastName, Name, Address, City, StateOrProvince, and ZipOrPostalCode fields to the design grid.

  e. In the ProductName Criteria box, type: Gizmo

  f. Run the query. Two records are displayed.

  g. Save the query naming it: Gizmo Customers

  h. Close the Select Query datasheet.

② **CREATE A NEW WORD DOCUMENT**

  a. Start Word.

  b. Create a new document, if one is not already displayed.

③ **CREATE A FORM LETTER**

  a. Select Tools → Letters and Mailings → Mail Merge. The Mail Merge task pane is displayed.

  b. In the Mail Merge task pane, select Letters if it is not already selected:

  c. Click Next: Starting document. Select Use the current document if it is not already selected:

d. Click <u>Next: Select recipients</u>. Select Use an existing list if it is not already selected and then click <u>Browse</u>:

e. In the Select Data Source dialog box, use the Look in list and the contents box below it to select the Widget database.

f. Select Open. The Select Table dialog box is displayed. Select Gizmo Customers:

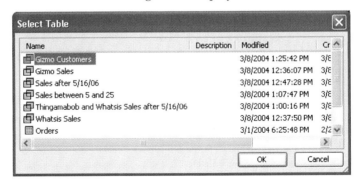

g. Select OK. The Mail Merge Recipients dialog box is displayed.

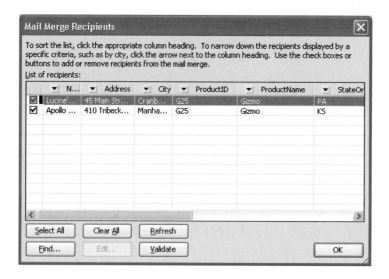

h. Select OK. The dialog box is removed.

i. In the Mail Merge task pane, click <u>Next: Write your letter</u>. The next set of options is displayed:

j. In the new Word document, press Enter 6 times to move the insertion point down about 1 inch (2.54 cm), type the following address and date, and then press Enter 4 times. Ignore the purple dotted line:

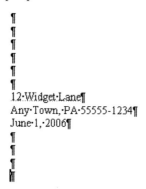

k. In the Mail Merge task pane, click <u>More items</u>:

The Insert Merge Field dialog box is displayed. Select ContactFirstName:

l. Select Insert. A merge field is inserted in the document.

m. Select Close. The dialog box is removed.

n. Type a space, click <u>More items</u>, and insert the ContactLastName merge field.

o. Close the dialog box.

p. Press Enter and then insert additional fields, pressing Enter and typing commas and spaces when necessary, to complete the letter opening:

q. Type the remainder of the letter and insert merge fields as shown below, substituting your name for Student Name and allowing Word to wrap the text:

```
Dear·«ContactFirstName»¶
¶
We·are·extending·a·special·offer·to·Gizmo·customers.·For·the·entire·month·of·June,·the·
«ProductName»·is·being·offered·at·25%·off·the·normal·wholesale·price.·But·hurry,·offer·
available·only·while·supplies·last!·Be·sure·to·specify·product·ID·«ProductID».¶
¶
Best·Regards¶
¶
¶
¶
Student·Name¶
The·Widget·Corporation¶
```

r. Save the form letter naming it: June Sale

④ *PREVIEW A MERGED COPY OF THE FORM LETTER*

In the Mail Merge task pane, click <u>Next: Preview your letters</u>. The next set of options is displayed and the letter for the first recipient is displayed in the Word window. Note that the merge fields are replaced by data from the Gizmo Customers query.

⑤ *VIEW THE MERGED DATA*

a. In the Mail Merge task pane, click >> :

The letter for the next recipient is displayed.

⑥ *PRINT THE MAIL MERGED LETTERS AND THEN CLOSE THE DOCUMENT*

a. Click <u>Next: Complete the merge</u>. The next set of options is displayed.

b. In the Mail Merge task pane, click <u>Print</u>:

A dialog box is displayed. Select All if it is not already selected:

c. Select OK. The dialog box is removed and the Print dialog box is displayed.

d. Select OK. Two letters are printed, with each personalized for the customer.

e. Save and close June Sale.

Mail Merge - Mailing Labels

The Mail Merge task pane can also be used to create mailing labels. Like a mail merge form letter, mailing labels are created in a document that includes merge fields.

To print mailing labels, place adhesive paper with multiple labels to a page in the printer. The Avery® brand of adhesive labels is widely used, and the dimensions of many of its labels have been included in Word. Therefore only the Avery product number needs to be selected for Word to automatically print labels in the appropriate format.

To create mailing labels select Tools → Letters and Mailings → Mail Merge or select Mail Merge from the Other Task Panes list. There are six steps to complete in the Mail Merge task pane:

1. Select the document type.

2. Select the starting document. Select the <u>Change document layout</u> link and then click the <u>Label options</u> link to display the Label Options dialog box. Choose the product name and product number from the dialog box. (Refer to the label packaging.)

3. Select the recipients. Names, addresses, and other data can come directly from an Access database table or query.

   Click the <u>Browse</u> link to display the Select Data Source dialog box where the Access database is selected. A dialog box lists the tables and queries in the database. After selecting the appropriate table or query, the Mail Merge Recipients dialog box is displayed. Click the check boxes of recipients to be removed, if any.

4. Arrange the labels. Insert fields, format the data, and arrange the information. Alternatively, click the <u>Address block</u> link to display a dialog box with options for creating an address label arrangement. Click [Update all labels] in the task pane when the first label is ready for replicating to the other labels.

5. Preview the merged labels. A sheet of labels is displayed in the Word window. The Mail Merge task pane contains options for previewing other labels and editing the recipient list.

6. Print the labels. The Mail Merge task pane contains options for printing and editing the labels.

Practice: June Sale Labels

You will create mailing labels for the mail merge documents created in the previous practice. Access should already be started with the Widget Database open.

① *CREATE A NEW WORD DOCUMENT*

② *CREATE MAILING LABELS*

    a. Select Tools → Letters and Mailings → Mail Merge. The Mail Merge task pane is displayed.

    b. In the Mail Merge task pane, select Labels.

    c. Click <u>Next: Starting document</u>. Select Change document layout if it is not already selected and then click <u>Label options</u>:

The Label Options dialog box is displayed. From the Product number list, select the Avery 5159 - Address label:

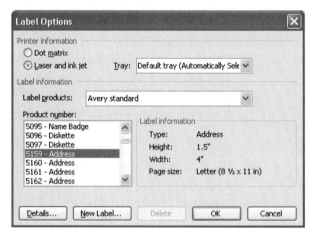

    d. Select OK. The Word document is modified to a layout that matches the sheet of labels.

e. Click <u>Next: Select recipients</u>. Select Use an existing list if it is not already selected and then click <u>Browse</u>.

f. In the Select Data Source dialog box, use the Look in list and the contents box below it to select the Widget database.

g. Select Open. The Select Table dialog box is displayed.

h. Select Gizmo Customers and then select OK. The Mail Merge Recipients dialog box is displayed.

i. Select OK. The dialog box is removed.

j. In the Mail Merge task pane, click <u>Next: Arrange your labels</u>.

k. In the Mail Merge task pane, click <u>More items</u>. The Insert Merge Field dialog box is displayed.

l. Select ContactFirstName and then select Insert. A merge field is created at the insertion point.

m. Select Close. The dialog box is removed.

n. Type a space and then click <u>More items</u> and insert the ContactLastName merge field.

o. Close the dialog box.

p. Press Enter and then insert additional fields, pressing Enter and typing commas and spaces when necessary, to complete the label. Bold the <<Name>> field:

«ContactFirstName»·«ContactLastName»¶
«Name»¶
«Address»¶
«City»,·«StateOrProvince»·«ZipOrPostalCode»¶
¤

q. In the Mail Merge task pane, click Update all labels . The label layout is duplicated.

r. Save the labels document naming it: June Sale Labels

③ PREVIEW A MERGED COPY OF THE LABELS

In the Mail Merge task pane, click <u>Next: Preview your labels</u>. The next set of options is displayed and the labels are displayed. Because there are only two records in the query, only two labels are displayed.

④ PRINT THE LABELS

a. In the Mail Merge task pane, click the <u>Next: Complete the merge</u>.

b. In the Mail Merge task pane, click <u>Print</u>. A dialog box is displayed.

c. Select All if it is not already selected and then select OK.

d. The Print dialog box is displayed.

e. Select OK. The labels are printed on regular paper. For actual mailing labels, insert the appropriate sheet of Avery labels into the printer before printing.

f. Save and close the modified June Sale Labels.

⑤ QUIT WORD

⑥ CLOSE THE WIDGET DATABASE

Parameter Query

A *parameter query* retrieves data that matches criteria, called a *parameter*, typed by the user when the query is run. A parameter query can include any of the fields from related tables in a database. For example, the following query selects the product name (from the Products table) and the order date (from the Orders table) where product name is what the user types when the query is run:

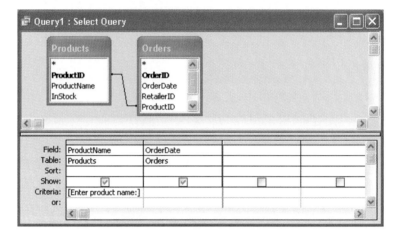

Instead of using actual data for comparison, a prompt enclosed by brackets is typed in the **Criteria** box. Click the Run button (!) on the toolbar to display a dialog box with the prompt:

Type a value, for example, Doodad, and then select OK to complete the query:

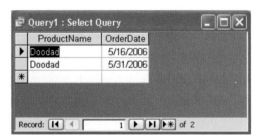

Practice: GADGET DEPOT – part 3 of 9

You will create a parameter query for the GADGET DEPOT database. Access should already be started.

① *CREATE A PARAMETER QUERY*

    a. Open GADGET DEPOT.

    b. Create a select query in Design view.

c. Add the Departments table and the Products table.

d. Add the Name field and Item field to the design grid.

e. In the Item Sort list, select Ascending.

f. In the Name Criteria box, type: [Enter department name:]

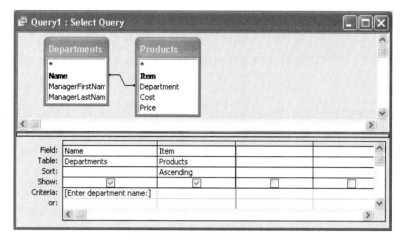

g. Run the query. A dialog box is displayed. Type: Garden

h. Select OK. The Select Query datasheet is displayed with Garden department items:

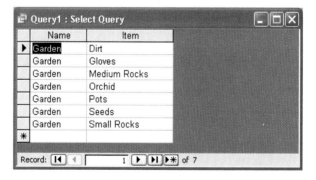

i. Save the query naming it: Department Items

j. Close the Select Query datasheet.

② *CLOSE THE GADGET DEPOT DATABASE*

The Update Query

An *update query* modifies, or "updates," records. Criteria can be specified to limit which records are updated. If no criteria is specified, then all records containing the update field are modified. For example, the following query updates InStock (from the Products table) to InStock – Quantity (from the Orders table):

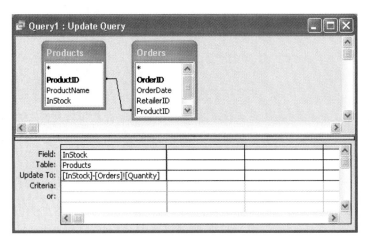

The relationship between the tables is used to match product names, and then the corresponding stock amount is decreased by the quantities ordered.

To create an update query, click ![Queries] in the Objects list in the Database window and then double-click the Create query in Design view icon. A new, empty query is displayed in Design view with the Show Table dialog box. Add tables to the Select Query window, click the arrow in the Query Type button (![Query Type]) on the toolbar, and then select Update Query. The button changes to ![Update] and an **Update To** row appears in the design grid. Drag fields into the design grid and type the update.

After defining the update query, click the Run button (![Run]) on the toolbar to update the records. To preview the records that will be modified, click the View button (![View]) on the toolbar before running the query. An update query cannot be reversed after it is run.

> **TIP** Update queries modify records each time they are run, even if records have been previously updated by the same query. Use caution when running an update query.

Practice: Widget – part 12 of 12

You will create an update query for the Widget database. Access should already be started.

  ① *OPEN THE WIDGET DATABASE*

    a. Open the Widget database.

    b. Display the Products table. Note the InStock amounts shown. To keep better track of inventory, an update query can be used to modify the in stock amounts to reflect orders.

    c. Close the Products table.

② CREATE AN UPDATE QUERY

    a. Create a select query in Design view.

    b. Add the Orders table and the Products table.

    c. On the toolbar, click the arrow in the Query Type button (▦▾) and then select Update Query. An Update To row is displayed in the design grid.

    d. Add the InStock field and the OrderDate field to the design grid.

    e. In the InStock Update To row, type: [InStock]-[Quantity]

    f. In the OrderDate Criteria box, type: >=5/1/2006 AND <=5/31/2006

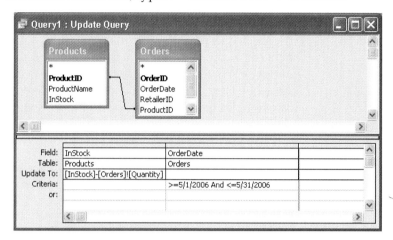

    g. Run the query. A warning dialog box is displayed:

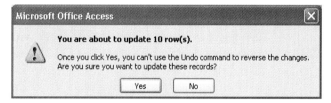

    h. Select Yes. The query is executed, but a datasheet is not displayed.

    i. Save the query naming it: May Stock Update

    j. Close the Select Query.

    k. Display the Products table. The stock amounts have decreased:

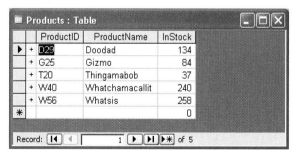

③ CLOSE THE WIDGET DATABASE

    Close the Products table and then close the Widget database.

④ QUIT ACCESS

Chapter Summary

In a relational database, each table must be related to another table by a field. Relationships between tables are defined using the Relationships button on the toolbar or the Relationships command. After relationships have been defined, subdatasheets are available in a table. A subdatasheet shows records from another table that are related to a particular record.

A select query can include fields from any table and uses the relationships between tables to determine which data to display. A sort order may also be specified. Select query results are displayed in a datasheet.

A range query has criteria that matches a range of values. Relational operators (>, >=, <, <=, <>) are used in the criteria expression. Complex queries have multiple criteria, which are specified with the AND and OR logical operators. The AND operator may be implied in the design grid for some complex queries. The or row in the design grid is used for complex queries involving OR.

Wildcards include the * and ? characters, and are specified in criteria to match any one or more characters. The * matches any number of characters or no characters at all. The ? matches any one character or no characters at all.

Select queries can include fields in their criteria by using the format [Table Name]![Field Name] to refer to a field.

Parameter queries prompt the user for criteria data. Update queries change data in multiple records at once.

A select query is modified in Design view. Tables and fields can be removed and added. To add a field between existing fields in the design grid, drag it to a column. Access automatically moves existing fields to the right. To delete a column, select it and then press the Delete key.

Use the Save As command to save a modified query using a new name. A select query is deleted by clicking its name in the Database window and then pressing the Delete key.

Mail merge is used to create personalized form letters. A form letter is a Word document that includes merge fields, which indicate where data from an Access table or query will go. Mail merge is also used to create mailing labels. Mail merge form letters and mailing labels are created using the Mail Merge command. Before printing mailing labels, special adhesive paper needs to be inserted into the printer.

Vocabulary

Asterisk (*) A wildcard character that matches any number of characters or no character at all.

Column selector The gray box at the top of a field in the design grid of a Select Query window.

Complex query A select query with multiple criteria.

Design grid The part of the Select Query window where fields and criteria are entered.

Form letter A Word document with merge fields.

Like Operator used to specify criteria that uses wildcards.

Logical operators AND and OR, which are used to specify complex query criteria.

Mail merge The process of integrating data in an Access database with a document to create personalized form letters.

Merge fields Placeholders in a Word document for data from an Access table or query.

Parameter A value used in a parameter query.

Parameter query A select query that retrieves data based on criteria typed by the user when the query is run.

Question mark (?) A wildcard character that matches any one character or no character at all.

Range query A select query with criteria that matches a range of values.

Related Two tables in a relational database with corresponding fields.

Relational operators Used to specify criteria in a range query. Operators include <, >, <=, >=, and <>.

Select query A database object that retrieves data that matches specified criteria.

Sorting Placing records in a specified order.

Subdatasheet Displays records from another table that are related to the current record.

Update query A query that modifies records based on criteria.

Wildcard A character used in criteria that matches any one or more characters.

Design Displays a query in Design view. Found on the Database window toolbar.

Mail Merge **command** Used to display the Mail Merge task pane. Found in Tools → Letters and Mailings.

Queries Displays the query objects. Found in the Database window.

Query Type button Clicked to choose Update Query. Found on the toolbar.

Relationships **command** Used to define or display the relationship between tables. Found in the Tools menu. The Relationships button on the toolbar can be used instead of the command.

Run button Clicked to run a query. Found on the toolbar.

Save As **command** Displays a dialog box used for duplicating a query. Found in the File menu.

Show Table **command** Used to add a table to a Select Query window. Found in the Query menu. The Show Table button on the toolbar can be used instead of the command.

View button Used to switch a table between Design view and Datasheet view and vice versa. Also used to preview records that will be affected by an update query. Found on the toolbar.

1. Explain the basis of a relationship between two tables.

2. Will a relationship need to be defined for two tables in which one table has a lookup field to another?

3. a) What is a subdatasheet?
   b) When is a subdatasheet available?
   c) How is a subdatasheet viewed?
   d) How is a displayed subdatasheet removed from view?

4. a) What is a select query?
   b) What is the design grid?

5. a) List the steps required to create and run a select query.
   b) List the steps required to run a previously created select query.

6. Consider the Widget database. The stock manager needs to know which items have less than 50 in stock.
   a) Which fields should be selected for the query?
   b) Which tables store the fields?
   c) What is the criteria expression?

7. A query similar to an existing query is needed. What is the most efficient approach to creating the new query? Explain.

8. In Design view, can a field be added between existing fields in the design grid of a select query? If so, how?

9. List the steps required to delete a column from the design grid of a select query.

10. a) What is a range query?
    b) List all the relational operators that create a range query.

11. In the explanation of complex queries using AND, the text states that in one case, the AND is implied. What is meant by this?

12. What is the or row of a select query design grid used for? How is this different from criteria involving AND?

13. List two criteria wildcards that can be used in a select query and explain when each would be used.

14. What does the LIKE operator in the design grid of a select query indicate?

15. How would a reference to the Grade field in the Student table be typed in the criteria?

16. a) What is mail merge?
    b) What is a form letter?
    c) What are merge fields?

17. a) What are mailing labels?
    b) Are mailing labels typically printed on plain paper? Explain.

True/False

18. Determine if each of the following are true or false. If false, explain why.
    a) A table does not need to be related to another table in a relational database.
    b) Subdatasheets are available before relationships are defined.
    c) A select query limits the data displayed to that which meets certain criteria.
    d) The > relational operator is used to specify criteria that is greater than a particular value.
    e) The AND logical operator requires a record to match both criteria in order to be displayed.
    f) The OR logical operator requires that a record not match any criteria in order to be displayed.
    g) The ? wildcard matches any number of characters.
    h) Mail merge documents allow multiple personalized documents to be created quickly.
    i) Addresses for mailing labels must be individually typed, even when a database of the names and addresses exist.
    j) A parameter query displays a dialog box at run time so that criteria can be varied.
    k) An update query cannot be reversed after it is run.

Designing Queries

19. Access converts a query in Design view to an SQL (Structured Query Language) statement, which is then used to query a database. SQL statements have a specific format as shown below. For each of the following questions, determine the fields, tables, and criteria required for a select query. Refer to the Widget database tables shown on the first page of this chapter and used in the practices. Write your answers as SQL statements, as in the following example:

What are the retailer IDs for retailers that purchased Thingamabobs?

SELECT RetailerID, ProductName
FROM Orders, Products
WHERE ProductName=Thingamabobs

a) How many Doodads are in stock?
b) What are the first and last names of the contact person for Apollo Sales Incorporated?
c) What items have Helena Unlimited ordered?
d) Which cities have Gizmos shipped to?
e) Which states have Whatsis items shipped to?

Exercise 1 ◈ ─────────────────────────Museum Exhibits

Sunport Science Museum wants to use queries to analyze the data stored in its Museum Exhibits database, which was created in Chapter 11, Exercise 1.

a) The Exhibits and Attendance tables are related by the ExhibitID field. Display the Relationships window and verify this relationship.

b) Create a select query that displays the ExhibitID, Name, Attendance, and Year fields of exhibits with an attendance over 1,500 in 2006. The query should sort the results in descending order by attendance. Save the select query naming it 2006 Attendance over 1,500. Print the select query datasheet.

c) Create a select query that displays the Name, Updated, Attendance, and Year fields of exhibits with an attendance less than 1,500 in 2006 and last updated before 1/1/05. Save the select query naming it 2006 Attendance < 1,500 & Updated before 05. Print the select query datasheet.

d) Create a select query that displays the ExhibitID, Name, Year, and Attendance fields. Specify criteria with the appropriate wildcard to display all the Exhibits with ExhibitIDs that begin WDH. Save the select query naming it Why Does That Happen Exhibits. Print the select query datasheet.

Exercise 2 ◈ ───────────────────────────── Library

The local library wants to use queries to analyze the data stored in its Library database, which was created in Chapter 11, Exercise 2.

a) The Books and Authors tables are related by the AuthorID field. Display the Relationships window and verify this relationship.

b) Create a select query that displays the AuthorID, FirstName, LastName, and Title fields of books authored by AuthorID TB22. Save the select query naming it Books by TB22. Print the select query datasheet.

c) Create a select query that displays the FirstName, LastName, Title, and Type fields of books that are of drama or mystery type. The query should sort the results in ascending order by the author's last name. Save the select query naming it Drama or Mystery. Print the select query datasheet.

d) Create a select query that displays the FirstName, LastName, Title, and ISBN fields. Specify the criteria with the appropriate wildcard to display all the authors with last names that begin with B. Save the select query naming it Authors beginning with B. Print the select query datasheet.

e) Create a parameter query that displays the FirstName, LastName, Title, and ISBN fields. The query should prompt the user for the title. Save the select query naming it Search by Title. Run the query and enter The Dog Wore a Red Coat. Print the query datasheet.

Exercise 3 —————————————————————————————————— Pizza Payroll

The owner of Pizza Palace wants to use queries to analyze the data stored in its Pizza Payroll database, which was created in Chapter 11, Exercise 3.

    a) The Employees and Payroll tables are related by the EmployeeID field. Display the Relationships window and verify this relationship.

    b) Create a select query that displays the FirstName, LastName, Date, GrossPay, and Taxes fields of all payroll checks where gross pay is less than $250 and taxes are less than $30. Save the select query naming it Gross Pay < $250 & Tax < $30. Print the select query datasheet.

    c) Create a parameter query that displays the EmployeeID, FirstName, LastName, Date, GrossPay, and Taxes fields. Have the query prompt the user for the employee ID. Save the select query naming it Employee Payroll Data. Run the query and enter E1. Print the query datasheet.

    d) Create a parameter query that displays the EmployeeID, FirstName, and LastName fields. The query should prompt the user for the employee last name. Save the select query naming it EmployeeID Lookup. Run the query and enter Warner. Print the query datasheet.

Exercise 4 —————————————————————————————————— Boat Storage

Sunport Boat Storage wants to use queries to analyze the data stored in its Boat Storage database, which was created in Chapter 11, Exercise 4.

    a) The Boats and Boat Owners tables are related by the OwnerID field. The Boats and Employees tables are related by the EmployeeID field. Display the Relationships window and verify these relationships.

    b) Create a select query that displays the Boat, OwnerID, FirstName of owner, LastName of owner, and Fee fields for those boats owned by OwnerID 2. Save the select query naming it OwnerID 2 Boats. Print the select query datasheet.

    c) Create a select query that displays the Boat, Fee, FirstName of owner, and LastName of owner fields of those boats with a monthly fee greater than or equal to $70. The query should sort the results in ascending order by the owner's last name. Save the select query naming it Fees >= $70. Print the select query datasheet.

    d) Create a select query that displays in ascending order by SlotNumber the FirstName of employee, LastName of employee, Boat, and SlotNumber fields of those boats stored in the first five slots. Save the select query naming Slots 1 through 5. Print the select query datasheet.

    e) Create a parameter query that displays the FirstName of employee, LastName of employee, Boat, and SlotNumber fields. The query should prompt the user for the slotnumber. Save the select query naming it Slotnumber Lookup. Run the query and enter 16. Print the query datasheet.

Exercise 5 ⟳ —————————————————————————————— Messages

The office manager wants to use queries to analyze the data stored in the Messages database, which was created in Chapter 11, Exercise 5.

    a) The Employees and Messages tables are related by the EmployeeID field. Display the Relationships window and verify this relationship.

    b) Create a select query that displays the FirstName, LastName, Date, and MessageID for employee Trey Jones. Save the select query naming it Trey Jones Messages. Print the select query datasheet.

    c) Create a select query that displays the FirstName, LastName, MessageID, Date, and Time fields for messages on 4/21/06 through 4/23/06. Save the select query naming it Apr 21 to Apr 23 Messages. Print the select query datasheet.

    d) Create a select query that displays the FirstName, LastName, CompanyName, and Package fields for messages regarding the delivery of a package. Save the select query naming Packages Delivered. The criteria for a Yes/No field is specified as either true or false. Print the select query datasheet.

    e) Create a parameter query that displays the LastName of employee and then all but the EmployeeID field from the Messages table. The query should prompt the user for the LastName. Save the select query naming it Message Lookup. Run the query and enter Jones. Print the query datasheet.

Exercise 6 ⟳ ————————————————————————— Media Collection

Use queries to analyze the data stored in the Media Collection database, which was created in Chapter 11, Exercise 6.

    a) The Media and Photographers tables are related by the PhotograperID field. Display the Relationships window and define this relationship.

    b) Create a select query that displays the Title, Event, Date, and MediaType fields for the Alaska trip event. Save the select query naming it Alaska Trip. Print the select query datasheet.

    c) Modify the Alaska Trip query created in part (b) to query for Montana trip media. Save the select query as Montana Trip. Print the select query datasheet. The Alaska Trip query should still be part of the database.

    d) Create a select query that displays the MediaType, FirstName, LastName, Title, and Description fields for media that includes bird in the description. Save the select query naming Bird Media. Print the select query datasheet.

Exercise 7 ————————————————————Coral Research

Researchers want to use queries to analyze the data stored in the Coral Research database, which was created in Chapter 11, Exercise 7.

    a) The Coral Sites and Growth Research tables are related by the SiteID field. Display the Relationships window and define this relationship.

    b) Create a select query that displays the CoralName, Color, Description, Date, and Size fields for the coral named Knobby Brain Coral. Save the select query naming it Knobby Brain Coral. Print the select query datasheet.

    c) Create a select query that displays the SiteID, CoralName, Date, and Size fields for all those corals larger than 1 meter in size. Save the select query naming it Size > 1. Print the select query datasheet.

    d) Create a select query to display the SiteID, CoralName, and Date fields for all those corals in sites with SiteID 1 or 2. Save the select query naming it Sites 1 or 2. Print the select query datasheet.

Exercise 8 ———————————————— Community Service

A local school needs to know specific information about the community service hours performed by their students. Use queries to retrieve the information needed from the Community Service database, which was created in Chapter 11, Exercise 8.

    a) The Students and Volunteer Hours tables are related by the StudentID field. The Organizations and Volunteer Hours tables are related by the OrganizationName field. Display the Relationships window and verify these relationships.

    b) Create a select query that displays the StudentID, FirstName, LastName, and Hours fields for students with less than 3 hours of community service. The query should sort the results in ascending order by Hours. Save the select query naming it Less than 3 Hours. Print the select query datasheet.

    c) Create a parameter query that displays the OrganizationName, StudentID, and Hours fields. The query should prompt the user for the OrganizationName. Save the select query naming it Organization Hours Lookup. Run the query and enter City Soup Kitchen. Print the query datasheet.

Exercise 9 ———————————————— Summer Camp

Use queries to retrieve information from the Summer Camp database, which was created in Chapter 11, Exercise 9.

    a) The Counselors and Activities tables are related by the CounselorID field. The Activities and Schedules tables are related by the ActivityName field. The Cabins and Campers tables are related by the CabinName field. The Schedules and Campers tables are related by the CamperID field. Display the Relationships window and verify these relationships.

    b) Create a select query that displays the Day, ActivityName, FirstName of the camper, LastName of the camper, and Location fields for the activities on the first day. The query should sort the results in ascending order by ActivityName. Save the select query naming it Day1 Schedule. Print the select query datasheet.

c) Modify the Day1 Schedule query created in part (b) to query for Day2 activities. Save the select query as Day2 Schedule. Print the select query datasheet. The Day1 Schedule query should still be part of the database.

d) Modify the Day1 Schedule query created in part (b) to query for Day3 activities. Save the select query as Day3 Schedule. Print the select query datasheet. The Day1 Schedule query should still be part of the database.

e) Create a select query that displays the CabinName, FirstName of the camper, LastName of the camper, FirstName of the counselor, and LastName of the counselor for all the cabins (no criteria needed). You will need to add the Campers, Cabins, and Counselors tables to the Select Query window. The query should sort the results in ascending order by CabinName. Save the select query naming it Cabin Assignments. Print the select query datasheet.

f) Create a select query that displays the FirstName of the counselor, LastName of the counselor, ActivityName, Location, and CabinName fields for all the counselors (no criteria needed). The query should sort the results in ascending order by LastName. Save the select query naming it Counselor Assignments. Print the select query datasheet.

g) Create a mail merge letter that is personalized for each of the camp counselors. Use the Counselor Assignments query created in part (f). Inform the counselors of their cabin assignment and the names of the campers assigned to their cabin. There is no need to include an address block at the top of the letter because counselors will receive the document at the camp orientation. Be sure the letter is upbeat in tone and remind the counselors of how much fun their experience will be, while still keeping the letter professional and to the point.

Exercise 10 ⟳ ——————————————————————— Travel Agency

A travel agency wants to use queries to analyze the data stored in its Travel Agency database, which was created in Chapter 11, Exercise 10.

a) The Clients and Booked Vacations tables are related by the ClientID field. The Booked Vacations and Vacations tables are related by the Package field. Display the Relationships window and verify these relationships.

b) Create a select query that displays the FirstName, LastName, and Package fields for those clients who have booked a Mountain Explorer or Summit Skiing vacation package. Save the select query naming it Mountain Explorer/Summit Skiing. Print the select query datasheet.

c) Create a select query that displays the ClientID, Date, Package, and Cost fields of those vacations booked by client with ClientID JU. Save the select query naming it Vacations Booked by JU. Print the select query datasheet.

d) Create a select query that displays the Package, Cost, and Date fields for all those vacations booked that are costing more than $500. Save the select query naming it Booked > $500. Print the select query datasheet.

e) Create a select query that displays the FirstName, LastName, Package, Cost, Location, Date, and Type fields for all those vacations booked which cost less than $1,000 and that are a relaxing Type. Save the select query naming it Booked Relaxing < $1,000. Print the select query datasheet.

f) Create a mail merge letter that is personalized for each of the travel agency clients. Inform them of an upcoming spring special to Jamaica. Let them know that the first 12 to respond receive a special travel kit. In the first paragraph of the letter, introduce the special, in the second paragraph give a few highlights of Jamaica, and in the closing paragraph summarize the special and remind them of how the travel agency works hard to give the best service. Type the letter in the block style as used in Chapter 4. Use the Internet or books to research Jamaica.

g) Print the first three mail merge documents.

h) Create address labels that are personalized for each of the travel agency clients. Print a sheet of labels on plain paper.

Exercise 11 ——————————————————— VIDEO STORE

The owners and customers of VIDEO STORE want to use queries to retrieve information about movies and rentals from its database modified in Chapter 11, Exercise 11.

a) Create a select query that displays the FirstName, LastName, and InDate fields of those members who have not returned a video. If a video has not been returned, the InDate field is blank. To display fields that are blank, type Is Null for the criteria. Save the select query naming it Not Returned. Print the select query datasheet.

b) Create a select query that displays the Title, Type, and OutDate fields for all those movies checked out before 2/7/06 that are Sci-fi movies. Save the select query naming it Sci-fi < 2/7/06. Print the select query datasheet.

c) Create a parameter query that displays the Title and Type fields. The query should prompt the user for the Title. Save the select query naming it Title Search. Run the query and enter ET. Print the query datasheet. Run the query again and enter Seabiscuit. Does the Video Store carry the movie?

Exercise 12 ◇ ——————————————————— INVENTIONS

The INVENTIONS database was modified in Chapter 11, Exercise 12. Open INVENTIONS and create the following queries:

a) Create a select query that displays the FirstName, LastName, BirthCountry, Invention, and Year fields of those inventions created after 1799 by inventors born in the United States. Save the select query naming it US > 1799. Print the select query datasheet.

b) Create a parameter query that displays the Invention and Year fields. The query should prompt the user for the Year. Save the select query naming it Year Search. Run the query and enter 1800. Print the query datasheet.

Chapter 13
Analyzing Data in a Database

Reports are discussed in this chapter. Calculated fields for displaying additional information in a query are also explained, as well as importing, exporting, and linking data.

What is a Report?

Reports present data from a database in an organized manner with a descriptive title, headings, and summaries. For example, in the GADGET DEPOT report below, both the Departments and Products tables are used and items have been grouped by department name:

Items by Department

Department	Item	Cost	Price
Garden			
	Dirt	$0.80	$1.50
	Gloves	$2.00	$4.00
	Medium Rocks	$0.75	$1.44
	Orchid	$8.00	$15.00
	Pots	$1.00	$1.99
	Seeds	$0.06	$0.15
	Small Rocks	$0.50	$0.95
Hardware			
	Heavy Hammer	$3.05	$5.13
	Light Hammer	$2.16	$4.22
	Nails	$0.38	$0.76
	Pliers	$2.08	$4.45
	Screws	$0.44	$0.80
Housewares			
	Knob	$3.00	$5.88
	Mushroom Brush	$0.99	$1.78
	Picture Hangers	$1.55	$2.90
	Shoe Brush	$1.19	$2.10
	Whatsis	$4.98	$10.50
	Widget	$0.50	$2.28
Lighting			
	Black Light Bulbs	$0.59	$1.18
	Ceiling Fan	$39.00	$52.99
	Florescent Bulbs	$4.13	$5.99
	Incandescent Bulbs	$3.09	$4.14
	Lamp	$18.00	$32.00
Paint			
	Drop Cloth	$0.30	$1.10
	Green Paint	$5.00	$8.00
	Medium Brush	$0.90	$3.50
	Red Paint	$5.00	$8.00
	Thick Brush	$1.10	$3.90
	Thin Brush	$0.80	$3.10
	Thingamajig	$1.20	$2.87
	Trim Brush	$2.29	$4.95
	Wide Brush	$2.10	$4.80

Page 1 of 1

Creating a Report

A report is based on the fields in a database. To create a new report, click [🗐 Reports] in the Objects list in the Database window and then double-click the Create report by using wizard icon. The Report Wizard displays dialog boxes for selecting fields, data grouping, sort order, layout, page orientation, and style. *Data grouping* organizes data based on a selected field and then indents the data in the report, making the report easier to comprehend, as in the "Items by Department" report on the previous page.

data grouping

Report Wizard

The Report Wizard makes creating a report simple and fast. Therefore, it is a quick process to generate several reports with different grouping, sorting, layouts, and styles until the best presentation for the data is achieved.

To open an existing report, click [🗐 Reports] in the Database window and then double-click a report icon. A report is generated each time it is opened. Therefore, changes to data in the tables used in the report are automatically reflected when the report is opened.

Practice: GADGET DEPOT – part 4 of 9

You will create a new report for the GADGET DEPOT database.

① *OPEN GADGET DEPOT*

    a. Start Access.

    b. Open GADGET DEPOT, which was last modified in the Chapter 12.

② *CREATE A NEW REPORT*

    a. In the GADGET DEPOT : Database window, click [🗐 Reports].

    b. Double-click the Create report by using wizard icon. A dialog box is displayed.

    c. In the Tables/Queries list, select Table: Departments, and then click [>] to move the Name field to the Selected Fields list:

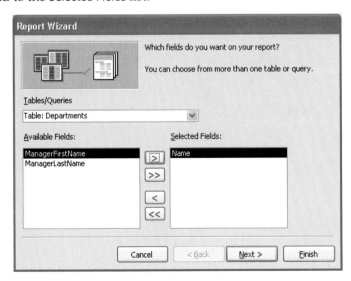

    d. In the Tables/Queries list, select Table: Products. Move the Item and Price fields to the Selected Fields list:

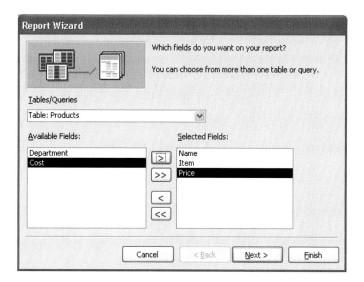

e. Select **Next**. View the report by Departments:

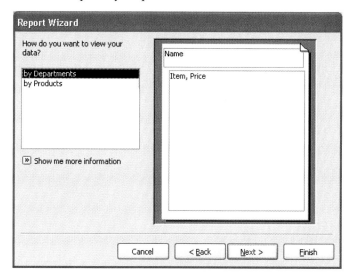

f. Select **Next**. The report data is grouped by Name. No other grouping is needed:

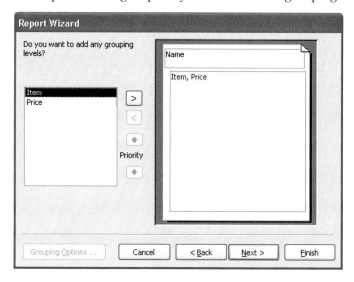

g. Select Next. Select Item from the first Sort list. Data will be sorted within each group:

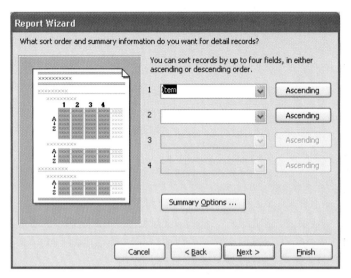

h. Select Next. Default layout options are already selected:

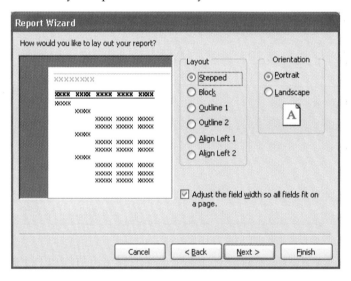

i. Select Next. A default style is already selected:

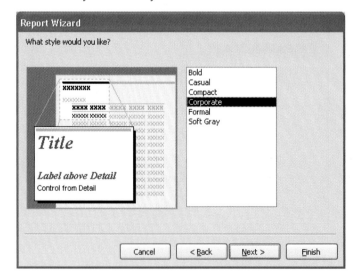

j. Select Next. In the What title do you want for your report? box, type Items by Department and then select Preview the report. if it is not already selected:

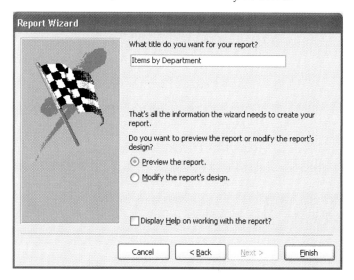

k. Select Finish. The report is displayed.

③ PRINT THE REPORT

a. Print the report.

b. Close the report.

Report Summaries

A *report summary* provides statistics on a number field, such as an average or minimum value. For example, the GADGET DEPOT report below includes summaries that show the maximum and minimum prices:

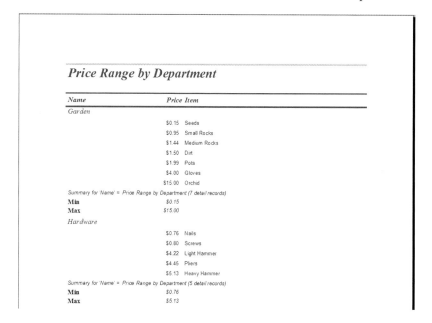

A summary can be added to a report that has at least one grouping level and at least one numeric field. Add a summary by clicking Summary Options... in the sort and summary Report Wizard dialog box.

Summary options include:

- the Sum check box computes the total for a group of values.
- the Avg check box computes the average for a group of values.
- the Min check box determines the smallest value in a group of values.
- the Max check box determines the largest value in a group of values.

Practice: GADGET DEPOT – part 5 of 9

You will create a new report with a summary. Access should already be started with the GADGET DEPOT Database window displayed from the last practice.

① *CREATE A NEW REPORT*

a. In the GADGET DEPOT : Database window, click [Reports].

b. Double-click the Create report by using wizard icon. A dialog box is displayed.

c. In the Tables/Queries list, select the appropriate tables and move the Name, Item, and Price fields to the Selected Fields list:

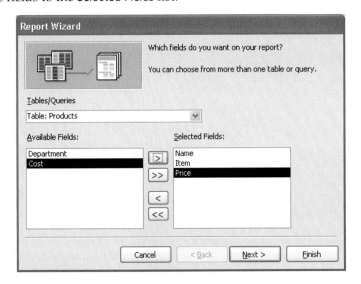

d. Select Next. View the report by Departments.

e. Select Next. The report data is grouped by Name. No other grouping is needed.

f. Select Next. Select Item from the first Sort list. Data will be sorted within each group:

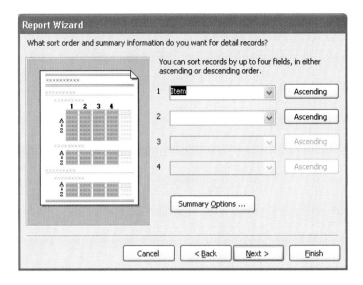

g. Click [Summary Options …]. The Summary Options dialog box is displayed. Select the Min and Max options:

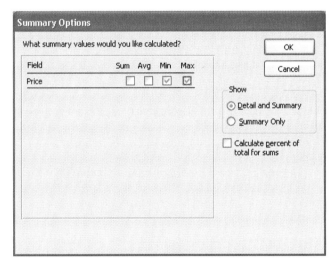

h. Select OK.

i. Select Next. Default layout options are already selected.

j. Select Next. A default style is already selected.

k. Select Next. In the What title do you want for your report? box, type Price Range by Department and then select Preview the report. if it is not already selected.

l. Select Finish. The report is displayed. Note the summary information.

② *PRINT THE REPORT*

a. Print the report.

b. Close the report.

Modifying a Report

A report is modified in Design view. To switch a displayed report to Design view, click the View button (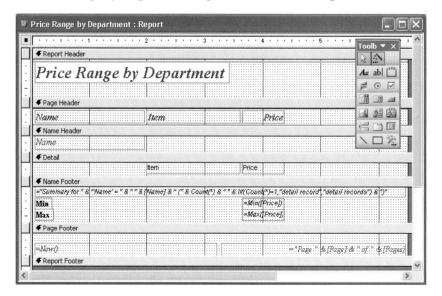) on the toolbar. To open a report in Design view, click 🔲 Reports in the Database window, select a report icon, and then click ✎ Design on the Database window toolbar. For example, the Price Range by Department report is shown in Design view:

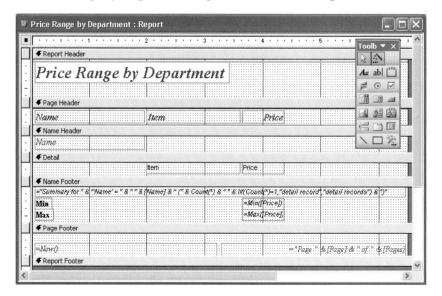

Click an object to select it. Drag a move handle to relocate an object or drag the center of an object to relocate it. Drag a size handle to change the object size.

The Toolbox is automatically displayed when a report is in Design view. Controls in the Toolbox are used to add labels, images, and other objects to the report. To add a label, click the Label control (**Aa**) in the Toolbox. Next, click the form to place the insertion point. Type text and then press Enter. Images are added with the Image control, also in the Toolbox. Click the Image control (🖼) and then click the form, which displays a dialog box for selecting the location of the image file.

adding a label

adding an image

When modifying a report, sections are sized by dragging the bottom border of the section.

When a report is displayed in Design view, the Formatting toolbar is displayed in the Access window:

Formatting can be applied to any selected object. Buttons include the Fill/Back Color (🎨), Font/Fore Color (**A**), Line/Border Color (✏), and Line/Border Width (▦). Change the background color of the form by clicking an empty portion of the Detail section and then selecting a color from the Fill/Back Color button (🎨) on the toolbar.

To switch a report from Design view back to Report view, click the View button (🔍) on the toolbar.

TIP Select View → Toolbars → Print Preview if the View button is not displayed when previewing the report.

Creating a Report in Design View

To create a report in Design view, with report objects selected, click 🔳 New on the Database window toolbar to display the New Report dialog box. In this dialog box, select Design View and then select a table or query from the list. Add fields to the report by dragging them from the displayed field list. Move field names to the **Page Header** section if names should appear only at the top of a page.

Choosing Colors

The more contrast, or difference in lightness and darkness, of the font color and background color, the easier a report will be to read. Bright colors are difficult to view for long periods of time and red is frequently associated with negative reactions.

You will modify an existing report. Access should already be started with the GADGET DEPOT Database window displayed from the last practice.

① *OPEN A REPORT*

    a. In the GADGET DEPOT : Database window, click [Reports].

    b. Double-click the Price Range by Department icon. The report is displayed.

② *MODIFY THE REPORT IN DESIGN VIEW*

    a. On the toolbar, click the View button ( ). The report is displayed in Design view and the Toolbox appears. Drag the Toolbox, if necessary, to move it. Size the window so that all the sections are displayed, if necessary.

    b. Click the "Price Range by Department" title object to select it.

    c. On the toolbar, click the Italic button. The text is no longer slanted.

    d. On the toolbar, use the Font box to change the title font to Tahoma.

    e. Drag the object's size handle so that the title is completely displayed:

    f. On the toolbar, click the arrow in the Fill/Back Color ( ) button and select the blue in the bottom row:

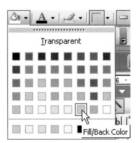

    g. Click the Report Header bar. The Report Header bar is solid black and there are no other objects selected.

    h. On the toolbar, click the arrow the Fill/Back Color ( ) button and select the blue in the bottom row. The section and the title background match.

    i. Click the gray bar just above the title in the Report Header section and then press the Delete key to remove it.

       Check – The Report Header should look similar to:

j. In the Name Header section, select the Name object.

k. On the toolbar, click the arrow in the Font/Fore Color () button and select the color black, which is the first color.

l. On the toolbar, click the Italic button. The object no longer contains slanted text:

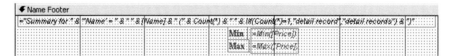

m. In the Name Footer section, format the bottom four objects with a dark blue font color and then move the objects to align similar to:

n. On the toolbar, click the View button (). The report is displayed.

o. Save and the modified report. The report looks similar to:

Price Range by Department

Name	Item	Price
Garden		
	Dirt	$1.50
	Gloves	$4.00
	Medium Rocks	$1.44
	Orchid	$15.00
	Pots	$1.99
	Seeds	$0.15
	Small Rocks	$0.95

Summary for 'Name' = Price Range by Department (7 detail records)

	Min	$0.15
	Max	$15.00

③ *PRINT AND THEN CLOSE THE REPORT*

Distributing a Report

Reports are often printed on paper for distribution. However, e-mail can be a faster and more efficient means of distribution. Posting a report to a Web site is another efficient means of making a report available to many individuals. Select File → Export to create an HTML document from a report. Select HTML Documents in the Save as type list and then select Export.

Exporting a report to HTML format creates an HTML file that can be published to the Web for viewing by many users. To send an HTML document to a limited number of viewers, select the report name and then select File → Send to → Mail Recipient (as Attachment). A dialog box is displayed. Select HTML in the displayed dialog box and then OK. Another dialog box is displayed. Select OK to display an e-mail window with the HTML document attached and ready for sending.

TIP A report snapshot file has the extension .snp.

report snapshot

A report exported as HTML may not look exactly the same as the one stored with the Access database. To electronically distrbute a report so that it looks exactly the same as the original, the report should be exported as a report snapshot. *Report snapshot* is a file format that requires the snapshot viewer, which is a free download at Office.Microsoft.com.

Practice: GADGET DEPOT – part 7 of 9

You will export a report as an HTML document and then view it in a browser. This practice requires browser software. Internet access is not required. Access should already be started with the GADGET DEPOT database displayed from the last practice.

① *EXPORT A REPORT*

   a. In the GADGET DEPOT : Database window, click [📋 Reports] and then click the Price Range by Department icon. The report is selected.

   b. Select File → Export. A dialog box is displayed.

   1. Use the Save in list and the contents box below it to select the appropriate location for the file to be saved.

   2. In the Save as type list, select HTML Documents.

   3. In the File name box, type Price Range by Department if it is not already entered.

   4. Select Export. Another dialog box is displayed.

   5. Select OK.

② *PREVIEW THE HTML DOCUMENT IN A BROWSER*

   a. Ask your instructor for the appropriate steps to start Internet Explorer or the browser you use in your classroom.

   b. Select File → Open. A dialog box is displayed.

   1. Select the Browse button and then open the Price Range by Department.html document created in the previous step.

   2. Select Open.

   3. Select OK. The first page of the report is displayed in the browser. Note that some of the formatting has been lost.

   c. Scroll to the bottom of the browser window and click <u>Next</u> to display the second page of the report.

   d. Close the browser window.

Calculated Fields

A *calculated field* displays the result of a mathematical expression that is defined in a select query. For example, the following query selects the item name (from the Products table) and the price (from the Products table) and displays another field named Profit, which displays the difference between the Price and Cost fields:

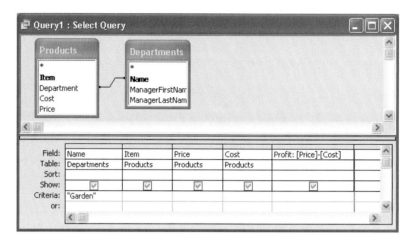

Use the format [Table Name]![Field Name] to refer to a field. If a field name is unique to the database, then the table name is not needed in the reference. When run, the select query displays the datasheet:

Calculated fields are not stored as part of a table and data cannot be directly entered into the field.

formatting a calculated field   To format the data in a calculated field, right-click the calculated field name in the design grid and select Properties. A dialog box with a Format box and Decimal Places box appears. Click in a box and select an option from the list.

Practice: GADGET DEPOT – part 8 of 9

You will create two calculation fields. Access should already be started with the GADGET DEPOT Database window displayed.

① *CREATE TWO CALCULATION FIELDS*

    a. Create a select query in Design view.

    b. Add the Products and Departments tables.

c. Add the Name, Item, Cost, and Price fields to the design grid. Have the query sort the results on Name.

d. In the next **Field** box, type: Profit: [Price]-[Cost]

e. In the next **Field** box, type: Markup: ([Price]-[Cost])/[Cost]

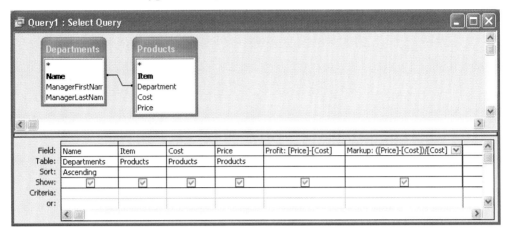

f. Right-click the Markup field and select **Properties** from the menu. A dialog box is displayed.

g. Click the **Format** box and select Percent and then select 0 from the **Decimal Places** box:

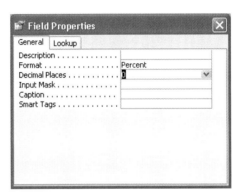

h. Run the query. The calculated fields are shown in a datasheet:

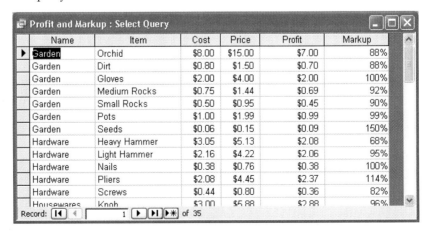

i. Save the query naming it: Profit and Markup

j. Print and then close the Select Query datasheet.

Exporting Access Data to Excel

Access data can be exported to Excel so that additional calculations can be performed, What If? questions asked, and charts created. To export a table, query, or report, click the arrow in the OfficeLinks button (⊞▾) on the toolbar and select **Analyze It with Microsoft Excel**. An Excel workbook with the same name as the selected database object is created and displayed.

Practice: Products

You will export data and analyze it with Excel. Access should already be started with the GADGET DEPOT Database window displayed from the previous practice.

① **EXPORT THE PRODUCT TABLE**

  a. In the Database window, click [▢ Tables].

  b. Open the Products table and sort the records in descending by Department.

  c. Save and then close the table.

  d. Select the Table icon in the Database window, if it is not already selected.

  e. On the toolbar, click the arrow in the OfficeLinks button (⊞▾) and select **Analyze It with Microsoft Excel**. A workbook named Products is displayed.

② **ASK WHAT IF?**

  a. The manager of the Garden department is planning a sale. Keep the rows in the worksheet with Garden in the Department column and delete the rest:

	A	B	C	D	
1	Item	Department	Cost	Price	
2	Medium Rocks	Garden	$0.75	$1.44	
3	Gloves	Garden	$2.00	$4.00	
4	Pots	Garden	$1.00	$1.99	
5	Dirt	Garden	$0.80	$1.50	
6	Seeds	Garden	$0.06	$0.15	
7	Small Rocks	Garden	$0.50	$0.95	
8	Orchid	Garden	$8.00	$15.00	
9					
10					

  b. In cell E1, type: Profit

  c. In cell E2, enter the formula: =(D2-C2)/C2

  d. Format the cell as Percent with 0 decimal places. 92% is displayed. This is the profit made on the sale of seeds.

  e. Copy the formula in cell E2 to cells E3 through E8.

  f. In cell D10, type: Markdown Amount:

  g. In cell F10, type: 10%

  h. In cell F1, type: Sale Profit

  i. In cell F2, enter the formula: =E2-$F$10

  j. Copy the formula in cell F2 to cells F3 through F8:

	A	B	C	D	E	F
1	Item	Department	Cost	Price	Profit	Sale Profit
2	Medium Rocks	Garden	$0.75	$1.44	92%	82%
3	Gloves	Garden	$2.00	$4.00	100%	90%
4	Pots	Garden	$1.00	$1.99	99%	89%
5	Dirt	Garden	$0.80	$1.50	88%	78%
6	Seeds	Garden	$0.06	$0.15	150%	140%
7	Small Rocks	Garden	$0.50	$0.95	90%	80%
8	Orchid	Garden	$8.00	$15.00	88%	78%
9						
10				Markdown Amount:		10%

k. The Garden department manager is planning a sale where evey item in the department is given the same markdown amount. However, to break even, there must be at least 50% sale profit on each item. What if the Markdown Amount were 20% or 30%? Change the Markdown Amount in cell F10 until the lowest sale profit amount on any one item is 50%.

③ *SAVE, PRINT, AND THEN CLOSE THE PRODUCTS WORKBOOK*

Importing an Excel Worksheet

Import Spreadsheet Wizard

An Excel worksheet can be imported to Access to create a new database table. In Access, select File → Get External Data → Import. Select the workbook from the displayed dialog box and then use the Import Spreadsheet Wizard dialog boxes to specify the field names, primary key, and table name. Before creating queries or reports that use the new table, display the Relationships window and define the table's relationship to the other tables in the database.

Practice: GADGET DEPOT – part 9 of 9

You will add a new table to the GADGET DEPOT database and create a query that selects data from the new table. Access should already be started with the GADGET DEPOT Database window displayed.

① *VIEW AN EXCEL WORKSHEET*

    a. Open GADGET DEPOT SALES, which is an Excel data file for this text.

    b. Note the sales records and then close the workbook and quit Excel.

② *IMPORT EXCEL DATA*

    a. Select File → Get External Data → Import. A dialog box is displayed.

        1. In the Files of Type list, select Microsoft Excel.

        2. Use the Look in list and the contents box below to select the GADGET DEPOT SALES file and then select Import. The Import Spreadsheet Wizard is started.

b. A portion of the spreadsheet is shown in the first dialog box:

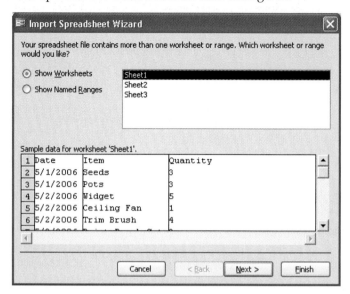

c. Select Next. The labels in the first row will be used for field names:

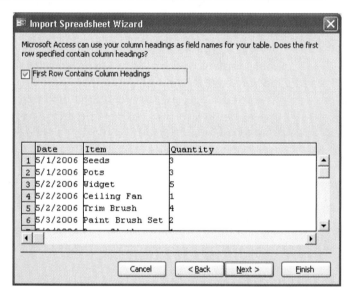

d. Select Next. The data should be used to create a new table:

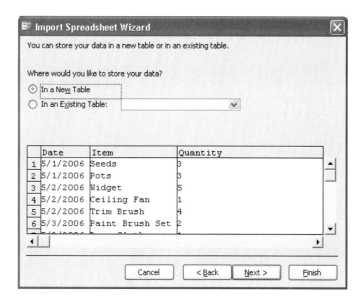

e. Select Next. No additional field options are needed:

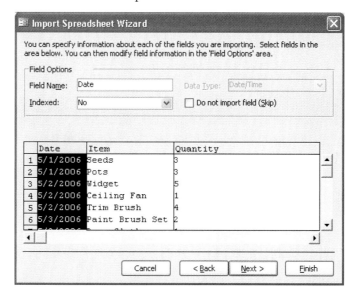

f. Select Next. Allow Access to add a primary key:

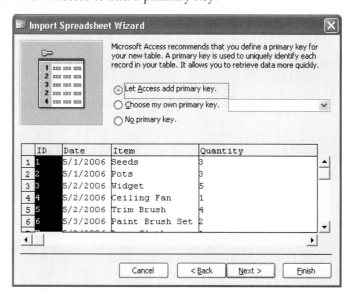

③ *DEFINE RELATIONSHIPS*

    a. Select **Next**. Type Sales for the table name:

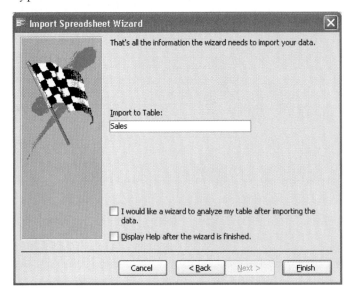

    b. Select Finish. A dialog box is displayed.

    c. Select OK. A new table has been added to the database.

④ *DEFINE A RELATIONSHIP*

    a. On the toolbar, click the Relationships button (▣). Relationships are displayed.

    b. On the toolbar, click the Show Table button (▣). A dialog box is displayed.

    c. Add the Sales table to the window and then close the dialog box.

    d. The Sales table is related to the Products table by the Item field. Drag the Item field from the Products table to the Item field in the Sales table. A dialog box is displayed.

    e. Verify the relationship and then select Create.

    f. Save the modified relationships and then close the Relationships window.

⑤ *CREATE A SELECT QUERY*

    a. Create a select query in Design view.

    b. Add the Sales and Products tables.

    c. Add the Date, Item, and Department fields to the design grid.

    d. Create a calculation field named Total that computes the total sale of an item by multiplying the price times the quantity purchased. Right-click the calculation field and format it as Currency:

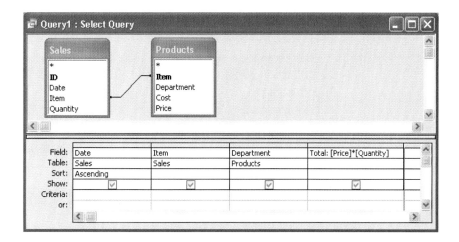

e. Run the query. The total amount for each transaction is displayed:

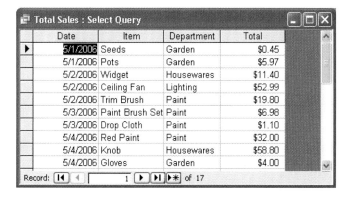

f. Save the query naming it: Total Sales

g. Print and then close the Select Query datasheet.

⑥ *CREATE A SALES REPORT*

a. Create a report using the Report Wizard.

b. Select Query: Total Sales and then add all the fields from the query to the Selected Fields list.

c. Group the data by Department.

d. Have the report display the sum for the amounts.

e. Select the Stepped layout.

f. Select the Corporate style.

g. Title the report: May Sales

h. Which department had the most sales?

i. Print and then close the report.

Linking Access Data to a Document

Data from a database is often used to support information presented in a Word document. To be sure the most current data is being presented, link the data from the Access table or query to the Word document. *Linked data* is updated in Word if there are changes to the Access table or query.

To insert linked data into a Word document, place the insertion point in the document and then select View → Toolbars → Database, which adds the Database toolbar to the Word window:

Database toolbar

Click the Insert Database button (⊞) on the Database toolbar, which displays a dialog box for selecting a data source. Next, select the table or query and then select the records to insert. The Insert data as fields check box must be selected in the last dialog box in order to link data. Inserted data is placed in a table.

TIP Press the F9 key to update linked data in a table.

To update data in Word, select the table of data and then click the Update Field button (⊞) on the Database toolbar. Before an update can occur, the source database window must be open and the table or query closed.

The Sort Ascending (⊞) and Sort Descending (⊞) buttons on the Database toolbar are used to sort records in the Word table. Place the insertion point in the key sort field and then click a sort button. The sort does not affect the Access database.

Chapter Summary

Data can be analyzed in many ways. Reports organize and summarize information, Excel worksheets can be used to ask What If?, and Word can be used to present data. Calculated fields offer additional information using existing data.

The Report Wizard is the quickest way to generate a report. The report can then be customized in Design view. Summaries can be included in a report to provide statistics.

Reports are often printed on paper for distribution, but e-mail and Web posting offer efficient means of distribution. Microsoft also provides a snapshot viewer for download to be used with report snapshot files. Reports in this format look exactly as they do when opened in Access. Other formats may not be able to preserve all the formatting.

An Access table or query can be exported to Excel where it is used to create a workbook by the same name as the table. An Excel workbook can be imported by Access to create a new table in the database. Access data can be linked to a Word document to ensure that the most current data is being presented.

Calculated field Displays the result of a mathematical expression that is defined in a select query.

Data grouping Organizes data in a report based on a selected field and indents the data in the report.

Linked data Data that is connected to data in another file.

Report Used to present data in an organized manner with a descriptive title, headings, and summaries.

Report snapshot A file format that maintains a report's formatting, but requires the snapshot viewer.

Report Summary Provides statistics on a number field.

Access Commands and Buttons

Database **command** Used to insert linked data into a Word document. Found in View → Toolbars.

⬚Design Opens a selected report in Design view. Found on the Database window toolbar.

Export **command** Used to create an HTML document from a report. Found in the File menu.

⬚ **Fill/Back Color button** Formats a selected object in a report in Design view with the selected color. Found on the Formatting toolbar in Design view.

⬚ **Font/Fore Color button** Formats the font or fore color of a selected object in a report in Design view with the selected color. Found on the Formatting toolbar in Design view.

⬚ **Image control** Clicked to add an image to a form in Design view. Found in the Toolbox.

Import **command** Used to import an Excel worksheet as an Access table. Found in File → Get External Data.

⬚ **Insert Database button** Used to insert a linked database table or query into a Word document. Found on the Database toolbar.

⬚ **Label control** Clicked to add text to a report in Design view. Found in the Toolbox.

⬚ **Line/Border Color button** Formats the outline of a selected object in a report in Design view with the selected color. Found on the Formatting toolbar in Design view.

⬚ **Line/Border Width button** Formats the outline of a selected object in a report in Design view with the selected width. Found on the Formatting toolbar in Design view.

⬚ **OfficeLinks button** Used to export a table, query, or report as a workbook. Contains the Analyze It with Microsoft Excel command. Found on the toolbar.

⬚ Reports Displays the report objects. Found in the Database window.

⬚ **Sort Ascending button** Orders records in a Word table from low to high based on the data in the active field. Found on the Database toolbar in Word.

⬚ **Sort Descending button** Orders records in a Word table from high to low based on the data in the active field. Found on the Database toolbar in Word.

⬚ Summary Options ... Displays the Summary Options dialog box. Found in the sort and summary Report Wizard dialog box.

⬚ **Update Field button** Used to update linked data in a Word document. Found on the Database toolbar.

⬚ ⬚ **View button** Used to switch a report between Design view and Report view and vice versa. Found on the toolbar.

1. What is a database report?

2. If a change is made to a table used in a report, is the change displayed the next time the report is viewed?

3. If a database contains five tables, fields from how many of the tables may be included in a report?

4. Explain how data grouping in a report can make the report easier to comprehend.

5. a) What is a report summary?
   b) What are the report requirements for adding a summary?

6. List three sections typically found in a report and explain how their objects are displayed in Report view.

7. List three buttons on the Formatting toolbar that are used for formatting a report in Design view and explain their purpose.

8. Give three examples of poor background/ foreground color combinations for a report. Explain why these combinations could affect usability.

9. List three ways to distribute a report.

10. List one advantage and one disadvantage of distributing a report by posting it to a Web site.

11. a) What is a calculated field?
    b) Can data be entered directly into a calculated field? Explain.

12. a) Explain the difference between importing and exporting data.
    b) What is one way data can be imported into Access? Explain what form the imported data takes.
    c) What is one way to export data from Access? Explain what form the exported data takes.

13. What is linked data?

True/False

14. Determine if each of the following are true or false. If false, explain why.
    a) A report can include fields from several different tables.
    b) A summary is displayed only at the very end of a report.
    c) A report can include images.
    d) The objects in Report view can be formatted with a different color.
    e) Reports should never be e-mailed.
    f) A calculated field cannot refer to a field in another table.
    g) A calculated field can be formatted as Currency.
    h) Field names are not exported with database field data to an Excel worksheet.
    i) A primary key can be selected when a worksheet is being imported to a database.
    j) Linked data must be copied and pasted again from a database when data is updated.

Exercise 1 ———————————————————————— Museum Exhibits

Sunport Science Museum wants to analyze the data in their relational database, which was last modified in Chapter 12, Exercise 1. Open Museum Exhibits and complete the following:

a) Create a report that displays the ExhibitID, Name, and Department fields from the Exhibits table and the Year and Attendance fields from the Attendance table. Have the report view the data by Exhibits, and group the data by Department. Have the report sort on Attendance in descending order, and include a summary that averages Attendance data. Select appropriate layout and style options. Title the report Exhibits Attendance Report. Print the report.

b) Create a report that displays all the fields from the Why Does That Happen Exhibits query. Have the report view the data by Exhibits and group the data by ExhibitID. Include a summary that totals Attendance data. Select appropriate layout and style options. Title the report Why Does That Happen Exhibits Report. Print the report.

c) Create a select query that displays the ExhibitID, Name, Department, Year, and Attendance fields for all exhibits in the year 2006 and includes a calculated field named Predicted2007Attendance. Sunport Science Museum predicts that the attendance in 2007 will be 10% higher than the attendance in 2006. Therefore, the predicted 2007 attendance is calculated by multiplying the Attendance field by 1.1. Format the calculated field as Standard with 0 Decimal Places. Format the select query datasheet appropriately. Save the select query naming it Predicted 2007 Attendance. Print a copy in the appropriate orientation.

Exercise 2 ———————————————————————— Library

The local library wants to analyze the data in their relational database, which was last modified in Chapter 12, Exercise 2. Open Library and complete the following:

a) Create a report that displays all the fields from the Books table. Have the report group the data by Type. Select appropriate layout and style options. Title the report Books Report. Format the report in Design view so that the ISBN and title information is displayed entirely. Print the report.

b) Create a report that displays the FirstName and LastName fields from the Authors table and the Title and Type fields from the Books table. Have the report view the data by Authors, and sort on Title in ascending order. Select appropriate layout and style options. Title the report Authors and Their Books. Print the report.

Exercise 3 ↻ ———————————————————————— Pizza Payroll

The owner of Pizza Palace wants to analyze the data in their relational database, which was last modified in Chapter 12, Exercise 3. Open Pizza Payroll and complete the following:

a) Create a report that displays the LastName, FirstName, Address, City, State, and Zip fields from the Employees table. Have the report sort on LastName in ascending order. Select appropriate layout and style options. Title the report Current Employees. Print the report.

b) Create a report that displays the EmployeeID, Date, GrossPay, and Taxes fields from the Employee Payroll Data query. Have the report view the data by Employees, and sort on Date in descending order. Include a summary that averages the GrossPay data and Taxes data. Select appropriate layout and style options. Title the report Employee EI Report. When the report is displayed, enter EI for the parameter value. Print the report.

c) Create a report that displays the FirstName and LastName fields from the Employees table and the Date, GrossPay, and Taxes fields from the Payroll table. Have the report view the data by Employees and sort on Date in descending order. Include a summary that totals the GrossPay data and Taxes data. Select appropriate layout and style options. Title the report Payroll Report. Print the report.

d) Create a select query that displays the EmployeeID, Date, GrossPay, and Taxes fields for all employees and includes a calculated field named NetPay. Net pay is calculated by subtracting the Taxes field from the GrossPay field. Format the query datasheet appropriately. Save the query naming it Net Pay. Print the select query datasheet.

Exercise 4 ↻ ———————————————————————— Boat Storage

Sunport Boat Storage wants to analyze the data in their relational database, which was last modified in Chapter 12, Exercise 4. Open Boat Storage and complete the following:

a) Create a report that displays the FirstName, LastName and Phone fields from the Employees table. Have the report sort on LastName in ascending order. Select appropriate layout and style options. Title the report Employee Phone List. Print the report.

b) Create a report that displays the FirstName and LastName fields from the Boat Owners table and the Boat, SlotNumber, and Fee fields from the Boats table. Have the report view data by Boat Owners. Include a summary that totals the Fee data. Select appropriate layout and style options. Title the report Boat Fees Report. Print the report.

c) Create a select query that displays the Boat, Fee, FirstName of boat owner, and LastName of boat owner fields for all boat owners and includes a calculated field named AnnualRenewal. The annual renewal charge is calculated by multiplying the Fee field by 30% (0.30). Format the calculated field as Currency with 2 Decimal Places. Format the datasheet appropriately. Save the select query naming it Annual Renewal Charges. Print a copy.

Exercise 5 ○ ——————————————————— Messages

The office manager needs to distribute an employee telephone directory. The directory can be in the form of a report from the company database, which was last modified in Chapter 12, Exercise 5. Open Messages and create a report that displays the LastName, FirstName, Department, Extension, and Email fields from the Employees table. Have the report sort on LastName in ascending order. Select appropriate layout and style options. Title the report Employee Directory and then print a copy.

Exercise 6 ○ ——————————————————— Media Collection

A report can be used to catalog items. Open Media Collection, last modified in Chapter 12, Exercise 6, and create a report that displays the Title, Event, Location, Date, and Time fields from the Media table. Have the report sort on Event in ascending order. Select appropriate layout and style options. Title the report Media Catalog and then print a copy.

Exercise 7 ○ ——————————————————— Coral Research

The Coral Research database last modified in Chapter 12, Exercise 7 contains information on coral sites and growth research. Open Coral Research and create a report that displays the CoralName field from the Coral Sites table and the Date and Size fields from the Growth Research table. Have the report view the data by Coral Sites, and sort on Date in ascending order. Select appropriate layout and style options. Title the report Coral Growth Report. Print the report.

Exercise 8 ○ ——————————————————— Community Service

A local school needs reports from the data in their database. Open Community Service, which was last modified in Chapter 12, Exercise 8, and create the following reports:

a) Create a report that displays the FirstName of the student, LastName of the student, OrganizationName, Date, and Hours. Have the report view the data by Students and group the data by OrganizationName. Have the report sum the Hours data and sort on Date in ascending order. Title the report Community Service Hours Report.

b) Edit the Community Service Hours Report in Design view. In the OrganizationName Footer, delete the object containing the "=Summary for …" label. Delete the object containing the "Sum" label and the object that will display the actual sum result. Close up the StudentID Footer section. Move the object containing the "Sum" label closer to the object that will display the actual sum results. In the StudentID Footer section, delete the object containing the "=Summary …" label. Move the object containing the "Sum" label closer to the object that will display the actual sum results. In the Report Footer section, move the object containing the "Grand Total" label closer to the object that will display the actual grand total.

c) Create a report that displays all the fields from the Organization Hours Lookup query. Select appropriate layout and style options. Title the report Literacy for the Little Report. When the report is run, enter Literacy for the Little, and then print the report.

Exercise 9 ——————————————————————— Summer Camp

A summer camp facility needs reports from the data in their database. Open Summer Camp, which was last modified in Chapter 12, Exercise 9, and create the following reports:

a) Create a report that displays the Location, ActivityName, FirstName, and LastName fields from the Day1 Schedule select query. Have the report group the data by ActivityName. Have the report sort on LastName in ascending order. Select appropriate layout and style options. Title the report Day 1 Schedule. Format the report in Design view so that the title and Locations are in a fun font, such as Comic Sans. Print the report.

b) Create a report using the Day2 Schedule that is similar to the Day 1 Schedule created in part (a).

c) Create a report using the Day3 Schedule that is similar to the Day 1 Schedule created in part (a).

d) Create a report that displays the fields CabinName, FirstName of the camper, and LastName of the camper from the Cabin Assignments query. Have the report group the data by CabinName and sort on LastName in ascending order. Select appropriate layout and style options. Title the report Camper Cabin Assignments. Format the report in Design view so that the title and cabin names are in a fun font, such as Comic Sans. Edit the Campers.LastName object to read LastName and edit the Campers.FirstName object to read FirstName. Print the report.

Exercise 10 ——————————————————————— Travel Agency

The Hot Spot travel agency wants to use a relational database to store travel bookings. Open Travel Agency, which was last modified in Chapter 12, Exercise 10 and create the following report and query:

a) Create a report that displays the FirstName and LastName fields from the Clients table, the Package and Cost fields from the Vacations table, and the Date field from the Booked Vacations table. Have the report view the data by Clients, and sort on Date in ascending order. Include a summary that totals the Cost field. Select appropriate layout and style options. Title the report Booked Vacations Report. Print the report.

b) Create a select query that displays the Package and Cost fields for all vacations and includes a calculated field named Discount. The discount is calculated by multiplying the Cost field by 0.20 and then subtracting that amount from the Cost field. Format the calculated field by right-clicking the formula in the design grid, selecting Properties, and then selecting Currency from the Format collapsible list. Format the select query datasheet appropriately. Save the query naming it Early Booking Discounts. Print the select query datasheet.

Exercise 11 ⟳ ─────────────────────── VIDEO STORE

The VIDEO STORE relational database contains information on a video store's members, videos, and rentals. Open VIDEO STORE, which was last modified in Chapter 12, Exercise 11, and complete the following steps:

a) Create a report that displays the FirstName, LastName, Phone, and Credit fields from the Members table. Have the report group the data by Credit, and sort on LastName in ascending order. Select appropriate layout and style options. Title the report Members Report. Print the report.

b) Create a select query that displays the TapeID, Title, Year, and Type fields of movies that are of drama type. Save the select query naming it Drama Movies.

c) Create a report that displays the Title and Year fields from the Drama Movies query. Have the report sort the data on Title in ascending order. Select appropriate layout and style options. Title the report Drama Movies Report. Print the report.

Exercise 12 ⟳ ─────────────────────── INVENTIONS

The INVENTIONS relational database contains information on inventions and inventors. Open INVENTIONS, which was last modified in Chapter 12, Exercise 12, and complete the following steps:

a) Create a select query that displays the Invention, Country, Year, FirstName, and LastName fields of all inventions created in the United States. Save the select query naming it United States Inventions.

b) Create a report that displays the Invention, Year, FirstName, and LastName fields from the United States Inventions query. Have the report sort the data on Year in ascending order. Select appropriate layout and style options. Title the report United States Inventions Report. Print the report.

c) Create a select query that displays the FirstName, LastName, Country, and Born fields for all the inventors born in the 1800s. You will need to enter >=1800 And <=1899 as the criteria for the Born field. Save the select query naming it Inventors Born in the 1800s.

d) Create a report that displays all of the fields from the Inventors Born in the 1800s query. Have the report group the data by Country, and sort on LastName in ascending order. Select appropriate layout and style options. Title the report Inventors Born in the 1800s Report. Print the report.

Chapter 14

Creating Presentations

PowerPoint is the Microsoft Office presentation graphics program. This chapter introduces PowerPoint for creating presentations that include text, charts, spreadsheet data, and pictures.

What is a Presentation?

A *presentation* is an informative speech that usually includes *visuals*, such as slides or transparencies, a flipchart, a white board, or handouts of printed material. *Presentation graphics* are slides created on a computer and usually projected onto a large screen while the presenter talks. A *PowerPoint presentation* is a collection of slides used to enhance an informative speech. The Microsoft PowerPoint 2003 window looks similar to:

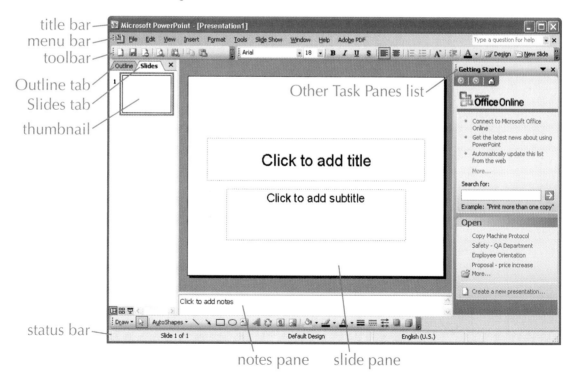

The PowerPoint window displays information about a presentation and includes tools for working with presentations:

• The file name of the current presentation is displayed in the **title bar**. The name Presentation1 is used temporarily until the presentation is saved with a descriptive name.

- Select commands from menus in the **menu bar**.

- Click a button on the **toolbar** to perform an action. Click the New button () to create a new presentation.

- View information in the **status bar** about the current slide and the total number of slides in the presentation.

- Links for opening a presentation or creating a new presentation are in the **Getting Started task pane**. Click the arrow in the **Other Task Panes list** to select a different task pane. Click the <u>Create a new presentation</u> link for new presentation options.

- The default view is **Normal view**, which divides the window into three panes. Click the **Outline tab** in the left pane to display an outline of the slide text similar to Outline view in Word. Click the **slides tab** to display smaller versions of the slides, called **thumbnails**. Type speaker notes that correspond to the displayed slide in the **notes pane**. Edit the current slide in the **slide pane**. Each pane can be sized by dragging its top or right border.

Planning a Presentation

Before typing text on slides, develop a plan for the presentation. A successful presentation is carefully planned so that it clearly conveys a message. The planning process involves three steps:

1. Carefully plan the lecture or speech that will accompany the presentation:

   - What is the purpose of the presentation? Determine the information to be communicated and what the effect should be on the audience, such as persuading opinions or presenting ideas.

   - Who is the audience? Identify characteristics of the audience and then determine appropriate language and speech styles. For example, young children require a different vocabulary than adult lawyers.

2. Determine the content and layout of the slides, and then sketch the slides using pencil and paper.

   - What will the content be? The *content* of each slide refers to the text, images, and other objects that appear on a slide. Make sure the content emphasizes key points of the lecture or speech. Separate content over several slides to avoid too many concepts and ideas on one slide.

   - What should the slides look like? Sketch the layout of each slide. The *layout* refers to the arrangement of text and images. The layout of the *title slide*, which is the first slide and usually includes the title and author, should be different from other slides to set it apart.

3. Create the presentation using PowerPoint.

   - Limit your design to three or less fonts, and avoid using all uppercase letters because they are more difficult to read.

The Outline Tab and Slides Tab

The tabs in the left pane may have icons instead of words if the pane is too narrow:

Dragging the right edge of the pane widens it.

Presentation Length

Keep remarks short and to the point. At the end of the presentation, the audience should want to hear more, not be relieved it is over.

Storyboard

A storyboard refers to sketches of the slides in a presentation arranged on a wall or table. A storyboard is created in the early development of a presentation, to help avoid major changes later.

- Format the text in a color different from the background, preferably a light color on a dark background or vice versa.

- Whether a new design is created or a design template is used, be sure it is appropriate for the purpose and the audience.

Adding and Deleting Slides

A new presentation contains one slide. To add a new slide after the current one, click `New Slide` on the toolbar, which adds a slide and displays the Slide Layout task pane:

TIP Another way to add a slide is to select Insert → New Slide, which adds a slide and displays the task pane.

More on Slide Layouts

Display the Slide Layout task pane by selecting it from the Other Task Panes list or Format → Slide Layout.

Selecting Reapply Layout from the arrow next to a layout removes any modifications made to the placeholders.

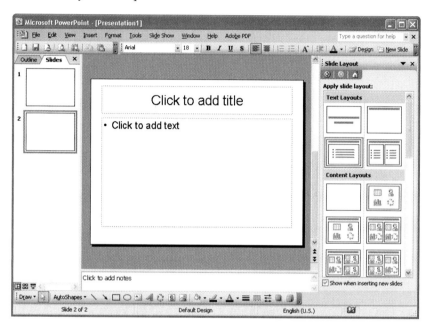

selecting a layout

The heavy outline around slide 2 in the left pane indicates that it is the slide currently displayed in the slide pane. Click a layout in the Slide Layout task pane to change the placeholders in the new slide.

Another way to add a slide after the current slide is to click the arrow next to a layout and select Insert New Slide:

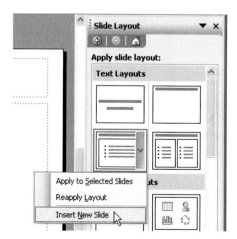

TIP Press the Delete key to remove slides that are selected in the Outline or Slides tabs.

deleting a slide

The current slide is deleted by selecting Edit → Delete Slide.

Editing a Slide

placeholders

Slides contain *placeholders* for holding text and other content such as pictures. Before content is placed, a placeholder appears as a box with a dashed-line border:

Outline tab

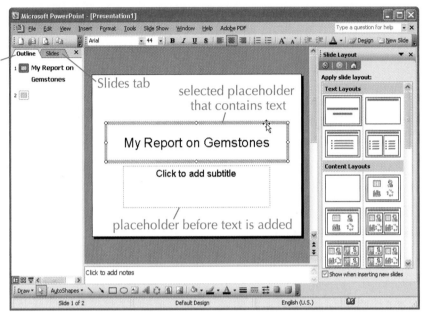

Automatic Spell Checking

Text in placeholders is automatically spell checked just as it is in Word. If a word is spelled incorrectly or is not in the dictionary file, a red wavy line appears below it. A misspelled word can be corrected by right-clicking, which displays suggested words, then clicking the correct spelling.

TIP Hold down the Shift key and click a slide to select multiple adjacent slides.

Click in a placeholder to place the insertion point and type or edit text. The border is no longer visible after text has been added. Text can also be added or edited next to the slide's icon (🖳) in the Outline tab in the left pane.

Clicking a placeholder selects it and displays handles. A placeholder is sized by dragging a handle. Pointing to a placeholder border changes the pointer to 🔁 and dragging then moves the placeholder.

Alignment, font, font size and other formats can be applied to selected text using toolbar buttons and commands in menus, similar to formatting text in Word.

PowerPoint has a feature called AutoFit that automatically resizes text as it is typed so that it fits in a placeholder. The AutoFit button (⬓) is displayed next to a placeholder when more text than can fit is typed. Click the arrow in the AutoFit button to display a list of options that include Stop Fitting Text to This Placeholder.

Click a layout in the Slide Layout task pane to change the placeholders on the current slide, even after text has been added. The text will be moved to the new placeholders. Multiple slides are selected by holding down the Ctrl key and clicking slides in the Slides tab or slide icons (🖳) in the Outline tab. A slide layout can then be applied to all the selected slides by clicking the arrow next to a layout and selecting Apply to Selected Slides.

Viewing a PowerPoint Presentation

Buttons in the lower-left corner of the PowerPoint window are used to change views:

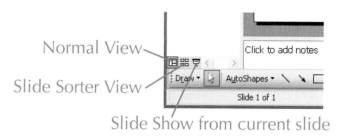

Normal View

Slide Sorter View

Slide Show from current slide

- **Normal View** is the default view that divides the window into the left pane, slide pane, and notes pane.

- **Slide Sorter View** displays thumbnails of all the slides in the presentation.

- **Slide Show from current slide** displays the current slide in full-screen size.

Normal view displays the current slide in the slide pane, and is best for editing the text on slides. Use the vertical scroll bars or press the Page Up or Page Down key to display the next or previous slide. The left pane can also be used to display a specific slide. Click a slide in the Slides tab or click a slide icon (▣) in the Outline tab to display that slide in the slide pane.

Slide Sorter view is useful for selecting multiple slides and changing the order of slides. In Slide Sorter view, drag a slide to another position to change the order in the presentation. Slide order can also be changed in Normal view by dragging a slide icon (▣) in the Outline tab or a slide in the Slides tab.

Slide Show view displays the presentation. Click the Slide Show from current slide button (▣) to start the presentation at the current slide. Select Slide Show → View Show or press the F5 key to start the presentation with slide 1, regardless of which slide is currently displayed. Once a presentation is started, the slides are displayed in full-screen size and the PowerPoint window is no longer visible. Navigate through the presentation using the keyboard and mouse:

- To display the next slide, click the left mouse button or press the N key, the Page Down key, or the spacebar.

- To display the previous slide, press the P key, the Page Up key, or the Backspace key.

- End the slide show by pressing the Esc key.

Move the mouse during a slide show to display a toolbar in the bottom-left corner. Buttons can be clicked to display the previous or next slide:

previous   menu   next

TIP Commands in the View menu and Slide Show menu can be used to change the view.

TIP The Previous Slide (▲) and Next Slide (▼) buttons below the vertical scroll bar display the previous or next slide.

More on Slide Show View

Right-click anywhere on the screen during a slide show to display a menu with commands such as Next, Previous, Go to Slide, and End Show.

You will create and view a simple PowerPoint presentation. The presentation plan is:

1. The purpose of the presentation is to present basic gemstone knowledge to an audience composed of peers.

2. The content will be all text. The layout will be similar on all slides, with a title at the top of the slide and a bulleted list below the title.

3. Create and format the PowerPoint presentation.

① *START POWERPOINT*

   a. Ask your instructor for the appropriate steps to start Microsoft PowerPoint 2003.

   b. Look at the PowerPoint window. Note the title bar, menu bar, toolbar, status bar, left pane, slide pane, notes pane, and Getting Started task pane.

② *ENTER TEXT ON SLIDE 1*

   a. In the slide pane, click the text "Click to add title." The text disappears and the insertion point is placed.

   b. Type: My Super Fantastic Report About Gemstones Around the World

     The AutoFit button is displayed as more text than can fit is typed.

   c. Click the AutoFit button (⯭ ▾) and select Stop Fitting Text to This Placeholder.

   d. Edit the title to read: My Report on Gemstones

   e. Place the insertion point in the "Click to add subtitle" placeholder.

   f. Type your name then click anywhere on the slide outside of the placeholder.

③ *ADD SLIDES*

   a. On the toolbar, click ▭ New Slide . The Slide Layout task pane is displayed.

   b. In the Slide Layout task pane, click the Title and 2-Column Text layout that looks similar to:

   c. Click ▭ New Slide five times. Five more slides are added with the default layout, and the status bar indicates that slide 7 of a total of 7 slides is displayed.

   d. In the left pane, click the Outline tab. Text is displayed next to the slide 1 icon.

④ *ADD TEXT TO THE SLIDES*

   a. In the left pane, click the Slides tab, then click slide 2 to display it.

   b. Replace the text "Click to add title" with: Introduction

   c. Place the insertion point in the "Click to add text" placeholder on the left side of the slide.

   d. Type the following text, pressing Enter at the end of each line. Note that PowerPoint adds bullets and hanging indents automatically:

     Made of minerals
     One type of mineral can form several types of gemstones
     Some are rare, others common

e. Type the following text in the placeholder on the right side of the slide, pressing enter at the end of each line:

> Found worldwide
> One type of gemstone can have several names

Check – Your slide should look similar to:

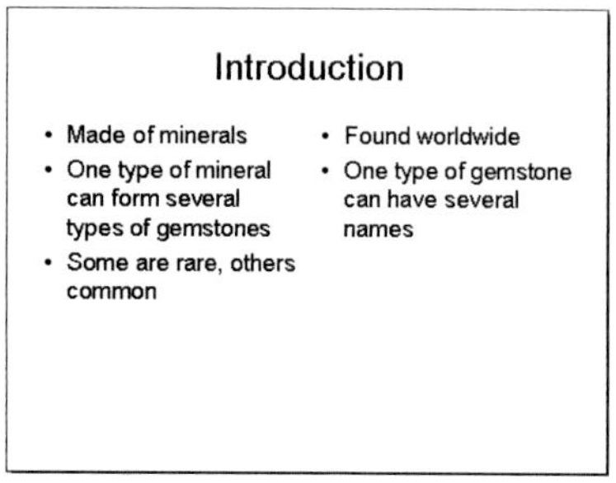

> ### Introduction
>
> - Made of minerals
> - One type of mineral can form several types of gemstones
> - Some are rare, others common
>
> - Found worldwide
> - One type of gemstone can have several names

⑤ *ADD TEXT TO MORE SLIDES*

a. If a placeholder is selected, click outside of the slide.

b. Press the Page Down key. Slide 3 is displayed.

c. In the title placeholder, type: Quartz

d. In the text placeholder, type the following items:

- Occurs in crystals
- Very common mineral
- Examples: amethyst, citrine

e. In the left pane, click the Outline tab, then click the slide icon for slide 4. Slide 4 is displayed in the slide pane.

f. Add the following title and text to the placeholders on slide 4:

> Beryl
> - Very large crystals
> - Found in Colombia, Australia, Russia
> - Examples: emerald, aquamarine

g. Display slide 5 and add the following title and text:

> Corundum
> - Aluminum oxide material
> - Found in USA, India, South Africa
> - Examples: ruby, sapphire

h. Display slide 6 and add the following title and text:

> Summary
> - Quartz: amethyst, citrine
> - Corundum: ruby, sapphire
> - Beryl: emerald, aquamarine

⑥ *DELETE SLIDES*

a. Display slide 7.

b. Select Edit → Delete Slide. The slide is deleted and slide 6 of 6 is now displayed.

⑦ *CHANGE THE ORDER OF SLIDES*

a. In the lower-left corner of the PowerPoint window, click the Slide Sorter View button (⊞). The presentation is displayed in Slide Sorter view.

b. Drag slide 5 to between slides 3 and 4. The "Corundum" slide is now slide 4.

c. In the lower-left corner of the PowerPoint window, click the Normal View button (⊞). The presentation is again displayed in Normal view.

⑧ *SAVE THE PRESENTATION*

Save the file naming it Gemstone.

⑨ *VIEW THE SLIDE SHOW*

a. In the lower-left corner of the PowerPoint window, click the Slide Show from current slide button (⊡). PowerPoint starts the presentation by filling the screen with the currently displayed slide (slide 6):

b. Press the Esc key. The slide show ends and the PowerPoint window is displayed.

c. Select Slide Show ➔ View Show. The presentation is started with slide 1.

d. Press the spacebar. The next slide is displayed.

e. Press the Backspace key. The previous slide is displayed.

f. Click the left mouse button. The next slide is displayed.

g. Right-click anywhere to display a menu, then select Next. Slide 3 is displayed.

h. Continue to view the presentation until a black screen with the words "End of slide show, click to exit." at the top of the screen is displayed. Click the left mouse button to end the presentation and display the PowerPoint window.

Design Templates and Color Schemes

A presentation will be more effective if the slides are designed for the audience and subject matter. To quickly change the design of a presentation, select a design template from the Slide Design task pane. A *design template* is a set of layouts, formatting, and backgrounds. Click [⊟ Design] on the toolbar to display the Slide Design task pane with Design Templates:

Click the arrow next to a design template and select Apply to All Slides to change the design of the entire presentation. Alternatively, select Apply to Selected Slides to change the design of only the selected slides.

color scheme

Once a design template is applied, the colors may be changed by applying a different color scheme to the template. A *color scheme* is the set of colors used in all elements of the presentation, such as the background and text. Click the <u>Color Schemes</u> link in the Slide Design task pane to display a list of color schemes. Click the arrow next to a color scheme and select Apply to All Slides to change the scheme of the entire presentation. Alternatively, select Apply to Selected Slides to change the color scheme of only selected slides.

Printing a Presentation

A presentation should be previewed before printing. Select File → Print Preview or click the Print Preview button (🔍) on the toolbar to display the Print Preview window. Once in print preview, the pages can be viewed in different ways:

- Press the **Page Up key** or **Page Down key** to display the previous or next page, respectively.

- Use the **vertical scroll bar** to view previous and next pages.

- Move the pointer onto the document and then **click the magnifying glass** (🔍) to zoom into that portion of the page. Click again to display the entire page.

Click 🖨 Print... on the toolbar to display a dialog box for the target printer. Options in the Print Range section affect how much of the presentation is printed.

Click Close on the toolbar or press the Esc key to return to the PowerPoint window.

The Print Preview toolbar can be used to change how a presentation is printed. Select an option in the Print What list to change how the presentation is arranged on the pages:

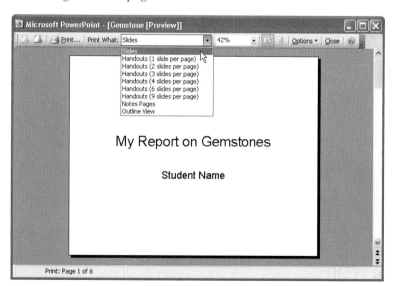

- **Slides** prints one slide per page.

- **Handouts** prints the indicated number of miniature slides on each page. Handouts of 3 per page includes lines for taking notes next to each slide:

Why Print?

A presentation may be printed for a peer to edit, as notes for the speaker to use when presenting, as a handout for lecture attendees, or on transparency film for use with an overhead projector.

Word Document from PowerPoint

A PowerPoint presentation can be exported to Word by selecting File → Send To → Microsoft Office Word. A dialog box contains several options for converting the presentation to a Word document.

TIP Select Frame Slides in the Options ▾ list to print an outline around each slide.

Formatting Handouts

When printing a presentation for handouts, consider how the audience will use them. A printout of 6 slides on each page may be enough to use as a reference. If the topic is such that the audience may take extensive notes, then 3 per page with lines for notes may be more appropriate. Also, always include pertinent information in the header and footer, because after the presentation all the attendee has is the handout.

TIP Click Options ▾ and then select Color/Grayscale to display a submenu of commands that affect the color of the printout.

- **Notes Pages** prints one slide in the top half of each page and any text that was typed in the notes pane in the bottom half of the page. Notes are discussed later in this chapter.

- **Outline View** prints the outline of the presentation as it appears in the Outline tab in Normal view.

Click Options ▾ to display a menu, and select Header and Footer to display a dialog box. Select the Notes and Handouts tab to display options that affect the printout:

- Type a date in the Fixed box, or select Update automatically to insert a time stamp. The location of the inserted date varies depending on the current Print What option.

- Type text for the top area of the page in the Header box and the bottom area of the page in the Footer box.

- Select the Page number check box to include a page number. Note that page numbers will not print if the Print What option is Slides.

Practice: Gemstone – part 2 of 2

You will apply a design template to the Gemstone presentation and add a picture to the presentation, add a footer to the printouts, and then print a copy. PowerPoint should already be started with the Gemstone presentation displayed from the last practice.

① *CHANGE THE DESIGN TEMPLATE*

    a. Click the Slides tab in the left pane if slide thumbnails are not already displayed.

    b. On the toolbar, click ☞ Design . The Slide Design task pane is displayed.

    c. In the Slide Design task pane, in the Apply a design template list, click the arrow next to any design, then select Apply to All Slides. Note in the Slides tab that the design is applied to the entire presentation.

    d. In the Slide Design task pane, in the Apply a design template list, scroll until green design templates are displayed. Pause the pointer over each of the green designs until the ScreenTip Glass Layers is shown.

    e. Click arrow next to the Glass Layers design, and then select Apply to All Slides. The design is applied to the entire presentation.

    Check – Slide 1 should look similar to:

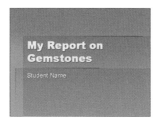

② CHANGE THE COLOR SCHEME

a. In the Slide Design task pane, click the <u>Color Schemes</u> link. A list of color schemes is displayed.

b. In the Slide Design task pane, in the Apply a color scheme list, click the arrow next to the orange color scheme, then select Apply to All Slides. The color scheme is applied to the entire presentation.

c. In the Slide Design task pane, in the Apply a color scheme list, click the arrow next to the purple color scheme, then select Apply to All Slides.

③ PRINT PREVIEW THE PRESENTATION

a. Save the modified Gemstone.

b. On the toolbar, click the Print Preview button (🖻). The first page is displayed in the Print Preview window.

c. Press the Page Down key. The next slide is displayed.

d. On the toolbar, in the Print What list select Outline View. The preview changes to display the outline of the presentation.

e. On the toolbar, in the Print What list select Handouts (2 slides per page). The preview changes to show 2 miniature slides on the page.

f. On the toolbar, in the Print What list select Handouts (6 slides per page). The preview changes to show 6 miniature slides on the page—this entire presentation.

④ ADD A FOOTER TO THE PRINTOUT

a. On the toolbar, click Options ▾ to display a menu, then select Header and Footer. A dialog box is displayed.

b. Select the Notes and Handouts tab if those options are not already displayed.

c. Set the options in the dialog box as follows:

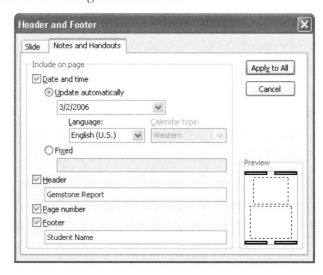

d. Select Apply to All. The dialog box is removed and the header and footer are added to the preview.

a. On the toolbar, click 🖨 Print... . A dialog box is displayed.

b. Select OK. The Gemstone presentation is printed on one page with a header and footer.

c. On the toolbar, click Close . The Print Preview window is closed and the presentation is displayed in Normal view.

⑥ *SAVE AND CLOSE THE MODIFIED GEMSTONE*

Slide Footers

Only Footers on Slides

Although the footer information placeholders on slides can be moved to the top and therefore resemble a header, helpful information is best displayed at the bottom of a slide, where it will not distract the audience. The top of a slide should only contain a title.

Information can be added in the footers of the slides. Select View → Header and Footer to display a dialog box, and select the Slide tab to display options that affect the footer:

• Type a date in the Fixed box, or select Update automatically to insert a time stamp.

• Select Slide number to include the slide number.

• Type text in the Footer box.

• Select Don't show on title slide to not have the information appear on the title slide.

Slide Masters

Instead of using a design template to change the look of a presentation, the Slide Master is used to create a custom look that applies to the entire presentation. Select View → Master → Slide Master to change the view to Slide Master view and display the Slide Master View toolbar:

Title Master

Some design templates have a Title Master in addition to a Slide Master. The Title Master is another slide in the left pane of Slide Master view. Formatting applied to the Title Master only applies to slides with the Title Slide layout.

Formatting applied on the Slide Master affects all the slides in the presentation. Select the text in a placeholder and then apply formatting. The changes are reflected in all the similar placeholders in the presentation. Click Close Master View on the Slide Master toolbar or click a view button in the lower-right corner to return to Normal view.

formatting the slide footer

Footer information on a slide can be formatted on the Slide Master. The location of the inserted date, text, and slide number is in the <Date/Time>, the <footer>, and the <#> placeholders on the Slide Master. Format or move the placeholders to modify the appearance of footer information.

Formatting Text and Backgrounds

Fonts, font size, alignment and other similar formatting can be changed on all the slides at once using the Slide Master. On a Slide Master, click the text in a placeholder to select it and then apply formatting using buttons on the toolbar or commands in the Format menu. Note that formatting applied to a Title Master only appears on slides with the Title Slide layout.

design considerations: text

Serif and Sans-Serif Fonts

Serif fonts have small strokes at the ends of characters:

The
Serif

The
No Serif
(Sans Serif)

Serif fonts are commonly used in large amounts of text. Sans-serif fonts lack the decorative strokes of serif fonts, and are often used in titles.

Care should be taken when formatting a presentation with different fonts. Choose no more than three different fonts for a presentation. A successful presentation is one that is easy to read. Sans serif fonts, such as Tahoma and Arial, are clean-looking and a good choice for titles and headings. Serif fonts, such as Times New Roman, have extra lines at the ends of the letters. A serif font is a good choice for large amounts of text. Large font sizes are easiest to read, such as 24 point.

To format the color of selected text, click the arrow in the Font Color button (A▼) on the toolbar to display a list of colors that match the current color scheme, and then click a color. The Automatic option in the list applies the formatting of the Slide Master. Select More Colors in the list to display a dialog box:

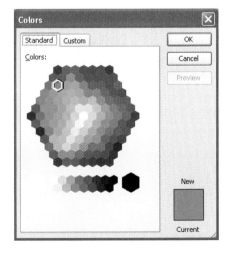

Click a color and then OK to apply the formatting. Once a color is applied, the bar below the "A" in the Font Color button changes to that color and the button can simply be clicked to apply the color to selected text.

WordArt

WordArt is a feature used to create text effects such as curved, 3-D, or skewed text. The resulting text usually has a casual, fun, and amateur-artist look. WordArt is therefore not appropriate for a professional presentation.

The Slide Masters are also used to change the background color on the slides. In Slide Master view, select Format → Background, which displays a dialog box. Click the arrow below the image to display a list of colors that match the current color scheme, and then click a color:

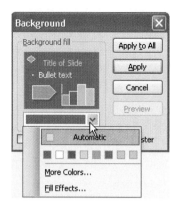

Room Conditions

If the presentation will be projected onto a screen in a room, consider the room conditions when making color choices. Lighting, room size, screen size, and the audience's viewing angle can all affect the readability of the projected presentation. If possible, try different color schemes in the room ahead of time.

design considerations: color

The More Colors option in the list displays a dialog box with additional colors. The Fill Effects option in the list displays a dialog box from which gradient, texture, and pattern formatting can be selected. The Fill Effects dialog box is also used to designate a picture as the background.

When choosing colors, use yellow or white text on a dark background, such as dark blue, for the best readability. In general, the more *contrast* or difference in lightness and darkness of the font color and background color, the easier it will be to read. Bright colors are difficult to view for long periods of time, and therefore should be avoided completely. The color red is frequently associated with negative reactions, and so should be used only as an accent color if at all.

Adding Images to a Slide

Images can be used to make a presentation more interesting and informative. Select Insert → Picture → From File to display the Insert Picture dialog box with a list of image files. Select Insert → Picture → Clip Art to display the Insert Clip Art task pane. Type a keyword in the Search text box, use the Search in list and Results should be list to narrow the search, and select Search to find all the clip art that have the keyword in their description. For example, type rabbit in the Search text box and select Search to display those pictures:

Clips

Clip art is a type of clip. A *clip* is a single media file, which is a picture, a sound, an animation, or a movie. Any type of clip can be added to a PowerPoint presentation.

Clips on the Web

The small globe (🌐) in the corner of three of the clips in the task pane shown to the right indicates the clips were found at a source on the Web. If the computer is not connected to the Internet, only the first clip would be found.

To place clip art on a slide, click the arrow to the right of the image and select Insert from the menu. Click a picture to select it and display handles. Size a picture by dragging a corner handle. Drag the center of an image (not a handle) to move the picture. Press the Delete key to delete the selected picture. Click outside the picture to remove the handles.

Creating and Printing Speaker Notes

In Normal view, notes for the speaker can be typed into the notes pane for each slide. Click the notes pane to place the insertion point, and then type text. Drag the top boundary of the pane to size it.

Notes Page view is used to add and format notes, add images to the notes, and format the layout of the Notes page. Select View → Notes Page to display one slide and the corresponding notes in Notes Page view. The notes can be printed by selecting Notes Pages in the Print What list in print preview.

Similar to the Slide Master, the Notes Pages Master can be used to change the look of printed speaker notes. Select View → Master → Notes Master to display the Notes Pages Master.

Practice: BETTER BURGER

You will use the Slide Master to change the look of a presentation, add a picture and speaker notes, and then print a presentation. PowerPoint should already be started.

① *OPEN BETTER BURGER*

Open BETTER BURGER, which is a PowerPoint data file for this text. This presentation has five unformatted slides with text.

② *VIEW THE SLIDE SHOW*

a. Select Slide Show → View Show. The presentation is started with slide 1.

b. Press the spacebar. The next slide is displayed.

c. Continue to view the presentation until a black screen with the words "End of slide show, click to exit." at the top of the screen is displayed. Click once to end the presentation and display the PowerPoint window.

③ *FORMAT THE BACKGROUND*

a. Select View → Master → Slide Master. The view changes to Slide Master view.

b. Select Format → Background. A dialog box is displayed.

c. Click the arrow below the image and select the More Colors option in the list. A dialog box of colors is displayed.

d. Select the bright blue in the top row, as shown on the next page:

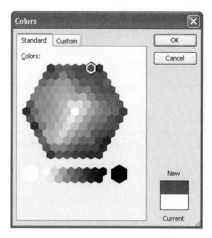

e. Select OK, and then select Apply to All to apply the blue background color to the entire presentation. The Slide Master is now blue.

④ *FORMAT THE SLIDE MASTER*

a. Click the text "Click to edit Master title style" to select it.

b. On the toolbar, click the arrow in the Font Color button (A) and select More Colors. A dialog box is displayed.

c. Select the medium yellow:

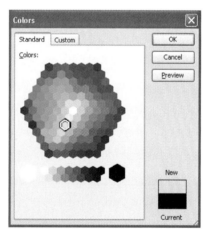

d. Select OK. Click outside of the placeholder. The text is formatted in a yellow color.

e. Format the "Click to edit Master title style" text as Tahoma.

f. Select all the text in the placeholder below the title, from "Click to edit Master text styles" to "Fifth level"

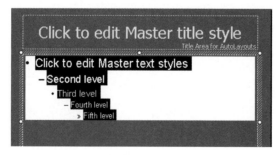

g. On the toolbar, note that the bar below the "A" in the Font Color button is the yellow that was just applied to text. Click the Font Color button (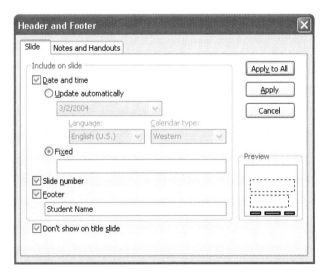) to apply the yellow color to the selected text.

h. Format the text as Times New Roman.

i. At the bottom of the slide, in the center placeholder click <footer> to select it.

j. Format the text as Times New Roman and in the yellow color.

k. At the bottom of the slide, in the right placeholder click <#> and format it as Tahoma and in the yellow color.

l. On the Slide Master toolbar, click Close Master View . The presentation is again displayed in Normal view. Note the colors.

⑤ *FORMAT TEXT ON THE SLIDES*

a. Display slide 3.

b. In the bulleted list on the left, place the insertion point in the text "Our Bun."

c. On the toolbar, click the Bullets button (⊞). The bullet is removed and the text is now formatted to be a title for the bulleted list.

d. In the bulleted list on the right, place the insertion point in the text "Alternative Bun."

e. On the toolbar, click the Bullets button (⊞).

f. Display slide 4.

g. Remove the bullet from the "Our Cheese" and "Alternative Cheese" items.

h. Display slide 5.

i. Remove the bullet from the "Our Best Seller" and "New Better Burger" items.

⑥ *ADD FOOTER INFORMATION TO THE PRESENTATION*

a. Display slide 2. Note the lack of footer information.

b. Select View → Header and Footer. A dialog box is displayed.

c. Select the Slide tab if those options are not already displayed.

d. Set the options in the dialog box as follows, typing your name instead of Student Name:

e. Select Apply to All. The dialog box is removed and footer information is displayed on all but the title slide.

⑦ *FORMAT TEXT ON SLIDE 1*

   a. Display slide 1.

   b. Format the text Building a Better Burger as bold.

   c. Format the text Making our best...choice as bold and italic.

⑧ *INSERT A PICTURE*

   a. Click anywhere outside the placeholders on slide 1 so that nothing is selected.

   b. Select Insert ➞ Picture ➞ From File. A dialog box is displayed.

      1. Select BURGER, which is an image data file for this text.

      2. Select Insert. The picture and the Picture toolbar is displayed.

   c. Point to the center of the picture. The pointer changes to ⬈.

   d. Drag the picture to be approximately centered above the title:

⑨ *CREATE SPEAKER NOTES*

   a. Display slide 2.

   b. Drag the top boundary of the notes pane upwards until the notes pane is about twice as tall.

   c. In the notes pane, click the text "Click to add notes" to place the insertion point.

   d. Type the following text, allowing the text to wrap:

      Currently our burger has 20% more calories and 3 more grams of fat than our competition. Carbohydrates are growing in popularity as a dietary concern and our burger is loaded with carbohydrates.

   e. Display slide 3 in Normal view.

   f. In the notes pane, type the following text, pressing Enter at the end of each line:

      Both buns have sesame seeds.
      Alternative bun costs 10% less!

   g. Display slide 4 in Normal view.

   h. In the notes pane, type the following text, pressing Enter at the end of each line:

      Both process cheese products are orange.
      Alternative cheese has a longer shelf life.
      Alternative cheese was preferred in taste tests.

⑩ *USE NOTES PAGE VIEW TO ADD NOTES*

    a. Display slide 5 in Normal view.

    b. Select View ➝ Notes Page. The slide is displayed in Notes Page view. Note the slide and the notes below it.

    c. Place the insertion point in the notes area and type the following text, allowing the text to wrap:

        Better burger has 30% less calories, 30% less fat, and 40% less carbohydrates than our best seller.

    d. Display the slide in Normal view.

⑪ *VIEW THE SLIDE SHOW*

    a. Select Slide Show ➝ View Show. The presentation is started with slide 1.

    b. View the presentation until a black screen with the words "End of slide show, click to exit." at the top of the screen is displayed. Click once to end the presentation and display the PowerPoint window.

⑫ *PREVIEW AND PRINT THE PRESENTATION*

    a. Save the modified BETTER BURGER.

    b. On the toolbar, click the Print Preview button (🔍). The first page is displayed in the print preview window.

    c. On the toolbar, in the Print What list select Handouts (6 slides per page).

    d. On the toolbar, click 🖨 Print... . A dialog box is displayed.

    e. Select OK. The presentation is printed on one page.

    f. On the toolbar, in the Print What list select Notes Pages. The preview changes to display the speaker notes below each slide.

    g. Press the Page Down key to display slide 2.

    h. On the toolbar, click 🖨 Print... . A dialog box is displayed.

    i. In the Print range section select Current slide and then select OK. The current slide is printed in Notes Pages view and the presentation remains in Print Preview.

    j. On the toolbar, click Close . The Print Preview window is closed and the presentation is displayed in Normal view.

⑬ *SAVE AND CLOSE THE MODIFIED BETTER BURGER*

Presentation Collaboration

A presentation may be the product of several individuals or departments. A presentation can be e-mailed from the author to a reviewer, and then the reviewer can make changes and add comments to any slide. When the original author receives the reviewed presentation, a change marker (🗋) appears where each change was made. The change markers are visible only to the original author, not the reviewer.

Revisions task pane   The Revisions task pane is displayed when a reviewed presentation is opened by the original author:

Collaborating with Multiple Reviewers

PowerPoint assigns a different color to each reviewer, which is reflected in the icons on the slides and in the Revisions pane. Different colors help to match comments and changes with each reviewer.

The Slide changes area indicates changes on the current slide and which slide has the next changes. The Previous and Next buttons display the previous or next revision, if any.

Clicking a change marker (⬜) on a slide displays details about the changes:

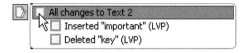

Note that changes must be selected to apply them.

Buttons on the Reviewing toolbar are used to select the previous (⬜) or next (⬜) edit. The Revisions task pane is also used to select the next change. The Apply button (⬜▾) and Unapply button (⬜▾) contain options for making or removing changes to the slide or the entire presentation. The Delete Comment button (✖▾) removes a selected edit or comment, and the Insert Comment button (⬜) allows the reviewer to type a comment.

E-mailing a Presentation

E-mail is a fast and efficient message delivery system. In PowerPoint, a presentation can only be e-mailed as an attachment. To e-mail a presentation as an attachment, open the presentation in PowerPoint and then select File → Send To → Mail Recipient (as Attachment) or click the E-mail as Attachment button (⬜) on the toolbar, which displays an e-mail window with the presentation included as an attachment file. Type the e-mail address of the recipient in the To box. The file name of the presentation automatically appears as the Subject. Type text in the body if additional information should appear in the e-mail message and then click ⬜Send to send the message with the attachment.

When collaborating on a presentation, select File ➔ Send To ➔ Mail Recipient (for Review) to send a presentation as an attachment that will include changes when opened by the recipient. After the reviewer has made edits, Reply with Changes... on the Reviewing toolbar is clicked to e-mail the presentation back as an attachment. The original author will be prompted to merge any changes into the existing file. Selecting Yes overwrites the existing file with the new. Selecting No displays the new presentation with a name similar to the old, allowing the new version to be saved separately from the existing version.

Practice: Butterflies

You will e-mail a presentation to a peer for collaboration. This practice requires Outlook and Internet access. You are also required to work with a classmate and exchange presentations through e-mail. PowerPoint should already be started.

① *CREATE A NEW PRESENTATION*

② *ENTER TEXT*

    a. Replace the text "Click to add title" with: Report on Butterflies

    b. Replace the text "Click to add subtitle" with the text Made by followed by your name.

③ *ADD A SLIDE*

    a. On the toolbar, click New Slide. A slide is added and the Slide Layout task pane is displayed.

    b. In the Slide Layout task pane, click the Title and Text layout that looks similar to:

    c. Replace the text "Click to add title" with: Butterfly Facts

    d. Replace the text "Click to add text" with:

        • Over 700 species in North America
        • Most active during the day

④ *SAVE THE PRESENTATION*

    Save the presentation naming it Butterflies *Name* where *Name* is your name.

⑤ *E-MAIL A PRESENTATION FOR COLLABORATION*

    a. Select File ➔ Send To ➔ Mail Recipient (for Review). After several seconds, an e-mail window is displayed with the Butterflies presentation as an attachment.

    b. If the e-mail window is not displayed, click the "Please review" button on the Windows taskbar. The e-mail window is displayed. Note that the body of the e-mail contains a "Please review the attached document." sentence.

    c. In the To box, type the e-mail address of a classmate.

    d. On the Outlook window toolbar, click Send. The e-mail is sent to your classmate for collaboration.

    e. Close Butterflies.

⑥ *COLLABORATE ON A PRESENTATION*

    a. Check your e-mail.

    b. Open the e-mail from your classmate. The e-mail message asks you to review the attached document.

    c. Open the attachment. The presentation is displayed in PowerPoint.

    d. Display slide 1 if it is not already displayed.

    e. Change Made to Prepared.

    f. Click outside the placeholder. The Placeholder is no longer selected.

    g. On the Reviewing toolbar, click the Insert Comment button (⬚). A comment is added in the upper-left corner of the slide and the insertion point is moved to the comment.

    h. Type I think Prepared sounds better- and then your name.

    i. On the Reviewing toolbar, click ⬚Reply with Changes... . After several seconds, an Outlook mail window is displayed.

    j. On the Outlook toolbar, click ⬚Send . The presentation is e-mailed back to the sender.

⑦ *REVIEW CHANGES*

    a. Check your e-mail.

    b. Open the e-mail reply from your classmate. The e-mail message includes the reviewed presentation as an attachment.

    c. Open the attachment. You will get a message about merging changes. Select Yes.

    d. On slide 1, click the change marker (⬚). Details are displayed and the Revisions task pane is displayed.

    e. Select All changes to Text 2. The changes are made.

    f. On slide 1, click the comment marker. The comment is displayed.

    g. On the Reviewing toolbar, click the Delete Comment button (✕▾). The comment is removed.

⑧ *SAVE THE MODIFIED BUTTERFLIES AND PRINT A COPY OF SLIDE 1*

⑨ *CLOSE BUTTERFLIES AND QUIT POWERPOINT*

Chapter Summary

This chapter introduced the presentation graphics program for creating presentations. PowerPoint is the presentation graphics program in Microsoft Office. A presentation usually includes visuals, and presentation graphics are slides created on a computer and projected onto a screen while a presenter talks.

The default view is Normal view, which divides the window into a left pane, notes pane, and slide pane.

A successful presentation is carefully planned so that it clearly conveys a message. The purpose and audience are defined and the appearance of the slides considered.

Slides contain placeholders for holding content. Text is typed or edited in placeholders or in the Outline tab in the left pane. Alignment, font, font size and other formats can be applied to selected text. The AutoFit feature automatically resizes text as it is typed so that it fits in a placeholder.

Click the New Slide button and then click a layout in the Slide Layout task pane to add a new slide. Slides are selected in the Slides tab. Select Edit → Delete Slide or press the Delete key to delete selected slides.

A presentation can be displayed in Normal view, Slide Sorter view, Slide Show view, and Notes Pages view. In Slide Show view, the presentation is controlled using the mouse or the keyboard.

A design template selected from the Slide Design task pane quickly changes the look of a presentation. The <u>Color Schemes</u> link in the Slide Design task pane displays a list of color schemes affecting the design template.

A presentation should be previewed before printing. Individual slides, notes pages, or handouts can be printed for a presentation. Select View → Header and Footer to add information in the footer of slides or in the header or footer of printouts.

Select View → Master → Slide Master to display the Slide Master, which is used to format the text, colors, backgrounds, and footer information of the entire presentation. When formatting, use fonts sparingly and choose colors for readability.

Select Insert → Picture → From File to add an image from a file, or Insert → Picture → Clip Art to insert clip art.

Notes for the speaker can be typed for each slide and then printed as Notes Pages.

A presentation can be e-mailed as an attachment for collaboration and peer editing.

Color scheme The colors used in all elements of a presentation, such as the background and text.

Content The text, images, and other objects that appear on a slide.

Contrast Difference in lightness and darkness of two colors.

Design template A set of layouts, formatting, and backgrounds that can be applied to a presentation to make it more appealing.

Getting Started task pane A task pane shown in the PowerPoint window with options for creating a new presentation.

Layout Refers to the arrangement of text and images on a slide.

Normal view The default view which divides the window into a three panes: a left pane, notes pane, and slide pane.

Notes Page view Used to format notes, add images to the notes, and format the layout of the Notes page.

Notes pane Contains any speaker notes that were typed to correspond to the current slide. Displayed in Normal view.

Placeholders Container on a slides that holds text and other content such as pictures.

PowerPoint presentation A collection of slides used to enhance an informative speech.

Presentation An informative speech that usually includes visuals.

Presentation graphics Slides created on a computer and usually projected onto a large screen while the presenter talks.

Slide Master A master slide of which the formatting applies to all slides in the presentation.

Slide pane Displays the current slide. Displayed in Normal view.

Slide Show view Displays the current slide in full-screen size.

Slide Sorter view Displays thumbnails of all the slides in the presentation.

Thumbnail A smaller version of a slide.

Title slide The first slide in a presentation, which usually includes the title and author.

Visuals Slides, transparencies, a flipchart, a white board, or handouts of printed material that are viewed while a speaker talks.

PowerPoint Commands and Buttons

Apply button Makes a change to the entire presentation when reviewing a presentation. Found on the Reviewing toolbar.

Apply to Selected Slides command Applies a slide layout to all the selected slides. Found in the menu displayed by clicking the arrow next to a layout in the Slide Layout task pane.

AutoFit button Displayed next to a placeholder when more text than can fit is typed, and offers options to stop PowerPoint from automatically resizing text so that it fits in a placeholder.

Background command Displays a dialog box used to change the background of slides. Found in the Format menu.

Clip Art command Displays a dialog box used to place a clip art image on a slide. Found in Insert → Picture.

Close Returns the view to the PowerPoint window. Found on the toolbar in the Print Preview window.

Close Master View Returns to Normal view. Found on the Slide Master toolbar.

Delete Comment button Removes a selected edit or comment. Found on the Reviewing toolbar.

Delete Slide command Removes selected slides from the presentation. Found in the Edit menu.

Design Displays the Slide Design task pane with Design Templates selected. Found on the toolbar.

End Show command Ends the slide show. Found in the menu displayed by right-clicking on the screen during a slide show.

Font Color button Used to format the color of selected text. Found on the toolbar.

From File command Displays a dialog box used to place a picture on a slide. Found in Insert → Picture.

Header and Footer command Displays a dialog box used to add headers and footers to a printout and add footers on slides. Found in the View menu.

Insert Comment button Adds a comment. Found on the Reviewing toolbar.

Insert New Slide command Adds a new slide after the current slide. Found in the menu displayed by clicking the arrow next to a layout in the Slide Layout task pane.

Mail Recipient (as Attachment) command Displays an e-mail window with the presentation as an attached file. Found in File → Send To. The E-mail as Attachment button on the toolbar can be used instead of the command.

Mail Recipient (for Review) command Displays an e-mail window with the workbook as an attached shared file that will be tracked for changes. Found in File → Send To.

New Slide Adds a new slide after the current one. Found on the toolbar.

Next button Selects the previous edit when reviewing a presentation. Found on the Reviewing toolbar.

Next command Displays the next slide in a presentation. Found in the menu displayed by right-clicking on the screen during a slide show.

Notes Page command Used to format notes, add images to the notes, and format the layout of the Notes page. Found in the View menu.

Options Displays a menu that contains commands for formatting the printout of a presentation. Found on the Print Preview toolbar.

Previous button Selects the previous edit when reviewing a presentation. Found on the Reviewing toolbar.

Previous command Displays the previous slide in a presentation. Found in the menu displayed by right-clicking on the screen during a slide show.

Print... Displays a dialog box with options for printing. Found on the toolbar in the Print Preview window.

Print Preview command Displays a presentation as it will appear when printed. Found in the File menu. The Print Preview button on the toolbar can be used instead of the command.

Reply with Changes... Sends the open presentation as an e-mail message back to the original sender. Found on the Reviewing toolbar.

Send Sends the message. Displayed after selecting the E-mail as Attachment button.

Slide Master **command**   Displays the Slide Master used to change the look of the entire presentation. Found in View → Master.

Slide Show from current slide button Starts the presentation with the current slide full-screen.

Unapply button   Makes a change to the entire presentation when reviewing a presentation. Found on the Reviewing toolbar.

View Show **command**   Starts the presentation with slide 1 and displays it full-screen. Found in the Slide Show menu.

1. a) What is a presentation?
   b) What are visuals? Include three examples in your description.

2. What information is displayed in the status bar?

3. a) In Normal view, what is displayed in the Outline tab in the left pane?
   b) In Normal view, what is displayed in the Slides tab in the left pane?

4. a) What does the content of a slide refer to?
   b) What does the layout of a slide refer to?

5. In addition to the new slide, what is displayed after a new slide has been added by clicking the New Slide button on the toolbar?

6. How is the current slide deleted?

7. Instead of editing text in a placeholder on a slide, where else can the text for the current slide be edited?

8. What does the AutoFit feature do?

9. a) Which view divides the window into three panes?
   b) Which view displays thumbnails of all the slides in the presentation?
   c) Which view displays the current slide in full-screen size?
   d) Which view is best for editing the text on slides?
   e) Which view is best for changing the order of slides?

10. a) List three ways to display the next slide of a presentation in Normal view.
    b) List three ways to display the next slide of a presentation in Slide Show view.
    c) What happens when the Esc key is pressed in Slide Show view?

11. List the steps required to move slide 8 to between slides 6 and 7.

12. What happens when ▣ Design is clicked on the toolbar?

13. List the steps required to change the color scheme of the current presentation.

14. List two ways to display the next page in Print Preview.

15. What is printed on each page if the following options are selected in the Print What list in the Print Preview window:
    a) Slides
    b) Handouts (3 slides per page)
    c) Handouts (2 slides per page)
    d) Notes Pages

16. a) List the steps required to add the text Widget to the footer on each page of a printout.
    b) List the steps required to add the text Widget to the footer on each slide of a presentation.

17. List the steps required to add the slide number and a time stamp to the footer on each slide of a presentation.

18. Describe the differences between changing the look of a presentation using the Slide Master and changing the look of a presentation by applying a design template.

19. A company wants an elaborate, fancy script font used for all the text in a presentation. What would your recommendation be about that decision, and why?

20. A company wants a dark blue background used in a presentation and would like to know what color would be best for the text. What colors would you recommend, and why?

21. List the steps required to place clip art on the currently displayed slide in Normal view.

22. List two ways to add speaker notes to a slide.

23. What is displayed when a reviewed presentation is opened by the original author?

24. Describe the steps involved in e-mailing a presentation to a peer for review.

True/False

25. Determine if each of the following are true or false. If false, explain why.
    a) Speaker notes are displayed when the presentation is displayed in Slide Show view.
    b) The content on a slide should include everything a speaker is going to say while that slide is displayed.
    c) The text on a slide should be typed in all capital letters.
    d) A new presentation contains three slides by default.
    e) There are only two slide layouts to choose from.
    f) A previous slide can be displayed in Slide Show view.
    g) Slide Sorter view displays all the slides in the presentation in one window.
    h) The colors in a design template cannot be changed.
    i) The number of slides that are printed on a single page can be changed.
    j) A footer can be placed on individual slides and on a printout.
    k) The Slide Master is used to create a custom look that applies only to the first title slide in a presentation.
    l) Pictures from a digital camera or scanned pictures can be used in a PowerPoint presentation.
    m) In Normal view, the notes pane can be sized.
    n) A PowerPoint presentation can be sent as an e-mail attachment.

Exercise 1 —————————————————————— Winter Trip Orientation

Create a new presentation. Save the presentation naming it Winter Trip Orientation and complete the following steps:

a) On slide 1, add the following text:

Marine Biology Winter Trip: The Florida Keys
Organized by the Biology Club and the Scuba Club

b) Add two more slides after slide 1 and apply the Title and Text layout to the slides:

c) Add the following text to slides 2 and 3:
What to Expect
- Long days in the sun and on boats
- Some classes at night
- Limited space for gear

What to Bring
- One duffle bag and one backpack
- Sleeping bag and mat
- Canteen and sunscreen
- Scuba gear

d) Change the background of all the slides to a dark blue.

e) Change the color of the text and footers on all slides to white.

f) Add your name and the current date in the footer of all slides.

g) Save the modified Winter Trip Orientation.

h) Print the presentation, with a footer that includes the current date, so that three slides with lines for notes are printed on each page.

Exercise 2 —————————————————————— MANAGEMENT PLAN

The MANAGEMENT PLAN presentation contains 6 slides with text. Open MANAGEMENT PLAN, which is a PowerPoint data file for this text, and complete the following steps:

a) On slide 1, change the text Student Name to your name.

b) Add a new slide after slide 1 and apply the Title and Text layout to the slide:

c) Add the following text to the slide:

Overview
- Vision
- Employees
- Team Building
- Risks

d) Apply an appropriate design template to the presentation.

e) Add the slide number and the current date in the footer of all slides except slide 1.

f) Change the background color of all slides, making sure that the text is still readable.

g) Save the modified MANAGEMENT PLAN.

h) Print the presentation, with a footer that includes your name, in Notes Pages view.

Exercise 3 ———————————————————— Catsharks

Create a new presentation. Save the presentation naming it Catsharks and complete the following steps:

a) Modify the presentation so that it contains five slides with the following text:

Catsharks
A Brief Introduction

Characteristics
- Bottom-dwellers
- Small, up to 1 meter long

Coral Catshark
- Found in the Pacific Ocean
- White spots on dark body

Swellshark
- Found in the Pacific Ocean
- Dark brown mottled color

Striped Catshark
- Found in the Atlantic Ocean
- Dark horizontal stripes

b) Apply an appropriate design template to the presentation.

c) Add the slide number and your name in the footer of each slide.

d) Save the modified Catsharks.

e) Print the presentation, with a footer that includes your name, so that all the slides are printed on one page.

Exercise 4 ———————————————— Festival Report

Create a new presentation. Save the presentation naming it *Festival Report Name* with your name as *Name* and complete the following steps:

a) On slide 1, add the following text, replacing Student Name with your name:

Fall Family Festival
Report by Student Name

b) On slide 1, add clip art of a leaf or leaves, above the title. Resize and move the picture as necessary.

c) Add three more slides after slide 1 and apply the Title and Text layout to the slides:

d) Add the following text to the slides:

Food Booths
- Problems with trash bins
- Not enough seating
- Profit:

Game Booths
- Need more games for young children
- Frisbee prizes caused problems
- Profit:

Craft Booths
- Most popular booths
- Not enough glue
- Profit:

e) Change the background of all the slides to a dark green.

f) Change the color of the text and footers on all slides to a light yellow.

g) Add the current date and slide number in the footer of all slides.

h) Save the modified *Festival Report*.

i) Print the presentation, with a footer that includes your name, so that four slides are printed on each page.

j) Collaborate with a classmate by e-mailing the presentation to them for review, and have a classmate e-mail their *Festival Report* to you for review.

k) Check your e-mail, open the e-mail from your classmate that you received for review and add the following dollar amounts after the *Profit:* text on the following slides:

Slide	Profit amount
Food Booths slide (slide 2)	$350
Game Booths slide (slide 3)	$315
Craft Booths slide (slide 4)	$405

l) E-mail the reviewed presentation back to your classmate by replying with changes.

m) Check your e-mail, open the reviewed presentation from your classmate, and accept and apply all the changes.

n) Save the modified Festival Report.

o) Print the presentation, with a footer that includes your name, so that four slides are printed on each page.

Exercise 5 ——————————————— Widget Sales Pitch

Create a new presentation. Save the presentation naming it Widget Sales Pitch *Name* with your name as Name and complete the following steps:

a) On slide 1, add the following text, replacing Student Name with your name:

Your Customers Want Our Gizmos

Student Name, your Widget Corporation Customer Service Representative

b) On slide 1, add the WIDGET LOGO picture, which is an image data file for this text. Move the picture as necessary so that it is not covering text.

c) Add four more slides after slide 1 and apply the Title and Text layout to the slides:

d) Add the following text to the slides, replacing Full Name with your full name:

Your Customer's Needs
• Quality
• Variety
• Durability

Our Gizmos
• Quality: we use the best materials and inspect twice
• Variety: 27 colors and 4 sizes
• Durability: tested to withstand over 4000 uses

Our Company
• Orders are filled when received
• Locations in six countries
• Direct lines to your representative

Full Name
• fullname@widget.lpdatafiles.com
• (561) 555-WIDG

e) Change the color of the text and footers on all slides to a dark blue.

f) Add a date that automatically updates, the text Widget Corporation centered, and the slide number in the footer of all slides. You may need to resize the text placeholder to accommodate all of the text by dragging a handle.

g) Save the modified Widget Sales Pitch.

h) Print the presentation, with a footer that includes your name, so that the entire presentation is printed on one page.

i) Collaborate with a classmate by e-mailing the presentation to them for review, and have a classmate e-mail their Widget Sales Pitch to you for review.

j) Check your e-mail, open the e-mail from your classmate that you received for review. On slide 1, change Your Customers Want Our Gizmos to read Your Customers Will Love Our Gizmos.

k) E-mail the reviewed presentation back to your classmate by replying with changes.

l) Check your e-mail, open the reviewed presentation from your classmate, and accept and apply all the changes.

m) Save the modified Widget Sales Pitch.

n) Print the presentation, with a footer that includes your name, so that the entire presentation is printed on one page.

Exercise 6 ——————————————— Etiquette Training

Create a new presentation. Save the presentation naming it Etiquette Training and complete the following steps:

a) On the Slide Master, add the WIDGET LOGO picture, which is an image data file for this text. Move the picture to the bottom-right corner of the slide. Leave a little space between the logo and the edges of the slide.

b) On slide 1, add the following text:

E-mail Etiquette
Widget Corporation

c) Add two more slides after slide 1 and apply the Title and Text layout to the slides:

d) Add the following text to slides 2 and 3:

Message Content
• Address the client as you would in person.
• Keep the message professional.
• Get directly to the point.

Message Formatting
• Do not type a message in all uppercase.
• Use a signature block.

e) Add the following notes in the notes pane of slide 2:

Address the client as if in person. For example, Client Z should be addressed as Ms. Z unless you would address her by her first name.
Be professional. Do not include jokes or emoticons.

f) Add the following notes in the notes pane of slide 3:

Using all capital letters is the equivalent of shouting.
Use a signature block with your full name, your title, and our company name.

g) Add a date that automatically updates and your name centered in the footer of all slides.

h) Save the modified Etiquette Training.

i) Print the presentation, with a footer that includes your name, in Notes Pages view.

Exercise 7 ——————————————— Cultural Awareness

The TRAINING document last modified in the practices of Chapter 5 has information about the Widget Corporation Life-Long Learning program. The program schedule includes a session on cultural awareness and you have been asked to be a speaker.

a) Determine the purpose and audience of the presentation and write down a list of their characteristics.

b) Research one aspect of cultural awareness using the Internet and library. Write a short lecture using the information gathered during your research, keeping in mind the purpose and audience.

c) Using pencil and paper, sketch the layout and content of each slide in the presentation. Keep in mind the purpose and audience and divide the content among the slides appropriately. Include notes about which colors and fonts to use.

d) Using PowerPoint, create the presentation. Save the presentation naming it Cultural Awareness. Include appropriate clip art and slide footers. Use the colors and fonts noted in your sketches. Create speaker notes for each slide. Print the presentation so that all the slides are printed six slides to a page with your name in the footer, and then print all the slide notes with your name in the footer.

e) Schedule a time to give a practice presentation to an audience of your peers. Use Outlook to create a meeting request and invite attendees.

f) Before the scheduled practice presentation, use Word to create a rubric that can be used by your peers for evaluating your presentation. Some criteria are listed below, include at least one more of your own. Be sure to include a scale where appropriate:

• Were the slides appropriately designed and easy to read?

• Did the presentation appear to be well-researched and did the speaker show an understanding of the topic?

• Were the speaker's mannerisms and voice level appropriate?

g) Prepare handouts for your practice presentation. Print the handouts and a copy of the rubric for each member of your audience.

h) Give the practice presentation. After the presentation, collect the rubrics. Based on your peer critique, make improvements to your presentation. In Word, write a paragraph about what you changed and why the change is an improvement. Print a copy of the document.

Exercise 8 ——————————————————————— Assertiveness

The TRAINING document last modified in the practices of Chapter 5 has information about the Widget Corporation Life-Long Learning program. The program schedule includes a session on assertiveness and you have been asked to be a speaker.

a) Determine the purpose and audience of the presentation and write down a list of their characteristics.

b) Research one aspect of assertiveness in the workplace using the Internet and library. Write a short lecture using the information gathered during your research, keeping in mind the purpose and audience.

c) Using pencil and paper, sketch the layout and content of each slide in the presentation. Keep in mind the purpose and audience and divide the content among the slides appropriately. Include notes about which colors and fonts to use.

d) Using PowerPoint, create the presentation. Save the presentation naming it Assertiveness. Include appropriate clip art and slide footers. Use the colors and fonts noted in your sketches. Create speaker notes for each slide. Print the presentation so that all the slides are printed six slides to a page with your name in the footer, and then print all the slide notes with your name in the footer.

e) Schedule a time to give a practice presentation to an audience of your peers. Use Outlook to create a meeting request and invite attendees.

f) Before the scheduled practice presentation, use Word to create a rubric that can be used by your peers for evaluating your presentation. Some criteria are listed below, include at least one more of your own. Be sure to include a scale where appropriate:

- Were the slides appropriately designed and easy to read?
- Did the presentation appear to be well-researched and did the speaker show an understanding of the topic?
- Were the speaker's mannerisms and voice level appropriate?

g) Prepare handouts for your practice presentation. Print the handouts and a copy of the rubric for each member of your audience.

h) Give the practice presentation. After the presentation, collect the rubrics. Based on your peer critique, make improvements to your presentation. In Word, write a paragraph about what you changed and why the change is an improvement. Print a copy of the document.

Exercise 9 ———————————————————— Organizational Skills

The TRAINING document last modified in the practices of Chapter 5 has information about the Widget Corporation Life-Long Learning program. The program schedule includes a session on organizational skills and you have been asked to be a speaker.

a) Determine the purpose and audience of the presentation and write down a list of their characteristics.

b) Research one aspect of organizational skills using the Internet and library. Write a short lecture using the information gathered during your research, keeping in mind the purpose and audience.

c) Using pencil and paper, sketch the layout and content of each slide in the presentation. Keep in mind the purpose and audience and divide the content among the slides appropriately. Include notes about which colors and fonts to use.

d) Using PowerPoint, create the presentation. Save the presentation naming it Organizational Skills. Include appropriate clip art and slide footers. Use the colors and fonts noted in your sketches. Create speaker notes for each slide. Print the presentation so that all the slides are printed six slides to a page with your name in the footer, and then print all the slide notes with your name in the footer.

e) Schedule a time to give a practice presentation to an audience of your peers. Use Outlook to create a meeting request and invite attendees.

f) Before the scheduled practice presentation, use Word to create a rubric that can be used by your peers for evaluating your presentation. Some criteria are listed below, include at least one more of your own. Be sure to include a scale where appropriate:

- Were the slides appropriately designed and easy to read?
- Did the presentation appear to be well-researched and did the speaker show an understanding of the topic?
- Were the speaker's mannerisms and voice level appropriate?

g) Prepare handouts for your practice presentation. Print the handouts and a copy of the rubric for each member of your audience.

h) Give the practice presentation. After the presentation, collect the rubrics. Based on your peer critique, make improvements to your presentation. In Word, write a paragraph about what you changed and why the change is an improvement. Print a copy of the document.

Exercise 10 ———————————————————— Persuade Investors

Plan a presentation in which you propose a business plan for a company you wish to start. Using PowerPoint, create the presentation. Save the presentation naming it Persuade Investors. Include appropriate clip art and footer text. Create speaker notes for each slide. Print the presentation so that all the slides are printed six slides to a page and then print all the slide notes.

Chapter 15

Advanced PowerPoint Presentations

T his chapter covers features that enhance PowerPoint presentations, including slide transitions, animation, and ink. Adding multimedia clips to presentations and publishing to the Web are also covered.

Adding Animation

Slide Design task pane

Animation is a visual effect that refers to the way items move onto a slide. Animation is applied to a slide so that separate items, such as bulleted list items, appear one by one in Slide Show view. For example, each item on a slide can appear by sliding in from the left side, or it can dissolve into place. Select Slide Show → Animation Schemes to display the Slide Design task pane with Animation Schemes:

In the task pane, click an animation in the Apply to selected slides list to apply the animation to the displayed slide or selected slides. Click Apply to All Slides to apply the selected animation to the entire presentation. Remove an animation by clicking the No Animation option in the Apply to selected slides list.

Animations are previewed by clicking the transition icon ( ) displayed next to each slide in the Slides tab and in Slide Sorter view.

The same animation is usually applied to the same elements on all the slides in a presentation. For example, bulleted list items may have the Fade in one by one animation applied, and slides with a graphic have the Fade in all animation applied. Too many different animations can confuse or distract the audience.

Adding Slide Transitions

Slide Transition task pane

A *slide transition* is the way one slide changes to the next in Slide Show view. For example, the current slide can appear to fall off the screen to reveal the next slide, or it can dissolve into the next slide. Select Slide Show → Slide Transition to display the Slide Transition task pane:

In the task pane, click a transition in the Apply to selected slides list to apply the transition to the displayed slide or selected slides. Options in the Speed list affect how fast the transition happens. A sound is selected in the Sound list. Click Apply to All Slides to apply the selected transition to the entire presentation. Remove transitions by clicking the No Transition option in the Apply to selected slides list.

A transition icon ( ) is displayed next to each slide in the Slides tab and in Slide Sorter view. Transitions are previewed by clicking the icon.

The same transition is usually applied to all the slides in a presentation. When viewing a presentation, the audience builds expectations and are uncomfortable when unexpected transitions occur. In addition, a presentation with varied transitions is perceived as choppy and disorganized, not polished and professional.

Some animation schemes have slide transitions associated with them and will override any slide transitions previously applied. Therefore, slide transitions should be applied after animation schemes.

You will add slide transitions and animations to a presentation.

①　*OPEN WEB CAREERS*

    a.　Start PowerPoint.

    b.　Open WEB CAREERS, which is a PowerPoint data file for this text.

    c.　On slide 1, replace the text Student Name with your name.

②　*ADD ANIMATION TO THE ENTIRE PRESENTATION*

    a.　Select Slide Show → Animation Schemes. The Slide Design task pane is displayed with Animation Schemes.

    b.　In the Slide Design task pane, in the **Apply to selected slides** list, select Faded wipe. You may need to scroll the list to find the animation. The animation is applied to the displayed slide.

    c.　In the Slide Design task pane, click Apply to All Slides . The animation is applied to all the slides in the presentation.

    d.　In the Slides tab, click the transition icon (⚝) next to slide 2. The slide is displayed and the animation is previewed.

③　*ADD TRANSITIONS TO THE ENTIRE PRESENTATION*

    a.　Select Slide Show → Slide Transition. The Slide Transition task pane is displayed.

    b.　In the Slide Transition task pane, in the **Apply to selected slides** list, select Cover Down. The transition is applied to the displayed slide.

    c.　In the Slide Transition task pane, click Apply to All Slides . The transition is applied to all the slides in the presentation.

    d.　In the Slides tab, click the transition icon (⚝) next to slide 3. The slide is displayed and the transition and animation are both previewed.

④　*SAVE THE MODIFIED WEB CAREERS*

⑤　*VIEW THE SLIDE SHOW*

    a.　Select Slide Show → View Show. The presentation is started with slide 1. Notice the subtitle is not yet displayed.

    b.　Press the spacebar. The subtitle fades in.

    c.　Press the spacebar again. Slide 2 drops down. Only the title of slide 2, "Web Developer," fades in.

    d.　Press the spacebar again. The first bulleted item fades in.

    e.　Press the spacebar again. The second bulleted item fades in.

    f.　Press the spacebar again. The third bulleted item fades in.

    g.　Press the spacebar again. Slide 3 drops down and covers slide 2.

    h.　Continue to view the presentation until a black screen with the words "End of slide show, click to exit" at the top of the screen is displayed. Press Esc to end the presentation and display the PowerPoint window.

Cut, Copy, and Paste

Creating a presentation may require moving and duplicating text and graphics. Text and graphics can be moved and duplicated within the same presentation or between two or more presentations.

The Cut ( ), Copy ( ), and Paste ( ) commands from the Edit menu are used to move and duplicate text and graphics:

1. Select the *source*, which is the text or graphic to be duplicated or moved.

2. Select either Cut or Copy. The source displays a moving dashed border.

3. Select the *destination*, which is the location where the text or graphic is to be pasted.

4. Select Paste. The text or graphic is pasted. Press the Esc key to remove the dashed border.

A copy of a slide or multiple slides can be created in the same presentation by first selecting the slide(s) in the Outline tab or Slides tab and then selecting Insert → Duplicate Slide.

Slides can be duplicated or moved from one open presentation to another open presentation. Select Window → Arrange All to display both presentations at the same time, then:

1. Click the source slide in the Slides tab to select it.

2. Right-click the selected slide and select Copy or Cut.

3. In the Slides tab of the destination presentation, select the slide that should be before the pasted slide.

4. Right-click the selected slide and select Paste. The copied or moved slides appear after the selected slide.

Adding a Chart to a Slide

Charts from an Excel workbook can be added to any slide. Open the PowerPoint presentation and the Excel workbook, then:

1. In the workbook, select the chart to be copied.

2. Select Copy. The chart shows a moving dashed border.

3. Display the PowerPoint window, and display the slide in the slide pane in Normal view.

4. Select Paste. The chart is pasted on the slide, and the Paste Options button ( ) is displayed.

Click the Paste Options button ( ) after pasting a chart into a slide to display a list of options that can be used to change the default paste option of Excel Chart (entire workbook) to Picture of Chart (smaller file size). Select Picture of Chart (smaller file size) if the chart on the slide will not need to be updated with new charted data.

On a slide, a chart can be dragged to move it. To size a chart, click the chart to select it and then drag a handle. Press the Delete key to remove a selected chart from the slide.

Creating a Chart in PowerPoint

Select Insert → Chart or click the Insert Chart button ( ) to place a chart on a slide. The Microsoft Graph program is started and a datasheet similar to an Excel worksheet is displayed. Type new data in the datasheet or select Edit → Import File to import data and modify the chart. Click outside the chart to close the Microsoft Graph program.

Using Ink During a Slide Show

annotations

Annotations are notes or markings made on a slide that help the audience better understand the content. During a slide show, the speaker adds annotations by drawing and highlighting on the current slide using a feature called *ink*. Move the pointer to display the Slide Show toolbar in the bottom-left corner of the slide, then click the pen-shaped button to display a menu with commands for using ink:

Select **Ballpoint Pen**, **Felt Tip Pen**, or **Highlighter** to change the pointer shape and then drag to draw on the slide. Select **Ink Color** to change the color of the ink. Annotations are removed using the **Eraser** or by selecting **Erase All Ink on Slide**. Select **Arrow** to return the pointer to an arrow. When the slide show is closed, a dialog box appears:

Select **Keep** to leave the annotations on the slides, or **Discard** to remove the annotations.

Practice: WEB CAREERS – part 2 of 3

You will copy and paste a chart from an Excel workbook onto a slide in a PowerPoint presentation and annotate a slide. PowerPoint should already be started with the WEB CAREERS presentation displayed from the last practice.

① *ADD A NEW SLIDE*

   a. Display slide 5 in Normal view.

   b. On the toolbar, click New Slide . A slide is added and the Slide Layout task pane is displayed.

   c. In the Slide Layout task pane, click the Title Only layout that looks similar to:

   d. In the placeholder, type: Salaries for Charlotte, NC

   e. Click outside of the placeholder.

② *OPEN A WORKBOOK AND COPY A CHART*

    a. Open WEB SALARIES, which is an Excel data file for this text. This workbook contains data on salaries for Web Careers.

    b. Click the chart to select it.

    c. On the toolbar, click the Copy button. The chart is copied to the Clipboard.

    d. Display the PowerPoint window. The WEB CAREERS presentation is displayed.

    e. On the toolbar, click the Paste button. The chart is pasted onto the slide.

    f. Click the Paste Options button (📋▾) and select **Picture of Chart (smaller file size)**.

    g. Size the chart larger and drag the chart until it is centered under the slide's title.

    h. Display the WEB SALARIES workbook.

    i. Close WEB SALARIES and quit Excel without saving changes.

③ *VIEW THE SLIDE SHOW AND USE INK*

    a. Select **Slide Show → View Show**. The presentation is started with slide 1.

    b. Press the spacebar until the "Create reports and databases" third bullet on Slide 2 (Web Developer) fades in.

    c. Move the pointer to display the Slide Show toolbar in the bottom-left corner of the slide.

    d. In the Slide Show toolbar, click the pen-shaped button, then select **Highlighter** from the menu.

    e. Drag the pointer across the word "Design" to highlight it. A yellow mark is drawn.

    f. In the Slide Show toolbar, click the pen-shaped button, then select **Felt Tip Pen** from the menu.

    g. Drag the pointer in a circle around the "Web Developer" title. A red mark is drawn.

    h. On the same slide, experiment with other ink options and change the ink color.

    i. Press the spacebar until the slide with the chart is displayed.

    j. Press Esc. A dialog box is displayed.

    k. Select **Discard** to remove the annotations and display the PowerPoint window.

④ *PRINT THE PRESENTATION*

    a. Save the modified WEB CAREERS.

    b. Print a copy of the presentation as Handouts with 6 slides per page.

⑤ *SAVE AND CLOSE THE MODIFIED WEB CAREERS*

Creating a Design Template

A *design template* is a set of layouts, formatting, and backgrounds that are used again and again whenever a presentation of that type is needed. For example, a company can create a design template that includes their logo, corporate colors and fonts, and slide footers. The design template would be used by employees when they create a presentation for the company, to ensure a consistent design.

A design template is created from an open presentation that has had formatting applied to the Slide Master. The formatting applied to the Slide Master will be included in the design template. Select File → Save As to display a dialog box. Type a file name in the File name box and select Design Template in the Save as type list. The Look In box changes to the Templates folder for PowerPoint. Select Save to save the design template.

The new design template appears in the Slide Design task pane in the Available for Use list the next time PowerPoint is started. To use the design template, select it in the Slide Design task pane like any other design template.

File Name Extensions

A PowerPoint presentation has a .ppt extension, and a design template has a .pot extension.

Practice: GUEST HOUSE – part 1 of 3

You will create a design template and apply it to an existing presentation.

① *CREATE A NEW PRESENTATION*

If a blank presentation is not already displayed, click the New Presentation button (🗋) on the toolbar.

② *FORMAT THE SLIDE MASTER*

a. Select View → Master → Slide Master. The Slide Master is displayed.

b. Select Format → Background. A dialog box is displayed.

c. Click the arrow below the image and select the More Colors option in the list. A dialog box of colors is displayed.

d. Click the dark purple on the right side:

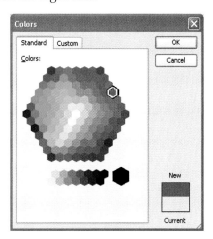

e. Select OK and then select Apply. The Slide Master is now purple.

f. Click the text "Click to edit Master title style" to select it.

g. On the toolbar, click the arrow in the Font Color button (A▾) and select More Colors. A dialog box is displayed.

h. Click the light blue near the center:

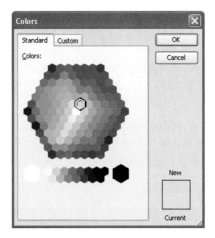

i. Select OK and then click outside of the placeholder. The text is a pale blue color.

j. Format the "Click to edit Master title style" text as bold.

k. Select all the text in the placeholder below the title, from "Click to edit Master text styles" to "Fifth level."

l. Click the Font Color button (⟨A⟩) to apply the blue color to the selected text.

m. At the bottom of the slide, format <footer> in the blue color.

n. Replace <footer> with your name.

o. Select Slide Show ➙ Animation Schemes. The Slide Design task pane is displayed with Animation Schemes.

p. In the Slide Design task pane, in the Apply to selected slides list, select Float. You may need to scroll to near the bottom of the list to find the animation.

q. On the Slide Master toolbar, click [Close Master View]. The presentation is displayed in Normal view. Note the colors.

③ *SAVE THE PRESENTATION AS A DESIGN TEMPLATE*

a. Select File ➙ Save. The Save As dialog box is displayed.

b. In the File name box, type Griffin and in the Save as type list, select Design Template. Note that the Save in list has changed to display the Templates folder.

c. Select Save. The presentation is saved as a template.

④ *CLOSE GRIFFIN AND THEN QUIT POWERPOINT*

⑤ *START POWERPOINT AND OPEN GUEST HOUSE*

a. Start PowerPoint.

b. Open GUEST HOUSE, which is a PowerPoint data file for this text. This presentation does not have any formatting applied to it.

⑥ *APPLY THE DESIGN TEMPLATE*

a. On the toolbar, click [Design]. The Slide Design task pane is displayed.

b. In the Slide Design task pane, in the Apply a design template list, scroll until a purple design template is displayed. Pause the pointer over the purple design template until the ScreenTip is displayed. Note that this is the Griffin design template.

c. Click arrow next to the Griffin design template, and then select Apply to All Slides. The design is applied to the entire presentation.

Check – Slide 1 should look similar to:

Griffin's Guest House

For Artists and Writers

⑦ *SAVE THE MODIFIED GUEST HOUSE AND VIEW THE SLIDE SHOW*

a. Save the modified GUEST HOUSE.

b. Select Slide Show → View Show. The presentation is started with slide 1. Notice the subtitle is not yet displayed.

c. Press the spacebar. The subtitle drops and fades in.

d. Press the spacebar again. Slide 2 appears with a dramatic animation. Only the title of slide 2, "Country Charm," drops and fades in.

e. Press the spacebar again. The first bulleted item fades in.

f. Continue to view the presentation until a black screen with the words "End of slide show, click to exit" at the top of the screen is displayed. Press Esc to end the presentation and display the PowerPoint window.

Adding Sound to a Slide

Sound is an audio file that can be added to a slide and played during a slide show. Display the slide in Normal view, then select Insert → Movies and Sounds → Sound from File to display the Insert Sound dialog box with a list of sound files. Select Insert → Movies and Sounds → Sound from Clip Organizer to display the Clip Art task pane with a list of sound files. Click the arrow to the right of a sound file and select Insert from the menu. A sound icon (🔊) is added to the slide and a dialog box is displayed:

> ### Multimedia
>
> Multimedia refers to using sound and/or video in a file of another type, such as a presentation or a Web page.

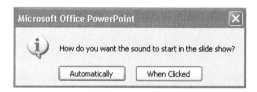

Select Automatically to have the sound play when the slide is displayed during a slide show. Select When Clicked to have the sound play when the sound icon is clicked during a slide show.

During a Slide Show, the sound stops playing when another slide is displayed or when the sound file ends, whichever occurs first.

> **TIP** Click the transition icon (📷) next to a slide in the Slides tab or in Slide Sorter view to hear the sound on a slide.

In Normal view, double-click a sound icon on a slide or right-click the sound icon and select Play Sound to hear the sound. Right-click and select Edit Sound Object to display a dialog box with options for the sound during a slide show:

TIP Select the Loop until next sound to have the sound repeat until another sound plays or another slide is displayed.

• Select Loop until stopped to repeatedly play a sound until a different slide is displayed.

• Click [🔊] to adjust the sound volume.

• Select Hide sound icon during slide show if the sound icon should not be visible on the slide during a Slide Show.

On a slide, a sound icon (🔊) can be moved and sized like a picture. Clicking the icon selects it and displays handles for sizing. Pressing the Delete key removes the selected sound icon from the slide. Click outside the icon to remove the handles.

When choosing sounds, make sure the sounds are appropriate for the audience and presentation topic. Sounds should enhance a presentation without annoying the audience. Too many sounds can have a negative effect on the audience.

Adding a Movie to a Slide

animated GIF

A *movie* is a digital video file that comes from various sources, including digital cameras and illustration software. An *animated GIF* is a file with several images that display in sequence and appear animated. Animated GIFs are supported by most browsers and are therefore a good choice for media on the Web. An animated GIF is not a movie but is treated as such in PowerPoint.

TIP A GIF file name has the .gif extension.

A movie can be added to a slide and played during a slide show. Display the slide in Normal view, then select Insert → Movies and Sounds → Movie from File to display the Insert Movie dialog box with a list of movie files. Select Insert → Movies and Sounds → Movie from Clip Organizer to display the Clip Art task pane with a list of movie files. Click the arrow to the right of a movie file and select Insert from the menu. The movie is added to the slide and a dialog box is displayed:

TIP Click the transition icon (⚡) next to a slide in the Slides tab or in Slide Sorter view to play the movie on a slide.

Select Automatically to have the movie play when the slide is displayed during a slide show. Select When Clicked to have the movie play when it is clicked during a slide show.

During a Slide Show, the movie stops playing when another slide is displayed or when the movie file ends, whichever occurs first. Animated GIFs continually play until another slide is displayed.

In Normal view, double click a movie on a slide or right-click the movie and select Play Movie to play the movie. Right-click and select Edit Movie Object to display a dialog box with options for the movie during a slide show:

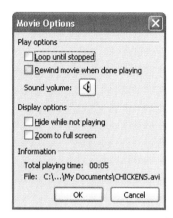

- Select Loop until stopped to repeat the movie until a different slide is displayed or until the movie is clicked.
- Click 🔊 to adjust the sound volume.
- Select Hide while not playing if the movie should not be visible on a slide until played.

Note that these commands and dialog boxes are not available for animated GIFs.

On a slide, a movie can be moved and sized like a picture. Clicking the movie selects it and displays handles for sizing. Pressing the Delete key removes the selected movie from the slide. Click outside the movie to remove the handles.

When choosing movies, make sure the movies are appropriate for the audience and presentation topic. Movies should add information or enhance a topic without distracting the audience from the topic.

Practice: GUEST HOUSE – part 2 of 3

You will add sound and a movie to the GUEST HOUSE presentation. You will need a sound card and speakers to hear the sounds in this practice. PowerPoint should already be started with GUEST HOUSE open from the last practice.

① *ADD A SOUND TO A SLIDE*

    a. Display slide 2.

    b. Select Insert → Movies and Sounds → Sound from File. A dialog box is displayed.

        1. Select ROOSTER, which is a sound data file for this text.

        2. Select OK. A sound icon is added to the slide and a dialog box is displayed.

        3. Select When Clicked. The slide is displayed and the sound icon is visible.

c. Drag the sound icon to the end of the "Actual working farm" phrase:

> • Actual working farm ◀

d. Double-click the sound icon. A rooster's sound is played.

② *ADD A MOVIE TO A SLIDE*

a. Display slide 4.

b. Select Insert ➜ Movies and Sounds ➜ Movie from File. A dialog box is displayed.

   1. Select CHICKENS, which is a movie data file for this text.

   2. Select OK. The movie is added to the slide and a dialog box is displayed.

   3. Select When Clicked. The slide is displayed and the sound icon is visible. If the AutomaticLayout options button is displayed, click it and select Undo Automatic Layout.

c. Drag the movie icon to be centered below the bulleted items:

d. Right-click the movie and select Play Movie from the menu. The five-second movie plays once.

③ *SET THE MOVIE TO LOOP*

Right-click the movie and select Edit Movie Object from the menu. A dialog box is displayed.

   1. Select the Loop until stopped check box.

   2. Select OK. The movie will continuously loop during a slide show until it is clicked.

④ *SAVE THE MODIFIED GUEST HOUSE AND VIEW THE MULTIMEDIA SLIDE SHOW*

a. Save the modified GUEST HOUSE.

b. Select Slide Show ➜ View Show. The presentation is started with slide 1.

c. Press the spacebar repeatedly until the last bulleted item of slide 2 appears, "Actual working farm."

d. Click the sound icon. The rooster sound is played.

e. Press the spacebar repeatedly to view slide 3 and then slide 4. Stop when the last bulleted item of slide 4 appears, "Charming views outside your window."

f. Click the movie. The movie plays continuously, over and over.

g. Press the spacebar to end the presentation. A black screen is displayed. Press Esc to end the presentation and display the PowerPoint window.

⑤ *PRINT THE PRESENTATION*

Print a copy of the presentation as Handouts with 6 slides per page.

packaging a presentation

Delivering a Presentation

There are many ways to *deliver a presentation*, which refers to the location and manner in which the audience experiences the presentation:

- A live speaker lectures or narrates while the presentation is projected onto a large screen in the same room as the audience. The presentation may be projected using a digital projector connected to a computer, or using an overhead projector with transparencies printed from the presentation.

- A live speaker in one location presents to audience members in other locations using collaborative meeting software such as Microsoft NetMeeting. Each audience member views the presentation on a computer at their location while listening to the speaker lecture or narrate. Everyone in the meeting sees the same presentation and can communicate with each other.

- The presentation is played in a continuous loop on an unattended computer, and viewed by anyone who chooses to watch it. For example, at a kiosk or in a museum exhibit.

- The presentation is distributed on CD or published to the Web, so that the presentation can be viewed at any time.

- The presentation is printed on paper in various layouts and given to the audience to read.

A PowerPoint presentation will need to be moved to the location where it will be delivered. To do this, the presentation and all the files associated with it, such as fonts and linked clips, can be *packaged* with the Viewer and copied to a CD or to a folder on a hard disk. The *Microsoft Office PowerPoint Viewer* will be required to show a PowerPoint presentation on a computer that does not have PowerPoint installed. Once packaged, the folder can be moved to other computers or the CD can be transported to another location or copied and distributed.

To package an open PowerPoint presentation, select File → Package for CD which displays a dialog box:

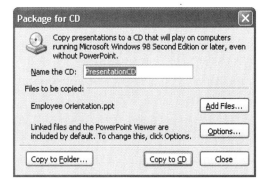

- Type a name for the CD in the Name the CD box if the presentation will be packaged to a CD.

- Click Add Files and select additional presentations to add to the package.

- Click Options, which displays a dialog box with options for the Viewer, linked files, embedding fonts, and passwords that restrict opening or changing the presentation. Sound files larger than 100 KB and any movies or animated GIFs are linked to a presentation by default and need to be included when packaging for CD.

Click Copy to Folder to package the presentation to a folder on a computer or network. Click Copy to CD to package the presentation to a blank, writable CD in a writable CD drive. Click Close to remove the dialog box without packaging the presentation.

Password Protection for a Presentation

Although passwords can be added when packaging the presentation to a folder or CD, passwords to restrict opening or editing the file can also be added to the PowerPoint file. Password protection is useful in many situations, such as when a presentation is distributed by sending the file to the recipients, but changes should not be made to it. To assign a password, select Tools → Options and select the Security tab to display those options:

- Type a password in the Password to open box to require a password to open the presentation.

- Type a password in the Password to modify box to require a password to make changes to the presentation.

Select OK to display the Confirm Password dialog box, type the identical password in the Reenter password box and select OK.

Choosing a Password

Passwords are case-sensitive and can include numbers, symbols, and lowercase and uppercase letters. A long combination is best, such as pi808wR6j6. Familiar words are not recommended.

Practice: GUEST HOUSE – part 3 of 3

You will package the presentation to a folder with the viewer. PowerPoint should already be started with GUEST HOUSE open from the last practice.

① *PACKAGE THE PRESENTATION*

    a. Select File → Package for CD. A dialog box is displayed.

    b. Select Options. A dialog box is displayed.

    c. Be sure that PowerPoint Viewer is selected.

    d. Select Linked files and Embedded TrueType fonts if they are not already selected.

    e. In the Password to modify each file box, type a password that you can remember.

    f. Select OK. The Confirm Password dialog box is displayed.

    g. In the Reenter the password required to modify files box, type the password and then select OK.

    h. Select Copy to Folder. A dialog box is displayed.

    i. In the Folder name box type: Griffin Guest House

    j. Select Browse to choose the location where you want the folder.

    k. Select OK. A folder is created and the files are copied.

    l. Select Close. The presentation, complete with viewer, fonts, and the linked movie, is in a folder and protected from modifications by a password.

② *CLOSE GUEST HOUSE*

Hyperlinks on a Slide

When a Web site address is typed in a slide, PowerPoint automatically turns it into a blue, underlined hyperlink. A reader viewing the PowerPoint presentation on screen can click the link, which displays the Web page in a browser window if there is Internet access.

PowerPoint also recognizes an e-mail address and formats it as blue underlined characters. An e-mail address on a slide is clicked to display a new e-mail message window.

The Insert Hyperlink dialog box contains options for inserting a hyperlink. To use this dialog box, select Insert → Hyperlink or click the Insert Hyperlink button (📇) on the toolbar. Select a type of link from the Link to list and then type a label in the Text to display box. For Web page links, type a URL in the Address box. For an e-mail address link, type an address in the E-mail address box. The label is placed at the insertion point, but the URL will be followed when the reader clicks the label.

removing a hyperlink

To convert a hyperlink to plain text, right-click the link and then select Remove Hyperlink from the menu.

Creating an HTML File and Publishing a Presentation to the Web

HTML is the file format for documents viewed using a browser, such as documents on the Web. A presentation in HTML format is more versatile because PowerPoint is not needed to view it, just a browser, such as Internet Explorer. *Publishing a presentation* means to place a copy of the presentation in HTML format on a Web server or in a folder. Select File → Save as Web Page to save a presentation in Web format. The Save As dialog box includes a Change Title button. Click Change Title and then type a descriptive *title*, which is text displayed in the title bar of the browser window. Select Publish to display a dialog box with options for publishing the presentation:

title

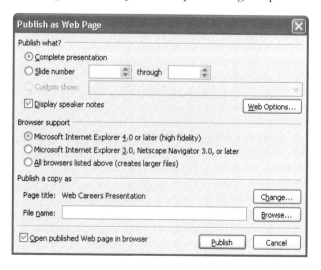

Click Browse to select the location where the presentation should be published, and give the Web page a name. Select the Open published Web page in browser check box to open the Web page in a browser after it is published:

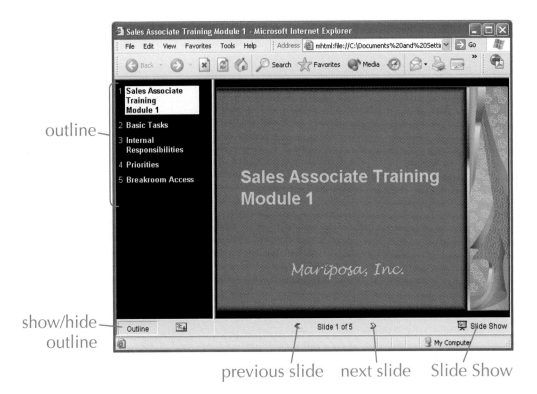

outline

show/hide outline

previous slide   next slide   Slide Show

- Click a link in the outline or click the previous or next slide button to display a slide.
- Click the Outline button to hide or display the outline.
- Click the Slide Show button to view the slide show full screen.

An open PowerPoint presentation can be previewed as a Web page by selecting File → Web Page Preview.

Saving a presentation as a Web page creates a copy of the file with the extension .mht. To view the file in a Web browser, open a browser, such as Internet Explorer and select File → Open.

MHTML

The Save as Web Page command saves a document in MHTML (MIME HTML) format, which means that all the information for the document, including pictures, is saved within one single file.

Practice: WEB CAREERS – part 3 of 3

You will add a hyperlink to a slide, publish the presentation to a folder, and view the file in a Web browser. PowerPoint should already be started.

① *OPEN WEB CAREERS*

Open WEB CAREERS and display slide 1 in Normal view.

② *ADD A HYPERLINK*

a. Place the insertion point in the subtitle at the end of the word "Counselor" and press Enter.

b. Type: www.lpdatafiles.com/careers.htm

c. Type a space. The Web site address turns blue and underlined.

③ *SAVE WEB CAREERS AS A WEB PAGE AND PUBLISH THE PRESENTATION*

a. Save the modified WEB CAREERS.

b. Select File → Save as Web Page. A dialog box is displayed.

1. Click **Change Title**. A dialog box is displayed.
2. In the Page title box type: Web Careers Presentation
3. Select **OK**.

c. Click **Publish**. A dialog box is displayed. Select options as follows:

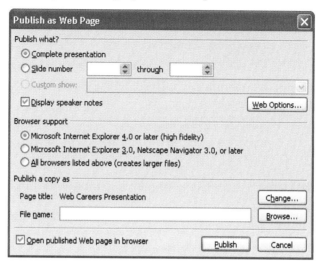

d. Click **Browse**. A dialog box is displayed.
1. Select the appropriate location for the file to be saved.
2. Select **OK**.

e. Click **Publish**. After a few seconds a browser window opens and the presentation is displayed.

f. Click the link on slide 1. The destination of the link is displayed in the browser window.

g. On the browser window toolbar, click Back. The presentation is again displayed.

h. View the presentation using the links in the outline or the ![«] and ![»] buttons at the bottom of the window.

i. Close the browser window when finished.

④ *SAVE AND PRINT THE PRESENTATION*

a. Save the modified WEB CAREERS.

b. Print a copy of the presentation as Handouts with 6 slides per page.

⑤ *CLOSE WEB CAREERS*

Creating a Photo Album

TIP Select Scanner/Camera in the Photo Album dialog box to insert pictures directly from a scanner or digital camera that is connected to the computer.

PowerPoint has a *photo album* feature that is used to create a slide show of pictures. Select Insert ➞ Picture ➞ New Photo Album which displays a dialog box. Select File/Disk to locate and select a picture file. Add pictures one by one to the list in the dialog box. Select a layout in the Picture layout list and then click Create to create a new presentation with a title slide and pictures on additional slides. The presentation can be formatted and edited like any other presentation. The photo album presentation can be packaged to a folder or CD to distribute, or published to the Web or another computer for viewing.

You will create and view a photo album. PowerPoint should already be started.

① *CREATE A PHOTO ALBUM*

   a. Select Insert → Picture → New Photo Album. A dialog box is displayed.

   b. Select File/Disk. A dialog box is displayed.

       1. Select AK BEAR, which is an image data file for this text.

       2. Select Insert. The picture is displayed in the preview and the image file name is added to the Pictures in album list.

   c. Select File/Disk. A dialog box is displayed.

       1. Select AK MOOSE, which is an image data file for this text.

       2. Select Insert. The picture is added.

   d. Use File/Disk to add the following four more pictures to the album:

       AK ORCAS

       AK OTTER

       AK SALMON

       AK SHEEP

   e. In the Picture layout list, select Fit to slide if it is not already selected.

   f. Click Create. After a few seconds a new presentation is created with a title slide and a slide for each picture. Slide 1 is displayed in Normal view.

② *EDIT THE PRESENTATION*

   a. In the Slides tab, select slide 7 and press the Delete key. Slide 7 is removed from the presentation.

   b. Display slide 1, and change the text Photo Album to: Alaska Wildlife

   c. Format Alaska Wildlife as bold.

   d. On slide 1, change the text below the title to your name.

③ *FORMAT THE BACKGROUND*

   a. Select Format → Background. A dialog box is displayed.

   b. Click the arrow below the image and select the More Colors option in the list. A dialog box of colors is displayed.

   c. Click the light blue near the center:

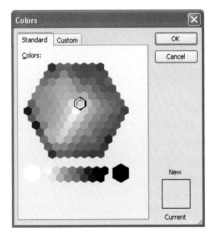

d. Select OK and then select Apply to All to apply the blue background color to the entire presentation.

④ *SAVE THE PRESENTATION*

Save the file naming it Alaska Photos.

⑤ *VIEW THE SLIDE SHOW*

a. Select Slide Show → View Show. The presentation is started with slide 1.

b. Press the spacebar. The next slide is displayed.

c. Continue to view the presentation until a black screen with the words "End of slide show, click to exit" at the top of the screen is displayed. Click the left mouse button to end the presentation and display the PowerPoint window.

⑥ *PRINT THE PRESENTATION*

a. On the toolbar, click the Print Preview button (🔍). The first page is displayed in the print preview window.

b. On the toolbar, in the Print What list select Handouts (6 slides per page).

c. On the toolbar, click 🖨 Print... . A dialog box is displayed.

d. Select OK. The presentation is printed on one page.

e. On the toolbar, click Close . The Print Preview window is closed and the presentation is displayed in Normal view.

⑦ *CLOSE ALASKA PHOTOS AND QUIT POWERPOINT*

Chapter Summary

This chapter covers features that enhance PowerPoint presentations and methods for distributing a presentation. Animation and slide transitions affect the way items move onto a slide and the way slides appear during a slide show. Selecting Slide Show → Animation Schemes displays the Slide Design task pane with Animation Schemes selected. Selecting Slide Show → Slide Transition displays the Slide Transition task pane. Animations and slide transitions are previewed using the transition icon, which is displayed next to slides in the Slides tab and in Slide Sorter view.

Text and graphics can be moved and duplicated within the same presentation or between two or more presentations using Cut, Copy, and Paste. Slides can be duplicated by selecting Insert → Duplicate Slide.

A chart in an Excel workbook can be copied in the workbook and pasted on a slide in PowerPoint. On a slide, a chart can be moved and sized.

Annotations can be made on a slide during a slide show using a feature called ink.

A design template is created from an open presentation by selecting File → Save As. The design template will appear in the Design Templates list the next time PowerPoint is started.

Sounds and movies can be added to a slide and played during a slide show. Sound icons and movies can be moved and sized on a slide.

There are many ways to deliver a presentation:

- Projected onto a large screen while a live speaker lectures.
- Presented using collaborative meeting software.
- Played in a continuous loop on an unattended computer.
- Distributed on CD or published to the Web.
- Printed on paper.

A PowerPoint presentation can be packaged with the Viewer and copied to a CD or to a folder on a hard disk. The Microsoft Office PowerPoint Viewer is required to show a PowerPoint presentation on a computer that does not have PowerPoint installed.

Passwords can be added to a PowerPoint presentation to restrict opening or editing the file. Passwords can also be added when packaging the presentation to a folder or CD.

Hyperlinks can be added to a slide, as well as e-mail addresses.

A PowerPoint presentation can be saved in HTML format and viewed using a browser. Publishing a presentation means to place a copy of the presentation in HTML format on a Web server or a folder.

PowerPoint has a photo album feature that is used to create a slide show of pictures. The photo album presentation can be packaged to a folder or CD to distribute, or published to the Web.

Vocabulary

Animated GIF   A file with several images that display in sequence and appear animated.

Animation   A visual effect that refers to the way items move onto a slide.

Annotations   Notes or markings made on a slide that help the audience better understand the content.

Deliver a presentation   The location and manner in which the audience experiences the presentation.

Design template   A set of layouts, formatting, and backgrounds that are used again and again whenever a presentation of that type is needed.

HTML   The file format for documents viewed using a browser, such as documents on the Web.

Ink   A feature used to draw and highlight on the current slide during a slide show.

Microsoft Office PowerPoint Viewer   Software required to show a PowerPoint presentation on a computer that does not have PowerPoint installed.

Movie   A digital video file from various sources, including digital cameras or illustration software.

Package PowerPoint feature that copies the presentation and all the files associated with it, including the Viewer, to a CD or to a folder on a hard disk.

Photo album   PowerPoint feature that creates a slide show of pictures.

Publishing a presentation   Placing a copy of the presentation in HTML format on a Web server or in a folder.

Slide transition   The way one slide changes to the next in Slide Show view.

Sound   An audio file that can be added to a slide and played during a slide show.

Title   Text in the title bar of the browser window.

PowerPoint Commands and Buttons

Animation Schemes command Displays the Slide Design task pane with Animation Schemes. Found in the Slide Show menu.

Arrange All command Displays all open presentations at the same time. Found in the Window menu.

Ballpoint Pen command Changes the pointer shape and draws on the slide when the pointer is dragged. Found in the menu displayed by clicking the pen-shaped button in the Slide Show toolbar.

Copy command Creates a duplicate of the selected text or graphic for pasting. Found in the Edit menu. The Copy button on the toolbar can be used instead of the command.

Cut command Removes the selected text or graphics. Found in the Edit menu. The Cut button on the toolbar can be used instead of the command.

Duplicate Slide command Creates a copy of the selected slide. Found in the Insert menu.

Edit Movie Object command Displays a dialog box with options for the movie during a slide show. Found in the menu displayed by right-clicking a movie.

Edit Sound Object command Displays a dialog box with options for the sound during a slide show. Found in the menu displayed by right-clicking a sound icon.

Erase All Ink command Removes all the ink on a slide. Found in the menu displayed by clicking the pen-shaped button in the Slide Show toolbar.

Eraser command Changes the pointer to remove ink when dragged. Found in the menu displayed by clicking the pen-shaped button in the Slide Show toolbar.

Felt Tip Pen command Changes the pointer shape and draws on the slide when the pointer is dragged. Found in the menu displayed by clicking the pen-shaped button in the Slide Show toolbar.

Highlighter command Changes the pointer shape and draws on the slide when the pointer is dragged. Found in the menu displayed by clicking the pen-shaped button in the Slide Show toolbar.

Hyperlink command Displays a dialog box used to create a hyperlink. Found in the Insert menu.

Ink Color command Changes the color of ink. Found in the menu displayed by clicking the pen-shaped button in the Slide Show toolbar.

Movie from Clip Organizer command Displays the Clip Art task pane with a list of movie files. Found in Insert → Movies and Sounds.

Movie from File command Displays a dialog box with a list of movie files. Found in Insert → Movies and Sounds.

New Photo Album command Displays a dialog box used to create a photo album presentation. Found in Insert → Picture.

Options command Displays a dialog box used to assign a password to a presentation. Found in the Tools menu.

Package for CD command Displays a dialog box used to package an open PowerPoint presentation. Found in the File menu.

Paste command Places the most recently copied or cut text or graphics at the insertion point. Found in the Edit menu. The Paste button on the toolbar can be used instead of the command.

Play Movie command Plays the movie once. Found in the menu displayed by right-clicking a movie.

Play Sound command Plays the sound once. Found in the menu displayed by right-clicking a sound icon.

Save As command Displays a dialog box used to save a presentation as a design template. Found in the File menu.

Save as Web Page command Saves a document in Web format. Found in the File menu.

Slide Transition command Displays the Slide Transition task pane. Found in the Slide Show menu.

Sound from Clip Organizer command Displays the Clip Art task pane with a list of sound files. Found in Insert → Movies and Sounds.

Sound from File command Displays a dialog box with a list of sound files. Found in Insert → Movies and Sounds.

Web Page Preview command Previews the open PowerPoint presentation as a Web page in a browser window. Found in the File menu.

1. a) What is animation?
   b) List the steps required to add the Faded zoom animation to slide 2 in a presentation.

2. a) What is a slide transition?
   b) List the steps required to add a Blinds Vertical transition to all the slides in a presentation.

3. a) Where is a transition icon displayed?
   b) What is a transition icon used for?

4. a) How can a copy of a picture on slide 2 be quickly put on slides 4, 6, and 8?
   b) List the steps required to move a slide from one open presentation to another open presentation.

5. List the steps required to place a copy of a chart in an Excel workbook on slide 3 in a PowerPoint presentation.

6. a) How is a chart on a slide moved?
   b) How is a chart on a slide sized?

7. a) What are annotations?
   b) How could annotations be useful? Give an example.

8. a) What is ink?
   b) How can the color of ink be changed?
   c) List the steps required to draw an x on slide 4 with the ink of your choice.

9. a) What is a design template?
   b) List the steps required to save the open presentation as a design template and then apply it to another presentation.

10. a) What is sound?
    b) List the steps required to add a sound from the Clip Organizer to slide 3 and have the sound play continuously during the slide show as soon as the slide is displayed.
    c) How is the volume of a sound changed?

11. Where does a sound icon appear?

12. Which would be better: a different sound plays every time a new slide is displayed, or the same sound plays every time a new slide is displayed? Explain your answer.

13. What is a movie?

14. What is an animated GIF?

15. List the steps required to add a movie from the Clip Organizer to slide 7 and have the movie play when clicked during the slide show.

16. a) List five ways to deliver a presentation.
    b) List the steps to package an open PowerPoint presentation to a CD.

17. List the steps required to password protect a PowerPoint presentation from being modified.

18. How is a hyperlink created on a slide?

19. a) What is publishing a presentation?
    b) List the steps required to publish the open PowerPoint presentation to the Web.

20. Describe what a PowerPoint presentation looks like when viewed in a browser.

21. a) Describe the photo album feature.
    b) Describe three scenarios for using a photo album presentation. Include a description of what you would need to do to the PowerPoint file for the scenario.

True/False

22. Determine if each of the following are true or false. If false, explain why.
    a) Animation is added the same way a movie or sound is added to a slide.
    b) A chart from an Excel workbook can be added to a slide.
    c) Annotations are added in Normal view.
    d) Sound can be played during a slide show by clicking a sound icon.
    e) Clicking the slide transition icon displays a slide in Slide Show view.
    f) A presentation can be viewed on the Web.

Exercise 1 ——————————————————— Maples, Maple Trees

Create a new presentation. Save the presentation naming it Maple Trees and complete the following steps:

a) Modify the presentation so that it contains five slides with the following text:

Maple Trees
Broad-leafed Tree Series

Sugar Maple
- Sap is used for maple syrup
- Height - 24 meters

Silver Maple
- Leaves have large teeth
- Height - 15 meters

Red Maple
- Bright red flowers and buds
- Height - 30 meters

Tree Heights

b) In a new Excel workbook, enter the tree names and their height data, and create a column chart titled Maple Trees. Save the workbook naming it Maples.

c) Place a copy of the chart on slide 5, the slide with the title "Tree Heights." Size and move the chart appropriately.

d) Apply an appropriate design template to the presentation.

e) Apply the Float animation scheme and then the Cover Down slide transition to all the slides.

f) Save the modified Maple Trees.

g) Print the presentation, with a footer that includes your name, so that all the slides are printed on one page.

h) Publish the presentation to a folder and then view and print the Web page.

Exercise 2 ——————————— Projectors, Digital Projectors

Digital projectors are commonly used in classrooms and in business to project presentations onto a screen. Common features that vary between projectors are:

> **Brightness** The greater the brightness, the farther the projector can be from the screen. Lumens is the unit used to express brightness.

> **Keystone Correction** A keystone effect refers to one side to the projected image being larger that the other side. Keystone effect usually happens when the projector is tilted. Some projectors have a feature that corrects the keystone effect.

> **Lamps** The lamp is the bulb that provides light in the projector. Replacement lamps vary by cost and life (how long they last).

> **Display Technology** Two of the most common display technologies are LCD and DLP.

Use the Internet and library to research and compare the cost and features of three digital projectors. Create a new presentation. Save the presentation naming it Digital Projectors and complete the following steps:

a) Include a title slide and at least one slide for each researched projector or one slide for each projector feature. Include pictures if possible.

b) Apply an appropriate design template to the presentation.

c) In a new Excel workbook, enter the names of the projectors and their cost, and create a column chart titled Digital Projector Costs. Save the workbook naming it Projectors.

d) Add a slide at the end of the presentation and place a copy of the chart on the slide. Size and move the chart appropriately.

e) Apply the Appear animation scheme and then the Box Out slide transition to all the slides.

f) Save the modified Digital Projectors.

g) Print the presentation, with a footer that includes your name, so that six slides are printed on each page.

h) Publish the presentation to a folder and then view and print the Web page.

Exercise 3 ——————————— Other Software, Presentation Software

There are other presentation applications in addition to Microsoft PowerPoint 2003. Use the Internet and library to research and compare the cost and features of three other presentation programs. In your research, compare cost and features.

Create a new presentation. Save the presentation naming it Presentation Software and complete the following steps:

a) Include a title slide and at least one slide for each researched presentation program or one slide for each feature. Include pictures if possible.

b) Apply an appropriate design template to the presentation.

c) In a new Excel workbook, enter the names of the presentation programs and their cost, and create a column chart titled Program Costs. Save the workbook naming it Other Software.

d) Add a slide at the end of the presentation and place a copy of the chart on the slide. Size and move the chart appropriately.

e) Apply the Dissolve in animation scheme and then the Comb Vertical slide transition to all the slides.

f) Add a slide at the end of the presentation with notes about when each presentation program would be best suited to be used. Include notes in the notes pane that explain your findings.

g) Save the modified Presentation Software.

h) Print the presentation, with a footer that includes your name, so that six slides are printed on each page.

i) Print the last slide with notes in Notes Pages view.

Exercise 4 ———————————————————Presentation Delivery

Choose one of the ways to deliver a presentation discussed earlier in this chapter and make a list of all the technology needed to deliver a presentation using that method. For example:

> A live speaker in one location presents to audience members in other locations using collaborative meeting software such as Microsoft NetMeeting. Each audience member views the presentation on a computer at their location while listening to the speaker lecture or narrate. Everyone in the meeting sees the same presentation and can communicate with each other.

> The technology for this method needed would be collaborative meeting software, and computers with speakers and microphones.

Use the Internet and library to research and compare the cost and features of the technology for the delivery method you chose. In your research, compare cost and features.

Create a new presentation. Save the presentation naming it Presentation Delivery and complete the following steps:

a) Include a title slide and at least one slide for each researched technology. Include notes for each slide that expand on the points on the slide.

b) Apply an appropriate design template to the presentation.

c) Apply the Fade in one by one animation scheme and then the Comb Horizontal slide transition to all the slides.

d) Add a slide to the end of the presentation, with the words The End. Add a sound to the slide from the Clip Organizer called "Claps Cheers" to the last slide. Make the sound play automatically when the slide is displayed.

e) Save the modified Presentation Delivery.

f) Print the presentation, with a footer that includes your name, so that the notes are included on each page.

g) Schedule a time to give a practice presentation to an audience of your peers. Use Outlook to create a meeting request and invite attendees.

h) Before the scheduled practice presentation, use Word to create a rubric that can be used by your peers for evaluating your presentation. In a new Word document, create a rubric. Some criteria are listed below, include at least one more of your own. Be sure to include a scale where appropriate:

- Were the slides easy to read?
- Was there too much or too little on the slides?
- What could you do to improve the slides?
- Did you speak too softly or loudly?
- What could you do to improve your mannerisms during the lecture?

i) Prepare handouts for your practice presentation. Print the handouts and a copy of the rubric for each member of your audience.

j) Give the practice presentation. After the presentation, collect the rubrics. Based on your peer critique, make improvements to your presentation. In Word, write a paragraph about what you changed and why the change is an improvement. Print a copy of the document.

Exercise 5 ———————————————————————————————Scuba Photos

Open PowerPoint and complete the following steps:

a) Create a new photo album with the following photos, which are image data files for this text:

```
SCUBA ANEMONE
SCUBA BUTTERFLY FISH
SCUBA CORAL
SCUBA GRAY ANGEL
SCUBA SPONGES
```

b) Save the presentation naming it Scuba Photos.

c) Include your name on slide 1, and change the title on slide 1 to Florida Scuba Photos

d) Add the BUBBLES sound, which is a sound data file for this text, to each slide that has a photo. Set the sound to not be visible during the slide show, and to play once on each slide as it is displayed.

e) Change the background of all the slides to a dark blue.

f) Apply the Uncover Down slide transition to all the slides.

g) Save the modified Scuba Photos.

h) Print the presentation, with a footer that includes your name, so that all the slides are printed on one page.

i) Package the presentation to a folder (or a CD if possible).

Using Microsoft Office Help

This appendix discusses how to effectively use the Microsoft Office help features.

Office Help Features

Microsoft Office has three help features that can be accessed while working in the Office applications. The Assistant provides tips in response to actions, Microsoft Office Help is a database of help topics that can be searched, and Online Help provides links to the Microsoft Office Online Web site.

The Assistant

When working in a Microsoft Office application, an animated character called the *Assistant* may appear:

The default Assistant is named "Clippit" and resembles a paper clip. The Assistant provides tips in response to actions performed, such as typing text or clicking a button. For example, as text is typed and edited in a Word document, a light bulb may appear above the Assistant, indicating that the Assistant has a helpful tip. Click the light bulb to display the tip in a balloon:

To cut text or graphic objects, click the Cut button on the Standard toolbar.

OK

The Assistant displays a tip, which explains how to cut text or graphic objects

Click OK to remove the balloon.

The Assistant also provides *Office Wizards*, which create a document automatically based on the user's answers to a series of questions. For example, the Office Assistant displays a helpful prompt when the Letter Wizard is selected:

Changing the Assistant

TIP Right-click the Assistant and select **Animate** from the menu to animate the Assistant.

The Assistant can be changed to a different character. Right-click the Assistant and select **Choose Assistant** from the menu to display a dialog box. Select the **Gallery** tab to display options for viewing and selecting a new Assistant:

Clippit can be changed to The Dot, F1, Office Logo, Merlin, Mother Nature, Links, or Rocky

Removing and Displaying the Assistant

To temporarily hide the Assistant while working, select Help → Hide the Office Assistant. Select Help → Show the Office Assistant to display the Office Assistant.

TIP If the Office Assistant is hidden when a tip is available, the Help button on the toolbar displays a light bulb (💡).

To turn off the Assistant, click the Assistant to display a balloon and then select Options in the balloon to display the Office Assistant dialog box:

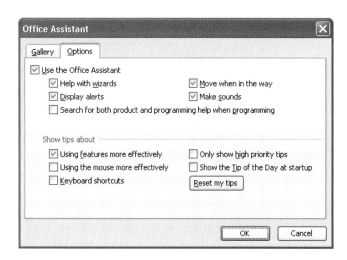

Click to clear the Use the Office Assistant check box and then select OK. Note that the Assistant will remain off even when Office is restarted. However, select Help → Show the Office Assistant while working to temporarily display the Office Assistant.

Program and System Messages

When the Office Assistant is on, program and system messages are displayed in the Office Assistant balloon, instead of a dialog box. For example, in Word, selecting File → Close displays either:

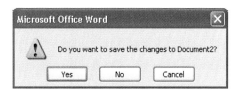

The way messages are displayed depends if the Office Assistant is turned on or turned off

Finding a Help Topic

The Assistant can be used to find helpful information. Click the Assistant to display a balloon with a What would you like to do? box:

Type a question and then select Search to display the Search Results task pane with a list of help topics:

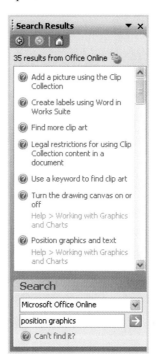

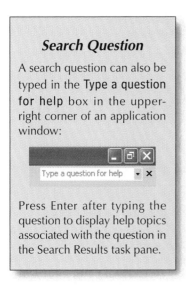

Search Question

A search question can also be typed in the **Type a question for help** box in the upper-right corner of an application window:

Press Enter after typing the question to display help topics associated with the question in the Search Results task pane.

Select a topic to display the application Help window next to the Search Results task pane:

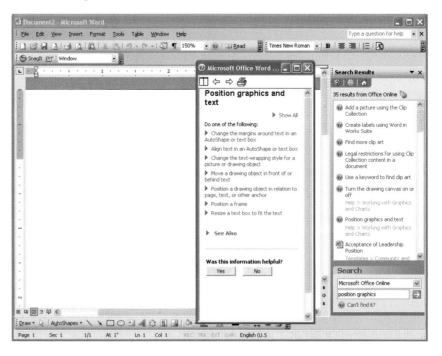

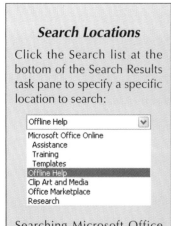

Search Locations

Click the Search list at the bottom of the Search Results task pane to specify a specific location to search:

Searching Microsoft Office Online requires Internet access but is advantageous over searching Offline Help because it provides access to up-to-date information and additional resources. Offline Help only searches the help database installed with the application.

In the example above, the Microsoft Office Word Help window displays a series of topics associated with the search question. Click a help topic to display information about the topic. Within the displayed information, keywords are displayed in a different color. Click a keyword to display the definition associated with the keyword:

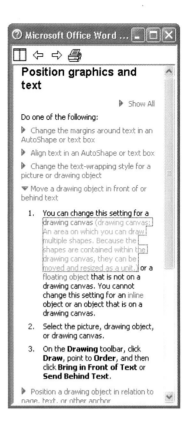

TIP Click the Maximize button in the upper-right corner of the application Help window to expand the size of the window.

Dialog Boxes

Dialog boxes contain a Help button ( ) in the top-right corner. Click the Help button to display help topics related to the dialog box.

Help topic with the "drawing canvas" definition displayed

Note that the information and keywords for all topics listed can be displayed by selecting Show All in the upper-right corner of the application Help window. Click the Print button ( ) to print the displayed topic. The ⇐ and ⇒ buttons can be used to scroll back and forth between previously viewed help topics. Click the Close button in the upper-right corner of the application Help window to remove the window.

browse help topics   It is also possible to browse search topics. Click the Help button ( ) on the toolbar to display the application Help task pane. Click the Table of Contents link to display a list of help topics:

TIP The application Help task pane can also be displayed by pressing the F1 key or selecting Help in the Other Task Panes list.

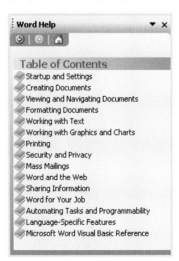

TIP To remove the application Help task pane, click the Close button in the upper-right corner of the task pane.

Click a book next to the topic to expand the list of topics. Click a topic to display it in the Microsoft Office application Help window.

Help topics vary depending on the active application. For example, Excel includes a Function Reference. Select the Table of Contents link in the Help task pane and then select Working with Data and then Function Reference to display a list of Excel Functions by category:

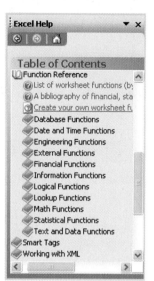

Keyboard Shortcuts

To display a keyboard shortcut reference sheet in Word, select **Tools → Macro → Macros** to display the Macro dialog box. Select **ListCommand** in the **Macro name** box and then click **Run** to display the List Commands dialog box. Select **Current menu and keyboard settings** and then click **OK**.

Using Online Help

An additional help resource that can be used when Internet access is available is the Microsoft Office Online Web site. In the application Help task pane, click the Microsoft Office Online link to open the Microsoft Office Online Web site in a browser window:

TIP The Microsoft Office Online Web site can also be displayed by selecting **Help → Microsoft Office Online.**

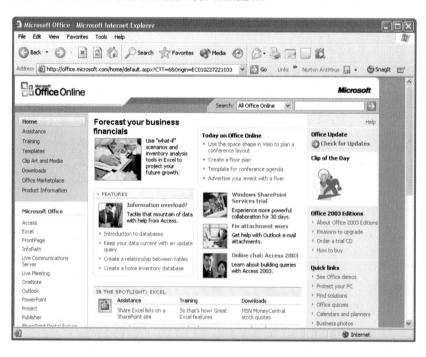

Links on the Microsoft Office Online Web site can be used to access assistance, training, templates, clip art and media, downloads, and product information. Content on this Web site is also searched when a search question is typed in an Office application and Microsoft Office Online is selected in the Search list at the bottom of the Search Results task pane.

Digital Images

Digital images are widely available and affordable. Even the least expensive digital cameras and scanners can produce images of acceptable quality for use in printed matter and on the Web. Digital cameras and scanners have settings that affect the image files produced by the camera. This appendix explains some aspects of digital image files.

Bitmap Images

Scanned and digital camera images are *bitmap images*, which are based on rows and columns of tiny dots that are square in shape. Each square is a *pixel* and is made up of one solid color. Many pixels of varying color create an image:

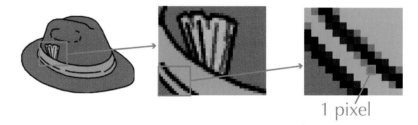

1 pixel

The number of *dots per inch (dpi)* is called the *resolution*. The larger the number of dpi, the better the quality of the graphic. Common bitmap image formats are BMP, JPG, TIFF and GIF.

Vector Graphics

Another type of graphic that is frequently used are *vector graphics*, which are composed of lines connected by points. Vector graphics can be resized smoothly, without developing a jagged-edge look that is common in low-resolution bitmap images.

Digital Image File Formats

digital camera

When a digital camera takes a photograph, a chip in the camera collects light and converts it to data. Settings in the digital camera determine what the camera does with the data that is collected. Common file settings in digital cameras are JPEG, TIFF, and RAW. The JPEG setting processes the data into a JPG file and the TIFF setting processes the data into a TIF file, which can then be transferred to a computer or printer. The TIF format has better quality than a JPG and is the better choice for printed matter such as newsletters, flyers, and brochures. The file size of a TIF is usually too large for use on the Web, so the TIF must be converted to a JPG for use in a Web page.

The RAW setting indicates that the data for a photograph has not been processed in the camera. The photograph's data must be transferred to a computer that has software installed that came from the camera manufacturer. The RAW file is manipulated using the software and saved in different image file formats, which is one reason why many professional photographers use the RAW setting. Manipulating a RAW file and saving the image in a different file format can be thought of as *processing* the digital film, because it allows adjustments such as exposure and color balance to be made. RAW file names have different extensions depending on the camera, for example .mrw is a Minolta camera RAW file, .crw is a Canon camera RAW file, and .nef is a Nikon camera RAW file.

scanner

A *scanner* is used to scan a photograph or drawing and create a digital image. The scanner can be operated through many applications, such as an image editing application. Common file formats of scanned images include TIF or TIFF, BMP, and JPG. Microsoft PowerPoint has a feature called Photo Album that includes options for selecting images from a scanner or digital camera connected to the computer.

Maintaining Image Quality in JPG Files

Setting a digital camera to process the photograph data as JPEG is a fast, convenient way to produce image files for use in a Web page. However, every time a JPG image is saved, it is compressed again and loses data because the JPG format has lossy compression.

To retain excellent image quality, the camera should be set to process the photograph data as TIFF, and then the TIF file can be modified on a computer as needed and saved in JPG format. This way, the image will have much better quality than if it was processed as JPG and then modified and saved a few times.

When using a high-resolution digital camera such as a 3 or more megapixel camera, processing the photograph data as JPG is acceptable. Because the image is at such as high resolution, it can be used in printed matter or saved at the proper resolution for use on a Web page.

Megapixels and Resolution

One megapixel is one million pixels. The megapixel specification for a digital camera is dependent on the number of pixels on the chip in the camera that collect light and convert it to data. For example, a camera with a chip that is 1,600 pixels wide and 1,200 pixels tall has a total of 1,920,000 pixels and is considered to be a 2 megapixel camera with a resolution of 1,600 x 1,200.

Digital Image Resolution

Digital cameras and scanners have settings that affect the resolution of the saved images. Scanner options are usually simply expressed in dpi. In a digital camera, these settings may be called something similar to "File Size" or "Quality" and have settings such as Large, Medium, and Small, which affect the resolution of the image file processed by the camera. For example, selecting Large may result in images that are 1600 x 1200 pixels, and Small may result in images that are 640 x 480 pixels. The file size (in kilobytes) of the Large image will be larger than the file size of the Small image because it contains more data.

Modifying an Image

Microsoft Word, Excel, and PowerPoint include the Picture toolbar, which can be used to modify an image. Selecting an image displays the Picture toolbar:

Click the Color button to change the image color.

Click the More Contrast and Less Contrast buttons to adjust the contrast.

Click the More Brightness and Less Brightness buttons to adjust the brightness.

Click the Crop button and then drag a handle to remove parts of an image.

Click the Rotate Left 90° button to rotate an image.

Click the Text Wrapping button to display a list of layout options, such as In Line With Text and Behind Text.

Click the Set Transparent Color button and then click a color in the image to make the color transparent. This button will be dimmed if the feature is not available for the image file type. For example, this feature is not available for JPG graphics.

Smaller, not Larger

The dimensions of a bitmap image should never be changed to a larger size because the software extrapolates data information to fill in additional pixels, which results in poor image quality. The resolution (dpi) also cannot be increased without resulting in poor image quality.

Another way to manipulate an image in Word, Excel, or PowerPoint is by right-clicking an image and selecting Format Picture from the menu to display the Format Picture dialog box. Select the Picture tab to display those options:

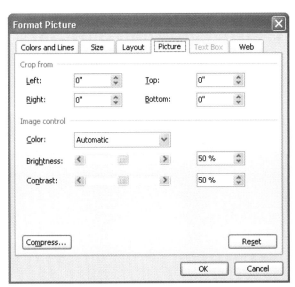

- The Crop from options hide parts of the image from view.

- The Image control options affect the appearance of the image.

Select the Size tab to display those options:

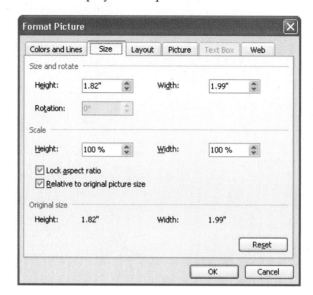

- The Size and rotate options affect the dimensions of the image in the document.

- The Scale options are used to size the image proportionally.

Changes made to an image in a document, workbook, or presentation only affect the embedded image, not the original.

Index

projectors, display technology 556
projectors, keystone correction 556
projectors, lamps 556
Promote button 181
Promote to Heading 1 button 181
proofreading 93
proposal 125, 161
Protect Sheet command 354
Protect Workbook command 354
protocol 319
Publisher 2003 1
publishing a presentation 547
purpose, brochure 191
Pyramid Diagram 189

Q

QT 543
query, complex 437
query, deleting 434
query, parameter 454
query, range 435
query, running 431
query, select 431
query, update 456
query criteria, fields 443
query criteria, wildcards 440
Query Type button 456
questions, What If? 482
question mark (?) 440
Quick Ratio 292
quitting an application 11
QWERTY 3

R

Radar chart 324
Radial Diagram 189
radio button 5
range 213
range, naming 343
ranges, naming 346
range query 435
RAW 565, 566
RDBMS 378
Reading Layout view 110
Reading pane 37, 47
Recently used file list 11
record 380
record, modifying 399
records, printing 395
records, printing specific 396
records, selecting 403
records, sorting 395, 431
records, unique 380
recordset 431
record controls 389
Record New Macro command 362
record selector 395
Rectangle ads 25
Recurrence button 67
red wavy line 93
Refresh button 27
Regular text 101

related 429
relational database management
    system 378
relational operators 270, 436
relationship, define in Access 429
relationships 379, 381, 430
relationships, illustrated 189
Relationships button 429
Relationships command 429
relative cell references 221, 268
Reminder window 65
remodeling project 294
Remove command 46
Remove Hyperlink 107, 349
Remove Page Break command 271
renovations 340
repaginates 131
Repeat command 89, 210
Replace command 95
Reply with Changes button 109,
    226, 517
report 527
report, Design view 476
report, distributing 478
report, e-mailing 478
report, posting 478
reports 87
reports, database 469
Reports button 470
report snapshot 479
report summary 473
Report Wizard 470
request letter 119
Research button 27
research papers 169, 172
Research task pane 27, 95
resize tab 2
resolution 565, 566
resolution, digital image 566
Restore button 2
résumé 87, 122
Reveal Formatting command 129
Reveal Formatting task pane 129
revenue 252
Reviewing toolbar 109
Revisions task pane 515
right-clicking 4
right aligned 105
Right tab stop 135
Roman number formats 185
room conditions 510
rotate handle 228
Rotate Left 90° button 567
ROUNDDOWN function 267
ROUNDUP function 267
ROUND function 267
rows 175, 208
rows, adding or deleting 176
row and column headings 214, 271
row height 176
rubric 167, 205, 530, 531, 532
rubric, creating 205

rubric, screenplay 166
rulers 88
Ruler command 136, 139
rules 43
Rules and Alerts command 43
running a macro 362
Run button 431, 456
Russell 2000 254, 337

S

S&P 500 337
sales pitch 527
sales revenue 335
salutation 91
sans serif fonts 117, 509
Save and Close button 66
Save As command 148, 233, 434, 539
Save as Web Page 151, 547
Save button 7
Save command 7
scannable resume 170
scanned images 146
scanner 19, 566
Scenarios command 259
schedule 245
schedule, organize 84
scheduling tool 60
schema 380
schema, database 380
schema design 380
screenplay 166
ScreenTip 5
scrolling sheets 278
scroll arrows 395
scroll bar 2, 27
scroll bars 208
sculptors 126
search, refining 95
Search button 27
search criteria 33
search engine 32
sections 184
section break 184
section break, deleting 184
section header 185
selected cell 208
Selected Chart command 320
Selected Legend command 320
selecting, vertical block 136
selecting text 98
selector, column 434
Select All button 213
Select All command 99
select query 431
select query, deleting 434
Send a Copy button 109
Send button 37, 516
Send Instant Message command 47
Send this Sheet command 225
Sent Items folder 43
serial values 353
series name 301

serif fonts 117, 509
service hours 375
Set Print Area command 271
Set Transparent Color button 173,567
share 291, 335
shared workbook 225
sheets 207
sheets, multiple 277
sheet tab 208
sheet tab color 277
Shift key 88
Short 379
shortcut 6
Show/Hide ¶ button 89
Show Table, command 434
Show Table button 434
Show the Office Assistant 560, 561
signature 41
signature line 92
Single 379
single spacing 138
size, field 379
sizes, using effectively 101
Skyscraper ads 25
slice 302
slide, adding a chart 536
slide, adding a movie 542
slide, adding hyperlinks 547
slide, adding sound 541
slide, add music from CD 542
slide, editing 500
slides, deleting 499
slides tab 498
slide background, formatting 509
Slide Design task pane 533, 539
slide footer, formatting 509
slide footers 508
slide layout, selecting 499
Slide Layout command 499
Slide Master command 508, 539
Slide Master view 508
slide pane 498
Slide Show from current slide 501
Slide Show toolbar 537
Slide Show view 501
Slide Sorter View 501
slide text, formatting 509
slide transition 534
Slide Transition command 534
SLN() function 294
smart tags 94
Smart Tag Actions button 94
smart tag indicator 94
snapshot 479
SND 542
.snp 479
software, presentation 556
software assessment rubric 205
solar energy 58
sorting 268
sorting, alphabetical 268
sorting, ascending 268

sorting, chronological 268
sorting, descending 268
sorting data 268
Sort Ascending button 268, 395, 488
Sort command 268
Sort Descending button 268, 395, 488
sort order 395
sound 534
sound file formats 542
Sound from File command 541
sound icon 541
source 220, 278
source, 536
Source command 25
Source Data command 319
Speakerphone 165
speakers 557
speaker notes 511
speaker notes, creating 511
speaker notes, printing 511
special characters, avoid 379
special effects considerations 545
Spelling and Grammar 37
Spelling button 209
spelling checker 93
spell checking, automatic 500
spider 32
spreadsheet 207
spreadsheet, planning 208
spreadsheet model 259
Standard & Poor's 500 254, 337
static 278, 309
static data 351, 405
statistics 473
status bar 2, 27, 88, 498
stocks 254
stock exchanges 335
stockholder's equity 246
stock indexes 337
stock portfolio 335
Stock tables 336
Stop button 27
Stop Recording toolbar 362
storage media 7
storyboard 498
style 178
style, columnar form 389
style, creating 179
style, Normal 178
styles, built-in 178
Styles and Formatting button 178
Styles and Formatting task pane 178
stylus pen 4
subdatasheet 430
subject tree 34
subnames 26
Subscript 102
Sum 474
summary, report 473
summary options 474
SUM function 260
superscript 102

Surface chart 324
surfing the net 24
symbols, operator 443
Symbol command 88, 92
synonyms 95
Synonyms command 95
system messages 561

T

tab, changing sheet 277
tab, sheet 277
table, creating 175, 382
table, formatting 135
table, selecting 176
tables 175, 378
table attributes 378
Table command 175
Table design window 382
table of contents 183
table of contents, updating 183
Tabs 135
Tabs command 136
Tab key 135, 209
tab leader 136
Tab Selection button 136
tab stop 135
taking test 125
Target Diagram 189
task 59, 71
task, completing 72
task, deleting or editing 72
taskbar 2, 12
TaskPad command 71
Tasks tool 71
task pane 2
task pane, Clip Art 146, 228
task pane, Getting Started 378
task pane, Help 563
task pane, Mail Merge 445, 451
task pane, New File 378
task pane, remove 146
task pane, Research 27, 95
task pane, Reveal Formatting 129
task pane, Slide Design 533, 539
task pane, Styles and Formatting 178
Task Panes list 498
Task Pane command 148
tear-off palette 5
telecommuting 159
temperatures 338
temperature conversion 247
template 148, 233
templates, formatting 233
text, body 178
text, entering into cells 176
text, finding 95
text, replacing 95
text, selecting 98, 99
text box 5
text color 102